Experimental Foundations
of Clinical Psychology

EDITED BY

Arthur J. Bachrach

EXPERIMENTAL FOUNDATIONS OF CLINICAL PSYCHOLOGY

BASIC BOOKS, INC., PUBLISHERS

NEW YORK

Third Printing

© 1962 by Basic Books Publishing Co., Inc.
Library of Congress Catalog Card Number: 61–15724
Printed in the United States of America
Designed by Nancy H. Dale

List of Contributors

HENRY E. ADAMS, Ph.D., Assistant Professor of Psychology, Louisiana State University, Baton Rouge.

ARTHUR J. BACHRACH, Ph.D., Associate Professor, and Director of Behavioral Science, University of Virginia School of Medicine.

IRWIN A. BERG, Ph.D., Professor of Psychology, Louisiana State University, Baton Rouge.

JOSEPH V. BRADY, Ph.D., Chief, Department of Experimental Psychology, Walter Reed Army Institute of Research, Washington, D.C.; Executive Director, The Institute for Behavioral Research, University of Maryland.

DANA BRAMEL, Ph.D., Assistant Professor of Psychology, University of Minnesota.

P. B. DEWS, Ph.D. (M.B., Ch.B.), Associate Professor of Pharmacology, Harvard Medical School.

LEON FESTINGER, Ph.D., Professor of Psychology, Stanford University.

ISRAEL GOLDIAMOND, Ph.D., Professor of Psychology, Arizona State University.

JOEL GREENSPOON, Ph.D., Professor of Psychology; Director, Clinical Training Program, The Florida State University.

RALPH F. HEFFERLINE, Ph.D., Associate Professor of Psychology, Columbia University.

WILLIAM A. HUNT, Ph.D., Professor of Psychology and the Biological Sciences, Northwestern University.

NELSON F. JONES, Ph.D., Assistant Professor of Clinical Psychology, University of Colorado Medical Center.

SEYMOUR LEVINE, Ph.D., Associate Professor of Psychiatry and Psychology, Stanford University.

ROBERT B. MALMO, Ph.D., Director, Laboratory for Psychological Studies, Allan Memorial Institute, McGill University.

JOSEPH D. MATARAZZO, Ph.D., Professor of Medical Psychology; University of Oregon Medical School.

LUIGI PETRULLO, M.A. Head, Group Psychology Branch, Department of the Navy, Office of Naval Research.

KARL H. PRIBRAM, M.D. Associate Professor of Psychiatry and Psychology, Stanford University.

MURRAY SIDMAN, Ph.D., Assistant Professor of Psychology in The Department of Neurology, Massachusetts General Hospital.

HANS H. STRUPP, Ph.D., Associate Professor of Psychology, University of North Carolina School of Medicine.

ROBERT I. WATSON, Ph.D., Professor of Psychology, Northwestern University.

JOSEPH WOLPE, M.D., Research Professor of Psychiatry, University of Virginia School of Medicine.

Preface

In 1958, the first University of Virginia Behavioral Science Symposium was held. The title of the symposium was "Experimental Foundations of Clinical Psychology," and among the speakers were a number of the contributors to the present volume, although their chapters are not the same as their original speeches. The relationship between the original symposium and the current volume bearing the same title is like Aristotle's jack-knife—a new blade and a new handle, but the same name. It also has the same goal as the symposium, that of acquainting experimentalists and clinicians alike with the mutuality of research with clinical problems and experimental methods. From the nucleus of the discussions held at the meetings there emerged an idea for an expanded and more comprehensive coverage of the experimental foundations of clinical psychology, eventuating in this volume.

Throughout the preparation and editing of the book there have been several people who have been of great help. Among these are my wife, Susan, whose ideas, interest, and encouragement were always a fine support. Two of the contributors, my friends, Irwin Berg and Murray Sidman, were also very generous with their suggestions with regard to material and plans for the book, in addition to the hard work they put in on their own chapters.

A.J.B.

Editor's Introduction

Although all psychologists presumably get the same training in graduate school—a training based in the experimental, scientific method—in the course of their subsequent careers they divide into two distinct groups in American psychology: the clinicians, concerned with therapeutic or testing practices; and the experimentalists, concerned first with academic and research responsibilities. The languages developed by these two groups are apparently different; their methods of functioning are more obviously different.

It can be—and has been—argued that the actual differences lie in the differences in role for each group. Peter Dews, on page 424 of this book, observes that it is in the nature of the work of the clinical psychiatrist and psychologist that they "are obliged constantly to make decisions as to the dispositions of their patients—decisions that usually cannot be made solely or even primarily on the basis of available scientific evidence. It is the clear duty of the clinician to make his decision on the basis of all available information. It is the equally clear duty of the basic scientist *not* to come to a decision until the scientific evidence justifies it."

The fundamental difference, then, lies in social obligations. Because the clinician must, out of human necessity, make decisions based on insufficient data, he is allowed a certain diplomatic immunity in his role on the ward. He is allowed to use such terms as "improvement," "therapy," "anxiety," without being required to specify the operational variables that go into them. The research psychologist, on the other hand, must assume the responsibilities, procedures, and criteria of the basic scientist.

Clinical practice has its own imperatives. The question then becomes: Is clinical *research* possible within the framework of the rigorous scientific method? And does such research have application to clinical practice?

Recognizing the traditional distinctions and barriers between clinician and laboratory worker, we feel that there are, nonetheless, areas of common interest. Many of these areas have received varying degrees of experimental attention. This book is an attempt to gather together in one place a summary of the present state of experimental progress in these areas of clinical research. Some are more advanced than others; some hold more promise than others. Although our primary purpose is to establish communication, the communication process must work in both directions. By becoming aware of the current state of research, the clinician will not only be better able to extract what is useful to him but will also be in a better position to offer constructive criticism. Hopefully, this survey will make it possible for clinicians and experimentalists to identify other areas that might be amenable to experimental research.

In a sense, *Experimental Foundations of Clinical Psychology* is in itself an experiment. If it helps to bridge the gulf between the two major groups in psychology by illuminating their common purposes and common roots, it will have achieved the aims of the editor and the contributors.

Contents

PART THREE: PSYCHOPHYSIOLOGY

PART FOUR: BEHAVIOR MODIFICATION:
EXPERIMENTAL BASES OF PSYCHOTHERAPY

PART ONE

General and Theoretical Aspects

1

The Experimental
Tradition and Clinical Psychology

ROBERT I. WATSON

A psychologist reading contemporary journal literature is being influenced unknowingly by an editorial decision that took place not too many years ago. The sheer productivity of the increased number of psychologists forced editors to eliminate or drastically curtail what at one time was an essential part of the research report—the historical introduction. Today, the first rule of article writing is to come immediately to the point. The setting for this point is often limited to no more than, "Since Brown (1959) has found that . . . then, . . . ," or the immortal phrase, "In a previous communication . . . ." It is not surprising then that readers, especially among younger psychologists, may slip into thinking that this work began with "Brown (1959)" or with the "previous communication," since this is the only work cited. Thus a valuable source of historical perspective has been lost, with no foreseeable chance that the custom will change. In the master's essay and the doctoral dissertation some attempt is still made to place a research problem in its historical context, but the value of these attempts is blunted by the sponsors' injunction to students; "When you prepare for publication, the first thing to eliminate is the historical introduction."

The change of policy about historical introductions may be both an effect of an ahistorical, or even anti-historical, attitude on the part of psychologists and one of the causes of the continued neglect of history.

This foreshortening of historical vision is perhaps one of the reasons that clinical psychologists are, to a considerable, degree, blithely oblivious to much of the content of experimental psychology on which their clinical efforts are based. The breach between "experimental" and "clinical" psychologists is obviously widened if no attempt is made to show that they are related. One of the sources of furthering *rapprochement* between these factions is attention to the historical antecedents of clinical work to be found in nonclinical settings.

Looking at historically rooted experimental antecedents of clinical psychology is a process similar to the clinical investigation of the investigation of the individual. A psychological problem viewed both in present context, as it is in the chapters to follow, and in historical perspective, as it is in this chapter, is like viewing the patient as reflecting both contemporary forces and past experiences. Most clinical psychologists, in attempting to understand a patient's current problem, feel that they need to know the individual's past history; so too should we be sensitive to the need for understanding current research in the light of its historical antecedents.

THE TRADITIONS OF CLINICAL PSYCHOLOGY

The history of psychology shows a cumulative advance by the building up of a body of research findings, theories, procedures, and techniques which are passed on from one generation of psychologists to the next. Because of this passage between generations it is proper to speak of a tradition of psychology. Within this general tradition, it is possible to discern several more specific traditions, each not completely separable and tending to blend one with another, but sufficiently distinguishable so that they have come to receive meaningful identifying labels.

As a field, clinical psychology originated in a matrix of older, already existing traditions within psychology. Indeed no tradition of psychology is so remote from clinical endeavor as to be ruled out completely as one of the foundations of clinical psychology. Discernible among these as particularly relevant to clinical psychology are the psychometric, the dynamic, the social, the biological-medical, and the experimental traditions.

The intent of this book requires that the experimental tradition be made central. Some of the other traditions are peripheral to this emphasis. What is meant by these traditions is already familiar. In a Presidential Address to the American Psychological Association, Cronbach (1957) focused on the contrast between experimental psychology and what he called correlation psychology. He was in fact contrasting the experimental and psychometric traditions. Bindra and Scheier

(1954), who wrote on the relation between what they called psychometric and experimental research, were also considering these two traditions. Omitted from this chapter is the psychiatric tradition as it is reflected, in the immediate past, in the field of the study of individual differences, stemming from Galton and Cattell, and the effect of this study upon psychology in general (Boring, 1957; Murphy, 1949), and upon clinical psychology in particular (Watson, 1953; Watson, 1959). This omission is justified, not because the study of individual differences is unimportant, but because it is sufficiently separable from the experimental tradition in the direction of the psychometric tradition to justify omission. The absence of much material on the human child illustrates this point, since so much research using children is dependent upon the use of already established differences. Some aspects of the psychometric tradition are discussed in the chapter by Berg on measurement and evaluation.

Clinical psychology also draws upon the dynamic tradition, epitomized in the work of Freud, James, Hall, and Janet. In a previous publication the writer (1953) explored historically the psychometric and dynamic tradition of clinical psychology. To write this chapter without further mentioning Freud (and the others in the dynamic tradition) except incidentally shows the selectivity of the point of view of this book. And yet it is fully justified. Despite his fecundity in stimulating research and thinking, Freud contributed nothing relevant to the *experimental* foundations of clinical psychology. It is convenient to refer to the biological-medical tradition in psychology as a more or less coherent, interrelated whole. Not only does this draw attention to the fact that medical research is rooted in biology, making them for present purposes essentially one, but it also serves to distinguish it from medicine's contributions to the dynamic tradition.

The social tradition, drawing unto itself social philosophy, sociology, and social psychology (as well as experimental and clinical psychology), is, in itself, a hybrid similar in this respect to clinical psychology. Insofar as these traditions draw upon experiment they are relevant to that which follows. Their rich contentual and theoretical heritage as well as their use of other methodologies must be neglected.

Each of these other traditions has a symbiotic relation with clinical psychology. Each tradition supplies content and approaches to the clinical field and receives in return content and procedures, but here attention is centered on the contribution from the experimental field. The reverse relation is another story.

Implicit in the title of this book is the contention that clinical psychological research has as one of its bases the contributions of experimental behavioral study. In this sense the entire history of experimental psychology bears relation to clinical psychology. No attempt has been made in this volume to limit the experimental tradition to a narrow definition. Rather, experimental psychology was interpreted as behavioral study oriented to and derived from the laboratory but not confined to it, providing that the concern in nonlaboratory settings attempted to preserve, insofar as the problem and setting permitted, the controls of the laboratory. Despite the broad context of the entire book, however, it would be absurd to try in the space of a few pages to sketch the history of experimental psychology.

This chapter instead presents selected historical material in settings that will bring out their contemporary significance. The illustrations used are drawn from the experimental tradition particularly relevant to some of the major problems discussed in later chapters. Selection of each topic was guided by its usefulness not only as an illustration of historical relationships as such but also by its capacity to deepen the value of knowledge of the history of psychology. Knowledge, for example, that contemporary investigation of clinical judgment is rooted in the very oldest of problems in the experimental tradition, that of psychophysics, helps us to understand the significance of the research and to gain some understanding of the direction it has taken. Moreover the possibility of showing that psychophysics which occupies one of the highest floors in the Ivory Tower is relevant to clinical psychology is a temptation that could not be resisted.

CLINICAL PSYCHOLOGY AND THE EXPERIMENTAL TRADITION IN THE PAST

Clinical psychology, as a separate discipline, arose some time after the turn of the century (Watson, 1953). This approximate date is used to differentiate its past from its historical period.

This past stretched back in time to the earliest known experimentally controlled research study of the Ancient World. In fact, the earliest psychological experiment known to the writer is relevant to the topic of Chapter 6, which is concerned with the effects of early experience on later behavior. As told by Herodotus, one Psammetichus, ruler of Egypt in the seventh century before Christ, wanted to enhance Egyptian national pride by proving that Egyptian was the oldest of languages. Accordingly, he ordered his herdsman to take two children "of the common sort" and to isolate them from birth onward in a hut, accompanied only by goats from which to draw nourishment; further, he gave strict instructions that no human beings be allowed to approach them. Two years later, when the hut was opened, the children rushed out crying, "becos." To the Pharaoh's chagrin, "becos" proved to be the Phrygian word for bread, forcing him to acknowledge that this, not Egyptian, was the oldest of languages.

To return to the period more than 2500 years later than Psammetichus—a considerable number of psychologists and other research workers can be considered possible early representatives of the experimental tradition in psychology. Some contributed so much to the intellectual climate of their times and influenced our own so forcefully that attention is forced upon them, despite the fact that they did their work before there was a clinical psychology. Representative of these are Darwin and Pavlov, towering above the others, who did not work with clinical problems and were, in fact, not even psychologists. But their contributions were so far reaching that they must be considered. Others, not so important, did experimental work which had direct relation with clinical problems, both in the past before clinical psychology emerged as a discipline and after the turn of the century when clinical psychology was beginning to emerge. By definition they were not clinical psychologists. Rather, they were individuals who contributed materially to experimental psychology but did so using clinical problems. Emil Kraepelin is representative of the past; Shepard Ivory Franz is representative of the period of emergence of clinical psychology.

Charles Darwin

Darwin was not the first biologist to concern himself with evolution. During the first half of the nineteenth century and even before, evolutionary theory excited considerable interest and furious discussion (Murphy, 1949). Darwin's genius rested not upon proposing the problem, but upon his long and painstaking collection of the relevant evidence. The period of preparation began in 1831 with the voyage of H.M.S. "Beagle" to the South Seas, lasted through the years of travel, and culminated with his reading of Malthus's *Essay on Population* in 1838. Thereafter he had a biological premise to work with and his own theory of evolution began to take shape in the doctrine of the transmutation of the species. Over the next *twenty* years he collected the necessary mass of relevant data. Only in 1859 did *On the Origin of Species* appear. What happened thereafter, we can assume, is generally familiar. We need be concerned only with Darwin's effect on psychology; there, his *The Expression of the Emotions in Man and Animals* was important.

For the remainder of the century, psychology clearly evidenced the influence of Darwin. His work shaped psychology in the direction of biology and function and away from the model of physics and chemistry and structure of the German psychologists. One facet of the biological orientation, as a matter of fact, was the line of development, from Galton through Baldwin and Hall, in the study of individual differences. Evidences of this biological orientation were manifested in other ways as well. A sign of Darwin's influence was found in the increasing tendency to interpret mental processes in terms of the functions they served. Moreover, the comparative viewpoint of a continuity of mental development became prominent because of his work. It has even been suggested by Beck and Molish (1959) that to Darwin we owe the beginning of "scientific clinical psychology." They reach this conclusion because of his recognition of the importance of the dynamics of behavior. These trends in the work of those influenced by Darwin will be apparent in later discussion.

It was Darwin's work that stimulated the study of comparative psychology immediately prior to the modern era (Warden, 1927: Watson, 1961). For some years after Darwin the anecdotal method, dependent upon casual observation of "clever" and unusual animals, was the dominating technique for collecting data. This inadequate method was accompanied by a tendency to anthropomorphize the lower animals. About 1890 the work of Jacques Loeb and C. Lloyd Morgan introduced the modern era in animal psychology. Loeb's work on tropisms helped to demolish the trend toward anthropomorphism. So too did Morgan's canon, which might be stated briefly as advancing the rule that no action should be interpreted as being due to a higher behavioral function if it is capable of being interpreted as the outcome of a behavioral function lower in the scale. This adaptation of the law of parsimony served to discourage extravagant interpretation of animal behavior.

Ivan P. Pavlov

In his autobiography, Pavlov (1955) acknowledged that he was enormously influenced by Darwin, first through the intermediary of Pisarev's expositions of Darwin and the theory of evolution (Pisarev was a Russian writer of the sixties and seventies) and later directly by Darwin's works. The second major influence he acknowledged was the writings of Sechenov, whom he called the "father" of Russian physiology.

Through his researches Sechenov had become convinced that spinal reflexes are capable of inhibition by the cerebral cortex. He further argued that thinking and intelligence were dependent upon exercise for their stimulation and that all psychological acts are reflexes. As Pavlov (1927) indicated, Sechenov's view was based on conjecture. Pavlov proceeded to carry out his well-known research studies to demonstrate the validity of this hypothesis.

Pavlov (1927) acknowledged that Thorndike's researches of 1898 were the first experiments in this general area, but he further indicated that at the time he began investigation he was not familiar with this work.

Before embarking on the study of conditioning, a detailed study of the digestive glands had occupied a considerable amount of his research time. While working on these glands, Pavlov (Wells, 1956) noticed that gastric juice was secreted by his experimental dogs not only when food was taken in the mouth but also when they saw it at a distance. Later on he found the same phenomena with the secretion of saliva. This "mouth watering" he first termed "psychical secretions," to distinguish this action-at-a-distance from direct stimulation of the nerve endings in the mouth. Heretofore, and indeed in his own early work, this and similar phenomena were considered in the then-current setting of introspective interpretation. The animal "judged" that it was food, that it "smelled good," and that he "desired" it. Pavlov's great contribution was to forego this introspective approach and treat the phenomena objectively. In other words, external stimulation and underlying nervous processes were studied experimentally by objective means. Pavlov followed this course by working on conditioned reflexes for his remaining thirty-five years.

His method, it should be noted, is extraordinarily flexible and has had far-reaching consequences. The conditioning referred to in later chapters, although perhaps initiated by problems quite alien to his range of interests, nevertheless all owe a debt to this physiologist. Vladimir Bechterev, too, beginning about 1907, studied the conditioning of motor responses (Bechterev, 1932, Rosenzweig, 1960). Bechterev's work (Rosenzweig, 1960) stimulated John B. Watson's (1916) enthusiastic presidential address in 1915, which was devoted to the topic of conditioning. However, as Hilgard and Marquis (1940) indicate, it was Pavlov's detailed approach to conditioning, not Bechterev's, which was accepted in the United States.

Emil Kraepelin

Born in 1856, Emil Kraepelin took a medical degree and subsequently was Professor of Psychiatry, first at Heidelberg and then at Munich. He is quite properly judged one of the founders of modern psychiatry—and sometimes described as the "father of descriptive psychiatry." This, in some circles, is dangerously close to epithet. What such critics forget is that his work on the classification and description of mental disorders made it possible for his successors to go further. Kraepelin himself seems to have been aware that it was too early to attempt more than description, for one of his papers (Kahn, 1956) ends expressly on the note that, once we have more knowledge, one can proceed to the main task—understanding the disorder.

He opened the first issue of his journal, *Psychologische Arbeiten*

(1895) with an account of his own previous researches. He then proceeded to write eloquently that the psychological experiment is not merely useful but indispensable. He indicated that every psychiatrist seemed to judge it his right, or, perhaps even his obligation, to construct his own psychological system and went on to ask what internist would dare to proclaim a new system of physiology without basing it on a laboriously acquired laboratory fact? All of this has a modern ring; it was written more than sixty-five years ago but might still be pertinent today as comment and question.

Nevertheless, because his contributions to descriptive psychiatry were so immense, other facets of his work, of more direct concern to psychiatry, are often neglected, and it is seldom pointed out that experimental laboratory research was a major interest to Kraepelin.

Wundt had taken over the word association technique from Galton, and several of his students, including Kraepelin, worked in this area. On the heels of Cattell's first work on reaction time, Kraepelin showed that characteristic alterations in association occurred when experimentally induced abnormal conditions, such as fatigue, hunger, and alcoholic intoxication, were introduced. Another area in which Kraepelin was a pioneer was the study of continuous work, such as adding. He was able to show the classic phenomena—the shape of the curve, the mutually opposing influence of fatigue and learning, warming-up, spurts, and so on—which were nearly always found in subsequent investigations.

Shepard Ivory Franz

A physician, Edward Cowles, founded at McLean Hospital the first psychological laboratory for the investigation of psychotic patients (Franz, 1919). A charter member of the American Psychological Association in 1892 (Dennis and Boring, 1952), Cowles became director of the McLean Hospital some years before the turn of the century (Hall, 1894).

In 1903 Cowles invited psychologist Shepard Ivory Franz to come to the hospital laboratory to carry out some research that earlier he had asked Franz to outline (Franz, 1932). This work had to do with relating the nerve physiology that Sherrington was then developing to problems of excitement and depression as formulated by Kraepelin. In 1907 after carrying out this research, Franz went to what is now St. Elizabeths Hospital in Washington, D.C., the federal mental hospital. He also had an appointment at George Washington University. His first task was to prepare a standard clinical psychological examination, adopted for use in the hospital in 1907 and expanded into a book, first published in 1912 (1919). This was almost certainly the first routine psychological examination program in the world. However, his work in the experimental tradition is more relevant to the present interest.

Before going to McLean Hospital, Franz, a Cattell Ph.D. from Columbia, had published his first paper in the field with which he was to become identified. This was the study entitled, "On the function of the cerebrum: the frontal lobes in relation to the production and retention of simple sensory-motor habits" (1902). His years at St. Elizabeths were productive in various fields. He studied, for example, the knee jerk in paretics. However, probably his most important work continued to have to do with cerebral function, especially in subjects in which brain areas were destroyed, and he published a considerable number of studies. Associated with him was Karl S. Lashley, and in 1917 they published together on the effects of cerebral destruction on habit formation in the white rat. From this point on the distinguished research work of Lashley continued along the lines thus laid down. Among his other younger associates was E. G. Boring, who spent the summer of 1913 with him, working in learning (and introspection) in dementia praecox (Boring, 1923 a, b).

Franz was by no means the only psychologist concerned with the abnormal person during these years. In a review of the experimental literature on psychotics through 1934 J. McV. Hunt (1936) reported on a considerable number of studies. After eliminating those irrelevant to present interests, such as psychometric and statistical studies, there were still about fifty experimental studies published before 1920. Among the other workers cited who used experimental methods with the psychotics before 1920 were J. W. Baird, A. Hoch, Grace H. Kent, T. V. Moore, E. W. Scripture, E. K. Strong, D. Wechsler, and F. L. Wells. Even this brief summary disproves the notion sometimes expressed that experimental study of the abnormal person was not taken seriously until more recent years.

CLINICAL PROBLEMS AND THE EXPERIMENTAL TRADITION

At this point, the approach of this chapter shifts to consider historically some of the major themes of the topics to follow. It is manifestly impossible in short compass to trace, one by one, the historical backgrounds for the topics of the chapters that follow. Instead, the general headings of the sections, each including several chapters, supply the remaining topics; the first of these is divided into two parts. The topic of *psychophysiology* is not discussed specifically since in considerable measure it draws upon the biological-medical tradition. Insofar as psychophysiology draws upon learning, that section is relevant. The topics, then, are *learning, communication,* and *behavior modification.*

The next chapter, concerned with clinical judgment, gives us the first topic of *psychophysics*. Each topic is examined in a different way in order to bring out its value in illustrating historically important issues.

Psychophysics

In Chapter 2 Hunt and Jones describe the experimental bases of clinical judgment. This discussion of its historical antecedents will center on the work of Hunt partly because of considerable familiarity with his work. So far as his contributions are concerned, research clinical selection procedures during and following World War II form the content. In the course of his duties as a clinical psychologist in the United States Navy, Hunt was faced with a practical clinical problem: psychologists' and psychiatrists' established practice of using clinical judgment in selecting, rejecting, and placing naval personnel. In his research, Hunt has applied a psychophysical analogue to this problem.

A short digression is necessary here; it also illustrates the value of knowledge of the experimental tradition. The history of psychology is replete with appeals to analogy. When the appeal stopped with the drawing of the analogy it was futile and essentially self-defeating. For example, the gigantic analogy between the individual—the microcosm and the world—the macrocosm plagued the history of intellectual development from the time of the pre-Socratic Greeks (Watson, 1961). The Platonic tripartite division of the individual soul as having the functions of reason, spirit, and sense corresponding to the ruling, warrior, and worker classes in the state is a specific instance of this analogy.

Hunt and his associates took the crucial and imperative step of going beyond analogy and testing it experimentally. Hunt, drawing on his knowledge of the history of psychology in general and the experimental tradition in particular, was able to see the experimental procedures of psychophysics as relevant to the problem.

The history of psychophysics (and the actuarial trend in the field of judgment) began with Weber's (1834–1846) and Fechner's (1860) classical work on the measurement of sensory mechanisms (Boring, 1957). Weber's statement that the just noticeable difference in a stimulus bears a constant ratio to that stimulus was expanded by Fechner into the formula, $S = k \log R$. Without going into the stormy history over the intervening years, let us move forward to the late twenties. One of the problems exciting considerable interest at this time was that of relative, as opposed to absolute, judgment in psychophysics as expressed, for example, by Wever and Zener (1928). As Hunt (1960) pointed out:

> The orientation in psychophysics at that time, and particularly so at Harvard, was a peripheral, end-organ one. More and more of us,

however, and I remember particularly Volkmann, Chapman, Cantril, and Sherif who were fellow graduate students at the time, were becoming convinced of the importance of "central" as opposed to "peripheral" processes.

If the processes producing psychophysical phenomena were central, and not confined to peripheral processes, then it followed that they might appear in areas other than that of classical psychophysics. Volkmann and Hunt (1937) found anchoring effects in affective judgment; Hunt (1941) found them in aesthetic judgment. In these two areas, far removed from that of classical psychophysics, they found that subjective standards are built up which in turn provide a standard against which other stimuli are judged.

With the demonstration of lawful predictable phenomena in judgment in different type of stimulus material, Hunt was encouraged to draw the analogy between psychophysical and clinical judgment.* An insightful transfer of knowledge and methodology derived from the experimental tradition to a clinical problem was effected.

Learning

In the nineteenth century some of the previously mentioned animal research of Morgan and Loeb, as well as that of Faber, Lubbock, and Verworn, was experimental in intent, but it was Edward L. Thorndike who introduced the modern laboratory type of experiment into animal psychology (Warden, 1927). Beginning in 1898, his pioneer studies of learning and imitation in chicks, dogs, cats, and monkeys began to appear. Work similar in spirit immediately became popular among psychologists. The animal work of Yerkes, Carr, and Hunter during the first twenty-five years of this century is illustrative. However, it was John B. Watson who made the most far-reaching innovations in his popularization of behaviorism.

Before dealing with his work, it is necessary to say something about functional psychology, which was a characteristic expression of psychology in the United States during the early years of the century. Many factors were at work in its development. There was, for example, the influence of James from the United States and Hoffding and Külpe from Europe (Murphy, 1949). Another important factor was certainly the Darwinian influence. At the risk of some oversimplification, it will be this influence that will be sketched.

It was through functional psychology that the Darwinian view extended beyond animal psychology to psychology in general. The philosopher of social change, John Dewey, was influential in developing

---

* The same general context that led to these studies was one of the elements entering into Sherif's studies (1936) of the assimilation of social norms in frames of reference as expressed in the autokinetic phenomenon.

the functional point of view. As Boring (1950) demonstrates, he had been influenced by Darwinian thinking. The paper by Dewey (1896) published in 1896 with the self-explanatory title, "The reflex arc concept in psychology," had considerable influence. After Dewey's simultaneous departure from the University of Chicago (for Columbia University) and from psychology (for philosophy), his work was carried on by Angell. Angell (1907), too, acknowledged a direct debt to Darwin (Boring, 1950), arguing that functional psychology was not new but had its modern impetus from the views of Darwin and Spencer (who also wrote in an evolutionary vein). As a "school," functionalism was relatively short-lived, and need not concern us further.

To return to Watson, who was trained at Chicago: much of the emphasis of functionalism lived on in behaviorism and in the neobehavioristic tendency, so prevalent today, to stress activity as contrasted with conscious states. Nevertheless, in one way functionalism strengthened Watson's rebellion—in this respect he was reacting as much against functionalism as against structuralism—in that functionalism, too, made no "clean break" with consciousness (Watson, 1929), and it was this break for which Watson argued. Watson himself stated that his debt was to C. Lloyd Morgan and Thorndike (Watson, 1929). The influence of Bechterev and Pavlov on Watson has already been mentioned. Watson began to formulate his views conversationally in 1903, gave them first public expression in 1905 to 1912, and first published them in 1913. Human behavior, learned and unlearned, with vigorous exclusion of introspective material, became a dominating force in American psychology under the enthusiastic sponsorship of Watson from about 1913 onward.

As behaviorism broadened, in the 1930's, from a school to a point of view without a school's ingroup manifestations, the next important figure to appear on the psychological scene was Clark L. Hull. In his autobiography (1952) Hull indicates how he came to his study of the quantitative laws of human behavior. He attributed his interest to his early training in the physical sciences; to being influenced favorably by Watson, although repelled by his dogmatism; and to reading Pavlov's *Conditioned Reflexes*, which had been translated in the late twenties. He goes on to indicate that about 1930 (after a considerable number of years of research endeavor on other problems) he came to the conclusion that the task of psychology as a natural science was the development of a "moderate" number of primary laws expressible quantitatively by means of ordinary equations, with the complex behavior of individuals to be derivable as secondary laws. His seminar became popular at the Institute of Human Relations at Yale University. Students, notably Kenneth W. Spence and Neal E. Miller, discussed this point of view with him, shared the general view, and conducted research along the lines laid down by Hull. It was to this program that he addressed the rest of the life work expressed in his three books (1940, 1943, 1951).

Of Hull's students Spence continued his work most directly; in a recent series of books surveying the present situation in psychology as a science a chapter is entitled, "The Hull-Spence Approach" (Logan, 1959). The work of Spence is highly systematic and detailed. He insists, more than did Hull, upon holding his theorizing more closely to the research data, extending his views only as new data become available (Logan, 1959). His general attitude, his techniques, and his methods are summarized in an article which shows by its title, his allegiance to a modified behaviorism (Spence, 1948).

Spence's collaborative studies with Janet A. Taylor serve to illustrate another historical point: sometimes the experimental foundations of clinical psychology are to be found in contemporary research which precedes the clinically significant research by only a few years. For example, Taylor and Spence, initiating their studies on the relation of manifest anxiety and learning, first reported on them in 1952 and 1953 (Taylor, 1953; Taylor and Spence, 1952). Taylor (1960) estimated that papers using the Manifest Anxiety Scale, published from 1952 through 1960, numbered about 300. Of these, 90 to 100 are quite directly concerned with the drive theory as proposed by Taylor and Spence. Their interest is and has been primarily in the role of drive in certain learning situations. Nevertheless, the extension of their work to the study of the phenomena of anxiety has also stimulated clinically oriented research—for example, that on the relationship of anxiety to stress.

Neal E. Miller, too, played an extensive role in the S-R reinforcement interpretation of learning. He has taken leadership in extending Hull's general point of view to approach-avoidance conflict behavior to psychotherapy and to social behavior. A recent account (Miller, 1959) covers his work on these problems.

B. F. Skinner is, of course, extremely important for much of the research reported in many chapters to follow. In 1959 he published a personal account of the development of his research approach. In his college days, although he had no courses in psychology, he had read about John B. Watson and studied Loeb and Pavlov. In his book he recounted these readings briefly, and next reported that he was at Harvard as a graduate student. It is plausible to infer, from this, that these men most influenced Skinner to follow a career in psychology. In another book (1953), which mentions remarkably few psychologists by name, Skinner refers only to Darwin, Freud, Pavlov, and Thorndike more than twice. All four men were cast in historical perspective and as initiating major developments in psychology. His dependence upon the work of Pavlov may be inferred from his early work, *The Behavior of Organisms* (1938). By 1938 he had some conception of his research plans for the future but had had only a few years to carry them out. As a consequence he had to depend upon the work of other men in his presentation. It would be no great exaggeration to say that in this work he referred to Pavlov as often as all other men combined.

Nevertheless, Skinner (1938, 1953) insists that the physiological activity which Pavlov thought he was studying was inferential. The processes being studied by Pavlov had not been reduced to neural events. No direct observations of the cortex are reported. In his view, Pavlov's achievement consisted, not in describing neural processes, but in formulating quantitative relations in behavior. It was in espousing the study of the behavior of the empty organism that he parted company with Pavlov. In short, it is unnecessary to concern oneself with physiological data in order to understand psychological phenomena. As Greenspoon put it, in introducing his chapter on verbal conditioning, Skinner made it possible to see verbal behavior as a response in its own right. Hefferline, in his statement of learning theory, speaks of work in the area less clogged with surplus meaning. Nevertheless, it should be noted in passing that this attempt to eliminate "physiologizing" has been criticized sharply by Pratt (1939), Kohler (1940) and Hebb (1949). The chapters in the section in this volume on psychophysiology show that there is still vigor to this approach. Moreover, the chapter by Hefferline attempts to demonstrate that Skinner's general approach is not vitiated by dealing with the internal environment.

It would appear that Pavlov's influence on relatively recent work in learning has been sufficiently demonstrated, but Darwin's more general influence has been neglected to this point. Before closing this discussion of learning some comment seems indicated.

As to the implications for later chapters of the work stimulated by Darwin, it is perhaps directly most pertinent to Levine's chapter on the effects of early experience upon adult behavior and to Wolpe's chapter on experimental approaches to neuroses. What began with the work following Darwin in the study of the continuity of mind in animals and man has reached such a degree of acceptance that these chapters are written without any except incidental reference to human subjects. Presumably only poorly controlled research exists with our species. Moreover, the feasibility of using much more radical experimental conditions than would be possible with humans is a compelling reason for the use of lower animals.

In his chapter Levine states that recent interest in his topic comes from Hebb's emphasis upon perceptual learning and the observations of European ethologists on early social stimulation and its later effect on various species of birds. This historical introduction should be significant to the clinician, who is apt to interpret present research in the perspective of his own interests. Hearing of the work on the effect of deprivation of animals and lacking historical information, the clinician might plausibly assume that the historical sequence was from Freud's theory of psychosexual stages to the work of Spitz, and thence to the animal work. He would thus be misled by what he thinks *should* have happened. The work on animal deprivation does indeed have clinical implications, but its historical roots are elsewhere. If the clinician does not appreciate the possibility that a problem with clinical significance may have a nonclinical origin, he would find much current work difficult to comprehend.

Communication

The chapter on small group research, by Petrullo, best illustrates the relation of communication research to clinical psychology. Clearly, in this area we are dealing simultaneously with a limited aspect of social psychology and with a special problem in learning. It is the social psychological aspect that will be stressed.

Murphy, Murphy, and Newcomb (1937) state that the first systematic studies of suggestion performed by Braid between 1841 and 1860 represent the inception of experimentation in social psychology. Braid (1899) rejected the concept of Mesmerism as magical in nature and invented the term "hypnotism" to describe the experimentally obtained phenomena. At one and the same time there occurred the beginning of experimentation in social psychology and the opening up of experimental research on a clinical problem. Following the work of Braid, there was a long procession of investigations concerned with related phenomena, including those by Ambroise-Auguste Liebeault, Hippolyte Bernheim, Jean Charcot, Pierre Janet, Boris Sidis, and Morton Prince. The work initiated by Bernheim had repercussions in other areas of psychology also. For example, Charcot's pupil, Gustave LeBon, stimulated by his teacher's doctrine of dissociation, found in it the explanation of crowd phenomena as a consequence of the splitting of personality (1895).

A slight trickle of experimental reports concerning group or communication problems appeared throughout the years until World War I. After the war, W. Moede and F. H. Allport independently advanced pleas that social psychology could and should be placed upon an experimental basis. Moede's work, beginning in 1913 with research on co-acting groups (as distinguished from face-to face groups), had priority over that of Allport (Allport, 1954). Moede (1920) studied the introduction of the social variable into standard experiments, such as the threshold of audibility. He did this by comparing the results obtained with subjects working alone with those found when subjects were working in groups of two or more. Using a similar experimental design, he studied imitation, fixation of attention, and learning. His work was not widely known in the United States, partly because the book that gives his major findings was not translated. Munsterberg, at Harvard, being familiar with his results, encouraged F. H. Allport to carry on studies in this area; these launched a whole series of studies (Allport, 1924).

Face-to-face studies were slower to appear than those on co-acting groups. In connection with priorities in this field, Allport (1954) states that the earliest experimental studies were performed by the Russians. They had been stimulated to this work by their concern for individual, as contrasted with collective, behavior—for example, the study of Bechterev and DeLange (1924). These studies, however, did not make much impression upon psychology in the United States.

Lewin's studies bring us almost to the present. His work, probably arrived at independently of the Russian work, stems directly from Gestalt tradition and to some extent from the work of Moreno (Moreno, 1952). Lewin and his co-workers introduced the concept of *social climate or group atmosphere* in a research setting. Thereafter this work was to have a pronounced effect on research in social psychology. Variation in productivity of subjects was studied under so-called "authoritarian," "democratic," and "laissez faire" working conditions (Lewin, Lippitt, & White, 1939). Despite the fact that unwarranted generalizations were derived from them, the studies have demonstrated that face-to-face groups could be studied under reasonably well controlled conditions.

Research expanded rapidly after the work of Lewin. Interest in research study spread to community, industrial, and therapeutic research settings. Group dynamics, group cohesion, group decision, and group conflict became intensively studied issues. In 1945 the Massachusetts Institute of Technology Research Center for Group Dynamics was established. In 1948, after the death of Lewin, the Center was moved to the University of Michigan. The Tavistock Institute, located in London, follows in some respects the Lewinian tradition. Under the joint sponsorship of the Center and the Institute a periodical, *Human Relations*, has appeared which is devoted to research in this area. Deutsch (1954) has written a very useful review of Lewin's work and that inspired by him in the setting of field theory as a way of thinking. These comments about small group research are extended in a later chapter in this volume by Petrullo. Because the "small group" includes within its rubric the face-to-face interaction of two individuals, this historical discussion is also relevant to the chapters by Matarazzo and by Strupp.

Behavior modification

"Behavior modification," as used as a section heading in this book, covers a multitude of approaches. It includes behavior modification as shown in the structured interview, in verbal conditioning, in the production of experimental neuroses, and in patient-doctor relationships. In a broader sense, the topic of behavior modification is related to the whole field of learning. Studies of behavior modification are studies of learning with a particular intent—the clinical goal of treatment. For example, Wolpe in his consideration of experimental approaches to the neuroses defines them as learned habits acquired in anxiety generating situations. In his chapter he discusses experimental neuroses and behavior therapy, including his own work in psychotherapy through reciprocal inhibition. In his book (1958) devoted to the topic Wolpe acknowledged his debt especially to Pavlov and to Hull, although Thorndike, Watson, Tolman, and Skinner are also specifically mentioned. The topic of behavior modification also has a close relation with communication in face-to-face pairs. It is, in fact, correct to say that the psychological study of behavioral modification began with the studies of Bernheim in the middle of the last century. Since his particular technique was that of hypnotic suggestion, a psychotherapeutic technique, his pioneer study is directly relevant.

The study of the behavioral effects of nonpsychological agents, such as drugs or operations, is an obscure and unwritten phase of the history of psychology. Although it is somewhat more peripheral in nature than the other matters considered here, it is fair to make at least one comment—in this area, the earliest work in the modern tradition was that of Kraepelin.

In a more specific way, recent research on behavioral modification is separable into two phases—the formal and the contentual. This is a distinction that we make in conversational behavior between *what* is said and *how* the speaker says it (Goldmann-Eissler, 1951). Formal analysis is concerned with how it is said and includes measurement of speed of talking, length of pauses, rate of talking, expressive movements, gestures, and facial expressions. Although studies of movements, gestures, and facial expressions are not unknown, in later chapters more attention is paid to the temporal relations in speaking.

Studies in the formal phase of behavioral modification were initiated by the work of Chapple (1939, 1940), an anthropologist, who published what he called the quantitative analysis of the interaction of individuals. At that time he was concerned neither with the interview nor with behavior modification. He saw the method of study he developed in the broader perspective of methodology for anthropological and social psychological study. Chapple (1939) saw as a weakness the fact that with the original primitive apparatus only two individuals could be studied simultaneously. The original studies (Chapple, 1939, 1940) were designed to give the durations of "actions" and "inactions" for calculation of the cumulative plot and the subsequent study and interpretation of the slope of the curves obtained. Later this interaction method was applied to the interview and behavior modification. By 1946 (Chapple, 1946) was referring to the period of time with the subjects as an "interview." This interaction method in the interview forms the basis for the studies reported in a later chapter by Matarazzo. Since this chapter contains a thorough review, attention hereafter will now be directed to the contentual phases of research on behavior modification.

The research study of the contentual phase of behavior modification by psychotherapy is a relatively new development. Its recent appearance cannot be attributed to a lack of an earlier literature on psychotherapy. Psychotherapy had been recognized as a specialized technique at least as early as the temple medicine of the Greeks in about the fifth century before Christ. Its rich history is attested to in various detailed accounts (e.g., Bromberg, 1954; Zilboorg and Henry, 1941). Nor was an extensive modern professional literature lacking. Individual psychotherapy has been a concern for a large number of clinical workers for a considerable number of years. A vast literature was already developing before 1940. Moreover, psychologists, as distinguished from other clinicians, had been engaging in psychotherapy and recounting their experiences with it since before 1910, as witness the work of Boris Sidis and Walter Dill Scott (Watson, 1953). Material was available on many issues and problems, even for as specialized a problem as group psychotherapy, for Slavson (1950) was able to cite forty articles published from 1905 to 1939. Nevertheless, until quite recently the published work relied on anecdotal methods supplemented by gross statistical findings. In evaluating psychoanalytic therapy as late as 1941, Knight (1941) reported an evaluation in which he had to fall back upon brochures of various institutes and a count of the number "cured," "better," and the like for his sources of information. Pleas for a research approach to the contentual phase of behavior modification had been made directly or indirectly in the twenties and thirties by Lasswell (1929, 1933, 1936, 1938), Rosenzweig (1937), Saul (1939), and Symonds (1939). In fact, Lasswell (1933, 1936) went beyond this appeal to report some data on electrically recorded psychoanalytic sessions.

It was a psychologist, Carl Rogers, who in 1942, through a book

(1942a) and an article (1942b), launched the research approach in behavioral modification through psychotherapy.*

Rogers' work needs no review here; we will move, instead, to a brief evaluation of early workers who influenced him. It is fashionable when speaking of Rogers to allege his debt to Otto Rank, to Jessie Taft, and possibly to Frederick Allen. All of these are nonpsychologists. To my inquiry concerning his indebtedness to psychology, Rogers (1960) replied, in a personal communication:

> So far as psychology goes, I guess I would say that Goodwin Watson and Leta Hollingworth of Teachers College, Columbia, both had real impact on me. E. K. Wickman of the Institute for Child Guidance was another psychologist whose thinking had some effect on me. Watson was very independent in his thinking and gave his students a great deal of freedom. Leta Hollingworth was an excellent clinician. Wickman was the careful, thoughtful, cautious researcher, though not a research man in a laboratory sense.

These three psychologists shared the tendency, which Rogers attributes to Wickman, to carry their research beyond the laboratory. None of them would be called an experimental psychologist in the narrow sense. Yet all three shared in that laboratory tradition through the training they themselves had received, and all three maintained familiarity with experimental work. It is as if Rogers had grandparents who were from among the experimentalists. Directly relevant to the issue at hand is a thoughtful article by Rogers (1955) written to describe the conflict and resulting gap that he felt existed between his work as a psychotherapist and his work as a researcher. His personal reconciliation, recounted therein, is an exercise in the reconciliation of the clinical and experimental traditions.

Rogers' work typifies still another way that the experimental tradition in psychology operates. He brought to the problem of psychotherapy neither a particular approach nor a problem analogous to an early experimental one, but a tendency to transfer his research training. He and his students, challenged by the problem of quantification of the process of psychotherapy, used ingeniously a variety of psychological tools—recording devices, rating scales, and so on—to attack the problem. They approached it with an internalized experimental tradition and, basing their methods on this tradition, proceeded to work with the materials of clinical psychology.

---

* Five years earlier (1937) Rogers had reported on three statistical surveys he had performed preparatory, he said, to the study of the treatment of child guidance clinic cases "as it is actually carried out" (1937, p. 48). The unpublished doctoral dissertation dated 1941 by E. H. Porter, Jr., carried out under Rogers' direction, developed and evaluated a measure of counselor responses (Rogers, 1942b).

Rogers' influence upon his own students and others is direct and obvious in many instances. It probably influenced many other psychologists who by no stretch of the imagination could be called "Rogerian." Many research studies bearing no direct obligation to his particular work but stimulated by it, came about once it was realized that Rogers had made a "breakthrough" in this area of research, although these studies were quite different in nature.

By definition this chapter has been concerned with the past. The experimental researches significant to the extended present are yet to come in the remainder of the book. Nevertheless, if we are to go beyond antiquarian interests, even this chapter has had to be concerned with the significance of the past for the present, and concerned with this in a variety of ways. Throughout, the author has tried to keep in the forefront the men and the issues to which they addressed themselves—the two major aspects of any historical account in psychology.

References

Allport, F. H. Social psychology. Boston: Houghton Mifflin, 1924.

Allport, G. W. The historical background of modern social psychology. In G. Lindzey (Ed.), Handbook of social psychology. Vol. 1. Reading, Mass.: Addison Wesley, 1954, 3–56.

Angell, J. R. The province of functional psychology. Psychol. Rev., 1907, 14, 61–91.

Bechterev, V. M. General principles of human reflexology. (Trans. 4th Russian ed.), New York: International Publishers, 1932.

Bechterev, V. M., & De Lange, M. Die Erbegnisse des experiments auf dem Gebiete der kollektiven Reflexologie. Z. angew. Psychol., 1924, 24, 305–344.

Beck, S. J., & Molish, H. B. Reflexes to intelligence: a reader in clinical psychology. Glencoe, Ill.: Free Press, 1959.

Bindra, D., & Scheier, I. H. The relation between psychometric and experimental research in psychology. Amer. Psychologist, 1954, 9, 69–71.

Boring, E. G. Introspection in dementia praecox. Amer. J. Psychol., 1913a, 26, 145.

Boring, E. G. Learning in dementia praecox. Psychol. Monogr., 1913b, 5, No. 63.

Boring, E. G. The influence of evolutionary theory upon American psychological thought. In S. Persons (Ed.), Evolutionary thought in America. New Haven, Conn.: Yale Univ. Press, 1950, 268–298.

Boring, E. G. A history of experimental psychology. (2nd ed.). New York: Appleton-Century-Crofts, 1957.

Braid, J. Neurypnology. (Rev. ed.), London: Redway, 1899. (Originally published 1843.)

Bromberg, W. Man above humanity: a history of psychotherapy. New York: Lippincott, 1954.

Chapple, E. D. Quantitative analysis of the interaction of individuals. Proc. Nat. Acad. Sci., 1939, 25, 58–67.

Chapple, E. D. "Personality" differences as described by invariant properties of individuals in interaction. Proc. Nat. Acad. Sci., 1940, 26, 10–16.

Chapple, E. D., & Donald, G., Jr. A method for evaluating supervisory personnel. Harvard Bus. Rev., 1946, 24, 197–214.

Cronbach, L. J. The two disciplines of scientific psychology. *Amer. Psychologist*, 1957, *12*, 671–684.

Dennis, W., & Boring, E. G. The founding of the APA. *Amer. Psychologist*, 1952, *7*, 95–97.

Deutsch, M. Field theory in social psychology. In G. Lindzey (Ed.), *Handbook of social psychology*. Vol. 1. Reading, Mass.: Addison Wesley, 1954, 181–222.

Dewey, J. The reflex arc concept in psychology. *Psychol. Rev.*, 1896, *3*, 357–370.

Franz, S. I. On the functions of the cerebrum: the frontal lobes in relation to the production and retention of simple sensory-motor habits. *Amer. J. Physiol.*, 1902, *8*, 1–22.

Franz, S. I. *Handbook of mental examination methods.* (2nd ed.). New York: Macmillan, 1919.

Franz, S. I. Shepard Ivory Franz. In C. Murchison (Ed.), *A history of psychology in autobiography*. Vol. II. Worcester: Clark Univ. Press, 1932, 89–113.

Goldman-Eissler, Frieda. The measurement of time sequences in conversational behavior. *Brit. J. Psychol.*, 1951, *42*, 355–362.

Hall, G. S. Laboratory of the McLean Hospital. *Amer. J. Insanity*, 1894, *51*, 358–364.

Hebb, D. O. *The organization of behavior*. New York: Wiley, 1949.

Herodotus. History (Trans. by G. Rawlinson.) In R. M. Hutchins (Ed.), *Great books of the western world*. Chicago: Encyclopaedia Britannica, 1952.

Hilgard, E. R., & Marquis, D. G. *Conditioning and learning*. New York: Appleton-Century-Crofts, 1940.

Hull, C. L. *Principles of behavior*. New York: Appleton-Century-Crofts, 1943.

Hull, C. L. *Essentials of behavior*. New Haven, Conn.: Yale Univ. Press, 1951.

Hull, C. L. Clark L. Hull. In Boring, E. G., *et al.* (Eds.), *A history of psychology in autobiography*. Vol. IV.

Worcester, Mass.: Clark Univ. Press, 1952, 143–162.

Hull, C. L., *et al.*, *Mathematico-deductive theory of rote learning*. New Haven, Conn.: Yale Univ. Press, 1940.

Hunt, J. McV. Psychological experiments with disordered persons. *Psychol. Bull.*, 1936, *33*, 1–58.

Hunt, W. A. Anchoring effects in esthetic judgment. *Amer. J. Psychol.*, 1941, *44*, 395–403.

Hunt, W. A. Personal communication, 1960.

Hunt, W. A., & Volkmann, J. The anchoring of an affective scale. *Amer. J. Psychol.*, 1937, *49*, 88–92.

Kahn, E. Emil Kraepelin, February 15, 1856–October 7, 1926–February 15, 1956. *Amer. J. Psychiat.*, 1956, *113*, 289–294.

Knight, R. P. Evaluation of the results of psychoanalytic therapy. *Amer. J. Psychiat.*, 1941, *98*, 434–446.

Kohler, W. *Dynamics in psychology*. New York: Liveright, 1940.

Kraepelin, E. Der psychologische Versuch in der Psychiatrie. *Psychol. Arb., Leipzig*, 1895, *1*, 1–91.

Lasswell, H. D. The problem of adequate personality records: a proposal. *Amer. J. Psychiat.*, 1929, *85*, 1057–1066.

Lasswell, H. D. Verbal references and physiological changes during the psychoanalytic interview: a preliminary communication. *Psychoanal. Rev.*, 1935, *22*, 10–24.

Lasswell, H. D. Certain prognostic changes during trial (psychoanalytic) interviews. *Psychoanal. Rev.*, 1936, *23*, 229–293.

Lasswell, H. D. A provisional classification of symbol data. *Psychiatry*, 1938, *1*, 197–204.

LeBon, G. *Psychologie des foules*. Paris: Olean, 1895.

Lewin, K., Lippitt, R., & White, R. Patterns of aggressive behavior in experimentally created "social climates." *J. soc. Psychol.*, 1939, *10*, 271–299.

Logan, F. A. The Hull-Spence approach. In S. Koch (Ed.), *Psychology: a study of a science, Study 1, conceptual and systematic:* Vol. 2, *general systematic formulations, learning and special processes.* New York: McGraw-Hill, 1959, 293–358.

Miller, N. E. Liberalization of basic S-R concepts: extensions to conflict behavior, motivation and social learning. In S. Koch (Ed.), *Psychology: a study of a science, Study 1, conceptual and systematic:* Vol. 2, *general systematic formulation, learning and special processes.* New York: McGraw-Hill, 1959, 196–292.

Moede, W. *Experimentelle Massenpsychologie.* Leipzig: Hirzel, 1920.

Moreno, J. L. How Kurt Lewin's "Research Center for Group Dynamics" started and the question of paternity. *Group Psychotherapy,* 1952, 5, 1–6.

Murphy, G. *Historical introduction to modern psychology.* (Rev. ed.) New York: Harcourt, Brace, 1949.

Murphy, G., Murphy, Lois B., & Newcomb, T. M. *Experimental social psychology.* (Rev. ed.) New York: Harper, 1937.

Pavlov, I. P. *Conditioned reflexes.* London: Oxford Univ. Press, 1927.

Pavlov, I. P. *Selected works.* (K. S. Kostoyants, Ed.) Moscow: Foreign Languages Publishing House, 1955.

Pratt, C. C. *The logic of modern psychology.* New York: Macmillan, 1939.

Rogers, C. R. Three surveys of treatment measures used with children. *Amer. J. Orthopsychiat.,* 1937, 7, 48–57.

Rogers, C. R. *Counseling and psychotherapy: newer concepts in practice.* Boston: Houghton Mifflin, 1942a.

Rogers, C. R. The use of electrically recorded interviews in improving psychotherapeutic technique. *Amer. J. Orthopsychiat.,* 1942b, 12, 429–435.

Rogers, C. R. Persons or science? A philosophical question. *Amer. Psychologist,* 1955, 10, 267–278.

Rogers, C. R. Personal communication, 1960.

Rosenzweig, M. R. Pavlov, Bechterev, and Twitmyer on conditioning. *Amer. J. Psychol.,* 1960, 73, 312–316.

Rosenzweig, S. The experimental study of psychoanalytic concepts. *Char. & Person.,* 1937, 6, 61–71.

Saul, L. J. Psychoanalytic case records. *Psychoanal. Quart.,* 1939, 8, 186–190.

Sherif, M. *The psychology of social norms.* New York: Harper, 1936.

Skinner, B. F. *The behavior of organisms: an experimental analysis.* New York: Appleton-Century, 1938.

Skinner, B. F. *Science and human behavior.* New York: Macmillan, 1953.

Skinner, B. F. A case history in scientific method. In S. Koch (Ed.), *Psychology: a study of a science, Study 1, conceptual and systematic:* vol. 2. *general systematic formulations, learning and special processes.* New York: McGraw-Hill, 1959, 359–379.

Slavson, S. R. Bibliography of group psychotherapy. *Group Ther. Brochure,* 1950, No. 32.

Spence, K. W. The postulates and methods of behaviorism. *Psychol. Rev.,* 1948, 55, 67–78.

Symonds, P. M. Research in the interviewing process. *J. educ. Psychol.,* 1939, 30, 346–353.

Taylor, Janet A. A personality scale of manifest anxiety. *J. abnorm. soc. Psychol.,* 1953, 48, 285–290.

Taylor, Janet A. Personal communication, 1960.

Taylor, Janet A., & Spence, K. W. The relationship of anxiety level to performance in serial learning. *J. exp. Psychol.,* 1952, 44, 61–64.

Warden, C. J. *A short outline of comparative psychology.* New York: Norton, 1927.

Watson, J. B. The place of the conditioned-reflex in psychology. *Psychol. Rev.,* 1916, 23, 89–116.

Watson, J. B. *Psychology from the standpoint of a behaviorist.* (3rd ed. rev.) Philadelphia: Lippincott, 1929.

Watson, R. I. A brief history of clinical psychology. *Psychol. Bull.,* 1953, 50, 321–346.

Watson, R. I. Historical review of objective personality testing: the search for objectivity. In B. M. Bass, & I. A. Berg (Eds.), *Objective approaches to personality assessment.* Princeton, N.J.: Van Nostrand, 1959a, 1–23.

Watson, R. I. *The psychology of the child: personal, social and disturbed child development.* New York: Wiley, 1959b.

Watson, R. I. *The great psychologists: from Aristotle to Freud.* New York: Lippincott, 1961. To be published.

Wells, H. K. *Ivan P. Pavlov: toward a scientific psychology and psychiatry.* New York: International Publishers, 1956.

Wever, E. G., & Zener, K. E. Method of absolute judgment in psychophysics. *Psychol. Rev.,* 1928, *35,* 466–493.

Wolpe, J. *Psychotherapy by reciprocal inhibition.* Stanford, Calif.: Stanford Univ. Press, 1958.

Zilboorg, G., & Henry, G. W. *A history of medical psychology.* New York: Norton, 1941.

2

The Experimental
Investigation of Clinical Judgment

WILLIAM A. HUNT and NELSON F. JONES

The contributors to this volume offer vivid testimony to the wide range of psychological interest in the experimental investigation of mal-adjusted behavior. As a rule clinicians have been concerned more with patient behavior than with their own behavior in the clinical situation. Yet the subjective decisions of the clinician himself—as instanced in the interpretation of projective tests, in the use of interview techniques, in diagnosis, and in the constant procedural decisions of therapy—are influenced by other factors than the patient's behavior.

The attempt to study the reliability and validity of the subjective processes of clinical judgment has met with some resistance, particularly from those clinicians who perform primarily service functions and rely heavily upon interpretive decisions in their daily duties. Such resistance would appear to stem from the normal expected insecurity in the individual who is frequently forced to make clinical decisions on his own responsibility with relatively little extraneous support or reinforcement, particularly where the decisions have im-

This study was done as part of a broader investigation of the nature of clinical judgment supported by the Office of Naval Research under contract 7 onr-450 (11) with Northwestern University. While the opinions expressed here are the responsibility of the authors, their gratitude is expressed to their colleagues, Stanley Blumberg, Harry Grayson, Roy Hamlin, Donald Johnson, Lee Sechrest, Frederick Thorne, and Ronald Walker, who, as members of a study group meeting on the Northwestern campus in August 1960 to discuss clinical judgment, were kind enough to offer their criticisms of some of the material contained herein.

portant consequences for other human lives. In clinical medicine the professional culture has developed buffer mechanisms to protect the doctor—for example, the concepts of medical authority and responsibility and the firm code defining malpractice. Psychology has not reached a like stage of professional maturity, however, and its defenses are apt to be expressed in an intellectual, philosophical position rather than in clearly defined codes of professional behavior.

Thus the clinical psychologist who is defending his intuitive procedures from experimental investigation tends to use rational argument designed to prove that such subjective processes are beyond the possibility of scientific research. Several notable psychological controversies have sprung up concerning the definition of intuition, the uniqueness of the individual and the inherent difficulties this offers to prediction, and the relative predictive efficiency of the "clinical" and "actuarial" approaches. As usual, much of this argument reduces to semantic confusion, but some basic issues are involved, issues on which the experimentally oriented clinical psychologist must take a stand before he can outline a comprehensive and consistent program of research in the area of clinical judgment. We propose to review these issues below, making clear the theoretical context within which our work has developed.

THE BASIC ISSUES

Perhaps the most basic issue for the psychologist doing research in the field of clinical judgment is whether or not the processes of judgment are open to scientific investigation. In the past there has been a tendency to view clinical judgment as a special means of knowledge different from the ordinary processes of human judgment. This has been encouraged by the phrase "clinical *intuition*," with intuition viewed as a direct means of understanding, an immediate, empathic revelation that bypasses the usual empirically based decision processes associated with evaluation in the other sciences.

This view of intuition is in the Germanic tradition and finds its main support in the work of the German cultural historians, such as Dilthey, who oppose the *Geisteswissenschaftlich* method of intuitive interpretation to the rigid documentary approach of the natural sciences or *Naturwissenschaften*. It becomes most explicit in the writings of Spranger on personality and value types. Spranger proposes a method of understanding or *Verstehen* which is direct and immediate as contrasted with the mediate processes of natural science.

The source of the problem lies in the fact that so much of the inferential activity of the clinician proceeds at an unconscious level and thereby exposes itself to a mystical interpretation if the clinician is so inclined. As we have said elsewhere, "Actually, intuition can never be divorced from its empirical backgrounds. This immediate act of knowledge is permitted to physicians, but only after many years of medical school and post-graduate residence. It is permitted to the clinical psychologist in interpreting his test results, but only after he has experienced the same testing situation with many subjects" (Hunt, 1951). Even in Spranger one finds that the act of understanding can come only after an extensive experience of the individual being understood. Factual knowledge concerning the person must be acquired and assimilated before the empathic evaluation can be rendered. This certainly smacks of the orderly processes of rational judgment, even though the experiential bases for the judgment may not be conscious at the time it is made.

Even Bruner, who gives intuition a sympathetic treatment as a process of immediate apprehension implying "the act of grasping the meaning, significance, or structure of a problem or situation without explicit reliance on the analytic apparatus of one's craft" and who views it as a complementary mode to analytic thinking, is quick to point out that "the rightness or wrongness of an intuition is finally decided not by intuition itself but by the usual methods of proof." He concludes that "In the end, intuition by itself yields a tentative ordering of a body of knowledge that, while it may generate a feeling that the ordering of facts is self-evident, aids principally by giving us a basis for moving ahead in our testing of reality" (Bruner, 1960).

Experimental evidence that rational inference can go on at an unconscious level has a long history, beginning with Helmholtz, who called it *unbewusste Schluss,* up to our modern work on probability learning. Certainly this history refutes the notion that intuition has a mystical element. As the mystical explanation decayed over the years, the use of the phrase "clinical intuition" diminished and has been supplanted by "clinical judgment" or "clinical decision." The clinician of today is on firm ground in viewing his judgmental processes as a natural behavioral phenomenon open to all the investigative procedures of experimental psychology. A like trend has developed in medicine (Ledley & Lusted, 1959). While such terms as unconscious, awareness, verbal report, etc., may need further careful differentiation before research in the area is given any exact interpretation, the general situation has been nicely stated by Eriksen in a recent article on "Discrimination and Learning Without Awareness," in which he concludes:

> A science of personality is not furthered by the frequent tendency of psychologists to discuss the "unconscious" with all the ambiguity and reverence that religions accord to the soul. There is great need to spell out explicitly the assumed characteristics of the unconscious and to search for explanations of so called unconscious phenomena

in terms of more commonplace psychological variables. To do so may destroy the titillating mystery that the unconscious seems to hold but then that is the business of science (Eriksen, 1960).

Having decided that clinical judgment is a lawful phenomenon amenable to experimental study, the investigator next comes face to face with two controversies that strike at the usefulness of the subjective judgmental processes of the clinician performing clinical services.

The first is the idiographic-nomothetic controversy, revolving around the uniqueness of the individual. If, as Gordon Allport proposes, the human being "is *inevitably, ineffably,* and *ineluctably* unique" (Allport, 1960), how can we gather the repetitive, nomothetic data that are demanded by science if we are to have valid prediction? Allport himself has never denied the possibility of prediction in the study and control of personality. With him it would be a matter of limits—of how much prediction, in what circumstances, and to what purpose. The idiographic argument, however, is seized upon by some defensive clinicians to deny any possibility of prediction, and hence to discourage the scientifically oriented clinician from the experimental study of a basic clinical technique, while encouraging the non-scientifically oriented clinician "in the carefree practice of a happy technique which necessitates no evaluative fore- or afterthought since it lies outside the realm of empirical validation" (Hunt, 1959). Fortunately the difficulty is largely a semantic one.

The case for uniqueness in human behavior has been grossly overstated. There is sufficient commonality in the behavior of any one patient over time, in the behavior of groups of patients at a given time, in the behavior of any clinician over time, or in groups of clinicians at a given time to make it possible to gather the repetitive data and establish the probability inferences required to make useful and valid predictions.

Although common and duplicable elements are present in many clinical situations, it is, nevertheless, difficult to evaluate prediction in an individual case. The clinician makes a diagnostic prediction involving a certain patient at a certain instant of time. The proponents of the idiographic position would argue that since the patient is unique and the particular instant of time will never be repeated we cannot obtain the sequential data demanded for a probability inference. We cannot answer the question "What are the chances of the clinician's prediction being correct?" On the surface, this seems true, but there is a way out of our dilemma. The logicians have a solution called the "transfer of meaning" whereby we transfer the actuarial locus from the patient to the clinician. Admittedly, we cannot obtain a probability estimate from the single case; however, the clinician makes many judgments in many cases, and, from a tabulation of his successes and errors, we can set up a probability weighting for his successes over a number of cases. This probability statement can then be transferred to the single instance. If he is correct nine times out of ten over a recorded series of judgments, we can then assume that the chances are 9 to 1 that he will be correct in any particular prediction.

In logical terms we have set the clinician up as a reference class from which can be obtained the sequential data demanded in order that we may establish a probability inference which we then attach through a "transfer of meaning" to the single case. To improve the accuracy of our probability inference we may narrow our reference class by limiting our observations more specifically. Instead of tabulating all instances of our clinician's predictions we may confine our tabulations to his predictions in a certain setting such as an outpatient clinic as opposed to a hospital, to predictions made where test results were available to be used in his decision, or to his judgments upon certain classes of patients, such as schizophrenics. As Reichenbach (1951) points out, such transfers are justified by expediency for purposes of action and represent the actual procedures used in applying statistics to individual cases. They successfully remove us from the horns of our predictive dilemma, and permit us to handle the idiographic prediction in nomothetic fashion.

Sarbin, Taft, and Bailey have summarized the danger of the idiographic position nicely in commenting on what they call the "clinician's" approach—"that his intentions are idiographic: that he is interested in the 'whole' personality, in 'understanding' rather than prediction; in the unique; in configurations of traits; in intuition; and that the test of knowledge is internal consistency, affective congruence, or logical coherence. This resolution only takes the idiographer out of the arena of science" (Sarbin, *et al;* 1960, p. 256).

Perhaps more damaging to morale is the attitude represented by such writers as Meehl and Cronbach who hold that the subjective techniques involving the use of clinical judgment cannot hope to compete in efficiency and validity with those objective techniques based upon the use of testing procedures whose results are interpreted through the use of actuarial tables. This is the clinical-actuarial controversy. It is best represented in Meehl's book, *Clinical versus Statistical Prediction,* where he states lucidly and convincingly the logical argument for the statistical approach backed by actuarial tables as a basis for making clinical decisions (Meehl, 1954). He also quotes comparative data from several studies showing the superior performance of actuarial methods. While his faith in these techniques has waned of late (Meehl, 1960), he is still a leading advocate of the actuarial or "cookbook" method (Meehl and Dahlstrom, 1960).

There is both a theoretical and a practical side to this argument, however. Theoretically, at a purely abstract level, it must be conceded that the actuarial technique is the one of ideal choice, although it, too, may have its limitations in any practical, operating situation. It would place all clinical decision-making firmly upon an objective, scientific footing and would give clinical prediction the same accuracy and authority as prediction in the physical sciences. Combined with modern computer practices it could automatize and render relatively foolproof much of clinical diagnosis and prediction. But this goal remains an ideal currently unattainable at this stage in the development of clinical psychology.

The main reasons would seem to be four:

1. To date the actuarial approach can be applied only in those limited areas where adequately developed tests permit its use. Ahead of us, if we are to use it widely, lies a tremendous task of test development and subsequent empirical construction of actuarial tables. Meehl presents the Minnesota Multiphasic Personality Inventory as the test best suited for actuarial purposes at present. But its development has taken years of effort and the expenditure of innumerable thousands of dollars, and it is still not a finished product. Of necessity we will have to rely on subjective clinical decision-making in many areas for many years.

2. New and creative discoveries cannot spring from actuarial procedures alone. Clinical "hunches" and "insights" will be necessary if we are to discover and explore new dimensions of behavior. In a very real sense clinical judgment as an exploring, probing technique is a necessary forerunner of any actuarial development. This is what Bruner means when he speaks of the complementary nature of intuitive and analytic thinking and depicts intuition as a "basis for moving ahead in our testing of reality" (Bruner, 1960).

3. As research continually improves our understanding of the judgmental processes, clinical judgment itself can be improved, can be rendered more objective and precise. By the introduction of scaling methods, for instance as we have done, subjective evaluation can be given objective numerical representation and the way prepared for the actuarial treatment of subjective clinical appraisals (Hunt, 1956).

4. Public opinion still distrusts the judgment of man by machine or by rote statistical formula, and demands that man be judged by man in many situations. It will take time to change this picture.

None of these points negates the value of the actuarial method in its proper field and where and when possible. They do point to the continued partnership of clinical and statistical techniques in any foreseeable future.

THE CHOICE OF METHOD OR MODEL

Having convinced ourselves that clinical judgment is a researchable phenomenon, we are faced with the problem of finding a model or method of approach to give our research direction and order. Any definition of intuition that would bring it within the range of scientific investigation would make it synonymous with judgment, which term has the advantage not only of being preferred usage today but of lacking the handicap of mystical surplus meaning carried by intuition.

A plausible choice would be the use of a model drawn from formal logic where clinical judgment would be patterned after the processes of syllogistic reasoning. An elegant and detailed treatment of such a model recently has been offered by Sarbin, Taft, and Bailey who adopt "the formal inference model to a description of the process of clinical inference . . . " (Sarbin, *et al.*, 1960, p. 46). They break down the inferential process into the following divisions: the postulate system of the person doing the inferring; the construction of a major premise; observation for the detection of occurrences (inputs or cues); the process of instantiation or categorization whereby the input is recognized as having class membership; the inferential product deriving from such class membership; and the prediction resulting therefrom. Crucial to the model are the concepts of the "cue" as an input unit critical to the process of instantiation, of the process of "instantiation" itself whereby the occurrence or cue is converted into an instance of a general class making possible an inferential conclusion, and the concept of "module" or cognitive organization (category, abstract, idea, etc.) which is the cognitive counterpart of the organization or objects in the environment. Instantiation occurs when the cue is aligned with the appropriate module.

Although this model enables the authors to make an excellent rational analysis of the process of clinical judgment, it offers little in the way of an experimental approach. The greater body of the experimental literature on judgment is not referred to and no attempt has been made to integrate it with the model, with the exception of the definition and delimitation of cognitive space as represented by the modules. Here, their uses of factor analytic techniques, the semantic differential, etc., for mapping modules are stimulating and suggestive, but the authors in general omit any other experimental emphasis.

Thus the inferential model not only remains on an abstract, rational level but has the added danger of removing the treatment of clinical judgment from the main stream of experimental psychology. We feel that any satisfactory model would be one that would pull the study of clinical judgment into the arena of experimentation rather than increase its isolation from it.

Actually, since the investigation of clinical judgment is still in an exploratory stage, the adoption now of any mathematical model would be premature. For example, it might seem profitable to adopt a mathematical model from current information theory as Hoffman (1960) has done, but more careful analysis of our current understanding of clinical judgment indicates that the cues or inputs crucial to the judgmental situation cannot yet be identified with enough accuracy to permit their experimental control. Thus our own work on the relationship between amount of information available and the reliability and validity of judgment is seriously handicapped by our inability to specify exactly how much of what is being varied (Jones, 1959). The same difficulty would appear to be true of any model available from current decision theory, although eventually fruitful analogies may be drawn from these fields and be valuable in the further understanding of the clinical process.

The mention of analogies is suggestive, and introduces our own solution to the problem. We wanted an approach that would draw clinical judgment out of its isolation as an independent clinical phenomenon and into the main stream of contemporary experimental psychology, that would relate it to other psychological functions and areas of research, thus offering us both new and applicable data for the further understanding of clinical judgment, and new and applicable designs and methods for its further investigation. This has led us to what we have chosen to call the Analogical Approach.

THE ANALOGICAL APPROACH

The assumptions underlying our analogical approach are first, that clinical judgment is related to other known phenomena studied in the psychological laboratory, and second, that the research techniques and experimental findings from these other areas may be applied to the clinical area. We have already drawn a fruitful analogy between clinical judgment and psychophysical judgment. It has been possible to apply some of the findings of psychophysics to the clinical situation, and in turn to apply some of the insights obtained in the clinical area to psychophysics (Hunt, 1959).

It is a well-established fact in psychophysics that errors in judgment may be caused by context effects. We have been able to demonstrate such context effects in clinical judgment as well, and to show that resistance to such errors is a function both of professional experience, and of experience in the performance of the specific rating task involved (Jones, 1957). In the course of our work with context effects we have uncovered a phenomenon of assimilation, opposed to the classical contrast effect, and this in turn has been demonstrated subsequently in a psychophysical setting (Campbell, *et al*, 1958).

The psychophysical analogy is not the only one available. We are currently investigating the applicability of learning theory to some aspects of the judgmental process (Hunt & Blumberg, in press). As yet, the results are perhaps more puzzling than enlightening, but the analogy is proving to be both promising and stimulating. A further analogy may well be made between clinical judgment and perception, although here, as in information and decision theory, the problem of cue isolation and definition must be solved first. The general approach by analogy is proving profitable, however, and it does succeed in firmly anchoring the processes of clinical judgment within the classical laboratory findings of experimental psychology.

In foregoing the choice of a formal logical or mathemathical model, we commit ourselves to a frankly empirical approach which lacks the elegance of a comprehensive, integrated structure such as the Sarbin, Taft, and Bailey logical model. But we feel that, at this stage of our knowledge, data is more important than theory. To put it frankly, at this point we would rather have data than a name for them. We advocate, not a sterile "dust bowl" empiricism, but an active program of experimental investigation. Whatever our analogical method may lack in subtlety, it is providing us with the usable findings that must be gathered before any fruitful systematic elaboration can be attempted.

In dealing with the relationship between the clinical and the psychophysical areas of judgment we have taken the position that:

> They are merely the opposite poles of a rough continuum, a quantitative continuum marked by the clarity and specificity with which the stimuli are defined, by the degree to which the judgmental setting is standardized through careful control of the known pertinent variables and the elimination of extraneous cues, and by the provision of uniform modes of reporting or response that lend themselves to convenient mathematical treatment (Hunt, 1959)

or, stated in more homely terms:

> The differences are ones of quantity rather than kind, that they are contrasting in amount rather than conflicting in nature, and that the clinical judgment is a culturally and educational handicapped country cousin of the psychophysical judgment, and not a different species of being.

The application of the psychophysical analogue will by no means furnish us with a complete and systematic body of knowledge. Too little is known about judgment in both its general and its specifically clinical aspects. While the result may be disappointing, it should not be disillusioning. The subject is researchable, and there is no better way to approach an area to be investigated than by mapping the areas of ignorance. That, in the field of clinical decision-making, these areas are vast should make the challenge more interesting.

THE PSYCHOPHYSICAL MODEL— STIMULUS IDENTIFICATION

Nowhere is the paucity of our information concerning the actual nature of clinical judgment more evident than in the matter of stimulus identification, description, and control. In psychophysics, we have extensive knowledge and exact control of the physical stimuli commonly used; in the the clinical situation we are dealing with largely unknown, or at best ill-defined, stimulus elements whose control and manipulation consequently must be rough and inexact. Under the heading stimulus identification we shall attempt to show how a number of recent studies, all dealing with the effect of the stimulus on judgment, illustrate the steps toward cue isolation which have actually been taken in clinical judgment. Efforts to sort out, from the necessarily global and complex stimulus situations with which the clinician must deal, the specific identifiable "part stimuli" which provide the real cues for judgment have led us to classify the source materials roughly as biographical data, test scores, and behavioral measures.

A number of questions arise concerning the use of biographical data in formulating clinical decisions. The first of these is whether the information is to be used as a collection of objectively verifiable vital statistics from which clinical decisions are to be made directly, or as information which is to modify and supplement test or behavioral data.

In the first case it would seem that the most reasonable means of treating biographical data is a purely actuarial combining. This could provide the most likely outcome for any given constellation of biographical facts, as well as identify other less likely possibilities which might arise out of them. We would thus assign confidence weights to any particular formulation much as the clinician does, while at the same time utilizing the advantages of the mechanical processes spelled out by Meehl (1954).

Generally, opinion holds that the clinician is better able to interpret related information if he has a background of biographical data about his patient. Some studies confirm this opinion; others have shown just the opposite. Kostlan (1954) showed by a system of progressive elimination of available information that better-than-chance decisions on the truthfulness of statements about a patient's behavior could be made with "minimal" information consisting of the patient's age, marital status, occupation, education, and source of referral. When test results were used as the basis for the same judgments, only the addition of a full social history allowed the clinician to make better inferences than he had done using the "minimal" information. This would indicate that biographical data alone may be sufficient for some judgments, and certainly indicates that it is a valuable addition to test interpretation. Similarly, Sines (1959) found that a biographical data sheet provided the basis for better-than-chance decisions about patients' personalities; and that interview data, not defined except as "historical," always added to accuracy when the same judgments were made on the basis of test results.

On the other hand, King, et al. (1952), found that background data on children being observed, when given to either or both of two judges observing them, lowered the initially high reliability with which the judges were able to agree upon the presence or absence of a number of socially relevant variables such as emotionality, aggression, anxiety, etc. Thus biographical data are not clearly established as either a help or a hindrance to effective judgment from test material or from observation. The notion that information from this source is inevitably helpful must be examined more closely. Possibly the question, of "How much and what kind of biographical data will be helpful in interpreting information from other sources?" is the proper one to be investigated. Cues included in biographical data may facilitate only certain kinds of information and inhibit other kinds.

A second major source of cues, that most frequently claimed by the clinical psychologist, is test results. Here too we must make a distinction. Test scores as "signs," or pathognomonic cues, and test results which are not so specified and simply represent a sample of the patient's behavior are the two major—and different—sets of cues obtained from tests. The difference between the two is that between the "three-M" sign coming out of Rorschach scoring (the pathognomonic cue) and the verbatim content of a Rorschach response (the sample of behavior). The two kinds of information yield different results when used as the basis for judgment. It may prove possible to take such sign information—for example, the number of M responses in the Rorschach, elevation of the Pd scale in the Minnesota Multiphasic Test, and presence or absence of buttons in the figure drawing test—and combine them by an actuarial formula to produce accurate statements about the patient making these responses. Certainly, this class of cue material has not provided the basis for spectacularly accurate judgments in current clinical practice.

The problem of cue identification in psychological test results has been the source of long-term, intensive research by Hamlin and his associates. Hamlin has surveyed a number of studies in which differing sources of cues were used (Hamlin, 1954). He concluded at that time that "psychometric signs" do not lend themselves to adequate clinical judgment. There are many other recent studies which support his contention, at least to the extent that they report negative results when this class of cue material is used (Elkins, 1958; Hamlin, 1955). Bourke and Fiske (1957), studying the use of data derived from observing, from listening, and from reading, found that all three were about equally good as bases for decision-making. They concluded that content rather than other cues was the effective agent. Our own program of research in the reliability and validity of clinical judgment has demonstrated that surprisingly reliable and valid judgments can be attained on a number of dimensions when verbal response protocols are used without reference to formal scoring (Hunt and Arnhoff, 1955; Hunt and Jones, 1958a, 1958b, et al; 1960).

Like biographical data, some test score information, particularly IQ scores, may be useful for the full appreciation of behavioral cues contained in total response protocols. Just what information is useful in this way has yet to be demonstrated, and certainly there is need for more experimental clarification before it can be assumed that interrelations between scores on one test and the content of another one are likely to be very significant.

Raw behavior as such is, of course, the clinician's basic datum. The cues contained in behavior must be systematized, however, if the clinician is to make efficient use of them. Psychological tests represent the major effort to systematize behavioral cues, but some effort has been devoted to the development of scales for formalizing observations on behavior. These observational scales are subjective, the result of the clinician's integration of a number of specific behaviors and not just a simple counting of specific acts. Here the observer gives the patient a rating of "hyperactive," rather than indicating that he got out of bed nine times during the night. A rating of 5 on a 7-point "activity" scale might then be a specifiable but relatively global cue which could be used in the compiling of behaviors contributing to any particular behavior syndrome.

One caution is in order in the construction of such behavioral scales. They should be descriptive rather than dynamic in order to avoid confusing observed behaviors with theory. That is, a rating on a scale of catatonia should represent what is seen in the patient's behavior at the time of observation and should not represent the end point of the theoretical historical chain of events beginning with early rejection, deprivation, or other possible etiological factors. We must not confuse observation with interpretation. Nursing behavior on the part of an infant should be reported as nursing behavior and not as oral gratification (Brady, Newman and Redlich, 1951). This requirement is in no sense an effort to minimize the importance of dynamic thinking, but simply points out a possible pitfall in the development of such a cue identification procedure.

Another approach to the identification and isolation of cues, apart from the categorization of sources, lies in the many studies which attempt to determine whether controlling the amount or kind of material presented to the judge has an effect upon the validity of the judgment. Certainly there are optimal combinations of kind and amount of material for given judgments. This is the one consistent finding of these studies. They do not, however, present us with the specific cues upon which judgments are made, but rather with a further indication that identifiable cues are included in the various cue sources which we have outlined and that the cues within them are specifiable.

Hamlin has shown the most consistent interest in the question of the effect on the subsequent judgment of the amount of material presented to the judge. In the aforementioned 1954 summary, Hamlin pointed out that the amount of test material useful to valid judgment depends in part upon the time to be devoted to making the judgment. Amounts of material as small as psychometric signs did not appear useful at all. That is, in making judgments of adjustment from Rorschach and figure drawing signs, consistently negative results were obtained. Amounts as large as a total Rorschach protocol were the basis for valid judgment only when extensive amounts of time were devoted to their analysis. For making judgments within an experimental situation he found that some amount between these two extremes was effective. Later studies by these same researchers support this finding and in addition indicate again that content rather than scoring categories may be the source of valid judgment (Powers and Hamlin, 1957, 1958). Other studies using Wechsler-Bellevue scores, vocabulary test scores, and Bender-Gestalt scores lend support to this point of view (Frehub and Scheener, 1958; Klehr, 1949; Nadler, et al., 1959).

Levine (1954) found validity was highest when he used, as data to be judged, specific items representing a very small amount of information; but when he selected information from more than one part of an interview, increasing the length of the passage to be judged did not affect the reliability. On the other hand, in investigating the effect of the amount of the material to be presented to the judge, we found that increasing the number of schizophrenic verbal responses to be judged from one half the total number of vocabulary responses to the entire vocabulary protocol lowered the reliability among the judges, but did not affect the over-all validity of the judgments of extent of schizophrenic pathology (Jones, 1959).

Studies of the kinds of material which are actually used in, or which best lend themselves to, a particular judgment include comparisons of listening, reading, and observing as sources of information (Bourke and Fiske, 1957; Luft, 1951; Cohen, 1960). Content which is obtained through reading is consistently associated with the best judgments. For some predictions the presence of voice cues is helpful, and when a voice different from that of the individual producing the judged response presents the material, the discrepancy shows up in poorer judgments. Direct observation of behavior, thus adding visual cues, to information available from listening or reading does not seem to contribute much toward improved judgment.

Starkweather reports that reliable judgments of aggressiveness and pleasantness were secured from judges who listened to verbal material screened through a low pass filter to render it content-free and meaningless (Starkweather, 1956, in press). In our laboratory Cohen has been unable, using like material, to obtain reliable and valid judgments of the degree of schizophrenia in patients (Cohen, 1960). Interview material was presented to undergraduate students in five modes —by playing back a recording, by playing a recording which had been filtered to render it content-free, by typescript, and by combinations of typescript and full recording, and typescript and filtered recording. Reliable and valid judgments of the amount of disorder present were obtained under all conditions except when the filtered material was presented alone. It is apparent that in this study the cues were coming from content and not from some vocal source. Of incidental interest is the fact that naïve subjects performed so well using content.

We have, then, in this collection of research, a start toward being able to isolate specific cues underlying any particular judgment. It will be necessary to further refine and control stimuli in a wide variety of judgmental situations in order to specify with the precision of psychophysics what cues are usable and what are not.

Our own effort at cue identification has been rather slow, but begins to bear some fruit. In offering clinical judges stimuli consisting of verbal responses to vocabulary and comprehension items, we have used highly restricted and in a sense specifiable stimuli. In varying the number of such verbal responses presented, we have also in a sense varied the number of cues available. But we feel that even within this delimited stimulus material there probably still are more specific indicators which we have not been able to point out to our judges and which are therefore uncontrolled.

In an earlier effort to extend the conditions under which reliable judgments could be made and to compare the judges' performance to known characteristics of the judged phenomena, we had schizophrenic verbal responses rated on four dimensions (Hunt and Jones, 1958a): intelligence, communicability, concreteness-abstractness, and extent of schizophrenia. We were able to show a correspondence between the judges' ratings of these dimensions and the typical structure of schizophrenic thinking, adding a type of contruct validity to our reliability findings. More important, however, is the point that, by defining more specific dimensions on which to rate schizophrenic test responses, we are approaching the problem of further defining and isolating specific relevant cues to schizophrenic thinking imbedded in the more general stimulus material. Among other possible interpretations, the fact that the correlation between the ratings for "schizophrenicity" and "intelligence" was very low might lead to the conclusion that cues relating to intelligence are not necessary for judgments of schizophrenia and might possibly be considered as part of the excess information which detracts from, rather than adds to, the efficiency of judgment as demonstrated by Hamlin, *et al.* In the same study, we found a phenomenally high correlation between the dimensions of communicability and schizophrenia. While it may be argued that the two dimensions are not separate, we choose to interpret this finding as an indication that cues relating to communicability are highly relevant to judgments of schizophrenia when using verbal material as a basis for the judgment. We are also in agreement with previous findings that the reliability and validity of our judgments vary with the type of test materials, i.e., vocabulary *vs.* comprehension items. Comparing the interaction between dimension and type of item should facilitate any cue analysis.

We are particularly interested in the isolation of further stimulus dimensions of a more specific nature than those we have used in the past. As an example of the stimulus refinement necessary if we are to achieve in the clinical field the clarity and objectivity of the psychophysical setting, let us look at the abstract-concrete dimension previously used in our experiments. We have found a low positive correlation between concreteness and schizophrenic tendency (Hunt and Jones, 1958a), bearing out the work of McGaughran and Moran (1956). This consistently has been a difficult dimension for our judges, both naïve and sophisticated, to handle, since even a trained clinician may have great difficulty in using it. For one thing, concrete and abstract sometimes seem to be confused with specificity and generality. Is a highly specific term always concrete and a highly general term always abstract? Can we clear up this confusion by clarifying our definition of the abstract-concrete dimension, and writing more careful instructions for our observers?

The root of our difficulty may well lie deeper than this in that "abstract-concrete" may not be a simple, unitary dimension. Because of their semantic polarity it is easy to assume that the terms represent opposite ends of a single continuum. The opposition may be purely semantic, however. Knowing schizophrenic thinking, it is plausible to assume that the schizophrenic is typified by extremes of both abstraction and concreteness, and that two dimensions are represented here rather than one. Thus, in a complex test response where both tendencies are markedly in evidence, the clinician is faced with an unfortunate alternative if he is given a single dimension on which to make his judgment. An example is the information test item, "Where is Egypt"; and the typically schizophrenic response, "In a manner of speaking it may be said to be an oasis, plenty surrounded by sand." Here, the words "oasis" and "plenty" might both represent abstractions, and the word "sand" a concrete response. No unidimensional scale would represent this adequately.

Moreover, it is possible that still another dimension would be appropriate here, one based upon the juxtaposition of the abstract and concrete. Certainly the abrupt transition from the abstract level of "oasis" and "plenty" to the concreteness of "sand" is inappropriate and unusual, and typical of much schizophrenic thinking. To add to the difficulty, one might even ask if the use of "oasis" is really an abstraction and not an example of concreteness; and if the use of "sand" is not possibly an abstract rather than a concrete response. It is the same sort of problem that plagues the clinician in interpreting responses on the Similarities test of the Wechsler intelligence scales, where a correct response may represent a genuine act of abstraction or the mere rote repetition of a learned verbal association.

We have no objective answer at present to such questions. They do point up the complexity of the stimulus materials when test responses are used, and to the intricate and possibly artificial nature of the dimensions used in our experiments. It is quite possible that the thinking of both experimenter and schizophrenic is marked by the use of inappropriate abstractions.

One promising further dimension which we wish to investigate in the future is one that we think of as "tangentiality," representing the indirect, circumlocutory nature of much schizophrenic thinking. We can illustrate this from our vocabulary test responses by the definition of the word donkey. Using a seven-point scale of schizophrenicity, the response, "A four-legged animal," is scaled as 1, or normal, by our judges. The standard deviation is zero, representing unanimous agreement. The response, "A type of four-legged animal," however, is scaled at 1.50 with a standard deviation of .52 (Hunt and Arnhoff, 1955). This is seen as a somewhat more schizophrenic response. A more extreme case would be the opening words of the response to the Egypt question mentioned above, "In a manner of speaking it may be said to be . . ."

At present such comments can be no more than conjectural, but they do point up the vast contrast between the clinical and the psychophysical situation in any attempt at the controlled study of human judgment. The experimental psychologist would shudder to think of a psychophysics which had not been preceded by physics, by the careful delineation of the physical properties of the stimuli involved; yet that is the situation in the field of clinical judgment, where a more detailed and penetrating descriptive psychiatry will be necessary before any great judgmental precision can be expected. Here our analogue poignantly points out the long, hard road ahead of us if we are to achieve the stimulus definition and control typical of the study of judgment in the psychophysical area, but the journey, while difficult, is by no means impossible.

THE JUDGMENTAL SITUATION

Perhaps the most difficult area in which to make our comparison, when one considers the practical necessities of clinical psychology, is the take-it-as-you-find-it judgmental situation presented by the clinical setting. It is extremely difficult to bridge the gap between the settings of clinical and laboratory judgments. How can the clinician's experience relevant to his task be controlled in the way that we would require experience to be controlled in order to evaluate a weight-lifting experiment? Johnson (1955, p. 282) has made much the same point in comparing judgment in general with laboratory judgment. But we, with Johnson, are convinced that similar problems inhere in or out of the laboratory and that qualitatively similar controls can be exercised to show the applicability of the same general principles in both situations.

As previously mentioned, our own research has related psychophysical principles of the effect of context to clinical judgment by demonstrating contrast and assimilation effects in the judgment of severity of schizophrenic verbal responses. These effects were shown as a result of varying the over-all severity of the background of other responses among which the experimentally distorted ones appreared. Those responses which had been judged moderately schizophrenic when presented in a group of responses comprising the full range of schizophrenic pathology, were judged less severe when they were presented in a context of severe items. Because of failure to deal properly with other situational variables, the one attempt in this program to demonstrate classical anchoring effects (Arnhoff, 1954) produced negative results and has not been attempted again. Arnhoff attributed the failure of his demonstration of anchoring effects to a lack of specificity in instructions, a problem we shall take up shortly.

In clinical judgment the effect of the context is more clearly a dual one than in laboratory psychophysics. There, the context or setting is presumed to affect the stimulus; the observer, a neutral instrument, simply responds to or reports the change. Adaptation level theory, with its concept of "residual" factors, brings in a subject variance which we must particularly consider in clinical judgment where the stimulus is both a potentially objectively measurable phenomenon affected by its background and an integral part of the judge's experience, past or immediate. The question then becomes: Is the effect of the context to produce a change in the qualitative field of the stimulus or a more sophisticated change in the observer? Can we separate the two?

Studying factors relating to resistance to the context effect (Jones, 1957) we found that each of three different kinds of experience contributed to a judge's stability level in the face of a distorting contextual force. The three kinds of experience studied were general level of clinical experience, number of times the particular judgmental task had been performed, and the experience with the particular stimuli which were being judged. Only the latter qualifies in the stimulus change paradigm of classical psychophysics, and it was the least effective of the three in forestalling distortion. This finding may be interpreted as support for our distinction between the places where the context operates and calls for additional research to clarify the role of experience, both here and in other judgmental situations.

Grigg (1958) and Cline (1955) found essentially the same thing that we did. The experienced clinical judge produces a more reliable rating than does the inexperienced individual. This is a further indication that, as an environmental or situational variable, experience acts as a residual phenomenon in adaptation level or context effects. However, Grigg's finding—that within the group designated "clinicians" varying levels of experience do not produce correspondingly varying levels in reliability of judgment—raises the additional question for clinical judgment of the kind and extent of experience necessary for various kinds of judgment. We ourselves have found (Hunt, et al., 1957) that while experienced clinicians are consistently more reliable in their judgments, naïve undergraduate students as a group can reach the same consensus, but do so somewhat less reliably. This matter of the relative effectiveness of varying kinds of experience may well be of crucial importance to the training of service personnel.

Closely allied to the problem of evaluating extent and kind of experience in the judge is that of the order of prior experience. Postman and Paige (1947) raised a question about the effect of order of experience in psychophysical judgments. They showed that interpolation of a similar judgmental series between two separate series of identical judgments produces a decrement in the accuracy with which the second of the two sets of identical judgments is made. They used judgments of two dimensions of a rectangle. If a judge were making estimates of the length of the rectangle in the first and third series of judgments, the interpolated series would consist of estimates of the rectangle's height. When the judge returned to estimates of length after the interpolated judgment of height, it was found that his estimates were less accurate than they had been in the first series of length judgments. This experiment shows a strong bond between psychophysics and learning theory, and it is one of utmost importance to clinical psychology. If the kinds of stimuli carrying judgmental cues differ from one judgmental situation to another, as they seem to, then the order of their consideration by the clinician may also be a critical factor in producing valid judgments.

In a series of preliminary studies we have found some evidence supporting the application of this psychophysical finding to clinical judgment (Jones, unpub.). In a prior study (Hunt and Jones, 1958a), we found that the dimension of communicability correlates more highly than that of intelligence with ratings of schizophrenia. Using undergraduate students as judges (although the distinctions between dimensions were not so clear for undergraduates as for clinicians), with schizophrenic verbal responses as a stimuli and the two sets of ratings of "how schizophrenic" as the basic judgment, we found that interpolating sets or series of judgments of intelligence, communicability, or the same judgment, "how schizophrenic," resulted in little interference, considerable interference, and facilitation, respectively, in the third series of judgments. These findings will, of course, have to be replicated using practicing clinicians as judges before we will be willing to place much confidence in them, but this beginning may lead eventually to some knowledge of optimal orders of consideration of cue materials by the clinician.

In a social rather than a clinical setting, Miller and Campbell (1960) have shown that primacy and recency effects, rather than being constant for any particular judgment, depend upon the time at which their measurement is taken, much as Underwood (1948) finds retroactive and proactive inhibition working in the verbal learning situation. Thus, it may be that in clinical judgment the effect of order of presentation of material is modified by passage of time and intervening events in a systematic way, knowledge of which might well be clinically useful. It is easy to see that Rorschach responses read yesterday might well exercise less influence on today's judgment than TAT responses taken an hour ago. The same relationship might not hold between these two sets of material, however, if the judgment were put off until tomorrow.

The Sines study quoted previously (Sines, 1959) found the effect of primacy to be greater than that of recency in the making of clinical judgments, indicating that undue weight may be given to the earliest material encountered in the making of a judgment. It may be, for instance, that a judgment of extent of schizophrenic pathology in a patient can best be made only on cues pertinent to that judgment, and that consideration of the patient's intelligence should be specifically reserved until after such a judgment is made. Unfortunately, this is still speculation; fortunately, it is a researchable question.

As important to clinical practice as it is to research studies in clinical judgment is the phrasing of the task to be accomplished. In both cases the instruction under which the clinician works should allow him the opportunity to integrate, not just to observe, the stimulus material. Donahoe (unpublished) found the clinician best able to judge if given meaningful behavioral dimensions to rate with specific instructions for making the ratings. In the study mentioned above, Arnhoff (1954) also found that while clinicians agree well on integrative dimensions without having to specify the precise basis of their decisions, some specificity of instructions is necessary to prevent self-instructions, which lead to ratings on dimensions different from the one which the experimenter had expected.

Aside from these specific sets produced by instruction are those produced by the environment. Both environmental sets and judgmental biases must be considered under the heading of judgmental situations. The tendency of a judge to see, in those he judges, exaggerated amounts of qualities lacking in himself is one of these. Both Campbell (1959) and Raines and Rohrer (1955) find this a judgmental tendency, and certainly it is one likely to produce clinical problems. We (Jones, 1959) and Campbell, Hunt and Lewis (1958) have identified what we call "assimilators" and "contrastors." These are judges who react against, as well as in direct response to, distorting effects of context. Thus in assimilators we have judges who are biased toward overcompensating for distorting factors which they recognize, while in contrastors we have a bias toward accepting the environment without questioning it. We would hypothesize that either, if recognized, can be brought under control in much the same way as in any comparable laboratory situation. Standards for judgment for predictable situations which will allow the assimilator or contrastor to maintain an unbiased frame of reference may be the answer. Also interesting is the fact that some judges show neither response bias, but recognize and control for such effects without apparent need for outside judgmental standards.

Johnson (1955, p. 361) has summarized a number of biases, such as the tendency to judge in even numbers, to use extremes of the judgmental scale, or to stay in the middle of the scale. He points out that these biases are more frequent when the instructions regarding categories of response are relatively nonspecific. These particular tendencies have not been specifically related to clinical judgment, but their pertinence seems obvious, and a thorough understanding of clinical judgment will require their systematic investigation.

An additional situational factor on which there has been little direct research is the effect of judgmental fatigue. Bendig (1955), working on this problem, found no decrease in reliability of rankings of food preference as a result of the length of the list of foods ranked or the number of trials at ranking, whereas Cummings (1954) and Hamlin (1954), getting different results, feel that failure of judges to respond as validly to large amounts of stimulus material as to smaller amounts is a function of "rater demoralization and fatigue." We would suggest that Bendig and Cummings mean different things by fatigue, and that Cummings' concept is more closely related to the problems discussed under the category of cue identification than to true fatigue effects. Although Bendig's findings are contrary to the hypotheses and findings of other researchers, we subscribe to his method of testing as offering the cleaner interpretation, and we feel that fatigue effects are an area in which further clinical judgmental research is due. The second problem, that of motivation of the judge as related to the size of the task facing him, is a separate but also an important and researchable question.

While our psychophysical analogue once more highlights our lack of detailed knowledge of the exact processes involved in clinical judgment, in this area of situational factors involving context effects, observer bias, self-sets, etc., it becomes obvious that psychophysics itself is plagued by the same problems. Whatever light we may shed on these matters as they affect clinical judgment is bound to shed some further and helpful illumination on the sister field of psychophysics. Here is one area where the analogical approach provides a two-way street for vital intercommunication and mutual progress.

CATEGORIES OF REPORT

The third of our areas of comparison is one in which psychophysics is of less help as a model. There has been relatively little interest in report categories in psychophysics simply because psychophysical categories are usually so clear and well established in everyday communication. A verbal report in terms of "feet or inches," "more or less," "equal or not equal" is relatively easy both for the experimenter to communicate to the subject as a task and for the subject to communicate to the experimenter as a report. In psychophysics, interest in the report itself arises only when a new scale must be established or in the rare case in which some new dimension is being investigated. An instance of this is Stevens' recent innovation of cross-modality testing of scales (Stevens, 1959) in which the subject adjusted his grip on a dynamometer to match the intensity of several different stimuli. Here the reliability of a new and exceedingly novel category of report had to be demonstrated, as frequently must be done in the clinical situation.

This area has a further difficulty: Whereas typical psychophysical judgments lend themselves readily to quantitative reports and, subsequently, to easy quantitative treatment, the clinical situation presents qualitative problems (along with special, although not essentially different, problems of quantitative treatment) in that some reports are highly specialized and far less commonly understood than those of psychophysics. Essentially, for clinical judgments, the response must be established in qualitative as well as quantitative classes, and frequently the qualitative classes are neither clear nor readily scaled.

If the nosology of a report system is not clear, it must impede judgment, and current psychiatric nosology is frequently subjected to this criticism. Studies like those of Mehlman (1952) and Ash (1949) have proved traditional diagnostic categories to be unreliable. In somewhat more sensitive designs Schmidt and Fonda (1956) found that agreement between judges was on the order of 80 per cent for major categories such as "organic," "psychotic," or "characterological," but when subtypes within these categories were demanded, agreement dropped to the order of 50. Hunt, et al. (1953), found essentially the same tendency. As diagnostic judgments became more specific, agreement between judges dropped. These latter findings indicate that it is probably not diagnostic nomenclature alone which is at fault but also the general lack of precision with which psychologists and psychiatrists use terms, as Grayson and Tolman (1950) demonstrated with categories other than diagnostic.

Thus, for the dual reasons that it is almost unshakably established and that it has not proved entirely false, we do not join the dissidents, like Sidman in this volume, who recommend scrapping the current nosology. On the contrary, we have been trying to establish the extent to which reliability can be expected in the various categories. The next constructive step in making a useful report system, as we have seen it, is to determine the dimensions on which any one of the nosological categories is based, first as a step toward cue isolation, and second as a step toward increasing reliability in the judgmental categories. In constructing dimensions, we have established quantitative scales on the assumption that the qualities to be judged in clinical situations are seldom completely present or completely absent. This makes our work considerably less elegant than that of Sarbin, et al. (1960), in their categorical treatment, but we feel that it reflects the reality of the patient behavior.

The problem of scaling in clinical judgment, at which we seem to have arrived, is again close to that found in psychophysics. If our basic processes are indeed similar to those of psychophysics, we can profit from an extensive literature on scale construction. In our own judgmental studies we have attempted the use of simple quantitative scales (i.e., the seven-point scale of schizophrenia mentioned earlier).

Obviously, in treating our ordinal scales as interval scales, as we do in obtaining means and standard deviations, we are pushing beyond the strict properties of an ordinal scale. There is much pragmatic justi-fication for this, as most psychological scales are indeed of the ordinal rather than the interval type. As Stevens (1951) points out, "strictest propriety" would forbid such practices, but the concept of strictest propriety is rapidly being extended by mathematicians and statisticians —as rapidly as any pragmatic value can be shown to accrue in the experimental market. In this case the evil certainly is supported within the temple as well as outside it. We can only hope that our heuristic behavior eventually will be justified by our experimental progress.

It is possible that some of the rough quantitative terms used in psychophysics may also be appropriate to clinical judgment. The dis-tinction is essentially that which Johnson (1955, p. 284) makes be-tween "exact judgments" and "estimations," and, as he also points out, the choice between them may be determined by the situation. Rough comparative terms have been used with success by Grayson, *et al.* (1958), who, incidentally, used the method of paired comparisons, rather than the more common method of absolute judgment which we have used, and employed actual patients as stimuli. They found the terms adequate and the method appropriate for their purpose in es-tablishing a criterion group of patients. Such methodological niceties may be demanded for and thoroughly appropriate to research prob-lems, but are less likely to be practical in an everyday clinical situation. The use of scale numbers in the clinical situation would seem a more appropriate technique.

Other efforts to isolate and scale response dimensions are represented in the studies of Trier (1958) and of Buss and Gerjouy (1957) who have isolated response dimensions on which personality descriptions can be reliably scaled. Klopfer, Crumpton, and Grayson (1958), too, have done extensive work in defining response dimensions. They have arrived at some 25 dimensions of ego functioning and defined scale points for each. In only a few cases have their scales been validated against external criteria, but they have been tested for reliability and scale intercorrelations and appear in all instances very promising.

These efforts are directed toward establishing categories other than those of standard diagnostic nomenclature, they are not aimed at re-placing it. There are many clinical decisions, as well as research prob-lems, which require such ratings, and we may be able to relate them to diagnostic categories. In contrast to the psychophysical field the investigation of categories of report in the field of clinical judgment is a lively, exciting area which promises much for the future.

It is our belief that the psychophysical analogy has been a helpful one in our investigation of clinical judgment, and that the extension of the analogical approach to such areas as learning, perception, etc., will increase our future understanding of the judgmental and decision making processes in clinical practice. True, the results in terms of concrete knowledge and theoretical understanding are not great to date, but ignorance must be pinpointed before it can be remedied. It is fitting and proper that this brief review has raised more questions than it has answered, for questions are the very fuel of research. The only criterion which such questions must meet is that they be amenable to answer by experimentation.

REFERENCES

Allport, G. W. Uniqueness in students. In W. D. Weatherford (Ed.), *The goals of higher education.* Cambridge, Mass.: Harvard Univ. Press, 1960.

Arnhoff, F. N. Some factors influencing the unreliability of clinical judgments. *J. clin. Psychol.,* 1954, 10, 272–275.

Ash, P. The reliability of psychiatric diagnoses. *J. abnorm. soc. Psychol.,* 1949, 44, 272–276.

Bendig, A. W. Rater reliability and judgmental fatigue. *J. appl. Psychol.,* 1955, 39, 451–454.

Bourke, Helen, & Fiske, D. W. Factors influencing the prediction of behavior from a diagnostic interview. *J. consult. Psychol.,* 1957, 21, 78–80.

Brody, E. B., Newman, R., & Redlich, F. C. Sound recording and the problem of evidence in psychiatry. *Science,* 1951, 113, 379–380.

Bruner, J. S. *The process of education.* Cambridge, Mass.: Harvard Univ. Press, 1960.

Buss, A. H., & Gerjuoy, H. The scaling of terms used to describe personality. *J. consult. Psychol.,* 1957, 21, 361–369.

Campbell, D. T. Varieties of projection in trait attribution. Progress report, NIMH project M-1544, January, 1959.

Campbell, D. T., Lewis, Nan A., & Hunt, W. A. Context effects with judgmental language that is absolute, extensive, and extra-experimentally anchored. *J. exp. Psychol.,* 1958, 55, 220–228.

Cline, V. B. Ability to judge personality assessed with a stress interview and sound film technique. *J. abnorm. soc. Psychol.,* 1955, 50, 183–187.

Cohen, A. Speech variables in judgments of schizophrenia. Unpublished master's thesis, Northwestern University, 1960.

Cummings, S. T. The clinician as judge: judgments of adjustment from Rorschach single card performance. *J. consult. Psychol.,* 1954, 18, 243–247.

Donahoe, J. W. A dimensional analysis of clinical judgment. Unpublished report.

Elkins, Elise. Diagnostic validity of the Ames "danger signals." *J. consult. Psychol.,* 1958, 22, 281–287.

Eriksen, C. W. Discrimination and learning without awareness: a methodological survey and evaluation. *Psychol. Rev.,* 1960, 67, 279–300.

Grayson, H. M., Cohen, L., & Mollo,

L. D. Validation of a method for rapid clinical appraisal in psychopharmacological research. In Transactions of the Third Research Conference on Chemotherapy in Psychiatry. Department of Medicine and Surgery, Veterans Administration, Washington 25, D.C. (no publication date, conference held at Downey, Ill., June 10–12, 1958).

Grayson, H. M., & Tolman, Ruth. A semantic study of concepts of clinical psychologists and psychiatrists. *J. abnorm. soc. Psychol.*, 1950, *45*, 216–231.

Grigg, A. E. Experience of clinicians, and speech characteristics and statements of clients as variables in clinical judgment. *J. consult. Psychol.*, 1958, *22*, 315–319.

Hamlin, R. M. The clinician as judge: implications of a series of studies. *J. consult. Psychol.*, 1954, *18*, 233–238.

Hamlin, R. M. Relationship between diagnostic category and deviant verbalizations on the Rorschach, *J. consult. Psychol.*, 1955, *19*, 120–124.

Hoffman, P, J. The paramorphic representation of clinical judgment. *Psychol. Bull.*, 1960, *57*, 116–131.

Hunt, W. A. An actuarial approach to clinical judgment. In B. Bass & I. A. Berg (Eds.), *Objective approaches to personality assessment.* Princeton, N.J.: Van Nostrand, 1959.

Hunt, W. A. Clinical psychology—science or superstition? *Amer. Psychol.*, 1951, *6*, 683–687.

Hunt, W. A. *The clinical psychologist.* Springfield, Ill., Charles C Thomas, 1956.

Hunt, W. A., & Arnhoff, F. N. Some standardized scales for disorganization in schizophrenic thinking. *J. consult Psychol.*, 1955, *19*, 171–174.

Hunt, W. A., & Blumberg, S. Manifest anxiety and clinical judgment. *J. clin. Psychol.*, 1961, *17*, 8–11.

Hunt, W. A., & Jones, N. E. Clinical judgment of some aspects of schizo-phrenic thinking. *J. clin. Psychol.*, 1958a, *14*, 235–239.

Hunt, W. A., & Jones, N. E. The reliability of clinical judgments of asocial tendency. *J. clin. Psychol.*, 1958b, *14*, 233–235.

Hunt, W. A., Jones, N. E., & Hunt, Edna B. Reliability of clinical judgment as a function of clinical experience. *J. clin. Psychol.*, 1957, *13*, 377–378.

Hunt, W. A., Walker, R. E., & Jones, N. E. The validity of clinical ratings for estimating severity of schizophrenia. *J. clin. Psychol.*, 1960, *16*, 391–393.

Hunt, W. A., Wittson, C. L., & Hunt, Edna. A theoretical and practical analysis of the diagnostic process. In J. Zubin and Hoch (Eds.), *Current problems in psychiatric diagnosis.* New York: Grune & Stratton, 1953.

Johnson, D. M. *The psychology of thought and judgment.* New York: Harper, 1955.

Jones, N. F. Context effects in judgment as a function of experience. *J. clin. Psychol.*, 1957, *13*, 379–382.

Jones, N. F. The validity of clinical judgments of schizophrenic pathology based on verbal responses to intelligence test items. *J. clin. Psychol.*, 1959, *15*, 396–400.

King, G. F., Ehrmann, J. C., & Johnson, D. M. Experimental analysis of the reliability of observations of social behavior. *J. soc. Psychol.*, 1952, *35*, 151–160.

Klehr, H. Clinical intuition and test scores as a basis for diagnosis. *J. consult. Psychol.*, 1949, *3*, 34–38.

Klopfer, B., Crumpton, Evelyn, & Grayson, H. M. *Manual for rating scales for ego functioning applicable to diagnostic testing.* Los Angeles: U.C.L.A Student Store, 1958.

Kostlan, A. A method for the empirical study of psycho-diagnosis. *J. consult. Psychol.*, 1954, *18*, 83–88.

Ledley, R. S. & Lusted, L. B. Reasoning foundations of medical diagnosis. *Science*, 1959, *130*, 9–21.

Levin, H. The influence of fullness of interview on the reliability, discriminability, and validity of interview judgments. *J. consult. Psychol.*, 1954, *18*, 303–306.

Luft, J. Differences in prediction based on hearing versus reading verbatim clinical interviews. *J. consult. Psychol.* 1951, *15*, 115–119.

McGaughran, L. S., & Moran, L. J. "Conceptual level" vs. "Conceptual area" analysis of object sorting behavior of schizophrenic and non-psychiatric groups. *J. abnorm. soc. Psychol.*, 1956, *52*, 43–50.

Meehl, P. E. *Clinical vs. statistical prediction.* Minneapolis: Univ. Minnesota Press, 1954.

Meehl, P. E. The cognitive activity of the clinician. *Amer. Psychologist*, 1960, *15*, 19–27.

Meehl, P. E., & Dahlstrom, W. G. Objective configural rules for discriminating psychotic from neurotic MMPI profiles. *J consult. Psychol.*, 1960, *24*, 375–387.

Mehlman, B. The reliability of psychiatric diagnoses. *J. abnorm. soc. Psychol.*, 1952, *47*, 577–578.

Miller, N., & Campbell, D. T. Recency and primacy in persuasion as a function of the timing of speeches and measurements. *J. abnorm. soc. Psychol.*, 1959, *59*, 1–9.

Nadler, E. B., Fink, S. L., Shontz, F. C., & Brink, R. W. Objective scoring vs. clinical evaluation of the Bender-Gestalt. *J. clin. Psychol.*, 1959, *15*, 39–41.

Postman, L., & Page, R. Retroactive inhibition and psychophysical judgment. *Amer. J. Psychol.*, 1947, *60*, 367–377.

Powers, W. T., & Hamlin, R. M. The validity, bases and processes of clinical judgment using a limited amount of projective test data. *J. proj. Tech.*, 1957, *21*, 286–293.

Powers, W. T., & Hamlin, R. M. A comparative analysis of deviant Rorschach response characteristics. *J. consult. Psychol.*, 1958, *22*, 123–128.

Raines, G. N., & Rohrer, J. H. The operational matrix of psychiatric practice. *Amer. J. Psychiat.*, 1955, *111*, 721–733.

Reichenbach, H. Probability methods in social science. In D. Lerner, & H. D. Larswell (Eds.), *The policy sciences.* Stanford, Calif.: Stanford Univ. Press, 1951.

Sarbin, T. R., Taft, R., & Bailey, D. E. *Clinical inference and cognitive theory.* New York: Holt, Rinehart, and Winston, 1960.

Schmidt, H. O., & Fonda, C. P. The reliability of psychiatric diagnosis: a new look. *J. abnorm. soc. Psychol.*, 1956, *52*, 262–267.

Sines, L. K. The relative contribution of four kinds of data to accuracy in personality assessment. *J. consult. Psychol.*, 1959, *23*, 483–492.

Starkweather, J. A. Content-free speech as a source of information about the speaker. *J. abnorm. soc. Psychol.*, 1956, *52*, 394–402.

Starkweather, J. A. Vocal communication of personality and human feelings. *J. communication.* In press.

Stevens, S. S. Mathematics, measurement and psychophysics. In S. S. Stevens (Ed.), *Handbook of experimental psychology.* New York: Wiley, 1951.

Stevens, S. S. Cross-modality validation of subjective scales for loudness, vibration and electric shock. *J. exp. Psychol.*, 1959, *57*, 201–209.

Trehub, A., & Scheerer, I. W. Wechsler-Bellevue scatter as an index of schizophrenia. *J. consult. Psychol.*, 1958, *22*, 147–149.

Trier, T. R. Vocabulary as a basis for estimating intelligence from the Rorschach. *J. consult. Psychol.*, 1958, *22*, 189–191.

Underwood, B. J. Retroactive and proactive inhibition after five and forty-eight hours. *J. exp. Psychol.*, 1948, *38*, 29–38.

3

The Experimental Bases
of Personality Assessment

IRWIN A. BERG and HENRY E. ADAMS

Early in the nineteenth century the German philosopher and psychologist Johann Herbart wrote that psychology was a science—and a mathematical science. He said, furthermore, that psychology was empirical but could not be experimental, for, as Boring (1950) remarked, Herbart saw no way in which experimentation could be done on the mind. Herbart was wrong, but by denying that psychology could be an experimental science he issued a challenge that stimulated scholars to attack the problem. A major breakthrough came in the form of the Weber-Fechner law, which showed that at least one aspect of mental phenomena—sensation—could be studied by means of physical responses to known stimuli. Although the law had only limited application, it pointed the way to other experimental investigations of behavior, which eventually included personality measurement.

The new interest in research on behavior led, of course, to blind alleys and false starts—for example, Lombroso's notion that criminality was inborn and that the criminal type could be identified by means of measurable and classifiable physical stigmata; or the theory advanced by Gall, a Viennese anatomist, that personality and other traits were reflected by bumps and other irregularities on the surface of the skull. These early (nineteenth-century) attempts to relate physical structure to personality were quickly rejected as pseudoscientific, although echoes of the theories linger on in the folkways.

Unfortunately, a by-product of the disillusionment with such theories seems to be a general indifference to and contempt for subsequent attempts in the twentieth century which were genuinely scientific. In particular, Kretschmer's work on constitutional psychology, initiated after World War I and greatly extended in recent decades by Sheldon, merits serious consideration. Hall and Lindzey (1957, Chap. 9) have an excellent discussion of work in this area.

But if there were blind alleys in the scientific study of behavior, there were also rich and rewarding leads. In the 1880's, as cases in point, Sir Francis Galton, ably followed by James McKeen Cattell, measured individual differences and devised some early statistical techniques for analyzing them. Out of this work came the first psychological tests in the modern tradition. At turn of the present century, Binet and Simon, taking another long step forward, developed the intelligence test. Their unique contribution probably lies in their concept of mental age as a basis for scaling intellectual performance. Significantly, current practice in intelligence assessment still utilizes their ideas. The remaining names and techniques which should be mentioned are relatively recent. The major contributors include E. L. Thorndike, R. S. Woodworth, L. M. Terman, Cyril Burt, L. L. Thurstone, Hermann Rorschach; the instruments developed include the Vocational Interest Blank, Murray's Thematic Apperception Test (TAT), Wechsler's intelligence scales, Kuder's Preference Record, Kent-Rosanoff Word Association Test, and Hathaway's Minnesota Multiphasic Personality Inventory (MMPI).

With this brief historical background in mind, we may go on to review present-day attempts to measure personality and personality change. The approaches differ widely and the evidence gathered varies in quality, but all are concerned with obtaining valid answers to crucial questions. There are a number of ways in which the many methods of personality assessment might be classified. The categories used here are modifications of those used by Berg (1952) in a review article. Because of the present stage of personality assessment research, a good many of the studies reviewed in following pages are not fully experimental, even within a charitable interpretation of the term. But because they are pertinent, we must include them if we are to understand the scope of assessment research today.

RATING METHODS

In assessing personality the most frequently used method is that of rating. Particular rating techniques vary immensely in form and content. They may be short and simple checklists or lengthily elegant scales. Usually they call for written responses such as words or check marks, but upon occasion the responses may be oral, gestural, or something else. The setting may require an immediate rating, as is the case during interviews or sociometric observations. At other times, a leisured recollection of past incidents may be required prior to rating. But in every instance one person judges another. He may pool his ratings with others and he may rate persons in a group; yet the basis of rating remains typically individual and subjective. The factor of subjectivity has justly troubled many researchers, because ratings in general have rather low reliability and their validity is difficult to establish. Yet in most clinical situations no other method is feasible. Despite their weaknesses, rating methods are convenient and often provide a useful comprehensive estimate of personality. In any case, whatever the yearnings of a scientifically oriented clinician may be, there is really no escaping ratings. More than one veteran researcher has smiled sourly when urged by a neophyte to use the MMPI or similar instrument as an objective personality measure in order to avoid ratings. The veteran knows that the MMPI is an excellent test, but he also knows that ratings were originally involved in identifying the MMPI criterion groups and in the subjects' self-ratings when responding to the test items, as well as in the interpretation of the scores. Ratings are indeed always with us; and our task becomes one of understanding and improving, not of decrying them.

Actually, rating techniques have a quite respectable scientific ancestry in classical psychophysics; the problems lie in how to use them neatly, with a maximum of rigor. As Stevens (1951) has noted, both psychological tests and rating methods may be viewed as psychophysical procedures. With this in mind, we may review the categories of persons who do the ratings and then examine the factors which, at times, lead them astray. Raters may be placed in one of three categories: *professional,* such as the staff members of a hospital; *self,* where the subject or patient evaluates himself; *others,* such as the family, friends, or co-workers of the subject.

Professional ratings

Professional raters are those who have some special competence in the behavioral area under investigation. Nurses and hospital aides, for example, usually have the most accurate information concerning a patient's daily ward behavior, while the social worker is often best able to rate the patient's relationship to his family. Behavioral dynamics or specific diagnostic judgments are best appraised by psychologists or psychiatrists. The most reliable ratings come about when the professional rates in the area for which his training and experience have best equipped him. Ratings from various sources are often pooled in order to increase reliability and validity. In clinic staff meetings for example, individual clinical ratings are reviewed collectively; in experimental studies summed ratings are employed in order to define or identify some variable. (Hunt and Jones in Chapter 2 of the present book and Matarazzo in Chapter 14 offer further discussion of these aspects of personality assessment.)

Self-ratings

Personality and adjustment may be affected by psychotherapy or by disease or injury. The technique most commonly employed for finding evidence of such personality modification is patient self-ratings, which are secured in a variety of ways. The crudest, most informal form would be an instance in which the patient's volunteered remark—"I feel better/worse today"—is woven into the fabric of someone else's rating. Still informal, but more deliberate, would be the probe in the form of the fatuous question, "How are we today?" But self-ratings typically involve more formal techniques, including perhaps oral reports derived from lengthy interviews and detailed rating forms; sometimes the ratings are obtained in before-, during-, and after-treatment appraisals, a desirable technique.

The value of many kinds of self-reports is reduced, however, by the influence of powerful cultural factors. For example, when asked, "How do you feel?" the out-patient who is still inter-acting socially in the outside world may respond, "Much better, thanks," simply because the acquiescent response is the rule in our society. Hathaway (1958) has discussed this response characteristic at some length as the "Hello-Goodbye" pattern. Or another factor may operate in this sort of situation: since no one enjoys being regarded as a fool, the patient may be unwilling to suggest that his and the therapist's time have been utterly wasted, and so claim a change for the better no matter how he really feels.

Opposed to this broad cultural set for acquiescence is the specific reinforcement of "sick" responses, particularly among hospitalized patients, of the sort described in some detail by Greenspoon in Chapter 15 of this volume. The patient who says he feels fine get little attention from the ward nurse or aide; the patient who mentions a Martian on his back or a bomb in his belly gets attention from the aide, the nurse, the ward physician, and perhaps even a consultant. It seems obvious therefore that the patient's self-ratings are unlikely to reflect personality changes with any validity.

Ratings by others

Occasionally a patient's family and/or others who know him have been asked to rate him on various personality dimensions. Because such ratings may be a source of embarrassment to the patient or to the person doing the rating, they are not usually trustworthy. Furthermore, the raters may ardently desire to have the patient back home or

at work or, with equal ardor, want him kept in the hospital. Such emotional involvement is more the rule than the exception among a
patient's family and friends. Thus, these ratings are of little value for
the experimental study of personality, unless the study is directed at
the raters rather than the patients who are being rated.

The reliability and validity of ratings

In our discussion thus far, ratings have been described as having
serious weaknesses. Yet—to repeat an earlier point—we cannot really
avoid them in personality assessment. Fortunately, ratings *can* be
reliable and valid, particularly when done by professionals under carefully structured conditions. The Hospital Adjustment Scale (HAS)
by McReynolds, Ballachey, and Ferguson (1952), for example, can
be filled out by a nurse or aide in about ten minutes; yet its reliability
is reasonably high, as is the Multidimensional Scale for Rating Psychiatric Patients (MSRPP) by Lorr, Singer, and Zobel (1951), designed for use by psychologists and psychiatrists. The two scales were
compared by Stilson, Mason, Gynther, and Gertz (1958) in a study
which required student nurses to rate 36 neuropsychiatric patients on
the HAS while psychologists rated the same patients on the MSRPP.
When the patients were re-rated by the same groups, the HAS had a
reliability of .79; the MSRPP, of .80. The correlation between HAS
and MSRPP ratings was − .57, indicating not only a satisfactory level
of reliability for the individual scales but also reasonable agreement
between the two sets of raters. It also appears that when the task is
properly structured for them, student nurses can do a competent job
of rating neuropsychiatric patients. Lorr (1954), one of the authors
of the MSRPP, has a comprehensive survey of rating scales which
will be useful to those contemplating research that involves these
methods.

Even self-ratings can be reliable under certain conditions. Webb
(1955) reported that the reliability of self-ratings *vs.* re-ratings for
normal subjects was only .19 when they were asked to give a quantative
rating of themselves along a single dimension. However, when he had
the subjects compare themselves with other members of the group, he
found that the reliability of their ratings was now at the respectable
range of .58 to .91, despite the fact that self-ratings were used. Of
course, subjects with severe emotional disturbances would probably
be less consistent in self-ratings.

Although professional personnel, by and large, do a better job of
rating, in terms of reliability and validity, than do other groups, even
professional ratings cannot always be trusted. In the hospital situation,
for example, the wise, experimentally oriented clinician is wary of

ratings of patient improvement as reflected in rates of patients discharged. This is particularly true of crowded state hospitals, where the rate of patients discharged as improved increases with increased pressure for new admissions. Occasionally a carefully designed research has failed simply because its success depended upon a professional rating which turned out to be slovenly. Schofield's (1950) carefully executed attempt to construct a "susceptibility to therapy" scale for the MMPI failed because patients in his criterion group were discharged from the hospital as improved when actually they were not.

But the pitfalls of rating techniques can be avoided and ratings can often make a surprisingly good showing. Intelligence measurement, for example, is often regarded as the unique province for particular tests. However, Hanna (1950) found that ratings of intelligence based upon material from carefully conducted interviews correlated .71 with the American Council on Education Psychological Examination and .66 with the Ohio State University Psychological Test. The two tests correlated .77 with each other; hence the intelligence estimate based upon ratings appears to be virtually as good as either test. Similar validity evidence for ratings is reflected in Wittson and Hunt's (1951) examination of 944 Navy neuropsychiatric (NP) discharges in relation to ratings by psychiatrists and psychologists as to degree of NP disability. Of those servicemen rated *mild* disability, only 6.5 per cent were later discharged as NP cases; of those rated *moderate*, 20.2 per cent were eventually NP discharges; but 89.7 per cent of those rated *severe* were later discharged for NP conditions. This study is a good example of how ratings may be effectively employed to achieve satisfactory validity and reliability, for the raters were professionally trained in the area they were rating, and no fine discriminations were demanded. Had they been required to rate severity of NP disability on a 20-point scale, the results would probably not have been so impressive. Indeed, Hunt, Wittson, and Hunt (1953) did something along these lines when they studied specificity of diagnostic rating and percentage of agreement among raters at a Navy precommissioning station and at a hospital. The subjects rated were 794 naval enlisted men. There was 93.7 per cent agreement for the rating "unsuitable for service"; however with somewhat greater rating specificity, the percentage of agreement was 54.1 for such categories as "psychosis," "psychoneurosis." When particular disorders were listed, such as "schizophrenia," "hysteria," or "anxiety state," the percentage of agreement was 32.6. If further specificity had been sought (for example, categories of *paranoid* schizophrenia), the level of agreement would undoubtedly have dropped even further. Berg (1954) and Hunt and Jones in Chapter 3 of the present book discuss this topic further.

The conditions of sound ratings

It seems clear that ratings may or may not be useful, depending upon who does them, and how. At this point it is worth while to examine the conditions under which useful, reliable, and valid ratings may be obtained. Those researchers who successfully employ rating methods have observed a few simple precautions. A fairly short distillation of the necessary guide lines, such as those suggested by Pinillos (1955), should be all that is needed for experimental-clinical purposes.

Careful selection of raters is essential. The rater must have compe- tence in the area he is appraising. Curiously, nearly everyone consid- ers himself to be an expert in the assessment of behavior. Beyond com- petence there are characteristics associated with good raters. Good judges tend to be task-oriented and socially detached, as Taft (1956) emphasized, whereas poor raters are less stable and introceptive. Thus the good rater in appraising sociability might give weight to the sub- ject's having been elected to office in a civic club, while the poor rater might be strongly influenced by his friendly smile. In other words, poor raters are more likely to generalize and exhibit the *halo effect* (Anas- tasi, 1954, p. 140). Other factors also contribute to poor ratings. For example, Taft (1956) has remarked that members of minority groups and rural dwellers do not rate well, although the reasons for this are not clear. Similarly, other characteristics of raters or rates can affect the kind of appraisal made. Intelligence and education, according to Bendig (1956) can influence ratings. So can the particular situation, as in Landfield's (1955) finding that subjects predicted their own behavior less accurately when in the presence of threatening persons than they did in the presence of nonthreatening persons. Rankin and Campbell (1955) found that white subjects exhibit a greater magni- tude of galvanic skin response to Negro than to white examiners. Pre- sumably, ratings taken under any of these conditions would be di- rectly affected by the conditions. However, such findings do not negate the use of ratings; rather, they underline the importance of selecting raters carefully.

It is essential that the rater have time and opportunity to observe the ratee. As crucial as careful selection of raters is the additional condi- tion that the raters know the pertinent behavior of the person being rated. More than one investigator has ignored this point while clearly defining the rater's qualifications in terms of training and experience. Occasionally this omission comes painfully to light only when an earnest rater writes on his form, "I think the patient is better, but I saw him only once for five minutes about a month ago." When such omis- sions do not come to light, the ratings may simply be condemned as useless and the study abandoned. Or worse—the study is published as a mélange of inconsistencies, to provide fresh ammunition for the non-clinical psychologists who gleefully collect examples of clinical non-sense mislabeled "research." Holzberg (1957) has stressed the importance of accumulating pertinent information before attempting to rate, but this sound injunction is often ignored on the dangerous assumption that a rater will not rate a person when he knows little or nothing about him. Some raters won't, of course, but some will and do. The only safeguards are to make certain that each rater understands the basis of personal knowledge upon which he is to make his judgment, and to make provision on the rating form for indications of the kind of information upon which the rating is based.

It is essential that rater bias be eliminated or controlled. This has already been mentioned in passing references to such factors as the "halo" effect wherein a favorable or unfavorable trait colors the rater's judgment of all other traits. But there are many other forms of bias: Specialized experiences or particular responsibilities, for example, may produce emotional identifications which interfere with valid ratings. Understandably, therefore, American scientists who are developing space missiles will rate our achievements ahead of the Russians, while the generals in charge of United States defense programs rate us lagging behind; or most American physicians may rate American medicine as the "best in the world," and our professional educators appraise American education in identical superlatives. The same physicians can usually validly and reliably assess the efficacy of one drug over another in treating a particular disease, and the same educators can often decide with reasonable objectivity that one method of teaching arithmetic is better than another. The latter ratings are in the area of their professional competence and, with a well-defined rating task, can be relatively free from bias. But being a member of a profession, like being a member of a family, has powerful emotional involvements, and it is too much to expect objectivity where emotional identification is primary. The possibility of such biases must be explored, and the biases controlled. Should bias exist, it does not mean that a rating cannot be made. The quality of American medicine could perhaps be appraised by members of kindred, but non-M.D., professions or another national group. For example, Swiss physicians might rate a large number of specific features on a paired-comparison basis in which first British and American, then French and American medicine were compared. Certain objective factors might also be included for assessment, such as death rate, epidemics, stillbirths. Thus, rater bias may be controlled or eliminated to a considerable extent, but one must first pinpoint it.

It is essential that the characteristics to be rated be expressed in simple, objective, and well-defined form.   Bias is not the only source of possible distortion in ratings; They may also be distorted simply because the rater does not know what he is supposed to rate. Worse, he may *think* he knows when actually something else is desired. Candidates for executive positions have frequently been rated on such characteristics as trustworthiness, future promise, stability; but unless such items are cast in behavioral and situational terms the ratings are likely to be meaningless. Thus *trustworthiness* can mean discharging all responsibilities on schedule, or accuracy and honesty in handling money. Which is to be rated? In the same way, *future promise* may be appraised only in situational terms—future promise *for what?* An engineer may be quite ordinary as an engineer but bear bright promise as an executive vice-president. Similarly, stability in bank presidents may be quite different from stability in sales managers. Such terms are obviously deceptive and require definition. To avoid misunderstanding, a description of the duties involved in the new situation should be spelled out before asking for ratings. For example, "This position is research director of an NP 2000 bed private hospital. The director supervises and coordinates the work of four assistant directors who are Ph.D.'s in psychology, and he deals directly with consultants in psychiatry, social work, anthropology, and statistics. He must be experienced in the design and appraisal of research with neuropsychiatric patients, particularly the treatment of schizophrenics and alcoholics. It is very important that he be able to present clear reports, both oral and written, to professional and lay groups, etc." The idea is to give details of the situation and the responsibilities of the job. Then, if the rater knows the person he is rating, he can do a much better job in his appraisal. He can even determine when he must say, "I don't know how he would perform in such a situation."

Occasionally, a rating form is overelaborate, and in this case, too, its purpose may be defeated. As Sorenson and Gross (1957) noted, complex rating forms often cause confusion. The confused rater does a poor rating job; the irritated rater usually abandons the task in frustration. Careful pilot testing will provide the means for identifying and correcting such sources of error.

There is, then, no escape from ratings. The experimental clinician would do well to recognize the usefulness of rating procedures for appraising any facet of personality and personality change. Ratings can be reliable and valid when biases are identified, controlled, or eliminated; rating scales can be confusing, but they need not be, for good scales can be prepared, often with less trouble than poor scales. The investigator in personality research must at some point deal with data obtained by rating methods; he may as well learn to use them effectively.

<h2 style="text-align:center">PSYCHOLOGICAL TEST METHODS</h2>

In a review which may be recommended to any serious student of the problem at hand, Super (1959) observed that fads and fancies appear in theories and techniques of personality assessment. Once the professional psychology journals were full of articles dealing with measures of *ascendance-submission, expressive-movement, introversion-extroversion,* but now such studies are rare. After a decade of virtual oblivion, a few studies of expressive movement have recently begun to reappear. During the past half-dozen years, Super notes, interest has waxed and then waned in research on personality characteristics such as authoritarianism, rigidity, empathy, motivation, and anxiety. A rash of studies has appeared in the past on each of these topics, followed by a gradual drop-off in frequency, as indicated by publication in *Psychological Abstracts* or *The Annual Review of Psychology.* Certain instruments, however, seem to endure the pounding of each newest tool, outlasting the fad as the anvil outlasts the hammer. The Minnesota Multiphasic Personality Inventory (MMPI), for example, has gained steadily in usefulness and clinical importance over the years. This is not too surprising in view of the amazing flexibility of this test. If social introversion is in the air, professionally speaking, or configural scoring of tests, Drake (1946) has a scale for the former and Meehl (1956) a method for the latter. One would be hard put to think of a new fad which the MMPI could not exploit by means of a new scale or new technique.

Projective techniques

In view of the firm foundation of supporting empirical evidence, it is not surprising that the MMPI has proved durable and useful; it is surprising that the Rorschach is still in the clinical armamentorium. Kelly (1954) wondered whether the adherence to such tests as the Rorschach, in view of the absence of demonstrated predictive validity, was not a phenomenon that should be studied by social psychologists. Super (1959) has observed that Eysenck (1955) reported abandoning the Rorschach as a clinical tool at the Maudsley Hospital in England, but that Columbia University continues to require a large block of graduate student time dedicated to projective techniques, despite dissatisfaction with them. In Super's words:

> We have agreed that they have no validity, but we retain the requirement. We do this for three reasons: (1) The unsatisfactory but practical consideration that such psychologists are expected to have

these skills and are likely to both feel and be handicapped if they do not, (2) the fact that they can learn something useful about clinical interaction by studying these procedures, and (3) the hope that familiarity with these methods may yet provide psychologists with a basis for some major breakthrough in the field of personality assessment (1959, p. 31).

It seems probable that Super's candid statement would be echoed by the staff members in many other clinical psychology programs where the research literature on projective techniques is known. Unquestionably, the validity of the Rorschach is very low, however, a new approach may emerge which will preserve the attractive, perceptual features of the Rorschach and still yield solid evidence for predictive validity. Perhaps the objective scoring approach of Holtzman (1959) or the stimulus analysis research by Baughman (1954) will provide the key. For the experimental clinician, the *Annual Review of Psychology* offers a year-by-year account of the status of research on the Rorschach and other projective techniques, as well as on new and provocative lines of inquiry.

Objective personality inventories

The adjective *objective* as applied to personality appraisal can be something of a problem. For present purposes, however, objectivity in personality measures may be considered achieved when the scoring of test responses by different persons shows little variance. As noted in the section on *Rating Methods,* the interpretation of such objectively determined scores may still be subjective, even though the scores are not. (Watson [1959] has an excellent discussion of the search for objectivity in testing.) Three procedures have generally been followed in developing objective measures of personality. Edwards (1959) has described them as: (1) *factor analysis techniques,* (2) the *criterion group method,* (3) *construct approaches.*

Factor analysis technique has been used by Guilford (1940) in his Inventory of Factors STDCR, and by Cattell (1950) in the 16 PF Questionnaire. The basic assumption of this approach is that a small number of factors will emerge from a large number of items. Just what these factors will be is not known in advance; hence close scrutiny of the content of those items which have high loadings for a particular factor is necessary. From such examination it is possible to get a more or less definite idea of what the items have in common. Then a label is applied which seems to be reasonably descriptive of the factor. It is at this point that difficulty is encountered, at least from the standpoint of clinical practice. A factor designated as sociability may mean various things to various clinicians, ranging from the overt manifestations of sociability exhibited by the backslapping politician to an undemonstrative but sincere enjoyment of just being with other people. A further description of the factor is usually supplied in order to clarify the term; however, the confusion is not necessarily dispelled, perhaps because the label, not the extended description, is what sticks in the mind of the clinician. As a result, some writers have used letters or numbers for their factors and then offered an explanation in terms of the content of the items which make up the factor. Cattell (1957) has frequently done this and given a description of negative and positive loadings, such as "impulsive, generous versus close, cautious." He also makes up words like *premsia, alaxia,* or *parmia,* apparently on the assumption that old associations will be less likely to be present in the new word. Whatever the drawbacks, factor methods do provide a means for scaling a single personality variable.

The criterion group method, called the "group difference method" by Super (1959, p. 35), requires two groups defined on some reasonably operational basis. The Strong Vocational Interest Blank, for example, used "men in general" for one group, and "engineers" for the other in preparing one of the occupational keys. The MMPI similarly employed a group of normal persons and a group of schizophrenics in the preparation of the Sc scale. With this method, after the groups have been appropriately identified, both are given a set of stimulus material, such as test items, and the responses are recorded. Those responses which differentiate the two groups at some agreed-upon level of statistical significance are then used as the basis for constructing a scale. This provides a straightforward empirical method of selecting items for measuring the variable under study. There are advantages and disadvantages to this approach. The experimenter has a scale based upon the responses of groups of known characteristics; thus when using the scale, he can predict with reasonable accuracy whether the scores indicate that a given subject responds like the members of one group or the other. The accuracy of this prediction, however, is limited to the representativeness of the groups originally used. This can be a problem, for contamination does occur despite careful application of controls. A large group of normal subjects, for example, is likely to include some persons who are "normal" only in the sense of not being hospitalized. Conversely, a group of schizophrenics will sometimes include patients who are really no longer schizophrenic but who, for various reasons, continue to be tagged with this NP classification. Another aspect of the problem of identifying criterion groups resides in locating meaningful operational definitions. Maturity in the sense of chronological age, for example, can be satisfactorily defined from birth certificates; however, something like delinquency is not amenable to convenient definition. Some who are called delinquents are merely neglected children, while others are schizophrenics, psychopaths, etc. Further information on the problem of criterion group definition will be found in Edwards' (1959) and Berg's (1961) discussions.

When using the *construct approach,* the investigator has a fairly definite idea of some variable that he wishes to study. He then devises items which are intended to sample its behavioral facets. Thus, if he is interested in behavior relating to religion, he may prepare items which deal with attendance at church, frequency of prayer, etc., and which are intended to tap aspects of a construct which might be termed, after Allport, Vernon, and Lindzey (1951), *religious values* or perhaps *religiosity.* The items thus obtained are administered to a heterogeneous group of subjects and the responses are analyzed, usually by factorial methods, in order to identify those items which relate most closely to each other and thus appear to be related to the construct. From such items a scale may then be prepared. Several tests, such as the Study of Values (Allport, Vernon, and Lindzey, 1951) and the Personal Preference Schedule (Edwards, 1953) were developed in this way.

The construct method has an advantage in that the investigator knows what he has striven to put into his items from the very beginning and he can employ factor analytical or other techniques to appraise the relation of particular items to the construct. Also, as Edwards (1959, p. 104) has observed, this is a form of the criterion group approach, with the important difference that item responses, not external criteria, identify the groups. Edwards goes on to note that different investigators may map a construct differently with the result that, while both use the same labels, the scales developed by each may be different. The same difficulty is reflected in the initial preparation of items. If an important area of the construct remains untapped, the scale will be inadequate. Factor analysis techniques have the advantage with regard to this point, for the large, commonly employed pool of heterogeneous items is much more likely to sample a broad range of behavior than the restricted content of items used in the construct approach. For such broader sampling, one pays a price in the form of an unwieldy factor matrix. But when it comes to labeling the variable, the construct method offers an advantage in that one may reasonably assume that what was put into the items should come out in the scale. It may be noted that neither statistical treatment nor labels are a problem in the criterion group approach *if the groups are validly defined.*

It is not feasible to examine in detail the many research and clinical uses of psychological tests, for the number of articles published is staggering. During the 20 years the MMPI has been in existence approximately a thousand studies dealing with the single test have appeared in print. The Rorschach is a considerably older test; hence it may not be surprising to learn that more than three thousand articles on it have been published. These are but two tests; and while they are among the most popular of all personality tests, there are hundreds of others about which many articles have been published. In clinical experimentation the tests are commonly used under test-retest conditions. That is, the test is given prior to the introduction of some new condition, such as therapeutic treatment, and then administered one or more times afterward. The usual pattern is testing once before and once after therapy. Rarely does a given study report follow-up testing after the formal therapeutic effort has been terminated.

The assumption underlying this test-retest procedure is that the tests will adequately measure the disturbed personality state prior to treatment, and the retest will reflect any personality changes which result from the treatment. Both assumptions are questionable. Even the best personality tests have a high percentage of false negative and false positive identifications. The researcher may work with a group of known adjustment characteristics—for example, in a group of schizophrenics; yet the test data will not identify all members of the group as schizophrenics. Furthermore, in the case of diagnostic categories, test score changes do not necessarily mean changes in the severity of the disorder. Thus, while schizophrenics usually earn standard scores above 70 on the MMPI Sc (Schizophrenia) scale, mild cases of schizophrenia may have very low or very high Sc scores, in the neighborhood of 73 or 93, because tests are rarely validated for severity levels in such situations. It is in fact difficult to establish reliably and validly the degrees of severity in psychopathological states, which brings into question the assumption that the test will adequately measure the disturbed behavioral state under investigation. Perhaps a fair appraisal would be to state that present tests identify behavior atypicalities, but not very well.

Even more troublesome is the assumption that test score changes will reflect personality changes, because again tests are not validated for personality changes resulting from intervention such as psychotherapy. Clearly, test scores *can* change as a function of psychotherapy, but we to date have no methods to find confirming evidence. Thus, when Muench (1947) administered several tests to a group of patients before and after psychotherapy, it was not clear whether the tests or the therapy were being validated. If one had good evidence that psychotherapy was successful, then the tests could be validated; conversely, the psychotherapy could be validated for efficacy if it were established that the test scores really changed with effective therapy— and we can recall here the failure of Schofield's research, which stumbled over that very point. Changes in test scores, incidentally, do occur in a test-retest situation; yet they may have nothing whatsoever to do with personality changes. A common phenomenon is regression toward the mean; hence with repeated testing, scores often increase or decrease depending upon whether they were originally below or above the mean. An elementary precaution against such problems is the use of control groups—an obvious safeguard which is lacking in a number of studies. One might also observe that virtually all research on personality change provides no control for the mere passage of time. Disturbed people do sometimes recover without therapy; thus a non-treatment control group is essential.

Another problem is that personality tests touch only a small sample of behavior; the range of behavior sampled may be too narrow to reflect adequately whatever changes do occur. Similarly, a particular personality dimension may be measured reasonably well in the normal person—but does it apply to psychopathological states? Is a sociability scale developed for normal persons meaningful when applied to schizophrenics? It may be, but we do not *know* that it is. There are many such problems, and they can be answered. But we do not have the answers yet. Perhaps the excitement for experimentally oriented clinicians in behavioral research lies precisely in these unanswered questions.

In summary, then—although personality tests have serious limitations, they are nevertheless useful for the clinician and the researcher so long as they are correctly applied and adequately understood—in terms of both what they can do and how they do it.

Verbal behavior

The relationship between speech and personality has long been recognized as close; however, most attention in this area of behavior has been directed to *what* is said or written, rather than to *how*. As Sanford (1948, p. 157) put it, "Language, traditionally, has been regarded as the 'vehicle of thought,' with the thought attracting far more attention than the vehicle." Jackson and Messick (1958) have more recently discussed content and style in relation to personality. The clinician notes the agreement between style and content when a patient slowly and laboriously utters, "I feel depressed, just no good—useless to the world," etc. But our professional habits are such that we typically are more closely attuned to *what* is said than to other language characteristics.

An example from Berg (1958, p. 130) is to the point:

> Let us suppose that a client were to say, "I wanted to see you because I know that my boss has it in for me. I know he hates me because of the things he does to me. Even my fellow workers say that my

troubles on the job are not *what I do* but rather what the boss does to me. I won't tell you what I think of him but just let me describe what I've had happen to me at work."

The alert therapist would undoubtedly recognize the paranoid flavor of this patient's remarks—to the ideational content—but would he also be aware that 15 of the 75 words, or 20 per cent in our sample, were the ego words *I, me,* and *my?* The chances are good that the therapist would not have noticed this language characteristic; for his training inclines him toward noticing the ideas expressed rather than the choice of words. Clinically speaking, this is probably sensible in a practical setting; for bizarre notions, thought fragmentation, delusions, etc., are readily apparent in the ideas conveyed by a patient and pertinent to clinical decisions. But for experimental purposes, other language characteristics can be a rich, if little-worked, mine of data for assessing personality and personality change. One of the early studies of this sort in which actual data were gathered was that of Buseman (1927), who found that an increase in verbs as related to adjectives among a group of school children was associated with teachers' ratings of instability among those pupils. Balken and Masserman (1940) employed the same verb-adjective ratio in an investigation of the language of 50 patients diagnosed as cases of conversion hysteria, anxiety state, and obsessive-compulsive reaction. They reported that adjectives were used more frequently by the conversion hysterics, while the obsessive-compulsive patients used more verbs and more total words. The anxiety-state patients used relatively fewer adjectives and were in between the other groups in frequency of verb usage. A somewhat more carefully executed study is that by Lorenz and Cobb (1953), who compared the spontaneous speech which accompanied TAT testing for 10 hysteric patients with that of 10 control subjects. When compared to the normal group, the hysteric patients were found to use more verbs and pronouns, fewer adjectives, prepositions, conjunctions, and articles. The patients also used the pronoun *I* with high frequency and used fewer different kinds of words per thousand words uttered. Another study by Lorenz and Cobb (1952) reported differences between speech samples of 10 manic and 10 control patients. The manics, like hysterics, used fewer different kinds of words and they repeated particular words with greater than normal frequency. They also used more pronouns, more main and auxiliary verbs, and fewer adjectives and prepositions. In general, the manic speech appeared to be relatively repetitive and homogeneous, unlike normal speech, which qualifies and individualizes.

Again many such studies unfortunately lack appropriate control groups for comparison purposes—for example, a number of language studies of the type-token ratio. These studies have compared the number of different words (the *types*) with the total number of all words spoken (the *tokens*) and there is probably something basic and potentially meaningful in such analyses of verbal behavior. Some of the results obtained thus far are tantalizing, although not yet convincing. Mann (1944) has shown that normal subjects have a higher type-token ratio (TTR) than schizophrenic patients, and Fairbanks (1944) has offered some support in his finding that schizophrenics use significantly fewer nouns, conjunctions, prepositions, and articles, but significantly more verbs, pronouns, and interjections than college students. Roshal (1953) used the TTR for the first and last of a series of psychotherapeutic interviews and found changes indicating that increased variability in verbal behavior had occurred, presumably as a result of the treatment. The majority of TTR researches have used college students as subjects or in control groups; and since speech is the response measure employed, it is difficult to assess the possible influence of vocabulary size, verbal fluency, education, etc. The possible existence of such influences does not, however, negate the usefulness of verbal behavioral measures. Speech is, after all, exclusively human and thus may well be a most fertile field for clinical research; but speech is so sensitive to cultural influences of class, education, and intelligence that such research requires controls which are considerably more thoroughgoing than usual.

Other approaches have examined verbal behavior in different contexts and with varying degrees of success. Dollard and Mowrer (1953) developed a discomfort-relief quotient (DRQ) to measure behavioral change. This method classifies words, clauses, and sentences as to whether they signify discomfort, relief from discomfort, or neither. Hunt (1949a, 1949b) carefully applied the DRQ to social casework settings and found that the ratings of improvement made by case workers failed to correlate significantly with the DRQ. An analysis of broader ideational units expressed by clients during therapeutic interviews was employed by Snyder (1945), who found that the client's discussion of future plans was virtually nonexistent during the first interview, but increased to approximately 12 per cent of the responses in the last interview. He also reported that the affective tone of responses changed from negative to positive during the same period. Seeman (1949) in a somewhat similar study also found an increase in positive and a decrease in negative attitudes as therapy progressed. Interestingly, however, he observed that positive attitudes tended to be expressed in the past tense and negative attitudes in the present.

While their method was rather qualitative, Mayers and Mayers (1946) did a novel study of the responses of various types of patients who were asked to make up stories. They assumed that the patients' conflicts would be reflected in their syntax and grammatical expression, and found some support for this notion in that insecure individuals used "might" and "if" frequently, whereas passive individuals avoided active verbs in favor of participles and passive expressions. Schizophrenics showed some tendency to omit articles and pronouns. Using a case published by Carl Rogers as his source of data, Berg (1958) analyzed a series of eight therapeutic interviews in terms of frequency of *ego words* (I, me, my, mine, etc.), *empathic words* (you, we, our, us, etc.), *negative expressions* (no, never, not, etc.), and the ratio of syllables to words. On the assumption that certain initial word sounds would be associated with profanity and obscenity, he then tabulated the number of words beginning with B, K, F, P, S, and Sh. It was found that, as the interviews progressed, the frequency of ego words decreased and empathic words increased. The frequency of B, K, F, etc., words also decreased with succeeding interviews. The correction of ego word frequency with this word analysis was .80. The negative word frequency showed a decrease as adjustment improved, and the word-syllable ratio showed no significant relationship to any of the measures taken.

Still another technique was that used by Chodorkoff and Mussen (1953) in a study of 40 schizophrenic patients compared with 40 normal persons, matched for age, education, and intelligence. The subjects were asked to select the best of four correct definitions on a vocabulary test, with each definition representing either class, example, description, or function. The schizophrenic selected more function and example definitions, whereas the normal subjects preferred class definitions.

One can speculate that careful, experimental study of verbal behavior may provide the basis for a much deeper understanding of personality and adjustment than now exists. But comprehensive analyses of verbal behavior, such as that occurring in an interview, are laborious and expensive. However, new recording methods and apparatus, such as that described by Matarazzo in Chapter 15, or new approaches like the verbal operant conditioning methods of Greenspoon in Chapter 16, may offer some solutions. It is likely that studies of verbal behavior will continue to require a high degree of effort, but the significance and value of the findings will increase with refined techniques.

PHYSIOLOGICAL AND ORGANIC MEASURES

Personality characteristics and emotional maladjustment are frequently associated with physiological dysfunction, organic damage, or bodily structural atypicalities. The tense, overactive victim of hyperthyroidism, the epileptic whose seizures are the product of brain scar tissue, and the saddle-nosed mongoloid child are obvious cases in point. Such physical indicators are often direct reflections of the personality variables under study and, at times, are causally related to them. Thus they are, potentially, more objective, pertinent, and sensitive, and simpler than the measures in common use. Indeed, there is ample evidence that the relationship of personality to such indicators is often quite close. But there are problems. For example, if the symptoms are treated without the investigator's knowledge, the symptoms may disappear, leaving unchanged the conflict or whatever personality facet is under study. Thus, one may try to find identifying characteristics of anxiety neurosis by measuring eyeblink rate, tics, tremors, etc., in a group of anxiety neurotics and in a control group. If, however, the anxiety-ridden patients have been given tranquilizers, they may blink, tic, and tremble no differently from the controls. Today, especially, it is almost impossible to find schizophrenic patients who are untranquilized and unshocked. Another problem is that the symptoms should relate directly and meaningfully to the personality characteristic under scrutiny. Tremors, for example, are often associated with anxiety reactions; yet various subjective and objective measures will sometimes indicate that the anxiety-neurotic patient is much improved, although the tremor remains. Whether the consequence of functional autonomy, a chance relationship, or sheer obstinacy on the part of the patient, the tremor persists, to the confusion of the earnest researcher who was using it as a response measure.

Symptom removal, of course, may be of prime importance to the patient. He comes for help because of general tension and skipped heartbeats, for example, and departs reasonably satisfied when his tension is relieved and the extra systoles have disappeared. It matters little to the patient, nor, in most cases, to the practitioner, whether pill, palaver, or neither produced the change. But it matters a great deal to the experimentalist, for he must know *why*, the answer to which is the reason for his professional existence. Curiously, while the practical treatment situation may offer pitfalls for the unwary researcher, the researcher himself often has his own blind spots. Do measurements taken in a laboratory setting, for example, apply to clinical problems? Then, when an actual treatment setting is employed, can the measures taken be generalized to other situations at work, play, or home? They may indeed, but few investigators have made any attempt to check this.

Still another question concerns the extent to which physiological measures may be meaningfully related to personality characteristics. Wenger (1948) in a careful study of a wide range of physiological variables with a large number of subjects, found difficulty in locating any significant correlations among the measures he used. In Part III of the present volume, Psychophysiology, the chapters by Brady, Dews, Malmo, and Pribram describe a great many studies dealing with physiological and organic measures which relate to personality. Thus, the following studies are presented chiefly as examples of the kind of measures which have been used for assessment purposes, not as an exhaustive review.

Most research dealing with physiological and organic factors in relation to personality has been concerned with deviant personality states and personality change rather than with the dimensions of the normal personality. Thus a great deal has been published on skin conductance, brain waves, muscle tension, etc., in schizophrenia, but very little on such measures as applied to general sociability or similar traits, as they occur in normal people. The measures actually used vary from direct, simple observation to elaborate records obtained from complex and elegant apparatus. In an observational study, for example, Altus (1946, 1950) found that enuresis and constipation were indicators of personality disturbance among illiterate soldiers. Some additional examples of such simple measures are worthy of consideration. Goddard (1902) and Doll (1916) used hand preference in studies of mental retardation, and found a limited relationship between left-hand preference and feeblemindedness. Olson (1929) measured nervous habits in children by recording the number of times the children picked their noses or put fingers into their mouths during a series of five-minute observation periods. More recently, Meyer, Bahrick, and Fitts (1953) tried to measure anxiety by determining eye blink frequency during short time periods, on the hypothesis that blink rate was positively related to anxiety. Although more complex in the sense of chemistry laboratory technique, direct observation was also employed in Fischer's (1953) report that a component in the urine of acute schizophrenics was of much greater toxicity than that of normal control subjects.

Examples of measures obtained through the use of apparatus are many and varied. One of the instruments in longest use is the psychogalvanometer, which has been used to measure galvanometric skin responses (GSR) in a variety of settings. Studies employing the GSR as measures of personality facets have frequently had disappointing results; yet there continues to be something tantalizing about them. Herr and Kobler (1953), for example, tried to distinguish between normal and neurotic subjects by means of the GSR with little success. Nevertheless, the greater variability of the neurotics and the direction of mean response change for certain empirically identified stimulus words indicated to the authors that it should eventually be possible to differentiate the two groups. The GSR varies with the therapist's permissiveness in a treatment situation, according to Dittes (1957), and thus seems to Dittes to represent a measure of anxiety or "mobilization" against any sign of punishment by the therapist.

The GSR magnitude of deflection does seem to bear a close relationship to subjects' estimates of the intensity of their experience and should eventually prove to be a valuable research tool. McCurdy (1950) makes this point in a highly readable review of GSR literature which should be a "must" for any researcher interested in this field. He recomputed data from a wide variety of studies and found the correlations of the intensity of experience and GSR magnitude of deflection to range from .45 to 1.00, with an average of .75, certainly an impressive relationship. The problem for personality assessment seems to be one of using the GSR appropriately. As Eysenck (1956) observed, little progress is likely to be made until fundamental problems of measurement are resolved.

Like the GSR studies, research with the electroencephalograph (EEG), electrocardiograph (EKG), and instruments designed to measure other physical responses such as muscle tension, skin temperature, and capillary blood saturation have provided provocative if inconclusive data. Faure (1950), for example, found in a study of anxiety patients that the degree of anxiety roughly paralleled the degree of perturbance of cerebral electrical potentials when a light was applied. In the more severe cases of anxiety the EEG was not modified by opening or closing the eyes. Morselli (1953) investigated a case of multiple personality with the EEG. During abnormal periods, the EEG records resembled those of Pentothal prenarcosis—that is, increased amplitude and irregular rhythm characteristics of partial sleep. When the normal personality was dominant, the EEG record was also normal. A hundred psychotic patients with various diagnoses were examined with the EEG by Lyketsos, Belinson, and Gibbs (1953). They found no slow wave foci, and the EEG sleep patterns of the psychotics were lower in voltage than those for normal controls. Levy and Dennard (1953) also used a hundred subjects in a study of the EEG records of penitentiary inmates compared to those obtained for a normal population. They found a significantly larger proportion of abnormal records among the prisoners, and some evidence which suggested that relatively good personality structure was related to normal EEG's.

Other measures, such as recordings of muscular tension, have been used in relation to personality adjustment. When hostility themes are discussed, for example, a high level of muscular tension is recorded in the forearms (Malmo, Smith, and Kohlmeyer, 1956) but discussion of sexual conflict is associated with similar tension in the legs (Shagass and Malmo, 1954). In another study of muscle tension, Stennett (1957) found that when motivating conditions are varied from low to high levels, muscle tension and palmar sweating also vary systematically with the changes in motivating conditions.

Some studies have employed highly specific bodily areas for measurement purposes. Mowrer, Light, Luria, and Seleny (1953), for example, measured fingertip sweating and found a relationship of this response to patient's self-ratings of tension during psychotherapy. Anxiety as identified by psychological tests, however, does not seem to relate to palmar sweating according to studies by Lotsof and Downing (1956) and by Calvin, McGuigan, Tyrrell, and Soyars (1956). Fingertip temperature as measured by a thermocouple was used by Flecker (1951) to demonstrate that a rise in finger temperature was associated with emotional security and a drop with states of conflict. The heartbeat has also been used as a measure in therapy situations. Di Mascio, Boyd, Greenblatt, and Solomon (1955) found a correlation of +.79 between patients' and therapists' heart rate during the initial stages of the interview but —.44 for the final stages. They also reported the rather provocative findings that one psychotherapist always produced a lower heart rate in all three subjects of one of their experiments.

Many studies of physiological and organic response measures in relation to personality could be reviewed. But the foregoing sampling gives at least the flavor of the kind of investigations reported within this area. Eventually—but a long time ahead—personality may be expressed in terms of blood and tissue components, the structure of organs, and the functioning of body cells. Somehow the present efforts seem vaguely reminiscent of the medieval alchemist's search for the philosopher's stone. Many investigators seem implicitly, if unconsciously searching for the *one* measure which will be the footrule for the personality trait under study. This is in no way intended to belittle their efforts; for some research has indeed come encouragingly within view of such a footrule. What is needed in the near future is an inspired theoretician who can assimilate the varied research findings and come out with a clear-cut general principle. Then a basic *science of personality* will emerge; it will probably introduce measurements based on chemistry and physics, not psychology.

ENVIRONMENTAL AND ACHIEVEMENT MEASURES

How one behaves in the social milieu is probably the major criterion used by others in appraising personality. The alcoholic, the schizophrenic, the juvenile delinquent, are commonly first identified by their social behavior. The same is true of positively valued responses such as the man who keeps his head in an emergency or who is liked by others and elected to high office. Praise, punishment, or treatment is meted out chiefly on the basis of behavior in the social environment. But if behavior in this context is the criterion employed for personality assessment by the general public, it is not often the criterion used in research studies when measuring therapeutic gain or personality change. Effective psychotherapy, of course, should produce altered responses in the problem area; that is, if treatment is to have real meaning, the chronic alcoholic should have quit drinking, the juvenile delinquent should have ceased his offenses, the oft-discharged worker ought to keep a job. Take the schizophrenic who no longer thinks he is God; there has been a remission of symptom, true, but then he may be sent home to mope in idleness. For the clinical record he is listed as successfully treated; in actuality the treatment is successful only in the sense of "off our backs and on the family's." The truer test is whether he *can* return to work and acceptably perform his duties. This observation minimizes neither the value of partial success in therapeutic effort nor the importance of even slight improvement. But the main goal of therapy is to return the patient to society as a useful, contributing, and self-sustaining member, although this admittedly is not possible for most patients at present.

A wide variety of environmental and achievement measures have been used at times to assess personality change, but their use has not been common. The problem is that such measures are both expensive and difficult to obtain. Job promotions, salary increases, absenteeism, accident rates, participation in social activities, to name but a few, are indeed useful criteria when properly employed. But to gather such data accurately over a period of years is exceedingly difficult. Former patients move to other cities, change jobs, exaggerate some information items and conceal others because of shame. Yet, if full information cannot be obtained over a period of time, some data on environmental and achievement correlates of personality can usually be assembled for assessment purposes.

Thus Friedman (1950) evaluated the effects of short-term therapy with 50 patients who complained of a phobia for travel by ascertaining whether, after treatment, they were actually able to travel. Twelve were unchanged, 15 showed improvement, and 23 were able to travel freely. One might, of course, like answers to other questions, such as whether other symptoms later replaced the phobia for travel. But the report at least measures improvement on one environmental criterion, and this is clearly a step in the right direction.

Environmental and achievement correlates to personality are not yet widely used, and the application of such criterion measures can be critized when they are used. Yet, such approaches are likely to provide the most useful criteria for many research situations. It seems appropriate, therefore, to review some of the investigations in this area.

Teuber and Powers (1951) wondered how effective psychotherapy would be with potential delinquents. With this question in mind, they matched a nontreatment control group with similar youngsters who were given psychotherapy. The number of court appearances over a period of time was totaled and compared for the two groups of potential delinquents. There were no significant differences.

Fox (1954) evaluated a prison counseling program by a variety of ratings and measures such as work records, school stability, financial budgeting, and reports from chaplains, cell block officers, and work supervisors, as well as successful discharge from, or violation of, parole. The counseled group did significantly better than the control group in terms of these environmental criteria. A similarly realistic study is that by Ludwig and Ranson (1947) who evaluated the success of treatment for combat-induced NP disability by the percentage of servicemen who could return to full combat duty. This is an obviously important criterion, because return to active duty as a kitchen hand, for example, is quite different from return to full combat duty.

Behavior in an institutional setting may be meaningful for evaluating the progress of a treatment program. Thus Cowden, Zax, Hague, and Finney (1956) evaluated the improvement made in a group of patients receiving group psychotherapy and chlorpromazine as compared to a nontreatment control group. As criteria for improvement, they used frequency counts of the times a patient required neural wet packs or electroconvulsive shock, engaged in fights or was transferred to less disturbed wards. Those receiving group therapy and chlorpromazine showed more improvement than the controls. Raush, Dittman, and Taylor (1959), using similar environmental events assessed change resulting from treatment administered to children in a residential setting. They standardized observations on the children's behavior during meal times, play periods, and arts-and-crafts sessions. With such measures they found that the most significant changes occurred in the children's relationship to adults, while their relationships with peers changed relatively little. These studies confirm the assumption that how an individual behaves as he moves about in his particular environment is a significant factor in the appraisal of adjustment.

In a study covering a seventeen-year period, Thorne (1958) found that the important measures of psychological health included a stable work history, broad range of vocational and avocational interests, socially approved habits such as sobriety and thrift, and, of course, freedom from chronic mental disorders. Interestingly and perhaps deterministically, the social classes which are less likely to meet Thorne's criteria are the ones which have the highest incidence of mental disorders. As Hollingshead and Redlich (1958) noted, not only do the members of the lower social strata contribute more NP patients but the treatment they get is likely to be different from that received by other classes. The lower classes are much more likely to receive electroconvulsive shock; the middle and upper classes more frequently receive psychotherapy. Kahn, Pollack, and Fink (1957) reported similar findings in an investigation of type of treatment of mental patients as related to age, education, and birthplace. The older, less educated, and foreign-born were more likely to receive electroconvulsive shock than other patients. Like Hollingshead and Redlich, they found that the patients who resembled therapists in their higher social background were more frequently given psychotherapy.

There is a problem in how to handle these measures and in understanding what they mean. As Berg (1952, p. 48) observed, "The use of environmental or achievement correlates requires a value judgment on the part of the investigator, namely, that the observed change validly indicates a better or poorer adjustment. At times this may be misleading. Lower academic grades, for example, may not signify poorer adjustment but merely that 'boy has met girl,' often a healthier symptom than higher grades." The same might be said of the ulcer-ridden, tremor-wracked sales executive who takes a lower paying job but thereby achieves better personal adjustment. In our culture we regard higher grades and increased salaries as signs of progress, but they do not always indicate better emotional equilibrium.

Problems exist not only in interpretation, but also in obtaining certain kinds of information. Information may be unavailable either because of policy or because it is unknown. Thus, company regulations may forbid supplying information on disciplinary action, absenteeism, or reprimands about an employee who was formerly under treatment. In a small business, after a year or two, personnel changes and an absence of formal records may similarly prevent the gathering of accurate data. Worse, an informant may deliberately mislead an investigator by indicating that an employee left voluntarily, perhaps for a better job, when actually he was *told* to find another job. But the informant is unwilling to prejudice what he regards as a new start for the former employee. Then, too, there are the limitations that the investigator must impose upon himself. In our culture many persons cling to medieval ideas about mental illness. Thus the investigator may have to exercise so much discretion in approaching those in contact with a discharged patient that it is hardly worth the effort, particularly in view of the difficulties even the most cautious inquiry may create for the ex-patient.

In general, the first caution in the use of environmental and achievement correlates would be that those selected are valid indications of improved adjustment. Second, multiple criteria are likely to be much more meaningful than single measures. (Zax and Klein [1960] have an excellent review of studies in this area.) Finally, the information sources must be closely scrutinized for maximum accuracy of report and for complete protection of the former patient. With these conditions met, it is probable that the most meaningful measures of therapeutic gain will be obtained if the measures can be repeated over a fairly lengthy period under conditions of before, during, and after treatment.

EXPERIMENTALLY INDUCED PERSONALITY CHANGE

The experimentally induced personality change requires that the changes or abnormal states be deliberately created, preferably along a single dimension. Various techniques have been used to produce appropriate changes for experimental study: *role playing*, in which an abnormal state such as mental retardation is simulated by a normal person; *psychological stress*, intended to arouse fear, anger, frustration, loss of self-esteem, etc.; *noxious stimuli*, either actual or impending, employed in the form of electric shock, etc., used to produce conflict or chaotic states in the subject; *deprivation or alteration of stimuli*, in which an absence or modification of stimuli causes behavioral changes; *drugs and biochemical components*, in which pharmaceutical and biochemical preparations create anxiety, depression, symptoms of mental disorder, etc.; *reactivation of a dormant conflict or state of maladjustment*, whereby a once-troublesome adjustment problem is again made a source of conflict.

In all of these procedures, measures are (or should be) taken before, during, and after the experimental condition, and any or all of the previously described methods of assessment may be used for this purpose—that is, rating, and psychological tests. Strictly speaking, such induction of personality change is a research design rather than a particular assessment method. Nevertheless, as an approach to the experimental study of personality it has great potential for definitive research. We might prophesy that the major breakthroughs in personality research will be brought about by these approaches in which personality changes are experimentally induced. But these procedures must be accompanied by caution and elaborate safeguards in order to avoid public misunderstanding of these techniques.

Much of the earlier work in this area was done with animals. Maier (1939) described a series of experiments in which he produced abnormal behavior in the rat by such techniques as forcing the animals to either brave a blast of air or jump across an open space and fall into a net. Landis and Hunt (1939) also summarized a long series of studies in which they used human as well as animal subjects in their investigation of the *startle pattern*. By means of sudden, intense stimulation, they produced catastrophic behavior in the organisms and measured the ensuing flexion (startle) response. While they produced a temporary upheaval which may legitimately be termed a state of maladjustment, their interest was limited to the startle pattern manifestations and did not include other possible associated personality effects.

Role playing or simulation

In role playing, the subject is instructed to respond to some measuring instrument, such as a psychological test, as if he had a particular personality characteristic or type of maladjustment. An essential condition, of course, is that the subjects have the necessary information to do a good job in their role. Usually, the experimenter has some purpose in mind other than the apparent or announced one. Thus Gough (1947, 1950) had persons familiar with clinical diagnosis simulate severe psychoneurosis and then paranoid schizophrenia when responding to the MMPI. He found that his subjects under such instructions produced MMPI profiles quite similar to those of genuine patients. Although interested in this finding, Gough was more interested in whether such faking could be detected. He found that the MMPI F, or validity, score minus the K, or test-taking attitude, score provided a means of detecting the fakers.

Using a similar approach, Goldstein (1945) and Pollaczek (1952) instructed subjects of normal intelligence to respond to intelligence test items as if they were mentally retarded. The responses thus obtained in both studies were then compared with the test responses of bona fide mental defectives. The malingerers showed definite patterns in their faking; for, while they were able to obtain low intelligence scores, how they answered various items provided a sound basis for detection. They missed many easy items which the true feebleminded cases were able to answer correctly; at times, they missed other items in a systematic manner—that is, as if they figured out the right answer and then deviated from it in a standard fashion. Both Goldstein and Pollaczek were each able then to prepare "malingering" keys for detecting faking on intelligence tests.

In another facet of role playing, the subject is not instructed in his role but rather assumes it voluntarily, usually for purposes of gaining some personal advantage. A clerical employee studied by Paterson (1946), for example, strongly desired a promotion to a personnel position, for which he was given both the Kuder and the Strong interest inventories. Although the employee slanted his responses to favor the promotion he wished to attain, the test data nevertheless indicated that the employee's interests were basically in clerical, not in personnel activities. Paterson's interest lay in observing whether the Kuder or the Strong was more easily faked in such situations; of the two, the Kuder appeared to be the more easily slanted. However, although situations in which the self-interest of subjects lead them to malinger are not common, it seems like that such self-imposed roles with natural conditions of motivation behind them could provide the framework for useful studies of personality change.

Psychological stress

In experimental stress situations, the subject is placed under pressure, and measures taken before and after the stress condition. Sarason (1957) found that subjects identified operationally as high in manifest anxiety performed poorly on a serial learning task when faced with pronounced threat of failure, whereas low anxiety subjects were not adversely affected. The high and low anxiety groups showed no differences when threat of failure was not present. Heath (1956) examined the effects of anxiety upon the intellectual performance of schizophrenic subjects by using test content constructed around anxiety themes. He found that there were individual thresholds for the appearance of anxiety responses in such subjects, and that severe anxiety had a disorganizing effect for the performance of intellectual tasks. Grinker, Sabshin, Hamburg, Board, Basowitz, Korchin, Persky, and Chevalier (1957) also employed psychiatric patients under conditions of stress in the form of interviews which, in nonreassuring fashion, probed the patients' most sensitive areas of conflict. The investigators were unable to control the degree of anxiety thus aroused nor were they able to grade the stimuli in relation to the anxiety produced. The possible forms of stress which have been employed at one time or another are many and varied, ranging from a physical examination to requiring subjects to cut off the head of a live rat. Whatever type of stress is used, it is essential that the stimuli utilized actually represent stress *for the subject*. A number of situations which would be regarded as distasteful, embarrassing, or threatening for the experimenter are nothing of the sort for many subjects.

Noxious stimuli

To the extent that potentially harmful stimuli are impending but not applied, the technique of noxious stimuli is essentially the same as the stress procedures already described. Perhaps it matters little whether the noxious stimuli are actually applied or merely threatened, since the effect upon the subject may be much the same in either case.

Threat alone should not be underestimated; young men in good health, as in the military services, have been known to faint at the prospect of a hypodermic injection. Schachter (1957), for example, subjected hypertensive and normotensive patients to various situations designed to arouse fear, anger, and pain. He found that a significantly greater rise in blood pressure occurred in the hypertensive patients as compared to the controls. Furthermore, the hypertensive subjects gave more overt indications of fear and anger than the normotensives. At times, conflicting results are reported for similar situations. For example, whereas Sarason (1957) found that subjects high in manifest anxiety performed relatively poorly in a serial learning task when threatened with failure, Silverman and Blitz (1956) found, by contrast, that high anxiety subjects who were threatened with shock did not exhibit poorer learning performance in learning tasks. Perhaps such differences occur as a function of the seriousness with which the subjects take the purported threatening condition. In any event, it would be desirable to have data on the nature and conditions of noxious stimuli. The recent burgeoning of space medicine research may well provide some of the needed information. Human subjects have been stressed with gravitational pull, high and low temperatures, confinement to small spaces, loud noises, etc. However, although such data are likely to be useful, personality measures are not usually included when appraising these stress effects.

Deprivation or alteration of stimuli

In deprivation or alteration of stimulus studies, the subject is deprived of sensory stimulation by some means, or the normal stimulus conditions are altered in some manner. Bexton, Heron, and Scott (1954), among others, used a soundproof room for this purpose, Lily (1956) immersed snorkel-equipped subjects in a tank of water. All sensory input was not eliminated, of course, since certain tactile and kinesthetic sensations could not be completely cut off; yet the results were striking. The subjects experienced auditory and visual hallucinations, and were unable to follow a connected line of thought. At times, a blank period occurred in which all mental content appeared to be absent. Certain of these effects appeared to linger in attenuated form for as long as twenty-four hours after the experiment ended. Stimulus alteration has also been achieved in other ways, such as in the use of tilting-chair and artificial horizon studies with airplane pilots or in the auditory feedback research on speech. Indeed, almost any form of illusion or change in stimulus property could be employed to study various facets of personality, although such has not often been the case. The usual measure taken is a decrement in performance, as on a verbal learning task, a pursuit rotor, or other perceptual motor activity. But the applications to personality study are both obvious and promising.

Several interesting studies have been reported wherein the usual conditions of auditory stimulation were modified, although the particular stimulus properties remained unchanged. Hassel, Magaret, and Cameron (1952) had a group of college students compose a five-minute story based upon one of the pictures in the Thematic Apperception Test (TAT). For half the group the stories were tape-recorded and then, while the subjects sought to composed a second TAT story, the first story which each had composed was played back to them by means of earphones. The other half of the group composed two stories, one after the other, without interference. It was found that the distraction resulted in a significantly greater amount of scattered speech by the subjects, but with increased meaningfulness in the story itself. Fairbanks and Guttman (1958) have used a somewhat analogous but more powerful technique in their studies of language disorganization. Their approach required the subjects to speak into a recorder; then, after a delay of 0, .1, .2, .4, and .8 seconds, the subjects heard what they had just uttered repeated through earphones while they read aloud a prose passage. The delay produced marked articulatory disturbances, phonetically illogical substitutions, and additions which were repetitive and apparently unpurposeful.

Drugs and biochemical components

Pharmaceutical preparations such as drugs or biochemicals are also used to change adjustment or personality characteristics. The assumptions underlying research of this sort are soundly based, for ordinary experience with the effects of such drugs as alcohol, barbiturates, or Benzedrine offer ample evidence of their capacity for modifying behavior. Anxiety states, depressions, hallucinations, have all been produced by the use of the appropriate drug. Because of the intense public interest in chemotherapy as a possible "cure" for mental disorder, the professional literature available in this field during the past decade is enormous, although many of the studies are poorly controlled and must be regarded as inconclusive. In general, what have been called *miracle drugs* in the public press are far less miraculous in their effects than the initial enthusiasm for them would have indicated. They are useful, yes, but neither *the key* nor necessarily the *ultimate answer* to personality aberration.

At the level of clinical description, however, a number of personality disorders are indistinguishable from symptomatology produced by drugs or toxic conditions. As Hoskins (1946, p. 71) observed, schizoid reactions can be produced by bulbocapnine, mescaline, alcohol, morphine, and even by breathing air of reduced oxygen content. Ex-

perimentally, the most widely used drug for producing psychopathological states is probably lysergic acid diethylamide (LSD). According
to Salvatore and Hyde (1956), this drug produces a series of behavioral changes which begin with bodily symptoms and anxiety reactions followed by perceptual distortions and feelings of unreality.
The final stage appears to be characterized by attempts to cope with
the feeling of unreality, during which various degrees of mental confusion result. After approximately six hours the symptoms dissipate. In
a critical review of LSD research, Clark (1956) questions whether the
LSD-induced experience is the same in form as any known natural
psychotic state. He notes that most studies either omit or have inadequate control groups, that observations are often unsystematic, and
that the experimenter and the subject may at times be biased, because
both have knowledge of the drug's behavioral effects.

The criticisms Clark leveled at LSD studies may with equal justice
be applied to research on glutamic acid. On the basis of reports which
indicated that learning performance in rats could be improved by the
administration of glutamic acid, this drug was used in attempts to
raise the level of intellectual functioning in human subjects. The reports were conflicting; however in an analysis of the various studies,
Astin and Ross (1960) showed that positive findings with respects to
raised intelligence after glutamic acid administration were definitely
associated with a lack of control data.

Another technique employs blood components of the victims of
psychopathological conditions. Heath and his colleagues have used
taraxein, a protein substance which is obtained from the blood of
schizophrenic patients (Heath, Martens, Leach, Cohen, and Angel,
1957; Heath, Martens, Leach, Cohen, and Feigley, 1958) to produce
schizophrenia experimentally. These investigators injected taraxein in
nonpsychotic prison inmates who volunteered for the study. All twenty
subjects developed primary symptoms of schizophrenia, including
autism, thought blocking, and depersonalization, as well as secondary
symptoms such as delusions and auditory hallucinations. They also
employed a rapid transfusion of blood from schizophrenic to normal
subjects and reported that the transfused subjects exhibited mild
schizophrenic symptoms which lasted for an hour or less. Freedman
and Ginsberg (1958) reversed this procedure and replaced about
60 per cent of the blood of schizophrenic patients with blood from
normal donors. Three adult schizophrenics showed no change and a
slight improvement was noted in one schizophrenic child. Hoagland
(1958) attempted to duplicate the Heath researches with taraxein, but
he was unsuccessful. Generally, the results of studies in this area have
been conflicting and thus far inconclusive. It seems likely that the research design is faulty in many of these investigations and that inade-

quate, qualitative assessment is employed in place of more quantitative measurement of behavioral change. There may very well be something of critical, perhaps of ultimate significance for the understanding of personality and maladjustment in future research which employs drugs or biochemical components. Certainly hormonal and other changes do seem to be present in psychopathological states. However, whether this is due to the disorder, a function of long hospitalization, or something else is not clear. Controls are needed but they are often difficult to attain. Just as an aside, it may be noted that it is frequently very difficult to locate patients who have not been given drugs or perhaps electroconvulsive shock treatment prior to NP hospital admission, so common has such prehospitalization practice become—all of which points up the pressing need for controls.

Reactivation of a dormant conflict or state of maladjustment

The reactivation of a previous conflict presumably permits study and/or treatment with the aim of understanding the processes involved and, perhaps, testing the efficacy of a treatment method. The technique is rarely used, probably because of the obvious difficulties and possible dangers involved. Indeed, the only carefully designed study is probably that by Keet (1948), which dealt with such minuscule problem areas that the technique may have limited applications at best. Keet used word association tests to identify conflict areas and then treated the miniature conflict by nondirective and directive procedures. The directive or interpretive techniques were found to be far more effective than nondirective methods—so much better that several investigators were led to replicate his study. However, replication was never accomplished. Merrill (1952), for example, did not find any difference between the two methods of treatment which would confirm Keet's results. Apart from the lack of support for Keet's results, the research *design* he used is ingenious and worth studying.

THEORETICAL EXPLANATIONS
OF ASSESSMENT

The material reviewed thus far demonstrates that a wide range of stimulus materials can be employed to produce a broad variety of responses which, in turn, can be used to assess personality and personality change. Furthermore, the evidence cited is but a small sampling of many thousands of similar studies. True, some of the assessment techniques described are considerably more effective than others for purposes of clinical prediction; but virtually all of them predict or otherwise identify personality characteristics at least to some degree. Hundreds of response measures have been used in thousands of personality investigations. Some of the measures do an adequate and needed clinical job of assessment, whereas the others predict only somewhat better than chance. Now, with so many and such varied techniques having at least some value for personality appraisal, the question remains: "Why? Why do so many different methods predict behavior?" In addition to the familiar inkblots, pictures, or verbal test items, one can employ the Archimedes spiral aftereffect (Price and Deabler, 1955), the autokinetic phenomenon (Voth, 1947; Rechtshaffen and Mednick, 1955), hand preference (Goddard, 1902; Doll, 1916), musical sounds (Cattell and Anderson, 1953), meaningless sounds (Adams and Berg, 1961), amount of body sway (Eysenck, 1947) and myriad other measures; yet all of them have varying degrees of value. In a discussion called "The Unimportance of Test Item Content" (Berg, 1959), it has been asserted that virtually any stimulus material and any sense modality could be employed for purposes of personality measurement. Not all such materials are of equal value—as, for example, not every item of the MMPI is just as good as any other for measuring the Hy (hysteria) or some other scale. But one could find a sound or an abstract design or some other stimulus material which would predict as well as a particular MMPI item for a given scale. In that sense, then, a particular type of test item content is unimportant.

In attempting to explain why personality assessment devices do measure, the oldest explanation is, by implication, that of *face validity*. Test materials were chosen because they obviously related to the variable under study; hence if one were interested in emotionality, he prepared items which inquired whether the subject was prone to "lose his temper easily" or whether he was "calm in emergencies," etc. Thus, although test item face validity was not systematized as an explanation of why psychological tests measured personality, the content used and the procedures followed in developing the older personality tests demonstrated that face validity was the basis for such assessment. During the last twenty-five years, although preoccupation with face validity was still evident in item construction, the actual basis for determining the value of a particular item gradually became empirical in orientation. Accordingly, a test item dealing with reading habits might be retained in a neurotic scale, even though its content seemed to be unrelated to neuroticism, because it was a differentiating factor. Another item with obvious face validity, such as a question about how often one felt jittery, would be rejected if it failed to differentiate neurotic from normal subjects to some degree. The usefulness of an item, therefore, was decided empirically, a simple *modus operandi*, yet one which was not always fully understood. Hutt (1945), for example, asserted that structured personality tests were based on the assumption that the items would have the same meaning for all subjects who took the test, a misunderstanding for which Meehl (1945) took Hutt sharply to task.

Under the onslaught of empirical approaches, interest in face validity was no longer paramount as the basis for constructing personality tests, leaving the question still open as to why personality tests measure. During the past decade, three explanations have been proposed as a first and partial step in resolving this question. These are explanations based upon (1) *Content and Style* (Jackson and Messick, 1958), (2) *the Social Desirability Variable* (Edwards, 1953, 1957) and (3) *the Deviation Hypothesis* (Berg, 1955, 1957, 1961).

Content and style in personality assessment

In studying behavior, one may examine the content (*what* is said or done) and the style or mode (*how* it is said or done). In denying a request, for example, a person may say "no" in soft, level tones unaccompanied by other bodily activity, or he may roar "no" while glaring balefully and leaning tensely forward. Jackson and Messick (1958) have remarked that although these two response characteristics are conceptually distinct, style is often overlooked. Therefore these writers propose that measures of response style, rather than content, are more likely to provide for adequate assessment of personality, and that such measurements may bridge the gap between personality theory and personality measurement. Most of the evidence they offer is based upon various studies of the California S scale which purports to measure authoritarianism, but actually seems to measure acquiescence. Jackson and Messick (1957), and Jackson, Messick, and Solley (1957), among other students of the problem, have shown that style rather than content is of chief importance in the F scale. These writers have been interested primarily in acquiescence as a characteristic response style; however, by extension they could apply their concept to other personality assessment techniques and thus offer an explanation of why and how various techniques measure. Cronbach (1946, 1950) has discussed various response style characteristics (he called them response sets) as they occur in psychological tests. In addition to *acquiescence*, Cronbach described a number of other styles—for example, *tendency to gamble, evasiveness*—however, he urged that such "sets" be identified and then eliminated in tests because of their influence on reliability and validity. Jackson and Messick propose to use, rather than eliminate, such response styles. Thus far, not too much evidence about the value of response styles has been accumulated, but it seems reasonable to predict that Jackson and Messick's confidence in such response characteristics will be justified. Certainly a large number of behavioral facets can be examined and tested experimentally within the content versus style framework.

The social desirability variable

Edwards (1957) has contended that almost any statement or item concerned with personality can be characterized in terms of its position on a single dimension. He calls this dimension the social desirability-undesirability variable, and further states that it appears to be the most important single dimension on which to locate personality statements. In his book on the social desirability variable in relation to personality assessment (1957), he presents a great deal of evidence on psychological tests to support his contention. For example, Klett (1957) found a relationship of .88 between social desirability scale values obtained for psychotic patients and college students, indicating that these subjects were rating the items in much the same way. Similarly, Hanley (1956) obtained correlations of .82 and .89, respectively, between probability of endorsement and social desirability ratings for samples of items from the MMPI D (symptomatic depression) and Sc (schizophrenia) scales.

With such evidence in mind, Edwards constructed a Personal Preference Schedule (1953) in which, he believes, the social desirability variable has been controlled. The studies of Silver (1957) and Kelleher (1958) support this belief. However, Goodstein and Heilbrun (1959) and Wiggins and Rumrill (1959) have raised doubts concerning the significance and pureness of this variable. Whatever the outcome of future studies on the SD variable, it seems likely that the approach is too narrow to explain more than a limited number of assessment methods. As noted earlier, an investigator may employ spiral aftereffects, autokinetic phenomena, eyeblink rate, and other stimulus-response conditions for assessing personality—all of them techniques whose effectiveness would not seem to be explained by the social desirability variable.

The deviation hypothesis

An approach which attempts to embrace a much broader spectrum of behavior is the *deviation hypothesis* (Berg, 1955, 1957, 1961). This conception is not limited to an explanation of why various techniques are able to measure, in varying degree, familiar dimensions of personality such as sociability, or psychopathological conditions such as schizophrenia. Although such personality facets are included in the formulation of the deviation hypothesis, many other behavior patterns, such as academic over- and underachievement, accident proneness, mental retardation, immaturity, and senescence are also included. Of the immense repertoire of all possible responses, according to this view, many responses are regarded as clustering or hanging together to form various patterns. Certain of these patterns are different or *deviant* in the sense that they are uncommon and may be objectively identified by simple statistical methods. They are not necessarily deviant in the sense of psychopathology; rather, they are deviant in the sense of a departure from the modal pattern, just as the literal meaning of *abnormal* is away from the norm or common pattern. Hence, a surgeon, an 80-year-old man, and a schizophrenic would each be deviant because most people are not surgeons, 80 years old, nor schizophrenics. What is important is that such deviant patterns be significant in some manner and be identified in an objective, operationally clean fashion. The deviation hypothesis makes the assumption that deviant responses are general; and if a deviant behavior pattern can be validly identified in a critical area of behavior (i.e., psychotic reactions), deviant behavior patterns can be identified in noncritical areas (i.e., responses to test items). This hypothesis has been stated as follows (Berg, 1957, p. 159): "Deviant response patterns tend to be general; hence, those deviant behavior patterns which are significant for abnormality (atypicalness) and thus regarded as symptoms (earmarks or signs), are associated with other deviant response patterns which are in noncritical areas of behavior and which are not regarded as symptoms of personality aberration (nor as indicators, signs, earmarks)." This does not mean, of course, that *every* response made by a deviant person will be deviant; obviously we are all deviant in a few areas. Yet most of our responses are quite like those of other people. But certain small patterns of deviant responses in a significant area of behavior (for example, schizophrenia) do appear to be associated with response patterns in unimportant areas of behavior (for example, marking a particular MMPI item *true* as opposed to *false*). If deviant responses are general in the sense outlined above the deviation hypothesis would explain why such a vast array of materials can be used to assess personality and other aspects of behavior. A sizable amount of evidence has been published in support of the hypothesis most of which has been reviewed by Berg (1961).

REFERENCES

Adams, H. E., & Berg, I. A. Deviant responses to auditory and visual stimulus patterns in the identification of schizophrenia. *J. Psychol.*, 1961. In press.

Allport, G. W., Vernon, P. E., & Lindzey, G. *Study of Values.* (Rev. ed.) Boston: Houghton Mifflin, 1951.

Altus, W. D. Some correlates of enuresis among illiterate soldiers. *J. consult. Psychol.*, 1946, *10*, 246–259.

Altus, W. D. Constipation and adjustment among illiterate males. *J. consult. Psychol.*, 1950, *14*, 25–31.

Anastasi, Anne. *Psychological testing.* New York: Macmillan, 1954.

Astin, A. W., & Ross, S. Glutamic acid and human intelligence. *Psychol. Bull.*, 1960, *57*, 429–434.

Balken, Eva R., & Masserman, J. H. The language of phantasy: III. The language of the phantasies of patients with conversion hysteria, anxiety state, and obsessive-compulsive neurosis. *J. Psychol.*, 1940, *10*, 75–86.

Baughman, E. E. A comparative analysis of Rorschach forms with altered stimulus characteristics. *J. proj. Tech.*, 1954, *18*, 151–164.

Bendig, A. W. Reliability of case history ratings and intellectual ability of graduate raters. *J. consult. Psychol.*, 1956, *20*, 142–144.

Berg, I. A. Measures before and after therapy. *J. clin. Psychol.*, 1952, *8*, 46–50.

Berg, I. A. Response bias and personality: the Deviation Hypothesis. *J. Psychol.*, 1955, *40*, 61–71.

Berg, I. A. Deviant responses and deviant people: the formulation of the Deviation Hypothesis. *J. counsel. Psychol.*, 1957, *4*, 154–161.

Berg, I. A. Word choice in the interview and personal adjustment. *J. counsel. Psychol.* 1958, *5*, 130–135.

Berg, I. A. The unimportance of test item content. In B. M. Bass and I. A. Berg (Eds.), *Objective approaches to personality assessment*. Princeton, N.J.: Van Nostrand, 1959.

Berg, I. A. Measuring deviant behavior by means of deviant response sets. In I. A. Berg and B. M. Bass (Eds.), *Conformity and deviation*. New York: Harper, 1961.

Bexton, W. H., Heron, W., & Scott, T. H. Effects of decreased variation in the sensory environment. *Canad. J. Psychol.*, 1954, *8*, 70–76.

Boring, E. G. *A history of experimental psychology*. New York: Appleton-Century-Crofts, 1950.

Bronfenbrenner, U. Circularity in relationships involving identification scores based on real or assumed similarity. In R. Tagiuri and L. Petrullo (Eds.), *Person perception and interpersonal behavior*. Stanford, Calif.: Stanford Univ. Press, 1958.

Busemann, A. Über typische und phäsiche unterscheide der kategoricalen Sprachform. *Z. pädag. Psychol.*, 1926, *27*, 415–419.

Calvin, A. D., McGuigan, F. J., Tyrrell, S., & Soyars, M. Manifest anxiety and the Palmar Perspiration Index. *J. consult. Psychol.*, 1956, *20*, 356.

Cattell, R. B. *The sixteen personality factor questionnaire*. Champaign, Ill.: Institute for Personality and Ability Testing, 1950.

Cattell, R. B., & Anderson, J. A. The measurement of personality behavior disorders by the IPAT Music Preference Test. *J. appl. Psychol.*, 1953, *37*, 446–454.

Cattell, R. B. *Personality and motivation structure and measurement*. New York: World Book, 1957.

Chodorkoff, B., & Mussen, P. H. Qualitative aspects of the vocabulary responses of normals and schizophrenics. *J. consult. Psychol.*, 1952, *16*, 43–48.

Clark, L. D. Further studies of the psychological effects of Frenquel and a critical review of previous reports. *J. nerv. ment. Dis.*, 1956, *123*, 557–560.

Cowden, R. C., Zax, M., Hague, J. R., & Finney, R. C. Chlorpromazine: alone and as an adjunct to group psychotherapy in the treatment of psychiatric patients. *Amer. J. Psychiat.*, 1956, *112*, 898–902.

Cronbach, L. J. Response set and test validity. *Educ. psychol. Measmt.*, 1946, *6*, 475–494.

Cronbach, L. J. Further evidence on response sets and test design. *Educ. psychol. Measmt.*, 1950, *10*, 3–31.

DiMascio, A., Boyd, R. W., Greenblatt, M., & Solomon, H. C. The psychiatric interview: a sociophysiologic study. *Dis. nerv. System*, 1955, *16*, 2–7.

Dittes, J. E. Galvanic skin responses as a measure of patient's reaction to therapist's permissiveness. *J. abnorm. soc. Psychol.*, 1957, *55*, 295–303.

Doll, E. A. Anthropometry as an aid to mental diagnosis. *Pub. New Jersey Trng. Sch.*, 1916, 8, 1–7.

Dollard, J., & Mowrer, O. H. A method of measuring tension in written documents. In O. H. Mowrer (Ed.), *Psychotherapy theory and research*. New York: Ronald, 1953.

Drake, L. E. A social I. E. scale for the MMPI. *J. appl. Psychol.*, 1946, 30, 51–54.

Edwards, A. L. The relationship between the judged desirability of a trait and the probability that the trait will be endorsed. *J. appl. Psychol.*, 1953a, 37, 90–93.

Edwards, A. L. *Manual for the Edwards Personal Preference Schedule*. New York: Psychol. Corp., 1953b.

Edwards, A. L. *The social desirability variable in personality assessment and research*. New York: Dryden, 1957.

Edwards, A. L. Social desirability and personality test construction. In B. M. Bass and I. A. Berg (Eds.), *Objective approaches to personality assessment*. New York: Harper, 1959

Eysenck, H. J. *Dimensions of Personality*. London: Kegan Paul, 1947.

Eysenck, H. J. La validité des techniques projectives. *Rev. de Psychologie Appliquée*, 1955, 5, 231–234.

Eysenck, S. B. G. An experimental study of psychogalvanic responses of normal, neurotic, and psychotic subjects. *J. psychosom. Res.*, 1956, 1, 258–272.

Fairbanks, G., & Guttman, N. Effects of delayed auditory feedback upon articulation. *J. Speech Res.*, 1958, 1, 12–22.

Fairbanks, Helen. The quantitative differentiation of samples of spoken language. *Psychol. Monogr.*, 1944, 56, 19–38.

Faure, J. L'épreuve de la lumière sur l'electro-encephalogramme de certains nevropathes. *Rev. Oto-Neuro-Ophtal.*, 1950, 22, 554–556.

Fischer, R. Stress and the toxicity of schizophrenic serum. *Science*, 1953, 118, 409–410.

Flecker, R. Skin temperature as a psychophysical variable. *Austr. J. Psychol.*, 1951, 3, 109–120.

Fox, V. The effects of counseling on adjustment in prison. *Soc. Forces*, 1954, 32, 285–289.

Freedman, A. M., & Ginsberg, V. Exchange transfusions in schizophrenic patients. *J. nerv. ment. Dis.*, 1958, 126, 294–301.

Friedman, J. H. Short-term psychotherapy of "phobia of travel." *Amer. J. Psychother.*, 1950, 4, 259–278.

Goddard, H. H. The height and weight of feeble-minded children in American institutions. *J. nerv. ment. Dis.*, 1902, 39, 217–235.

Goldstein, H. A. A malingering key for mental tests. *Psychol. Bull.*, 1945, 42, 104–118.

Goodstein, L. D., & Heilbrun, A. B., Jr. The relationship between personal and social desirability scale values of the Edwards Personal Preference Schedule. *J. consult. Psychol.*, 1959, 23, 183.

Gough, H. G. Simulated patterns on the Minnesota Multiphasic Personality Inventory. *J. abnorm. soc. Psychol.*, 1947, 42, 215–225.

Gough, H. G. The F minus dissimulation index for the MMPI. *J. consult. Psychol.*, 1950, 14, 408–413.

Grinker, R. R., Sabshin, M., Hamburg, D. A., Board, F. A., Basowitz, H., Korchin, S. J., Persky, H., & Chevalier, J. A. The use of an anxiety-producing interview and its meaning to the subject. *Arch. Neurol. Psychiat.*, 1957, 77, 406–419.

Guilford, J. P. *An inventory of factors STDCR*. Beverly Hills, Calif.: Sheridan Supply Co., 1940.

Hall, C. S., & Lindzey, G. *Theories of personality*. New York: Wiley, 1957.

Hanley, C. Social desirability and responses to items from three MMPI scales: D, Sc, and K. *J. appl. Psychol.*, 1956, 40, 324–328.

Hanna, J. V. Estimating intelligence by interview. *Educ. psychol. Measmt.*, 1950, *10*, 420–430.

Hassel, L., Magaret, A., & Cameron, N. The production of language disorganization through personalized distraction. *J. Psychol.*, 1952, *33*, 289–299.

Hathaway, S. Some consideration relative to non-directive counseling as therapy. *J. clin. Psychol.*, 1948, *4*, 226–231.

Heath, D. H. Individual anxiety thresholds and their effect on intellectual performance. *J. abnorm. soc. Psychol.*, 1956, 52, 403–408.

Heath, R. G., Martens, S., Leach, B. E., Cohen, M., & Angel, C. Effects on behavior in humans with the administration of taraxein. *Amer. J. Psychiat.*, 1957, *114*, 14–24.

Heath, R. G., Martens, S., Leach, B. E., Cohen, M., & Feigley, C. A. Behavioral changes in non-psychotic volunteers following the administration of taraxein, the substance obtained from the serum of schizophrenic patients. *Amer. J. Psychiat.*, 1958, *114*, 917–920.

Herr, V. V., & Kobler, F. J. A psychogalvanometric test for neuroticism. *J. abnorm. soc. Psychol.*, 1953, *48*, 410–416.

Hoagland, H. Biochemical aspects of schizophrenia, *J. nerv. ment. Dis.*, 1958, *126*, 211–220.

Hollingshead, A. B., & Redlich, F. C. *Social class and mental illness.* New York: Wiley, 1958.

Holtzman, W. H. Objective scoring of projective techniques. In B. M. Bass and I. A. Berg (Eds.), *Objective approaches to personality assessment.* Princeton, N.J.: Van Nostrand, 1959, 119–145.

Holzberg, J. D. The clinical and scientific methods: synthesis or antithesis? *J. proj. Tech.*, 1957, *21*, 227–242.

Hoskins, R. G. *The biology of schizophrenia.* New York: Norton, 1946.

Hunt, J. McV. The problem of measuring the results of psychotherapy. *Psychol. Serv. Cent. J.*, 1949a, *1*, 122–135.

Hunt, J. McV. A social agency as the setting for research. *J. consult. Psychol.*, 1949b, *13*, 68–91.

Hunt, W. A., Wittson, C. L., & Hunt, Edna B. A theoretical and practical analysis of the diagnostic process. In P. H. Hoch and J. Zubin (Eds.), *Current problems in psychiatric diagnosis.* New York: Grune and Stratton, 1953.

Hutt, M. L. The use of projective methods of personality measurement in army medical installations. *J. clin. Psychol.*, 1945, *1*, 134–140.

Jackson, D. N., & Messick, S. J. A note on "ethnocentrism" and acquiescent response sets. *J. abnorm. soc. Psychol.*, 1957, *54*, 132–134.

Jackson, D. N., & Messick, S. J. Content and style in personality assessment. *Psychol. Bull.*, 1958, *55*, 243–252.

Jackson, D. N., Messick, S. J., & Solley, C. M. How rigid is the "authoritarian?" *J. abnorm. soc. Psychol.*, 1957, *54*, 137–140.

Kahn, R. L., Pollack, M., & Fink, M. Social factors in the selection of therapy in a voluntary mental hospital. *J. Hillside Hosp.*, 1957, *6*, 216–228.

Keet, C. D. Two verbal techniques in a miniature counseling situation. *Psychol. Monog.*, 1948, *62*, No. 294.

Kelleher, D. The social desirability factor in Edwards' PPS. *J. consult. Psychol.*, 1958, *22*, 100.

Kelley, E. L. Theory and techniques of assessment. *Annual Review of Psychology*, Vol. 5, Palo Alto: Annual Reviews, 1954, 281–311.

Klett, C. J. The social desirability stereotype in a hospital population. *J. consult. Psychol.*, 1957, *21*, 419–421.

Landfield, A. W. Self-predictive orientation and the movement interpretation of threat. *J. abnorm. soc. Psychol.*, 1955, *51*, 434–438.

Landis, C., & Hunt, W. A. *The startle pattern.* New York: Farrar and Rinehart, 1939.

Levy, S., and Dennard, Margaret. A study of the electro-encephalogram as related to personality structure in a group of inmates of a state penitentiary. *Amer. J. Psychiat.,* 1953, *109,* 832–839.

Lilly, J. C. Mental effects of reduction of ordinary levels of physical stimuli on intact, healthy persons. *Psychiat. Res. Rep.,* 1956, No. 5, 1–9.

Lorenz, Maria, & Cobb, S. Language behavior in manic patients. *Arch. Neurol. Psychiat.,* 1952, *67,* 763–770.

Lorenz, Maria, & Cobb, S. Language behavior in psychoneurotic patients. *Arch. Neurol. Psychiat.,* 1953, *69,* 684–694.

Lorr, M., Singer, M., & Zobel, H. Development of a record for the description of psychiatric patients. *Psychol. Serv. Cent. J.,* 1951, *3,* No. 3.

Lorr, M. Rating scales and check lists for the evaluation of psychopathology. *Psychol. Bull.,* 1954, *51,* 119–127.

Lotsof, E. J., & Downing, W. L. Two measures of anxiety. *J. consult Psychol.,* 1956, *20,* 170.

Ludwig, A. O., & Ranson, S. W. A statistical follow-up of effectiveness of treatment of combat-induced casualties: 1. Returns to full combat duty. *Milit. Surg.,* 1947, *100,* 51–62.

Lyketsos, G., Belinson, L., & Gibbs, F. A. Electro-encephalograms of non-epileptic psychotic patients awake and asleep. *Arch. Neurol. Psychiat.,* 1953, *69,* 707–712.

McCurdy, H. G. Consciousness and the galvanometer. *Psychol. Rev.,* 1950, *57,* 322–327.

McReynolds, P., Ballachey, E. L., & Ferguson, J. T. Development and evaluation of a behavioral scale for appraising the adjustment of hospitalized patients. *Amer. Psychologist,* 1952, *7,* 340 (abstract).

Maier, N. R. F. *Studies of abnormal behavior in the rat.* New York: Harper, 1939.

Malmo, R. B., Smith, A. A., & Kohlmeyer, W. A. Motor manifestation of conflict in interview: A case study. *J. abnorm. soc. Psychol.,* 1956, *52,* 268–271.

Mann, Mary B. The quantitative differentiation of samples of written language. *Psychol. Monogr.,* 1944, *56,* 41–74.

Mayers, A. N., & Mayers, E. B. Grammarrhetoric indicator. *J. nerv. ment. Dis.,* 1946, *104,* 604–610.

Meehl, P. E. The dynamics of "structured" personality tests. *J. clin. Psychol.,* 1945, *1,* 296–303.

Meehl, P. E. Configural scoring. In G. S. Welsh and W. G. Dahlstrom (Eds.), *Basic reading on the MMPI in psychology and medicine.* Minneapolis, Minn.: Univ. Minnesota Press, 1956.

Merrill, R. M. On Keet's study, Two verbal techniques in a miniature counseling situation. *J. abnorm. soc. Psychol.,* 1952, *47,* 722.

Meyer, D. R., Bahrick, H. P., & Fitts, P. M. Incentive, anxiety, and the human eye blink rate. *J. exp. Psychol.,* 1953, *45,* 183–187.

Morselli, G. E. Personalita alternante e pathologia affettiva. *Arch. Psicol. Neur. Psich.,* 1953, *14,* 579–589.

Mowrer, O. H., Light, D. H., Luria, Zella, & Seleny, Marjorie P. Tension changes during psychotherapy. In O. H. Mowrer (Ed.), *Psychotherapy: theory and research.* New York: Ronald, 1953.

Muench, G. A. An evaluation of nondirective psychotherapy. *Appl. Psychol. Monog.,* No. 13, 1947.

Olson, W. C. *The measurement of nervous habits in normal children.* Minneapolis, Minn.: Univ. Minnesota Press, 1929.

Paterson, D. G. Vocational interest inventories in selection. *Occupations,* 1946, *25,* 152–153.

Pinillos, J. L. Tests de personalidad: II

calificaciónes. *Rev. Psicol. gen. apl.*, Madrid, 1955, *10*, 601–633

Pollaczek, P. P. A study of malingering on the CVS abbreviated individual intelligence scale. *J. clin. Psychol.*, 1952, *8*, 75–81.

Price, A. C., & Deabler, H. L. Diagnosis or organicity by means of spiral aftereffects. *J. consult. Psychol.*, 1955, *19*, 299–302.

Rankin, R. E., & Campbell, D. T., Galvanic skin response to Negro and white experimenters. *J. abnorm. soc. Psychol.*, 1955, *51*, 30–33.

Raush, H. L., Pittman, A. T., & Taylor, T. J. The interpersonal behavior of children in residential treatment. *J. abnorm. soc. Psychol.*, 1959, *58*, 9–26.

Rechtschaffen, A., & Mednick, S. A. The autokinetic word technique. *J. abnorm. soc. Psychol.*, 1955, *51*, 346.

Roshal, J. J. G. The type-token ratio as a measure of change in behavior variability during psychotherapy. In W. U. Snyder (Ed.), *Group report of a program of research in psychotherapy.* State Univ., Pa.: Pa. State Univ. Press, 1953.

Salvatore, S., & Hyde, R. N. Progression of effects of Lysergic Acid Diethylamide (LSD). *Arch. Neurol. Psychiat.*, 1956, *76*, 59–59.

Sanford, F. H. Speech and personality. In L. A. Pennington and I. A. Berg (Eds.), *An Introduction to clinical psychology.* New York: Ronald, 1948.

Sarason, J. G. The effects of anxiety and two kinds of failure on serial learning. *J. Pers.*, 1957, *25*, 383–392.

Schachter, J. Pain, fear, and anger in hypertensives and normotensives. *Psychosom. Med.*, 1957, *19*, 17–29.

Schofield, W. Changes in responses to the MMPI following certain therapies. *Psychol. Monogr.*, 1950, *64*, No. 311.

Seeman, J. A study of the process of nondirective therapy. *J. consult. Psychol.*, 1949, *13*, 157–168.

Shagass, C., & Malmo, R. B. Psychodynamic themes and localized muscular tension during psychotherapy. *Psychosom. Med.*, 1954, *16*, 295–314.

Silver, R. E. The Edwards Personal Preference Schedule and social desirability. *J. consult. Psychol.*, 1957, *21*, 402–404.

Silverman, R. E., & Blitz, B. Learning and two kinds of anxiety. *J. abnorm. soc. Psychol.*, 1956, *59*, 301–303.

Snyder, W. U. An investigation of the nature of nondirective psychotherapy. *J. gen. Psychol.*, 1945, *33*, 193–223.

Sorenson, A. G., & Cross, C. F. Interrater reliability from the viewpoint of the rater. *Personnel Guid. J.*, 1957, *35*, 365–368.

Stennett, R. G. The relationship of performance level to level of arousal. *J. exp. Psychol.*, 1957, *54*, 54–61.

Stevens, S. S. Mathematics, measurement, and psychophysics. In S. S. Stevens (Ed.), *Handbook of experimental psychology.* New York: Wiley, 1951, 1–49.

Stilson, D. W., Mason, D. J., Gynther, M. D., & Gertz, B. An evaluation of the comparability and reliabilities of two behavior rating scales for mental patients. *J. consult Psychol.*, 1958, *22*, 213–216.

Super, D. E. Theories and assumptions underlying approaches to personality assessment. In B. M. Bass and I. A. Berg (Eds.), *Objective approaches to personality assessment.* Princeton, N.J.: Van Nostrand, 1959, 24–41.

Taft, R. Some characteristics of good judges of others. *Brit. J. Psychol.*, 1956, *47*, 19–29.

Teuber, H. L., & Powers, E. Evaluating therapy in a delinquency prevention program. *Res. Publ. Ass. nerv. ment. Dis.*, 1951, *31*, 138–147.

Thorne, F. C. Life record criteria of psychological health. *J. clin. Psychol.*, 1958, *14*, 123–132.

Voth, A. C. An experimental study of mental patients through the autokinetic phenomenon. *Amer. J. Psychiat.*, 1947, *103*, 793–805.

Watson, R. I. Historical review of objective personality testing: the search for objectivity. In B. M. Bass and I. A. Berg (Eds.), *Objective approaches to personality assessment.* Princeton, N.J.: Van Nostrand, 1959, 1–23.

Webb, W. B. Self-evaluations, group evaluations, and objective measures. *J. consult. Psychol.,* 1955, *19,* 210–212.

Webb, W. B. A procedure for obtaining self-ratings and group ratings. *J. consult. Psychol.,* 1956, *20,* 233–236.

Wenger, M. A. Studies of autonomic balance in Army Air Force Personnel. *Compar. Psychol. Monogr.,* 1948, *19* No. 4 (Serial No. 101).

Wiggins, J. S., & Rumrill, C. Social desirability in the MMPI and Welch's factor scales A and R. *J. consult. Psychol.,* 1959, *23,* 100–106.

Wittson, C. L., & Hunt, W. A. The prediction value of the brief psychiatric interview. *Amer. J. Psychiat.,* 1951, *107,* 582–585.

Zax, M., & Klein, A. Measurement of personality and behavior changes following psychotherapy. *Psychol. Bull.,* 1960, *57,* 435–448.

PART TWO

Learning and Communication

4

Learning Theory and Clinical Psychology— An Eventual Symbiosis?

RALPH F. HEFFERLINE

The statement that learning theory is a support of clinical psychology will receive general, albeit bored, assent. A livelier reaction seems in order to an assertion that such support is too much—and spurious. The late David Rapaport made this claim as a spokesman for psychoanalysis in *Psychology: A Study of a Science* (1959). He says:

> Learning theory seems to be the academic theoretical backbone of the majority of recent, mass produced clinical psychologists. But since this theory cannot guide their clinical work, they rely there increasingly upon psychoanalytical propositions, whose theory they have not studied (p. 144).

Although learning theory is considered impotent to guide clinical work, it can at any rate make trouble in the Freudian camp. Rapaport conceded that present-day psychoanalytical theory cannot on empirical grounds account for behavior attributed to conditioning. Concerning experimental analogues of "Freudian mechanisms" he stated:

> These . . . . would be neither embarrassing to nor incompatible with psychoanalytic theory if no claim were made that in man, too, the mechanism of the primary process and of the defenses are products of conditioning. . . . Psychoanalytic theory at present

Preparation of this chapter was supported by research grant M-2961(C)S1, National Institutes of Health, U.S. Public Health Service.

cannot escape this embarrassment, since it has no learning theory of its own to pit against conditioning. . . . Psychoanalysis will be totally free of embarrassment from this quarter only when it has a learning theory which not only fulfills its own empirical and theoretical requirements, but is also broad enough to account for conditioning phenomena—including the conditioned analogues of "unconscious mechanisms"—as special cases (p. 145).

In other words, learning theory will be supplanted eventually, but only by another learning theory—one presumably originating in psychoanalytic theory—which will dispose of "conditioning phenomena . . . as special cases." Proponents of conditioning, in the meantime, expect that eventually their formulation will assimilate everything that is nutritious in psychoanalysis.

This chapter, of course, has a thesis: that although psychologists tend to join or split on many issues—pure versus applied, academic versus professional, individual versus social, systematic versus eclectic, behavioristic versus phenomenological—they are all bound by the common family tie of a concern for the problems of psychology. This chapter attempts to point up evidence that there is, today, special opportunity for increased collaboration between learning theorists and clinicians. Learning theorists may continue to regard clinical implications as none of their concern, and clinicians may construe this proposal as a callous affirmation of the trend toward lumping together rats, robots, and men, toward violation of the human personality by brain washing, toward spread of epidemic gadget psychosis.

In sober fact, this presentation merely suggests that much may be accomplished for humanity if we—experimentalist and clinician together—exploit to the utmost the advanced technology achieved in other fields in the service of other objectives. Emphasis will be, therefore, not on what learning theory has already turned up that may be useful to clinical psychology, but on the newly available tools, techniques, and research situations now available for common exploitation. Part of what is new is the opportunity to up-date the old. What was plausible in the past on introspective grounds, but later rejected when we could no longer stomach subjectivism, gets restated in operational terms whenever we can directly observe what previously had to be guessed at. Dangerous side-effects, such as rekindling old sentimentalities about Man, presumably get balanced out by opposing new tendencies to computermorphize.

In 1945 a symposium on operationism, suggested by Edwin G. Boring, was conducted in the September issue of the *Psychological Review*. Boring espoused the position of methodological behaviorism and asserted, "Science does not consider private data" (1945, p. 244).

Skinner, on the other hand, took the stand that one may, as a radical behaviorist, "in some cases consider private events (inferentially perhaps, but none the less meaningfully). . . . The irony of it is that, while Boring must confine himself to an account of my external behavior, I am still interested in what might be called Boring-from-within" (1959, p. 285).

In 1960 Miller, Galanter, and Pribram after a year of free discussion in the "think tank" at Stanford, published *Plans and the Structure of Behavior* (1960). Their frolicking style, rarely found in scientific publications, seemed to say, "We don't know how much we want to be held responsible or to hold ourselves responsible for what we're saying." They concluded:

> As our debate progressed and our conception of Plans became clearer, a conviction grew on us that we were developing a point of view toward large parts of psychology. . . . We did not feel that we were behaviorists, at least not in the sense J. B. Watson defined the term, yet we were much more concerned . . . with what people did than with what they knew. Our emphasis was upon processes lying immediately behind action, but not with action itself. On the other hand, we did not consider ourselves introspective psychologists, at least not in the sense Wilhelm Wundt defined the term, yet we were willing to pay attention to what people told us about their ideas and their Plans. . . . It suddenly occurred to us that we were subjective behaviorists. When we stopped laughing we began to wonder seriously if that was not exactly the position we had argued ourselves into. At least the name suggested the shocking inconsistency of our position (p. 211).

Their position can be made consistent, although still sufficiently shocking, if "subjective"—connoting the "mind" of the mind-body dichotomy, as they certainly don't intend—is replaced by "private." When they concern themselves with "processes lying immediately behind action," they deal with overt behavior's invisible substrate. These processes themselves are a form of action, involving receptor-effector relations which will herein be called covert behavior. Instead of being subjectivists, as they laughingly call themselves, they are, I believe, a viable mutant of the radical behaviorist, who could like Skinner be interested in "Boring-from-within."

Hebb, assailed by similar giddy fancies, reacted with playfulness of a more belligerent brand. In a paper called *Alice in Wonderland or Psychology Among the Biological Sciences* (1958) he verbally flayed those psychologists who retain an antiphysiological position. Two years later, in more mellow vein, he presented to the American Psychological Association a presidential address entitled *The American Revolution* (1960). This revolution, a psychological one, is now victoriously through its first phase, but it is time, Hebb declares, to get on with the second. This he takes to be "a behavioristic or learning-theory analysis of the thought process" (p. 735). In facing up to this challenge he does not shrink from lending his support to the study of such long-recoiled-from-as-untouchable topics as "hallucination, body image, and the self" (p. 740).

While heartily in accord with the research objectives stated, my view on how to achieve them is different. Perhaps this is *my* vertigo. Instead of taking what people say about their Plans at face value, I believe that verbal report itself urgently needs empirical investigation. Instead of taking, as Hebb does, intervening variables as conceptions that cannot be avoided, I believe the variables important for psychology, even when they operate beneath the skin, to be presently or potentially accessible to direct or indirect observation and measurement. To win the second phase of Hebb's revolution calls for no change of basic strategy, it seems to me, but resourceful use of new and improved weapons now coming into our hands.

There is no intention to applaud the psychologist turned gadgeteer. However, although instrumentation of itself cannot solve the problems of psychology, it may be remembered that astronomy found the telescope helpful and that the study of fine structure took a turn for the better with the invention of the microscope. Modern instrumentation, when intelligently used in psychology, permits improved specification of stimulus and response, provides automatic programing of experimental operations too fast or too slow for manual execution, and processes voluminous data with superhuman speed and accuracy. With artificial eyes, ears, and hands, recording impartially and without lapse of attention, the psychologist, as he deals with a complex situation, gets a fuller and more trustworthy answer to the question of what is going on.

That the experimentalist needs equipment is obvious. But of what use can it be to the clinician? It can supplement his present instruments—diagnostic tests and interviews—and enter directly into the treatment process. As one example, consider the psychotherapist's problem of determining whether a patient has been moved emotionally at some particular juncture. Is he really untouched or merely hiding behind a poker face? A clear answer could be had were the therapist monitoring a suitable variable, say, the galvanic skin response.

The necessary equipment no longer requires a tangle of wires running from messy electrodes to a cumbersome galvanometer. Preparation can now be reduced to having the patient pull on a special pair of socks and strapping a small box comfortably over one of his ankles. The socks contain dry plantar electrodes, made of silver conductive cloth, individually sewed in (Levy, Thaler, and Ruff, 1958). The box contains a tiny FM-transmitter, which broadcasts to an ordinary FM-tuner located anywhere within a hundred feet. The GSR, continuously recorded, may be presented to the therapist on a moving paper chart or projected on a screen. If desired, this record can be readily synchronized with a tape recording of the therapeutic interview.

What's more, suppose it is important that the patient, "alienated from his feelings," should have objective evidence of his affect. Then he too can view the record and be publicly informed of his own poker face, which otherwise might mislead him as well as the therapist.

With such instrumentation the therapist interested in research can have a consulting room which is at the same time a laboratory. Or any recordings obtained as an adjuvant to therapy can supply data for someone else's scientific use. The feasibility of arrangements of this sort is what leads me to speak of symbiotic relations which could obtain between experimental and clinical psychology.

Work with subhuman species is by no means finished. It will go on, as it does as a mainstay of medical sciences. Although it seems to have class-standing of its own, most experimental psychologists today, while taking it as a matter of course that animal work will continue, feel prepared to tackle the "king-sized rat" without too much loss of experimental rigor. Beyond confirming that the same behavioral principles hold good to the top of the phyletic scale, they wish especially to investigate the species-specific behavior which results from undergoing socialization in a human community—namely, verbal behavior and all its myriad ramifications and derivatives.

The clinical setting is one of the few which contain a pool of human subjects with enough time and motivation to tolerate intensive, prolonged study. Some of these, moreover, present for benevolent manipulation behavioral repertoires of the most interesting sort, acquired under environmental variables so bizarre or cruel as to preclude ever setting them up deliberately for investigation.

Such a cold-blooded announcement of the erstwhile animal worker's readiness to intrude himself upon the clinical scene serves notice that, where admitted, he comes because he finds this the next step to take in the development of a science of behavior. He will be pleased, to be sure, when a case with which he has been connected shows improvement, but his joy will be enhanced should the improvement result from control gained for the first time over some important variable.

For experimentalists and clinicians to join forces on any large scale must itself involve experimentation of a sort and also constitute something of a clinical problem. Benefits for each party will need to be demonstrated. Without them experimental effort may for some time to come be more effectively expended in the human engineering aspects of space travel, defense measures, industrial situations, and the school system. Successes there—with teaching machines, for instance —will inevitably find clinical application, but probably on a basis less congenial to clinicians than if they had themselves participated wholeheartedly in shaping the new developments.

To discuss these issues intelligibly in what follows, such technical terms as may be called for will be those of a single theoretical formulation. The one developed by B. F. Skinner and his followers seems least clogged with surplus meaning and, since also the one most familiar to me, will constitute the reference system. Besides, its criteria of scientific progress—improved prediction and control of behavior— seem particularly appropriate with respect to the practical endeavors of clinical psychology. Work done under formulations other than Skinner's I take to be equally relevant and shall cite when apropos. "Reinforcement theory," "learning theory," and "conditioning" appear interchangeably. Readers still innocent of the concepts of operant and respondent behavior may look into Skinner (1938), Keller and Schoenfeld (1950), or Sidman (1960).

WALDEN TWO VERSUS CLINICAL PSYCHOLOGY

Several aspects of Skinner's psychological stance must be examined in order to make clear what is involved in this concept of an experimental-clinical symbiosis. This would be presumptuously *ad hominem* were it not essential to indicate that, while I align myself unreservedly with his experimentalism and take his methodology as the core of the present approach, I place a different bet on how, as a man of good will, a psychologist may best spend himself in bringing about a better world.

Skinner regards concern with "remedial work" as one version of the misspent life, as shown in these comments about Albert Schweitzer:

> He has earned the gratitude of thousands, but we must not forget what he might have done instead. If he had worked as energetically for as many years in a laboratory of tropical medicine, he would almost certainly have made discoveries which in the long run would help—not thousands—but literally *billions* of people (1959, p. 250).

Men spend themselves in remedial work, Skinner believes, "because personal gratitude is a powerful generalized reinforcer" (p. 249). "We can scarcely hold it against psychologists that they want to help their fellow men," he acknowledges, "but we must not forget that the remedial step is necessarily a short-term measure and that it is not the only step leading to the same goal. The lively prosecution of a science of behavior, applied to the broad problem of cultural design, could have more sweeping consequences" (pp. 249–250).

Skinner is an inverse Omar Khayyam, bidding us "take the credit and let the cash go." Lacking prescience, he admits the choice to be a gamble, as shown by the contingent clause which starts this statement:

> If such a promising alternative is actually feasible, anyone who is capable of making a long-term contribution may wisely resist the effect of other consequences which, no matter how important they may be to him personally, are irrelevant to the scientific process and confine him to short-term remedial action (1959, p. 250).

The tone of this passage reminds one of old-fashioned appeals to a decision-making "inner agent," long since exorcized by Skinner. Noting that the behavior of wise resistance is but weakly conditioned, he adds a warning about the "danger of a cultural design which does not harness some personal reinforcement in the interests of pure science" (1959, p. 250). For the present he must resort to the ethical "should":

> The young psychologist who wants above all to help his fellow men should be made to see the tremendous potential consequences of even a small contribution to the scientific understanding of human behavior. It is possibly this understanding alone, with the improved cultural patterns which will flow from it, which will eventually alleviate the anxieties and miseries of mankind (1959, p. 250).

Skinner's policy statements in other contexts too reveal this paradoxical combination of unrestrained extrapolation of experimental findings (obtained in limited situations) to his proposed social engineering *and* untiring advocation of ascetic adherence to pure science. Between these extremes of pure and applied science one finds, for the most part, a vast excluded middle. Work in a number of specialties which regard themselves as attempts to build a bridge from an insufferable present to a more tolerable future he would discourage as irrelevant, self-indulgent, or miserably retail—whereas, if such effort were now devoted exclusively to study of operant conditioning, ultimate application might be magnificently wholesale.

In 1958 Skinner exhorted experimental psychologists not to join "the flight from the laboratory" (1959, pp. 242). This deplorable exodus he sees taking place in several directions, among them "the flight to real people" (clinical psychology) and "the flight to the inner man" (physiology). What will be proposed here, on the contrary, is that a science of behavior, whether for the benefit of mankind at large or for mere intellectual enjoyment, can be most speedily and comprehensively advanced by extending the outlook and practices of the behavioral laboratory to the clinic and by rechristening as psychology some areas now conventionally assigned to physiology. If this constitutes a flight of any sort, it is not from but rather *with* the laboratory.

It is tempting to conjecture whether Skinner's weighting of variables which control behavior might not have been appreciably different had he ever exposed himself to the clinical situation. He has worked consistently with intact organisms, naïve at the start of the experiment. In conjunction with O. R. Lindsley he has, it is true, experimented with psychotic human subjects, but that project apparently has to date consisted mainly of confirming that psychotics, like rats or pigeons, may be conditioned by operant procedures (Lindsley, 1956). The general formulation antedated this work, and seems to have been little influenced by it.

Skinner's rats and pigeons have, over the years, behaved under "the special control of variables attainable only in laboratory experimentation" (1959, p. 243). Starting with fresh animals, he has by suitable programing provided them with the specific reinforcement histories required for the problem at hand. By these methods he has achieved spectacular success in bringing animal behavior under control. However, an unevaluated factor in this technical and scientific triumph is the thoroughness with which he has also excluded from any important degree of differential control the whole range of interoceptive and proprioceptive stimulation. Outside the laboratory or in a laboratory more closely simulating the conditions of everyday life as lived by man and other species, such types of stimulation, as I shall try to show later, play a sizable role in determining behavior. They are unquestionably of critical concern for the clinical psychologist, preoccupied as he is with problems of emotion.

In contrast to his productiveness elsewhere, Skinner has made sparse contributions to the study of emotion. He recognizes the problem's magnitude, to be sure, and in *Walden Two* (1948) has Frazier, the genius who set up the utopia, describe its elaborate program for conditioning children to control emotion. That Skinner nevertheless remains uneasy on this score may be inferred from comments which he has the book's narrator make about Frazier's report: "I began to realize, also, that he had not really wanted to tell this story. He was vulnerable. . . . I was pretty sure he had not established the value of these practices in an experimental fashion" (p. 90).

Skinner's lack of assurance in dealing with emotion may be traceable to his early decision to restrict the definition of behavior to "what the organism is doing to the environment"—in other words, to operant behavior (1938, p. 428). He does not deny respondents the status of behavior—they receive systematic, albeit brief, treatment in his general accounts (1938, 1953)—but he deals with them almost distastefully. In reviewing his early efforts to find lawful behavioral processes, he says, "Pavlov had shown the way, but I could not then, as I cannot now, move without a jolt from salivary reflexes to the important business of the organism in everyday life" (1959, p. 80). Elsewhere he raises the question of "whether respondent behavior, which is chiefly involved in the internal economy of the organism, may not reasonably be left to the physiologist." (1938, p. 438). Yet emotion continues for Skinner to be an important problem, and it is in large part undeniably respondent. Must he not, then, eventually, if he is to complete his formulation, retrieve from the physiologist the unasked-for gift and study respondents in their own right?

In view of the tremendous thrust of Skinner's undertaking—who can doubt his ambition to transform the cultural design?—it is readily comprehensible that he should wish for strategic reasons to narrow the investigative field as much as possible. A scientific crash program can ill afford the luxury of self-indulgent scientific curiosity. However, a science of behavior, as worked at by the sort of scientist who cannot "wisely resist the effect of . . . consequences . . . important . . . to him personally," retains a broad reach and tolerates regions of useful blur with sister disciplines. May it not also stand as good, or perhaps even better chance, of hastening the advent of utopia?

ENVIRONMENT IS WHERE RECEPTORS ARE

The beginner in psychology learns that this science concerns itself with the behavior of the organism in its environment. The environment stimulates and the organism responds. Stimuli affect the organism through receptors. These are classified as extero-, intero-, and proprioceptors, depending on whether they are activated by events outside or inside the skin. The student, already aware of the importance of eyes and ears, now learns that "somesthesis" is important, too. His textbook may even quote this passage from Stevens' *Handbook of Experimental Psychology* (1951):

> In some ways the somesthetic senses are biologically of greater importance than the special senses of sight, hearing, taste, and smell. Helen Keller provides an example of a useful life without sight and hearing, and no doubt she could have managed without taste and smell. But it is hard to imagine how anyone could survive, let alone act like a human being, if totally devoid of kinesthesis for the control of position and movement (p. 1172).

From such a start the student might reasonably expect to hear a great deal more about kinesthesis (proprioception) and the other "body senses." He doesn't. Actually, little is known of them in an experimental way. Receptors under the skin are inconveniently located. How get to them to stimulate? Eyes and ears are readily accessible, and physics has helpfully analyzed the dimensions of light and sound. Isn't it better, then, to leave the internal environment to physiologists and let them, if they wish, cut their way in?

Stopped short by the organism's skin-barrier, the behaviorist has for decades played dog-in-the-manger with the clinical psychologist, who continues a bootleg traffic in introspectionism. Clinicians display uneasiness in this regard, but so do behaviorists about their own out-of-hand condemnation of the verbal report. On this score Skinner (1953) comments: "The verbal report is a response to the private event and may be used as a source of information about it. A critical analysis of the validity of this practice is of first importance" (p. 282).

With improved instruments and new techniques perhaps the way is open at last to begin this critical analysis, or maybe it has begun already. It consists of "the private made public" (Skinner, 1953, p. 282). Instruments which detect the same events as do the organism's internal receptors offer an independent means of checking the verbal report of events beneath the skin. That this, when more fully developed, will constitute a "breakthrough" for experimental psychology seems self-evident. That it will benefit the clinician as well will be argued later.

At this point it may be worth while to clarify what an instrumented approach implies for the relationship between psychology and physiology, if only to clear away certain admonitions which have lost pertinence. Psychologists who become interested in subdermal behavior suffer renaming as physiological psychologists or psychophysiologists. Simply to adopt the technique of recording electrically from the organism, regardless of the problem under study, makes one an electrophysiologist. This has not deterred psychologists in general, including clinical psychologists, from "fooling around" with the galvanic skin response, but this "physiological" measure has been kicked about so much and for so long that it apparently has passed into the public domain.

Why should a psychologist be stigmatized for "going physiological"? Actually, he isn't except by a small but highly articulate group of his fellows. They make two well-known points, both irrelevant in the present context. One is that "naïve physiologizing" appeals to a "conceptual nervous system." Skinner has proscribed this as an "explanatory fiction," for it arbitrarily invests the nervous system with precisely the explanatory properties needed. One way to counter this argument might be to engage only in *sophisticated* physiologizing.

The other argument rests on the distinction between "molar" and "molecular." Physiology works at the "molecular" level of observation, while psychology is busy—or should busy itself—one degree higher at the "molar" level. Skinner (1959) has maintained this position, too. I shall quote him rather fully here, since it seems desirable to make quite clear that what he is condemning is *not* what I am recommending:

> The *physiological* inner man is, of course, no longer wholly inferential. New methods and instruments have brought the nervous system and other mechanisms under direct observation. The new data have their own dimensions and require their own formulations. The behavioral facts in the field of learning, for example, are dealt with in terms appropriate to behavior, while electrical or chemical activities occurring at the same time demand a different conceptual framework. Similarly, the effects of deprivation and satiation on behavior are not the same as the events seen through a gastric fistula. Nor is emotion, studied as behavioral predisposition, capable of being analyzed in terms appropriate to pneumographs and electrocardiographs. Both sets of facts, and their appropriate concepts, are important—but they are *equally* important, not dependent one upon the other. Under the influence of a contrary philosophy of explanation, which insists upon the reductive priority of the inner event, many brilliant men who began with an interest in behavior, and might have advanced our knowledge of that field in many ways, have turned instead to the study of physiology. We cannot dispute the importance of their contributions, we can only imagine with regret what they might have done instead (p. 253).

I agree fully with Skinner that the physiological approach he refers to, is not, as such, a direct study of behavior. Its importance to a science of behavior is the description it affords of the *internal behavioral environment!* The physiologist here is beginning to do for intero- and proprioceptors what the physicist and chemist have long since done for exteroceptors. He is sounding and plumbing and charting that part of the psychological environment which lies beneath the skin. Only by such work, at first indirectly and then more and more directly, can we learn to specify those internal stimulus events which, by themselves or in company with exteroceptive stimuli, elicit respondents and/or provide discriminative stimuli for operants.

This is not reductionism, for behavior remains at whatever is its own appropriate level and is conceptualized in the self-same fashion as when the controlling stimuli are delivered from the outside. The terminological trouble—about which something must be done sooner or later—is that the organism itself is in part the source of stimuli which control its own behavior—and, worse still, is, as will be developed later, itself a crucial part of the environment on which its operants operate.

The traditional dichotomy between organism and environment has long been rejected in various quarters, all the way from transcendental thinkers to cellular biologists. For the cytologist the two-way traffic across the permeable membrane is the focus of his investigations, just as action at an interface or boundary is the subject matter of many other specialties. The skin of the organism may be construed in similar fashion, though the point will not be argued here. It seems sufficient for present purposes to note that the functional living system comprises the contents of the skin and the immediate surroundings.

On the grounds offered above, the psychologist need turn physiologist when he studies the environment of the internal receptors *no more and no less* than he need turn physicist when he tests with visual or auditory stimuli the discriminative capacities afforded by the exteroceptors. Unfortunately, the internal environment is still, relatively speaking, a jungle, and psychologists may for particular problems be obliged for some time to come to do *ad hoc* physiologizing.

Another troublesome dichotomy, this time an incomplete one, is that between respondents and operants. A glib distinction is that operants are skeletal responses, while respondents are under the control of the autonomic nervous system, with perhaps a few overlapping instances of two otherwise independent types (Skinner, 1938, p. 112). That this is gross oversimplification seems indicated by the manner in which respondents raise or lower operant strength. More directly Fulton (1939) states: "It is indeed unlikely that there is such a thing as a pure somatic reflex unaccompanied by a parallel autonomic adjustment" (p. 221).

The autonomic nervous system traditionally has been regarded as exclusively effector in its action, despite early and continued reports of visceral afferent fibers leading from the activated viscus. While these, it is true, were appealed to in support of the James-Lange theory of emotion, their significance only now is beginning to be fully appreciated. The following quotation from Lacey (1958), together with his citation of Dell, suggest the direction taken in recent studies:

> The accumulating evidence is becoming ever more convincing that the autonomic nervous system has a role in behavior far more important than it has been given by being restricted mainly to the topics of emotion or stress. As Dell (1952) puts it in his thorough review of the relationships between the somatic and vegetative systems: ". . . to the conception of a vegetative nervous system, chiefly bulbo-spinal, broadly autonomous and solely an effector— data now enable us to oppose the conception of a vegetative system

organized, along its main lines, like the somatic system, represented at all the levels of the central nervous system, and possessing afferent pathways, homologous to the great sensory pathways, and sharing numerous central formations with the somatic system." The autonomic and somatic systems, Dell says, are "two systems closely bound together in a single functional unity, homologous in their organization, regulated in part by the same mechanisms and synergistically controlling numerous common pathways" (pp. 201–202).

Lacey (1958) further states that "feedback via visceral afferents and reticular formations, or via the baroreceptors, implies that *an autonomic response becomes a stimulus*" (p. 202). That he is fully aware of what this means for a science of behavior is shown in his parenthetical comment: "Such a sequence of events in which a response produces or becomes the stimulus for the next response in a chain, it should be noted, is by no means unfamiliar to the behavior theorist" (p. 202).

Recent translations of Soviet work (Brazier, 1958; *Central Nervous System*, 1959; Simon, 1957) reveal similar views. While the Russian workers continue along Pavlovian lines, making no sharp distinction between respondents and operants, their methodology and results are impressive. Razran is preparing a whole review volume of their experiments and applications of interoceptive conditioning. He cites Chernigovsky as having declared in 1953 that "we may confidently assert that there is not an organ or tissue in the body that has no receptors of its own."

Regardless of whether or not this claim is extravagant, Razran has come across Russian evidence of interoceptors "in the red marrow, lymphatic nodes, adventitia, pericardium, endocardium, epicardium, mesentery, cisterna chyli, testes, ovaries, uterus, kidneys, urinary bladder, liver, gall bladder, bile ducts, spleen, lungs, salivary glands, mammary glands, pancreas, suprarenals, thyroid gland—not to mention the main portions of the vascular and digestive systems such as the aortic arch, carotid sinuses, abdominal aorta, pulmonary artery, vena cava, esophagus, duodenum, caecum, rectum, etc."

The Russians have also, Razran reports, studied assiduously the differential distributions and gradients of the several classes of interoceptors in different organs and in different regions of the same organ. The types of receptor, while limited to three main classes—mechano-, chemo-, and thermoreceptor—are divided into many subclasses. A variety of techniques, some quite ingenious, have been invoked.

Razran concludes his introductory considerations with the following evaluation:

> It is clear that unconditioned exteroceptive and interoceptive stimulations share the common problems of searching and studying their respective morphology and electrophysiology; that students of extero-

ception are by no means uninterested in correlated systemic involvements; and that in at least a few studies conscious correlates of interoceptive stimulation have been reported and preliminarily investigated. The two fields are thus really true natural complements in understanding total organismic reactivity: interoception as the hinterland of largely unconscious (or unverbalized) registration of reverberations in vital organs, and exteroception as the foreground of largely conscious (or verbalized) reception and perception of external events and forces, each permeating and influencing the other in ways long suspected and guessed at by the nonexperimental clinicians of human behavior but hardly touched by experimentalists. The experimental neglect of interoception, no doubt due primarily to methodological and technical difficulties, has heretofore been indeed very glaring, and the Russian psychophysiologists are surely to be congratulated for opening and broadening the field, overcoming many difficulties, and getting closer to solutions.

The purpose of the foregoing discussion has been to suggest that the stimulation affecting internal receptors of the organism constitutes an environment sharing many of the properties of the external environment and exerting a control over behavior which should be admitted as significant even prior to securing empirical data with which to evaluate this issue. That data relevant for this purpose can be obtained is demonstrated by reports that they *are being* obtained, notably by the Russians. Early returns do *not* support a judgment of minor importance.

COVERT BEHAVIOR—BASIS OF "INTERNALIZATION"

Behavior is covert when invisible and overt when plain to see. Respondents, comprising smooth muscle and gland activity, are, with few exceptions, necessarily covert. Operants, consisting of skeletal muscle activity, are, at least when large enough to have discriminable effects upon the physical and social environment, usually overt. However, they may diminish in size until undetectable by an external observer, while still exercising some effect, even full effect, upon the internal environment. This is the basis of privacy, including what Cameron (1947, 1951) calls "behavioral duplicity" whereby one may "think" one thing and "say" another.

With both verbal report and "listening with the third ear" (Reik, 1948) barred as acceptable means of direct scientific access to covert behavior—whether respondent, operant, or a compound of both— resort must be had to special techniques for amplifying some indicant, usually electrical, of the behavior in question. An incomplete solution is reached by such devices as the lie-detector, which merely exploits the supposed fact that it is exciting to tell a lie and that excitement or "arousal" may be detected by altered breathing, pulse-rate, blood-volume, skin-resistance, muscular tension, and the like (Woodworth and Schlosberg, 1954).

More precise information on small operants is supplied by electro-myography. In the classical work of Jacobson (1932) the subject, with surface electrodes attached, was told to "think of" or to "imagine" performing a particular action. While carrying out the instructions he produced no directly visible movement. Nevertheless, the instrumental recordings showed that the appropriate muscles had run through a patterned sequence of activity which was the same, except for magnitude, as would have been involved in performing the action "in reality."

The fact that faint behavior may be invisible to an external observer does not necessarily indicate that it is so faint as to be unobservable by the subject himself. He is in a privileged position, not with respect to seeing his own behavior as others see it, but with respect to "feeling" it proprioceptively. On the basis of stimuli impinging on receptors embedded in muscles, joints, and tendons, he may respond to his own movements, to patterns of tension, or even to diffuse changes in his over-all tonus or readiness for action. Such responding, further discussed in the next section, has by many been taken to be—especially when in the form of subvocal talking—an important part of what traditionally has been called consciousness.

Until recently investigation of covert operants—often called implicit movements—has largely concerned the running off in miniature of response-sequences conditioned earlier at the overt level under exteroceptive stimulus control. Since such responses, while under the control of a series of external discriminative stimuli, are accompanied by a concurrent series of discriminable proprioceptive stimulations, the latter can acquire control sufficient to program the response-chain even after the exteroceptive stimuli, originally essential, are discontinued. A dramatic example of such proprioceptive control—in this case maladapted—is presented when a typist attempts to use a machine with a nonstandard keyboard.

The importance of investigating systematically such proprioceptively controlled covert behavior which is already in the repertoire (as heir apparent, it may be, to what were formerly called the "higher mental processes"), is now generally conceded. Also, the technical arrangements necessary for prosecution of such studies are fairly well understood.

The conditioning of such behavior de novo—that is, the process of its acquisition—deserves even more intensive investigation for the light it may throw upon the problem of "internalization." Transfer of behavior control from exteroceptive to internal stimuli must, it seems, lie at the core of this matter. Its study should illuminate Freud's (1950) notion of the superego as the "internalized parents," Piaget's (1952) account of child development in terms of "assimilatory schemata," Hebb's (1949) speculations on "cell assemblies and phase sequences" and all the other attempts to account for the organism's *acquired limited independence* of immediate external stimulation. Simply to find out that many theorists have made good sense on non-objective grounds would be small gain. What is important is to discover how the organism's behavior gets "packaged" in the repertoire and to learn how to get specific "packages" out at a later time when the external environment provides but a fragment of the variables originally present. This matter will be returned to in the next section, where the role of covert responses in providing the substrate for perceptual and verbal behavior will be discussed.

Something needs to be said at this point about the covert substrate itself—those responses which are precursors to perceptual or verbal or otherwise "meaningful" responses. The admirable experimentation of R. C. Davis in this area, extending over a number of years, is just now beginning to have its significance fully recognized. In 1952 he gave the notion of "stimulus trace," as involved in judgment responses, an empirical grounding by revealing sustained muscular responses in the relevant effectors. More recently, in collaboration with Buchwald and Frankman (1955), he has studied autonomic and muscular responses, and their relation to simple stimuli, when the instructions to the subject are simply to "do nothing." He introduces this monograph with the following statements:

> Rather than being hopeful of homologies between the somatic responses and psychological concepts built from other materials, we should be surprised by their discovery and rather astonished at the simplicity of the universe. Nevertheless, somatic responses abound. One has but to observe them on a set of recording instruments to believe that they are by far the most numerous responses of the organism. It is clear that any overt response, vocal utterance, or bodily movement, is surrounded by a wide penumbra of them, and it may not be too bold a guess to say that whenever there is any evidence of a stimulus affecting the individual, something in his periphery or viscera is set into motion. Not infrequently these may be seen when there is no other means at hand for detecting that the person has been stimulated. In point of time, the somatic responses may lead up to an overt response, accompany it, or follow it. In this area of somatic responses an occasional wave breaks into an external response. To understand these breaks we suppose that a study of the waves in general would be a great help. Or, to leave the figure of speech, we would say that confronted with problems about the last of a chain of events, we propose the

study of events immediately before it, and of similar events which are not followed by the same conclusion (pp. 1–2).

An uncommitted investigator may well have qualms about plunging himself into this "sea of somatic response." Furthermore, he will receive no reassurance from reports by Lacey (1953), Malmo (1950), Wenger (1941), Jost and Sontag (1944), and others, that autonomic responses tend to be peculiar to the individual, although this might have been suspected from the many clinical observations of "psychosomatic" cases.

Davis and his colleagues (1955) have made some headway in establishing certain response patterns as the characteristic reaction of the organism to specific types of stimuli. However, that much remains to be ordered is emphasized by their putting the whole following quotation in italics:

> So far as response patterns are different the state of a single response variable cannot serve as an index of the size of a response or the general conditions of the organism. On the other hand, where one has reason to believe that the responses being compared are reasonably similar, as they are under variations of auditory intensity, one response variable might serve well. To make decisions of this sort in general clearly requires more knowledge than so far exists (p. 66).

Behavior turns out to be even more complex than we had supposed, but this is scarcely the time to grow faint-hearted. While we can no longer entertain the hope that it will suddenly turn simple if we but hit upon the right explanatory principle, we do have powerful new tools and procedures with which to pursue the scientific venture, and it is not unreasonable to expect fairly quick returns in terms of major practical applications, particularly in the field of clinical psychology, even though a relatively full account from the standpoint of pure science may still be far in the future.

SECONDARY BEHAVIOR—KEY TO PERCEPTION AND VERBAL REPORT

That responses may produce eliciting or discriminative stimuli for succeeding responses is a familiar notion (Dollard and Miller, 1950; Guthrie, 1952; Keller and Schoenfeld, 1950; Skinner, 1953). The characteristic scalloping of the cumulative response curve under fixed ratio Skinner (1938) attributed to discrimination of rate of responding. That he takes increased interest in such matters may be inferred from these introductory statements to *Schedules of Reinforcement* (1957) done in collaboration with Ferster:

> The primary purpose of the present book is to present a series of experiments designed to evaluate the extent to which the organism's own behavior enters into the determination of its subsequent behavior. From a formulation of such results we should be able to predict the effect of any schedule (p. 3).

As mentioned earlier, behavior acquired under exteroceptive control may come to be controlled in whole or in part by response-produced stimuli, and, when this occurs, it constitutes the process spoken of in other contexts as "internalization." As such, it would appear to supply an experimental approach to the question of just how the reinforcement history—in subjective terms, the previous experience—of the organism exerts its influence on present behavior. Vigorous development of such an approach should supply information on the precise manner in which external and internal stimuli may come to substitute for each other, blend, conflict, or "transact" (Dewey and Bentley, 1949) in both transient and sustained control of the organism.

Response-produced stimuli may be most readily studied when the behavior in question consists of a tightly chained, repetitive sequence of discretely specifiable movements, as in locomotion or stereotyped, assembly-line tasks. In tracking a regularly moving spot of light the practiced subject can ordinarily continue accurately for a few cycles after the target is turned off.

Technically, any response determined by a previous response could be called secondary. However, I shall reserve the term for something more in line with what is implied in Freud's (1939) notion of "primary and secondary process," Pavlov's (1957) formulation of "first and second signal systems," Skinner's (1957) "autoclitic behavior," Piaget's (1952) hierarchy of "circular reactions," Carmeron's (1947, 1951) "self-reaction," and the many other accounts which postulate something like two levels of response, with the second contingent on occurrence of the first.

To my knowledge the only writers thus far to make a carefully explicit analysis of what is involved are Schoenfeld and Cumming (in press) in their chapter entitled "Perception and Behavior," which has long awaited publication. They start with the general basic formula:

$$R = f(S),$$

where R is the response (dependent variable) and S is a controlling independent variable (usually a stimulus operation). Immediately it develops that $f(S)$ is not a simple relation. Its complexity may reside in its parameters, of which some may be partly or wholly unknown, thus requiring an expansion of the initial expression [as performed, for example, by Graham (1952)] into:

$$R = f(a, b, c, \ldots).$$

This indicates that adequate stimulus specification may involve many variables operating in combination. Furthermore, the response also is complex. This statement from Schoenfeld and Cumming is italicized in the original:

> R is relatively complex, with either identifiable component responses having individual conditioning histories more clearly known than R itself, or with conditional probabilities among component responses arising from special circumstances of reinforcement.

After a remarkably lucid treatment of the thorny problems encountered in stimulus discrimination, including psychophysics, these authors go on to say:

> Many behaviors dubbed perceptual are not adequately described by the simple S→R paradigm . . . . and for these we shall need to use a more intricate schema. This new paradigm may be written $S \rightarrow R_1 \cdot R_2$, in which R_1 is an initial response to S, and R_2 is conditional upon the occurrence of R_1. . . . We may now turn to behaviors which, though often regular enough to permit ignoring R_1, still would be misconceived were the existence of R_1, and the dependence of R_2 upon it, not explicitly acknowledged.

R_2 has the status of a *reporting response*, and may be attached to R_1 by training. In relating R_2 to R_1 by the expression $R_2 = f(R_1)$, Schoenfeld and Cumming refrain from committing themselves with respect to the precise nature of the relationship. If R_1 produces stimuli which determine R_2, then the mediational relationship would be of the type made familiar by, among others, Osgood (1953), and the paradigm might be written:

$$S \rightarrow r \rightarrow s \rightarrow R.$$

My supposition would be that this is the typical case, and would assuredly account for the kind of "self-awareness" to be discussed later. However, the magnitude of R_1 and whether or not R_2 occurs may depend on parametric conditions of the organism requiring additional specification. These would include, as Schoenfeld and Cumming are careful to point out, the presence of a continuing activity or condition of the sort usually implied in the notion of "set."

The experimental reality of R_1 is evidenced by studies such as those of Davis previously cited (1940, 1949, 1952, 1957). No stress was laid, when they were mentioned earlier, on the conditioned or unconditioned status of the "somatic responses." For the human infant, Schoenfeld and Cumming state, "at birth and for some period thereafter, a multiplicity of stimuli, singly or in combination, indiscriminately produce a multiplicity of responses, giving James' adult's-eye view of an infant's-eye view of the world as blooming, buzzing confusion." Selective reinforcement of "responses in, and differentiable from, this pool of behavior" is brought to bear by nature or society, "in correlation with the presence or absence of relevant stimuli." The accumulating history of selective reinforcement gradually produces increased specificity of response with respect to one sense-modality as opposed to another, and with respect to stimulus dimensions within a particular modality.

R_2 corresponds to Skinner's (1957) "tact," the type of verbal response which, loosely stated, "names" or "reports" a stimulus situation. Since its conditioning is strictly contingent on selective reinforcement by those members of the "verbal community" who, to put it crudely, "already speak the language," it is obvious that the $R_1 \cdot R_2$ correlation will be set up for the new member of the "verbal community," not in all the instances which are theoretically possible, but only in those where the "teacher" has a clear basis for selective reinforcement—and has in the past undergone such selective reinforcement himself. This means, ordinarily, that tacts will be acquired only with respect to stimuli which can simultaneously impinge on the receptors of the "teacher"—that is, exteroceptive stimuli. In the history of the race there has been no basis on which members of the community could acquire unambiguous tacts with respect to discriminated intero- and proprioceptive stimuli.

The consequence—a serious one, I believe—has been that man's great achievement, verbal behavior, has had only a one-sided application to the behavioral environment. One can verbalize freely with respect to the external environment, but only slightly with respect to the individually "private" one beneath the skin. A potential corrective for this situation, and its relevance to clinical psychology, will be dealt with later.

SET—TRANSIENT OR ENDURING SUBSTRATE OF BEHAVIOR

Despite its ubiquity as a psychological term, set is usually inferred, not observed. Notable exceptions occur in the work of R. C. Davis (1940) and G. L. Freeman (1948). The former a number of years ago demonstrated electromyographically the dependence of simple reaction time on the muscular tension produced by the ready signal in the relevant effector. However, the general problem obviously has by no means received the intensive investigation in keeping with its key explanatory position in many formulations.

Technically, it is now relatively easy to study the sustained contractions of one or a number of muscle groups, and to measure their facilitating or interfering effects upon phasic responses. This experimental point of entry bears also on what may be the same problem in another guise—namely, the question of how the reinforcement history, as somehow cumulated in the organism, operates currently in the control of behavior.

The importance of set—whether called attitude, predisposition, postural organization, or any other of set's many synonyms—has been attested to on a multitude of nonexperimental grounds. As chronic readiness or unreadiness for various types of behavior it has been foundational for various theories of emotion and personality.

Conversely, techniques for modifying the set of a patient or even training him to manipulate his muscular status has been involved in a number of formal and informal therapies. Some of this material will be collated here, and in the final section a program for verifying it experimentally and organizing it for effective clinical application will be described.

A basic claim to be substantiated is that the organism's operants—so defined because they operate on the environment—may be just as effectively reinforced when they operate on the environment of the internal receptors as when they operate on the environment of the exteroceptors, and that clinical psychology may appropriately direct its attention and remedial efforts not only to the patient's interpersonal situation but also to his intrapersonal arrangements. To put it extremely, take care of movement and the constraints to movement and the "feelings" will take care of themselves.

The concept of set has a long history and a sizable literature. Much of the latter has a speculative rather than an experimental basis. In such writings, to give a flavor of established fact, appeal is frequently made to the tonic posture-regulating mechanisms as studied by Magnus (1924), Sherrington (1952) and, more recently, by the workers concerned with the wonders of the reticular formation (French, 1960). That such considerations are highly relevant cannot be doubted. Patterns of tonic facilitation, altering thresholds for phasic response, have been catalogued extensively in both experimental and clinical medicine. Some psychiatrists and clinical psychologists have been alert to the implications for their own work.

Apart from investigation of species-specific modes of postural regulation, recent work has emphasized temporary or chronic modifications of such regulation by deliberately or unwittingly produced conditioning effects. For instance, Sperry in 1955, after deploring the physiologist's neglect of the psychologist's "anticipatory set" or "expectancy," undertook to remedy the matter as follows:

We are led to postulate as an important aspect of the conditioning process the intermediation of complex high level patterns of central nervous facilitation, i.e., the neural counterparts and derivatives of the psychological expectancies and anticipatory sets. The pattern of central excitation aroused in the brain by the conditioned stimulus can then be assumed to be governed by an intermediate pattern of transient facilitation, rather than being channeled directly by neural engrams or traces as traditionally conceived. Unlike the dynamic traces of earlier theory, the central facilitory pattern or "set" is not a simple vestige or trace of cerebral excitation involved in an earlier pairing of conditioned stimulus and response. It represents, rather, a novel and relatively independent organization arising out of high level cerebral activity such as insight, expectancy and the like. In this hypothesis, the permanent structural changes for long-term retention do not help directly to form new associations between sensory and motor centres. Instead they reinforce the intermediate expectancy or facilitory set (p. 42).

Statements not unlike Sperry's have been made repeatedly in the past. The important difference is that they now appear in the context of a rapidly increasing pool of direct experimental findings, as displayed, for instance, in the first three volumes of the new *Handbook of Physiology* (Field, 1960); all of them devoted to neurophysiology.

The altered situation is pointed up by noting that when Gibson in 1941 made "a critical review of the concept of set in contemporary experimental psychology," his gloomy conclusion was that "no common meaning can be discerned." Davis (1946) took issue with this position, commenting:

Literally taken, this is perhaps an over-statement. For a definition of sufficient generality (e.g., "a set is a determining tendency in the organism, subject to change under certain conditions") would probably apply to all usages. Although this would include enough territory, it certainly would not exclude enough to satisfy most. It is in their subdivision of this broad territory that accounts differ and conflict (p. 388). (This is possibly what Gibson meant.)

In a long series of experimental studies G. L. Freeman treated set as "the postural substrate." These he summarized and developed into a general theory in 1948 in *The Energetics of Human Behavior*. Floyd Allport followed in 1955 with what is thus far the most comprehensive treatment of set, presented under the title *Theories of Perception and the Concept of Structure*. There, having praised Freeman for his pioneering efforts, he chides other psychologists for having allowed such fruits "to wither on the vine." He then proceeds to elaborate his own detailed account of set, treating it as "subthreshold version of the behavior itself," which may be raised to the overt level by current stimuli or parametric conditions of the organism. In thus making set, in a sense, "the place where memory dwells," he is strikingly in accord with the position of Sperry (1955), who says in this connection:

> In considering the problem of the patterning of the brain engrams, it is all-important that one does not lose sight of the primary role played by the above dynamic factors. Even after a long rest interval, or electroshock treatment, the conditioned response is still dependent upon a preliminary rearousal of the anticipatory set (p. 43).

What has been said about set above, even if still rather diffuse, carries at least the reassuring aroma of the laboratory. Fuller explication would involve more than can be attempted here. What now follows is still more tenuous, since selected from a welter of verbal reports of varying credibility. It includes folklore, cultistic practices, medical anecdote, and, at best, only semicontrolled observation.

Somatic regimens conducted for supposed effects upon "mind" or "spirit" have been a frequent component of religious practice—e.g., yoga (Behanan, 1937), Zen (Senzaki and McCandless 1953), and multitudinous forms of trance-induction (Huxley, 1957). According to report, these may impart to the devotee voluntary control of processes ordinarily involuntary and establish subjective states not otherwise deliberately attainable. Whether such effects could be brought under experimental observation and manipulation is a fascinating question, but remote from more immediate considerations to be dealt with here.

Apart from religious connections, body culture has been practiced for purposes of general health and also—usually under the stigma of quackery and official disbelief—as a mode of psychotherapy. Several types, still extant, will be briefly described.

F. Matthias Alexander (1932) developed a training procedure for establishing correct "use of the self." His most distinguished pupil, John Dewey, wrote appreciative forewords for several of his books, and it appeared at one time that the British army would convert its basic training to a version of Alexander's method. In brief, the technique calls attention to the nearly universal misuse of the body by modern man in locomotion, sitting, standing, and manipulation of objects. "Wrong" movement sequences have come to feel "right" through familiarity, and the pupil thus strongly resists correction. A crucial correction is for the head, which needs to go "forward and up" in order to produce a beneficial redistribution of tonus throughout the body. Etiology is ignored, and the faulty "use of the self" attributed simply to "habit-formation."

Aldous Huxley, inveterate tryer-out of everything excitingly new (from the Bates methods for correcting defective vision without glasses to induction of mescaline euphoria), was another of Alexander's pupils. He made literary capital of the method in *Ends and Means* and *Eyeless in Gaza*.

Alexander's son-in-law, an English physician named Barlow, published an "experiment" (1952) in which he reported success, by criteria of physical measurement and subjective judgment, in improving the theatrical performance of students in a school of acting. Currently, Frank P. Jones, at Tufts University, is conducting experiments and teaching courses in "kinesthetic perception," based upon Alexander's training procedures (Jones, 1958, 1959, 1960).

A somewhat similar interpretation of the ills which have befallen mankind and what should be done to cure them was made by the late Trigant Burrow, whose work is continued by the Lifwynn Foundation, which he established. Apart from his general speculative account of man's situation, Burrow in the laboratory found measurable differences in physiological functioning for two subjectively discriminable "modes of attention"—"ditention" (the habitual tension pattern taken to be characteristic of the socially neurotic condition) and "cotention" (the tensional pattern, attainable with practice, supposedly characterizing the biologically integrated condition of the human organism). Such differences were apparently established conclusively with respect to electroencephalographic patterns, respiration, and frequency and kind of eye-movement (Hefferline, 1958b). Hans Syz (1960), scientific director of the Lifwynn Foundation, is hopeful that the new technology will permit verification of the main tenets of Burrow's formulation.

Edmund Jacobson's technique of progressive relaxation is well known and finds increasing application (Jacobson, 1938). By learning to relax chronically tense skeletal musculature the patient at the same time relaxes spastic smooth muscle, with resulting improvement or cure of a variety of so-called psychosomatic ailments. Etiologically, tense musculature is, as it was for Alexander, simply a matter of "habit-formation." The significance of the fact that not all patients could benefit from his method was overlooked by Jacobson, and receives attention only in those systems, to be mentioned later, which deal directly with the problem of anxiety.

Progressive relaxation finds incidental application in the work of many masseurs, physiotherapists, and psychotherapists. It is systematically used as an adjuvant to therapy, formal or informal, by Gutwirth (1957), Haugen, Dixon and Dickel (1958), Rathbone (1943), Read (1946), and Wolpe (1958).

In 1932, shortly after publication of Jacobson's *Progressive Relaxation*, a German author published a book on a method of "concentrative autorelaxation" (*konzentrative Selbstentspannung*), which, like Jacobson's, was the result of over twenty years of investigation—*Das Auto-gene Training*, by J. H. Schultz (1932). Relaxation exercises as carried out in Schultz's "training" are supposed to give the subject self-regu-latory control of otherwise autonomic functions.

Twenty-six years later, in 1958, Schultz, in collaboration with W. Luthe, published in English a revision of the earlier book under the title *Autogenic Training: A Psychophysiologic Approach to Psycho-therapy* (1959). The authors claim their method to be "one of the most widely applied psychotherapeutic methods in central Europe," and, in fact, base the new book on a survey of more than 600 publica-tions dealing with autogenic training. Perhaps there is also a Russian version of these relaxation techniques, since Schultz and Luthe refer to the "related approaches" of I. Z. Velvoski and A. P. Nikolajew. Felden-krais (1949), in Israel, makes use of a somewhat similar method.

Set, in the sense of chronic postural arrangements, has been a matter of intense concern also for a number of psychoanalytic workers. These include some of the early and eminent Freudians—Ferenczi (1950), Fenichel (1953), Landauer (1926), Reich (1949), and others. Today most orthodox and para-Freudians seem oblivious to this strand of psychoanalytic theory and practice, but there are indications of re-awakening interest (Braatøy, 1954; Lowen, 1958).

Fenichel (1928) called attention to "the remarkable fact . . . that most healthy people, at least in our culture, display in greater or lesser degree a remarkable condition of muscle tonus" (p. 128). Apart from the hypertonus, "the degree of which varies with the muscle group and with the individual, and which may occasionally reach complete rigidity," he noted that "movements may involve not only unneces-sary muscle groups (associated movements), but innervations which are unsuitable and of unnecessary intensity" (p. 128). Fenichel at-tributed these phenomena to "organ libidinization accompanying the defense against drives."

The behavioral core of these diverse muscular manifestations may be readily demonstrated even in the animal laboratory without resort to high-level interpretations. I have dealt with this matter elsewhere (1958) as proprioceptively controlled avoidance behavior. Similar formulations are widely available in the conditioning literature, and Mowrer (1960) has recently spelled out the general process in tremen-dous detail. However, to make sure that in the present context the generalization to the human level is fully comprehensible, a brief statement follows on conditioning the "holding" response in the white rat:

> Light aversion was the drive employed. . . . As soon as a rat pressed down a small, movable bar, a bright overhead light went out. The bar press constituted an effective escape response from

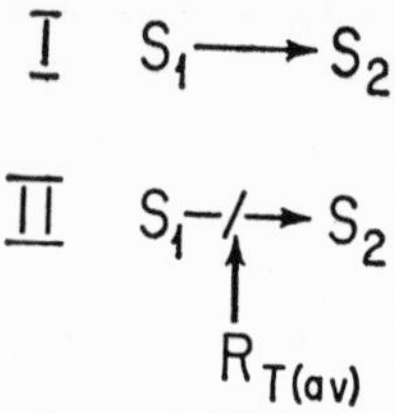

$$\underline{\text{I}} \quad S_1 \longrightarrow S_2$$

$$\underline{\text{II}} \quad S_1 \text{--/} \rightarrow S_2$$
$$\uparrow$$
$$R_{T(av)}$$

Figure 1. Schoenfeld's paradigm for the general use of avoidance.

noxious stimulation. However, the switch was rigged so that when the animal released the bar the light immediately relit. In other words, bar-releasing behavior was negatively reinforced (punished.)

Under these conditions the rat learned to hold the bar down without once releasing it for as long as 45 minutes. . . .

In the analysis of these prolonged "holds" it was assumed that the animal made incipient releasing movements. However, the least motion in the direction of bar release would presumably present discriminable proprioceptive stimuli to the rat. Such stimuli, since they always occurred just prior to the onset of aversive light, would become aversive (punishing) in their own right on the basis of simple Pavlovian conditioning. Therefore, any response that reduced or put an end to the now aversive proprioceptive stimuli would be positively reinforced (rewarded). Such a response might be a mere discontinuance of the release movement or, more likely, activation of antagonistic muscles.

Schoenfeld (1950) has written the paradigm for the general case of avoidance as shown in Figure 1. S_1 is originally a neutral stimulus and S_2 a noxious one. However, if S_1 characteristically precedes S_2 it will become noxious also on a conditioned basis. In the holding experiment S_2 is the glaring light and S_1 the proprioceptive stimuli accompanying bar release.

The animal will now be motivated to take action sooner in the sequence of events. Whereas the rat previously worked to escape S_2, it will now, given the chance, work to escape S_1. In the second part of the paradigm R^T is a terminating response. The additional symbol (Av) is included to indicate that, in addition to terminating S_1, it also avoids S_2. The transverse bar shows that the correlation between S_1 and S_2 is broken. In the holding experiment R^T (Av) is resumption of bar pressing. This simultaneously escapes the conditioned aversive effect of the proprioceptive stimuli, thus immediately reinforcing the response, and it also has the derivative effect of avoiding S_2, the bright light (Hefferline, 1958a, pp. 742–743).

In later work Winnick (1956) followed with a demonstration that the holding was not immobilization but vacillation between release movements and compensatory renewals of forward thrust, and Eldridge (1954) finally established the presence of an aversive state of "anxiety" set up in the animal by its own proprioceptive stimuli. (Eldridge used conditioned respiratory changes as his indicator of "anxiety.")

The most casual inspection of child-training procedures reveals them to be, in large part, training in a variety of avoidances. "Bad" behavior is punished. Traditionally it has been supposed that punishment annihilates further tendencies to such behavior, but experimental evidence (Dinsmoor, 1954; Estes, 1944; Skinner, 1953) now seems conclusive that punishment does not expunge responses from the repertoire.

Punishment's effect is, instead, to condition a holding back response. While the punishable behavior may be effectively restrained from overt manifestation, it is not extinguished, and, in cases where the conflict remains chronic, is not replaced by alternative responses more acceptable to parental or other social authority:

> Instead, there appears to develop a kind of low-grade, chronic deadlock comparable to the conflicts described in animals. Whole areas of behavior apparently may be affected, particularly those that constitute sexual behavior, aggression, or even, in some families, merely "getting excited."
>
> Much of what is punished in childhood, however, seems to be merely the precocious appearance of behavior not only sanctioned in the adult but actually demanded of him. For a child to be thoroughly conditioned either to accept unquestioningly or to resist blindly what may be arbitrary (or, indeed, nonsensical) parental demands suggests that, although later he might meet the criteria of maturity in many conventional respects, he would remain overrestricted in his behavior. His effectors would chronically be partially engaged in restraining behavior now appropriate to adult status. This would be the situation clinically called "residual tension" (Hefferline, 1958a, p. 746).

From the above it appears that a conditioning account can be given of the chronic sets noted by the psychoanalysts to whose work we shall now return. Those who might reject Freudian theory per se, will not, I presume, question the veracity of descriptive statements made by psychoanalysts about their patient's directly observed behavior.

Reich's (1949) concept of "muscular armor" is widely familiar. It is unfortunate that his search for "orgone" in later life tended to discredit his earlier clinical work. By present standards his therapeutic procedure with muscularly tense patients may seem brutal and ill-advised, since he would on occasion, when he found a spastic condition, attempt to break the cramp by physical force. An alternative procedure, as used, for example, by Lowen (1958), is to analyze the conflict, ventilate the affects (permit conditioned respondents to extinguish), and allow the patient to resolve the muscular block himself.

A formulation which combines the elements of psychoanalysis, clinical medicine, and conditioning theory is that of E. J. Kempf. His well-known 1921 monograph, "Autonomic functions and the personality", and his later writings, down through his 1958 monograph, "Basic Biodynamics," have consistently and with scholarly documentation developed his views on the "physiology of attitude," which for him subsumes the psychological aspects as well. His account of the "emergence of the ego-organization" makes the Freudian ego itself a kind of super set. Possibly because of his rather obscure style, his work has not received due attention. His over-all position is that "our postural tensions reveal our way of holding our affective pressure so as to fit it to our situations as we see them. . . . Often the form of the postural tensions reveals the nature of the suppressed or repressed affect" (Kempf, 1931).

The clinical approach to chronic muscular dystonus most nearly in keeping with the general tenor of this chapter is the work of the several Institutes for Gestalt Therapy. Their use of the term gestalt to characterize their work is, in my opinion, misleading, since it ties them to a movement with which they share little other than the use of such phrases as "figure and ground." They will be mentioned again in the final section in connection with a series of "informal experiments in self-awareness."

The upshot of this cursory account of set, as studied in the laboratory and as extrapolated to the chronic muscular conditions found in clinical practice, is to suggest once more, as Floyd Allport did earlier, that as psychologists we have here a broad spectrum of behavior, largely tonic, which has extreme importance in determining the strength of the more conspicuous phasic responses. With the tighter formulation which may now be developed and with the technical arrangements which are more nearly adequate to the task, it is suggested that it is high time to conduct intensive and extensive investigation.

TWO NEW SPECIALTIES — CLINICAL EXPERIMENTALIST AND EXPERIMENTAL CLINICIAN

The experimentalist can appropriately follow some of his problems into the clinic and take behavioral data from patients undergoing diagnosis or treatment. Correspondingly, the clinician can equip himself with the tools of the laboratory and monitor some of the autonomic and skeletal variables which may at times be better indicants of the patient's status than his verbal report to the clinician or than the clinician's verbal report to himself.

Due to space limitations a series of illustrative studies from the American and Russian literature will not be reviewed. Fortunately, it is now possible to refer the reader instead to Razran's (1961) remarkable one-man issue of the *Psychological Review* entitled, "The Observable Unconscious and the Inferable Conscious: Interoceptive Conditioning, Semantic Conditioning, and the Orienting Reflex." This monograph, although not stressing clinical implications, parallels closely the basic position taken here.

Proprioceptive studies using unanesthetized animals have usually involved passive flexion. Unless immobilized, the animal tends to fight electromyographic leads. Even if it does not, its gross movements ordinarily swamp electrically any small signal that may be of interest. Equipment of advanced design minimizes these problems, as mentioned earlier, by utilizing tiny transistorized amplifiers and perhaps even a miniaturized FM transmitter. These may be strapped to the animal without any entangling leads, and the signal detected and recorded at a remote location. Similar arrangements are feasible for the human subject and have been used for example, in monitoring cardiac function, brain waves, and autonomic variables from a passenger in a racing car.

Technological advance has been greatly spurred by the crash program directed at telemetering a man in space. Improved transducers, amplifiers, and recorders, developed for use in satellites, are already available commercially at reasonable prices. Obviously, such devices can be used efficiently with earthbound experimental subjects.

For many problems it appears that a new type of force transducer may bypass many of the inconveniences, technical problems, and expense of an electronic setup. My colleagues and I (Hefferline, Birch, and Gentry) have prototyped a number of devices making use of pressure sensitive paint or pressure cells of the type called "microducers." A description of some of them together with preliminary calibration data, is now in press. The sensitive element is manufactured by processing certain of the rare earths with zirconium tetrachloride. The resulting resins or plastics undergo tremendous change in electrical resistance upon physical compression. The force applied may be read from an ohmmeter by suitable calibration of its scale, or, after insertion of a flashlight battery into the circuit, on a 0–1 recording milliameter. Without amplification the output is sufficient to operate relays, recorders, scopes, tube circuits, or even to control the speed of miniature motors. With amplification the force changes may be measured at the microgram level.

The potential applications of this remarkable product seem unlimited. Thus far we have checked its feasibility in a pressure bar for rats or other small mammals, a pecking-target for pigeons or other birds, touch spots for sheer bodily contact, and as a heart-rate and respiration indicator. A pressure cell can be made small enough for insertion in a hypodermic needle, and could obviously be embedded surgically in animal tissue for continuous recording. Of considerable importance in possible multichannel applications is its elimination of the troublesome cross-talk problem encountered in electronic systems.

As might be expected, we are vigorously pressing the development of these and other devices, and we invite others to do likewise, with a view to sharing the improved designs which are sure to follow when a number of investigators begin experimenting with this pressure sensitive product.

Such devices are immediately applicable to the problem of set considered as sustained response. We have readily conditioned rats to maintain, within rather narrow limits, a stipulated pressure on a lever, with reinforcement contingent on holding the lever within this pressure range for a certain length of time. Automatic timing is provided by voltage-sensing switches which start or stop the clocks as the range limits are under- or over-shot.

Comparable results are obtainable for human subjects when these simple transducers are used. Furthermore, when slight contraction of a particular muscle produces and maintains the discriminative stimulus for some phasic response, the subject quickly acquires control of this discriminative stimulus without "knowing" that it is he, and not the experimenter, who "has charge" of it.

It has been the standard position of learning theorists that there is no qualitative difference between the behavior of man and that of subhuman organisms, the seeming difference being produced by the fact that man alone possesses verbal behavior. A further assumption is that this verbal behavior itself may be accounted for by the very same principles that apply to nonverbal behavior. Skinner's *Verbal Behavior* (1957) is a nonexperimental attempt to make good on this claim. Experimental verification would be greatly facilitated, of course, if man as a laboratory subject could be studied with the variables controlling his verbal behavior somehow rendered temporarily inoperative.

Such a technique seems to have been demonstrated in a preliminary way (1959) by the success which my associates and I recently had in conditioning escape and avoidance responses in human subjects without their observation of this behavior. Because this study establishes a kind of baseline for further work of immediate importance to clinical psychology, it will be quoted at some length:

When the human subject has "voluntary control" of the response to be conditioned, experimental results are in general less predictable and reproducible than those obtained from animals. This is commonly attributed to "self-instruction"—that is, to variables experimentally uncontrolled. In the present study this problem was circumvented by working with a response so small as to preclude a history of strengthening through discriminable effect upon the environment—in fact, so small as to occur unnoticed by the subject. . . .

The subject sat in a shielded enclosure in a reclining chair. Recording electrodes were attached to the palmar base of the left thumb and to the medial edge of the left hand. Three additional sets of dummy electrodes were applied in some instances, to suggest that a comprehensive study of body tensions was being conducted. Muscle action-potentials across the left hand were amplified by a factor of 1 million and rectified, and their average momentary values were displayed on a meter. They were also permanently recorded by an Esterline-Angus recording milliameter. . . .

Results are reported from eight men and four women ranging in age from 18 to 50 and divided into four groups of three each.

Group 1, with four sets of electrodes attached, were told that the study concerned the effects on body tension of noise superimposed on music. Their task was to listen through earphones and, otherwise, do nothing. Group 2, also with all electrodes attached, were told that a specific response, so small as to be invisible, would temporarily turn off the noise or, when the noise was not present, postpone its onset. Their task was to discover and make use of the response. Group 3, with recording electrodes only, were informed that the effective response was a tiny twitch of the left thumb. Group 4 were given the same information as Group 3 but had, in addition, a meter before them during the first half-hour of conditioning, which provided a potential basis for them to use the visual presentation of their response as a "crutch" for proprioceptive observation of the response. . . .

While the subject relaxed and listened to tape-recorded music through earphones, the experimenter watched the meter on his panel for 5 to 10 minutes to select for later reinforcement a response of a size occurring not more than once in 1 or 2 minutes. It was a ballistic swing of the pointer up and back over a few scale divisions.

After the operant level for this response had been recorded for 10 minutes [OL 1 in Figure 2], conditioning was begun by superimposing on the music an aversively loud 60-cycle hum. Whenever the experimenter saw on the meter an instance of the selected response, he pressed a key. This turned off the noise for 15 seconds or, when it was already off, postponed noise resumption for 15 seconds. . . .

After an hour of conditioning, with a 5-minute intermission at the half-hour point, 10 minutes of extinction occurred during which the subject's response was ineffective in terminating continuously present

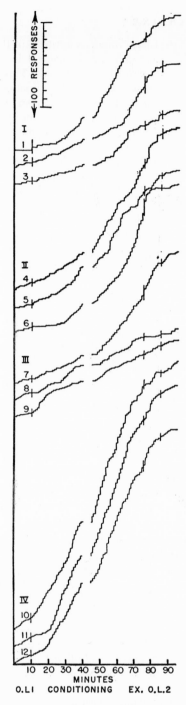

Figure 2. Cumulative response curves for adult human subjects in a situation where a small and unnoticed thumb twitch either terminated or postponed noise stimulation. *OL 1* and *2*, initial and terminal operant level determinations, respectively; *EX.*, extinction.

noise. During final 10 minutes of music only, the extent of recovery of the original operant level was recorded.

Figure 2 presents a cumulative response curve for each subject. Conditioning is clearly indicated by the positive acceleration in the rate of responding for all subjects except 2 and 3 in group 3. These two kept so busy producing voluntary thumb-twitches that the small, reinforceable type of response had little opportunity to occur.

When interviewed later, all members of group 1 still believed that they had been passive victims with respect to the onset and duration of noise, and all seemed astounded to learn that they themselves had been in control. Subject 1 and 2 of group 2 reported that they early gave up searching for an effective response and thus, in effect, transferred themselves to group 1. Subject 3 of group 2 professed to have discovered an effective response sequence, which consisted of subtle rowing movement with both hands, infinitesimal wriggles of both ankles, a slight displacement of the jaw to the left, breathing out— and then waiting! Subject 1 of group 3 gave evidence of conditioning perhaps because he misconstrued the instructions. Instead of making the response a quick contraction, he spent his time very gradually increasing pressure on an imaginary switch button. This may have kept deliberate activity at a level low enough for the correct response to break through and be reinforced.

Group 4 subjects, provided with their own meter, obtained many more reinforcements than the others, an effect which continued through the second half-hour of conditioning with the meter removed. While the meter did not enable them to achieve direct control of the discrete response, it seems to have provided a basis for rapid responding within a range which included the reinforced size. This showed on the meter as rapid oscillation (Hefferline, Keenan, and Harford, 1959, pp. 1338–1339).

Unpublished data indicate that small, unobserved responses may be conditioned just as readily with a secondary reinforcer, such as a score increment on a numerical readout mounted in the subject's enclosure at eye level (Hefferline, Keenan, and Birch).

The theoretical and practical importance which we attribute to conditioning under this technique is that it enables us to approach the adult human subject just as we would an animal of another species. Since he does not discriminate his own behavior in the manner called conscious, he is not in a position to introduce the confusing array of variables which are the product of the socialization process. It is as if his "human" behavior had been functionally dissected out of the repertoire, leaving his "animal" behavior to be independently manipulated.

In further work we plan to introduce systematically variables of the sort which may lead the subject to discriminate and report his "animal" responses, thus providing the secondary behavior which we have discussed earlier. This would be the R_2 responding of Schoenfeld and Cumming's advanced paradigm.

Suppose, for example, we condition a small response, such as the tiny thumb twitch described above, with reinforcement consisting of an increase in score (secondary reinforcement) whenever the appropriate response is made. The response is much too small for the subject to produce voluntarily or even to observe when it occurs. Can we make its occurrence an effective discriminative stimulus for a reporting response? The latter could have the form of pressing a key, if so instructed, or merely saying aloud, "I did it."

There are various procedures which could be invoked. We might tell the subject, "Henceforth you will not be reinforced unless you state that you are eligible for reinforcement; you must tell us whenever you make what you think is a reinforceable response." If the subject now makes the thumb response and then, with short latency, makes the key press or the vocal reporting response, as the case may be, he will see his score increase. Should he omit to report a reinforceable response, he will receive no reinforcement. This, of course, is the standard procedure for establishing a discriminated operant. If the subject reports the thumb twitch when it occurs and ceases to report it when it has not occurred, he will have become "aware" of the thumb twitch in the ordinary sense of the word—that is, he can now talk about the thumb twitch to the extent of "tacting" or "naming" it. Perhaps he can say nothing else about it, such as describing his criteria for the reporting response, but he and the experimenter now share a common language about his "private" stimuli, even though it has but a single word in its vocabulary.

Suppose the above procedure fails and the subject does not come to discriminate his thumb twitch or, if he does discriminate it as above, suppose we wish him to form discriminations of subtler aspects of the response. In such case there are a number of "crutches" available by which the reporting response may be facilitated. For instance, he may "watch" his response on a meter or scope, and thus be able to match the unmistakably clear visual aspects with the vaguer proprioceptive "feel," and perhaps come to say something about the behavioral context in which the response occurs.

The artificial feedback channel may be auditory. In conditioning a sustained response, as contrasted with a momentary twitch, we have integrated the output and fed it back to the subject as discrete "beeps" of an audio oscillator. The frequency of beeps correlates with the degree of muscle contraction, and the subject more speedily learns to hold the required tension than is the case when the feedback is proprioceptive only. Furthermore, once such crutches have been

used in response acquisition, they may be disposed of, with the subject getting along just as well, or nearly as well, with what remains
of the previously compound discriminative stimulus—namely, the
proprioceptive component.*

My reason for going into some detail with respect to the technique
by which previously "unaware" responses may come to be reported
is to establish its feasibility for wider experimental and clinical use.
It may seem a far cry from the unverbalized thumb twitch, as mentioned here, to the "unconscious" or the "repressed" as talked about in
psychoanalysis, but there is a possible continuity. However, before
leaving the topic of simple supplementary feedback to the subject, it
might be appropriate to mention two practical examples which have
come to my attention.

Dickel, Wood, and Dixon (1957) permit their tense patients to
observe on an oscilloscope their output of muscle action-potentials before and after treatment with a "tranquilizer" such as meprobamate.
These investigators report the technique useful to them and to the
patient in demonstrating "an increase in capacity to co-ordinate
and respond to given signals."

Dental researchers (Hickey, Stacey, and Rinear, 1957; Moyers,
1950, 1956) have long made intelligent use of electromyography in
connection with subjective and objective problems of the patient's
"bite." William Shpuntoff (1959) employs the oscilloscope to demonstrate to patients the manner in which excessive jaw tensions may
damage their teeth or recently acquired dentures. Such contractions,
when intense, are diagnosed as bruxism, a rhythmic clenching or
gnashing of the teeth which may occur while one is asleep or awake.
In a number of patients short periods of observing tension and relaxation as indicated on the 'scope, and noting the accompanying proprioceptive "feel" of the jaw, have been sufficient to reduce or eliminate this tendency. How they then dispose of "inward aggression," of
which bruxism is supposed to be an expression (Stolzemberg, 1953),
Shpuntoff apparently does not consider his responsibility.

In order to tackle more directly and yet comprehensively the question of how laboratory and clinical procedures may be combined with
gains for both pure science and therapy, I should like to return to
the topic of chronic sets or tensional patterns discussed in the preceding section. There the emphasis was simply upon the existence of such
conditions on a widespread basis. Therapy was mentioned only in
terms of conventional psychoanalysis or other forms of practice. The

* As this goes to press it is possible to report that we have now demonstrated
that stimuli from a response too small for the experimental subject to produce
deliberately, or to be "conscious of" the sense of making conventional verbal
report, may acquire discriminative control over another covert response in a
distant part of the body or over an overt response such as a key-press.

following attempts a preliminary statement of a proposed application
of the discrimination procedure, as discussed in the context of the
thumb twitch, to the resolution of neurotic conflict.

It will be recalled that punishment may lead to the active withholding of previously punished behavior. Such behavior may be of supra-
threshold strength, but the conditioned aversive proprioceptive stimuli
which are generated when it is on the point of being emitted lead to
intense contraction of the antagonistic musculature. Since the skeletal
muscles are voluntary muscles, one might presume that the individual,
if his attention were directed to the conflict, might deliberately terminate the conflict in one direction or the other. Paradoxically, he can do
this only indirectly, by the roundabout procedure of making a kind of
proprioceptive inspection of this situation in the internal environment
and then, with persistence and some luck, discovering *how* he maintains the muscular conflict. It is usually only after some increased
mobility develops—the typical accompaniment of discrimination of
slight changes in the contracture—that the question of *why* is likely
to receive an answer.

More than ten years ago, on the assumption that the condition of
the musculature could be taken to be part of the world of things and
events and thus susceptible to observation and verbal report, I prepared mimeographed instruction sheets entitled *Informal Experiments
in Self-Awareness* and distributed them to undergraduates enrolled in
courses in abnormal psychology.* In the course of about seven years,
sets of reports were collected from more than a thousand students. A
general statement of procedure is quoted here from a previous summary account:

> As part of his assignment the subject was encouraged to make what
> amounted to a systematic proprioceptive survey of his own body,
> conducted in private with minimum external distractions. A person
> neither dead nor in flaccid paralysis presumably should be able to
> discriminate the tonic condition of all or of any part of his skeletal
> musculature. The first report of a subject is likely to be that he can
> do this. He can feel, he says, every part of his body. When further
> inquiry is made, it often turns out that what he took to be proprio-
> ceptive discrimination of a particular body part was actually a visuali-
> zation of the part or a verbal statement of its location. Or else, to
> discriminate the part, he may have had to intensify proprioception by
> making actual movements.

* A version of this material, together with verbatim excerpts from written
reports submitted by students, was published in 1951 as the first half of a
collaborative book entitled *Gestalt Therapy* (Perls, Hefferline, and Goodman).
The title, along with some of the printed statements, were somewhat alien
to my own way of speaking but necessitated by the fact that this was a
collaborative effort. The approach was phenomenological and an attempt was
made to make the general tone nontechnical and rather intimate.

With further work, if he can be persuaded to continue, the subject may report certain parts of his body to be proprioceptively missing. Suppose it is his neck. He may discriminate a mass that is his head and a mass that is his trunk with what feels like simply some empty space between. At this stage the subject is apt to remember more important things to do and his participation in the silly business ends.

Some subjects, however, apparently made curious by blank spots and hopeful of recovering some lost degree of freedom in their system of voluntary control, do whatever is involved in paying closer attention to and acquiring interest in this peculiar private situation. A blank spot, they say, may gradually fill in. Or it may suddenly become the locus of sharp pain, paresthesias of one sort or another, "electric" sensations, or the unmistakable ache of muscular cramp.

Then what formerly was a blank may become as demanding of attention as an aching tooth. Further and more detailed discriminations may be made. It soon becomes imperative to relax the cramp, but the subject says that he does not know how to do so; he is concerned with so-called voluntary muscles, but these are reportedly not under voluntary control. The subject is somewhat in the position of the elementary psychology student who is assured that he has the voluntary muscles needed to wiggle his ears. The difference, of course, is that in the case of ear-wiggling he has never acquired control, whereas, in the case of the cramped muscles he has somehow lost control.

As soon as the question becomes one of how to acquire or regain control, problems for investigation sprout in all directions. A host of variables, direct or indirect in their effect, become relevant. One involves merely the instruction to continue to pay sustained attention to the blocking, regardless of discomfort, and to be on the alert for subtle changes of any sort. This seems to give rise to what previously was called ideomotor action, and may in itself bring a loosening of the reported muscular clinch.

Another instruction is to increase the clinch deliberately, if possible, and then, while relaxing from this added intensity, to learn something about relaxing still further. Also relevant are procedures that make use of proprioceptive facilitation—for instance, those used in training polio victims, partial spastics, and others to make better use of whatever healthy muscle they still possess. Kabat (1950) has developed these methods systematically.

When a muscular block is definitely resolved, it is frequently claimed by the subject that there occurs vivid, spontaneous recall of typical situations, perhaps dating back to childhood, where he learned to tense in this particular manner. Should a correlation between recovered movements and recovered memories be found and turn out to be high, it would afford substantial support to a motor theory of the so-called higher mental processes. It would generalize in ways not clearly foreseeable Davis's basic experimental finding that the "stimulus trace" is conserved in the differential activity of muscles (Davis, 1952).

Such subjective accounts of proprioceptively controlled events, although they may be revealing and fully convincing when made at first hand in observing one's own behavior, are obviously not to be taken at face value as scientific data. They have merely introspectionistic standing unless or until they can be corroborated objectively in the laboratory. A first step in this direction, it is believed, is the attempt to achieve quantitative measurement of proprioceptive stimuli and to lay foundations for a method of checking verbal report against instrumentally obtained data (Hefferline, 1958a, pp. 747–749).

For the past three years my efforts have been directed toward developing a research facility where such work can be undertaken. A host of prior problems have been encountered, and short-term, limited studies are still the order of the day. For the most part they have been methodological or concerned with the development of reliable, low-cost equipment. While full instrumentation remains costly, a sensitive channel of electromyography can now be set up, including a recording system, for a few hundred dollars.

In concluding this rough account of potential symbiotic relations between learning theory and clinical psychology I am keenly aware of leaving the scene untidied. Perhaps that is as it should be. What I have done most definitely is to argue for extension of learning theory's viewpoint and methodology into the domain of clinical psychology and to urge that clinical psychology become thoroughly behavioristic in a broad sense which includes objective study of events previously considered inescapably private.

In my opinion the region under the skin, where covert behavior, both operant and respondent, takes place, is psychology's new frontier, and this environment needs to be coordinated with the external environment by whatever means can be contrived in order that a scientific account of the stimulus control of the organism may be completed. The organism's reinforcement history seems to be conserved, at least to an important degree, in the sustained behavior called set, and resolution of the stalemate between antagonistic sets is a means of recovering repressed content and, more important, of remobilizing blocked forms of action.

What is most characteristically human in behavior is conditioned during the socialization process. It is secondary behavior, largely verbal, and is the carrier of those properties which have given rise to the notion of consciousness. Secondary behavior is acquired exclusively from transactions with the external environment or with the internalized versions of such transactions. As such, it is subject to extinction or to reshaping by withholding or rearranging reinforcements. This is man's strength or his weakness, depending on whether one speaks of therapy or brainwashing. That it may be the former and not the latter is what I conceive to be the special urgency for an effective program of experimental-clinical research conducted by men of good will.

REFERENCES

Alexander, F. M. *The use of the self.* New York: Dutton, 1932.

Allport, F. H. *Theories of perception and the concept of structure.* New York: Wiley, 1955.

Barlow, W. Postural homeostasis. *Annals Physical Med.,* 1952, *1,* 77–87.

Behanan, K. T. *Yoga: a scientific evaluation.* New York: Dover, 1937.

Boring, E. G. The use of operational definitions in science. *Psychol. Rev.,* 1945, 52, 243–245.

Braatøy, T. *Fundamentals of psychoanalytic technique.* New York: Wiley, 1954.

Brazier, R. A. B. (Ed.). The central nervous system and behavior. *Trans. First Conf.,* 1958; *Second Conf.,* 1959; *Third Conf.,* 1960. New York: Josiah Macy, Jr., Foundation.

Cameron, N. *The psychology of behavior disorders.* Boston: Houghton Mifflin, 1947.

Cameron, N., & Magaret, A. *Behavior pathology.* Boston: Houghton Mifflin, 1951.

The central nervous system and behavior: Selected translations from the Russian medical literature. Washington, D.C.: G.P.O., U.S. Dept. of Health, Education and Welfare, Public Health Service, 1959.

Davis, R. C. Set and muscular tension. *Indiana Univ. Science Ser. No.* 10, 1940. Bloomington, Ind: Indiana Univ. Press.

Davis, R. C. The psychophysiology of set. In F. L. Harriman (Ed.), *Twentieth century psychology.* New York: Philosophical Library, 1946.

Davis, R. C. The stimulus trace in effectors and its relation to judgment responses. *J. exp. Psychol.,* 1952, *44,* 377–390.

Davis, R. C. Response patterns. *Trans. N.Y. Acad. Sci.,* 1957 (Ser. II), *19,* 731–739.

Davis, R. C., & Buchwald, A. M. An exploration of somatic response patterns: stimulus and sex differences. *J. comp. physiol. Psychol.,* 1957, *50,* 44–52.

Davis, R. C., Buchwald, A. M., & Frankmann, R. W. Autonomic and muscular responses, and their relation to simple stimuli. *Psychol. Monogr.,* 1955, *69,* (No. 405).

Davis, R. C., Lundervold, A., & Miller, J. D. The pattern of somatic response during a repetitive motor task and its modification by visual stimuli. *J. comp. physiol. Psychol.,* 1957, *50,* 53–60.

Dell, P. Corrélations entre le système végétatif et le système de la vie de rélation. Mésencéphale, diencéphale et cortex cérébral. *J. de Physiol.* (Paris), 1952, *44,* 471–557.

Dewey, J., & Bentley, A. F. *Knowing and the known.* Boston: Beacon Press. 1949.

Dickel, H. A., Wood, J. A., & Dixon, H. H. Electromyographic studies on meprobamate and the working, anxious patient. *Annals, N. Y. Acad. Sci.,* 1957, *67,* 780–787.

Dinsmoor, J. Punishment I: The avoidance hypothesis. *Psychol. Rev.,* 1954, *61,* 34–46.

Dollard, J., & Miller, N. E. *Personality*

and psychotherapy. New York: Mc-Graw-Hill, 1950.

Eldridge, L. Respiration rate change and its relation to avoidance behavior. Unpublished Ph.D. dissertation, Columbia Univ., 1954.

Estes, W. K. An experimental study of punishment. *Psychol. Monogr.*, 1944, No. 263.

Feldenkrais, M. *Body and mature behavior.* New York: Internat. Univs. Press, 1949.

Fenichel, O. Organ libidinization accompanying the defense against drives. In *Collected papers of Otto Fenichel: First Series.* New York: Norton, 1953.

Ferenczi, S. Thinking and muscle-innervation. In *Further contributions to the theory and technique of psycho-analysis.* London: Hogarth, 1950.

Ferster, C. B., & Skinner, B. F., *Schedules of reinforcement.* New York: Appleton-Century-Crofts, 1957.

Field, J., Magoun, H. W., & Hall, V. W. (Eds.). *Handbook of Physiology.* Vols. I–III. Washington: Amer. Physiol. Soc., 1960.

Fisher, S., & Cleveland, S. E. *Body image and personality.* Princeton, N.J.: Van Nostrand, 1958.

Freeman, G. L. *The energetics of human behavior.* Ithaca, N.Y.: Cornell Univ. Press, 1948.

French, J. D. The reticular formation. In J. Field, H. W. Magoun, & V. E. Hall, (Eds.), *Handbook of physiology. Vol. II.* Washington, D.C.: Amer. Physiol. Soc., 1960, 1281–1305.

Freud, S. *The ego and the id.* London: Hogarth, 1950.

Freud, S. The interpretation of dreams. In A. A. Brill, (Ed.), *The basic writings of Sigmund Freud.* New York: Modern Library, 1939, 181–549.

Fulton, J. F. Levels of autonomic function with particular reference to the cerebral cortex. *Res. Publs. Assn. Res. nerv. ment. Dis.*, 1939, *19.*

Gibson, J. J. A critical review of the concept of set in contemporary experimental psychology. *Psychol. Bull.*, 1941, *38,* 781–817.

Graham, C. H. Behavior and the psychophysical methods: an analysis of some recent experiments. *Psychol. Rev.*, 1952, *59,* 62–70.

Guthrie, E. R. *The psychology of learning.* (Rev. Ed.). New York: Harper, 1952.

Gutwirth, S. W. *You can stop worrying.* Chicago: Regnery, 1957.

Haugen, G. B., Dixon, H. H., & Dickel, H. A. *A therapy for anxiety tension reactions.* New York: Macmillan, 1958.

Hebb, D. O. Alice in Wonderland or psychology among the biological sciences. In H. F. Harlow & C. N. Woolsey (Eds.), *Biological and biochemical bases of behavior.* Madison: Univ. Wisconsin Press, 1958, 451–467

Hebb, D. O. The American Revolution. *Amer. Psychologist,* 1960, *15,* 735–744.

Hebb, D. O. *The organization of behavior.* New York: Wiley, 1949.

Hefferline, R. F. An experimental study of avoidance. *Genet. Psychol. Monogr.*, 1950, *42,* 231–337.

Hefferline, R. F. The role of proprioception in the control of behavior. *Trans. N.Y. Acad. Sci.*, 1958a, *20,* 739–764.

Hefferline, R. F. Trigant Burrow: a life in letters. *Main Currents*, 1958b, *15,* 21–23.

Hefferline, R. F., Birch, J. D. & Gentry, T. Simple transducers to detect or record operant amplitude. *J. exp. anal. Behav.* 1961. In press.

Hefferline, R. F., Keenan, B., & Harford, R. A. Escape and avoidance conditioning in human subjects without their observation of the response. *Science*, 1959, *130,* 1338–1339.

Hefferline, R. F., Keenan, B., & Birch, J. D. Conditioning small operants in human subjects without their observation by means of secondary reinforcement. Unpublished.

Hickey, J. C., Stacy, R. W., & Rinear, L. L. Electromyographic studies of mandibular muscles in basic jaw movements. *J. prosthetic Dent.*, 1957, 7, 565–570.

Huxley, A. The history of tension. *Annals N.Y. Acad. Sci.*, 1957, 67, 675–684.

Jacobson, E. Electrophysiology of mental activities. *Amer. J. Psychol.*, 1932, 44, 677–694.

Jacobson, E. *Progressive relaxation.* Chicago: Univ. Chicago Press, 1938.

Jenkins, W. L. Somesthesis. In S. S. Stevens (Ed.), *Handbook of experimental psychology.* New York: Wiley, 1951, 1172–1190.

Jones, F. P. Head-balance and sitting posture: An X-ray analysis. *J. Psychol.*, 1960, 49, 289–293.

Jones, F. P., Gray, F. E., Hanson, J. A., & O'Connell, D. N. An experimental study of the effect of head balance on patterns of posture and movement in man. *J. Psychol.*, 1959, 47, 247–258.

Jones, F. P., & O'Connell, D. N. Posture as a function of time. *J. Psychol.*, 1958, 46, 287–294.

Jost, H., & Sontag, L. W. The genetic factor in autonomic nervous function. *Psychosom. Med.*, 1944, 6, 308–310.

Kabat, H. Central mechanisms for recovery of neuromuscular function. *Science*, 1950, 112, 23–24.

Keller, F. S., & Schoenfeld, W. N. *Principles of psychology.* New York: Appleton-Century-Crofts, 1950.

Kempf, E. J. Basic biodynamics. *Annals N.Y. Acad. Sci.*, 1958, 73, 869–910.

Kempf, E. J. Neuroses as conditioned, conflicting, holistic, attitudinal, acquisitive, avoidance reactions. *Annals N.Y. Acad. Sci.*, 1953, 56, 307–329.

Kempf, E. J. Postural tensions for normal and abnormal behavior, their significance. *California & West. Med.*, 1931, 35, 182–184; 272–274.

Kempf, E. J. The autonomic functions and the personality. *Nerv. and ment. Dis. Monogr.*, No. 28, 1921.

Lacey, J. I. The relationship of resting autonomic activity to motor impulsivity. In *The brain and human behavior. Proc. Assn. Res. nerv. ment. Dis.*, 1958, 36, 144–209.

Lacey, J. I., Bateman, D. E., & Van Lehre, R. Autonomic response specificity: an experimental study. *Psychosom. Med.*, 1953, 16, 8–21.

Landauer, K. Die Kindliche Bewegungsunruhe. *Int. Z. Psa.*, 1926, 12, 388.

Levy, E. Z., Thaler, V. H., & Ruff, G. E. New technique for recording skin resistance changes. *Science*, 1958, 128, 33–34.

Lindsley, O. R. Operant conditioning methods applied to research in chronic schizophrenia. *Psychiat. Res. Rep.*, 1956, 5, 118–139.

Lowen, A. *Physical dynamics of character structure.* New York: Grune & Stratton, 1958.

Magnus, R. *Körperstellung.* Berlin: Springer, 1924.

Malmo, R. B., Shagass, C., & Davis, F. H. Specificity of bodily reactions under stress: a physiological study of somatic symptom mechanisms in psychiatric patients. *Res. Publ. Ass. nerv. ment. Dis.*, 1950, 29, 231–261.

Miller, G. A., Galanter, E., & Pribram, K. H. *Plans and the structure of behavior.* New York: Holt, 1960.

Mowrer, O. R. *Learning theory and behavior.* New York: Wiley, 1960.

Moyers, R. E. Physiologic considerations of centric and other jaw relations. *J. prosthetic Dent.*, 1956, 6, 183–194.

Moyers, R. E. An electromyographic analysis of certain muscles involved in temperomandibular movement. *Am. J. Orthodontics*, 1950, 36, 481–515.

Osgood, C. E. *Method and theory in experimental psychology.* New York: Oxford Univ. Press, 1953.

Pavlov, I. P. *Experimental psychology and other essays.* New York: Philosophical Library, 1957.

Perls, F. S., Hefferline, R. F., & Goodman, P. *Gestalt therapy.* New York: Julian, 1951.

Piaget, J. *The origins of intelligence in children.* New York: Internat. Univs. Press, 1952.

Rapaport, D. The structure of psychoanalytic theory: A systematizing attempt. In S. Koch (Ed.), *Psychology: a study of a science. Vol. 3.* New York: McGraw-Hill, 1959, 55–183.

Rathbone, J. L. *Relaxation.* New York: Bureau of Publications, Teachers College, Columbia Univ., 1943.

Razran, G. *Interoceptive conditioning: A review of Russian experiments and applications.* In preparation.

Razran, G. The observable unconscious and the inferable conscious in current Soviet psychophysiology: interoceptive conditioning, semantic conditioning, and the orienting reflex. *Psychol. Rev.* 1961, *68,* 81–147.

Read, C. D. Correlations of physical and emotional phenomena of natural childbirth. *J. Obst. & Gynaec. Brit. Emp.,* 1946, *53,* 55–61.

Reich, W. *Character-analysis.* (3rd Ed.). New York: Orgone Institute Press, 1949.

Reik, T. *Listening with the third ear.* New York: Farrar, Straus, 1948.

Schoenfeld, W. N. An experiemental approach to anxiety, escape and avoidance. In P. J. Hoch and J. Zubin (Eds.), *Anxiety.* New York: Grune & Stratton, 1950, 70–99.

Schoenfeld, W. N., & Cumming, W. W. Perception and Behavior. In S. Koch (Ed.), *Psychology: a study of a science. Vol. 5.* New York: McGraw-Hill. In press.

Schultz, J. H. *Das autogene training.* Leipzig: Thieme, 1932.

Schultz, J. H., & Luthe, W. *Autogenic training: a psychophysiological approach to psychotherapy.* New York: Grune & Stratton, 1959.

Senzaki, B., & McCandless, R. S. *Buddhism and Zen.* New York: Philosophical Library, 1953.

Sherrington, G. S. *The integrative action of the nervous system.* New Haven, Conn.: Yale Univ. Press, 1952.

Shpuntoff, W. Personal communication, 1959.

Sidman, M. *Tactics of scientific research.* New York: Basic Books, 1960.

Simon, B. (Ed.). *Psychology in the Soviet Union.* Stanford, Calif.: Stanford Univ. Press, 1957.

Skinner, B. F. *The behavior of organisms.* New York: Appleton-Century-Crofts, 1938.

Skinner, B. F. *Walden Two.* New York: Macmillan, 1948.

Skinner, B. F. *Science and human behavior.* New York: Macmillan, 1953.

Skinner, B. F. *Verbal behavior.* New York: Appleton-Century-Crofts, 1957.

Skinner, B. F. *Cumulative record.* New York: Appleton-Century-Crofts, 1959.

Sperry, R. W. On the neural basis of the conditioned response. *Brit. J. Anim. Behav.,* 1955, *3,* 41–44.

Stolzenberg, J. Case reports on bruxism and periodic hysterical trismus. *J. clin. and exp. Hypnosis,* 1953, *1,* 67–70.

Syz, H. Personal communication, 1960.

Wenger, M. A. The measurement of individual differences in autonomic balance. *Psychosom. Med.,* 1941, *3,* 427–434.

Winnick, W. Anxiety indicators in an avoidance response during conflict and nonconflict. *J. comp. physiol. Psychol.,* 1956, *49,* 52–59.

Wolpe, J. *Psychotherapy by reciprocal inhibition.* Stanford, Calif.: Stanford Univ. Press, 1958.

Woodworth, R. S., & Schlosberg, H. *Experimental psychology.* New York: Holt, 1954.

5

The Effects of Infantile
Experience on Adult Behavior

SEYMOUR LEVINE

It is always tempting when introducing an area of investigation to cull appropriate quotes from antiquity in order to show that the particular problem under discussion has concerned eminent scholars throughout the ages—and thus establish its importance, as well as give the reader confidence in the scholarliness of the author.

Certainly, when the subject matter is the importance of the ex-perience of infant organism upon subsequent behavior a plethora of such references is available. What is striking, however, is not that the importance of environmental factors during infancy has been com-mented on and discussed for many centuries, but that in spite of these many references the systematic experimental laboratory in-vestigation of this problem is no more than a decade and a half old. Throughout the history of psychology there has of course been a consistent interest in the ontogenesis of behavior. A number of early studies by Small (1899) and Yerkes (1907) were directly concerned with the ontogenetic aspect of behavior; there is also the large body of normative data collected by developmental psychologists through cross-sectional studies on behavioral development and more data collected largely by naturalists on development of behavior of animals in their natural habitat. In spite of the existence of this material, laboratory investigators almost completely resisted the temptation to

This paper was prepared while the author was a Fellow of the Foundations' Fund for Research in Psychiatry. Most of the author's research was supported by Research Grant PHS M-1630 from the National Institute of Mental Health.

bring this problem into the laboratory. Additional impetus should have been given by the tremendous emphasis placed on infantile experiences by the doctrine of psychoanalysis, but with the exception of a few studies related to the restriction of food supply in young animals (Levy, 1934, 1938), the verification of Freudian theory was left mainly to the poorly controlled clinical observations of children and retrospective analysis. Perhaps this should serve as a commentary and *raison d'être* for the present book, for in spite of the tremendous impact Freudian theory had on many aspects of psychological thought, the recent interest in this area can be traced primarily to the nonclinically accented theories of Hebb (1949) and the observations and theories of the European ethologists (Lorenz, 1952) who have studied the influence of early social stimulation upon the adult behavior of various species of birds.

Regardless of the theoretical impetus, the research over the past years has yielded information which permits us to state with confidence that *infantile experience profoundly affects later behavior.* The difficulties and complexities arise, however, when we look critically at each of the words in this apparently straightforward statement. Certainly one would assume that there would be agreement on the concept of infancy, and yet in the literature we find the term infantile used for the neonatal, postnatal and preadolescent organism. For the purpose of this paper infancy will be defined as that period immediately following birth during which the organism exhibits complete dependence upon the maternal object for survival and fulfillment of its biological needs. Even this definition is not without its problems for in some organisms—for example, most fowl and some mammals—the period of maternal dependency is extremely brief. The guinea pig is able to sustain itself almost completely shortly following birth, in marked contrast to the human's extremely long period of maternal dependence. However, many animals with long periods of maternal dependency have highly developed sensory and motor capacities at birth. Ungulates, for example, are capable of walking at birth; olfaction and vision are much more highly developed than in most rodents, primates, and humans. Although we shall return to this problem later, in considering the general problem of critical periods, it should be pointed out here that the extent and manner in which environmental factors affect the subsequent behavior of the organism must be dependent largely on the organismic factors—in other words, on the constitutional genetic organization of the infant interacting with the environment. Thus we may expect and indeed will show that similar environmental conditions differentially affect species, strains within species, and sex within strain. Although this may appear to limit the generality of the effects of infantile experience on later behavior, we

believe that such limitations are dependent not on genetic considerations but on the nature of the environmental stimuli which the organism experiences in the laboratory or in its natural surroundings.

At this point let us consider the problem of what constitutes experience (the second term in our previously simple statement). The
kinds of environmental manipulations presented in the literature are
almost as varied as the number of available experiments. King (1958)
classified three categories: (1) stress, which includes a variety of
"traumatic stimuli," (2) environmental, which generally includes
manipulation of the living conditions of the organism either by a
change in the conditions themselves or by altering the organism's ability to perceive the environment, and (3) social, which involves experiences concerning animal–animal interactions. Although these
categories seem relatively descriptive, they represent an interpretation of the environmental factors with respect to the phenomenological
experiences of the infant organism. Unfortunately there is little in
the way of objective criteria to indicate what is and what is not stressful to the infantile organism. Indeed, there is much controversy over
the interpretation of certain manipulations, such as handling (Bovard,
1958). Thus, whereas King includes handling and restriction under
the classification of environmental experiences, they may well be
classified as stress, as may competition and aggression which King
includes as social experiences. We propose a different order of classification based upon the actual manipulations imposed upon the organism—namely, physical or mechanical and nonmechanical or environmental. If the technique employed in the laboratory consists of im-
posing upon the animal stimulation from an external source, such
stimulation would be classified as physical—for example, electric
shock, loud sound, extreme temperature variations, mechanical rotation, handling, etc. Such experiences are usually brief, occurring at
regular intervals, and in general fairly intense. In contrast if the environment is experimentally structured so that the nature of the
environment involves changes in general living conditions including
housing, feeding, and contact with other animals in the environment,
these may be considered as environmental and would include such
experiences as restriction or free environment, alterations in feeding
and drinking, in group living and competition, etc. The environmental
experiences are usually constant and long acting and vary markedly
in their degree of sensitivity. This system of classification is an
attempt to avoid interpretation of an animal's response to environmental occurrences—in other words, the classification should describe only the events themselves, in an operational sense. Unfortunately, almost any classification scheme is going to include interpretive

elements, because many aspects of many categories overlap with the other.

Some means of classifying behavior are needed, however, to create some order in the discussion to follow. Although many dimensions of behavior have been investigated, we shall in general limit the discussion to the general classes of social behavior, behavior related to emotionality including learning, and the patterns of behavior in response to novel and noxious stimuli in adulthood. These limitations are abitrary and made solely for the sake of convenience, although there is also the implicit value judgment that these forms of behavior are more relevant to the general purpose of this book. It should be noted however that it is within these general classes of behavior that the most profound effects of infantile stimulation have been observed.

In 1954, after reviewing the literature related to the "Effects of Early Experience on Later Behavior of Animals," Beach and Jaynes stated:

> Reviewing the studies in the foregoing pages has left the authors with two basic convictions. The first is that a fuller understanding of the effects of early experience upon subsequent behavior is fundamentally important for a science of psychology and the broader field of animal biology. A second and equally strong impression is that much if not most of the presently available evidence bearing upon this problem is equivocal and of undetermined reliability.

In the ensuing years although there has been considerable work in this area one is still unable to contradict the latter conclusion of the writers. In so important an area one would expect to find rigid requirements placed upon design and conclusions, and yet we find gross errors in design persisting throughout the years, as though a result of mass fixation.

To illustrate: Hall and Whiteman (1951) subjected infant mice to intense sound stimulation. Then, using mice which had been placed in the same situation but not subjected to sound stimulation, they compared these mice with the stimulated organisms for frequency of eliminative responses when the mice were later placed in the same environmental setting where the intense stimulation had occurred. Since the mice subjected to sound defecated more, it was concluded that infantile "trauma" resulted in an increase in "emotional instability." Griffiths and Stringer (1952) exposed infant rats to a variety of stimuli which they assumed to be traumatic. Comparing the various traumatized groups with a control group, which although presumably not traumatized did receive some form of treatment which was not clearly specified, and finding no differences in these groups in adulthood, these authors concluded that infantile (pre-weaning) trauma had *no* effect upon later behavior. A subsequent study (Levine, Chevalier, and Korchin, 1956) demonstrated that if an infant rat is subjected to intense stimulation during infancy (electric shock), this animal does not differ consistently from control animals which, although not subjected to the same intense *stimulation* (as defined by the experimenter), were subjected to the same *procedures;* that is, removal from the nest, placement in the shock apparatus without shock, and return to the nest. If, however, the shocked and manipulated groups are compared with a *"strictly"* nontreated group the differences are dramatic. The nontreated group when confronted as adults with novel and noxious stimuli show the most severe disturbances of behavior in terms of the criteria usually defined as emotional. Thus when we examine the studies of Hall and Whiteman, Griffiths and Stringer, Stanley and Monkman (1956), Scott (1955), to mention only a few, it can be found in all of these experiments that the control (?) group was treated in some manner. (Parenthetically, "nontreated" animals would be those subjected to none of the handling procedures in the laboratory.)

Since there is now sufficient evidence that even the "mildest" and most innocuous treatment can have significant effects on later behavior, when compared with no treatment, all that can be said of any study which attempts to learn the effects of infantile experience without a nontreated control group is that at best such experiments have investigated the effects of different treatments in infancy upon subsequent behavior. Yet, as late as 1960 one still finds experiments being reported which draw broad conclusions concerning the effects of infantile experiences when the experimenters have not used a nontreated control group (Lindzey, Lykken, and Winston, 1960).

It is apparent that when restrictions are placed upon (1) the type of adult behavior to be discussed, and (2) the design of the experiment which is considered essential, the available information becomes significantly less. We shall impose yet another restriction—namely, age. If the major concern of this paper is with the effects of infantile experience, then the experiments considered should be with reference to the infant organism within the limits of our previous definition.

CRITICAL PERIODS

Any consideration of the effects of early experience on later behavior must be concerned with the temporal aspects of the onset of such stimulation. Underlying this concern with age is the general concept of critical periods, which assumes specific periods in ontogeny during which the organism is particularly sensitive to certain types of stimulation which shape and mold its subsequent behavior. The concept of critical periods as applied to behavior was certainly explicitly stated by Freud (1940) in his concept of discrete stages in psychosexual development and the effects of fixation at one or another level. Lorenz concluded as early as 1935 that "there are specific and restricted periods during which the stimuli which will evoke certain instinctive responses are permanently determined. After the critical period has passed, the environment cannot alter the nature of the effective stimulus."

The concept of critical periods has received a lot of attention recently, with some interesting consequences. One of the early attempts to explore the critical period hypothesis was by Scott and co-workers at the Jackson Memorial Laboratory. Scott (1945) first noted that lambs removed from the mother during the first ten days of life and reared in association with humans were subsequently unable to make adequate social adjustments to the flock. Such inabilities to become associated with the flock lasted several years. The problem of critical periods with regard to socialization was extensively investigated in dogs by the Bar Harbor group. Scott, Fredericson, and Fuller (1951) divided the developmental sequences of the puppy into distinct periods, starting with the neonatal period, lasting about ten days, during which the principal activities of the puppy are nursing, defecation, and urination. During this period, since the animals are essentially blind and deaf, it was assumed that they were isolated from the environment. The second period, the transition period which begins at about the age of ten days and terminates at three weeks, is characterized by the development of perceptual motor capacities which now make the puppy vulnerable to environmental changes. Period three, the period of socialization, lasting to ten weeks, is described as the critical period during which socialization takes place. Then there ensues a juvenile period, which lasts from weaning at ten weeks to sexual maturity.

Similar sequences of development have been worked out for the mouse (Williams and Scott, 1953). The experimental evidence for the critical period hypothesis with reference to socialization is fairly clear, and generally indicates that if there is some disturbance in the social environment, i.e., removal from the litter, isolation, etc., during this period critical for socialization, there then appears a marked destruction of the social capacity of the organism (Scott, 1958; Freedman, Elliot and King, 1958). It is important to note that so far as critical periods and socialization are concerned, no experience occurring during the neonatal period of dog development appeared to have any permanent effect on subsequent behavior. That this is in contrast to the earlier study on lambs is understandable; Scott and Marston (1950) point out the lamb is born with the ability to walk, its eyes and ears

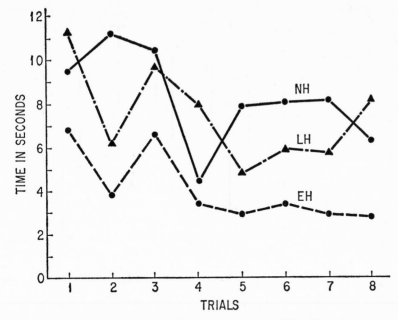

Figure 1. Mean latency for eight criterion trials. *EH* refers to preweaning handling, *LH* to postweaning handling, *NH*, nonhandled. [From Levine, 1956, courtesy of *Journal of Personality*.]

are functional at birth, and within ten days it is eating solid food. Thus the lamb at birth is already in what has been described as the transitional period of development and isolation may be expected to have a profound and prolonged effect. However, when one examines the critical period hypothesis in the rat and mouse—which have a developmental pattern like the dog, but collapsed in time—it can be found that experiences occurring at the neonatal stage do indeed have their effects.

The early attempts at determining critical periods in the more common laboratory animals were gross and merely tended to indicate that stimulation of animals prior to weaning had a significantly greater effect than postweaning stimulation. Thus Levine (1956) (see Figure 1) and Levine and Otis (1958) found that animals receiving stimulation during infancy developed better avoidance learning, and showed less defecation and freezing than did animals receiving postweaning stimulation or no stimulation. Further, rats stimulated in infancy were significantly heavier and survived a severe stress longer than the other groups did. Stimulation in these experiments was started at birth and continued until weaning, thus including all the stages of development described by Scott, *et al.*

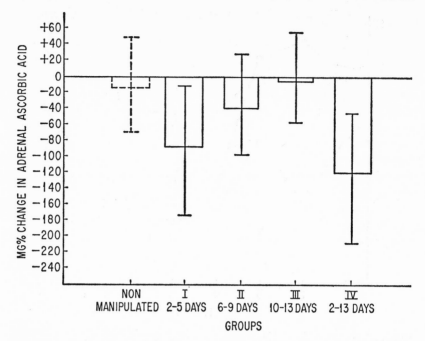

Figure 2. Comparison of depletion in AAA in the various groups of infant albino rats of the study. The bar represents the mean depletion; the lines, the range. The dotted bar and dotted line represent untreated animals that had previously been tested. [From Levine and Lewis, 1959, courtesy of *Science*.]

Schaefer in 1957 set out to investigate systematically a number of variables related to the effects of infantile stimulation on later behavior in an open field situation. In this experiment, groups of animals were stimulated for 1–7 days, 8–14 days, 15–21 days, and 1–21 days. The following measures were used: (1) length of time it took the animal to reach a wall after being placed in the center of the open field; (2) number of guide lines crossed before and after a loud sound stimulus; (3) defecation and urination; (4) crouching time before and after a loud click. The general finding was that the infants stimulated from day 1–7 and day 1–21 were significantly less emotional as defined in terms of the above measures, than were the other groups. Since the animals stimulated throughout the three-week nursing period behaved similarly to rats that were manipulated during the first seven days of life, it was reasonable to assign the reduced emotionality produced by stimulation throughout the entire nursing period to the stimulation that occurred during the first week only. These results were indeed surprising, for if, as Scott, *et al*, proposed, the neonatal period represents the period during which the organism is insulated from environmental stimulation, then it would be expected that stimulation during the neonatal period should be without effect. There are now significant data (Levine and Lewis, 1959; Denenberg and Bell, 1960) from other sources—based on measures which include avoidance learning in mouse and rat and maturation of the hypothalamo-adrenal system in the rat—to indicate that, for these animals, there is a critical period which is even more restricted than the first week and is somewhere within the first five days of life (see Figure 2).

How then do we reconcile the data obtained for the dog with the data obtained on rat and mouse with reference to critical periods? The obvious answer, but the least satisfactory, is that there are different critical periods for different species. This is undoubtedly true, but the statement is based not merely on the fact that species differ but also on the fact that they differ in their developmental stage at birth; it is thus reasonable to assume that critical periods are critical only when defined in terms of the developmental status of the organism at the time of stimulation. In the case of the species under discussion this is not so; although the temporal aspects of the sequence of development are different, the same phases are present following birth. The crucial difference seems to lie in the type of behavior being investigated. Thus, Scott, *et al.*, were concerned with social behavior and the early developmental factors related to such behavior, whereas the investigations which demonstrated extremely early critical periods were concerned with parameters of behavior which appear more closely related to the emotional status of the organism. This would indicate therefore the existence of, not *one* critical period, but of several critical periods during which environmental stimuli have the most profound effects; it indicates further that the behavior which is modified by these environmental stimuli will differ according to the development stage of the organism at the onset of stimulation and the type of environmental stimuli which are imposed upon this developing organism. A similar point of view has been advanced by Denenberg and Karas (1959).

Infantile stimulation and adult behavior

If, as late as five years ago, one examined the literature concerning the effects of infantile experience with noxious stimuli on later emotional stability, the conclusions reached would have been similar to those of Cruikshank (1954) when she wrote: "The studies discussed here have confirmed the fact that infantile experience *may* affect later behavior. However this effect is not necessarily inevitable and it is quite possible that the animal will react after initial readjustment in a manner similar to that of the nonstimulated animal."

Thus some investigators reported the infant organism subjected to stimulation assumed to be noxious exhibited more emotional instability than unstimulated organisms, whereas other authors claimed that stimulation of an intense quality had no demonstrable effect on subsequent emotionality and in turn on behavior that might be affected by the emotional status of the organism. Although it was difficult to compare many of these experiments, because they differed in so many parameters, there was no evidence which reasonably would lead to the conclusion that noxious stimulation in infancy resulted in reduced emotionality.

However, at about this time annoying experimental noises were being heard indicating all was not well in this area. In a preliminary experiment by Otis and Hunt at the University of Chicago, infant rats which were handled twice daily from age 7 through 21 days were found as adults to be much less "timid" about emerging from their living cages onto a runway placed in front of the open cage door when hungry than were animals that received no such handling. Emergence from the cage has been shown to be associated in general with emotionality; thus, this study indicated that some form of stimulation during *infancy* could result in reduced emotionality. This experiment presented no real problem for the camp followers of the *trauma → emotional instability* camp, since what experimenter would dare to assume that simple handling of the infant animal is in any way noxious?

However, these same investigators (Hunt and Otis, 1955) repeated the original experiment and added other groups in a more extensive study. One group of handled rat pups was removed from the mother and maintained on a daily 10–12-hour deprivation schedule from the fifth day following birth until weaning at 24 days. Another group received two electric shocks in addition to deprivation. A third group was presented with two electric shocks daily; the remaining group received only daily handling. When tested as adults on the emergence from the cage test, there was no significant difference between any of the experimentally treated groups. All groups did differ significantly, however, from the control nontreated animals on this test of emotionality. One would have expected the infants receiving what might be thought of as "traumatic" infantile experience to be more emotional in view of the results available at the time, or at least that there be no differences between the groups. The finding of reduced emotionality as a function of noxious stimulation in infancy was indeed surprising. The *crucial* difference between these experiments and others is that these authors did not assume that what appeared to be nontraumatic stimulation—handling—was without effect and therefore included an additional control group, the nontreated animals.

At about the same time, at the Institute for Psychosomatic Research

at Michael Reese Hospital, the author set out to investigate the effects
of noxious infantile experiences on later behavior, in this case, conditioned avoidance learning. Working on the same misapprehension
that beset prior investigators, it was expected that infant rats given
daily experiences of a painful electric shock which was sufficient to
cause evasive random movements and squeaking in the infant would
result in greater emotional instability, which would in turn affect conditioned avoidance learning in adulthood. Thus the usual two groups
were employed, a shocked group and a nonshocked but otherwise
identically treated group. In addition, like Hunt and Otis, a completely
nontreated group was included in the design. When the shocked group
was compared with the nonshocked group, only slight and marginally
significant differences emerged, with the nonshocked group exhibiting
slightly better avoidance learning. However, the nontreated group
differed markedly both qualitatively and quantitatively on the avoidance learning situation. These animals were significantly poorer than
their treated counterparts on avoidance learning, and the poorer learning appeared to be a function of the extreme emotionality exhibited
by these animals when confronted with noxious stimuli as adults. Thus,
instead of running and jumping in response to shock, the nontreated
subjects exhibited a marked tendency to freeze and defecate, a response which is indeed incompatible with efficient avoidance learning (Levine, Chevalier, and Korchin, 1956) (see Figure 3).

Subsequent experiments (Levine, 1958, 1959) using shock have led
to the conclusion that stimulation in infancy results in the capacity for
the organism to respond more effectively when confronted with novel
situations or, in other words, to exhibit a diminished emotional response
to such novel stimuli whether the stimulus change be either exteroceptive or interoceptive. Using the same design involving a shocked, nonshocked, and nontreated group, it was found that at 60 days of age the
nontreated rats consumed considerably less water in a minute-period
following 18 hours of deprivation than did either of the two experimentally treated groups. This difference was greatest after the first
three days, and by the fourth day the groups were equal and remained
so for a period up to 14 days. Following this period of stable drinking
each of the groups was divided into two. Prior to the drinking tests
all the animals were placed in a grid box. One subgroup in each of the
major groups was then given shock and the other subgroup merely
remained there for an equivalent time. The results of the drinking
test following the grid box experience revealed the following information: (1) Although there was a significant decrement in drinking in
all groups, by far the greatest and most persistent decrement occurred
again in the nontreated group; (2) The decrement in drinking for the
infantile treated groups was the same regardless of whether or not

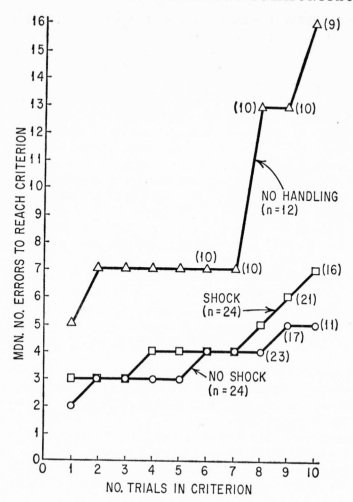

Figure 3. Errors for successive fixed criteria of learning. (Parenthesized figures denote the number of subjects included). [From Levine, Chevalier, and Korchin, 1956, by courtesy of *Journal of Personality*.]

they were shocked in the grid box, and this decrement was transitory, whereas in the nontreated subjects the decrement in drinking following adult shock was significantly greater than in the nonshocked counterparts and persisted throughout the experiment. Other measures such as defecation and freezing indicated that the nontreated animals were indeed more "emotional," since they defecated significantly more and exhibited much more freezing behavior.

It should be pointed out that in these experiments the phenomenon of stimulation reducing emotionality appears to be independent of the mode of stimulation employed. These experiments also indicated that the effects of infantile stimulation could be demonstrated in the absence of any additional handling in adulthood. However, common to these methods is that animals are handled in some fashion in infancy for varying periods of time, and in the usual stimulation procedures also involve some manipulation of the mother.

The question of whether it is the stimulation per se or whether the effect is due to some maternal disturbance was investigated recently by Schaefer (1957) and Levine (1959). Schaefer removed the mother from the pups for varying periods of time up to six hours and found that the procedure had no demonstrable effects upon subsequent emotionality. Similarly Levine compared nontreated animals where the mother was removed daily for five minutes with other nontreated animals where the mother was not disturbed, and again found no difference. It can be concluded that the effects of stimulation are not directly due to maternal interference, but most likely represent a direct action upon the infant. As to the question of handling, it has been found that stimulation which involved no contact with the experimenter, that is, shaking the living cage, had effects which could not be distinguished from other modes of stimulation which did involve handling; this finding eliminated experimenter contact (handling) as a critical variable.

Other studies which shall be discussed later when the subject of genetics and ontogenetics is considered have in general substantiated the finding that experience with noxious stimulation tends to reduce subsequent emotionality.

Aside from the statement of the functional relationship between infantile noxious stimulation and alterations in emotionality that has just been made, what more can be concluded from these data? It would be foolhardy to conclude that Freud's notions concerning infantile trauma and later behavior have been hereby disproven, since one has no way of knowing what constitutes trauma for the infant rodent and in fact what constitutes trauma for the infant human. An example of this dilemma can be found when the data related to infantile trauma and maternal deprivation are examined. Spitz (1945), Ribble (1941), and Bowlby (1951) have described a pattern of events which has been assumed to be associated with the "trauma" of maternal deprivation, among these being a retarded rate of development, greater susceptibility to disease and less adaptability in adulthood. Yet similar patterns are found in rats which have all the maternal care but have been deprived of extra stimulation. Is it not possible that the observations made on children deprived of mother and placed in foundling homes could have been the result of deprivation of stimulation, which after all is in most humans provided principally by the maternal figure? Are we then to assume that reduction in what appears to be a vital factor in development and on later behavior—namely, stimulation—is traumatic? It seems apparent that unless an objective criterion of trauma is available the term has indeed little meaning.

A further example of the chaos can be found in the "simple" interpretation of the data obtained in the rat. The effects of painful stimulation, or for that matter any stimulation provided by the experimenter, have been interpreted (Levine, 1956) as being stressful and in turn such experiences with stress in infancy "condition" the organism's ability to adapt to later stressful experiences (reduced emotionality). Hunt (unpublished manuscript), however, interprets these very same data as indicating that painful stimulation is not traumatic and states, "The finding of the effects of shock calls seriously into question the notion that early infancy is a period when mammals are most easily traumatized by strong and painful stimulation." Whether the animals are stressed, traumatized, or not traumatized, or whether the trauma lies not in the painful stimulation but in the lack of stimulation is the sort of question that leads to a large number of publications which hotly debate the various merits of opposing points of view but lead us no closer to the solution of the main question: What are the mechanisms whereby stimulation or, more broadly, experiences are translated by the organism into the long-range behavioral and physiological changes which have been reported? The notions of stressful or traumatic stimuli all convey the idea that one has some way of knowing the meaning of the stimulus to the stimulated organisms. Not only does such information not exist but there has been no attempt to investigate the problem. If it is not possible to specify what is trauma or what stimuli are traumatic, there remain two courses to follow: one can continue arbitrarily to define trauma in terms either of the stimuli or of the behavioral effects, and then proceed to consider any stimuli which fail to produce the expected results on any a priori basis as not being traumatic; or conversely to reject the concept of trauma as being of little value, full of surplus meaning, and highly subjective. Even in its extreme the latter course seems much more desirable.

Rejection without an alternative is hardly a constructive approach. However, in this area of research the alternatives are all too numerous. To mention only a few: first, to describe fully the parameters of stimulation in terms of their physical characteristics; second, to determine whether there exists a threshold for stimulation; third, to determine the range of behavior which is affected by stimulation, etc. Only when many of these parameters are worked out will we have the proper experimental armament to attack the problem of mechanism.

In spite of their superficial simplicity, the type of stimulation used in all the studies described has been complex and massive. Shock, shaking, handling, etc., all involve thermal changes, proprioceptive and kinesthetic stimulation, and tactile stimuli. Since the organism's visual and auditory capacities are almost nonexistent during the critical periods when the type of stimulation used appears to have its most profound effects, it seems reasonable to rule out these sensory routes as critical, particularly in view of recent experiments (Levine, unpublished) which produced no differences between nontreated animals reared in constant bright light and control nontreated subjects. The thermal changes which occur during the usual stimulation procedures also do not appear to be important, since animals stimulated in their home cages where thermal conditions are assumed to be constant still show the same behavioral and physiological changes as do otherwise stimulated organisms.

What emerges is that the effects on stimulation appear to depend upon the earliest tactile and kinesthetic stimulation. The importance of tactile stimulation for yet another aspect of infantile experience and later behavior has been demonstrated in a most convincing manner by the recent research of Harlow (1958) and associates.

There is however another dimension of stimulation which may be more critical. When one examines the usual laboratory environment of the organisms which have been studied, the striking quality of these environments is that they are barren. Depending of course upon the elegance and financial status of any particular laboratory, temperature, light, sound, and housing are kept rigidly controlled, with as little variation as possible. This environment, in marked contrast with the natural environment, has been stripped of most of the environmental changes which are so common in the natural habitat. When the organism is experimentally stimulated the introduction of these procedures represents sudden and usually drastic change in the environment. It cannot by any means be concluded that the nontreated animals are without stimulation, for their environment includes the mother, siblings, and usually laboratory routines. What may be lacking is this dynamic quality of stimulation. A similar analogy can be found in the work of Rheingold (1956). She concluded that children in institutions receive more stimulation than noninstitutionalized children. If, as we have previously suggested, the effect of such institutionalization arises from lack of stimulation, then Rhiengold's observations would tend to contradict this proposition. If however the important dimension is not merely the quantitative aspects of stimulation but in addition the qualitative dynamic properties of the environment, then it is possible to reconcile the fact that more stimulation may exist in an environment but still possess a static quality. When stimuli are reduced it generally follows that the dynamic aspect of stimulation is also reduced, but even this is not an irrefutable relationship, for it is possible that the more barren the environment the more dynamic a small amount of stimulation may be.

Conversely, if a large but constant amount of stimulation is present in an environment, the amount of change necessary to make a stimulus dynamic would be larger. This notion, like many others, has not yet been subjected to experimental scrutiny. However, it has always been a source of amazement that a procedure which usually takes no more than three minutes per day or less and which represents a total of .2 per cent of the total day in the life of the rat can have such a potent effect. Since what seems to be such a minimal change in the environment does indeed result in such a marked change in the organism, the question of the critical property or properties of the environment deserves much more study. Implicit in this discussion is the problem of thresholds, which will be discussed in more detail in the next section of the chapter.

With but a few exceptions investigations of the effects of infantile experience on adult behavior have tended to examine that behavior of the animal which has been assumed to be the most affected by the type of environmental manipulation employed. Thus, when the environment is manipulated so as to affect the social structure of the environment, the dependent variable has usually been social behavior; in contrast, if the organism is subjected to physical stimulation which has been assumed to affect some affective state of the organism, the later behavioral observations are usually made in situations which are designed to best illustrate these affective differences. Even when the exceptions exist, the investigation of the data is related to the affective processes. Levine (1959b) tested C57/B110 mice for aggressive behavior in adulthood following infantile stimulation produced by handling. In this experiment the mice stimulated in infancy proved to be significantly more aggressive in terms of the number of pairs fighting and the latency to fight. However these aggressive differences seemed related to the fact that the nontreated mice behaved in their "typical" fashion; when confronted with another mouse, the fighting arena, and the noise involved in testing, these mice tended to freeze. Insofar as freezing cuts down on the contact with the other mouse, it in turn reduces aggressive behavior; obviously, therefore, the interpretation of the differences in social behavior was based upon the differences in the emotional status of the animal (see Figure 4).

Since the emotional status of the animal can affect many aspects of behavior, the question arises as to whether the differences observed in behavior as a function of infantile stimulation are a result of a unidirectional action of such stimulation upon the alterations in emotionality, which in turn affects other behavior patterns, or whether the effects of different kinds of stimulation at different critical periods have multiple

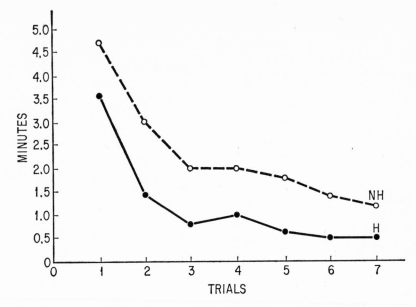

Figure 4. Mean fighting response latency. [From Levine, 1959b, courtesy of *Journal of Genetic Psychology*.]

and differential effects, as was suggested previously when the problem of critical periods was discussed. The relevant information here is equivocal. An examination of the experiments reveals that when the effects of stimulation on infancy are tested in situations which involve noxious stimuli, the differences are striking and fairly permanent. When, however, the adult testing situation does not have as apparent an aversive quality, differences still appear but are transitory. (Levine, Staats, and Frommer, 1958). These initial differences appear to depend upon the novelty of the testing situation, and once the nontreated animal has adapted to the situation the behavior observed cannot be differentiated from the stimulated animal.

Since it would be expected that emotionality would be more directly involved with performance under aversive conditions, the proposition that the effects of infantile stimulation affect principally the emotionality of the organism seems reasonable. Nevertheless, a series of recent studies (Levine, unpublished) does not fit in with this conception. If the differences obtained are solely a function of emotional differences, it should be possible to make certain predictions concerning responses to noxious stimulation. Thus, in an avoidance learning situation, it would be expected that the more emotional organisms (nontreated) should respond to a lower level of shock, and, assuming a curvilinear relationship between emotionality and intensity of the noxious stimu-

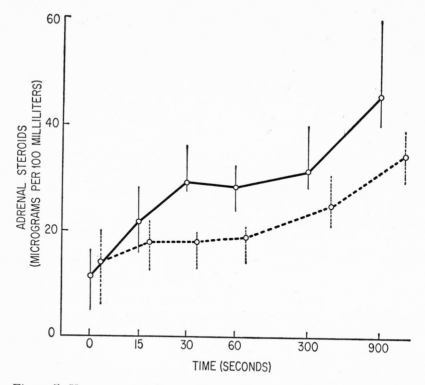

Figure 5. Upper curve indicates the steroid output of stimulated subjects following adult shock. Lower curve represents the values for nonstimulated subjects. [From Levine, 1960, courtesy of *Scientific American*.]

lation in adulthood (given at a higher level of shock), a decrement of performance should ensue. The converse should be true of less emotional animals. What is found however is in direct contradiction to expectations. At a lower level of shock the stimulated animals are significantly better avoidance learners, whereas at a higher level of shock this situation is reversed. Further, one should expect the physiological reaction to noxious stimulation to be reduced in the less emotional organism, and, although initial studies (Levine and Otis, 1958) using some chronic stress indicated this to be true, more recent evidence (Levine, 1960) again shows the stimulated organism to be significantly more responsive to acute stress (see Figure 5).

Either the simple proposition of a unidirectional action—infantile stimulation → emotionality—is in error, or our preconceived notions of how emotionality affects behavioral or physiological responses are in error. At the moment there is no clear available solution to this dilemma. However these data do suggest that the effects of infantile stimulation are significant beyond the changes in emotionality which have been observed. It appears that one of the major consequences of infantile stimulation may be to endow the organism with the capacity to make finer discriminations concerning the relevant aspects of the environment and to allow it to make responses more appropriate to the demands of the environment, including appropriate responses to stress.

To further complicate the issue, there exists evidence that alteration of the social milieu not only affects subsequent social behavior but also produces changes in emotionality similar to those seen with stimulation by physical means. Seitz (1954) raised a group of infant rats in small litters of six pups per cage, and another group of rats in large litters of twelve rats per cage. The results revealed that small litter rats showed more exploratory behavior and less "anxiety" than large litter rats. In addition large litter rats were more vicious and more resistant to handling in adulthood. De Mato (1960) however recently reported no differences in discrimination learning between large and small litter rats, and Levine and Broadhurst (1961) found no differences between small (< 4) and large (> 8) litters in open field behavior.

Further evidence comes from a study by Freedman, Elliott, and King (1958) who, although principally concerned with critical periods for socialization, report that dogs reared in the absence of any human contact and manipulation reacted the most to being placed in a harness and presented with various noxious stimuli. They conclude, in fact, that the absence of human contact beyond a critical point results in an irreversible pattern of fearfulness of humans and, it appears, of many other aspects of the environment. The evidence, although sparse, points to a relationship between social stimulation and subsequent emotionality. It should be pointed out again, and emphasized, that the division of various types of stimulation or lack of stimulation is an arbitrary one. The evidence points to the likelihood that there may be common elements in all forms of stimulation; if these are given at the proper time and have the appropriate characteristics and intensity, they produce similar results.

It is obvious that as yet there exists no complete answer to the question: What are the principal behavioral alterations which result from infantile stimulation? There still exists the possibility that the changes are principally affective. From our current knowledge of the effects of affective states on behavior there appear to be inconsistencies; nevertheless, such inconsistencies may simply reflect our lack of knowledge concerning the manner in which emotionality affects behavior. This is another major problem that will be avoided for obvious reasons.

GENETICS AND ONTOGENETICS

Throughout this chapter thus far we have included in our discussion studies which have used such subjects as mice, rats, dogs, and monkeys and humans. References and cross-references have been made without any of the usual platitudes and precautions known too well to all of us concerning the question: "What can one say from studies done on animals about man?" The cautions are no doubt necessary, but they also reflect man's own perception of his role in nature. As a matter of fact, the cautionary comments need to be extensively broadened to include the question: What can we say about the rat from studies done on humans, mice, dogs, crocodiles, kiwi birds, or what have you? The evolutionary process has produced species which are tailored to adapt to the environments in which they survive. Each species is unique in many aspects of its behavioral and physiological adaptive processes. Of course the above statement no doubt reinforces and brings joy to the hearts of those among us who believe (1) that because of these wide species differences comparative research is doomed from the onset and (2) that since human behavior is the principal concern of psychology, comparative investigations are even more pointless. As far as the clinician is concerned the behavior of the human is undoubtedly the primary point of reference, but from the point of view of the biologically oriented behavioral scientist these species differences present some of the most exciting problems. Each individual within a species is similar to but also unique to the species, depending upon its genetic constitution and variations in the environment. The same analogy holds for species differences: species are unique in the biological universe but also there exist similarities between species. If we are ever to be able to arrive at universal psychological principles, both the uniquenesses and similarities of species must eventually be known. It is the assumption of similarities that makes comparative research possible.

Within the specific area of the effects of infantile experiences of later behavior, there is ample evidence that the infantile environment affects a wide variety of mammalian and nonmammalian organisms. The puzzling fact is not that infantile experiences affect many species but that the effects of similar forms of stimulation depend very much on the organismic factors. Depending thus on many organismic factors, most of them as yet unknown, the same physical stimulation can have no effect or a profound effect in any given direction. This study of the genetics of behavior is by no means new, but interest in psychogenetics has also taken on new life in recent years. With the growth of psychogenetics it has become apparent that investigations into the genetic-environment problems are now possible in a much more con-

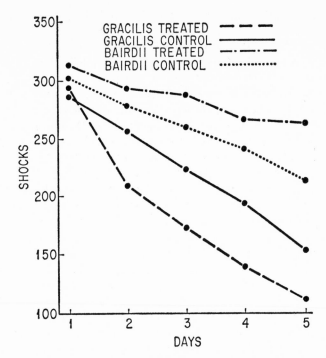

Figure 6. Number of shocks received by four groups of *Peromyscus* during five days in an operant-conditioning apparatus. [From King and Eleftheriou, 1959, courtesy of *Journal of Comparative and Physiological Psychology*.]

trolled and systematic fashion. Some striking results have been obtained when the effects of infantile stimulation are studied using organisms with different genetic backgrounds. As was discussed previously, the problem of whether certain infantile experiences reduced or increased emotionality has preoccupied many investigators in the field. The answer now seems to be that the same stimulation can result in either effect, depending upon the organism stimulated. King and Eleftheriou (1959) have presented a striking example of this. These investigators took two species of deermice (*Peromyscus*) and subjected them to mechanical stimulation as infants. When the performance of the adult mice of both subspecies was examined, it was found that the avoidance learning (Skinner Box) of the treated subspecies Gracilis was significantly better than the control nontreated animals, whereas the converse was true of the subspecies Bairdii (see Figure 6).

Ginsburg (1960) and his associates have been systematically investigating the effects of infantile stimulation on several inbred strains of mice. As adults these mice have been tested for activity and defecation on an elevated runway. Ginsburg has found all possible effects.

Some inbred strains show no effect of stimulation; others are more active on the runway as a function of stimulation; others are significantly less active. If the assumption is made that activity is related to emotionality, then all effects are possible with infantile stimulation. The mouse has been a favorite animal for many of these studies primarily because of the greater availability of pure genetic lines. Even in the absence of rigid genetic control, similar evidence is available in both the rat and the dog. Using the substrain of hooded rats and one strain of albino rat, it was found that although there were significant differences between the strains in their avoidance learning scores, the two hooded strains still showed significantly better learning as a function of infantile stimulation, whereas the albino strain showed the reverse (Levine, unpublished). Recently Denenberg and Karas (1960) showed that rats of the Wistar strain were significantly superior in avoidance learning from day 11 through 20 if they had been stimulated during the first 10 days, but that rats stimulated from days 1 through 20 were no different from the control nontreated animals. The failure to find differences between the birth-through-weaning stimulated group is in contrast to the reports of Levine and Schaefer and may be due in part to strain differences, since such strain differences have been reported between Sprague Dawley and Wistar rats.

Freedman (1958) reported that the same treatment which involved "indulgence"—defined as lack of punishment—and "discipline"—which consisted of punishment and training—had markedly different effects on later behavior in the dog. Shetland sheep dogs and Basenjis showed little or no effect of the early treatment, whereas the wire-haired fox terriers and beagles were indeed affected by the treatment (see Figure 7).

All these experiments show differences as a function of genetic constitution of animals within the same species. What of differences between species? There exists only the most meager evidence of such differences. The most likely reasons for this paucity of information is the fact that comparative analysis depends upon the availability of many species in a single setting. Such settings are rare; even when they do exist the tendency is to concentrate on one species rather than a cross-sectional analysis of many. Unfortunately, even the small amount of available evidence is not behavioral. Denenberg and Karas (1959) subjected mice and rats which had been manipulated in infancy to the severe stress of total food and water deprivation. Rats which had been stimulated showed a greater resistance to this stress and lived significantly longer than nontreated rats; in contrast, the treated mice succumbed significantly faster. Similarly, stimulated mice die sooner than nonstimulated mice following the injection of a transplantable leukemia; whereas stimulated rats of the Fisher strain

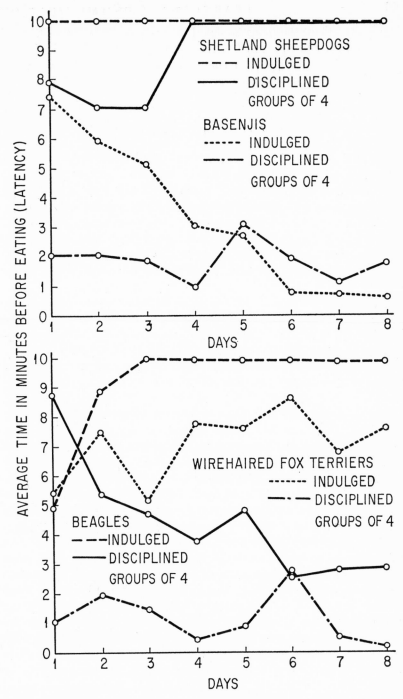

Figure 7. Performance of eight-week-old puppies on the "inhibition-to-eating" test. [From Freedman, 1958, courtesy of *Science*.]

live longer than the nonstimulated animals following injection of leukemia cells (Levine and Cohen, unpublished). Ideally, the break-through on this problem of species-environment interactions will come only when a truly comparative program is systematically evolved.

That the effects of stimulation are dependent on genetic factors is clear enough. But beyond this statement of a functional relationship, what do we really know? There are no indications of the mechanisms of such an interaction either genetically or ontogenetically. What are the critical genetic factors which will determine the action of any environmental event? Some suggestions have been made. Ginsburg has postulated a gene or genes related specifically to stress. If the process of stimulation is indeed aversive and constitutes a stress, then the direction of the effects of stimulation would be dependent on the genetic factors related to the response to stress. Implicit in this proposi-tion is the concept of thresholds of stimulation, for if the genetic con-stitution related to stress is different in different species, then both quantitative and qualitative aspects of the stimulation necessary to prove effective will depend upon the organism's response to such stimulation. This notion of differential thresholds of stimulation as a function of genetic differences has been examined by Scott and Charles (1954). The term effective is used only in the sense that a particular set of environmental stimuli produce an organism which differs from the appropriate control animals.

What has been done thus far in all the studies related to genetics and infantile experience is to take a fixed set of stimulus parameters and vary the genetics. If the concept of thresholds has any validity, it might be expected that different parameters of stimulation—intensity, dura-tion, etc.—might still produce the same effect on animals with varied genetic structures. We need then not only to vary the genetics but at the same time to vary the environmental factors within and between strains and species. But perhaps before this sort of investigation can produce meaningful results it is necessary to return once again to the important question of parameters of stimulation.

Any discussion of genetics-environment must imply to some readers a rehash of the nature-nurture question. We should like to state more emphatically than usual that the nature-nurture question as such has no meaning. The organism from the moment of conception exists in an environment which is constantly impinging on it and interacting with constitutional factors. One of the clearest statements of this position was made by Ginsburg (1958): "In the normal course of events the environment provides substance, energy and milieu for the unfolding of the organism's potentialities: in the extreme, environmental in-fluences can determine whether the process of development will con-tinue and produce an organism."

DEVELOPMENT AND INFANTILE
STIMULATION

Throughout this paper we have been concerned, particularly with reference to critical periods, with problems of development, and we have pointed out that the effects of stimulation are intimately concerned with the developmental stage of the organism. Thus, when discussing the differences between the effects of isolation in lambs and in puppies, the problems of infancy, and the stages of development have appeared to be a major variable. It should be pointed out that, when comparing mice and rats, developmental difference may be critical since the mouse develops much more rapidly than the rat. Such differences in development may account for the results of King and Eleftheriou. The subspecies Gracilis which shows the effects of stimulation which have been reported in the rat exhibit a developmental process in time similar to the rat, whereas the Bairdii develop at a much more rapid rate. How these developmental rates are related to the effects of stimulation is yet another of the many unanswered questions.

In addition it has been found that the rate of development is itself dependent upon the infantile environment. It has been observed consistently that stimulated organisms are heavier at weaning and maintain these weight differences through adulthood. The time of the opening of the eyes in the rat is approximately 15–16 days. Stimulated rats open their eyes at about 13–14 days, and eye opening has been observed as early as 12 days (Levine, 1959). These developmental differences in gross morphological characteristics precipitated a series of investigations into the effects of stimulation on other physiological aspects of development. The first of these studies the maturation of the hypothalamo-hypophysial-adrenal system (Levine, Alpert, and Lewis, 1958, Figure 8). One response of the rat adrenal to stress is the depletion of the ascorbic acid present in the adrenal. A measure of adrenal function and in turn of pituitary release of adrenocorticotrophic hormone secretion following stress is ascorbic acid secretion. It has been shown previously that infant rats do not respond to environmental stress until about 16 days of age. This was true also of our nontreated animals. However, stimulated infants showed a significant adrenal response as early as 12 days of age. In another study Levine and Alpert (1959) showed that, measuring the maturation of the central nervous system in terms of the process of myelination, the stimulated infant was developing at a more accelerated rate—or, conversely, and perhaps interpreting these results more correctly, the nontreated infant was developing at a slower rate. What the

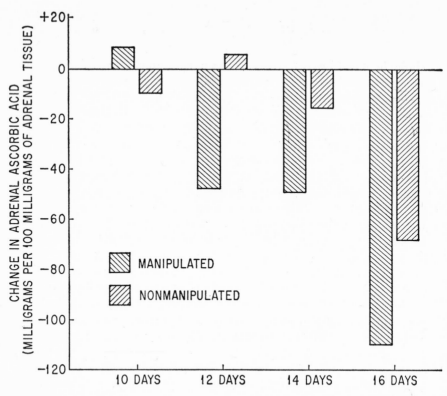

Figure 8. Adrenal ascorbic-acid depletion in manipulated and nonmanipulated infant rats. [From Levine, Alpert, and Lewis, 1958, courtesy of *Journal of Comparative and Physiological Psychology*.]

significance, if any, of rate of development is in relation to later behavior is not known.

The changes in development reported as a function of infantile stimulation appear to be general and not species specific (Meier and Stuart, 1959), although specific changes related to the structure and chemistry of the retinal nerves has been found by Riesen and co-workers (unpublished manuscript) following a period of deprivation of visual stimuli in the infant primate.

CONCLUSION AND COMMENTS

Infantile experience profoundly affects later behavior. We return then to our original opening statement, which has by now been excessively qualified and modified but remains unaltered in essence. The extent and direction of the behavioral changes that occur with infantile experience depend on many factors, some of which have been pointed out; many no doubt are as yet unknown. Although there are many more qualifications that should have been made, one more seems necessary. Throughout this chapter the concept of emotionality has been used freely and glibly, as though an agreed-upon specific criterion of emotionality exists. This is far from the truth. Some agreement of what constitutes emotionality exists in specific situations such as the open field test. The effects of emotionality on behavior other than activity, timidity, startle, defecation, and urination are still questions that are being actively investigated, and the solution to the problem of infantile stimulation and subsequent behavior will only come when both independent and dependent variables are adequately specified. If we avoid the use of the concept of emotionality then the statement related to the effects of the environment during infancy would be as follows: In some circumstances some kinds of stimulation to certain organisms facilitate performance, produce a decrement of performance, or produce no change.

Lest the reader be left with an entirely negative approach to these problems we should state, as an article of faith, that no understanding of the organism either as an infant or adult can ever be achieved without an awareness and understanding of ontogenetic and genetic factors—which after all *are* the organism. The importance of this problem to the problems of the clinical psychologic and personality theorists is so apparent as to make further elaboration redundant, although we might emphasize its obvious relevance to our ideas about child rearing.

We have avoided either presenting a new "theory" to account for the data or evaluating any of the existing theories. Theories are dependent on information, and, where the effects of infantile experiences are concerned, the information, although it seems extensive, is pitifully sparse. This area of research is unfortunately no different from many others.

That there are many methodological and logical difficulties is all too obvious, but as Beach and Jaynes conclude:

> It can be said that the longitudinal approach to the study of animal life is obviously more beset with methodological problems than studies concerned with any one portion of the life span. Experimental control in this area is more difficult to realize because the animals, by the very nature of the problem, are exposed to numerous variables, some of which may not yet be recognized or capable of isolation. These difficulties, however, are more than offset by the general interest and *wide significance* of the problems that may be studied.

Although throughout the chapter we have enumerated problem after problem and have displayed, much to our dismay, many signs of ignorance, the future of this area of research actually looks bright. The experimental beachhead has been established and the major difficulty confronting the field at this moment is really that of choosing the line of attack to follow; so many are apparent. The particular avenues along which the research is directed depend principally on the avenues along which the research is directed depend principally on the research worker's own interests. However, some problems present themselves as needing special attention. One of the major problems is the analysis of the parameters of stimulation. Before many other questions related to thresholds, critical periods, etc., can be tackled, the problem of the crucial factors, both quantitative and qualitative, of the stimulus events must be solved. This information will not only permit us to produce a reliable effect which can be used to then study other aspects of the problem but also give us a vital link in the solution of the problem of mechanism. Another major line of investigation is the detailed study of genetic and ontogenetic relationships. The comparative study of the effects of infantile stimulation superficially seems relatively straightforward. However, the mere comparison of strain within species as species comparison is no longer sufficient. A more imaginative and systematic analysis is needed to give the vital information concerning these major determinants of behavior. Yet another challenging question is that of "therapy." Thus far in all the studies discussed there has been little attempt to investigate factors which may be capable of reversing the effects produced by the absence of extra stimulation. How general are the effects? Are there aspects of behavior that are affected more permanently than others? And so forth.

It is apparent that one could go on ad infinitum, with problem after problem. In the final analysis, this may be the most promising aspect of the future, for perhaps we have finally arrived at the stage where one can begin to ask the appropriate questions. The progeny of research is research and many exciting problems have yet to emerge. There is little doubt and every hope that the closer we come to the experimental solutions to many of these problems, the closer we come to the understanding of the behavior of organisms, regardless of species.

REFERENCES

Beach, F. A., & Jaynes, J. Effects of early experience upon the behavior of animals. *Psychol. Bull.*, 1954, *51*, 239–263.

Bovard, E. W. The effects of early handling on viability of the albino rat. *Psychol. Rev.*, 1958, *65*, 257–271.

Bowlby, J. Maternal care and mental health. *World Health Organization Monogr.*, 1951, No. 2.

Cruikshank, Ruth. Animal infancy. In Carmichael (Ed.), *Manual of child psychology.* New York: Wiley, 1954, 186–209.

De Mato, M. R. Effects of litter size on brightness discrimination and reversal. *Psych. Rep.* 1960, 7, 91–97.

Denenberg, V. H., & Bell, R. W. Critical periods for the effects of infantile experience on adult learning. *Science,* 1960, *131,* 227–228.

Denenberg, V. H., & Karas, G. G. The effects of differential handling upon weight gain and mortality in the rat and mouse. *Science,* 1959, *130,* 629–630.

Denenberg, V. H., & Karas, G. G. Interactive effects of age and infantile experience on adult learning. *Psychol. Rep.,* 1960, 7, 313–322.

Freedman, D. G. Constitutional and environmental interactions in rearing of four breeds of dogs. *Science,* 1958, *127,* 585–586.

Freedman, D. G., Elliott, O., & King, J. A. Developmental capacities for socialization in puppies. Paper presented at the A.P.A. Meeting, 1958.

Freud, S. *An outline of psychoanalysis.* New York: Norton, 1949.

Ginsburg, B. E. Genetics as a tool in the study of behavior. *Perp. Biol. & Med.,* 1958, *1,* 397–423.

Ginsburg, B. E. Genetic control of the ontogeny of stress behavior. Paper presented at the A.P.A. meeting, 1960.

Griffiths, W. J., Jr., and Stringer, W. F. The effects of intense stimulation experienced during infancy on adult behavior in the rat. *J. comp. physiol. Psychol.,* 1952, *45,* 301–306.

Hall, C. S., & Whiteman, P. H. The effects of infantile stimulation upon later emotional stability in the mouse. *J. comp. physiol. Psychol.,* 1951, *44,* 61–66.

Harlow, H. H. The nature of love. *Amer. Psychologist,* 1958, *13,* 673–685.

Hebb, D. O. *The organization of behavior.* New York: Wiley, 1949.

Hunt, H. H., & Otis, L. S. Restricted experience and "timidity" in the rat. *Amer. Psychologist,* 1955, *10,* 432 (Abstr.).

Hunt, J. McV. Investigations of the effects of early experience in subhuman animals. Unpublished manuscript.

King, J. A. Parameters relevant to determining the effects of early experience upon the adult behavior of animals. *Psychol. Bull.,* 1958, *55,* 46–58.

King, J. A., & Eleftheriou, B. E. The effects of early handling upon adult behavior in two subspecies of deermice, Peromyscus maniculatus. *J. comp. physiol. Psychol.,* 1959, *52,* 82–85.

Levine, S. A further study of infantile handling and adult avoidance learning. *J. Pers.,* 1956, *25,* 70–80.

Levine, S. Infantile experience and resistance to physiological stress. *Science,* 1957, *126,* 405.

Levine, S. The effects of differential infantile stimulation on emotionality at weaning. *Canad. J. Psychol.,* 1959a, *13,* 243–247.

Levine, S. Emotionality and aggressive behavior in the mouse as a function of infantile experience. *J. genet. Psychol.,* 1959b, *94,* 77–83.

Levine, S. Infantile stimulation. *Scientif. Amer.,* 1960, *202,* 81–86.

Levine, S., & Alpert, M. Differential maturation of the central nervous system as a function of early experience. *Arch. gen. Psychiat.,* 1959, *1,* 403–405.

Levine, S., Alpert, A., & Lewis, G. W. Differential maturation of an adrenal response to cold stress in rats manipulated in infancy. *J. comp. physiol. Psychol.,* 1958, *51,* 774–777.

Levine, S., & Broadhurst, P. L. Genetic and ontogenetic influences on later emotionality in the rat. Paper presented at the Brit. Psychol. Assoc., 1961.

Levine, S., Chevalier, J. A., & Korchin, S. J. The effects of early shock and handling on later avoidance learning. *J. Pers.*, 1956, *24*, 475–493.

Levine, S., & Lewis, G. W. Critical periods of infantile experience on the maturation of a stress response. *Science*, 1959, *129*, 42–43.

Levine, S., & Otis, L. S. The effects of handling before and after weaning on the resistance of albino rats to later deprivation. *Canad. J. Psychol.*, 1958, *12*, 103–108.

Levine, S., Staats, S. R., & Frommer, G. Studies on "response by the rat to environmental change." *Psychol. Rep.*, 1958, *4*, 139–144.

Levy, D. M. Experiments on the sucking reflex and social behavior in dogs. *Amer. J. Orthopsychiat.*, 1934, *4*, 203–224.

Levy, D. M. On instinct satiation: an experiment on the pecking behavior of chickens. *J. gen. Psychol.*, 1938, *18*, 227–248.

Lindsey, G., Lykken, D. T., & Winston, H. D. Infantile trauma, genetic factors and adult temperament. *J. abnorm. soc. Psychol.*, 1960, *61*, 7–14.

Lorenz, K. Z. Der Kumpan in der Umvelt des Vogels. *J. Ornithol.*, 1935, *83*, 137–213.

Lorenz, K. Z. *King Solomon's ring.* New York: Crowell, 1952.

Meir, G. W., & Stuart, A. L. Effects of handling on physical and behavioral development of Siamese kittens. *Psychol. Rep.*, 1959, *5*, 497–501.

Rheingold, H. L. The modification of social responsiveness in institutional babies. *Monogr. Soc. Res. Child Developm.*, 1956, *21*, No. 63 (No. 2).

Ribble, Margaret A. Infantile experience in relation to personality development. In J. McV. Hunt (Ed.) *Personality and the behavior disorders, Vol. II.* New York: Ronald, 1954.

Riesen, A. H. Effects of stimulus deprivation on the development and atrophy of the visual sensory system. Unpublished manuscript.

Schaefer, T. The effects of early handling: infant handling and later behavior in the white rat. Unpublished Ph.D. dissertation, Univ. of Chicago, 1957.

Scott, J. H. Some effects of maturity of gentling, ignoring, or shocking rats during infancy. *J. abnorm. soc. Psychol.*, 1955, *51*, 412–414.

Scott, J. P. Social behavior, organization, and leadership in a small flock of domestic sheep. *Comp. Psychol. Monogr.*, 1945, *18*, 1.

Scott, J. P. Critical periods in the development of social behavior in puppies. *Psychosom. Med.*, 1958, *20*, 42–54.

Scott, J, P., & Charles, Margaret S. Genetic differences in the behavior of dogs: a case of magnification by thresholds and by habit formation. *J. genet. Psychol.*, 1954, *84*, 175–188.

Scott, J. P., Fredericson, E., & Fuller, J. L. Experimental exploration of the critical period hypothesis. *Personality*, 1951, *1*, 162–183.

Scott, J. P., & Marston, M. V. Critical periods affecting the development of normal and maladjustive social behavior in puppies. *J. genet. Psychol.*, 1950, *77*, 25–60.

Seitz, P. F. D. The effects of infantile experiences upon adult behavior in animal subjects: I. The effects of litter size during infancy upon adult behavior in the rat. *Amer. J. Psychiat.*, 1954, *110*, 916–927.

Small, W. S. Notes on the psychic development of the young white rat. *Amer. J. Psychol.*, 1899, *11*, 80–100.

Spitz, R. A. Hospitalism, An enquiry into the genesis of psychiatric conditions in early childhood. In *Psychoanalytic study of the child,* Vol. I. New York: Internat. Univs. Press, 1945, 53–74.

Stanley, W. C., & Monkman, J. A. A test for specific and general behavioral effects of infantile stimulation with shock in the mouse. *J.*

abnorm. soc. Psychol., 1956, 53, 19–22.

Williams, E., & Scott, J. P. The development of social behavior patterns in the mouse in relation to natural periods. *Behavior,* 1953, 6, 35–64.

Yerkes, A. W. *The dancing mouse.* New York: Macmillan, 1907.

6

Operant Techniques

MURRAY SIDMAN

Traditionally areas of human pathology received clinical attention long before the laboratory could make its contribution. Human misery makes its demands immediately felt, and science is slow. This is as true of behavioral pathology as it has been of liver disease or endocrine malfunction or any of the other more obviously biological problems to which man is subject. The clinical psychologist is impatient; the press of immediacy impels him to build his clinical house as best he can before an experimental foundation is available.

From simple analogy with the various medical disciplines we can expect that an appropriate laboratory science will indeed prove useful to the behavioral clinician. No more subtle argument than this need be made for the desirability of an experimental foundation. Similarly, we can expect the clinician to welcome this help when it does arrive. But what kinds of help is he to expect from the laboratory?

There are a number of areas of potential contact between the clinic and the laboratory: investigative techniques, basic research and theory, classification and diagnosis, and therapeutic practices. I shall discuss each of these areas and, wherever possible, shall provide detailed examples selected from the available literature.

INVESTIGATIVE TECHNIQUES

One of the claims of experimental psychology is that it can help sharpen the methodological and evaluative tools of clinical investigation. Experimentalists have offered the clinician two major contribu-

This chapter was prepared while the author was with the Walter Reed Army Institute of Research.

tions: the control group, and statistics. As a result, analysis of variance is now almost as common a tool in clinical behavioral research as is the stethoscope in clinical cardiac research.

I have argued elsewhere, and at some length, that control groups and statistical evaluation of data are among the least desirable features of much current laboratory research (Sidman, 1960b). The same may be said of clinical research except, of course, where the interest is in normative or epidemiological problems. Clinically derived knowledge is, in the last analysis, subject to the same pragmatic criteria that are used to evaluate laboratory findings. When enough practitioners of research, diagnosis, or therapy have been able to replicate or use a finding, that finding then becomes an established datum, a bit of knowledge.

It is in using the results of his research that the clinician will recognize the sterility of statistical evaluation. For he cannot, in his practice, deal with a mythical average individual, a group composite. He cannot diagnose a group nor can he treat one—a statistical group, that is to say. He must apply his research findings to individuals.

What else does experimental psychology have to offer the clinician? My brief criticism of the relevance of statistical methodology leads directly to a discussion of operant conditioning techniques, with which I shall be concerned in the remainder of this chapter. The methodology of operant conditioning has several features that the clinical investigator will find congenial: It obtains its data from the individual; it uses the individual as his own control; it evaluates data in terms of its replicability and utility; it uses techniques that have species generality; it *examines* instances of variability. But most relevant of all are the contributions made by operant conditioning to our fund of *techniques of behavioral manipulation*. Such techniques are the unique province of a science of behavior, and if experimental psychology cannot provide these the clinician may justifiably conclude that his experimental foundations have yet to be built.

The bulk of operant conditioning work has been carried out with species lower than man on the phylogenetic scale. This has undoubtedly contributed to the existing gap between clinician and experimentalist. Furthermore, the basic experimental interest has been in normal, rather than pathological, behavioral processes. The assumptions have been that (1) the increased rigor of experimental control permitted by work with lower animals makes it possible to discover and isolate behavioral processes whose relevance to humans may then be assessed under more complex circumstances; and (2) an understanding of normal behavior is a prerequisite for the adequate evaluation of malfunctioning behavioral processes. How well have these assumptions stood up?

I shall begin by summarizing the technical foundation that has been built upon animal studies, and illustrate the techniques by describing some of the extensions that have been made to normal human behavior in the laboratory. The exposition is intended to serve three functions: The first is to indicate to the clinical investigator some of the techniques that are available to him for manipulating a subject's behavior in controlled investigation. These are basic tools with which every student of behavior should be acquainted, for they give him direct access to his subject matter. The second function is to indicate the range in which the techniques have been found applicable to human subjects. Not all of them have been so applied, and certain difficulties have been encountered, but there is a sufficient weight of evidence to demonstrate that the animal work is both practical and relevant in principle to human behavior; I shall emphasize the technical practicality in this section. The third function is simply to provide the reader with a knowledgeable background for the topics to be covered in the final portion of the chapter, where the techniques I have described will be seen in action.

The establishment of behavior

The first manipulative task faced by an experimenter is to get his subject to behave, to interact with the environment so that the experimenter can observe, record, and alter the nature of the interaction. With normal human subjects there is usually no problem in establishing behavior; the experimenter can use verbal instructions or other methods that take advantage of the subject's behavioral history. The task can be difficult, however, if the subject is a psychiatric or neurological patient, a retarded or preverbal child, or a lower animal.

Shaping. By applying the principle of reinforcement in an artful manner, the experimenter can shape the desired behavior out of the mass of responses available to his subject. Shaping is accomplished by reinforcing successively closer approximations to the behavior with which the experimenter ultimately wants to work. The experimental situation, for example, may be one in which a monkey is to be reinforced with food for pressing a lever. If the monkey just sits quietly at first, the experimenter will wait until the animal moves and will then immediately deliver the food. By continuing to reinforce all movements, the experimenter will soon have an active animal with which to work. He then reinforces only those responses which bring the animal closer to the lever. Within a few reinforcements, the monkey will have moved close to the lever, as if drawn by an invisible string. The experimenter now directs his attention to the animal's hand. He delivers the food whenever the hand moves closer to the lever, and it is not long before the animal places its hand on the lever and depresses it. The experimenter can then turn the rest of the job over to his automatic apparatus, which will deliver the food only when the animal actually depresses the lever.

The shaping process is by no means species specific. It is applicable not only to a great variety of lower animals but also to humans who may range widely in intelligence, in the integrity of their nervous systems, or in the debilitating effects of psychiatric illness. Unless deliberate shaping of a patient's behavior has been attempted, it is unwise to conclude that he is unable to behave in a certain way. The process is particularly important in occupational therapy, where the establishment of behavior is a primary goal. We have much to learn about the shaping process, and a considerable amount of art is involved in shaping an organism's behavior, but there are a number of well-established practical rules that will help to ensure success:

1. *Reinforce the behavior immediately.* If the reinforcement is delayed, even by a fraction of a second, it is likely to be preceded by some behavior other than that which the experimenter intended to reinforce.

2. *Do not give too many reinforcements for an approximation of the desired final response.* Behavior that is initially reinforced must ultimately be extinguished as we move closer to the end point. If we reinforce intermediate forms of behavior too much, these once-reinforced but now-to-be-discarded responses will continue to intrude and will unduly prolong the shaping process. There is, unfortunately, no quantitative method for predicting how many reinforcements are too many or, as we shall see below, how many are too few. The experimenter must take the subject's behavior as his guide, and if the subject tells him he has made a mistake he must be prepared to modify his own behavior accordingly.

3. *Do not give too few reinforcements for an approximation of the desired final response.* This is the most common difficulty in shaping behavior; the experimenter moves too fast. He abandons a response before he has reinforced it enough and, as a consequence, both the response and the variations which stem from it extinguish before he can mold the next closer approximation to the final behavior. The subject may then return to his original behavior, as if he had never gone through a shaping process at all.

When this happens, the experimenter may be tempted to evade his responsibility by calling the subject stupid. What he must do is to start again and move the subject once more through the successive steps of the shaping process, taking care this time not to move too rapidly. If the experimenter is patient and willing to learn, he will usually find the subject equally willing.

4. *Carefully specify the response to be reinforced in each successive*

step. Before abandoning one response and reinforcing the next approximation to the final behavior, the experimenter must watch the subject closely to determine what behavior is available for reinforcement. He should then specify that behavior as quantitatively as possible and adhere rigorously to the specification he has established. Otherwise he may inadvertently reinforce a slightly different but highly undesirable form of response and unnecessarily prolong the shaping process.

The maintenance of behavior

Reinforcement variables. Once the experimenter has established some behavior in his subject, he is faced with the problem of maintaining the behavior and keeping it available. A number of factors will influence his success in maintaining the subject's behavior: the state of deprivation of the subject; the type of reinforcement he uses; the size, or amount, of reinforcement; and the schedule that he follows in delivering reinforcements.

One of the first problems is satiation. If he has shaped the desired behavior with food reinforcement, for example, the experimenter can be certain that his subject will behave as usual in the experimental situation whenever he has been sufficiently deprived. Conversely, he can be certain that the subject will not behave as usual if he has been fully or partially satiated.

A problem related to satiation is the size of the reinforcements received by the subject. If these are too small, they will not maintain his behavior for any great length of time; if they are too large, the subject will quickly become satiated. The experimenter must find a useful compromise.

Food and other primary reinforcements are not always the most convenient types to use. Conditioned, or secondary, reinforcements may be more practical, particularly with human subjects. Environmental stimuli, not normally reinforcing in themselves, that control various segments of a subject's behavioral repertoire (see p. 185) will eventually acquire a reinforcing function. For example, if a monkey is reinforced whenever a buzzer is sounding, we can then use the buzzer as a reinforcement to shape and maintain some other behavior in the animal. But just as food is a reinforcer only to an organism that has been deprived of food, a conditioned reinforcer that has been established through its control over food-reinforced behavior will be relatively ineffective unless the organism is food deprived. If there were no way around it, this dependence of a reinforcer upon a specific state of deprivation in the organism would severely limit the utility of behavioral control through reinforcement.

Fortunately both for laboratory investigation and for the richness of life outside the laboratory, conditioned reinforcers do not have to be so limited. A given stimulus can set the occasion for varied kinds of reinforcements: money, for example, and stimuli arising from the social environment, verbal stimuli, and others provided by friends, family, or institutional sources. Such stimuli have been termed "generalized reinforcers" (Skinner, 1953), for they are effective in a wide variety of environmental contexts and under a wide variety of deprivation states. Money will be an effective reinforcer at almost any time because a person is likely to be in at least one of the many deprivation states with which it is associated.

Even in the animal laboratory, when the experimenter begins to work with a new species of organism one of the major initial problems he will face is the selection of an adequate reinforcer. Standard food reinforcers are now available for rat, monkey, chimpanzee, and pigeon, but the problem has not yet been solved adequately for cat and guinea pig, for example. When the experimenter moves to human subjects the problem becomes even more acute, for he does not usually have sufficient control over the subject's state of deprivation to make food reinforcement practical. He must find other reinforcing agents that will still be powerful enough to generate and maintain stable behavioral patterns. When humans fail to replicate the orderliness of behavior shown by lower animals, the reason is often an inadequate reinforcer.

Long, Hammack, May, and Campbell (1958), using trinkets as reinforcers for children, found a deterioration in the orderliness of their subjects' behavior after several sessions of experimentation. Since the altered performance was similiar to that of lower animals which had become satiated after insufficient deprivation, Long and his co-workers substituted new trinkets, thereby ameliorating the deteriorated performance. Stoddard (unpublished data), using candy reinforcement with children, observed similar changes, and was able to reverse them by varying the nature of the reinforcements within each experimental session, the children receiving candy, pennies, any of a wide variety of trinkets, or tokens that could be exchanged later for more valuable toys.

Ultimately, exchangeable tokens are probably the most feasible solution. If the experimenter cannot achieve adequate control over deprivation conditions, he should turn completely in the other direction and make use of generalized reinforcers. By using tokens, which can be exchanged for a wide variety of reinforcers, he can take advantage of whatever deprivation is currently effective in his subject. Generalized reinforcers have been used to advantage by Stoddard, Sidman, and Brady (1960), working with normal and with psychotic adults in a hospital setting. They set up what was essentially a variety store, in which the subjects could trade their tokens for such objects as cigarettes, candy, magazines, books, records, art pictures, pipes, clothing, gift items, and many others. They could also trade their tokens for commercial trading stamps, which they could save and then trade for any of the items in the catalogue of the trading stamp company. Many of the subjects in this study came into the experimental cubicle almost daily, and performed in a consistently lawful fashion over a period of three years.

Morse and Dews (unpublished data), working with a prison population, have found that cigarettes are an effective generalized reinforcer in such an environment. The prisoners use them as a medium of exchange among themselves, and in this instance the experimenters do not have to maintain a supply of exchangeable items.

Bijou and Sturges (1959), in reviewing some of the ways reinforcers have been used in studies with children, have pointed out that interactions between subject and experimenter can markedly alter the degree of control exercised by an ostensible reinforcer. The child brings with him into the laboratory a history of social interaction, and socially mediated factors such as signs of approval or expectation from the experimenter may override the effects of reinforcers like candy or trinkets. For example, a child may be spacing his responses in a manner appropriate to a temporal conditioning procedure (see p. 181) with candy as reinforcement; but if the experimenter has also indicated his approval of the child's performance, the same behavior may continue even after the procedure has changed to one in which spaced responding is no longer efficient. The reinforcement from the experimenter may be more powerful than the candy, and the child's behavior may not come entirely under the control of the candy reinforcement. Bijou and Sturges suggest that human subjects be given minimal instructions, that all reinforcers be presented by mechanical or electronic means, and that the experimenter have as little contact with the subject as possible.

The point is well taken, but, as the writers themselves recognized, it may be difficult for the experimenter to isolate himself from the subject when the experiment itself is concerned with social interaction. Studies of verbal behavior, in which the reinforcement is also verbal, illustrate this difficulty very nicely. The effectiveness of any individual as a reinforcer will inevitably depend upon the subject's conditioning history. I mention the problem only briefly, for it is discussed at greater length in Chapter 15.

It is possible, by appropriate instructions to the subject, to take advantage of types of conditioning history that are relatively consistent in the culture to which the subject belongs. We characterize the products of such conditioning histories with such common terms as competitiveness, self-respect, ambition, desire to please, etc. These terms are actually more descriptive of certain classes of generalized reinforcers than of any specific forms of behavior. The "signal detection" procedure devised by Holland (1958) has proven to be an extremely effective method for using a generalized reinforcer that is based upon instructions to the subject; the instructions, in turn, derive their effectiveness from an unspecified, but evidently general, set of cultural reinforcing practices.

Holland's subjects were asked to report whenever the pointer on a dial was deflected from its normal resting position. Their instructions were only to make as many detections as possible and to reset the pointer as rapidly as possible whenever a deflection was observed. At the end of each experimental session, the subject was told how many detections he had made and the average time taken per detection. This verbal interaction with the experimenter was sufficient to establish and maintain the pointer deflection as a reinforcer, and behavior was generated in the following way:

The subjects, working in the dark, could see the pointer only when they pressed a key that illuminated the face of the dial for a fraction of a second. When the subject observed that the pointer was deflected, he reported it by pressing another key, which reset the pointer. The deflections of the pointer were programed so as to make possible various schedules of detections, or reinforcements. By recording the rate at which the subjects pressed the first button, thereby illuminating the dial, Holland was able to measure objectively the subjects' observing behavior.

Reinforcement schedules. In general, the greater the deprivation, the larger the reinforcement, and the more appropriate the type of reinforcement, the more successful we will be in keeping the subject behaving for long periods of time. Given adequate reinforcement variables, the schedule of reinforcement then becomes critical. I shall describe some of the more commonly used reinforcement schedules in order to illustrate the advantages and shortcomings of each, and to demonstrate the gross behavioral changes that may be brought about by some rather subtle alterations in the schedule of reinforcement. In these schedules the student of behavior has some powerful tools at his disposal, and he should be equipped to use them. I shall present only a few examples of published records for comparison with the known animal data, in order to provide some indication of the generality of the techniques.

1. *Continuous reinforcement.* The simplest technique is to reinforce the subject each time he responds appropriately. In one sense this is the most powerful technique, for it will keep the subject responding even when he is minimally deprived and when the size of

each reinforcement is relatively small. But the continuous reinforce-ment schedule has at least one major disadvantage for experimenta-tion; the subject is reinforced so frequently that he is likely to become satiated, making it impossible for the experimenter to observe his behavior over any substantial period of time.

Fortunately, we need not reinforce the subject for every response in order to maintain his behavior. Occasional reinforcements may maintain the response even more effectively than if we reinforced it every time. In fact, if we want to extinguish a subject's behavior, we must be absolutely consistent in withholding reinforcement. But, it should be noted, although we can maintain a subject's behavior by reinforcing only intermittently, we must then pay even more atten-tion to deprivation and amount of reinforcement. Deprivation, rein-forcement size, and reinforcement frequency are interlocking variables, and we must compensate for any decrease in one of these by increas-ing the others.

2. *Fixed-interval reinforcement.* One method of arranging rein-forcements intermittently is to make them available to the subject only after a fixed period of time has elapsed; at the end of this period, the subject's next response will produce a reinforcement and the time interval will start again. If the experimenter has been able to secure an optimal arrangement of the important contributory variables the subject will adjust his behavior to the schedule in the manner shown in Figure. 1.

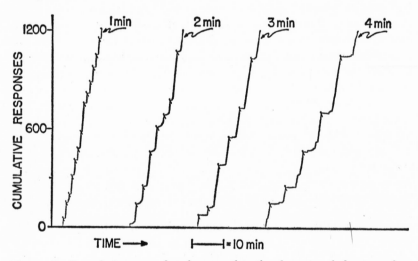

Figure 1. Cumulative records of one subject's observing behavior when reinforced on fixed-interval schedules of 1, 2, 3, and 4 minutes. The di-agonal marks indicate reinforcements. [From Holland, 1958, courtesy of *Science.*]

Holland (1958) has reported fixed-interval data obtained from Navy enlisted men. These subjects pressed a key which illuminated a dial, and the reinforcement for key pressing was a deflection of the needle on the dial. Figure 1 is a set of cumulative records from one subject for whom dial deflections were scheduled to occur, in different sessions, at fixed intervals of 1, 2, 3, and 4 minutes. The curves are very similar to those reported for lower animals (e.g., Ferster and Skinner, 1957). Each reinforcement is followed by a pause, the length of which is related to the duration of the fixed interval; as time elapses, the subject begins to respond and reaches a high rate before the next reinforcement. Curves for extinction after fixed-interval reinforcement also confirmed the animal data.

Working with children four to eight years of age, who received trinkets, pennies, or projected pictures as reinforcement for pulling a lever or pressing a key, Long and his associates (1958) replicated some of the usual features of fixed-interval behavior, but were not able to maintain consistent performances on this schedule.

Stoddard, Sidman, and Brady (1960a) have also obtained fixed-interval data that differs from the animal data usually reported. Their subjects were military personnel, both attendants and staff members, employed in a closed psychiatric ward in a military hospital. Generalized token reinforcers were used to maintain the subjects' lever-pulling behavior. The subjects behaved very efficiently on the fixed-interval schedule, pausing almost the full duration of each interval and then responding once or twice to procure the token almost on time. Many of the subjects used watches, however, and it is possible that if their behavior of looking at the watches could have been recorded, this would have yielded a typical fixed-interval picture, as did Holland's subjects when their observing behavior was recorded. When the experimenters placed an upper limit on the fixed interval, so that the subjects would miss an opportunity for reinforcement if they delayed their response as little as 0.5 second after the end of the interval, the records took on an appearance more like the expected one.

In general, the indications have been that the fixed-interval schedule is the least stable of all the reinforcement schedules in controlling human behavior. In animal work, too, however, fixed-interval behavior is notoriously sensitive to other variables, such as deprivation, reinforcement size, and novel stimuli. Holland's work suggests that stable and species-consistent fixed-interval behavior can be obtained in humans with appropriate techniques.

3. *Variable-interval reinforcement.* We can make reinforcements available to the subject at variable rather than fixed periods of time. The irregular spacing of reinforcements in time will eliminate the cyclic changes in response rate that characterize the subject's per-

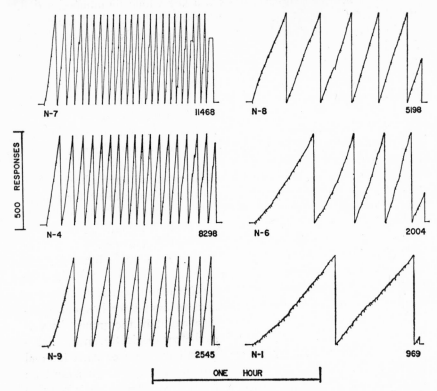

Figure 2. Cumulative records of the behavior of six subjects reinforced with nickels on a variable-interval schedule. [From Lindsley, 1960, courtesy of *Diseases of the Nervous System, Monograph Supplement.*]

formance on a fixed-interval schedule. If the variable-interval schedule is efficiently constructed (see Sidman, 1960b), the subject will respond at a steady rate. The performance will be sensitive to the effects of many experimental operations, and because of its stability it will pose fewer measurement problems for the experimenter.

Figure 2 shows records obtained by Lindsley (1960) from six normal adult subjects who were reinforced with nickels on a one-minute variable-interval schedule. The response was lever pulling. Although there are wide individual differences in response rate, each individual's rate is steady and, although not shown here, is relatively consistent during many successive experimental periods. The curves resemble the animal data very closely. Holland (1958), too, reports similar consistent response rates when the observing responses of his subjects are reinforced on a variable-interval schedule and, in addition, presents a more quantitative replication of the animal work. The response rates of his subjects decrease as the average interval of the variable-interval schedule is increased from fifteen seconds to two minutes.

The performance by children on variable-interval schedules in the experiments of Long, Hammack, May, and Campbell (1958) also closely resembles that of other organisms. These investigators, however, noted that the construction of the variable-interval program was an important factor in determining the regularity of the children's performance. If there were too few short intervals in the program, there was considerable pausing and the records were generally irregular. This is to be expected, since too few short intervals will make the program more like fixed interval and will tend to generate a fixed-interval performance; experimenters working with lower animals have also noted this phenomenon.

4. *Differential reinforcement of low rates.* Reinforcement availability can be programed simultaneously by a fixed-interval timer and by the subject's own behavior. For example, the timer may make reinforcement available every ten seconds, but only if the subject has not responded for ten seconds. Each response of the subject resets the timer and starts the ten-second period all over again. Every time the subject waits for ten seconds without responding, he will produce a reinforcement with his next response. Since responses that occur at a rate higher than one per ten seconds are extinguished, the schedule is characterized as the *differential reinforcement of low rates,* often abbreviated *DRL*. The resulting behavior is sometimes called timing behavior, or delayed response, for the subject must be able to delay his response for a specified period of time if he is to procure reinforcements.

Even with animal subjects, the DRL schedule can produce an empathic feeling of intense and painful concentration in the human observer. Experimenters who have themselves worked on this schedule report that it is extremely difficult for them to refrain from responding until the required time interval is judged to have elapsed. Nonetheless, the DRL schedule has proved extremely effective in maintaining stable and efficient behavior in human subjects. The frequency distributions of Figure 3 are from two of the children in Stoddard's investigation (unpublished data). The children had to space their lever-pulling responses at least ten seconds apart to procure candy; if they pulled the lever too soon, the ten-second interval began anew without any reinforcement; if they waited ten seconds or more since their last lever pull, their next response produced the candy.

The schedule was effective in generating low response rates in children ranging in age from 2.5 to 12 years. The older children were more precise in timing their responses, producing interresponse-time

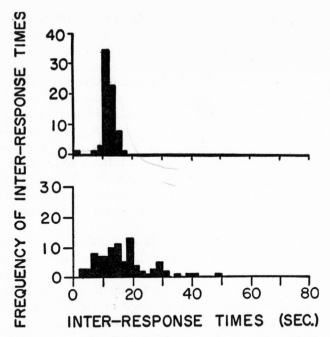

Figure 3. Frequency distributions of interresponse times, obtained from two children reinforced with candy on a DRL schedule. The upper record is from a ten-year-old child, the lower from a 2.5-year-old.

distributions with much less variability than is usually found with rats, but which are comparable with the performance of monkeys.

When the DRL schedule was shifted from ten to twenty seconds, the children decreased their response rates, and the interresponse-time distributions shifted appropriately. Also, many of the children were observed to go through a "superstitious" chain of responses between each lever pull; such behavior has also been reported with lower animals (Wilson and Keller, 1953).

Holland (1958) found similar orderliness when his subjects' observing behavior was reinforced according to a DRL schedule that required them to pause at least thirty seconds between each observing response. He also confirmed an additional detail of the DRL performance that has been reported in several animal studies; when the subject responded just a little sooner than the required interval he often emitted a short burst of responses at a rapid rate (Sidman, 1956).

Lane (1960) combined the Holland technique with the DRL schedule, but required a vocal utterance, the sound, "oo," as the observing response. His subjects were male and female undergraduates. Like animal subjects, they produced low response rates that were close to the value that would maximize the frequency of reinforcement. He also found appropriate shifts in response rate when he altered the length of the required pause.

Dews and Morse (1958) used a more complex version of the DRL schedule with male medical students who were reinforced with four nickels for pressing a telegraph key. Some subjects had to space their responses 2.5 seconds apart, and received their coins every hundredth time they did this; other subjects had to space their responses 25 seconds apart and were reinforced every tenth time they did so. The subjects were informed of the schedule. They were extremely efficient in spacing their responses; again the interresponse-time distributions were more like those of monkeys than of rats. Dews and Morse also gave their subjects amphetamine, and the results were again consistent with those obtained from lower animals; the interresponse-time distributions were shifted in the direction of shorter interresponse times.

5. *Fixed-ratio reinforcement.* If we require the subject to respond a fixed number of times for each reinforcement, the availability of reinforcement will depend solely upon his own behavior. When we establish a fixed ratio of responses to reinforcements, the subject will behave as is shown in Figure 4; if he does not respond at a near maximal rate he does not respond at all. The pauses, when they occur, usually come just after a reinforcement.

In the investigations of Long and his coworkers (1958), the children were also exposed to fixed-ratio schedules. Figure 4 illustrates two performances that confirm the findings from lower animals. In record 1, the subject had to respond 60 times for each reinforcement; in record 2, the ratio was shifted to 90 responses per reinforcement. These

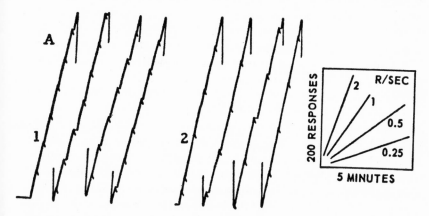

Figure 4. Cumulative records of the behavior of a child reinforced on fixed-ratio schedule of 60 (record 1) and 90 (record 2) responses per reinforcement. [From Long, Hammack, May, and Campbell, 1958, courtesy of *Journal of the Experimental Analysis of Behavior.*]

investigators also observed deteriorative changes similar to those previously described for the fixed-ratio behavior of lower organisms when the ratio size was increased too rapidly or when the subjects had accumulated large numbers of reinforcements (Ferster and Skinner, 1957).

Holland (1958), in his investigations of observing behavior in humans, also observed fixed-ratio performances characteristic of those obtained from lower animals with conventional reinforcement. And when he extinguished the observing response of his subjects, their extinction behavior exhibited the same special characteristics that are normally seen in the extinction records of animals after fixed-ratio reinforcement (Skinner, 1938).

6. *Variable-ratio reinforcement.* We can also make reinforcements available to the subject after variable rather than fixed numbers of responses. This schedule will generate the highest response rates of any described, and if the schedule is efficiently constructed the subject will hardly pause in his responding at all, even after receiving a reinforcement.

Variable-ratio schedules have not been used frequently with human subjects. Orlando and Bijou (1960) are the only investigators who have reported on this schedule and their work was with developmentally retarded children. Like infrahuman subjects, these retarded children responded at high steady rates on the variable-ratio schedule, with pauses being infrequent and not obviously related to the receipt of reinforcement.

Making behavior available

For reasons both of experimental convenience and control, the experimenter builds into his subject the behavior he wishes to investigate. First he shapes the behavior and then sets up the conditions to maintain it for the duration of the observation period. When he places the subject in the experimental situation, the desired behavior will appear.

But if the clinician is impatient, so is the experimenter, in his own way. He is not satisfied to have a single sample of behavior with which to work but wants to push on to greater complexity, to build several types of behavior into his experimental organism and study them all. There is the problem, then, of establishing a complex behavioral repertoire in a subject and subsequently making each component of the repertoire available for individual observation at the experimenter's convenience.

Stimulus control. An organism's behavior is governed not only by its reinforcing consequences but by the current environmental stimuli as well. This is vividly illustrated by the phenomenon of stimulus generalization. A pigeon, for example, is first reinforced on a variable-interval schedule for pecking a disk that is illuminated with a particular wavelength of light. Then, during extinction, the illumination on the disk is changed periodically so that the bird is exposed to a number of other wavelengths in addition to the one that was present during reinforcement. The pigeon's rate of pecking will decrease as the stimulus differs more and more from the original one (Guttman and Kalish, 1956). The more the subject's environment changes, the less likely it is to behave in its usual fashion.

We can make deliberate use of environmental stimulus control to bring out the various components of a subject's built-in behavioral repertoire. When shaping the response and setting up the various conditions for its maintenance, we simply change some aspect of the environment to correspond with each of the separate maintenance conditions. For example, we may sound a tone while the subject is working on a fixed-interval schedule; when the subject is working on a fixed-ratio schedule we change the tone to a buzzer; and when the subject is avoiding shock we replace the auditory stimuli with a light. Eventually each of these stimuli will come to control its own form of behavior; whenever we turn on one of the stimuli the subject will respond appropriately to the experimental conditions correlated with the particular stimulus. The behavior is "on call," so to speak, at the experimenter's command.

It appears quite feasible to build more than one sample of behavior into the human subject and to place each form of behavior under stimulus control. Stoddard, Sidman, and Brady (1960a) set up a multiple schedule with fixed-interval and fixed-ratio components; when a green light was turned on above the lever, the subjects were reinforced on a one-minute fixed-interval schedule, and when a red light was on, the reinforcement schedule was a fixed ratio of 50 responses per reinforcement. The schedule changed each time the subject received a reinforcement. Later, an upper limit was placed on the fixed interval, so that the subjects had to respond within 0.5 second after the end of each interval or else miss the reinforcement. Figure 5 illustrates the precision of the control exercised by the stimuli over the interval and ratio patterns of behavior. When the red light came on, the subject responded rapidly until he received a reinforcement and the light changed to green. With the onset of the green light, the subject paused for a while and then responded rapidly until reinforced. Both samples of behavior were thus available for observation in close temporal juxtaposition, and the effect of other variables could be assessed on each. Multiple stimulus control of fixed-interval and fixed-ratio behavior in the signal detection situation has also been shown by Holland (1958) to be of comparable precision.

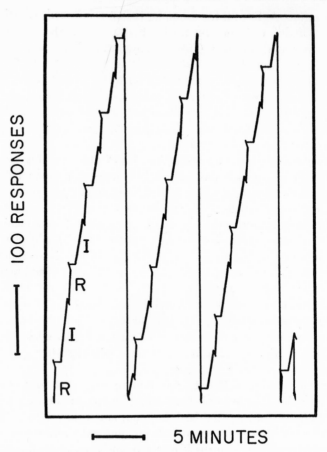

Figure 5. Cumulative records of one subject's behavior on a multiple fixed-interval, fixed-ratio schedule. The pen is deflected downward during the fixed-ratio schedule. The schedule changed after each reinforcement. The first two interval segments are indicated by the letter *I*, and the first two ratio segments by *R*.

With children as subjects, Stoddard (unpublished data) used a multiple schedule with variable-interval and DRL components. Competing effects from the subjects' reinforcement histories and a decline in the reinforcing power of the candies used as reinforcement in this study prevented good schedule control in some of the subjects, but where the schedule control was adequate, control by the corresponding stimuli was also precise.

Behavioral control through aversive stimuli

Aversive stimuli will reinforce, not the behavior by which the organism produces them, but rather the behavior which permits the subject to escape from them, or to terminate them. The most common stimulus of this type in the laboratory is electric shock, but others such as bright lights, loud noises, and excessive cold have also been used.

Conditioned suppression. The initial effect of a strong electric shock is to produce a general cessation of an animal's ongoing behavior. This disrupting effect of shock can, however, be placed under stimulus control. For example, we may first shape a monkey's lever-pressing response with food reinforcement and maintain the behavior with a variable-interval schedule. Then we shock the animal every ten minutes, but before each shock we turn on a tone for five minutes. The shock at first disrupts the monkey's lever-pressing behavior, but the disruption soon becomes channeled into the periods during which the tone is sounding; during these periods the animal ceases pressing the lever but returns to its normal performance after the shock. We now have available a technique for studying both the contributory and therapeutic effects of other variables upon a well-controlled behavioral disruption, a technique that will be particularly valuable if this phenomenon does indeed have relevance to "anxiety," a term that is frequently applied to it (see Chapter 10).

Escape behavior. Aversive stimuli may be used not only to suppress behavior but also to generate and maintain new responses. The simplest way to do this is to allow the subject to terminate, or escape from, the aversive stimulus whenever it is administered. Like food-reinforced behavior, escape-reinforced behavior can be maintained by various reinforcement schedules (e.g., Kaplan, 1956; Dinsmoor, 1958). The subject may succeed in turning off the shock only after the lapse of fixed or variable intervals of time (interval schedules), or after he has responded a fixed or variable number of times (ratio schedules).

Experimenters have been understandably reluctant to use electric shock with human subjects, and a number of other aversive stimuli have demonstrated their utility in a variety of experimental situations. Azrin (1960), for example, used periods of rest from strenuous work. He instructed subjects to turn a handwheel against a friction clutch to the limit of their physical ability. When the subjects were reinforced by a two-minute rest period after every 85 revolutions of the handwheel, they increased the rate at which they turned the wheel and actually performed 50 per cent more work than when the rest periods were given independently of their behavior.

Avoidance behavior. Another way for organisms to deal with aversive stimuli is to prevent their occurrence—to avoid them. To generate avoidance behavior, we simply administer brief shocks to the subject, on either a fixed or irregular temporal schedule, and arrange conditions so that the subject postpones the shock each time he presses a lever. By pressing frequently enough, he could successfully prevent any shocks from occurring. With this procedure, the subject will respond at a steady rate for long periods of time, with the response rate being an inverse function of the amount of time the shock is postponed by each lever press. This behavior, too, can be brought under stimulus control to form an element in the experimental organism's multiple behavioral repertoire.

Using shock as an aversive stimulus for medical students, Ader and Tatum (1961) generated avoidance behavior which closely resembled that obtained with lower species. The subjects were given brief periodic shocks unless they pressed a button; each time they pressed the button, shock was postponed for a fixed period of time. Some of the subjects simply left the experimental situation, an escape response that is not usually available to animal subjects, but of those who remained, the majority learned to press the button within the first session. These subjects not only responded at the stable rates characteristic of avoidance behavior under this procedure (see Figure 6), but their response rates were also inversely related to the amount of time each response postponed the shock, as has been found in animal studies (Sidman, 1953). The subjects had no instructions on how to deal with the shock.

Azrin (1958), using military personnel as voluntary subjects, generated escape and avoidance behavior with intense noise as the aversive stimulus. His basic technique was the signal detection procedure of Holland (1958), the subjects' button-pressing responses being reinforced by needle deflection on a three-minute fixed-interval schedule. This produced the usual type of fixed-interval behavior, the subjects pausing after each reinforcement and then responding more rapidly until the next signal detection.

Once the fixed-interval baseline had been established, Azrin turned on an intense noise, allowing the subject to terminate the noise for five seconds (escape) with each observing response, or to postpone the onset of noise for five seconds (avoidance) each time he pressed the button when the noise was off. When these aversive contingencies were programed concurrently with the fixed-interval schedule of signal detection, the temporal pattern of the subjects' behavior changed markedly. Instead of pausing after each signal detection, they pressed the button often enough to prevent the onset of noise. Near the end of the fixed interval, the usual high fixed-interval rate emerged from this initial avoidance behavior. Azrin was thus able to demonstrate avoidance and fixed-interval behavior concurrently in human subjects, replicating earlier data in which shock was used in a similar fashion with rats (Ferster and Skinner, 1957).

Azrin was also able to place this behavior under multiple stimulus

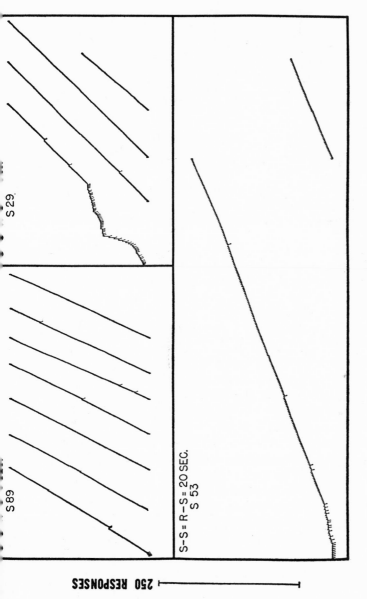

250 RESPONSES ⊢————————————⊣

⊢——— 10 MINUTES

Figure 6. Cumulative records of avoidance behavior during the first conditioning session. The oblique markers indicate shocks. Shocks come at different frequencies (S-S) for each subject, and each subject avoided shock for a different period of time (R-S). [From Ader and Tatum, 1961, courtesy of *Journal of the Experimental Analysis of Behavior.*]

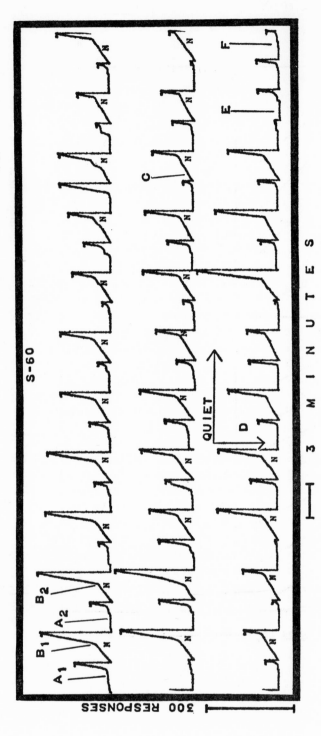

Figure 7. Cumulative records of a subject's performance when reinforced by signal detection on a three-minute fixed-interval schedule. In the alternate periods marked *N*, each response also avoided an intense noise for five seconds. [From Azrin, 1958, courtesy of *Journal of the Experimental Analysis of Behavior*.]

control, with the noise acting as both aversive and discriminative stimulus. He did this by alternating three-minute periods with and without noise. Figure 7 shows some sample results; without noise, the subject displayed the typical fixed-interval performance, but when the noise was scheduled during alternate three-minute periods the records are typical of the concurrent fixed-interval and avoidance patterns. This experiment is most encouraging with respect to the feasibility of extending to humans some of the techniques that have been developed in the animal laboratory for working with complex behavior.

Hefferline, Keenan, and Harford (1959) have been able to condition an avoidance response that is so small as to occur unnoticed by the subjects, adult humans. A tiny twitch of the subject's left thumb, recorded electromyographically, served to terminate or to postpone noise that was superimposed upon music to which the subject was listening. This work is described in greater detail in Chapter 4.

Lindsley (1957) used a pure tone to generate escape and avoidance behavior in an adult subject. Each time the subject closed a switch with his thumb, he reduced the intensity of the tone slightly. By operating the switch rapidly, the subject could quickly reduce the tone to zero intensity, and could then avoid the tone by continued responding. By operating the switch slowly, the subject could keep the tone at a moderate intensity. If the switch was not operated, the tone rose to and was maintained at its full intensity (30 db.). Lindsley used this technique in a sleep-deprived subject to measure the duration and depth of sleep.

If animals are permitted to postpone the onset of a stimulus that is correlated with nonreinforcement, or extinction, the response by which they can do so will be successfully conditioned and will display the usual characteristics of avoidance behavior (Morse and Herrnstein, 1956). A similar technique has been used by Baer (1960) with preschool children. The children were permitted to watch cartoons, but occasionally the cartoons were interrupted. By pressing a lever, a child could reinstate the cartoon, and if he pressed the lever while the cartoon was still on he could postpone the next interruption. The technique of using a period of time-out from positive reinforcement as an aversive stimulus seems a promising one for human experimentation.

BASIC RESEARCH FINDINGS OF
CLINICAL INTEREST

Despite its emphasis on the resemblances between animal and human behavior in the laboratory, the preceding section was not intended to belittle the special problems of human behavior. My purpose was simply to demonstrate the applicability to human behavior of operant techniques that were developed in the animal laboratory. The evidence is more than merely suggestive.

Once it is known that the techniques are generalizable from subhuman to human, we can then place greater confidence in the generality of the findings that come out of these and related techniques. The following pages, therefore, will contain a selection—not by any means a thorough review—of some basic problems of clinical interest that have been raised, or even clarified, by the use of lower animals in the operant conditioning laboratory.

Stimulus generalization

Whenever an organism is reinforced or punished it is always in some environmental context, physical or social. The next time the organism encounters that same environment it will behave in the way for which it was previously reinforced, or in the same manner by which it was successful in dealing with the punishment; for example, by escape or avoidance. This may be considered a somewhat loose statement of a general behavioral principle. My concern here is with a related principle: the organism will also behave similarly when it encounters a situation that differs in some respects from the original one. This, again loosely stated, is the principle of stimulus generalization.

When a laboratory-derived behavioral phenomenon catches the attention of the clinical investigator or theoretician, he is rarely interested in those quantitative aspects of the data which are so dear to the experimenter's heart. He uses the experimental findings only in a qualitative way; the phenomenon is or is not relevant to a particular clinical problem. Stimulus generalization is an exception to this custom. Some of its most interesting and controversial extrapolations to clinical problems are based upon a quantitative assumption about the nature of the generalization gradient: namely, that behavior controlled by punishment will generalize in a quantitatively different manner, either more or less widely, than behavior controlled by positive reinforcement. Miller, for example, has based an ingenious theory of displacement on the assumption that the avoidance gradient is steeper than the approach gradient (Miller, 1944, 1948). Although no other theory has been stated as quantitatively as Miller's, the opposite assumption, that avoidance behavior generalizes more widely than approach behavior, is often invoked implicitly to explain the occurrence of phobias and other types of neurotic anxiety.

A most convincing demonstration that the latter assumption is correct has been provided by Hearst (1960), who obtained simultaneous generalization gradients for punishment-controlled and reward-controlled behavior in individual monkeys. There were two responses available to the monkey concurrently; each time it pressed a lever it postponed shock for ten seconds, and when it pulled a chain it was occasionally rewarded with food on a variable-interval schedule. During subsequent generalization testing, both shock and food reward were discontinued, and the intensity of the cage illumination was systematically varied. The animal's rate of lever pressing (the avoidance response) did not change, regardless of how much the cage illumination varied from its original level. It pulled the chain (food-reinforced response) progressively less frequently, however, as the cage illumination differed more and more from its original intensity. The avoidance gradient was flat and the reward gradient was relatively steep, with both gradients being measured simultaneously in the same animal.

The effectiveness of punishment in eliminating behavior

Punishment is a prevalent method of behavioral control in most cultural groups. Yet its role in the etiology of behavior disorders is a hotly debated issue, as is its utility in therapeutic techniques. Operant conditioning studies, however, as far as they have gone in this area thus far, yield a relatively clear picture of the effects of punishment. It is well established that the immediate consequence of punishment is to stop the organism from performing the punished behavior. There are also certain nonspecific effects of punishment: other responses than the punished one will also decrease in probability, a phenomenon that has been studied extensively by means of the conditioned-suppression technique (Estes and Skinner, 1941): the effects of punishment will generalize to other situations than the one in which the organism was initially punished—stimulus generalization (Sidman, 1961); if it is possible for the organism to avoid the punishment it will develop the behavior that permits it to do so (Azrin, 1956), thereby, perhaps, substituting an even more undesirable response for the one that was initially punished.

But what are the long-term consequences of punishment with respect to the punished behavior itself? By using punishment, can we actually eliminate a response permanently from a subject's repertoire of behavior?

Azrin (1959, 1960), using pigeons as subjects and electric shock as the aversive stimulus, has shown that if the organism continues to be reinforced with food for the punished behavior it will eventually begin responding again. The initial suppression of the punished response does not last. This is so even when the organism is shocked every time it responds and the food reinforcement is delivered only intermittently. Only when the shock intensity is extremely high will there be some permanent reduction in the animal's rate of response. Such high intensities, of course, are also most likely to generate the undesirable side effects of punishment, thereby increasing the cost at which we purchase the elimination of a particular response. Azrin also noted that when the shock is discontinued, the animal will respond for a while at a much higher rate than it ever did before being punished.

Even when other sources of reinforcement are eliminated, and the animal receives only punishment for its response, the initial suppression of the punished behavior is not likely to be permanent. Estes (1944) shocked rats while extinguishing their previously food-reinforced lever-pressing behavior. After they had stopped pressing the lever, he discontinued the shock. Soon the animals began to respond again, even though there was still no food reinforcement.

Both Estes and Azrin report a number of other corroborative and additional findings. The conclusion would seem to be that punishment is not a very efficient method for permanently eliminating behavior except via certain side effects like generalized suppression or avoidance.

Adventitious reinforcement

The principle of reinforcement is so pervasive in the experimental control of behavior that we sometimes take it for granted and fail to give it the respect it deserves. The experimenter sometimes sets up a contingency between the response of an organism and a subsequent reinforcement and then proceeds blithely to assume that he need only consider the particular contingency he has established. But the action of reinforcement is automatic, and independent of the intentions of the experimenter. Any behavior, whether or not he observes and measures it, that precedes the delivery of a reinforcement to the organism will be affected by the reinforcement. There need be no causal correlation between response and reinforcement; even when reinforcement follows a response adventitiously it will have the same effect upon that response as if the connection were a necessary one.

Skinner (1948) first demonstrated this by delivering food to pigeons at regular intervals, regardless of what they were doing at the time. Because a bird was necessarily doing something when the reinforcement came, its current behavior was "caught" and became a stereotyped performance, even though no such specific performance was necessary to produce the food. Skinner called this a superstition, because the animal's behavior was being maintained by a reinforcement over which it actually had no control; just as the rituals of the rainmaker are maintained by occasional rainfalls.

Since Skinner's original experiment, adventitious reinforcement has come to play an increasingly important role in experimentation not only as a technical problem that is often difficult to solve but also as the key to a number of phenomena that would otherwise be difficult to understand.

For example, we may want to set up a discrimination experiment in which the animal is to respond only when a light is on. We turn the light on, let us say, every two minutes, and reinforce the animal only when it responds in the presence of the light. But we observe that the animal also responds when the light is off; furthermore, its temporal pattern of responses is typical of fixed-interval behavior. This is not simply a breakdown of behavioral lawfulness, an instance of behavior being maintained without reinforcement. The light in this experiment is a conditioned reinforcer, and because the animal happened to respond just before the light came on, the response was reinforced adventitiously, and began to occur more frequently when the light was off. And because the light was presented on a fixed-interval schedule of two minutes, the subject's adventitiously reinforced behavior assumed the appropriate temporal pattern. Such behavior can easily be eliminated by arranging that the light will never come on if the animal has just responded.

Morse and Skinner (1957) have demonstrated yet another way in which a stimulus can develop adventitious control over an organism's behavior. Their baseline procedure was a variable-interval reinforcement schedule, with pigeons as subjects. The experimental operation was simply to turn on a blue light for four minutes once every hour. The blue light eventually assumed some control over the subjects' behavior, even though the variable-interval schedule remained the same, whether the light was on or off. Some of the subjects, for example, increased their rate of responding when the light was on. This happened because of accidental correlations between the light and the variable-interval program of reinforcement. Sometimes the light happened to come on when the schedule provided several closely spaced reinforcements, so that there was an adventitious correlation between the light and a higher-than-usual frequency of reinforcements delivered to the subject. The principle of reinforcement respects such a correlation, regardless of its utility, or lack of it, for the organism.

Behavior may become controlled adventitiously by aversive stimuli, also. In an experiment in which monkeys could obtain food by pulling a chain and, concurrently, could avoid shocks by pressing a lever, Sidman (1958) has shown that the food-reinforced response became involved adventitiously in the avoidance contingency, even though the response actually had no connection with shock avoidance. Simple temporal juxtaposition of the animal's chain pull and lever press, with the subsequent avoidance of shock, was sufficient to establish a spurious but powerful connection between chain pulling and shock avoidance.

A subject's behavioral history may contribute to the likelihood of adventitious control. Herrnstein and Sidman (1958), working with monkeys, first developed a conditioned suppression of the animals' food-reinforced lever-pressing behavior. Then they trained the animals to press the lever to avoid shock. When the animals were again exposed to the conditioned-suppression procedure, they reacted by increasing their rate of lever pressing—just the opposite of suppression. The key to this phenomenon is the history of avoidance behavior that had been built into the animals. Because of this history, they reacted to the shock as if they could avoid it; an unreal and ineffective mode of adaptation, to be sure, but appropriate to their reinforcement history.

From these and other experiments there emerges at least one trend. The more complex the experiment—the more responses, stimuli, and types of reinforcement that are involved, and the more extensive the organism's behavioral history—the greater will be the likelihood of adventitious control over the behavior. The moral is evident, for what experimental situation involves more of these complexities than do the ordinary life situations of the behaving human? Because adventitious control is, in one sense, unrealistic control, its existence may give an impression of disorderliness in behavior, but the disorder is only in our interpretation, not in the behavior itself (Sidman, 1960a).

So much for basic research findings of clinical interest. More unified presentations of related material are to be found in other chapters of this book. Let us now turn to some areas in which the laboratory has made closer contact with the clinic. The work I shall discuss in the following sections is still, in one sense, basic, for it is largely untried clinically, and is even occasionally speculative. But it is at least one step removed from "the study of behavior for its own sake and ultimately, perhaps, also for clinical relevance," and is in the direction of the study of behavior for its immediate clinical relevance.

CLASSIFICATION, DIAGNOSIS, AND THERAPY

There are numerous pathways through which an organism's behavior may be influenced. Anatomical structure, nerve chemistry, endocrine function, environmental input—to mention but a few—may all play a role in maintaining the stability and adaptiveness of one's behavior, or in producing malfunction—behavioral pathology. Behavioral breakdown, therefore, may originate in any of the systems and processes that are relevant to the normal functioning of the organism.

But regardless of their starting point all behavioral pathologies must pass through a final common pathway. Whether the pathology springs from a person's malfunctioning nervous system or from an unusual conditioning history, we can observe it only in the way he responds to and deals with his environment, both physical and social. The final common pathway, then, comprises the set of behavioral processes that govern the relations of the organism to his environment.

Here, then, is where the analysis of behavioral pathology must make its beginning. We must first be able to classify the patient's behavior in a fashion that will permit us to identify the behavioral processes involved in his particular problem. Once a useful behavioral classification has evolved, we may then go on to seek other correlates that will help to define the disease process.

Our gross preliminary observations tell us little more than that the patient is not behaving as he should. Perhaps he finds himself involved in a paranoid plot; or walls himself off in autistic silence; or develops an aphasic inability to name objects. Such classifications—paranoia, autism, aphasia—are too general to form a maximally useful diagnostic base. Patients given one label are found to differ among themselves in the etiology of their breakdown, in their response to similar treatments, in their specific patterns of behavior. What is required is a set of general behavioral principles which will serve to regroup behavioral pathologies into classes that may be differentiated in terms of the behavioral processes involved.

For example, we may have a patient who cannot say nouns. Can this symptom be the basis for a class of neurological disease? What status do nouns have in the elucidation of behavioral processes? In themselves, they have no status at all. They are verbal responses, and as such may participate in many different behavioral processes. We may hold up a pencil and ask the patient to tell us what it is, and he may be unable to name it. Yet if we ask him to write his name he may immediately say, "Give me a pencil." The response, pencil, is under two different forms of behavioral control in this example. One of these forms of control is defective; the other is intact. The case may be no different in principle from that of a rat which, after it has undergone an experimental brain lesion, will no longer press a lever if we give it food for doing so, but will continue pressing a lever that serves to avoid shocks. The animal's response is the same, but it is under two forms of environmental control; the brain lesion affected only one of these.

APPROACHES TO CLASSIFICATION

Operant techniques and the principles derived from them have only just begun to be applied to problems of classification. The validity of the attempts has yet to be established, and perhaps it is even too soon to try this, for the range of phenomena that have been touched upon is still narrow and no single problem has yet been analyzed in depth. The approaches to classification may themselves be subdivided in terms of their methods of analysis.

The educated guess

This is a strictly clinical approach, in that it relies upon direct observation of the patient in a nonexperimental setting. As in the best clinical tradition, however, the observations are made against a background of existing knowledge. In the present instance, this background consists of laboratory-acquired knowledge of the processes by which a person's behavior is established and maintained. Ferster (1958) has given an excellent exposition of this approach, based upon Skinner's (1953) extensions of operant principles to problems of social interaction.

One begins simply by observing the patient's current behavior, analyzing his performances in terms of known behavioral processes, and then making guesses about the ways these processes might have been historically manipulated so as to produce the patient's particular difficulties. Ferster elaborates a number of ways of classifying the psychiatric patient in terms of such a functional analysis, with emphasis upon the role of the social environment.

For example, the patient may lack "parts of the complex repertoire necessary to achieve reinforcement from the complicated social environment" (Ferster, 1958, p. 107). He may be deficient verbally, or unable to engage in everyday social intercourse. This could have come about through an inadequate reinforcement history. The behavior may simply not have been built into the person. If the behavior is not established at the appropriate time it may be very difficult to do so later. A child's initial approximations to socially desirable behavior will be accepted as part of the shaping process, but society demands greater precision from the adult and will not reinforce his "childish" approximations.

The person can actually possess the required behavior but fail to engage in it because the current reinforcement conditions are not optimal with respect to amount, frequency, or schedule. The behavior is available but cannot be maintained. Or excessive punishment may have generated avoidance behavior that successfully competes with more adaptive forms of response.

When behavioral classification is made by means of educated guesswork, its ultimate validation must come via therapeutic success. The therapist must actually manipulate the variables he suspects are relevant in any particular case. As Ferster points out:

If the therapist is ultimately to be successful, he must alter the relationship between the patient's performance in a wide variety of social situations and the reinforcement and punishment which will result. . . . It is possible that many of the symptoms which bring the patient to therapy are largely a by-product of inadequate positively reinforced repertoires; that the disposition to engage in the psychotic, neurotic, and pathological behaviors may seem strong when compared to weak existing repertoires but would disappear as soon as alternative effective ways of dealing with some accessible environment are generated (Ferster, 1958, pp. 105, 117).

This is, indeed, an active conception of therapy. It is based upon the assumption that a patient's behavior, whatever historical factors may have been responsible for its present state, is manipulable through variations in the concurrent controlling environment. And, insofar as it is feasible, it extends therapeutic practice from the therapist's office out into the community of which the patient is a member, the community whose reinforcing practices will eventually pronounce judgment upon the success or failure of the therapy.

Ferster and DeMeyer (1961) have undertaken a detailed analysis of autistic children's performance and have described several kinds of historical circumstances which might have brought about their behavioral deficits. Based on his preliminary classification, which he stated in terms of a functional analysis of operant behavior rather than the usual diagnostic categories, Ferster made an intensive study of the practices which might be effective in developing a behavioral repertoire in the autistic child. In a controlled environment, he used the techniques of shaping, reinforcement schedules, stimulus control, extinction, conditioned reinforcement, and generalized reinforcement. Through these techniques, the children learned to manipulate various automatic devices, starting with a simple electrical switch for which they were reinforced with food. More complex performances were built up gradually, the children finally behaving with great accuracy on a matching-to-sample procedure. Various kinds of reinforcers were used: food, candy, music, an opportunity to play a pinball machine, a picture viewer, etc. Later, coins were established as generalized reinforcers, and the children could use these to operate devices that allowed them to watch cartoons, to get a trained animal to perform, to play with an electric organ, a motor-driven rocking horse, an electric train, or a television set, or to obtain a life jacket and go to the swimming pool. They also learned to save up coins and to use them only when appropriate stimuli indicated that the coins would be effective for "purchasing" something.

After considerable refinement of the techniques, the autistic children exhibited essentially normal behavior in the experimental environment for several hours at a time. Therapy, of course, was far from complete. Outside the controlled environment the children were still autistic, and even within the environment they still had not developed a repertoire of social behavior. It remains to be seen whether operant techniques can accomplish these extensions.

The educated guess has also received some experimental-therapeutic validation in a few other areas. Flanagan, Goldiamond, and Azrin (1958, 1959) were able to control stuttering in chronic stutterers through operant techniques. They succeeded in increasing the frequency of stuttering by permitting the subject to turn off or to avoid a loud tone (105 db.) with each nonfluency; conversely, they also decreased the frequency of stuttering by punishing each nonfluency with the same loud tone. As they point out, stuttering is open to an operant analysis, and the direct operant control of stuttering may be a more profitable line of therapy than attempts to treat it as a by-product of "anxiety." Again, however, there is the problem of generalizing the therapeutic effect from the laboratory to the normal environment.

Ayllon and Michael (1959), analyzing the ward behavior of hospitalized psychiatric patients, concluded that many of the problems these patients presented were the direct result of reinforcement in the hospital setting. They were concerned, not with the behavior that led to the patients' admission to the hospital, but rather with the annoying and disturbing behavior displayed by some patients in the hospital setting and which ". . . may become so persistent that it engages the full energies of the nurses, and postpones, sometimes permanently, any effort on their part to deal with the so-called basic problem,"—such behavior as "failures to eat, dress, bathe, interact socially with other patients and walk without being led, hoarding various objects, hitting, pinching, spitting on other patients, constant attention-seeking actions with respect to the nurses, upsetting chairs in the dayroom, scraping paint from the walls, breaking windows, stuffing paper in the mouth and ears, . . ." (Ayllon and Michael, 1959, p. 323). They instituted a specific program of operant control to reduce the frequency of such disruptive activities, with psychiatric nurses playing the role of "therapists."

By extinguishing the undesirable behavior, for example by refusing to give a patient attention when she habitually entered the nurses' office, or by not reacting in any way to a patient's delusional talk, the nurses were able to reduce the incidence of such behavior to the point where it was no longer troublesome to them in their routine duties. Another technique they used with a violent patient was to reinforce incompatible behavior. Escape and avoidance conditioning were used with two patients who consistently refused to eat unless aided by the nurses. Since both of these patients were extremely concerned with keeping their clothes neat and clean, the nurses instituted the practice of spilling some food on the patients' clothing whenever they insisted on being spoon fed. The patients could avoid this by feeding themselves. In both cases, the program ultimately resulted in complete self-feeding by the patients.

Slack (1960) has applied operant shaping techniques to the problem of introducing hitherto unreachable adolescent delinquents to psychotherapy. By working with the boys not as patients but as experimental subjects, Slack created a situation in which he was able to pay them for participating in the project. But long before any therapeutic relationship could develop, the problem of maintaining reliable contact with the subjects had to be solved. Schwitzgebel (1960) has described the technique that was developed:

> Following the initial contact, the boy may arrive at any time during the day. Whenever he arrives and for whatever reasons, his attendance is immediately reinforced by the sharing of food such as cokes, fruit, or sandwiches. Immediately after his talking into the recorder he is paid in cash. He may then help to build electronic equipment, listen to music, take driving lessons, or participate in other rewarding activities. When his hour or so is up, a time convenient for him is set for the next day. At first the experimenter is not particular about his early or late arrival. Only after attendance becomes dependable is there an attempt to get him to arrive on time. This is done by paying the boy more the nearer he arrives to the correct time or by using unexpected bonuses. Gradually, then, a time more convenient for the experimenter is set. Within 15 to 30 meetings the boys generally arrive very dependably, on time, and at the experimenter's convenience.

The shaping procedure has proved to be efficient in establishing consistent attendance. Subsequently, and at the subjects' own pace, the major source of reinforcement shifts from the salary to the interpersonal relationship that develops between experimenter and subject. The work is still in an early stage, but there are strong indications that once the initial hostility and suspicion are overcome the delinquent is as capable of accepting therapy as is the ordinary middle-class neurotic.

Laboratory testing for behavioral deficit

The educated guess provides, at best, a nonquantitative classification of behavioral pathology. An autistic child, for example, may be a victim of a history of general nonreinforcement; a delusional patient may be a product of too much reinforcement; stuttering may be an instance of reinforcement that has been inappropriately applied. These are all-or-none classifications. This is not to deny their potential value, which is likely to be especially great in the hands of a practitioner who is familiar with operant principles and at the same time has considerable clinical experience. But the techniques of operant conditioning in the laboratory permit a precision of behavioral analysis far greater than the educated guess can provide. There have, therefore, been a number of attempts to correlate behavioral pathology with the patient's performance in relatively well-controlled laboratory settings.

Perhaps the most extensive program of this sort is one that was initiated by Lindsley, Skinner, and Solomon (1956) with hospitalized chronic psychotics. Through long-term testing of the operant behavior of individual patients, they have been attempting to identify syndromes of behavioral deficit, in the hope that such syndromes would define subclasses of psychosis. In the basic technique (Lindsley, 1956), the subjects voluntarily enter a small room. The room contains a panel on one wall, and on the panel are located a plunger the patient can pull and a small aperture through which reinforcements can be delivered. Most of the data thus far have been obtained by reinforcing the patients with candy for pulling the plunger, the reinforcement schedule being a one-minute variable interval.

Approximately 15 per cent of the adult patients refused to enter the room, either initially or after a few days of testing. Shaping eventually brought in several of the most deteriorated members of this group. Only 10 per cent of the patients pulled the plunger at normal rates for this reinforcement schedule—above 800 responses per hour. The remaining 75 per cent of the patients responded at low, irregular rates, with frequent pauses. This initial success in achieving a gross differentiation between psychotic and normal populations, even with such a simple technique, encouraged the investigators to undertake a further analysis of the low response rates characteristic of the psychotic patients.

The first, and perhaps the most striking observation, was that each patient engaged in his characteristic psychotic symptom during the pauses in plunger pulling. "For example, the pacer paced, the hallucinator berated the empty room, the destructive patient tore his clothing, the compulsive patient made patterns out of his candies on the floor, the depressed patient just sat, etc." (Lindsley, unpublished report). This observation suggests that psychotic processes function as competing response systems in the operant testing situation; that the frequency and duration of pauses in the patient's operant performance can be used as an index of the frequency and duration of discrete psychotic episodes or incidents.

Since inadequate reinforcers can also produce low and erratic response rates, the investigators explored a variety of reinforcers with a group of male chronic psychotics: candy, female nude pictures, male nude pictures, five-cent pieces, feeding a hungry kitten, and extinc-

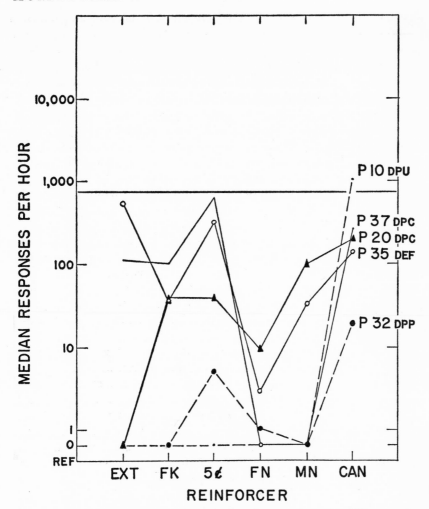

Figure 8. Response rates for five subjects when working for different rein-forcers. *EXT*, no reinforcements; *FK*, feeding a kitten; *5¢*, nickels; *FN*, female nude pictures; *MN*, male nude pictures; *CAN*, candy. [From Linds-ley, Skinner, and Solomon, 1955, *Annual Technical Report 3*.]

tion (no reinforcement). In general, candy emerged as the most ef-fective reinforcer, but the most interesting data with respect to classi-fication were the "motivation profiles" that were constructed for each individual patient. Examples of five such profiles may be seen in Figure 8. Patient P10 responded only for candy; patient P32 responded for candy and for the generalized reinforcer, nickels; all of these patients responded at low rates for female nude pictures, but two of them, patients P20 and P35, responded at higher rates for male nudes—

both of them had been observed engaging in homosexual practices within the hospital; patients P35 and P37 responded at high rates in extinction, when no reinforcement was being provided at all.

Other types of profiles, too, were obtained from the group of patients tested. What we have here is the beginning of a behavioral subclassification, based upon the types of reinforcers that are effective for each individual. Some of the patients show a deficiency in the extent to which their behavior is controlled by generalized reinforcement (nickels), or by specific types of conditioned reinforcers (male or female nude pictures, or feeding a kitten), or by lack of reinforcement (extinction). None of these, by itself, is likely to define a class of psychosis that will be useful to the diagnostician or therapist; but when these profiles can be examined in combination with others for different variables, useful clusters are likely to emerge. The clusters may show little correlation with current schemes of psychiatric diagnosis, but such correlations should not be the goal of behavioral classification. A behavioral classification of behavioral deficit, based upon objective, manipulable variables, will single out those factors to which the therapist must give his attention; again, as with the educated guess, therapeutic success will be the final criterion of the effectiveness of such a classification.

Lindsley has extended the study of the variables relevant to psychotic behavior in a number of directions, and I can do no more than mention some of these. He has studied long-term rhythms in response rate of patients who came to the laboratory almost daily for several years and has correlated these rhythmic variations with psychiatric diagnosis, ratings of ward behavior, drug treatments, social variables, and physical disease. In the analysis of psychosis as a competing response system, vocal hallucinatory symptoms have been recorded and manipulated concurrently with the operant plunger-pulling behavior of the patients. Extensive studies have been made of patients who appeared to be insensitive to extinction; that is to say, who never stopped responding after reinforcement was discontinued. The mode of adjustment of several patients was studied when the reinforcement schedule was changed from variable interval to fixed ratio. Drugs and other types of therapy were evaluated with respect to their effects upon the patients' performance in the operant situation.

Extensive as these investigations have been, they are as yet only a beginning. They do little more than suggest that a purely behavioral classification of psychosis is possible, and indicate some of the lines an attempt at such classification may follow. More extensive sampling of the psychotic population is still required, not for statistical purposes but to ensure evaluation of all possible varieties of the illness; more extensive investigation of behavioral variables must be undertaken in order to ensure that all possible avenues of behavioral control are included in each patient's profile; and when a workable classification begins to emerge, therapeutic validation must be attempted.

Some initial applications of operant techniques to the problem of classification have been made with populations other than the chronic psychotic adult. Lindsley has demonstrated the applicability of the techniques to psychotic children (Lindsley, Skinner, and Solomon, 1956). Orlando and Bijou (1960) have shown that simple and multiple reinforcement schedules can maintain the behavior of retarded children, and they suggest that these behavioral baselines are well suited to the study of discrimination, generalization, and motivation in such children. Ellis, Barnett, and Pryer (1960) have made similar observations, even with retardates of a type usually labeled "untestable," and have, in addition, found a positive relation between response rates and mental age in retarded children. They also noted that the performance of severely defective children was characterized by frequent pauses, similar to those found in Lindsley with adult psychotics. This observation underscores the need for more detailed profiles for each patient; a single indicator may suggest pathology but is not likely to differentiate subclasses of pathology.

Laboratory testing of specific behavioral variables

Lindsley has pointed out that psychotics are not always psychotic: "Psychosis, defined in terms of the behavior that hospitalizes a person, is most often highly infrequent" (Lindsley, 1960, p. 3). Similarly, clinical neurologists are well aware that behavioral deficits or abnormalities are highly variable in a given patient, sometimes showing up in one examination and then being absent in an examination at a different time. Such observations require that we look more closely at the concept of "deficit." If the patient sometimes has a particular response or set of responses, and sometimes does not, in what is he deficient?

It is highly likely that the deficiency exists not in the patient's behavior but in some variable or set variables that controls the behavior. If we do not recognize the different variables that may control a given response, we may easily fail to recognize differences in our behavioral tests. In one situation we may try to elicit the behavior by applying the variable whose control is defective; in another situation we may apply a variable whose control is intact and the behavior may appear where it was previously absent. This is surprising to us only so long as we do not have an adequate classification of the relevant variables. A second type of laboratory test of operant behavior, then, will look not for behavioral deficit but for unusual functional relations between behavior and its controlling variables.

In his analysis of verbal behavior, Skinner (1957) has outlined a number of classes of relation that may exist between verbal responses and their controlling variables. Even though the *form* of a verbal response may be the same on different occasions, it cannot be treated as the same operant if it is determined by different factors. Hughlings Jackson (1958) made a rough distinction of a similar sort when he differentiated between two kinds of speech, emotional and propositional: patients with motor aphasia who were unable to say voluntarily more than a few words could nevertheless swear exceedingly well; or an aphasic who could say almost anything "by accident" could not say the same thing when he wished. Skinner's classification goes into considerably more detail, and only a brief summary can be given here of some of the types of functional relations he describes.

Take, for example, the vocal response, "water." One form of this response may be largely controlled by a person's state of water deprivation; if he is unable to emit the operant, "water," when thirsty, we may assume that the control of deprivation is deficient. A different type of control is involved when we show the person some water and ask him to name it. The naming of objects is largely under stimulus control, and the consequences of such behavior are often of more immediate benefit to the listener than to the speaker. A patient in whom the functional relation between deprivation and the response, water, is intact, may nevertheless show a deficiency in stimulus control and be unable to identify water on demand. Still other types of behavioral control are involved when a person is asked to echo the response, water, after it has been pronounced by someone else, or to read it aloud from a text. But because textual and echoic responses have usually been strongly conditioned—they are among the earliest forms of control established in the child—these functional relations may remain intact when at the same time the patient may be unable to fill in the blank in the statement, "The boat hit an iceberg and rapidly filled with ——." The response in this instance is under the control of other verbal responses, and such intraverbal control, usually less strongly conditioned than textual or echoic control, may be deficient.

As Skinner points out, this ". . . is not a classification of forms of response, since we cannot tell from form alone into which class a response falls. . . . In order to classify behavior effectively, we must know the circumstances under which it is emitted" (Skinner, 1957, p. 186). There have as yet been no definitive tests of Skinner's classification of verbal behavior, but with the experimental material already at hand in the form of a large aphasic population, we may look forward to the increasing application of operant techniques and principles to the pathology of verbal behavior.

There has, however, been a small beginning made in a similar direction with respect to nonverbal operant behavior. Stoddard, Sidman, and Brady (1960), working with acute psychotics in a military hospital, have been attempting to identify the lines along which behavioral control has fractured in these patients. The variable upon which they have concentrated thus far has been reinforcement frequency. They used a complex procedure consisting of the following elements: The subjects had two plungers available, and obtained token reinforcements for pulling one of them (the reinforced response). The basic token-reinforcement schedule was a multiple fixed interval, fixed ratio. When the subjects were working on the interval schedule, however, the length of the interval doubled after they received each token; similarly, when they were working on the ratio schedule, the number of times they had to respond to obtain a token doubled each time they received one. Thus, the reinforcement frequency on each schedule decreased whenever the subject obtained a token.

By pulling the second plunger (the switching response), the subject could change the schedule from interval to ratio or *vice versa*, and when the schedule changed, the progressively increasing sequence began anew at the lowest interval or ratio value. The likelihood that the subjects would switch from one schedule to the other was manipulated by placing the switching response on a ratio schedule. A fixed number of switching responses was therefore required before the subject could change the schedule and return the reinforcement frequency to its highest level.

When a large number of responses was required to switch the schedule, the subjects could maximize the reinforcement frequency by switching less often. For example, if the subject had to respond 88 times to change the schedule from fixed ratio to fixed interval, it would not be very efficient for him to switch when he could obtain the next token after only 11 responses. He could obtain more tokens in a shorter period of time if he postponed the changeover until the ratio schedule for the reinforced response was more nearly equal to the ratio schedule for the switching response. On the other hand, if only 11 responses were required to change the schedule, the subject could increase the frequency of reinforcement by switching more often.

The nonhospitalized subjects and several of the patients were found to adjust their behavior in such a way that they maximized the frequency of reinforcement each time the switching requirement was increased. The behavior of several patients, however, was not under the control of reinforcement frequency; as the number of responses required to change the schedule increased, they failed to adjust their switching behavior in such a way as to keep reinforcement frequency at its highest possible level. Their efficiency curves, measured in terms of reinforcement frequency, declined as the switching requirement increased.

Here was a clear indication that a basic variable was not controlling the behavior of some of the patients in a manner consistent with normal behavioral control. Interestingly enough, these patients were assigned the least favorable psychiatric prognosis—arrived at independently of the experimental findings—at the end of their treatment period. But again, it is unreasonable to expect an adequate classification on the basis of one variable alone. We can anticipate not only that some patients will be controlled normally by reinforcement frequency but that some otherwise efficiently functioning people will exhibit abnormal control. Techniques will have to be developed for checking other basic variables, both singly and in interaction with each other, and any valid classification will have to be based upon complete profiles of behavioral control. Again, too, the classifications are not likely to conform closely to current psychiatric categories. The ultimate validating step will come from therapeutic attempts to restore the normal functional relations between a patient's behavior and those variables whose control has been found to be deficient.

References

Ader, R., & Tatum, R. Free-operant avoidance conditioning in human subjects. *J. exper. anal. Behav.*, 1961, 3, 275–276.

Ayllon, T., & Michael, J. The psychiatric nurse as a behavioral engineer. *J. exper. anal. Behav.*, 1959, 2, 323–334.

Azrin, N. H. Some effects of two intermittent schedules of immediate and non-immediate punishment. *J. Psychol.*, 1956, 42, 3–21.

Azrin, N. H. Some effects of noise on human behavior. *J. exper. anal. Behav.*, 1958, 1, 183–200.

Azrin, N. H. Punishment and recovery during fixed-ratio performance. *J. exper. anal. Behav.*, 1959, 2, 301–305.

Azrin, N. H. Effects of punishment intensity during variable-interval reinforcement. *J. exper. anal. Behav.*, 1960a, 3, 123–142.

Azrin, N. H. Use of rests as reinforcers. *Psychol. Rep.*, 1960b, 7, 240.

Baer, D. M. Escape and avoidance response of pre-school children to two schedules of reinforcement withdrawal. *J. exper. anal. Behav.*, 1960, 2, 155–159.

Bijou, S. W., & Sturges, P. T. Positive reinforcers for experimental studies with children—consumables and manipulatables. *Child Develpm.*, 1959, 30, 151–170.

Dews, P. B., & Morse, W. H. Some observations on an operant in human subjects and its modification by dextro amphetamine. *J. exper. anal. Behav.*, 1958, 1, 359–364.

Dinsmoor, J. A. Shock intensity in variable-interval escape schedules. *J. exper. anal. Behav.*, 1958, 1, 145–148.

Ellis, N. R., Barnett, C. D., & Pryer, M. W. Operant behavior in mental defectives: exploratory studies. *J. exper. anal. Behav.*, 1960, 3, 63–69.

Estes, W. K. An experimental study of punishment. *Psychol. Monogr.*, 1944, 57, 1–40, No. 263.

Estes, W. K., & Skinner, B. F. Some

quantitative properties of anxiety. *J. exper. Psychol.*, 1941, *29*, 390–400.

Ferster, C. B. Reinforcement and punishment in the control of human behavior by social agencies. *Psychiat. Res. Repts.*, 1958, *10*, 101–118.

Ferster, C. B. Positive reinforcement and behavioral deficits of autistic children. *Child Developm.*, 1961, *32*, 437–456.

Ferster, C. B., & DeMeyer, M. K. A method for the experimental analysis of the behavior of autistic children. *Am. J. Orthopsychiat.*, 1961. In press.

Ferster, C. B., & Skinner, B. F. *Schedules of reinforcement.* New York: Appleton-Century-Crofts, 1957.

Flanagan, B., Goldiamond, I., & Azrin, N. Operant stuttering: the control of stuttering behavior through response-contingent consequences. *J. exper. anal. Behav.*, 1958, *1*, 173–177.

Flanagan, B., Goldiamond, I., & Azrin, N. H. Instatement of stuttering in normally fluent individuals through operant procedures. *Science*, 1959, *130*, 979–981.

Guttman, N., & Kalish, H. I., Discriminability and stimulus generalization. *J. exper. Psychol.*, 1956, *51*, 79–88.

Hearst, E. Simultaneous generalization gradients for appetitive and aversive behavior. *Science*, 1960, *132*, 1769–1770.

Hefferline, R. F., Keenan, B., & Harford, R. A. Escape and avoidance conditioning in human subjects without their observation of the response. *Science*, 1959, *130*, 1338–1339.

Herrnstein, R. J., & Sidman, M. Avoidance conditioning as a factor in the effects of unavoidable shocks on food-reinforced behavior. *J. comp. physiol. Psychol.*, 1958, *51*, 380–385.

Holland, J. G. Human vigilance. *Science*, 1958, *128*, 61–67.

Jackson, J. H. Notes on the physiology and pathology of language. In J. Taylor (Ed.), *Selected writings of John Hughlings Jackson, Vol. 2.* New York: Basic Books, 1958, 121–128.

Kaplan, M. The maintenance of escape behavior under fixed-ratio reinforcement. *J. comp. physiol. Psychol.*, 1956, *49*, 153–157.

Lane, H. Temporal and intensive properties of human vocal responding under a schedule of reinforcement. *J. exper. anal. Behav.*, 1960, *3*, 183–192.

Lindsley, O. R. Operant conditioning methods applied to research in chronic schizophrenia. *Psychiat. Res. Repts.*, 1956, *5*, 118–139.

Lindsley, O. R. Operant behavior during sleep: a measure of depth of sleep. *Science*, 1957, *126*, 1290–1291.

Lindsley, O. R. Characteristics of the behavior of chronic psychotics as revealed by free-operant conditioning methods. *Dis. nerv. System, Monogr. Suppl.*, 1960, *21*, 66–78.

Lindsley, O. R., Skinner, B. F., & Solomon, H. C. Periodic project reports, Metropolitan State Hospital, Waltham, Mass. June 1953–Aug. 1956. Microcard No. FO-57-524-527, L. C. No. MicP 57-30.

Lindsley, O. R., Skinner, B. F., & Solomon, H. C. Annual Technical Report 3, Sept. 1955–Nov. 1956.

Long, E. R., Hammack, J. T., May, F., & Campbell, B. J. Intermittent reinforcement of operant behavior in children. *J. exper. anal. Behav.*, 1958, *1*, 315–339.

Miller, N. E. Experimental studies of conflict. In J. McV. Hunt (Ed.), *Personality and the behavior disorders.* New York: Ronald, 1944.

Miller, N. E. Theory and experiment relating psychoanalytic displacement to stimulus–response generalization. *J. abnorm. soc. Psychol.*, 1948, *43*, 155–178.

Morse, W. H., & Herrnstein, R. J. The maintenance of avoidance behavior using the removal of a conditioned positive reinforcer as the aversive stimulus. *Am. Psychologist*, 1956, *11*, 430. Abstract.

Morse, W. H., & Skinner, B. F. A second type of superstition in the pigeon. *Am. J. Psychol.*, 1957, *70*, 308–311.

Orlando, R., & Bijou, S. W. Single and multiple schedules of reinforcement in developmentally retarded children. *J. exper. anal. Behav.*, 1960, *3*, 339–348.

Schwitzgebel, R. A new approach to understanding delinquency. *Fed. Probation*, March, 1960, 5 pp.

Sidman, M. Two temporal parameters of the maintenance of avoidance behavior by the white rat. *J. comp. physiol. Psychol.*, 1953, *46*, 253–261.

Sidman, M. Time discrimination and behavioral interaction in a free operant situation. *J. comp. physiol. Psychol.*, 1956, *49*, 469–473.

Sidman, M. By-products of aversive control, *J. exper. anal. Behav.*, 1958, *1*, 265–280.

Sidman, M. Normal sources of pathological behavior. *Science*, 1960a, *132*, 61–68.

Sidman, M. *Tactics of scientific research: evaluating experimental data in psychology.* New York: Basic Books, 1960b.

Sidman, M. Stimulus generalization in an avoidance situation. *J. exper. anal. Behav.*, 1961, *4*, 157–169.

Skinner, B. F. *The behavior of organisms: an experimental analysis.* New York: Appleton-Century-Crofts, 1938.

Skinner, B. F. "Superstition" in the pigeon. *J. exp. Psychol.*, 1948, *38*, 168–172.

Skinner, B. F. *Science and human behavior.* New York: Macmillan, 1953.

Skinner, B. F. *Verbal behavior.* New York: Appleton-Century-Crofts, 1957.

Slack, C. W. Experimenter-subject psychotherapy: a new method of introducing intensive office treatment for unreachable cases. *Ment. Hygiene,* 1960, *44*, 238–256.

Slack, C. W., & Schwitzgebel, R. A handbook: reducing adolescent crime in your community. Privately printed.

Stoddard, L. T., Sidman, M., & Brady, J. V. Conditioning and maintenance of human behavior by multiple schedules of intermittent reinforcement. Paper delivered at Eastern Psychological Association Convention, New York, 1960a.

Stoddard, L. T., Sidman, M., & Brady, J. V. Reinforcement frequency as a factor in the control of normal and psychotic behavior. Paper delivered at Psychonomic Society Meetings, Chicago, 1960b.

Wilson, M. P., & Keller, F. S. On the selective reinforcement of spaced responding. *J. comp. physiol. Psychol.,* 1953, *46*, 190–193.

7

Small Group Research

LUIGI PETRULLO

This chapter is an attempt to bring some of the experimental literature on small groups out from the back of the stage where it is seen only by the specialized student and hold it up to the view of the clinical psychologist. It directs itself to research on questions and issues which may have relevance to, and may serve as background for, clinical practice. It is not a review of the whole group behavior field, for that is too large for a single chapter to cover with any degree of satisfaction for anyone. In addition, very excellent reviews of segments of the field do exist and these will be cited and discussed.

The small group can be viewed as the mediator between the inner cognitive man and the external world of objects, relations, and people. It facilitates the exchange and flow of information which the individual needs in order to shape his life—and to gain insight into the very nature of his *self*. It is the vehicle which transmits potential knowledge about the two important aspects of life—love and work; love which springs from the individual, and work which is demanded by society.

The clinical psychologist can also use the small group to gain information and insight into the self, not only the self of his client but also his own. This he gains through observation and analysis of persons in a variety of situations and group settings, some of which he contrives himself. When in interaction with his client, he observes himself and the other in both real and imagined settings. Quite often, he finds himself an actor in the same group with his patient. He need not be a scientist to influence the behavior of the other person; many seem to do this in ways we call intuitive. Nevertheless, on top of this aptitude, if aptitude it is, or warmth or empathy as some have held, he needs to develop skills, understanding, and practical techniques. These cannot be little tricks that work for the moment, nor should they be of a hit-or-miss type. On the contrary, they must be embedded in a context of basic psychological and cultural processes so as to ensure proper and long-range beneficial effects. He must also be aware of the dangers and limitations of his skills and techniques and know how and when to use them. Because at present there are no mechanical short cuts to diagnosis and treatment (psychological tests in the hands of inexpert people are unquestionably harmful) clinical methods must rely upon training, experience, and constant reference to the contemporary body of research.

The psychologist and the client form a small group, and the relationship within this small community may help the course of treatment if handled skillfully, or it may hinder progress. For example, the patient's reciprocal perception of the therapist can hinder or assist therapy; it is wise to know something about this reciprocal process and the conditions under which it operates, as well as the direction it may take.

Following World War I, experimental psychology became much more concerned with the social behavior of man than it had been previously. An increasing number of social facilitation experiments were being performed; the existence of the "group" mind was a popular subject of controversy; and much research was done comparing the productivity of individuals and groups. Social factor variables were used more and more in experimental studies of such subjects as learning, motivation, leadership, and memory.

But social man was not an easy subject to study in the laboratory. New research models and equipment were needed; new methods of research design and analysis had to be developed. The ideal laboratory man, deprived of contact with all inner and outer forces except those the experimenter wished to study, did not exist. Man was an interacting, dynamic force who never remained still long enough to be observed, recorded, and analyzed. He changed while he was being observed. As the social facilitation experiments implied, he changed perhaps as a result of being observed. He even seemed to influence the "objective" experimenter who was observing him. The subject of research perceived the experimenter and often manipulated him in more subtle ways than he himself was being manipulated. Upon careful thought, the situation in the laboratory often seemed no different than in the outer world of reality where students influenced their teachers, followers their leaders, and patients their doctors, perhaps as much as they were themselves influenced. To try to rule out these effects, some experimenters moved further and further from real life and invented new kinds of simple laboratory life for study. While this produced quantitative results, it did not produce much knowledge about social behavior. Gradually, the need to study man in interaction with other men—as he behaved in the external world—became very strong. In his search for methods to study social man in the laboratory, the psychologist discovered experimental group psychology.

While psychology was struggling to bring social man into the laboratory, social scientists were looking for ways to study culture and society in a more objective way. Governments, institutions, cultures could be observed and talked about, but more than just observation and speculation was needed; systematic observations and analyses of social behavior were required. The small group seemed more accessible to such study and began to be seen as a natural bridge between the individual man and the large national or cultural group. Comte, Durkheim, Cooley, and others saw in the small primary group—the family, the work group, the military group, the classroom group—a new significance. These natural, face-to-face groups seemed to carry with them the history of mankind, and if they could be understood, perhaps cultures and societies could be better understood. Field experimental methods came into being even while opinions about classifications of groups were discussed. By the time psychology had developed its experimental laboratory methods for studying social behavior, social scientists had improved the method of field experimentation enough to make possible a series of rich studies.

The turn of the century was not only a time of great speculation and invention, it was also a time of action. How to modify the behavior of others as well as one's own was an end pursued by many in a variety of disciplines. Educators faced with an increasing population eager for knowledge searched for methods to make the teacher more effective. Psychiatrists saw hope that deviant behavior might be normalized by some kind of influence technique. In its search for more efficient methods of production, industry became concerned with methods for restructuring situations and work groups. Military methods of training and fighting were being found outdated and new ideas were sought. Politics, business, religion—there was no field that did not seek methods to influence others. Where large groups were difficult to handle and keep in existence for any length of time, and where man-to-man persuasion was too time consuming, the small group seemed to be a readily accessible unit that involved the masses of people.

Thus by 1920, history had discovered in the small group a means for studying not only natural groups but the individual personality as well as societies and cultures;* furthermore, the desire to use the

---

* Today, this seems to be taken for granted. Thus, Gordon W. Allport, in his preface to a volume of Lewin's essays (1948), states that "the group to which an individual belongs is the ground for his perceptions, his feelings, and his actions"

small group for various practical ends grew greater. Experimental research activity on group behavior likewise grew, and today there exists a large body of writing as an indication of the wide interest in the subject. Because of its comparatively late start, experimental research is just beginning to contribute to adequate theories of group behavior.

There are two large categories of experimental work—field oriented and laboratory oriented. This is evidenced, for example, in a symposium on social psychology held at the University of Chicago in 1947. The volume which resulted was called *Experiments in Social Process* (Miller, 1950). In it were included two important reports on small group work: the role of group belongingness, by Leon Festinger; and changing group productivity, by John R. P. French, Jr. The first was a laboratory type experiment and the other a field type experiment. In 1950 also appeared two other books which illustrated laboratory and field experimental approaches involved in theory building—Bales' *Interaction Process Analysis*, and Homans' *The Human Group*, to be discussed later. This interest in both kinds of experiment is characteristic of present-day research on small groups. Festinger's statement (1950) concerning this is worth quoting:

> The controlled laboratory experiment is *not* an attempt to duplicate in miniature, a real-life situation. It is rather an attempt to set up the pure case. In other words, it is an attempt to take a factor or cluster of factors which we have good reason to believe are important and systematically vary them in a context where other factors are well controlled. By such means we may begin to build up a body of knowledge concerning the precise functional relationships between these factors and the behavior of human beings in social situations.
>
> The laboratory experiment can give us the empirical laws of behavior. It does not immediately tell us how to apply these laws to the real-life situation. To permit application we must proceed to the diagnosis and measurement of factors which operate in real-life situations, and to the determination of which laws do and to not apply. We must, however, know the laws before we can apply them (p. 34).

The laboratory experiment is not, of course, the only avenue to the development of empirical laws of behavior. As Homans (1950), follow-

---

(p. vii). Similarly Faris (1953), a sociologist, states: ". . . the small intimate group . . . is the center of concern in the study of personality" (p. 155). Schutz (1961) takes a very intriguing position when he states: "The parallel existing between ego and leader is expressed by the general proposition: *a person is a group and a group is a person.* (The word 'is' is used in the sense of 'follows the same laws as.')" He then presents persuasive evidence that the small group presents unique opportunity for studying the individual. Hare, Borgatta and Bales (1955) support the view that small group study furnishes a method for studying personality, social systems, and culture.

ing the logico-experimental method developed so painstakingly by V. Pareto, demonstrated in his analysis of five studies of natural groups, field experiments can be so designed as to lead to the development of fruitful hypotheses which can be cross-validated on other groups, as well as added to. The hypotheses can in time lead to generalized concepts and finally to theory.

It would seem that these two kinds of research reflect the sociological tradition on the one hand and the psychological tradition on the other. Somewhere in the middle there would seem to be the third tradition which is action oriented in the spirit of psychiatry, training, and education. This third group includes sociodrama, psychodrama, *National Training Laboratory* Training Groups, therapeutic communities, and various other kinds of training and therapeutic groups. The interesting thing about all of these approaches is that they seem to come together in the study of the small group. The sociologist is really interested in studying institutions, cultures, and societies in general, but in order to learn about them he has had recourse to study of the small group which is the smallest unit of social behavior that can be studied. The psychologist, on the other hand, has been concerned with the behavior of the individual, but in studying the individual it has been necessary for him to determine the influence that the other individuals have on him. This means again that the small group must be studied in order to understand the individual. The therapist and the trainer have been interested in the small group because of their interest in problems of motivation as well as in techniques to modify behavior. The small group is something very manageable, whereas large cultures and institutions can not be observed for their immediate effects on changing the behavior of an individual. On the other hand, the individual cannot be considered as an isolated unit. Even where the trainer or the therapist works with a single subject there is still the effect of the teacher or trainer on the student or patient, as well as prior and outside experience. The two-person influence group and the multiperson natural group must be understood if therapy or instruction is to be maximally effective.

The need for consideration of a variety of variables in the correlation of social psychological variables with mental health and mental illness is indicated by a review of studies on these correlates by Scott (1958). Scott reviewed and summarized the literature which deals with such correlates of mental health and mental illness as demographic and environmental factors (urban-rural differences, socioeconomic factors, ethnic differences, and intracity differences), and interpersonal factors (group cohesiveness, social isolation, group involvement, etc.). Even though his survey failed to disclose generalizations across studies because of differing concepts of mental health and for other reasons, the review is useful for its content, and for its caution about the need for considering a multitude of important determiners necessary in clinical judgments. In this area, validation and criterion problems are very much with us.

Since there are a number of bibliographies, reviews, and texts on small group research, and since several excellent attempts at integration of various aspects of small group behavior have been made, it would be expedient to review these and then proceed with an analysis of what today is considered the most important aspect of the small group process, namely, interaction. The plan of this section, then, is to cite some primary sources of information about experimental work on small groups to which the clinical psychologist can go for more detailed information, then to discuss some of the more pertinent and major results, and finally to indicate what trends and implications can be derived from past and current work.

Until the 1950–1960 decade opened, the primary sources which reported on small group research were a number of social psychology textbooks written by psychologists and sociologists. To be sure, much had been written about small groups before this time, but much of it was speculative and not experimental, and the experimental studies existed in scattered journals. Allport (1924), Dashiell (1935), and Murphy, Murphy, and Newcomb (1937) may be mentioned among the early experimenters who brought together much of this scattered literature. The first two textbooks in social psychology reflected the psychological concern on the one hand (McDougall, 1908, with emphasis on motivation) and the sociological on the other hand (Ross, 1908, with emphasis on interaction). Several sources which can be consulted for the philosophical and sociological background of events leading to the experimental study of small groups are Wilson (1945), Churchman and Ackoff (1950), Shils (1951), and Faris (1953).

The period before 1930 was dominated, in so far as small group research was concerned, by a controversy over the existence of the "group mind" (e.g., McDougall, 1920; Allport, 1924); by the entrance of psychoanalytic thinking into American psychology with overtones for group psychology (Freud, 1922); by Frederic Thrasher's classic study of the Chicago boys' gang which presented a systematic study of the informal organization of a small group (Thrasher, 1927); by the Hawthorne studies in 1927–1932 which were to be written up later and which served as models for many field industrial studies (see Roethlisberger, Dickson and Wright, 1939).

Interest in small groups picked up markedly in the nineteen thirties. In 1934 Moreno published *Who Shall Survive?* and introduced the sociometric technique which is today an indispensable part of much small group research (see Jennings, 1950; Moreno, 1956; Criswell, 1961). Sherif during this period was busy both with field type studies and with laboratory work which substantiated his results on the development of social norms (Sherif, 1935, 1936, 1956). Influenced by both the Gestalt movement in psychology and by anthropology and sociology, Sherif held that culture and the particular environmental factors had significant effect on the nature of perception. The individual, the group, and the culture had to be studied not separately, but as a unit. In 1935, Sherif published the results of an important experiment on apparent movement as reported by individuals and by groups. The well known autokinetic effect—the apparent movement of a single small light in complete darkness—provided the start. When individuals were tested alone, each reported movement and "subjectively established a range of extent (a scale) and a point (a standard or norm) within that range which is peculiar to the individual" (Sherif and Sherif, 1956, p. 253). When individuals were put in groups, however, they began to develop new norms which were the product of the convergence of different members' opinions. Again, each group developed its own peculiar norms. These results in the laboratory, added to by Sherif and some of his collaborators (Rohrer, 1951; Sherif and Harvey, 1952) have their counterpart in field experiments carried out by Sherif in boys' camps and villages (Sherif and Sherif, 1953, 1956) as well as studies by Thrasher (1927), Whyte (1943), and Newcomb (1943).

Newcomb's four year study, started at Bennington College in 1935 (Newcomb, 1943), employed considerable psychological ingenuity and sociological sophistication to unravel the social and psychological factors which are involved in attitude change. Newcomb found that, on the one hand, such factors as intelligence and motivation to achieve freedom from parental authority seemed to prepare and dispose the individual to be receptive to outside influences; on the other hand, the cultural milieu, the kind of faculty and intellectual opportunity, family setting, reference groups, and norms, were likewise indispensable in making possible such change. Newcomb in his later work has consistently held to this position that the study of the development of the individual must involve at all stages both psychological and social factors, that separating the fundamental unit of behavior—the interaction unit—leads to artificiality and little progress.

In the 1930's there appeared another powerful figure who was to have the greatest influence on the development of group psychology. Kurt Lewin, who had already firmly established for himself a reputation in experimental psychology, had upon emigration to this country concerned himself with the application of psychological principles and methods to the study of social action problems. Lewin was a thorough experimenter and he must have been an inspiring and enthusiastic teacher, for he and his students (Lewin died in 1947 just as the group psychology movement was beginning to gather momentum) have done a great deal to show how necessary the analysis of social interaction is to the development of psychology as a science (See Lewin, 1948, 1951, 1959; Deutsch, 1954; Cartwright, 1958).

World War II saw an intensification of work directed at social action programs. Notable among them may be mentioned Lewin's work on such programs as changing attitudes toward food habits (with Radke, Mead, Festinger, and others), and increasing industrial productivity through participative techniques (with French); the work of Stouffer and his colleagues on the American Soldier (1950); the OSS studies which introduced situational tests as predictive instruments (1948); and the Ohio State leadership studies started in 1944 (Shartle, 1956). By the end of the war, a number of research programs were being generated which were to have important consequences for small group research. For example, the Lewinian work, continued at MIT in 1944 with the establishment of a group dynamics laboratory there, moved to the University of Michigan in 1947, where R. Likert had started a social science institute devoted to a large extent to survey research (Cartwright, 1958). The Michigan Laboratory was one of the first of perhaps more than thirty major laboratories which exist today which are concentrating their energies on the study of small groups and organizations.

Readings in Social Psychology (Newcomb and Hartley, 1947; Swanson, Newcomb, and Hartley, 1952; Maccoby, Newcomb, and Hartley, 1958) represents a series of volumes which have included an increasing number of small group reports—as has the *Annual Review of Psychology*, which started publication in 1950.

In 1951 a great deal of the experimental research on small groups which had been sponsored by the Office of Naval Research, was brought together in one volume (Guetzkow, 1951). The topics included were: Cattell's work on syntality, a concept referring to the "personality" of the group; work on communication in small groups by Festinger; research on small group productivity by French; the decision-making conference by Marquis, Guetzkow, and Heyns; projects on human relations problems by Katz, Kahn, Jacobson, Morse, and Campbell; Margaret Mead's work on contemporary cultures; leadership studies by Shartle, Stogdill, Carter, and Sanford; and a series of studies on individual behaviors in group context—Asch's conformity work, McClelland's work on the achievement motive, Cofer's work on verbal behavior, Swanson's report on mass communication effects, and two therapy oriented projects by Harris on the tuberculous and Hunt on neuropsychiatric screening procedures. Darley, Macmillan, and Page summarized, critically evaluated the work, and cited possible applications.

This important volume was followed by a major attempt to integrate research and findings in group dynamics by Cartwright and Zander in 1953. This book not only brought together in one place a number of the most important writing on small groups but developed generalizations and trends resulting from analysis of the related parts of the research. This volume was revised and brought up to date in 1960.

In their revision, Cartwright and Zander (1960) have expanded the scope of the group dynamics area to include group cohesiveness, group pressures, group standards, goals, leadership, the structure of groups and motives—"the field of inquiry dedicated to advancing knowledge about the nature of group life" (p. 5). For Lewin (1948), such a study also meant the study of changes in individual behavior brought about by changes in group structure. This latter aspect of Lewin's work has sometimes been emphasized in such work as that conducted by the National Training Laboratories in training individuals in group techniques such as conference management, role playing for problem solving purposes, group decision, etc. But group dynamics should be considered in its broader sense and not as a cluster of techniques; as such the field has made many contributions to the experimental foundations of clinical psychology.

In 1953 also appeared Roseborough's review of 169 publications of experimental studies on small groups (less than thirty of which had been published before 1940). This review excluded theoretical and interpretive articles and studies on social facilitation and it included studies which provided "the possibility of intragroup communication." Studies were classified in terms of *independent variables* specified and discussed under five headings: (1) studies contrasting individual and group behavior; (2) studies involving manipulation of social structure variables; (3) studies of effect of culture variables; (4) studies involving manipulation of situation variables; (5) studies of personality variables.

Strodtbeck and Hare's (1954) bibliography of small group research covering the period 1900–1953 provided additional historical perspective. This bibliography listed "research reports which place emphasis on the nature and consequences of face to face interaction in small groups." Indicative of the tremendous growth of interest are the figures which show almost as many articles written in the 1950–1953 period (610) as in the entire period preceding 1950 (787).

In 1954, G. Lindzey edited the *Handbook of Social Psychology* (quite different from the *Handbook of Social Psychology* edited by Murchison in 1935) which included a number of very fine chapters on a variety of subjects relevant to small group research. This was followed in 1955 by the first comprehensive book devoted to all aspects of research on small groups, *Small Groups* by Hare, Borgatta, and Bales. This consisted of many of the most important reprints of writings on small groups, abstracts of almost six hundred others, and commentaries by the editors.

In 1957, McGrath reported on the beginning of an ambitious study devoted to an integration of the small group literature. The second product in this series was a bibliography of 2200 titles in 1960 (Terauds, Altman, and McGrath). New publications aimed at the further development of a system for the organization of knowledge in this field are expected from this source. In 1959, Raven published a bibliography of 1445 titles with author and subject indexes, and a punched card method for keeping the bibliography current. This perhaps represents a straw in the wind indicative of the need of information storage and retrieval methods so necessary in scientific areas where data are accumulating at such a tremendous rate.

In addition to the above, a number of systematic attempts have been made at integration and theory building. G. C. Homans' book on the *Human Group* (1950) represents one of the best sociological attempts.

Homans (1950) analyzed five studies of groups which had been completed by various investigators (the "bank wiring observation room" from the Western Electric studies; Hilltown by D. L. Hatch; the Norton St. Gang by W. F. Whyte; R. Firth's Tikopia; and the electrical equipment study by C. M. Arensberg and D. MacGregor) in terms of four interdependent variables called interaction, sentiment, activities, and norms in a context of structure, process, and function, and within the constraints of the internal and external systems of the group. These are elaborated upon as a result of the analysis, and a system of hypotheses developed and cross checked. At the time of publication, Robert Merton called this the most important contribution to the sociological theory of small groups since Simmel's work a half century before. The importance of the study was in the system of hypotheses developed and in their careful check from group to group for pertinent generalizations. The following quotation illustrates the manner in which Homans was able to bring together a large number of relationships in a succinct manner.

We have seen that the more frequent the interaction between people, the stronger in general their sentiments of liking or affection for one another. But in the interaction between people we have also seen that, as one person gives orders that another must obey, the interaction between them tends to decrease toward the amount required by the external system—interaction is largely "on business"—and the emotional attitude of the subordinate toward the superior tends to be one of respect rather than close friendship. The relationship between a given leader and his follower will be determined by both of these hypotheses. To the extent that the two merely interact with one another, sentiments of affection will grow up between them, and their interaction will increase "socially" beyond the amount required by the external system. To the extent that one gives orders that the other must obey, social interaction will be held down, and sentiment will move in the direction of respect or at worst, antagonism (p. 444).

Several other important integrative attempts have been made since Homans developed his. Among the most important are the following: Josephine Klein, *The Study of Groups* (1956); M. S. Olmsted, *The Small Group* (1959); J. W. Thibaut and H. H. Kelley, *The Social Psychology of Groups* (1959); F. Heider, *The Psychology of Interpersonal Relations* (1958); B. Bass, *Leadership, Psychology, and Organizational Behavior* (1960); D. Stock and H. A. Thelen, *Emotional Dynamics and Group Culture* (1958); W. C. Schutz, *FIRO: A Three-Dimensional Theory of Interpersonal Behavior* (1958); T. Parsons, R. F. Bales, and E. A. Shils, *Working Papers in The Theory of Action* (1953); R. Tagiuri and L. Petrullo, (Eds.), *Person Perception and Interpersonal Behavior* (1958); L. Petrullo and B. M. Bass (Eds.), *Leadership and Interpersonal Behavior* (1961). In addition, there have been important textbooks in social psychology such as M. Sherif and C. Sherif (*An Outline of Social Psychology*, 1956, 2nd edition) which include major attempts at integration of small group research. Some of these will be discussed more fully in the following section on the interaction process.

THE INTERACTION PROCESS

The three primary streams from which small group research has acquired its objectives, methods, and impetus have today contributed heavily to the new stream known as group interaction. The psychological inheritance which stressed the study of the personality of the individual has been modified by the sociological tradition of looking at the whole picture of culture and by the action-oriented disciplines with their emphasis on change of the person as well as change of societies. T. M. Newcomb (1959), in narrating the history of his career, gives us a beautiful illustration of how this process has influenced a person in the development of a theory.

The quarrels of McDougall and Floyd H. Allport (in which both sides eventually gave ground) concerning the existence of a group mind, have given way to a new dynamic and interactive point of view as represented by such men as Kurt Lewin, Fritz Heider, Dorwin Cartwright, Leon Festinger, J. W. Thibaut, and H. H. Kelley. The older points of view have not been altogether discarded, for they have made great contributions to current theory. The theoretical systems of Simmel, Cooley, and Ross, with sociological emphasis on cultural interactions, have been modified by the Dewey and Mead points of view, and have developed into the currently used interaction analysis methods of E. D. Chapple, R. F. Bales, and J. Matarazzo. The Moreno-inspired sociometric movement, originally therapy directed, is enlarging its scope and showing interest in the structure and analysis of task-oriented as well as affiliative groups (Jennings' socio- and psyche-groups), and in the process has moved in the direction of interaction analysis. The therapeutic groups and communities of Bion have been taken over by H. A. Thelen, W. C. Schutz, and D. Grant, who have developed theories and instruments for composing compatible groups for various purposes—educational, task oriented, and therapeutic. The Gestalt-inspired Lewinian movement has been advanced by a brilliant group of Lewin's colleagues and students who have developed both laboratory and field experimental techniques, and have enriched the small group literature with a wealth of new concepts and new measurement techniques (F. Heider, A. Bavelas, R. Lippitt, J. R. P. French, Jr., D. Cartwright, M. Deutsch, M. Horwitz, J. Thibaut, A. Pepitone, and others).

The clinical psychologist who is not familiar with this literature faces a challenging problem in trying to understand and apply it to his work. Most research-oriented psychologists in this area think in terms of interactions rather than in terms of the dependent and independent variables the clinician is accustomed to deal with— for example, if he wants his patient to be less shy or more productive or less defensive, he not only tries to understand the personality but also looks for a method to bring about the desired change. But research people have not tried, as a rule, to develop techniques for bringing about cures; they have tried to develop concepts which would enable them to understand behavior—sometimes to predict it. Today they think that their best approach to such an understanding lies in an analysis of the interaction unit. From the theoretical point of view, it is more satisfactory, as Thibaut and Kelley (1959) point out, to view group process in terms of social interaction where "each subject's behavior is at the same time a response to a past behavior of the other and a stimulus to a future behavior of the other; each behavior is in part dependent variable and in part independent variable; in no clear sense is it properly either of them" (p. 2).

It is necessary to think in terms of interaction in order to understand the small group literature of today. This will therefore be discussed in this section; it will be followed, however, by a section which does deal with dependent and independent variables in a discussion of the relationship of personality to small group behavior.

An explanation is necessary concerning the several uses of the word interaction. Sometimes it is used to refer to the interaction of tendencies within the individual (Heider, 1958); sometimes it refers to the process within the group—person-to-person interaction (Thibaut and Kelley, 1959). At other times it refers to the interaction of variables at various levels, as for example, the interaction of organismic, individual, group, cultural, and societal factors. Sherif and Sherif (1956, p. 12) has listed relevant social situation factors which can interact under four headings: (1) those related to persons; (2) those related to problems; (3) those related to environment; and (4) those pertaining to relations of the person to the problems and environment. Stimson (1960), using the Bales Interaction Process techniques as revised by E. F. Borgatta, reports experimental work on small groups involving interaction across levels (that is, on the influence of norms on action) as thus accounting for more of the variance in behavior as well as for behavior in more situations.

The conceptual scheme developed by Horwitz (1953) deals with interaction within and among individual, group, and institutional systems. Homans in his analysis of the *Human Group* refers to the internal system of the group within which interaction occurs, and also to an external system which influences these interactions. Similarly, Berrien has developed a homeostasis theory (Berrien, 1961) where the internal system maintains equilibrium by readjustment of its parts within certain constraints imposed by the boundaries of the system. The distinction between within-group and among-levels interaction is important, but quite often theories which deal with within-group interaction fail to account for outside-the-group factors.

A. Paul Hare has developed a conceptual scheme to account for the various dimensions of within-group social interaction that he found in the literature (Hare, 1960). Behavior is designated as either interpersonal or personal (this latter includes intrapersonal behavior as well as individual performance).

Interpersonal behavior has dimensions referring to both *form* and *content*. The dimension of *form* includes (1) the communication network, and (2) the amount of interaction. The *content* dimension

includes task behavior (with subcategories of observing, hypothesiz-
ing and formulating action) and social-emotional behavior (with
subcategories of control and affection). Input and output characteristics can be described, then, in the above terms as defined and oper-
ationalized. For the communication network, one can, for example,
specify the number and direction of the channels. Interaction profiles
can be used for describing the content variables.

Personal behavior is described by measures such as intelligence and
social sensitivity, as well as age, sex, strength, etc.

Interpersonal and personal factors involved in group activities can
be observed, measured, and predicted for both the personality (the
tendency to act) and the role (the expectation for behavior).

A number of theoretical systems have been built around the interaction model. In the ensuing discussion of research on group interaction, reference to Hare's model may help the reader in categorizing
the multitude of variables with which this field must contend.

Equilibrium

The concept of interaction leads inevitably to the concept of
equilibrium or homeostasis, and indeed all theories of group interaction as they develop grapple with the problem of how equilibrium
is disturbed and regained. Such concepts have been applied to groups
as follows: equilibrium models by Homans (1950), Bales (1950), Miller (1955), and Berrien (1961); Blake's (1958) application of Hel-
son's "adaptation level" theory to social perception; Festinger's theory
of cognitive dissonance (1957); cognitive balance models by Cartwright and Harary (1956); Abelson and Rosenberg (1958) and
Heider (1958); and Newcomb's "system strain" model (1959). Since
so much research concerns itself with varieties of equilibrium models,
it is desirable to discuss a number of these theories as they relate
to small group research and the individual.

A distinction should be made among the various models presented.
For example, Homans, Bales and Berrien are concerned with equilibrium within groups in contrast, say, with Heider's model which is
strictly concerned with the achievement of balance and imbalance
within the individual. For Homans, as with Bales and Berrien, groups
must achieve equilibrium in order to survive, and such groups are
capable of handling disturbances in the within-group system by corresponding changes in relations and interactions.

Within-group equilibrium

Chapple and Coon (1942) define a state of equilibrium as follows:
"If a small force is impressed upon a system, a change or adjustment

takes place within the system, and once this force is removed, the system returns to approximately its previous state."

For Chapple and Coon, equilibrium as thus defined is dependent upon the rates of interaction among the members of a group. Constant rates reflect equilibrium; any disturbance in the rates is eliminated if the group is in equilibrium. Groups which exist in equilibrium for long periods are stable groups which can resist environmental stresses better than other groups. Berrien (1961) adheres to a similar view concerning groups; for him, "if the group needs, satisfactions, and formal achievement remain relatively constant and at acceptable levels over a period of time, in the presence of fluctuating demands, it has been assumed that homeostatic processes are taking place." As with Chapple and Homans, Berrien believes that what the group does in the presence of some stress indicates the survival potentiality of the group. Survival means return to a steady state.

In order to give operational meaning to his ideas concerning interaction, Chapple developed a method of interaction analysis which was published in collaboration with Arensberg in 1940. The method is today applicable to natural, as well as to laboratory, groups—for example, Chapple has used it with industrial and psychiatric groups, and Saslow and Matarazzo have made extensive use of it in their studies.

This was one of the first comprehensive attempts made to develop precise methods for measuring human interaction in order to understand, as well as to predict, future interaction. This work grew out of sociological and anthropological research devoted to the observation and analysis of behavior of communities and societies. Today their methods find additional application in small group research in the laboratory as well as the field. The method is based upon observation of individuals as they act to stimulate other people, or as they respond —an operational method. In this method, a unit of interaction is a sequence of units of actions by people. Action is defined as "a period of activity recorded from the initial change in muscular state until a second brings the activity to an end." (Chapple and Arensberg, 1940, p. 26). From these units, ordered sequences and events are built up. Chapple then developed his method for observing and recording units of interaction, events, sequences, origination of action, origin-terminus relations, and equilibrium. These in turn are built into sets, components, and systems, and described algebraically. From this base, he went on to develop an interaction chronograph which was a device used by an observer to record all actions and pauses (see Heyns and Lippitt, 1954). From these time sequences, scores are obtained on tempo (frequency of action initiation), dominance, adjustment to the other, etc. This method has been used in vocational guidance, industrial situations, and psychiatric interviews. Matarazzo, in Chapter 14, gives examples of such use. In addition, it is the basis for the development of concepts concerning, for example, the development of societal hierarchies.

In 1950, Bales published his theory and method for the study of small groups, called *Interaction Process Analysis*. It was a method which he had used for some time and which has many uses today, for example, in the study of family relationships. His book followed a period of theory development as well as a period of concern with the development of operational definitions to test a series of hypotheses concerning small group behavior, as studied in its own right and as a possible model of society. In contrast with the Chapple interaction observation process which was based exclusively on the skilled observation of movements, gestures, pauses, etc., Bales' method as finally developed required the observation of activity in a group and recording of interactions on a set of twelve categories (e.g., solidarity, tension release, agreement)—in other words, of interpretations of the actions of the participants observed. (It is interesting to note, in view of what has been said previously, that one of the groups observed by the use of this method, and reported in the 1950 volume, was a discussion group on the Group Mind!) In the course of development, the discovery that many categories of behavior used in former analyses could be combined within a single frame of reference, reduced the large number of categories with which Bales had started to a manageable number—twelve—which covered both the task area and the positive and negative aspects of the social-emotional area.

Individual and group profiles could be derived from scores obtained from the observation of the group in interaction, and these have been used for a wide variety of purposes in studying the structure and functions of many different kinds of groups.

Bales differentiated four theoretical dimensions of social structure of role differentiation: (1) access to resources (property); (2) control over other (authority); (3) status (prestige); and (4) solidarity. These have been translated into empirically based roles of talking, guidance, and liking.

It is with respect to these roles that Bales has postulated an equilibrium model. Changes in one or more of these roles or dimensions lead to changes in the others, so that the social system maintains a steady state of equilibrium. In addition, there is constant interaction between the problem-solving aspects of group behavior and the social-emotional aspects, and as external forces are imposed upon the group, constant adjustment in these variables takes place.

The two theories and methods of interaction analysis which have been described grew out of anthropological and sociological attempts at understanding societies. Interestingly enough, they both started out with interest in the development of theoretical conceptualization of the societal process, and both found in the small group a means of operationalizing these concepts. Today both Chapple and Bales have progressed to the stage where their methods focus as much on *individual* behavior in the group (e.g., Chapple's interest in the industrial worker, and Bales' analyses of the leader and of the family) as they do on the group process. Homans' equilibrium model which was discussed in the historical section represents the purer sociological approach; the Chapple and Bales theories in so far as they have moved toward analysis of individual behavior have begun to include techniques, methods, and research attitudes which have been traditionally regarded as psychological.

The study of the small group has also been approached from the psychological side, and again where interest was at first directed at the analysis of individual behavior, work with the small group led to the inevitable feeling that here was also a key to the study of organizations and societies. Newcomb (1959), Guetzkow (1959, 1961), Bavelas (1948), Sherif (1935, 1936), Lewin (1948, 1951), McClelland, *et al.* (1953), and many others whose original work was directed on individual behavior were able to relate psychological work to small groups as well as to investigation of organizations and cultures (industrial, military, organizational, national, etc.).

Some approaches which have remained psychological and retained a sound theoretical base will now be discussed, for they are basic to much current research on small groups.

Heider's cognitive balance theory (1958) is concerned strictly with intraperson perceptual process. His concepts, relative to the perception of the other person, of *ought, can, value, causality, want,* etc., are interwoven in a balanced Lewinian structure of field forces. His model is a Gestalt conceptualization of intraperson forces or tendencies which lead to perceptual changes required to convert a state of imbalance to balance. Heider defines a balanced state as "a harmonious state, one in which the entities comprising the situation and the feelings about them fit together, without stress" (Heider, 1958, p. 180); and again, "a situation in which the relations among the entities fit together harmoniously; there is no stress toward change" (p. 201). Tension arises when imbalance remains because, for some reason, a change is not possible. Heider gives many examples of such balance and imbalance in dyads and triads.

Heider was tremendously influenced by Kurt Lewin, and his work should be studied in connection with Lewin's field-theoretical approach. His balance theory has relevance to much current research on cognition and affect. For example, a great deal of the work on attitudes (Peak, 1958; Carlson, 1956; Rosenberg, 1960a, 1960b) concerns the congruity of affective and cognitive components of attitudes.

Newcomb's (1959) ideas on orientations (attitudes), communication and system strain likewise involve the central concept of balance as the device which explains change in attitudes and actions. In integrating aspects of communication behavior which involves the genesis of a primary unit of behavior called the A-B-X model (wherein A communicates with B about an object X) Newcomb has developed a concept of "system strain" through which perceived discrepancy in attitude and communicative behavior provides the energy to cause a system to maintain itself in equilibrium. In his theory, he utilizes three main sets of variables—communication, systems of orientation, and system strain. Communication is defined in terms of exchange of information; systems of orientations as "intra-individual representors of the objective interactional systems in which individuals are psychologically involved at any given moment" (p. 387). System strain is regarded "as corresponding to a state of tension . . . induced by the judged state of the cocommunicator's orientations in regard to one's own" (p. 393). "Balance" is achieved by the movement of systems from states of greater to lesser strain; communicative behavior provides the means.

Newcomb has applied this model to a number of his studies—it might more properly be said that it is the product of his studies—on norms, reference groups, and attitude changes. The vital issues he is concerned with involve the dynamic interaction process between perception, affect, cognition, and social influences. The person in this drama emerges as a forceful actor who perpetually buffets and is buffeted by a strain nourished as much by inner as by outer forces. The context of group within which this struggle takes place is important. Although the theory has not been applied clinically, it would seem promising in the hands of an experimental clinical psychologist.

The above do not exhaust by any means theories making use of an equilibrium model; reference will be made to the concept in discussing other work later on under other headings.

Group dynamics

Current research in group dynamics has resulted from the efforts of behavioral scientists to pool their objectives and resources to understand group behavior and to learn how to make it productive and satisfying for natural groups. In the beginning, some twenty years ago, Kurt Lewin was instrumental in developing field theory out of various Gestalt concepts and in applying it to social psychology. Today, his basic ideas have been adopted by many of his students and colleagues; but, in addition, much has been added from other sources so that under group dynamics we find not only the application of field theory but also the use of the sociometric test of mutual preference expression, of personality tests for optimum group composition, of measures of need for achievement and for affiliation, of role theory, of such concepts as level of aspiration, trust, defensiveness, hostility and power—many of which Lewin touched on or worked with. Unquestionably the group dynamics field has been indebted to Lewin for many central ideas, for his vision in seeing the possibilities of field theory application to social problems, and for his energy in carrying out so much experimental work in getting the group dynamics movement started with the help of colleagues such as those mentioned previously. Nevertheless, the infusion of ideas from many other sources must also be acknowledged.

Lewin's formulation of field theory has been written up in a number of sources which have been cited. For our present purpose it is not necessary to present it in any complete form here but rather it is considered better to discuss some of the major work which represents an extension and expansion of some of the central concepts.

Lewin postulated the psychological field as a mathematical spatial construct within which dynamic forces operated with positive and negative valences, in various regions and through barriers. Locomotion in the field was necessary for the satisfaction of drives and motives. These life spaces could correspond with reality or not; time perspective was a factor in the attainment of goals.

The complete theory, of which the above represent some key concepts, seemed to help Lewin and others in formulating problems not only in the realm of individual psychology but also in the psychology of groups. The individual, in this theory, was represented as a dynamic force who was in turn influenced by the social field of force. In dealing with problems, such as the wartime problem faced in persuading the population to eat foods to which they were not accustomed, in introducing a change in industrial technology without detriment to worker performance, etc., the Lewinian model seemed to help the investigator in operationalizing his concepts and in the measurement of variables and their relations so as to find the determiners of change in the person in order to make appropriate application.

It was after he came to the United States that Kurt Lewin, during the thirties, increased his interest in the dual role of social science— its scientific development and its practical applications. With a number of students and collaborators at Cornell, Iowa State, and M. I. T. he conducted research on children and adults on such topics as the training of leaders of youth groups (with Bavelas), styles of leadership and group atmosphere (with Lippitt and White), group decision in industrial production (with French and Marrow) and group decision in changing food habits (with Margaret Mead and Marian Radke). The Research Center in Group Dynamics which was founded in 1944 at M. I. T. moved to the University of Michigan in 1947 (Cartwright, 1958).

Out of these beginnings has emerged a large body of research on group processes by a number of experimenters (see Cartwright and Zander, 1953 and 1960; Jackson, 1956; Faucheux, 1957). The topics dealt with have included leadership, affiliation, group productivity, the influence of the group on personality, cohesiveness, communication patterns, etc. The two fundamental objectives of Lewin—scientific and applied—are still much in evidence in this work. Work with both laboratory groups and natural groups in field situations is conducted with a constant exchange of ideas from both kinds of experiment. Sometimes the research has a predominantly applied objective, as for example the work of the National Training Laboratories in such areas as defensive behavior (Gibb, 1961), hostility (Horwitz, 1958), attitude change (Coch and French, 1948), etc. Sometimes, the research is oriented toward systematic theory building (Festinger on cognitive dissonance, 1957; Heider on interpersonal relations, 1958; Deutsch on cooperation and trust, 1949, 1960; Cartwright on power, 1959; Schachter on affiliation, 1959). For these formulations much of the experimental evidence is derived from laboratory studies with artificially contrived groups, with field experimental substantiations in several cases.

The research is characterized by intensive analysis of the interaction process. Lewin's field concepts provided the initial influence, but much that is new has been added, and one important unit of analysis is the interaction unit (see, for example, Thibaut-Kelley, 1959).

Growing out of the group dynamics approach (as defined broadly), Thibaut and Kelley (1959) have developed a tightly knit theory of group behavior based upon interdependency and readjustment of individual members as they participate in the group process for some needed reward. They begin their theory development with two-person interaction behavior analyzed in terms of behavior sequences or sets —acts directed toward the attainment of some goal eventuating in rewards received and costs incurred. Interaction which can be started for a variety of reasons—even accidentally—can only continue willingly if it is reinforcing (rewarding). The standard used in making the judgment of adequacy is a concept Thibaut and Kelley call the comparison level (CL), "by which the person evaluates the rewards and costs of a given relationship in terms of what he feels he 'deserves' "—satisfying if above the CL and unattractive below; and $CL_{(alt)}$ as the "lowest level of outcomes a member will accept in the light of available alternative opportunities" (p. 21). The various outcomes of dyadic interaction can be represented by a reward-cost matrix, and from these interactions arises a model of behavior to explain the initiation, development, evaluation, and maintenance of the dyadic relationship and its relation to power, dependence, norms, roles, and tasks. Interdependence in larger groups is then considered in relation to coalitions, status, conformity to norms, goals and roles (such as leadership). In the functional analysis of roles, task functions and maintenance functions are described in terms similar to those of Bales' equilibrium model; that is, the group is dependent upon these functions for survival. Again, maintenance here refers to the social emotional aspects of interaction, whereas the task function involves problem solving.

Although Thibaut and Kelley do not discuss their theory in terms of equilibrium, it seems to fit the constraints usually defined for such a state. For example, they speak of interaction in terms of necessary readjustments as the dyadic relationship is disturbed, of a balance of task and maintenance functions within the groups, and of reinforcing conditions necessary to keep a relationship in existence. It is at this level that the clinical psychologist can begin to see where eventually he may derive some assistance from the further expansion of this theory. In the group context, how does a specific individual with a known history behave so as to preserve the goals of the group, maintain its functions, and react to disturbances so as to reap rewards he needs, rewards which can be obtained only through the survival of the group? Although the theory is not prepared to answer such questions now—indeed, as designed at present it is more immediately useful in the analysis of organizational structures and roles—it is a sound foundation for the orderly investigation of factors which will lead to the understanding of individual problems.

A good source of much of the literature in group dynamics is the volume *Group Dynamics,* by Cartwright and Zander (1953, 1960) cited earlier. In addition to reprints of many original articles, it includes original analyses by the two editors who have been identified with group dynamics from its early beginnings.

Reinforcement

Psychologists have been concerned with problems associated with social response reinforcement for some time (see Allport, 1924), Dashiell (1935), Murphy, Murphy, and Newcomb (1937), and Lambert (1954). From its experimental beginnings, problems of imitation in animals and children, of social response facilitation, and of learning in social and nonsocial situations have presented certain methodological problems, the solution of which has led to the current laboratory techniques. These early studies were not studies in reinforcement, but they were a necessary prelude to the development of methods characterized by careful control and measurement of the complex social stimulus situation.

Skinner's notion of verbal behavior as behavior reinforced through the mediation of another person would indicate that a large segment of psychology could be profitably reviewed under this heading. Such a review is beyond the scope of this chapter; reference should be made to Skinner's writings as well as to Taffel (1955), Greenspoon (1955), Rotter (1954), Verplanck (1955), Estes (1957), Krasner (1958), Salzinger (1959), Salzinger and Pisoni (1960), and Bachrach, Candland, and Gibson (1961). Krasner's review of 31 studies of operant conditioning of verbal responses and Salzinger's review of studies involving manipulation of verbal behavior can serve as a starting place for information concerning trends in such research. Krasner reviewed the "verbal behavior" studies in terms of setting, verbal response, reinforcing stimuli, population, controls, length of experimental sessions, relationship to personality variables, results, and "awareness." He concluded that these studies do indicate that the use of generalized conditional reinforcers (verbal and nonverbal) such as nods, smiles, "good" and "mmmm-hmm" produces positive results (p. 166). It is interesting to speculate whether if verbal behavior can be modified by operant conditioning techniques, this in turn may lead to general reorientation of other aspects of a person's behavior.

Salzinger (1959) provides not only a conceptual scheme for the experimental manipulation of verbal behavior within a learning theory framework but also a program of research. The variables he deals with may be categorized under the following headings: (1) the response; (2) the type, amount, number, delay, and schedule of reinforcement; (3) awareness of conditioning; (4) type of discriminative stimulus; (5) reinforcement history and state of the individual. Important implications may be drawn from such a program of research, as for example, the utilization of reinforcement techniques during the interview in a therapeutic situation (Salzinger and Pisoni, 1960).

Among current examples of social reinforcement research with implications for the clinical psychologist are the work of A. Bachrach (University of Virginia), O. K. Moore (Yale University) and David Shapiro (Harvard University). The work done thus far by these investigators is of a preliminary exploratory nature, since many methodological problems must be solved before experiments can be set up with conditions as precise as those required.

Bachrach, Candland, and Gibson (1961) call attention to problems involved in obtaining data under the categories of (1) reinforcement history of the group and of the individual, (2) the reinforcement contingencies (nature, amount and schedule of reinforcement), (3) discriminative stimuli, and (4) individual response. Although they have selected verbal behavior in social situations as the most efficient to study (in terms of control and manipulation of variables) the large number of variables involved and the need for precision scaling make the task of operationalizing concepts and designing experiments a very difficult one.

The work that has been reported thus far has involved the eliciting of verbal behavior-response rate in a multiperson situation under conditions of (1) operant level, (2) acquisition, (3) extinction, and (4) re-acquisition. The results indicate that the response rate of the subject can be manipulated by varying the social stimulus condition. These results, added to Taffel's (1955), Greenspoon's (1955), Salzinger's (1959), and others' have encouraged Bachrach to explore further problems of conformity and deviation as results of types and schedules of reinforcement and to plan a new series of experiments in the context of social situations.

O. K. Moore's work at Yale has involved the use of a person to reinforce certain responses of children in learning to type and in concept formation. Startling results have been obtained with children as young as three years of age. Additional work has started with a group of hard-of-hearing children in order to develop appropriate types and schedules of reinforcement to assist in the learning of speech.

Reinforcement techniques which have been used by Lindsley (1960) in a psychiatric situation in an effort to teach a patient to communicate with the outside world are being extended by Shapiro at Harvard Medical School by the introduction of a social context. Lindsley developed schedules of reinforcement for his subjects (by use of a candy-vending type of machine) to evoke motor responses. Shapiro's experiments will involve social type reinforcements to produce desired verbal behavior. Methods are being developed to study the same individual in isolation and in a group situation. If interaction is an important factor in the determination of behavior, lack of participation in interaction or exclusion from interaction may have as profound effects as sensory deprivation has been shown to have. One of the techniques of brainwashing seems to revolve around systematic deprivation of an individual's social and cultural anchorages (Schein, 1956). The suggestion that this period of extinction followed by reinforcement of new social and cultural anchorages be studied does not seem to have produced much, if any, published research but the guide lines for such research seem clear.

The Shapiro-Leiderman studies utilize, in a laboratory situation, techniques to reinforce or extinguish the rate of initiative attempts per subject, average number of verbal responses per trial, number of interpersonal disagreements, rates for occurrences of particular body movements, speech patterns, linguistic elements, etc. Their preliminary results, substantiating hypotheses in this area, have encouraged them to extend their studies to individuals in isolation as well as in groups, and to include physiological as well as psychological reinforcements. Reinforcement and extinction schedules are being systematically developed and tried out for such phenomena as "scapegoating," "sacrificing," "pairing," "role taking," and learning "without awareness" in a number of social situations. This is a promising line of research viewed with a great deal of interest.

Sociometric

J. L. Moreno conceived the central idea in sociometrics some time following World War I (Moreno, 1923) and developed a method of application and research, in that sequence (see Moreno, 1934). The method, with innumerable variations, is widely used today. One of Moreno's central ideas was the sociometric test or technique which involves the selection by a person of another person with whom he desires to share some activity—work, play, companionship, etc. From these choices, groups can be composed for therapy or for work purposes which, according to Moreno, lead to optimum results for the individual, and hence for society.

The sociometric approach is well known and need not be described here. Furthermore, many of its principles and techniques are used routinely by the experimental psychologist as well as by the practitioner in many professions. The use of such techniques in small group research is well accepted and has led to important contributions. For example, Jennings' work with natural groups led directly to the development of a theory of leadership and group behavior. Her development of the concepts of psychegroups and sociogroups, roughly, affiliative and task-oriented groups, and her analysis of the leader's role in the two kinds of social groups have provided support for hypotheses on leadership and group behavior tested through other approaches, as for example, the work of Shartle and his associates (1956) on initiating structure (task aspect) and consideration (person orientation).

Jennings (1953) has written that "sociometric study of the choosing process . . . suggests that it is no less than the process by which the individual becomes what he becomes" (p. 332). This is related to the belief by such differently oriented investigators as Bion, Thelen, Schutz, and Fiedler that individuals' life styles determine the associates with whom productivity and satisfaction can be achieved, and from whom emotional support is received. Therapy or problem solving can best be achieved, according to these views, by composing groups of compatible individuals. The theory underlying such compatibilities differs from investigator to investigator, ranging from Fiedler's concern with ASo (assumed similarity of opposites) to Schutz's conceptualization of three basic needs as affiliation, control, and integration. These approaches will be discussed further later on.

The sociometric point of view not only indicates that the individual's personality is influenced by the choices he makes but also that his ability to maintain relations with others influences the creativity and productivity of the other person. Fundamentally, it is an approach which stresses human relations as the ultimate source of productive and affiliative behavior. Its applications are not only in therapy, but in personnel administration, institutional organization, community applications, military organization, education and training, prisons, etc. (See Lindzey and Borgatta, 1954; Criswell, 1949; Jennings, 1953; Moreno, 1956, 1960).

Perceptual

There is a great deal of research in group psychology concerned with relationships between external events and perception. Muzafer Sherif's work, for example, has been characterized by (1) the modification of perception by cultural and group norms, and (2) the reciprocal process between perception and action. Asch's work on conformity (1956) grew out of a sustained interest in perception; Jerome Bruner has participated in considerable fine research relating personality, perceptual, and social variables (Bruner, 1951, 1957; Bruner, Goodnow, and Austin, 1956). Whereas Sherif has concentrated on the effect of group norms on an individual's perceptions (as well as on the formation of group norms), Bruner's work has studied the intricate intraperson process involved in the relationship between perception and expectations or "readiness."

The whole area of interpersonal perception is one which strangely has not received the concentrated experimental attention which it should have. Tagiuri and Bruner have called attention to this gap (Tagiuri and Bruner, 1954; Tagiuri and Petrullo, 1958) and today there is a heartening effort to bring such study into the laboratory. H. Cantril, A. Ames, and their associates have likewise labored in this area with astonishing results (see Kilpatrick, 1952; Ittelson and Slack, 1958; Wittreich, 1955; Wittreich and Radcliffe, 1956). Still, nothing but the barest beginning has been made.

How we come to know, perceive, and judge other persons is a central problem not only to the clinical psychologist but to all of psychology. MacLeod (1960) states, ". . . the central problem of all psychology is that of understanding ourselves and other people. Basic to the problem of understanding is the problem of perception" (p. 226).

Tagiuri (1956) has discussed the relevance of person perception to personality diagnosis and indicated the need for studying: (1) the process of clinical judgment formation; (2) individuals' misperceptions and methods of changing; and (3) relationship of perceptions to action. The value of pursuing these research ends is illustrated by important research reported by Jones and Thibaut in 1958. Jones and Thibaut related intra-individual processes to interpersonal perception in terms of inferential sets. Three kinds of sets—value maintenance, causal-genetic and situation-matching—were postulated, resulting from three different kinds of goals. Since the clinical psychologist's goal is to understand his patient and find out what causes him to behave as he does, he needs to adopt a causal-genetic set. Newcomb's (1958) analysis of humans who cognize other persons as cognizers, and the relation of this to the selection of friends, is another example of fruitful study of the cognition of persons.

The subject of interpersonal perception provides a good transition to the next section on personality and group behavior. Some of the work discussed in this section could as well be discussed under personality, and vice versa. Work such as Thelen's, Schutz's, Cattell's, and Fiedler's, for example, deals with personality disposition, but the process of group formation with which they are concerned is definitely an interaction process. Their work lends itself more easily to personality analysis, and it may be more useful to the clinical psychologist when discussed in that context.

PERSONALITY AND THE SMALL GROUP

The "Review of the Relationship between Personality and Performance in Small Groups" by Mann in 1959 provides the best single integration of research on this subject. In an attempt to determine what the major conclusions were, Mann reviewed some 1400 results of studies reported during the period 1900–1957.

A first task of integration of this kind is the reduction of number of variables, not only for ease of handling, but more important to see whether a smaller number of factors actually encompasses the larger number of variables. Since the 1400 studies involved over 500 personality tests and a wide assortment of status and behavior variables, Mann's task was large. He was able to isolate three conceptual approaches: (1) the first is based on the satisfaction of needs through interaction with others; (2) the second focuses on the relationship between personality and the way an individual is perceived and judged; (3) the third highlights the processes involved in the individual's performance in solving problems confronting the group.

Examination of various factor analytic studies led Mann to arrive at seven primary clusters into which he was able to group the majority, but not all of the personality measures. These seven clusters he called: (1) intelligence; (2) adjustment; (3) extroversion-introversion; (4) dominance; (5) masculinity-femininity; (6) conservatism; and (7) interpersonal sensitivity. The status and behavior variables, with which the personality measures were related, Mann was able to classify under the following six groups of dependent variables: (1) leadership; (2) popularity; (3) total activity rate; (4) task activity; (5) social-emotional activity; and (6) conformity.

The trends resulting from integrations of results of the various studies were then presented by Mann in a number of tables. In view of his extensive analysis, it is considered worthwhile to present a number of his major syntheses.

> The best predictor of an individual's performance is intelligence. In order of the proportion of positive results, intelligence is found to be positively related to total activity rate, leadership and popularity. In addition, it is positively related to the number of task contributions made by an individual, but, controlling for the total activity rate, it is negatively related to the proportion of his total activity falling in the task contribution area. Intelligence is positively related to both the amount and proportion of positive social-emotional activity, whereas it is negatively related to negative social-emotional activity.
>
> Adjustment is found to be positively related to leadership, popularity, and total activity rate, in that order. It is positively related to the total number of task contributions, but negatively related to the percentage of the total number of acts which are task contributions. Adjustment is positively related to positive social-emotional activity and negatively related to negative social-emotional activity. Although subjects who tend to conform to group opinion see themselves as better adjusted, other measuring techniques indicate a negative relationship between adjustment and conformity. Except for the fact that intelligence has not been related to conformity a sufficient number of times to be reviewed, adjustment is related to behavior and status variables in much the same way as intelligence.
>
> Extroversion is positively related to popularity, total activity rate, and leadership. Although it is positively related to the total number of task contributions, this result cannot be considered as independent of the relation between extroversion and total activity rate. While individuals who conform more than others to group opinion tend to see themselves as more extroverted, techniques other than self ratings fail to show any significant association.

Dominance is positively related to the total number of task contributions initiated and to leadership. It is negatively related to an individual's tendency to conform to group opinion.

Masculinity bears a low positive relationship to leadership and popularity. A positive association is found between masculinity and the total number of task contributions, although there is some slight indication that this relationship is reversed when the total activity factor is controlled.

Conservatism is negatively related to leadership, but positively related to popularity. A positive association is found between conservatism and the raw number of task contributions. Finally, conservatism is positively related to conformity; those who tend to conform to the opinions of others are more conservative or authoritarian.

The measures of interpersonal sensitivity relate positively to both leadership and popularity. Both relationships are of low magnitude, and, in the case of the latter, there is a possibility that the number of the results which are spuriously positive is sufficient to cast doubt on the whole trend."

Although Mann could not report on many of the studies which he examined, it is doubtful that much can be added to the above generalizations by including a large number of specific findings. It is worth while to call attention in this section to several additional important recent contributions.

Social influence

Much work has been done on social influence resulting from group interaction. This work ranges all the way from concern with, say, temporary change of attitude to so-called "brain-washing" (Schein, 1961) where presumably deep-seated personality changes resulting in fundamental orientations to life may be induced. The clinician is rightly interested in the phenomenon of social influence; here again small group research seems to offer some promise for helping to understand the process. Concepts such as group norms, conformity, and person-to-person communication networks which have resulted from small group research will provide useful constructs in a theoretical structure of individual-group-environment interaction systems.

Katz and Lazarsfeld in their book on *Personal Influence* (1955) have done an admirable job in explaining the relation of norms and networks to persuasion. The mass communications process could not be understood without some understanding of small group behavior because fundamentally social interaction must ultimately be reduced to a person-to-person interaction. The individual is both the object of influence and the instrument.

Kelman (1961, and in press) has described three processes of social influence—compliance, identification, and internalization—and their antecedent and consequent conditions, which are directly related to personality dynamics.

These three processes can be, perhaps, viewed as three stages of acceptance of some value or orientation, though it would not follow that such acceptance would necessarily proceed through each consecutively. Internalization of some belief, for example, could be almost instantaneous if it fitted into the individual's existing orientation.

Kelman's antecedents and consequents of these three processes are summarized in Table 1.

This model has value because of its experimental implications, and Kelman has utilized it in testing the relationships postulated as well as in the study of personality factors in social influence.

Personality compatibility

The sociometric method which was discussed earlier is based upon the concept that an optimum community can be constructed of people who choose each other for one reason or another. Such choice, it is argued, leads to the formation of groups within which the individual can achieve spontaneity and creativity. He can also influence others to fulfill their needs in these directions, through the release of some peculiar human energy not too well defined in the works of the sociometrists.

Group compatibility has been approached from other directions than voluntary choices. Fiedler's concept of ASo (assumed similarity of opposites), Schutz's three-dimensional theory of interpersonal behavior (inclusion, control, and affection), and Thelen's theory of work and emotionality are examples which make use of the method of personal choice in group formation, but which develop theoretically quite differently.

Fiedler has differentiated between the personality that might be called therapeutic and that which is task-oriented. Assumed similarity is defined as a measure of personal distance; the therapeutic personality perceives other persons as somewhat similar to himself; the task-oriented person sees most and least preferred coworkers (by himself) as quite different. The perceived distance of others from one's self and the perceived distance between the most and least preferred lead to interesting combinations of attitudes in group members. Attitudes establishing more social distance (high ASo) can make for productivity, while warmer orientations (low ASo and high assumption of similarity to self) tend to create "a country club atmosphere" (Fiedler, 1958; Godfrey and Fiedler, 1957). Were there a taxonomy of situations and organizations it would be possible, utilizing Fiedler's methods, to select individuals for every situation so as to maximize the

TABLE 1

Summary of the Distinctions Between the Three Processes

	COMPLIANCE	IDENTIFICATION	INTERNALIZATION
Antecedents			
1. Basis for the importance of the induction	Concern with social effect of behavior	Concern with social anchorage of behavior	Concern with value congruence of behavior
2. Source of power of the influencing agent	Means-control	Attractiveness	Credibility
3. Manner of achieving prepotency of the induced response	Limitation of choice behavior	Delineation of role requirements	Reorganization of means-ends framework
Consequents			
1. Conditions of performance of induced response	Surveillance by influencing agent	Salience of relationship to agent	Relevance of values to issue
2. Conditions of change and extinction of induced response	Changed perception of conditions for social rewards	Changed perception of conditions for satisfying self-defining relationships	Changed perception of conditions for value maximization
3. Type of behavior system in which induced response is embedded	External demands of a specific setting	Expectations defining a specific role	P's value-system

SOURCE: From Kelman, H. C. Processes of opinion change. *The Public Opinion Quarterly*, 1961, *25*, 57–78.

particular function of the group. Needless to say, there is no such taxonomy as yet. Yet, Fiedler's patient work with natural groups— military, industrial, competitive, sports, etc.—has enabled him to construct the elements of a respectable theory which may have real application.

Schutz's theory (1958), similarly, is concerned with group compatibility based on mutual need satisfaction. Schutz postulates three basic needs—for inclusion, for control, and for affection—derived not only from his own work, which has been extensive, but also from other experimenters. These needs have been conceptually as well as operationally defined, and Guttman type scales have been developed for their measurement. The needs are further broken down, for example, into the need for control and the need to be controlled. Measures (the FIRO scales—fundamental interpersonal relations orientation) of these needs are basic to the formation of groups of persons most compatible for a given purpose. This theory is derived from research on (1) interpersonal behavior in small groups; (2) environmental and cultural influences on behavior; (3) cognition; and (4) developmental and clinical history. The subjects for this research have included students, naval personnel, superintendents of schools, and teachers; the research program has succeeded in the development of a theory which holds promise for effective application wherever groups are needed.

In further work Schutz has discussed his FIRO theory in relation to the concept of the individual as a group (1961). The three interpersonal needs are equated to self-preservation, aggression, and the sexual urge. For instinctual urge he substitutes interpersonal need. Thus, the ego develops (partly) through dealing with interpersonal needs and their interaction, and partly through autonomous factors, comprising the conflict-free ego sphere and their interaction. Ego functions are equated with leadership; and the leader becomes a completer. Schutz recommends that the group be studied in order to learn about individual behavior.

Like Schutz, Herbert Thelen was influenced by the work of W. R. Bion, an English psychiatrist who developed a method for using the small group as a therapeutic device. Bion noticed what has always been known—that some people seem to find certain individuals easier to get along with than others. His attempts to compose compatible groups led to the development of concepts which have been developed and made more explicit by Thelen. Whereas Bion was concerned with hospital groups, Thelen did his work with educational groups.

Thelen (1959) believes the small group can serve to meet individual needs and to help in producing work or solving problems. This can best be done by the combination of individuals with compatible emotionality needs and purposes. To discover these basic needs and purposes, Thelen observed the behavior of many groups at a variety of tasks; Bion's concepts of fight, flight, dependency, and pairing seemed to be useful in describing personal as well as group needs.

Under task conditions, or under stress, individuals take action to solve their problems, achieve their goals, and reduce or eliminate stress. Stress arises from the conflict between trying to achieve warm human relations and at the same time to deal critically and analytically with the problem at hand. The ensuing interaction can be successful or not, depending on whether there is a proper matching of individual to individual, and to group purpose.

Thelen's approach has gone beyond theory. He has used not only the small group laboratory to develop, test, and try out his ideas but the community and the classroom as well.

Some trends and implications

Research on small group behavior is accumulating at a great rate, from both the laboratory and field, and from many disciplines. Some of the research, such as that at the Group Dynamics Center of the University of Michigan, has pursued systematic and sustained effort since World War II; independent investigators like Heider, Newcomb, and Sherif who have had considerable influence on theoretical as well as experimental developments have also pursued systematic programs for more than several decades, but most current research has had a recent start. It is safe to say that there is at this moment more research waiting for publication than all the research that has been published up to this time. Much of it is in mimeograph form, much is awaiting replication—a healthy sign that the field is maturing and the rush to get into print with first results has slowed down, much is in manuscript form as part of a larger work, quite often some theory in various stages of development. Under these circumstances, it may not be sufficient to merely review the current published literature; it would be a real service to attempt to determine the trends, as Jackson (1956) and Thelen (1959) have done to some extent. Yet this is a difficult task in view of the fact that there is more significant unpublished work going on than has been published to date.

It is obviously not possible to cover the wide range of topics related to small group research which is now being worked on. Just to list a few of the major publications on aspects of small group research which have been published recently gives some glimpse of this growing area: the achievement motive (McClelland, 1953); affiliation (Schachter, 1959); leadership (Shartle, 1956; Bass, 1960; Petrullo and Bass, 1961); power (Cartwright, 1959); communication (Bavelas, 1951; Festinger, et al., 1950); interpersonal perception (Tagiuri and Petrullo, 1958); interpersonal relations (Heider, 1958); group composition (Schutz, 1958; Thelen, 1959); satisfaction (Morse, 1953); interaction (Thibaut and Kelley, 1959); group dynamics (Cartwright and Zander, 1960);

morale (Gardner and Thompson, 1956); assumed similarity (Godfrey and Fiedler, 1957; Fiedler, 1958). This list is only partial and omits the larger part of the research which appears in the journals and which is abstracted in the *Annual Review of Psychology.*

The *Annual Review* is a good source to get an idea of the trends in small group research. The first volume, published in 1950, had very little on small group research; the 1959 volume has an entire chapter. Textbooks in social psychology are also reflecting this growth, with the more recent books devoting more and more space to this area. Sociology and psychology texts show the same trend.

A number of attempts aimed at systematic development of theoretical positions have been made. The efforts of McDougall and Freud, nonexperimentally based, have been mentioned. Sociologists also developed systematic positions which today are exercising influence in experimental derivations. What is currently lacking are theories based upon experiment; some exceptions have been noted in the earlier text, but even these are in need of support from experimental work.

T. M. Newcomb in his statement of development of his ideas on group behavior (1959) has given us an interesting history with implications for future developments. Since the early thirties, he has influenced and been influenced by the leading psychologists and sociologists of our times. These influences show in his work—his work on balance, system strain, norms, reference groups, etc., and his incorporation of concepts such as dissonance and role indicate this interaction. In his development, he has been very conscious of the importance of organismic, social, and cultural variables at work in the shaping of a personality, and has tried to incorporate these influences in his systematic philosophy. To measure the variances in behavior and relate these precisely to antecedent conditions is the very difficult task of the experimenter. To design experiments so as to shape a body of theory that will be not only a model for explanation but prove heuristic is a need of our times. Newcomb, in trying to meet these objectives, is giving us some notion of the direction in which small group research is heading. This is a direction that requires the systematic collection of many facts, the ordering of these data, and the conceptualizing of them into small and related categories.

Bales (1959) has called attention to the problem of amount of data required by small group research, so great that computers and computer techniques will have to be worked out in order to bring together, organize, and reduce to manageable size the amount of information needed to complete an adequate study. Experimental replication will be routine in the future, and as the pace of research hastens and as more and more factors are studied in interaction it is inevitable that mechanization in research will arrive. We may also expect that, in the future, clinical psychologists (like research psychologists) will develop mechanical aids which will help them to select the particular information that they need in their work, refine it so as to select only relevant material, and develop the relationships that would hold for a particular set of variables (personality, situations, culture, etc.). This is not a dream for the distant future; we are already committed to this course of action.

The growing body of research on specialized topics means also that the time is coming when the clinical psychologist will be able to refer to a number of sources for material on specific topics relating to small groups just as he is able today to refer to a rich literature on intelligence, or on projective techniques, etc. For example, Jack Gibb has been working for a number of years on defensive behavior and will issue within the next few years a series of volumes on this subject; Murray Horwitz at New York University and A. Pepitone at the University of Pennsylvania have done a great deal of research on hostility; R. deCharms at Washington University in St. Louis has much data on the achievement motive; J. R. P. French, Jr., at the University of Michigan, and Bert Raven at UCLA have much data on power relations; Vincent Nowlis at the University of Rochester has worked on mood, drugs, and group behavior for many years and has developed techniques and hypotheses; Ronald Lippitt at the University of Michigan has much material on aspects of personality development; Helen Peak at the University of Michigan, M. Rosenberg at Yale, O. J. Harvey at the University of Colorado, and H. Schroder at Princeton have worked on various aspects of changes in attitudes and belief systems—and much of this is unpublished.

All of these investigators, and many more, have manuscripts in various degrees of completion. These books, when published, will be of great help to the clinician—provided he finds the time to read them, of course.

The large volume of research also points to the need for integration of information on small group research. McGrath (1957), Terauds, Altman and McGrath (1960), and Raven (1959) have made starts in developing systems for information storage, integration, and retrieval. A. Paul Hare has devoted considerable time and skill in integrating small group research (publications mentioned earlier). Cartwright and Zander have led the way in integrating the results of group dynamics research. Again many others can be cited; the significance of this is to make a large amount of material and techniques available to the clinical psychologist.

As fast as research results are integrated, new needs arise for more data and more integration. There are definite trends towards "systems" research with requirements for the collection, assimilation and comparison of tremendous quantities of data. The techniques of the past with emphasis on studying the relations among a few variables will give way to multivariate techniques dealing with many variables and many outcomes. Of course, this is precisely what the clinician will need before any of the results of small group research can hope to find application. The variance among individuals, the variance among situations, and the interactions possible simply cannot be handled by a few generalizations.

Related to systems type research where many variables within the system are studied and external stimuli related to changes within the system have been the invention and use of "models" to study behavior of individuals and groups. These models are often invented to stimulate some real life situation or situations—not precisely, but in some manner that will promote the study of specific factors. The model is simpler to handle, and the expectation is that observation of it will develop information useful in the real life situation. Mention has already been made of Schutz's attempt to demonstrate that the study of the group can be helpful in the study of the individual. The small group can be set up in such a way as to simulate various aspects of the personality which are not easily observable in the individual, but which can be observed as functioning in a group. There will undoubtedly be a great deal more of this work, but again these models will require the accumulation of much data, too much to handle without the use of new computers and machine techniques.

The use of models in research, the systems approach, the rise of computers and computer programs, all of these mean that the small-group laboratory is in for a great deal of modification. Already there are plans for series of small group laboratory rooms, wired for sound and recording, lighted for observation, to be used in multiples; data are immediately fed into computers, and interaction results computed even while the group is still under observation. One effect of this kind of laboratory is the invention of a new method of research. Even while individuals are interacting their responses become quickly known, interaction indexes are computed, and new stimuli can be fed into the experiment on a sequential basis. Exploratory studies can be hastened and experiments quickly replicated by the use of these devices—and much time saved.

The emphasis on the interaction process has put great pressure on the development of these techniques, equipment, and methods, but as a result, laboratory experiments will not only be sped up, but they will begin to resemble more the life process than is the case in much of today's research on small groups.

Nor is this trend only evidenced in laboratory work. Portable equipment is being built—compact computers, small booths, and interaction analyzers—which can be taken out to the field and used in the live situation. More and more of this will be done and the anthropologist, sociologist, political scientist, or psychologist of the future might very well have all his data analyzed by the time he is ready to return from a field experiment. Again, these techniques will be useful to the clinical psychologist who has very much the same kind of problem in his interactions during his interviews.

Strupp (1960) has called attention to the need for research in what he calls the functional situation. Many laboratory experiments on group behavior are performed with nonfunctional groups—and even though the situation may resemble a real-life one, it is hazardous to over-generalize from one to the other.

Several things are being done to remedy this situation. One is the initiation of research comparing results obtained in contrived and actual situations (see, for example, Borgatta, 1955). More of this kind of research is needed.

A second effort has been to form research teams of psychologists and sociologists (a good illustration is at the Social Science Institute, Washington University in St. Louis) to conduct research in both laboratory and natural settings. One of the functions of laboratory research is for the exposure of clues which can assist in the conduct of field research. Sometimes research can be so designed as to make possible a ready translation from one context to another.

Similarly, interdisciplinary teams have come into existence to work on various aspects of a problem. For example, O. K. Moore's work on problem solving at Yale has involved sociologists, psychologists, linguists, logicians, and psychiatrists. The interdisciplinary team approach has grown within the past few years and appears to offer a needed research technique for dealing with the varied aspects of a problem.

Another growing concern is the need for a taxonomy of situations to enable the study of interaction between personality variables and situational variables. Raymond B. Cattell, who has developed a taxonomic system of personality profiles, has called attention to this need and has started some work in this direction (e.g., Cattell and Stice, 1953). Saul B. Sells, Texas Christian University, has held a symposium recently on aspects of task taxonomy which is a promise of research to come.

The interdisciplinary-team research has another aspect—international co-operative research. Cross-cultural studies are on the increase. For example, the University of Michigan has for a number of years exchanged research professors with the University of Norway at Oslo. This has made possible the replication of studies on a number of national groups. H. Gullicksen of the Educational Testing Service in

Princeton, New Jersey, reported at the Bonn International Psychological meetings in 1960 about work on the scaling of values done in a number of countries. This type of work is very much on the increase, with replications being reported from all over the globe.

Enough has been said already to indicate the changing nature of today's theory on small group behavior. The great lack up to the present has not been a lack of theory, but a lack of theory substantiated by empirical and experimental data. With the increase in the amount of data reported and with the new methods for speeding up the collection and analysis of data, there will be a corresponding increase in theory development.

Most of the theories on small group behavior, at least those based on some experimental evidence, have already been discussed. At best, they represent guide lines to future work; none of the authors claims that he has developed any sort of comprehensive system. They are all frank about their shortcomings, but real beginnings have been made, and it is not too much to expect that theoreticians are even now preparing their next steps. Much of today's experimental work is really a prelude to the development of a body of knowledge; it is exploratory of methods, it searches for vulnerable areas to dissect, and it is developing guide lines for the conduct of future fruitful work. Theory can point the way. For example, the Heiderian models have helped in planning experiments in a variety of social processes. Thibaut and Kelley's ideas are being used to develop new experiments. As data come in, the theory will grow and produce new ideas. In the process, a technology will develop which should be useful to the clinical psychologist. The interaction of technology and theory, both in their infancies now, will show accelerating progress; the difficult times are the present when attempts are being made to get the model "off the ground."

References

Abelson, R. P., & Rosenberg, M. J. Symbolic psycho-logic: a model of attitudinal cognition. *Behav. Sci.*, 1958, 3, 1–13.

Allport, F. H. *Social psychology*. Boston: Houghton Mifflin, 1924.

Annual review of psychology. Stanford, Calif.: Stanford Univ. Press (Annual since 1950).

Asch, S. E. Studies of independence and conformity. 1. A minority of one against a unanimous majority. *Psychol. Monogr.*, 1956, No. 416.

Bachrach, A. J., Candland, D. K., & Gibson, J. T. Experiments in verbal behavior. I. Group reinforcement of individual response. In I. Berg and B. Bass (Eds.) *Conformity and deviation*. New York: Harper, 1961, pp. 258–285.

Bales, R. F. *Interaction process analysis. A method for the study of small groups*. Reading, Mass.: Addison-Wesley, 1950.

Bales, R. F. Small-group theory and research. In R. K. Merton, L. Broom, &

L. S. Cottrell, Jr. (Eds.), *Sociology today*. New York: Basic Books, 1959, 293–305.

Bass, B. M. *Leadership, psychology, and organizational behavior*. New York: Harper, 1960.

Bavelas, A. Some problems of organizational change. *J. soc. Issues*, 1948, *3*, 48–52.

Bavelas, A. Communication patterns in task-oriented groups. In D. Lerner & H. Lasswell (Eds.), *The policy sciences*. Stanford, Calif.: Stanford Univ. Press, 1951.

Bavelas, A. Leadership: Man and function. *Adm. Sci. Quarterly*, 1960, *4*, 491–498.

Berrien, F. K. Homeostasis theory of groups—implications for leadership. In L. Petrullo & B. M. Bass (Eds.), *Leadership and interpersonal behavior*. New York: Holt, Rinehart and Winston, 1961.

Blake, R. The other person in the situation. In R. Tagiuri & L. Petrullo (Eds.), *Person perception and interpersonal behavior*. Stanford, Calif.: Stanford Univ. Press, 1958.

Borgatta, E. F. Analysis of social interaction: actual, role playing, and projective. *J. abnorm. soc. Psychol.*, 1955, *51*, 394–405.

Bruner, J. S. Personality dynamics and the process of perceiving. In R. R. Blake & G. V. Ramsey (Eds.), *Perception: an approach to personality*. New York: Ronald, 1951.

Bruner, J. S. On perceptual readiness. *Psychol. Rev.*, 1957, *64*, 123–152.

Bruner, J. S., Goodnow, J. J., & Austin, G. A. *A study of thinking*. New York: Wiley, 1956.

Carlson, E. R. Attitude change and attitude structure. *J. abnorm. soc. Psychol.* 1956, *52*, 252–261.

Cartwright, D. Some things learned. An evaluative history of the Research Center for Group Dynamics. *J. soc. Issues*, supplement series No. 12, 1958.

Cartwright, D. (Ed.) *Studies in social power*. Ann Arbor, Mich.: Univ. of Mich., 1959.

Cartwright, D., & Harary, F. Structural balance: a generalization of Heider's theory. *Psychol. Rev.*, 1956, *63*, 277–293.

Cartwright, D., & Zander, A. *Group dynamics: research and theory*. Evanston, Ill.: Row, Peterson and Co., 1953. (Rev. ed.), 1960.

Cattell, R. B., & Stice, G. F. *The psychodynamics of small groups*. Urbana, Ill.: Laboratory of Personality Assessment and Group Behavior, 1953.

Chapple, E. D., & Arensberg, C. M. Measuring human relations: an introduction to the study of the interaction of individuals. *Gen. Psychol. Monogr.*, 1940, *22*, 3–147.

Chapple, E. D., & Coon, C. S. The equilibrium of groups. In A. P. Hare, E. F. Borgatta, & R. F. Bales (Eds.), *Small groups*. New York: Knopf, 1955. (Taken from E. D. Chapple & C. S. Coon, *Principles of anthropology*. New York: Holt, 1942.)

Churchman, C. W., & Ackoff, R. L. "Social science: The nature of the social group," *Methods of inquiry*. St. Louis, Mo.: Educational Publishers, 1950, 476–507.

Coch, L., & French, J. R. P., Jr. Overcoming resistance to change. *Hum. Relat.*, 1948, *1*, 512–532.

Criswell, Joan H. Sociometric concepts in personnel administration. *Sociometry*, 1949, *12*, 287–300.

Criswell, Joan H. The sociometric study of leadership. In L. Petrullo & B. M. Bass (Eds.), *Leadership and interpersonal behavior*. New York: Holt, Rinehart, and Winston, 1961.

Dashiell, J. F. Experimental studies of the influence of social situations on the behavior of individual human adults. In C. C. Murchison (Ed.), *Handbook of social psychology*. Worcester, Mass.: Clark Univ. Press, 1935.

Deutsch, M. A theory of cooperation

and competition. *Human Relations,* 1949, *2,* 129–152.

Deutsch, M. Field theory in social psychology. In G. Lindzey (Ed.), *Handbook of social psychology.* Reading, Mass.: Addison-Wesley, 1954, 181–222.

Deutsch, M. Trust and suspicion. *Conflict resolution,* 1958, *2,* 265–279.

Deutsch, M. The effect of motivational orientation upon trust and suspicion. *Human Relations,* 1960, *13,* 123–139.

Estes, W. K. Of models and men. *Amer. Psychologist,* 1957, *12,* 609–617.

Faris, R. E. L. Development of the small-group research movement. In M. Sherif & M. O. Wilson (Eds.), *Group relations at the crossroads.* New York: Harper, 1953, 155–184.

Faucheux, C. La dynamique de groupe. *L'Année psychologique,* 1957, *2,* 425–440.

Festinger, L. The role of group belongingness. In J. G. Miller (Ed.), *Experiments in social process.* New York: McGraw-Hill, 1950.

Festinger, L. *A theory of cognitive dissonance.* Evanston, Ill.: Row, Peterson, 1957.

Festinger, L., Back, K., Schachter, S., Kelley, H. H., & Thibaut, J. *Theory and experiment in social communication.* Ann Arbor, Mich.: Univ. Michigan, Inst. for Soc. Res., 1950.

Fiedler, F. E. *Leader attitudes and group effectiveness.* Urbana, Ill.: Univ. Illinois Press, 1958.

Freud, S. *Group psychology and the analysis of the ego.* London. Hogarth, 1922.

Gardner, E. F., & Thompson, G. G. *Social relations and morale in small groups.* New York: Appleton-Century-Crofts, 1956.

Gibb, J. R. Defense level and influence potential in small groups. In L. Petrullo & B. M. Bass (Eds.), *Leadership and interpersonal behavior.* New York: Holt, Rinehart and Winston, 1961.

Godfrey, E. P., & Fiedler, F. E. *Boards, management and company success.* Danville, Ill.: Interstate Printers & Publishers, 1957.

Greenspoon, J. The reinforcing effect of two spoken sounds on the frequency of two responses. *Amer. J. Psychol.,* 1955, *68,* 409–416.

Guetzkow, H. (Ed.). *Groups, leadership and men.* Pittsburgh, Pa.: Carnegie Press, 1951.

Guetzkow, H. A use of simulation in the study of inter-nation relations. *Behav. Sci.,* 1959, *4,* 183–191.

Guetzkow, H. Organizational leadership in task-oriented groups. In L. Petrullo & B. M. Bass (Eds.), *Leadership and interpersonal behavior.* New York: Holt, Rinehart and Winston, 1961.

Hare, A. P. The dimensions of interaction. *Behav. Sci.,* 1960, *5,* 211–215.

Hare, A. P., Borgatta, E. F., & Bales, R. F. *Small groups. Studies in social interaction.* New York: Knopf, 1955.

Heider, F. *The psychology of interpersonal relations.* New York: Wiley, 1958.

Heyns, R. W., & Lippitt, R. Systematic observational techniques. In G. Lindzey (Ed.), *Handbook of social psychology.* Reading, Mass.: Addison-Wesley, 1954.

Homans, G. C. *The human group.* New York: Harcourt, Brace, 1950.

Horwitz, M. The conceptual status of group dynamics. *Rev. Educ. Res.* 1953, *23,* 309–328.

Horwitz, M. The veridicality of liking and disliking. In R. Tagiuri & L. Petrullo (Eds.), *Person perception and interpersonal behavior.* Stanford, Cal.: Stanford Univ. Press, 1958.

Ittelson, W. H., & Slack, C. W. The perception of persons as visual objects. In R. Tagiuri & L. Petrullo (Eds.), *Person perception and interpersonal behavior.* Stanford, Cal.: Stanford Univ. Press, 1958

Jackson, J. M. *Current trends in group dynamics research and theory.* Ann

Arbor, Mich.: Research Center for Group Dynamics, 1956.

Jennings, Helen H. *Leadership and isolation.* New York: Longmans, Green, 1950. (2nd ed.).

Jennings, Helen H. Sociometric structure in personality and group formation. In M. Sherif & M. O. Wilson (Eds.), *Group relations at the crossroads.* New York: Harper, 1953, 332–365.

Jones, E. E., & Thibaut, J. W. Interaction goals as the bases of inference in interpersonal perception. In R. Tagiuri & L. Petrullo (Eds.), *Person perception and interpersonal behavior.* Stanford, Cal.: Stanford Univ. Press, 1958.

Katz, E., & Lazarsfeld, P. F. *Personal influence.* Glencoe, Ill.: Free Press, 1955.

Kelman, H. C. *Social influence and personal belief: A theoretical and experimental approach to the study of behavior change.* New York: Wiley. (In press).

Kelman, H. C. Processes of opinion change, *The public opinion quarterly,* 1961, 25, 57–78.

Kilpatrick, F. P. (Ed.). *Human behavior from the transactional point of view.* Princeton, N.J.: Institute for Associated Research, 1952.

Klein, Josephine. *The study of groups.* London: Routledge & Kegan Paul Ltd., 1956.

Krasner, L. Studies of the conditioning of verbal behavior. *Psychol. Bull.,* 1958, 55, 148–170.

Lambert, W. W. Stimulus-response contiguity and reinforcement theory in social psychology. In G. Lindzey (Ed.), *Handbook of social psychology.* Reading, Mass.: Addison-Wesley, 1954.

Lewin, K. *Resolving social conflict.* New York: Harper, 1948.

Lewin, K. *Field Theory in Social Science: selected theoretical papers* (Ed. by D. Cartwright). New York: Harper, 1951.

Lewin, K. *Psychologique dynamique.*

Les relations humaines. Paris: Presses Univérsitaires de France, 1959.

Lindsley, O. R. Characteristics of the behavior of chronic psychotics as revealed by free-operant conditioning methods. *Dis. nerv. System Monogr. Suppl.* 21, Feb. 1960.

Lindzey, G. (Ed.). *Handbook of social psychology.* Reading, Mass.: Addison-Wesley, 1954.

Lindzey, G., & Borgatta, E. F. Sociometric measurement. In G. Lindzey (Ed.), *Handbook of social psychology.* Reading, Mass.: Addison-Wesley, 1954.

Maccoby, Eleanor, Newcomb, T. M., & Hartley, E. L. *Readings in social psychology.* (3rd ed.) New York: Holt, 1958.

MacLeod, R. B. Person perception: A commentary. In H. P. David & J. C. Brengelmann (Eds.), *Perspectives in personality research.* New York: Springer, 1960.

Mann, R. D. A review of the relationship between personality and performance in small groups. *Psychol. Bull.,* 1959, 56, 241–270.

McClelland, D. C., Atkinson, J. W., Clark, R. A., & Lowell, E. L. *The achievement motive.* New York: Appleton-Century-Crofts, 1953.

McDougall, W. *Introduction to social psychology.* London: Methuen, 1908.

McDougall, W. *The group mind.* New York: G. P. Putnam, 1920.

McGrath, J. E. *A framework for integration of small group research studies.* Arlington, Va.: Psychological Research Associates, 1957.

Miller, J. G. (Ed.). *Experiments in social process. A symposium on social psychology.* New York: McGraw-Hill, 1950.

Miller, J. G. Toward a general theory for the behavioral sciences. *Amer. Psychologist,* 1955, 10, 513–531.

Moreno, J. L. *Das Stegreiftheater.* (Spontaneity theater). Potsdam: G. Kiepenheuer Verlag, 1923.

Moreno, J. L. Who shall survive?

Nerv. ment. Dis. Monogr. No. 58, 1934, Washington, D.C.

Moreno, J. L. (Ed.). *Sociometry and the science of man.* New York: Beacon House, 1956.

Moreno, J. L. (Ed.). *Sociometric reader.* Glencoe, Ill.: Free Press, 1960.

Morse, N. C. *Satisfactions in the white-collar job.* Ann Arbor, Mich.: Institute for Social Research, 1953.

Murchison, C. C. (Ed.) *Handbook of social psychology.* Worcester, Mass.: Clark Univ. Press, 1935.

Murphy, G., Murphy, Lois B., & Newcomb, T. M. *Experimental social psychology.* New York: Harper, 1937.

Newcomb, T. M. *Personality and social change.* New York: Dryden, 1943.

Newcomb, T. M. The cognition of persons as cognizers. In R. Tagiuri & L. Petrullo (Eds.), *Person perception and interpersonal behavior.* Stanford, Cal.: Stanford Univ. Press, 1958.

Newcomb, T. M. Individual systems of orientation. In S. Koch (Ed.), *Psychology: A study of the science.* New York: McGraw-Hill, 1959, Vol. 3, 384–422.

Newcomb, T. M., Hartley, E. L., & others. *Readings in social psychology.* New York: Holt, 1947.

Nowlis, V. Methods for the objective study of drug effects on group functioning. In J. G. Miller & L. Uhr (Eds.), *Drugs and behavior.* New York: Wiley, 1961.

Olmsted, M. S. *The small group.* New York: Random House, 1959.

OSS Assessment Staff. *The assessment of men. Selection of men for the Office of Strategic Services.* New York: Rinehart, 1948.

Parsons, T., Bales, R. F., & Shils, E. A. *Working papers in the theory of action.* Glencoe, Ill.: Free Press, 1953.

Parsons, T., & Shils, E. A. *Toward a general theory of action.* Cambridge, Mass.: Harvard Univ. Press, 1951.

Peak, Helen. Psychological structure and person perception. In R. Tagiuri & L. Petrullo (Eds.), *Person perception and interpersonal behavior.* Stanford, Cal.: Stanford Univ. Press, 1958.

Petrullo, L., & Bass, B. M. (Eds.). *Leadership and interpersonal behavior.* New York: Holt, Rinehart, and Winston, 1961.

Raven, B. *A bibliography of publications relating to the small group.* Los Angeles, Cal.: UCLA, 1959.

Raven, B. The dynamics of groups. *Rev. educ. Res.,* 1959, *29,* 332–343.

Roethlisberger, F. J., Dickson, W. J., & Wright, H. A. *Management and the worker.* Cambridge, Mass.: Harvard Univ. Press, 1939.

Rohrer, J. H. and Sherif, M. *Social psychology at the crossroads.* New York: Harper, 1951.

Roseborough, Mary E. Experimental studies in small groups. *Psychol. Bull.,* 1953, *50,* 275–303.

Rosenberg, M. J. Cognitive reorganization in response to the hypnotic reversal of attitudinal affect. *J. Personality,* 1960a, *28,* 39–63.

Rosenberg, M. J. A structural theory of attitude dynamics. *Public Opinion Quarterly,* Summer, 1960b.

Rosenberg, M. J. An analysis of affective-cognitive consistency. In M. J. Rosenberg, C. I. Hovland, W. J. McGuire, R. P. Abelson, & J. W. Brehm, *Attitude organization and change.* New Haven, Conn.: Yale Univ. Press, 1961.

Ross, E. A. *Social psychology.* New York: Macmillan, 1908.

Rotter, J. B. *Social learning and clinical psychology.* Englewood, N.J.: Prentice-Hall, 1954.

Salzinger, K. Experimental manipulation of verbal behavior: a review. *J. gen. Psychol.,* 1959, *61,* 65–94.

Salzinger, K., & Pisoni, Stephanie. Reinforcement of verbal affect responses of normal subjects during the interview. *J. abnorm. soc. Psychol.,* 1960, *60,* 127–130.

Saslow, G., & Matarazzo, J. D. A technique for studying changes in interview behavior. In *Res. Psychother.* Washington, D.C.: Amer. Psychol. Assoc., 1959.

Schachter, S. *The psychology of affiliation.* Stanford, Cal.: Stanford Univ. Press, 1959.

Schein, E. H. *Coercive Persuasion.* New York: Norton, 1961.

Schutz, W. C. *FIRO. A three dimensional theory of personal behavior.* New York, Rinehart, 1958.

Schutz, W. C. The ego, FIRO theory and the leader as completer. In L. Petrullo & B. M. Bass (Eds.), *Leadership and interpersonal behavior.* New York: Holt, Rinehart, and Winston, 1961.

Scott, W. A. Social psychological correlates of mental illness and mental health. *Psychol. Bull.,* 1958, *55,* 65–87.

Shartle, C. L. *Executive performance and leadership.* Englewood Cliffs, N.J.: Prentice-Hall, 1956.

Sherif, M. A study of some social factors in perception. *Arch. Psychol.,* 1935, No. 187.

Sherif, M. *The psychology of social norms.* New York: Harper, 1936.

Sherif, M. and Harvey, O. J. A study in ego functioning: elimination of stable anchorages in individual and group situations. *Sociometry,* 1952, *15,* 272–305.

Sherif, M., & Sherif, Carolyn. *Groups in harmony and tension.* New York: Harper, 1953.

Sherif, M., & Sherif, Carolyn W. *An outline of social psychology.* New York: Harper, 1956.

Shils, E. A. The study of the primary group. In D. Lerner & H. Lasswell (Eds.), *The policy sciences.* Stanford, Cal.: Stanford Univ. Press, 1951.

Stimson, J. Some religious-ethnic differences in interaction rates. *Psychol. Repts.,* 1960, *7,* 345–356.

Stock, Dorothy, & Thelen, H. A. *Emotional dynamics and group culture.*

Washington, D.C.: National Training Laboratories, 1958.

Stouffer, S. *et al. The American soldier.* Princeton, N.J.: Princeton Univ. Press, 1949.

Strodtbeck, F. L., & Hare, A. P. Bibliography of small group research (from 1900–1953). *Sociometry,* 1954, *17,* 107–178.

Strupp, H. H. Nature of psychotherapist's contribution to treatment process. *Arch. gen. Psychol.,* 1960, *3,* 219–231.

Swanson, G. E., Newcomb, T. M., & Hartley, E. L. *Readings in social psychology.* New York: Holt, 1952.

Taffel, C. Anxiety and the conditioning of verbal behavior. *J. abnorm. soc. Psychol.,* 1955, *51,* 496–501.

Tagiuri, R. Perception of persons: report of the interuniversity summer research seminar. *Item,* 1956, *10,* 2–5.

Tagiuri, R., & Bruner, J. S. The perception of people. In G. Lindzey (Ed.), *Handbook of social psychology.* Reading, Mass.: Addison-Wesley, 1954.

Tagiuri, R., & Petrullo, L. (Eds.). *Person perception and interpersonal behavior.* Stanford, Cal.: Stanford Univ. Press, 1958.

Terauds, A., Altman, I., & McGrath, J. E. *A bibliography of small group research.* Arlington, Va.: Human Sciences Research, Inc., 1960.

Thelen, H. A. Work-emotionality theory of the group as organism. In S. Koch (Ed.), *Psychology: a study of the science.* New York: McGraw-Hill, 1959. Vol. 3, 544–611.

Thibaut, J. W., & Kelley, H. H. *The social psychology of groups.* New York: Wiley, 1959.

Thrasher, F. M. *The gang.* Chicago: Univ. Chicago Press, 1927.

Verplanck, W. S. The control of the contents of conversation: Reinforcement of statements of opinion. *J. abnorm. soc. Psychol.,* 1955, *51,* 668–676.

Whyte, W. F. *Street corner society.* Chicago: Univ. Chicago Press, 1943.

Wilson, L. Sociography of groups. In Gurvitch & W. E. Moore (Eds.), *Twentieth century sociology.* New York: Philosophical Library, 1945. Ch. 7, 139–171.

Wittreich, W. J. The influence of simulated mutilation upon the perception of the human figure. *J. abnorm. soc. Psychol.,* 1955, *51,* 493–495.

Wittreich, W. J., & Radcliffe, K. B., Jr. Differences in the perception of an authority figure and a nonauthority figure by Navy recruits. *J. abnorm. soc. Psychol.,* 1956, *56,* 383–384.

8

The Reactions of
Humans to Cognitive Dissonance

LEON FESTINGER and DANA BRAMEL

The idea that an individual strives for "consistency" among his opinions, attitudes, and values is neither particularly new nor particularly dramatic. All of us, for example, have at one time or another experienced the discomfort of having someone point out to us during some discussion that we have made two or more contradictory statements. The existence of such contradiction usually makes us feel that something must be done about it, something is wrong. We also, of course, assume that other people feel the same way about contradictions or "inconsistencies." Finding some inconsistency among the opinions and values of another person is, usually, a very effective beginning step in the process of persuading him to change his opinion. The converse has also been frequently recognized. For example, many people feel that one of the difficulties of doing psychotherapy with a person who has a paranoid delusion is the fact that the delusion usually is internally consistent.

There is probably no one whose behavior, opinions, beliefs, and values comprise a perfectly consistent system. And although the inconsistencies which exist may be bothersome, frequently there is little one can do to eliminate them. This may be the reason for the widespread popularity of the reassuring quotation that "foolish consistency is the hobgoblin of little minds." This may be a way of reducing the discomfort of the inconsistencies which exist. Usually people forget that the first word in that quotation is the word "foolish"; and rarely does one hear anyone ask how one distinguishes foolish consistency from other kinds.

Only within the last ten years have psychologists begun seriously to concern themselves with questions about inconsistency—such as what is and what is not inconsistent psychologically and how do people react to such inconsistency. Rogers (1951) has emphasized the importance of inconsistency involving the self concept; Heider (1946) has discussed the consequences of inconsistency in the perception of relations among persons; Osgood and Tannenbaum (1955) have presented a theory concerning changes of opinion as a result of inconsistency between the source of a persuasive communication and its content. All of these authors have emphasized specific inconsistencies and have discussed how people cope with them. An attempt to state a very general theory about such inconsistency and reactions to it has been made by Festinger (1957). Because of its more general formulation, this theoretical statement had the advantage of being able to deal with a wide variety of seemingly dissimilar situations, all of which had inconsistency at their core. This theory of cognitive dissonance has proved useful in accounting for certain aspects of communication and influence processes, consequences of decisions, effects of forced compliance, and others. In the following discussion we will present the theory of cognitive dissonance in brief outline along with some examples of supporting empirical evidence. Special attention will be given to those aspects of the theory, and to those studies, which seem especially relevant to the problems of interest to clinical psychologists.

The word "dissonance," in its ordinary meaning, refers to an inharmonious, inconsistent, discrepant relation between two things. The usage in the theory is similar to this. A cognition is something a person knows about himself, about his behavior, or about his surroundings. Dissonance is said to exist when two cognitions, occurring together, are inconsistent with each other according to the expectations of the person. If, for the person, the obverse of one cognition would follow from the other, there is dissonance. These expectations of what goes with what are built up on the basis of past experience, including notions of logical relations, cultural mores, and learned empirical correlations among events. Thus, if a person's consciously hostile and insulting behavior toward a stranger were responded to with kindness and affection, the cognitions representing these facts would be dissonant with one another because he knows from experience that retaliation, not affection, follows from insult. Two cognitions are said to be consonant if, considering them alone, one follows from the other. If a cognition leads to no implications about another cognition, then the two are defined as irrelevant in the theory. For most people, the cognition that the sun is shining is irrelevant to the cognition that it is Wednesday.

The central hypothesis of the theory is that the presence of dissonance gives rise to pressure to reduce that dissonance, and that the strength of this pressure is a direct function of the magnitude of the existing dissonance. There are three major ways in which dissonance may be reduced. The person may change one or more of the cognitions involved in dissonant relations; he may add new cognitions that are consonant with already existing cognitions; and he may decrease the subjective importance of the cognitions which are involved in the dissonant relations. Dissonance is conceived as a motivating state comparable to other drive states. Successful reduction of dissonance is, for example, comparable to successful reduction of a state of hunger.

From this outline of the core of the theory, it can be seen that the individual is conceived as seeking for consistency among his opinions, attitudes, knowledge, and values. Research growing out of the theory has been aimed at specifying the antecedent variables affecting the magnitude of dissonance and at discovering the kinds of dissonance reducing processes most likely to occur in response to different dissonance producing situations. The usefulness of the theory is best illustrated by the specific derivations that have been made from it, a number of which are contrary both to "common sense" and to what one would expect from other theoretical formulations.

THE CONTENT OF RUMORS: AN INSTRUCTIVE EXAMPLE

Most theories in psychology assume, explicitly or implicitly, that persons avoid unpleasant things such as pain, discomfort, the arousal of anxiety, and the like. And, certainly, the validity of such a notion is usually borne out by data and observation. Sometimes, however, one may observe behavior which looks as though it is contradictory to this widely accepted assumption. Let us examine one study which presents data showing that, at least under some circumstances, instead of reducing and avoiding anxiety, persons actively seemed to arouse anxiety in themselves and others.

Prasad (1950) recorded rumors which were widely circulated immediately following an especially severe earthquake in India in 1934. The quake itself, a rather prolonged one, was felt over a large geographical area. Actual damage, however, was quite localized. The rumors were collected in the area where people felt the shock of the earthquake but did not suffer or see any damage.

Prasad reports little concerning the emotional reactions of people to the quake but it is probably plausible to assume that these people, who knew little about earthquakes, had strong reactions of fear to the violent and prolonged shaking of the ground. We may also assume that such a strong fear reaction did not vanish immediately but probably persisted for some time after the actual shock of the quake was over. Thus, while these people had a strong and persistent fear reaction, they could see nothing different around them, no destruction, no further threatening things. In short, a situation had been produced where dissonance existed between the cognition corresponding to the fear they felt and the knowledge of what they saw around them which, one might say, amounted to the cognition that there was nothing to be afraid of.

The vast majority of the rumors which were widely circulated were rumors which, if believed, provided cognitions consonant with being afraid. One might call them "fear-provoking" rumors, although if our interpretation is correct, they would more properly be called "fear-justifying" rumors. The following are typical of many of the rumors which Prasad reports:

"There will be a severe cyclone at Patna between January 18 and January 19." (The earthquake occurred on January 15.)

"There will be a severe earthquake on the lunar eclipse day."

"A flood was rushing from the Nepal borders to Madhubani."

"January 23 will be a fatal day. Unforeseeable calamities will arise."

If this explanation is correct in accounting for the prevalence of these "fear-justifying" rumors, one would expect that if rumors had been collected among persons living *in* the area of destruction, few, if any, such rumors would have been found. People who were in the area of destruction were, undoubtedly, also frightened. Indeed, their fear reaction would very likely have been even stronger than that of the persons who merely felt the shock of the quake. But for the people in the area of destruction, the things they could see around them (the destruction, the wounded and killed) would produce cognition which would be consonant with feeling afraid. There would be no impulse or desire to acquire additional cognitions which fit with the fear, and fearful rumors of the type so prevalent outside the area of destruction should have been absent.

Unfortunately, Prasad presents no data on rumors which circulated inside the area of destruction following the earthquake. There is, however, another study reported by Sinha (1952) which bears on this. This study reports rumors following a disaster in Darjeeling, India, a disaster which was comparable to the earthquake in terms of destruction and loss of life but which arose as a result of a landslide. Nevertheless, it must have produced considerable fear among the people. Sinha directly compares the two when, in describing the landslide disaster, he states:

"There was a feeling of instability and uncertainty similar to that which followed the Great Indian Earthquake of 1934." (p. 200)

There is, however, one important difference between the study reported by Prasad and the one reported by Sinha. While the rumors following the earthquake were collected among persons outside the area of destruction, the rumors which Sinha reports were collected from persons who actually were in the area and witnessed the destruction. Since for these people there would have been no dissonance—what they saw and knew was quite consonant with being afraid—we would not expect disaster rumors to arise and spread among them.

Actually, in Sinha's report, there is a complete absence of rumors predicting further disasters or of any type of rumor that might be regarded as supplying cognition consonant with being afraid. The contrast between the rumors reported by Sinha and those reported by Prasad is very strong. Of course, the uncontrolled nature of these provocative findings allows for many alternative interpretations. Nevertheless, the interpretation from the theory of dissonance that the rumors might be fear-justifying seems interesting and plausible. We will now turn to some less ambiguous data bearing upon the theory of dissonance.

THE CONSEQUENCES OF DECISIONS

A considerable amount of theory has been developed in psychology concerning conflict and decision situations and a considerable amount of experimental work has been done on the behavior of people in decision situations. Very little, however, has been said or done concerning the behavior of a person subsequent to the making of a decision. The making of a decision may terminate the conflict situation for a person, and theories concerning conflict behavior may no longer be relevant to the person's behavior, but there still exist interesting questions which may be raised. Let us examine carefully the situation in which a person finds himself after he has made a decision, let us say, between two alternative courses of action.

In most situations, the course of action which the person chose will have some favorable and some unfavorable aspects to it, at least in the cognition of the person who chose it. The rejected course (or courses) of action also undoubtedly has both favorable and unfavorable aspects to it. To the extent that this is true, we must accept the fact that, subsequent to having made a choice, the person has a considerable amount of knowledge which is dissonant with his cognitions concerning the choice he has made. If one considers solely his knowledge concerning the unfavorable aspects of the chosen alternative and his knowledge concerning the favorable aspects of the rejected alternative, it is clear that these represent cognitions which are dissonant with his cognition concerning his behavior.

If such postdecision dissonance exists, we would expect to observe evidence of tendencies to reduce the dissonance after a decision has been made. There are, as always, a number of ways in which such postdecision dissonance may be reduced. The person may persuade himself that aspects of the rejected alternative which had previously appeared as favorable are, in reality, not favorable at all; he may persuade himself that seemingly negative aspects of the chosen alternative are, after all, advantages; and he may also find new considerations favoring the chosen alternative which he had never thought of before. Imagine, for example, a student who, after considerable conflict, decides to go out on a date rather than study on the night before an examination. After having made his decision he may be expected to try to convince himself that studying more would not have helped him; that, in fact, last-minute cramming might be positively harmful; that the girl is really extremely attractive; and that the movie he will take her to is one that he very much wants to see. The net effect of all this, whatever the specific form of the dissonance reduction, would be to increase the attractiveness of the chosen alternative and/or to decrease the attractiveness of the rejected alternative after a decision has been made.

Brehm (1956) tested this hypothesis in the laboratory by giving subjects a choice between objects and by measuring the change in attractiveness of the objects from before to after the decision was made. Each subject was told that the experimenter was engaged in market research for a number of manufacturers of various kinds of products. As a reward for participation, the subject was told she would be given a rather valuable gift from one of the manufacturers. The experimenter then arranged eight objects, each worth approximately twenty dollars, in front of the subject. These included electrical appliances and art objects. The subject was asked to rate each object as to its desirability. Then it was explained that she was to receive one of these objects as a gift, and that she would be given a choice between two selected by the experimenter. After she had made her choice she was again asked to rate each of the objects.

Half of the subjects were given a choice between two objects which they had rated as differing only a small amount in attractiveness. The other subjects were asked to choose between two objects which they had rated as very different in desirability. According to the theory, there should be more dissonance for subjects in the condition where the rejected alternative was close to the chosen alternative in desirability, since for them there would be more favorable aspects of the rejected object. The results showed clearly that chosen objects increased, and rejected objects decreased, in attractiveness as a result of the choice. Further, these changes were greater for the subjects who chose between objects of similar desirability. Data from a control group, who were given a gift without having made a choice, revealed that the changes were not attributable to statistical regression or to tendencies simply to like things which one owns.

In a study by Brehm and Cohen (1959) it was found further that greater postdecision dissonance resulted from having to choose from among more than two alternatives. This might be expected from the theory, since the more alternatives rejected, the more knowledge there would be concerning favorable characteristics of these rejected alternatives. If all these cognitions concerning the favorable aspects of rejected alternatives are dissonant with the cognition concerning the choice that was made, one would expect more dissonance reduction when a choice is made of one among several alternatives than when the choice is made just between two alternatives. The study by Brehm and Cohen clearly shows this to be the case.

THE WILLINGNESS TO EXERT EFFORT OR ENDURE INCONVENIENCE

If some goal is sufficiently attractive to a person, he may be induced to exert considerable effort or to suffer considerable pain and inconvenience in order to reach the goal. Sometimes such goals, when reached, do not turn out to be as desirable as had been anticipated. Thus, for example, a student might work very hard in order to obtain an idealized Ph.D. degree and then discover, when the degree is obtained, that the advantages it confers on him are less than he had expected. If we examine the cognitions which a person would have under such circumstances, we may infer the existence of dissonance. The cognitions concerning the effort expended and the inconvenience which was endured would be dissonant with the knowledge of some of the exact characteristics of the goal which has been obtained. In order to reduce the dissonance the person may do either of two things—he may persuade himself that the effort and inconvenience were negligible or he may persuade himself that the goal really is, after all, terribly attractive. Thus, the student of our example above might persuade himself that the life of a student was really fun and the Ph.D. degree was an extremely important thing. Or to take another hypothetical, and slightly facetious, example, let us imagine a person who, because of various problems which he has, is sufficiently motivated to spend large sums of money in order to consult a psychoanalyst. Let us pretend that, far from receiving help, he finds that the analytic sessions leave him even more troubled than he had been before. Such a person, in order to reduce dissonance, might persuade himself that psychoanalysis and psychoanalytic theory represent indisputable truth and that the analyst himself is someone to be loved and revered.

In order to test these implications of dissonance theory, an appropriate kind of situation was simulated in a laboratory experiment by Aronson and Mills (1959). In this experiment college women volunteered to join a group for the purpose of participating in a series of discussions on the psychology of sex. The subjects were randomly assigned to one of three experimental conditions: a *severe initiation* condition, a *mild initiation* condition, and a *no initiation* condition. In the *severe* and *mild initiation* conditions each subject was told that, in order to gain admission to the group, she would be required to demonstrate that she was sophisticated enough to participate freely and frankly in a sexually oriented discussion. An "embarrassment test" was then administered in which the subject read aloud some sexually oriented material in the presence of the male experimenter. The experimenter explained that he would judge from her performance whether or not she qualified for admission to the group. In the *severe initiation* condition the "embarrassment test" consisted of the reciting of a number of obscene words plus some lurid sexual passages from contemporary novels. In the *mild initiation* condition the subjects were simply required to recite a short list of rather genteel sexually oriented words. In the *no initiation* condition the subject was allowed to enter the group without going through any initiation.

Each of the subjects then listened to the same tape recording of a group discussion which she believed was a live discussion being conducted by the group she had just joined. The recordings was a rather dull, banal, and irrelevant discussion of the secondary sex behavior of lower animals. The participants spoke haltingly, inarticulately, and unenthusiastically. Immediately after listening to the tape recording, each subject was asked to rate the discussion and the group members on several evaluative scales: e.g., dull-interesting, intelligent-unintelligent.

The experimenters reasoned that, in the *severe initiation* condition, the subjects would experience dissonance; their cognition that they had undergone an extremely embarrassing experience to become a member of a group would be dissonant with their cognitions concerning the negative aspects of the group. They could reduce the dissonance by distorting their perceptions of the discussion in a positive direction. In the *no initiation* and *mild initiation* conditions, however, the subjects made relatively little investment in order to enter the group and, hence, would not be expected to experience much dissonance. The results show clearly that the subjects in the *severe initiation* condition rated the group as being more attractive and the discussion more interesting than did the subjects in either the *mild* or *no initiation* conditions. The results thus strongly supported the theoretical predictions.

There are many occasions on which pressure is exerted on a person to behave overtly in a certain way or to state publicly a certain opinion. Obviously, if the person is already inclined to engage in the given behavior or if his private opinion already agrees with the public statement he is urged to make, there is little problem involved and little or no pressure is required to produce the overt action. An interesting situation is produced, however, if the person's private opinions or private inclinations disagree with the overt actions in which he is urged to engage. If sufficient pressure in the form of offers of reward for compliance or threats of punishment for noncompliance is brought to bear on the person, he will undoubtedly engage in the overt action, but dissonance will then exist. The knowledge that he believes one thing will, of course, be dissonant with the knowledge that he has done or said the opposite.

If such dissonance is created in a compliance situation, one should be able to observe some of the effects of dissonance reduction. Frequently, particularly if the overt behavior cannot be easily changed or revoked, the dissonance will be reduced by changing the private opinion so as to bring it closer to what the person has overtly said. For example, imagine a child who really enjoys school work but who, because of a desire for the social approval of his peers, publicly states, again and again, that he hates school. One would expect from the theory of dissonance that such a child would gradually change his opinion in the direction of actually disliking school.

In the overt compliance situation there will, of course, be some cognitions consonant with knowledge of the overt behavior. The knowledge that one is receiving a reward or avoiding a punishment is consonant with the knowledge that one has performed the requested behavior. That is, considering these cognitions alone, the knowledge that one will be rewarded or will avoid punishment implies that one does what is requested. The greater the reward or threatened punishment, the more weight this consonance will have in the person's thinking. Consider, for example, a situation where a man came up to you and said he would give you a million dollars if you publicly stated that you liked reading comic books. Let us assume, for the sake of the example, that you believe him and that you do not like reading comic books. Very likely you would publicly announce your preference for comic books, pocket the million dollars, and be quite content. There is some slight dissonance, to be sure. You said you liked comic books and you really do not. But there are some very important elements that are consonant with having uttered this public statement—namely, the knowledge of the money now in your pocket. Relative to this, the dissonance is negligible and one would expect little or no opinion change in order to reduce the dissonance. Only if the pressure which produced the compliance was relatively small would the magnitude of dissonance be large.

Suppose a number of people have had an experience to which they reacted negatively. Each of these persons, then, let us say, is offered a different amount of money to tell someone else that the experience was very pleasant and enjoyable. In each case, let us further imagine, the amount of money offered is at least large enough so that the person accepts the money and engages in the overt behavior required. Certainly, after telling someone that the experience was enjoyable, there is dissonance between his cognition of what he has said and his own private opinion.

This dissonance could be reduced if the person persuaded himself that the experience was, indeed, fairly pleasant and enjoyable; that is, if he changed his private opinion so that it corresponded more closely with what he had said. The greater the dissonance, the more frequently should one observe such subsequent attitude change. We would expect then that, after the person had told someone else that the experience was pleasant and enjoyable, he would change his private opinions concerning the experience to some extent. We would further expect that the more money he was given to induce him to make the public statement, the smaller would be the subsequent opinion change, because a lesser magnitude of dissonance had been created initially. The more important the consonant relations (being rewarded for the behavior), the less the over-all magnitude of dissonance.

This prediction was tested in a study by Festinger and Carlsmith (1959). In this experiment, subjects performed a series of extremely boring and tedious tasks for one hour. After they had finished the tasks, the experimenter falsely "explained the purpose of the experiment." The subjects were told that the purpose was to see whether people perform better if they are told beforehand that the tasks are interesting and enjoyable than if they are not told anything. The experimenter explained that, in the experimental condition, an accomplice poses as a subject who has just finished the experiment and tells a waiting subject that the task was a lot of fun. The experimenter then appeared very uncomfortable and explained to the subject that a girl was now waiting to be tested and the accomplice had not shown up yet. He then asked the subject if he would do him a favor by substituting for the accomplice and telling the waiting subject that the tasks are interesting and fun. He offered to pay the subject for doing this and for serving as a substitute accomplice in case of future emergencies.

Each subject was assigned to one of three conditions: (1) A one-dollar condition, in which the subject was paid one dollar for serving as an accomplice; (2) a twenty-dollar condition, in which the subject was paid twenty dollars for the same job; and (3) a *control* condition in which the subject was not asked to lie to the waiting subject.

Each subject was interviewed after he had complied with the request, and was asked to rate how enjoyable the tasks were. The results supported the predictions made from the theory. In the control condition and in the twenty-dollar condition, the subjects felt the tasks were rather unenjoyable; there was no difference between the ratings made by the subjects in these two conditions. In the one-dollar condition, however, the subjects rated the tasks as rather enjoyable. The ratings of the tasks by the subjects in the one-dollar condition were significantly more positive than those in either the twenty-dollar condition or the control condition. In short, inducing a person to make a public statement which was contrary to his private belief introduced considerable dissonance when the reward offered for making the public statement was small. If too much pressure is applied to elicit the overt behavior, the dissonance aroused is correspondingly less and private change of opinion does not occur.

THE EFFECTS OF TEMPTATION

Let us consider a person who is tempted, by anticipation of a reward. to perform some act which he regards as immoral. If he performs the act, there may be dissonance between his knowledge that the act is immoral and the knowledge that he has done it. One way in which he might reduce this dissonance would be to change his attitude toward the behavior, that is, to convince himself it is not really so very immoral. Since his cognitions about the reward he receives for performing the act are consonant with performing the act, the over-all dissonance is less the greater the reward. One would, therefore, expect on the basis of the theory that there would be less attitude change the greater the reward anticipated or received.

How about the person who is tempted, but resists the temptation and refrains from committing the immoral act? For him the cognition that the act is immoral is probably consonant with his knowledge that he refrained from performing it. However, his knowledge that he is giving up a reward is dissonant with cognitions about his behavior. The over-all dissonance may be reduced by increasing the number and importance of cognitions consonant with the behavior to which the person has committed himself. In the case of the individual who resists temptation this can be done by convincing himself that the act is extremely immoral, thus justifying his behavior.

Whereas the person who succumbs to temptation has less dissonance the greater the reward he gains, the person who resists temptation has more dissonance the greater the reward he forsakes.

These hypotheses were tested in an experiment by Mills (1958). Sixth-grade students were first given a questionnaire intended to measure the severity of their attitudes toward cheating. They then participated in a contest in which each subject individually worked at a task involving eye and hand coordination. Some groups were told the winners would receive a large reward, while other groups were led to expect only a small reward for winning. The task was constructed in such a manner that cheating was possible but could be secretly detected by the experimenter. In each condition, as it happened, there were some subjects who cheated and some who did not.

One day later the subjects were again asked to indicate their attitudes toward cheating. On the average, those children who cheated became more lenient toward cheating, while those who did not cheat became more severe in their moral attitude toward cheating. Again, the magnitude of this effect was a function of how much dissonance was introduced experimentally. Those children who cheated for a small prize changed more toward feeling lenient about cheating than did those who cheated for a large prize. Among those who did not cheat, the changes in the direction of greater severity toward cheating were larger for those who gave up a large prize by not cheating than for those who gave up only a small prize.

REACTIONS TO DISAGREEMENT

One of the most widely explored areas in the field of social psychology is that of how people react to disagreement from others and the nature of the ensuing persuasive influence process. In many ways, the usual psychotherapeutic situation can also be seen as one involving social influence to a major extent and, for this reason, research on how people react to dissonance-producing communications from others should be of particular interest to clinical psychologists.

Although this is not the place to embark upon a review of the state of knowledge concerning determinants of opinion change, it is appropriate to outline some of the clarifications suggested by the theory of cognitive dissonance.

When a person is confronted with an opinion contrary to his own which is held by people whom he respects, he experiences dissonance. Considering these two cognitions alone, the knowledge that a favorably evaluated person holds a given opinion implies subjectively that one

also holds that opinion. There is considerable evidence from laboratory experimentation that the magnitude of the dissonance thus introduced will depend upon the importance of the person or group that
voices the disagreement and on the importance and relevance to the
individual of the issue concerning which the disagreement exists (Festinger, 1957).

According to the theory the magnitude of dissonance increases with
increasing discrepancy between one's own belief and the belief being
advocated by a respected person. If greater extent of disagreement
creates greater magnitude of dissonance, then one should observe more
attempts at dissonance reduction as the extent of disagreement increases. Since opinion change is one means of reducing dissonance,
one might expect greater opinion change resulting from greater disagreement.

Experimental work on the relation between extent of disagreement
and amount of opinion change has not, however, yielded very consistent results (Hovland, 1959; Hovland and Pritzker, 1957). Sometimes greater disagreement seems to result in more opinion change and
sometimes in less opinion change. A possible explanation is that, as
the extent of disagreement increases, the tendency to reduce dissonance primarily by derogating the disagreeing person also increases. If
this were true, then an experiment which only measured opinion
change and did not control the ease with which the disagreeing person
could be derogated might indeed be expected to show variable effects,
since these two are alternative methods of reducing dissonance.

Zimbardo (1960) performed an experiment designed to throw some
light on this problem. In his study he attempted to minimize the possible use of derogation of the disagreeing person as a dissonance reducing technique by always having the disagreement come from a
very close friend. The subjects, eighty college girls, volunteered for the
experiment in such a way that each was paired with a friend. The two
subjects were told that they were to evaluate some aspects of the
problem of juvenile delinquency. After reading a case history, each
subject privately indicated her opinion concerning the locus of blame
for the youth's crime. Forty of the subjects were told that their response to the case study material would be a good indicator of their
basic social values and their personality (*high involvement*). The
other forty were led to believe that the task would not effectively reveal important aspects of their personality (*low involvement*).

At the same time, half the subjects were led to believe that the
opinion of each's friend was extremely discrepant from their own while
the other half believed each's friend's opinion to be only slightly discrepant from their own. "Extremely discrepant" in this study was de-

fined as being in a range which the subject had previously indicated was unreasonable and indefensible.

On the assumption that derogation of a close friend would not occur, change in opinion was used as an index of dissonance reduction. The results showed clearly that (1) the more involved a subject was, the more she tended to shift her opinion in the direction of that of her friend; (2) the greater the discrepancy between a subject's opinion and her friend's opinion, the more she tended to shift her opinion in the direction of that of her friend.

In short, the experiment by Zimbardo presents clear evidence that the magnitude of dissonance introduced by disagreement increases, even where the disagreeing person voices an opinion outside of the range that the person considers acceptable and reasonable. If alternative methods of dissonance reduction, such as derogating the source of the disagreement, are made difficult, then there results a clear relationship: the greater the amount of disagreement, the greater the amount of resulting opinion change.

Bergin (1960) recently noted the conceptual similarity between "depth interpretation" in certain kinds of therapy and "degree of discrepancy" in the study of the effects of persuasive communications. That is, he points out that usually what is meant by a "deep" interpretation is a statement by the therapist which is highly discrepant from the client's own opinion in the same sense in which Zimbardo used the term "extremely discrepant." Theorists of psychotherapy vary greatly in their recommendations regarding the most effective depth of interpretation. They range from Rogers (1951), who advocates paraphrasing the client's own responses, through the classical psychoanalytic position (e.g., Fenichel, 1941) that interpretations should be "moderate" in depth, to the position of those (e.g., Klein, 1937) who argue that "deep" interpretations should be made even early in therapy. Fenichel suggests that "deep" interpretations are likely to alienate the client. A tentative generalization from Zimbardo's experiment would suggest, on the other hand, that "deep" (highly discrepant) interpretations would produce more change than "moderate" ones, providing that the client had great respect for the therapist's competence.

In order to determine whether Zimbardo's finding would be reproduced in a situation more closely approaching therapy, Bergin designed an experiment involving two levels of credibility (respect for competence) and three degrees of discrepant communications. The content of the discrepant communications was chosen so as to be important to the subjects and related to an opinion which is rather resistant to change. Specifically, they dealt with the subject's standing on the personality dimension of masculinity-femininity. If Zimbardo's findings were replicated when the source of the communication was difficult to derogate but were not replicated if the source was easy to derogate, this would throw light on the problem of depth of interpretation in relation to influence processes.

In the high credibility condition, subjects reported individually to the Psychiatry Department at the impressive new Stanford Medical Center where the experimenter played the role of the director of a personality assessment project. The subject, after rating himself on a masculinity-femininity scale and indicating those points acceptable and not acceptable as descriptions of himself, also took a battery of impressive personality tests while being hooked up to three electrical recording devices. When the subject returned for the second session, he was shown an elaborate set of diagrams purporting to be analyses of all his previous responses. The subject was specifically told where this analysis placed him on the masculinity-femininity dimension. For different subjects, chosen at random, this information involved a "moderate," "high," or "extreme" discrepancy between his self-rating and the test results on the masculinity-femininity dimension. This was the persuasive communication. Subjects in the "moderate" discrepancy condition were told that their true position was at a point they had previously rated as "also acceptable," whereas subjects in the "extreme" discrepancy condition were led to believe that their actual position was at the point they had rated as "most contrary" to their self-rated masculinity-femininity. After receiving this information, the subject took another simple test (to provide a time gap between communication and measure of change) and was then asked to rate his masculinity-femininity again.

In the low credibility condition subjects reported to a standard small room in the laboratory section of the Psychology Department. During the first session they simply filled out a set of self-rating scales and were reminded when to report for the second session. In the second session the subject was introduced to a person, purportedly another subject, who was actually a confederate of the experimenter. The confederate was a 14-year-old male high school freshman.

The same three degrees of discrepancy were produced by having the confederate pretend to rate the subject, the actual ratings having been made in advance by the experimenter. The ratings were then shown to the subject and it was pointed out that there was a discrepancy on the masculine-feminine scale between the subject's self-rating and the position assigned to him by the other person. After a brief interpolated test, the subject was again asked to rate himself on the masculinity-femininity dimension.

The results in general confirmed the hypotheses derived from dissonance theory. In the high credibility condition there was increasing attitude change with increasing discrepancy between original self-

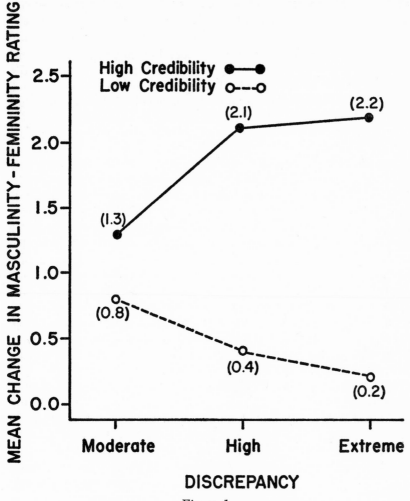

Figure 1.

rating and the persuasive communication. In the low credibility condition there was decreasing attitude change with increasing discrepancy. Figure 1 shows the results obtained. It seems clear that the impressive setting in the high credibility condition successfully prevented discrediting the communicator as a means of reducing dissonance. Under these conditions Zimbardo's results were replicated.

The "extreme" discrepancy communications used by Bergin in the high credibility condition were, of course, not as extreme as they might have been. Consequently, it is difficult to say whether attitude change would continue to increase with even greater discrepancies. We are unable to say at what point the communicator or therapist might begin to be discredited. There was some evidence in Bergin's experiment that increments of attitude change were decreasing at the "extreme" discrepancy level. Nevertheless, taking Bergin's and Zimbardo's results together, there appears to be a considerable range of discrepancies within which there is increasing attitude change with increasing dissonance, providing the perceived competence of the communicator is high, and providing that certain other avenues of dissonance reduction are effectively closed off.

DEFENSIVE PROJECTION AS
DISSONANCE REDUCTION

Many readers will by now have noted some similarity between certain mechanisms for dissonance reduction and certain "defense mechanisms" discussed in psychoanalytic theory. Many of the processes which we have described as dissonance reducing look very much like what others might call "rationalization" or "defensive denial," for example. Obviously, it is interesting to speculate about the reasons for such similarity of mechanisms in two theoretical approaches which were developed in different contexts.

One possible reason for this similarity immediately suggests itself. If certain mechanisms such as rationalization, repression, or projection are available to an organism, there is, of course, no necessity for their use to be restricted to one realm of situations. Once these mechanisms are available and developed for a person, perhaps they can be used to reduce dissonance just as readily as they can be used to avoid and reduce other kinds of psychological discomfort and pain. Another possible reason for the similarity of "mechanisms" may be that the concept of dissonance and the psychoanalytic notion of conflict have overlapping meaning. Let us look at this latter possibility a bit more closely to see if a clear distinction can be made between these two conceptual notions.

Psychoanalytic theory deals at considerable length with situations in which the individual's perception of some aspect of himself is contrary to his internalized standards of right and wrong (the superego). Imagine a person who considers homosexuality to be a bad and disgusting thing. For some reason he is suddenly exposed to information strongly implying that he has homosexual tendencies. According to psychoanalytic theory, his perception of this information arouses fear of punishment, perhaps especially a fear of painful guilt feelings (Fenichel, 1945). In order to avoid further anxiety and guilt feelings, the ego is said to initiate defensive measures, of which the most common appear to be various forms of denial of the threatening information.

In order to determine the relevance of dissonance theory to this problem it is necessary to ask whether dissonant relations would be expected to exist among the cognitions involved. Is the cognition that one has homosexual tendencies necessarily dissonant with the belief that such tendencies are bad and that one *should not* have them? The answer is no. These particular cognitions would be dissonant only for those persons who believed that they consistently lived up to their internal standards. For some people (we assume) the knowledge that a trait is undesirable does not strongly or necessarily imply in itself that one does not possess it. It follows that some people who are threatened in the psychoanalytic sense will also experience considerable dissonance, while others will not. In other words, according to psychoanalytic theory the conflict sufficient to produce defensive behavior does not necessarily include what we would define as dissonance.

This is not to say that dissonance would be completely absent from the cognition of the person who does not expect himself always to live up to his own standards. For example, when he discovers he has homosexual tendencies this knowledge may be dissonant with his belief that he is really quite masculine, even though it may not be dissonant with his conviction that homosexuality is a bad thing. In any concrete case to which the psychoanalytic theory is applied, it is quite unlikely that dissonance will be completely absent. Nevertheless, close examination reveals that any contribution which dissonance might make to defensive behavior would be in addition to the factors emphasized by psychoanalytic theory. Perhaps the key difference between the approaches at this point is highlighted by the lack of concern for the self-concept in classical psychoanalytic theory. Dissonance theory would place more emphasis upon the individual's concept of *what he is* rather than his concept of *what he should be* (superego).

The question arises whether the Freudian defense mechanisms against anxiety could also be used to reduce dissonance in the type of situation we have been discussing. Let us consider, as an example, the defense mechanism of projection, which is especially interesting to social psychologists because of its interpersonal implications. For purposes of exposition we continue with homosexuality as an example of threatening material. In order to ensure that dissonance will be great, we choose a hypothetical person who has high self-esteem, with many cognitions favorable to himself and very few which are unfavorable. He considers homosexuality a very bad thing and a matter of considerable importance. He is suddenly confronted with information that he is sexually attracted to members of his own sex. This cognition will be strongly dissonant with his cognitions concerning what a good person he is and also dissonant with his belief that he is actually quite a masculine person.

Can this dissonance be reduced by attributing homosexuality to other people? One possible way to do this would be to attribute homosexuality to people who are liked and respected in order to be able to re-evaluate homosexuality as such. If liked and respected persons possess the trait, then perhaps the trait is not so bad after all. Then possession of the trait would no longer be contradictory to a favorable level of self-esteem, and dissonance would have been reduced. A further possibility is that the person, by attributing homosexuality to members of his reference or comparison group, may be able to convince himself that he does not deviate from the persons who are most important to him. If he is only *average* in his possession of the trait, then subjectively it does not so strongly negate his favorable self-esteem.

These possibilities suggest that projection may indeed be used as a means of reducing dissonance. There are several studies in the literature (Wright, 1942; Murstein, 1956; Bachman and Secord, 1959) which are relevant to the question, but all leave certain important issues unresolved. Consequently, an experiment was recently conducted by Bramel (1969) to test whether projection is used to reduce dissonance and to throw some light on the particular ways in which this reduction may be mediated.

Each of the undergraduate male subjects who signed up for the experiment appeared individually for the first session. He was told that the first part of the experiment was designed to discover what kinds of people had insight into themselves. He was asked to take a number of personality tests which, he was told, would be carefully analyzed by members of the clinical psychology staff. After the tests were scored, he was to learn the results in an interview, during which time his self-insight would be measured. The tests included in the booklet were selected for their impressiveness (the Rorschach, for example) and variety.

At the beginning of the second session (about a week later) the subject was told that the second part of the experiment was concerned with forming impressions of personality, and that he would be asked, in addition to other things, to make some judgments about another subject. For this second session, two subjects were scheduled to appear simultaneously and, prior to the reporting of the results of the tests, the two subjects were introduced to one another. The experimenter asked each in turn (in the presence of the other) a set of questions about himself and his attitudes toward certain current events. This was to enable the two strangers to gain some impression of each other in preparation for a later measurement of their attitudes toward each other. At the conclusion of this introduction, the subjects were separated and the appropriate personality test report was communicated to each of them privately.

Unknown to the subject, the "results" which he received had been prepared with no reference whatsoever to his actual test performance. There were only two test reports, one very favorable (the *Favorable* condition), and the other very unfavorable (the *Unfavorable* condition). The reports covered the personality "dimensions" of originality (creativity), hostility, egocentricity, and over-all maturity. Each section of the report gave a rather detailed discussion of the test results bearing upon the particular dimension. The tone was objective and the general favorability (or unfavorability) quite consistent throughout the report. One subject of each pair was assigned randomly to the *Favorable* condition and the other to the *Unfavorable* condition. Thus, experimentally, the self-esteem of one subject was enhanced while the self-esteem of the other was reduced somewhat.

After receiving the "results" of their personality tests, the two subjects were brought together into a room containing a long table, an opaque slide projector, and a projection screen. On the table in front of each subject was a small plywood box containing a dial facing the subject. Issuing from the box were two wires with electrodes on the ends. Each box, with its dial, was completely shielded from other persons in the room. Thus, each subject perceived his apparatus immediately in front of him and could not see the other subject's apparatus.

The subjects were first asked to make some judgments of each other, using eleven adjective scales which could be scored for general favorability. A self-concept measure followed, consisting of sixteen polar adjective pairs similar to those included in the prior rating of the other person. The favorability score derivable from this scale provided a check on the effectiveness of the experimental manipulation which had attempted to influence their level of self-esteem.

Next, the experimenter read a set of instructions to set the stage for introducing undesirable cognitions which, presumably, should create considerable dissonance for subjects in the "favorable self-esteem" condition but should not produce much dissonance for subjects in the "unfavorable self-esteem" condition. These instructions were largely of a deceptive nature. It was explained that psychologists were especially interested in whether or not people could estimate "deeper and more personal aspects of the personality" on the basis of a first impression, and that this part of the experiment would be concerned with the perception of sexual arousal. An elaborate explanation of the physiology of sexual arousal and the sensitive techniques for their measurement followed. Considerable emphasis was placed upon the unconscious nature of sexual arousal and the impossibility of exerting conscious control over its expression in the "psychogalvanic skin response." The subject's task was to observe his own sexual arousal response on his galvanometer for each of a series of photographs of men which would be projected onto the screen. He was to record this figure on a page of a small anonymous booklet. After he had recorded his own arousal level for the particular picture on the screen, he was to make an estimate of the dial indication of the other subject's apparatus for the same photograph. The subjects were explicitly told that movements of the dial indicated homosexual arousal to the photographs. As a precaution against excessive threat, the subjects were told that persons with very strong homosexual tendencies would consistently "go off the scale." Further, the anonymity and privacy of the situation was carefully spelled out, with the intention of convincing the subject that only he would know what his own responses had been.

Unknown to the subject, the supposed "psychogalvanic skin response apparatus" was not actually responding to the changes in his own level of sexual arousal to the pictures. Rather, the galvanometers were controlled remotely by the experimenter. He exerted complete control over the movements of the needles, which were identical for the two subjects. Each photograph had been assigned an "appropriate" scale value in advance, so that those depicting handsome men in states of undress received more current than did those depicting unattractive and fully clothed persons. Both subjects were thus led to believe that they were sexually aroused by certain pictures and not by others, according to a consistent pattern.

It was hoped that the instructions would be so impressive to the subjects that denial of the fact that homosexual arousal was being indicated would be very difficult. According to our hypothesis, the subjects in the *Favorable* condition should experience considerable dissonance when observing their needle jump in response to photographs of unclothed males. Having a strongly undesirable trait is quite dissonant with believing you are an extremely fine person. Subjects in the *Unfavorable* condition, on the other hand, would have many cognitions consonant with the new information concerning homosexuality, and not so many dissonant cognitions. Discovering you have a very undesirable trait is consonant with believing you are an undesirable person. Subjects would also, no doubt, experience some dissonance due to their prior belief that they are not homosexual, but the two conditions would not differ in this respect. If projection is a positive function of the magnitude of dissonance, then subjects in the *Favorable* condition should attribute more homosexual arousal to others than those in the *Unfavorable* condition. It should be noted also that the two groups, while differing in dissonance, presumably did not differ in the degree to which the homosexual information was threatening to the superego (standards of good and bad).

After the subjects had estimated each other's arousal for each of fifteen photographs and had answered a few questionnaire items, the purpose of the experiment and the deception used were carefully discussed until it was quite clear that the subjects were satisfied and had regained their composure.

The results showed clearly that subjects in the *Favorable* condition attributed significantly higher arousal to their partners than did subjects in the *Unfavorable* condition. The average subject in the *Favorable* condition estimated that his partner had the same arousal level as he himself had; those in the *Unfavorable* condition generally estimated that the other person had less arousal than they themselves had. This difference between the groups was specific to the trait of homosexuality. There was no difference between conditions in the general favorability with which subjects rated their partners. In short, it would appear that projection occurred in order to reduce dissonance, since there was more projection where dissonance was high than where it was low even though "threat to superego" was the same for both conditions.

Some of the results derived from internal analyses were especially interesting. It was found, for example, that an identified projection effect tended to occur mainly when self-esteem was exceptionally high—in other words, when the dissonance introduced by the issue of homosexuality was quite great. Even within the *Favorable* condition projection occurred relatively consistently only when measured self-esteem was above the average for that group.

Let us now proceed to look at what the data show regarding selection of an object for projection and the particular ways in which projection may reduce dissonance. It will be recalled that it seemed plausible that the major dissonance-reducing effects of projection would occur only if the person onto whom the trait was projected was liked or favorably evaluated. By projecting onto respected persons an individual might succeed in making homosexuality appear a less undesirable trait, and by projecting onto his reference or comparison group he might conclude that he is no worse than average in the degree to which he possesses an undesirable trait. The occurrence of processes of this type should be revealed in the data by a tendency for subjects with more dissonance (the *Favorable* group) to project more than those with less dissonance particularly if they liked the person with whom they were paired.

The relevant comparison can be seen in Figure 2. It appears that subjects in the *Unfavorable* condition attributed homosexual arousal in accordance with a halo effect, that is, they attributed more of the undesirable trait to people they did not respect. Subjects in the *Favorable* condition also followed the halo pattern when their partner

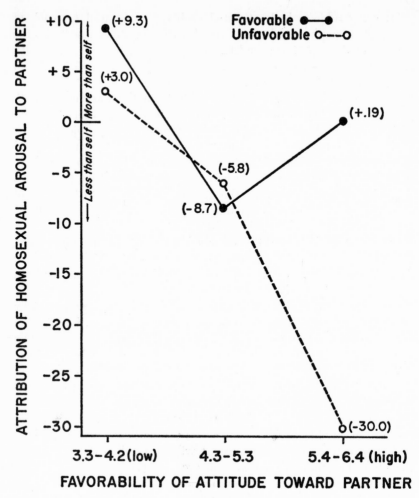

Figure 2.

happened to be evaluated poorly or moderately. However, the halo effect disappeared when these dissonant subjects happened to be with a partner whom they respected. Considering only those subjects who rated their partner very favorably, there is a significant difference between the *Favorable* and *Unfavorable* conditions in the expected direction.

It is worth emphasizing that subjects in the two conditions differed in attribution of homosexuality *only* when their partner was rated favorably. At the other points in Figure 2, there is no clear difference between the groups. This suggests that defensive projection occurred only when the available social object was favorably evaluated.

The contrast between this conclusion and certain common usages of the concept of defensive projection is striking. Writers in the psychoanalytic tradition (e.g., Fenichel, 1945; Ackerman and Jahoda, 1950) frequently call upon projection to explain phenomena of prejudice toward out-groups, for example. It is important to note that in most cases the projection is said to be aimed at persons and groups who are disliked and considered incomparable and inferior to the projector. This, of course, is directly contrary to the kind of projection whose effects were observed in the present experiment. The term "projection" has been applied very freely in explaining the derogatory content of attitudes toward out-groups, often without any clear attempt to distinguish between defensive attribution of own traits, halo effects, and rationalizations of displaced hostility. It is indeed difficult to decide in an individual case whether a particular attribution represents a defensive projection of own traits or some other type of motivation. The decision is perhaps easiest when, as in this experiment, derogatory traits are attributed to liked and respected persons, thus ruling out explanation by reference to halo effects and rationalization of hostility.

It is interesting to speculate about the conditions under which dissonance with the self-concept will lead to projection onto favorably evaluated persons. In Bramel's experiment the dissonance-producing information was probably quite striking and unambiguous to the subjects. The experimenter had taken pains to explain that movement of the needle in response to looking at the photographs was a clear and indisputable sign of homosexual arousal. The situation was such that outright denial of the meaning of the needle movements would have been quite difficult for persons in reasonable touch with reality. We are dealing, probably, with subjects who were forced to accept the information as implying some degree of homosexual arousal in themselves. Under these circumstances of self-ascription, a good way to reduce the dissonance remaining was to try to get desirable people "into the same boat."

However, if the subjects had been able to deny the direct implications of the galvanic skin response, then a different pattern of attribution might have been observed. If the information were sufficiently ambiguous, so that denial occurred, then it would no longer be so comforting to attribute the undesirable trait to persons with whom the subject ordinarily classes himself. That is, when one is attempting to avoid self-ascription, it does not help to ascribe the trait to others who are seen as generally similar to oneself. Whether, when denial is possible, attribution tends to be increased toward *undesirable* persons or out-groups, is an interesting question for further experimental exploration.

POSTSCRIPT

We have tried, by discussing a wide variety of examples of areas to which dissonance theory is relevant, to give a picture of the usefulness of the theory. Some of the examples were chosen, of course, because they seem particularly relevant to problems which are of concern to the field of clinical psychology. There is little question concerning the relevance of projection, for example, to the concerns of the clinical psychologist. Some may also see clear relevance to clinical problems in the examples of research on reactions to disagreement and change in moral values following temptation. Certainly, there is less clear relevance to clinical psychology of research on the reduction of post-decision dissonance or reactions to forced compliance situations. It is to be hoped, however, that any increased understanding of human behavior and human thought processes are potentially relevant to clinical psychology and that someone will see the relevance of these more remote areas also.

We would like to add a note of caution. While it seems that the theory of dissonance is useful in a wide variety of contexts, it should not be imagined that dissonance explains everything. Indeed it does not. There are many other motives and many other considerations which affect and determine human behavior. One may hope that dissonance theory may prove useful when added to these other psychological theories.

REFERENCES

Ackerman, N. W., & Jahoda, Marie. *Anti-semitism and emotional disorder.* New York: Harper, 1950.

Aronson, E., & Mills, J. The effect of severity of initiation on liking for a group. *J. abnorm. soc. Psychol.,* 1959, 59, 177–181.

Backman, C. W., & Secord, P. F. Effects of dissonance in the self-concept on the perception of other persons. Unpublished manuscript, 1959.

Bergin, A. Personality "interpretations" as dissonant persuasive communications. Unpublished doctoral dissertation, Stanford Univ., 1960.

Bramel, D. Some determinants of defensive projection. Unpublished doctoral dissertation, Stanford Univ., 1960.

Brehm, J. Post-decision changes in de-

sirability of alternatives. *J. abnorm. soc. Psychol.,* 1956, 52, 384–389.

Brehm, J., & Cohen, A. R. Re-evaluation of choice alternatives as a function of their number and qualitative similarity. *J. abnorm. soc. Psychol.,* 1959, 58, 373–378.

Fenichel, O. *Problems of psychoanalytic technique.* Albany, N.Y.: Psychoanalytic Quarterly, 1941.

Fenichel, O. *The psychoanalytic theory of neurosis.* New York: Norton, 1945.

Festinger, L. *A theory of cognitive dissonance.* Evanston, Ill.: Row, Peterson, 1957.

Festinger, L., & Carlsmith, J. Cognitive consequences of forced compliance. *J. abnorm. soc. Psychol.,* 1959, 58, 203–210.

Heider, F. Attitudes and cognitive organization. *J. Psychol.*, 1946, *21*, 107–112.

Hovland, C. Reconciling conflicting results derived from experimental and survey studies of attitude change. *Amer. Psychologist*, 1959, *14*, 8–17.

Hovland, C., & Pritzker, H. Extent of opinion change as a function of amount of change advocated. *J. abnorm. soc. Psychol.*, 1957, *54*, 257–261.

Mills, J. Changes in moral attitudes following temptation. *J. Pers.*, 1958, *26*, 517–531.

Murstein, B. I. The projection of hostility on the Rorschach and as a result of ego-threat. *J. proj. Tech.*, 1956, *20*, 418–428.

Osgood, C. E., & Tannenbaum, P. H. The principle of congruity and the prediction of attitude change. *Psychol. Rev.*, 1955, *62*, 42–55.

Prasad, J. A comparative study of rumors and reports in earthquakes. *Brit. J. Psychol.*, 1950, *41*, 129–144.

Rogers, C. *Client-centered therapy.* Boston: Houghton Mifflin, 1951.

Sinha, D. Behaviour in a catastrophic situation: a psychological study of reports and rumours. *Brit. J. Psychol.*, 1952, *43*, 200–209.

Wright, Beatrice A. Altruism in children and the perceived conduct of others. *J. abnorm. soc. Psychol.*, 1942, *37*, 218–233.

Zimbardo, P. G. Involvement and communication discrepancy as determinants of opinion conformity. *J. abnorm. soc. Psychol.*, 1960, *60*, 86–94.

9

Perception

ISRAEL GOLDIAMOND

A recent textbook considers perception as "becoming a central unifying study linking the laboratory with the clinic" (Ittelson, 1960). The relationship expressed has considerable historical support. The logic and procedures of early laboratory investigations in perception underlie many of the diagnostic procedures currently used in the clinic. In addition, research in perception and theoretical positions relevant to such research have often entered into theoretical and methodological formulations in clinical psychology.

During the past decade, laboratory experimentation in psychology and developments in communications systems have led to considerable reformulation of classical perceptual problems. Such reformulations may have implications for clinical procedures, investigations, and formulations based upon perceptual formulations made prior to this period. It will be a purpose of this discussion to present some of these

This report was written under contract with the Operational Applications Office of the Electronic Systems Division, U. S. Air Force Systems Command, L. G. Hanscom Field, Bedford, Mass., and is ESD Technical Report 61–21. The research reported herein was performed under contract with the E.S.D., A.F.C.-C.D.D., and A.F.C.R.C., from 1959–present, to whom the author is indebted for generous support.

The author also wishes to express his appreciation to the National Science Foundation for grants G-2088 and G-3259, for support of research reported and performed prior to 1959. Support from the Illinois Psychiatric Training and Research Authority, and the Cooperative Research Program of the Department of Health Education and Welfare is also gratefully acknowledged.

Opinions expressed are those of the author and do not necessarily reflect the views of the granting agencies involved.

reformulations and the evidence upon which they are based, and to discuss some of their implications for perception, for clinical psychology, and for other relevant branches of psychology.

SOME HISTORICAL RELATIONS

It is no accident that a classic textbook on psychometrics and mental testing (Guilford, 1954) starts out with the classical psychophysical procedures used to obtain visual, auditory, tactual, and other thresholds. Binet applied the formal logic of psychophysical perceptual research to intelligence testing. For the *threshold intensity* of a stimulus, that is, the intensity at which the stimulus would produce stipulated responses 50 per cent of the times it was presented, there was substituted the *mental age* of a question, that is, the age at which the question would produce stipulated responses in 50 per cent of the children asked. Thurstone made similar application to attitude testing. For the *more heavy than* in weight judgments, there was substituted the formally equivalent *more desirable than* for nationalities as neighbors or spouses. The formal procedures relating responses to measurements supplied by mechanical scales were applied to supply scale values to nationalities.

The quantifiability of some objective mental tests may be related to the fact that investigators in one branch of perception limited the questions they asked to those providing ready quantification, such as frequency of Yes responses. Such restriction was regarded as oversimplification, and other branches of perception tolerated more latitude in the subject's range of responses, as exemplified by projective tests such as the Rorschach.

Where laboratory concepts have been applied to clinical activity, therapy has often been related to learning formulations, and diagnosis to perception. Since the threshold is a diagnostic statement, it would have been surprising if rigorous methods, developed in the laboratory, to obtain the threshold should not have been applied by psychologists interested in rigor in other areas. The application has not only been of the formal logic of psychophysics (mental tests) but also of the laboratory procedures of psychophysics (the recognition thresholds of perceptual defense), and of relationships investigated in perception (Gestalt closure, Archimedes spiral, Necker cube, [*cf.* Eysenck, Granger, and Brengelmann, 1957]). These tests assume normative or other data with which they can be compared; the development of perception in children is the subject of considerable investigation (Wohlwill, 1960). Hallucinations and distorted perceptions enter into the diagnosis of schizophrenia. Psychophysical and recognition procedures are used in routine audiometric and visual testing, and a recognition difficulty is considered involved in aphasia and dyslexia. These are but samples of the use of perceptual procedures in the clinic.

A theory to unify learning and perception has been considered desirable (Hilgard, 1948). There have been attempts to explain perceptual data and the development of perception in learning terms (Hebb, 1948); Gestalt psychology represents at least one attempt to subsume the data of learning under a theory with perceptual emphases (Koffka, 1935). A further issue separates the two areas: much learning today is behaviorist in orientation, and much perceptual research makes use of an intervening experiential state, since perception seems to imply this by its very subject matter (seeing, hearing, etc.), as do the responses used in much perceptual research (Yes = "I see the light"). Since clinical responses are often also of this type, this may be a source of affinity between perceptual research and personality theories.

"Dynamic" theories of personality are concerned with motivational variables, and where such theories have suggested laboratory research, perceptual procedures have often been used. Such experiments have often been interpreted as suggesting motivational influences, some unconscious (but see Bartley, 1958, p. 387), and therefore necessary considerations for research and theoretical formulations in perception.

Recent research relevant to communications systems and to the laboratory control of behavior may bear on some of the issues raised. One of the most significant advances in psychophysical research, the Theory of Signal Detection, is related to advances in communications research. Much of the research in the experimental analysis and control of behavior bears directly on classical problems of perception, although a conditioning terminology is used. These areas have extended the practical application of experimental psychology considerably beyond the diagnostic. These two areas have further commonalities in their utilization of advances in technology in the physical sciences, which have provided new ways of attacking classical perceptual problems. Use of mechanical devices has also necessitated *explicit* definition of the psychological problems and variables involved, since explicit specification is required for machine definition.

When an environmental change produced by an output affects further output, such control characterizes feedback devices. In the Theory of Signal Detection, the responses of an organism in the presence of signal ensembles (perceptual displays) are governed by consequences attached to the responses (the pay-offs of a utility matrix). In operant conditioning research such discriminative responses are similarly governed by their consequences (reinforcing or aversive stimuli). The commonalities in these approaches are evident. It should also come as no surprise that both the perceptual behavior of organisms and the systematic alteration of such behavior (learning) are considered by both areas. Further, when another organism is the environment in this feedback paradigm, the responses of the one are the stimuli for the other, and the conditions are established for the investigation of communication within the existing frameworks.

Some of the procedures and problems of perception will be considered in the light of developments in these two areas and in related areas. To the extent that the procedures and problems can thereby be reformulated, and to the extent that the extensions discussed in this introduction are based upon the classical formulations, such reformulation may have relevance for the procedures, problems, and formulations of clinical psychology.

METHODOLOGICAL RESEARCH

In perceptual research, the experimenter is typically concerned with three classes of arbitrary representations which can be related to his observations. One class, *the dependent variable,* is designated in perceptual research as the perceptual response, or response indicator, and another, *the independent variable,* may have a variety of designations, including stimulus presentation variables (*cf.* Graham, 1950). The perceptual response temporally follows the stimulus presentation, and the major object of such research is to establish functional relations between the two. In Rorschach investigation, for example, the occurrence of certain responses when a colored card is presented is designated as "color shock." In psychophysics, there has been a concerted effort to express this functional relation mathematically, an example being Fechner's Law, $R = c \log S$, or Stevens' suggested revision of this relationship to a power function (Stevens, 1961). Such relationships are obtained under carefully controlled conditions, and these *conditions* constitute the third class of representations in an experiment. Any functional relations established hold only for certain conditions. A major task of much scientific research has been to specify the conditions under which the functional relations hold.

It had been noted in psychophysical research that the curves obtained, which related stimulus presentation and response, were a function of the psychophysical procedure used. Variations in procedure which affected results included order of stimulus presentations (ascending, descending, randomized), stimulus presentation single or accompanied by comparison stimuli, experimenter or subject control of the stimulus presentation, and fixed presentation (absolute) or changing, among others. What are called the various psychophysical methods are but a few of the many possible different combinations of these. Much *methodological* research has been concerned with the effects of such procedures upon the functional relations obtained.

Another type of research can be called *substantive* research; it generally applies a psychophysical method for a different problem, such as thresholds for scotopic and photopic vision. The two types of research are related since it is apparent that if variation in procedure produces differences in substantive results, the results must be stated as limited to the procedure used (Graham, 1950), rather than as a general rule of perception for the populations or phenomena studied. Further issues are raised, such as which of the differing results and procedures are to be accepted, can rules be established for assessing procedural validity (Blackwell, 1953), what invalidating variables are involved and to what extent can they account for the results obtained? Among the attempts to resolve these issues have been greater laboratory control, and the isolation and elimination of "errors." The Mental Test Equation (Guilford, 1954) extends this logic to mental testing. The equation (with the perceptual issue in brackets) states that Test Score (indicator score) = True Score (perception) + Error Score (constant and variable errors). Needless to say, classical psychophysics has not been alone in attempting to measure a perceptual process which is independent of the examining procedures and is to be inferred from them. To the extent that error is eliminated in the equation given, correlation between Test and True Scores, or indicator *validity*, is increased. To the extent that the True Score is characteristic of the individual, such elimination of error will eliminate fluctuation, and session to session *reliability* is increased.

Recent research stemming from the Theory of Signal Detection is explicitly concerned with the issues of true perception and error, which are crucial to the historical perceptual substrates of the mental test. Psychophysical methodology, within this framework, consists of a systematic investigation of explicitly specified parameters and variables. Using such procedures, investigators have been able to rationalize some of the differences obtained between classical psychophysical methods. This theory will now be considered.

THE THEORY OF SIGNAL DETECTION AND ITS IMPLICATIONS

Psychophysical procedures are often used in substantive investigations in sensation and perception, and the concept of the threshold as a descriptive measure of these processes has been useful. The threshold is typically considered as the stimulus energy level which divides absence of these processes from their presence, or is the best estimate of this conceptual divide. Absence and presence are inferred from or operationally equated with responses such as No and Yes, Inaccuracy and Accuracy, or absence and presence of other responses. The equation of such a sensory change (the terms *sensory* and *perceptual* will be used interchangeably, *cf.* Graham, 1952, p. 59) with a change in verbal response poses some semantic problems which underlie the notion of discrimination without awareness, which will be discussed later. One solution for the validity of verbal response in classical psychophysics was the *Vexierversuch* (Boring, 1942, p. 479), in which blank presentations were introduced. The number of Yes responses during blank presentations was used as a correction factor for Yesses during stimulus presentation. Wrong responses were subtracted from correct responses in other experiments as well; the relation to the corrective procedures of mental testing requires no elaboration.

The Theory of Signal Detection questions the concept of a sensory threshold (as opposed to a response threshold), as well as the wrongness of Yes responses to blanks and the logic of related correction procedures. It has other implications for perceptual (Swets, Tanner, and Birdsall, 1961; Swets, 1961b) and psychophysical (Swets, 1961a) research, as well as mental testing, some of which will now be considered.

An example by Tanner (1959) may serve to illustrate the treatment and some of the psychological variables involved. It will be assumed that the background sound (or illumination of a screen) fluctuates randomly around some level set by the experimenter. On stipulated occasions, a tone (or flash of light) is superimposed upon the background, and the subject is to report Yes and No with regard to the presence or absence of added tone, that is, to detect it. Fluctuations in the background (called *noise*, or *N*) can be exemplified by outcomes from tosses of two dice, which vary randomly from 2 to 12; 7 will be the mean. The tone to be detected (called *signal*, or *S*, and since it is superimposed upon *N*, is *SN*) can be exemplified by a third die, with a 3 on three faces (*S*) and a blank (or a contribution of O to *N*, or *N*) on the other three. The subject is given each *total* score from the three dice, and is required to detect the 3, or state whether or not a signal was presented. The following table indicates the relationship of the scores obtained to the presentation of *N* or *SN*. The first row presents the sum of the readings from the three dice, and is analogous to the stimulus presentation (*SN* or *N*). The second row presents the number of ways such a reading can be theoretically obtained (out of 36 possible combinations) when the contribution from the third die is O, that is, no signal is presented. In the third row the third die is 3, that is, the score from signal is superimposed on the other two dice.

Presentation (total score from the three dice)	2	3	4	5	6	7	8	9	10	11	12	13	14	15
No. of ways of occurrence when N alone		1	2	3	4	5	6	5	4	3	2	1	0	0	0
No. of ways of occurrence when SN		0	0	0	1	2	3	4	5	6	5	4	3	2	1

It will be observed from this example that certain presentations provide no problems (2, 3, 4, and 13, 14, 15) for stating when the presentation included signal and when not. Further, if the signal to noise ratio is high enough (the third die, for example, having 15 on each face), there will also be no problems in signal detection. Returning to Tanner's example, however, what happens when a 9 is presented? Did the experimenter put in a signal, or did he not? The presentation is the same in both cases, and whether the subject's Yes is recorded as a *hit*, and evidence of signal detection; or is recorded as a wild guess or a *Vexierversuch* error (a *false alarm*); or whether the subject's No is recorded as a *miss* of the signal, and evidence of insensitivity; or is recorded as a true report of no presentation (a *quiet*)—these do not reflect upon the subject's perception or sensitivity (in the intuitive sense), since they are independent of them. If the

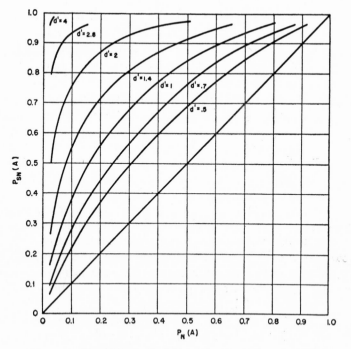

Figure 1. $P_{SN}(A)$ *vs.* $P_N(A)$ with d' *as the parameter.*

subject says Yes whenever a 10 or above is presented (the response criterion), and No for 9 and below, the odds that he will be called a detector rather than a hallucinator are 21 to 6. He will, however, let 15 of each 36 signal presentations go by unreported. If he is to increase detection (report, say, 33 of 36), his criterion for saying Yes should start at 7. However, the detection-hallucination odds will now shift from 21–6 to 33–21. Greater "sensitivity" has been purchased at the price of tremendous increase in false alarm rate. Is it worth it?

Figure 1 departs from the dice example given and presents R.O.C. (Receiver Operating Characteristic) curves. These depict the probability, $P_{SN}(A)$, on the ordinate of reporting Yes when SN was presented, as a function of the abscissa, $P_N(A)$, the probability of reporting Yes when N alone was presented. The parameter, or the family of curves, labeled as values of d', represents different signal to noise ratios (the third die ranging from 0 to 10, say). For a given S/N ratio, it can be seen that detection can be increased only at the the cost of increasing false alarms.* Whole families of psychophysical curves can be drawn by going across the parameter, starting at the straight line with 45° slope, where the signal contribution to SN is 0, This corresponds to the zero stimulus point of classical psychophysics, and the number of Yesses at this point corresponds to *Vexierversuch* blank Yesses. These are actually false alarm rates at this point. A subject can shift his curves, and thereby his threshold, by shifting his response patterns, as discussed (Tanner and Swets, 1954). The more he shoots (trigger-happy), the more enemy planes he shoots down—and also American planes. The more cautious he is with regard to the latter, the more enemy planes go through.

The threshold is classically the energy level of 50 per cent detection on the psychophysical ogive. Any number of threshold shifts and classical ogives can be generated from these R.O.C. curves *without shift in sensitivity*, and purely as a function of shift in false alarm rate. Variables that govern such rate, which are pertinent to this discussion, will now be considered; other variables of concern to the Theory of Signal Detection are presented by Licklider (1959).

Utility functions. The subject can make two types of responses,

---

* For example, at d' equals .5 (analogous to a given intensity), if the subject detects 30 per cent of the signals presented (0.3 on the ordinate), he will also report as signals 15 per cent of the blanks (the corresponding 0.15 point on the abscissa. To detect 60 per cent of the signals, at the *same stimulus level*, he will produce a 40 per cent false alarm rate. He can improve detection only by increasing false alarm rate. At the next energy level, d' equals .7, there will be more detection, but there will still be a dependence of detection upon false alarm rate. The threshold (0.5 on the ordinate) can be d' equals .5, .7, 1, 1.4, 2 (in this example) depending not on sensitivity, but upon comparative costs of false alarms, compensations for detection, and the like, or, so to speak, risk taking history and behaviors.

Yes and No, and the experimenter can make two types of presentations, SN and N. The interaction produces a utility table, presented below, with names of cell entries given:

		E presents	
		N	SN
S responds	Yes	a. False alarm	b. Detection (Hit)
	No	c. Quiet	d. Miss

Monetary values are assigned as *consequences* of the location of a response in a given entry. If, for example, the subject is (a) fined one cent for a false alarm, (b) given five cents for a hit, with (c, d) no values, during one series, and is (a) fined five cents for a false alarm, (b) given five cents for a hit, with (c, d) no values on another series, he will produce less false alarms during the second series, and therefore, since detection rate is a function of false alarm rate, will score less hits and obtain a higher threshold. His ogive will be displaced to the left, as expected from the R.O.C. curves. Experimental subjects shift as the utility entries are shifted.

A priori probabilities. In the dice example given by Tanner, the 3 was on half the faces. If the 3 is on five-sixths of the faces, utility will be optimized by different response patterns.

Deprivation variables. A subject for whom every penny counts may be expected to operate differently from one for whom it does not.

Signal-noise ratios. Changing the face value of Tanner's signal die (from 3 to 6 to 12, for example) will also produce different curves as will changes in noise, indicated by the values of d', given on the R.O.C. curves.

This change in signal-noise ratio is analogous to the stimulus energy values of classical experiments. Since any number of curves can be produced depicting response change as a function of energy change (a classical psychophysical concern), depending on the utility table entries and a priori probabilities, it is evident that any particular ogive produced (under similar conditions) holds only for particular settings of such variables, and is not a general sensory function depicting the sensitivity of the transducer (ear or eye) involved to discriminate signal from noise at different ratios. A power of the Theory of Signal Detection is that it renders *explicit* variables in signal detection, which are either implicit in classical psychophysical research or, by virtue of not having been made explicit, were not built into the experiment. Accordingly, in classical research comparisons between experiments becomes difficult, and the curves become limited to the procedures used. A position which can systematize the differences as functions of explicitly statable experimental variables, and can control them, has obvious merits. Rather than being focused on the classical Methods, the Theory of Signal Detection is focused on systematic investigation of the variables, parameters, and conditions that govern signal detection behavior, and relevant substantive investigations.

Forced choice and Yes-No differences. Differences obtained between these two methods have a considerable experimental history, and define the subliminal perception effect, where the Yes-No threshold is higher than a forced-choice threshold obtained for the same subject. In a forced-choice experiment, N may be presented three times (or in three positions), and SN once, with the subject required to indicate which of the four was SN. In the dice example given, response utility will be optimized by consistently responding at the highest toss. Where a Yes or No is required at every toss, if the conditions are such as to optimize a low false alarm rate, it becomes evident how a person can accurately *locate* the signal presentation at a signal-noise ratio that produces very few hits in a Yes-No experiment. Prediction has been possible from one type of experiment to the other (Swets, 1959).*

The ideal observer. For stipulated a priori probabilities, entries in the utility table, signal-noise ratios, and so on, there is obviously an optimal performance, designated as the ideal observer. The actual behavior patterns under similar conditions of a particular signal detection system or observer can be compared to the ideal observer, and its *efficiency* thereby described as the ratio between these performances (Tanner and Birdsall, 1958).

Implications for perception and mental tests. For both psychophysical and perceptual methodology, the Theory of Signal Detection has implications bearing upon perceptual response validity and the related notion of correction for error to increase the correlation of the response with a perceptual process assumed to underlie it. According to the Theory of Signal Detection, there can be obtained from the same subject equally *valid*, but *differing*, modes of response to the *same* stimulus presentations, producing thereby different functional relations. Accordingly, the notion of a curve representing a sensory threshold is questionable, since the subject's response in all cases is

* The contribution by utility functions present in Yes-No responses (the "criterion problem") can be lessened in forced choice tasks, suggesting this method for psychophysical research (Blackwell, 1952a, 1952b, 1953; Swets, 1961b). That such behavior is under control by pay-offs is evident from malingering data. Stated otherwise, this response, too, is an operant.

governed by utility variables, as well. *The consequences of his responses are entering into the curves produced.* Differences in thresholds obtained under similar conditions may, accordingly, reflect differential control over the responses by their consequences, and by other variables.

With regard to the standard classical correction for error, false alarms represent as valid a mode of responding as a hit, and penalization of scores seems unwarranted. The classical curves present signal detection (Yes) as a function of signal-noise ratio, and misses can be derived (No when SN was presented) from them, but the other two entries of the utility table are lost. The R.O.C. curves involve no such loss in data, since all four entries are presented. Subtracting false alarms from the signal detection scores post hoc would seem to involve a further loss in information. Penalization of error results in restricted detection, an experimental phenomenon which parallels others noted in the clinic. In the forced-choice situation, there is often correction for error, as exemplified by subtracting Wrongs from Rights in True-False tests. Swets, Tanner, and Birdsall (1956) report that, in a forced-choice task, when the subject is not correct on the first choice, he is likely to be correct, above chance, on the second choice. This can be derived from the dice example presented earlier and is in direct contradiction to the implied working assumptions of current forced-choice procedures, which grade accuracy on all-or-nothing basis.

Multiple choice examinations make a similar all-or-nothing assumption in their grading procedures. The author allowed subjects in a psychology multiple-choice examination to make second, third, and fourth choices. Students whose accuracy was high on their first choices, also performed above chance on their second choices when first choices were inaccurate, and so on for other choices. Students who scored on their first choices, also did so on the other choices. In other words, if the students had information, it was continuous. In a perception experiment, where a stimulus presentation is being made, a variable which must be considered is the number of responses allowed the subject. In an experiment by the author (1954), subjects who reported signal presence on an eight-point scale detected far more signals (and gave more false alarms) than subjects using a three-point scale, who detected more than those using a two-point scale (Yes-No).

Within the framework of the Theory of Signal Detection, Egan, Schulman, and Greenberg (1959) have rationalized results using binary and multiple ratings. These suggest that the theory discussed has implications extending beyond the research thus far undertaken. Describing the detection presentations in terms of SN and N distributions can be considered an example of the more classical figure-ground description, restated in explicit and mathematically specifiable terms. The author's study superimposed a skeleton triangle on white light; although this S/N ratio was not quantified, utility variables were operative. Egan (1957b) has extended the theory to speech communication involving spondees and other message sets (1957a); recognition memory (Egan, 1958) and a theory of recognition (Tanner, 1956) are also considered. Analysis of a recent (early 1960) bibliography by Creelman suggests a geometric progression of investigations, with an approximately equal number of references (40) for the 4 years 1953–1956, the 2 years 1957–1958, and the 1 year 1959.

The clinical literature is characterized by an extensive use of formulations in perceptual terms, accompanied by a corresponding lack of investigations which might cleanly support such formulations. The Theory of Signal Detection seems to have at least two implications for this discrepancy. First, it suggests that the notion of sensory or perceptual (in the intuitive sense) thresholds is difficult to justify, or ascertain, since the response indicator is always under the control of other stimuli, as well. Since differing responses which are equally valid can be obtained, if perception is to be defined by or inferred from a given response, an infinite number of definitions or inferences is possible. Secondly, the theory suggests that considerable control and prediction can be obtained from one psychophysical method to another, using the proper procedures. Further, the ideal observer provides a ready reference point for the operating characteristics (rather than the perception) of a given subject, and for changes in such behavior.

It should be noted that among the variables made explicit by this research and which govern behavior in a signal detection experiment are the utility functions of pay-offs attached to the responses possible. These are explicitly considered in operant conditioning. Operant behavior is that class of responses the probability of which is governed by stimuli explicitly made contingent upon them. It is apparent that the signal detection responses discussed are operants by this definition, as are most verbal responses, and values and costs (penalties) attached to the responses are reinforcing and aversive stimuli, respectively.

OPERANT CONDITIONING, DISCRIMINATION, AND GENERALIZATION

Conditioning procedures may be classified into two types, respondent and operant, and currently the main difference between them can be conceptualized as follows: Where stimuli are paired with reinforcement, in operant conditioning the reinforcement is made explicitly contingent upon the response, whereas in respondent conditioning it is not. In respondent conditioning, both the conditioned and unconditioned (reinforcement) stimuli, tone and food, *precede* the salivary response. In operant conditioning, the discriminative stimulus, the tone, precedes the response, but reinforcement (food) is presented *only if* the response occurs. The response, for example, pecking, is necessary for the reinforcement, but it may not be sufficient, since a reinforcement may be scheduled upon every fiftieth response (producing thereby a high rate of response) or three minutes after the last reinforcement (producing thereby pauses close to that time), and so on, depending upon the schedules of reinforcement (Ferster and Skinner, 1957). Since most perceptual responses are operants, this discussion will open with a consideration of operant discrimination and generalization.

Should the experimenter manipulate the stimulus conditions, and occasionally reinforce a response made in the presence of certain stimuli, but never reinforce responses made when other stimuli are presented, discrimination may be established—that is, the response will occur when certain stimuli are presented, but not when others are presented. Using the word "red" in the presence of one wavelength will produce consequences which differ from those when it is used with another wavelength, and the first wavelength may come to control the response *"red"* (Graham, 1959). Similarly, that wavelength can be brought to control the pecking response of a pigeon (Guttman and Kalish, 1956; Blough, 1961). If different wavelengths are now *added*, in whose presence the response had not been reinforced, the control over the response by the original stimulus may be attenuated—that is, there may be less responding, and a "generalization gradient" of response may be produced. As more and more green light is added to the red, making it yellow, there will be fewer responses of "red," or fewer pecks. Similarly, there may be fewer Yes responses as the light is dimmer on a continuum from light (Yes) to no light, or from high S/N ratio to low. The general subject matter of an operant conditioning experiment in discrimination or generalization is, accordingly, the general subject matter of psychophysical and perception experiments.

The discriminative stimuli, that is, those in the presence of which (S^D) the response is occasionally reinforced or never reinforced (S^Δ), are *defined by the experimenter*, since he controls the differential reinforcement which distinguishes them. The organism, on the other hand, may initially respond differentially in some other way. Differential responding defines different *stimulus classes;* examples of differential (verbal) responses which define different stimulus classes are Cat,

Bulb, Number, Even Number, or, for that matter, Red, since any color manual will contain hundreds of different chips which control the response Red. The object of much discrimination training is to make the organism's *stimulus classes congruent with the discriminative stimuli* of the experimenter, and this is established through the differential reinforcement which defines the discriminative stimuli. It might then be stated that the organism has understood the experimenter's intent, that there has been successful communication, that the experimenter's concepts and abstractions (the rule for inclusion in the set, or the definition of the set) are now the organism's, as defined by his differential behaviors in relation to the stimulus presentations.

Discrimination and concept formation

A logical set may be defined by the explicit rules whereby elements are included and excluded from it; any element may simultaneously be a member of different sets, that is, it may also meet different definitions. A presentation of a light may be described (and may vary independently) in terms of hue, saturation, brightness, film, gloss, position, duration, number, and so on (Evans, 1948), and the experimenter may establish his rule for inclusion or exclusion in terms of any one or more of these, and through differential reinforcement form discriminative stimuli; whether they can also be made stimulus classes for the organism is an empirical matter.

The stimulus classes may be in the psychophysical terms discussed, or may be equipment and commodities. Thus, chairs, books, tables, and relay racks are in one stimulus class, and chalk, paper, pencils, and relays are in another by virtue of the differential forms required by a purchasing office for their acquisition; the consequences of sending the wrong form through are familiar. For a scientist made berserk by these procedures, the elements may be members of the classes combustible-noncombustible, in which case chairs, books, wooden tables, paper, and pencils would be in one class, and metal tables, relay racks, relays, and chalk would be in the excluded class. In all events, stimulus classes may be established through similar (for members of the same class) and differential (for different classes) contingencies, and may also be disestablished by altering the contingencies. For a very fine discrimination, S^D must be very small, and $S^\triangle$ large.

Pigeons can be trained to peck only in the presence of a perfect pill and not to peck (reject) all others; they are currently being trained for quality control of minute electrical components (Verhave, 1959). They may thereby free inspectors for less tedious tasks, creating a form of technological unemployment which might be called bestiological unemployment. The discrimination can be in terms of matching to a varying sample. The psychophysical Method of Average Error, in which a human subject *adjusts* a stimulus to match another, has been programed for pigeons placed in the cones of missiles. For the pigeon, S^D is the crosshairs over the approaching target viewed through a window. The pigeon's pecking changes the course of the missile so that it can be kept on a perceptual dead center (Skinner, 1960). The discrimination training may be broadened so that chimpanzees respond to concepts such as threeness (Kelleher, 1958). The terms abstraction, concept formation, discrimination, and generalization refer, accordingly, to similar operant procedures. This parallels the relationship between perception and cognition stressed in experiential formulations.

The relationship of an operant response to a perceptual stimulus will, accordingly, be governed by past and present differential reinforcements and the schedules of reinforcement. The issue is further complicated by a set of variables related to reinforcement, which have been subsumed under names such as "motivation," "drive," "need," and "state variables" (the term to be used here). Since commonsense language differs from scientific language, it would be expected that some commonsense terms which are complex are simplified in scientific terminology (for example, the abstraction-conceptualization dimension discussed, which simplifies to discrimination procedures), and on the other hand, some commonsense terms which are simple turn out to be quite complicated when considered scientifically. Drive is in this category. If drive is defined behaviorally as those *procedures which make a given reinforcement effective*, the complexity becomes evident. The thirst drive can be increased, or *water can be made an effective reinforcer*, by depriving the organism of water, by feeding salt, by exercise in the sun, by administering a diuretic, by appropriate brain stimulation or ablation, by paying the subject to drink, by showing Sahara travelogues, and so on. One commonality which these procedures have is their description by a word containing letters with the alphabet order 4, 18, 9, 22, 5 (or 14, 5, 5, 4). The common term conceals the procedural differences. Behaviorally, they share the commonality of making a particular reinforcement effective, and thereby influence the establishment and maintenance of discriminative behavior.*

The operant paradigm. The paradigm for perception, where the response is an operant, can now be presented; it is the paradigm for any operant or instrumental behavior. Dollard and Miller (1950) list the four variables of learned behavior as "drive, response, cue, and

---

* Although these procedures share this commonality, it should be reiterated that the differing procedures may produce differing functional relations.

reinforcement" (pp. 25–26), which are identical with the classes of variables of the paradigm presented below:

$$\ldots\ldots\ldots\ldots\ldots \text{SV (state variables)}$$

Controlling stimuli:
S^D–$S^\triangle$ (discriminative) $\Big\}$ — R (response) $\longrightarrow$ S^r–S^o (differential
SS^C (constant) reinforcement) †

According to this paradigm, presentation of the discriminative stimulus, S^D (in the presence of other stimuli, SS^C, also present when $S^\triangle$ is presented), may occasion the response, R, depending upon the consequences, S^r, of that response (under these conditions) and the state variables, SV, which make the consequences effective in establishing such control. This situation reiterates, in conditioning terminology, the case previously presented in discussion of the Theory of Signal Detection, when equally valid but differing responses could be obtained to the same S/N presentations, as a function of pay-off consequences and other variables. Differences in operant responses can reflect differences in conditioning history, effects of reinforcement, state variables, and other experimental conditions rather than differences in discrimination or sensory thresholds inferred from them.

A perception experiment is a behavioral experiment, and the perceptual response is subject to control by the same variables which govern other operant responses. The investigator in vision may use instruments such as a Macbeth illuminometer normally not used in conditioning research, and develop a technology, procedures, and related problems which differentiate his area of research from operant conditioning research, or for that matter, from acoustical or algesic research. Consequences contingent upon behavior will still govern the behaviors studied, a variable explicitly considered by the Theory of Signal Detection. Similarly, the investigator in conditioning may be involved in a technology, procedures, and related problems which define his area, but the stimuli in the differential presence of which differential reinforcement occurs will enter to control the behaviors which are his dependent variables.

Stimulus change

Conditioned behavior is very sensitive to the conditions (SS^c) under which it has been established. The buzzing of a bee in Pavlov's

† The differential reinforcements, S^r (reinforcement) and S^o (no reinforcement), are paired with S^D and $S^\triangle$, respectively, and define the latter terms. Aversive stimuli (S^a) may be substituted for S^r (Appel, 1960) in establishing and maintaining operant behaviors, and the reinforcement may be positive or negative. In the paradigm, S^r should be considered as *exemplifying* those response contingent stimuli which alter response probability, rather than as defining this class of stimuli.

laboratory disrupted a previously established conditioned response. In a study of the effects of noise, which reconciles many conflicting data in that field, Azrin (1958) disrupted temporal discrimination by presenting noise. Where the operant behavior had been established under noise, introducing quiet was disruptive. Such disruption through change of the stimuli in the presence of the conditioning which has been established is the referent of the commonsense term, distraction, and is technically referred to as *stimulus change;* this differs from the systematic stimulus alteration related to differential reinforcement which is involved in stimulus discrimination. That the perceptual operant response can be manipulated by this variable as well as the discriminative stimulus, suggests that control of "irrelevant" stimuli is quite relevant.

The specificity of conditioning to stimuli in the presence of which it has been established raises the problem of explaining behavior under varying conditions. In the noise experiment cited (Azrin, 1958), when noise and quiet were continually interspersed, the disruption eventually ceased, since the same contingencies upon temporal discrimination were operating throughout. This phenomenon of habituation or adaptation to disruption may be attributed to the fact that the contingency relation (or lack of it) to the old behaviors is maintained under the new conditions. Eventually the response will be reestablished, but under the control of more stimuli than before. That is, the SS^c class has been broadened. This is one usage of the term *stimulus generalization.* Another usage refers to the occurrence of the response when novel stimuli (that is, without a conditioning history), between S^D and S^Δ are presented. Such responses are typically lower in strength (Keller and Schoenfeld, 1950), and one possible explanation for the lowered stimulus control is that the discriminative stimulus is attenuated. The extent to which such change is critical enough to disrupt behavior, or merely to produce attenuation, may depend upon the procedures employed. Recently, Pierrel and Sherman (1960) obtained *augmented* response by such procedures; a 30-decibel tone was S^D, and a 10-decibel tone was S^Δ. Response was augmented when a novel 40-decibel tone was initially presented, suggesting that location of the stimulus in relation to a S^D–S^Δ continuum was involved in its control of the response. That the rise in the psychophysical curve as a function of stimulus energy rise may be related to such a continuum rather than a stimulus intensity dynamism (Hull, 1951; Blough, 1959) is suggested by the fact that the same authors obtained results opposite to what might be implied from the Fechner Law. In this case S^D was 10 decibels and S^Δ was 30 decibels; the novel tone of 0 decibels produced more responding than 10 decibels, and the novel 40 decibel tone produced *less* responding than did 30 decibels. By the seventh day, the peak was at 10 decibels, suggesting that the rat's *stimulus class* was becoming congruent with the discriminative stimuli. Wolf (1961) employed S^D's from different modalities in separate series, a tone and light. When both were presented simultaneously, response frequency (bar presses) was considerably greater than the sum of responses for each S^D, for certain conditions employed. Similar results, of course, may be obtained by unidimensional addition—that is, when the brightness of a light is increased by adding more light. Taken together, these experiments suggest that the dimensional control of behavior associated with stimulus dimensions can be a property of differential reinforcement which is paired with points on the stimulus dimension, rather than being a property of absolute stimulus values. Accordingly, the experiments suggest the importance of differential reinforcement in psychophysical, perceptual, and generalization investigations.

The research cited may have a further implication for providing an alternative explanation (or restatement) of the Gestalt experiments on responding to relations between stimuli (patterns) rather to absolute stimulus values. If response is along an S^D–$S^\triangle$ continuum, then presentation of S^{D+}, a novel stimulus outside the range, with S^D, should produce greater responding for S^{D+} than for S^D in the transposition experiment.

Forced-choice, Yes-No, and conditioning

Where animal perception has been investigated, the procedures utilized have generally been discrimination training, involving forced-choice procedures. One form or color may be S^D, and one or more others are $S^\triangle$. Generalization gradients (psychophysical curves) have been obtained by varying the S/N presentation between S^D and $S^\triangle$. These procedures have been extended, one example being the use of the Method of Average Error by the pigeon in the guided missile (Skinner, 1960). A characteristic of this method is that the subject varies the stimulus presentation along the experimental dimension. The Békèsy audiometer (1947) varies auditory dimension automatically, with the human subject instructed to respond when the tone becomes audible. This reverses the direction, and now the subject's responses (at inaudible) provides a further reversal, and so on. This Yes-No procedure, hitherto considered a human prerogative, has been ingeniously adapted for pigeons by Blough (1958), who has thereby obtained curves resembling the rod-cone shift (1957). Gourevitch, Hack, and Hawkins (1960) have related changes in such Yes-No auditory behavior by rats to ototoxic drugs; Weitzman, Ross, Hodos, and Galambos (1961) report the use of similar procedures for pain in monkeys. Perception in human subjects, such as mentally retarded children, is often difficult to investigate; the Blough procedures have been adapted for obtaining auditory curves from such subjects by Meyerson and Michael (1960).

Space does not permit discussion of the use of other explicit operant conditioning procedures for discrimination research nor of the considerable amount of other research in animal discrimination (e.g., Meyer, 1960; Kimble, 1961) which bears upon the establishment and maintenance of human perceptual responses. Another source of generalization gradients has been respondent conditioning, where the curve is formed by responses to stimuli on a continuum with the conditioned response (Woodworth and Schlosberg, 1954, pp. 576–577). Where the CR is a tone, this procedure has been adapted for human audiometry, and has been considered "more objective" than other procedures. Recently, Atkinson (1959a) has utilized such eyelid responses as avoidant operants to a discriminative tone, rather than as a CR. He reports overcoming several difficulties inherent in respondent audiometry. Curves obtained by differing methods were compared (1959b).

Where the subjects are human, verbal instructions are typically employed. That animals and humans can be trained using these procedures to produce curves similar to those obtained when verbal instructions are used, suggests that the verbal instructions are experimentally equivalent to the training procedures used with animals, and that the experimenter telescopes into a few seconds of verbal instructions the variables operating in training sessions. These sessions, in animal research, involve making the animal's stimulus classes congruent with the experimenter-defined S^D and S^Δ. As was discussed earlier, communication can now be considered to have occurred, the animal has "understood" the instructions, and so on. In all events, discrimination or generalization tests can now be run—that is, when the subject is under the stimulus control of S^D rather than other stimuli. This is precisely the hoped-for result of verbal instructions; the subject responds to (is under the stimulus control of) the perceptual stimuli rather than to those "extraneous" to the experiment. His responses can now be related to the independent variables of the experiment. "Rapport" is now achieved, the subject "understands" the instructions, he is "motivated" to respond, and the like. A few "trial sessions" typically precede the test; human subjects may have a long history of control by verbal instructions (the experimenter is considered the "generalized reinforcer" by Skinner, 1953). The presence or absence of reinforcement during the test sessions can influence the observing responses (Holland, 1958). A slight change in nuance or tone may be the equivalent of a gross change in the larger scale map which is the training procedure. As Keller and Schoenfeld (1950) put it:

Nothing seems more reasonable on the surface than to ask a person whether he can or cannot perceive a stimulus or stimulus difference. In this case, however, . . . common sense does not reveal the actual complexity of the experiment or the tacit assumptions upon which we proceed. . . . These experimental situations include far more than the stimuli to be discriminated (pp. 132–133).

VERBAL BEHAVIOR AND WORD VARIABLES

Perceptual experiments often involve two sources of verbal statements. One source of these is the instructions given by the experimenter; the other is the verbal statements by the subject.

Verbal behaviors are often the perceptual responses which the experimenter seeks to relate to his stimulus presentations. In psychophysical experiments, the subject may be instructed to say Yes when he sees the light; in recognition or intelligibility experiments, he may be asked to name the word he hears; in other perceptual experiments, he may be asked to describe his visual experience. Some of these statements can be replaced by button presses and other manual behaviors. The verbal and manual responses are operants, that is, are controlled by the variables governing operant responses. Responses to S^D, it will be recalled, are established and maintained by variables other than the perceptual variables S^D may represent to the experimenter.

Although turning a light on and off may produce a subjective response of seeing and not seeing the room, a relationship between behavioral responses and light alteration can be produced by the experimenter without his having to refer to the subject's experience in any way, as was suggested in the preceding section. The point being made is not that seeing (experiential) is not involved, but that it is the procedures the experimenter sets up which define the experiment as being a visual experiment, rather than any explicit reference to seeing made by experimenter or subject. Instructions to "report what you see" are condensation procedures which telescope results of a long history of training procedures and related variables. The "simple" verbal instructions may have come to control these behaviors in much the same manner that the order "Charge!" by an officer controls a highly complicated set of behaviors. Since there are a variety of reasons why a platoon does not charge, inferring differential hearing of orders from differential numbers of soldiers going over the top is questionable. These considerations may enter into perceptual inferences drawn from investigations with populations such as psychotics and children. The peculiar perceptual responses ("hallucinations") of psychotics may refer to the same lack of stimulus control which is exhibited in their other behaviors, rather than to a visual abnormality. The reported development of child perception to adult standards as a function of age may reflect increasing exposure to differential reinforcements for adult behaviors occasioned by instructions, rather than perceptual or conceptual development. Similar control over behavior is no more guaranteed by identical instructions than it is by the application of identical training periods, since the past histories of the organisms with respect to such conditioning may differ.

Responses such as Yes (= I see), or Green, or "I see movement and dots coming in, then bursting" are similarly products of a complex prior history of training in verbal behavior (Graham, 1959), and experimental variables related to these. A verbal response is an operant, *even when it has semantic reference to subjective experience*, that is, not only can it be manipulated by stimuli irrelevant to its semantic referent, but it is *dependent on such stimuli for its history and maintenance.* Accordingly, verbal responses (or any operants) are *always* under the control of such stimuli. Consideration of the verbal response as an operant (Skinner, 1957) is the subject of a growing body of research (Krasner, 1958; Salzinger, 1959; Verplanck, 1955).

For precautions and differing results obtained under different conditions, see Azrin, Holz, Ulrich, and Goldiamond, 1961; for control of verbal questionnaire responses, see Azrin, Holz, and Goldiamond, 1961). Other investigations have applied the experimental analysis of behavior to control formal aspects of operant verbal behavior (e.g., Lane, 1960a, 1960b; Flanagan, Azrin, and Goldiamond, 1958, 1959; Bilger and Speaks, 1959; Goldiamond, 1960a, 1960b). In Skinner's analysis, the audience supplies both the reinforcing and aversive contingencies for verbal behaviors and thereby to a considerable extent defines the discriminative stimuli for such behavior. The experimenter may be the audience in a perceptual experiment.

Recognition and intelligibility

These experiments are identical, but their referent differs. In intelligibility experiments, the referent is the stimulus, for example, if presentation of *cat* produces greater accuracy than *gat*, the former word is considered more intelligible. In recognition experiments, if John is more accurate than Mary when *gat* is presented, John is considered as having a lower recognition threshold than Mary for that word. While the stimulus presentation need not be a word (it may be a geometric form, an airplane, a face), the response typically is a word, and its accuracy is the dependent variable of the experiment. Accuracy is usually regarded as the congruence between responses and the stimulus presentation; hence the perceptual inference. In actuality, it is defined as "the congruence between S's response and E's score sheet" (Goldiamond, 1958, p. 396). Accordingly, if elements in a set of presentations appear equally on a score sheet, those words corresponding to them which have a higher frequency will score more hits—that is, have greater congruence with score-sheet entries than will words with lesser frequencies. Similar considerations led Solomon and Howes (1951) to state that "any variable that is a general property of linguistic responses must also be a property of any perceptual concept that is based upon these responses" (p. 257), a statement similar to that made in the preceding paragraph. The occasion for this comment was a demonstration, using correlational procedures, that certain systematic differences in thresholds obtained in a recognition experiment might be accounted for on the basis of systematic differences in the word frequency of the words used.

This response bias hypothesis (Goldiamond, 1958) was tested by Goldiamond and Hawkins (1958), who trained subjects in nonsense syllables with differential frequency, and then instructed them that these words were to be flashed on a screen for them to recognize. A regular score sheet was used, and the differential word frequency was relatable to differential accuracy, but since the flashes were blanks, the results could be attributed to response bias rather than to perceptual dependency upon frequency. Since then, Brown and Rubinstein (1961) have demonstrated that there is a stimulus contribution, relatable to frequency, in such experiments, and Howes (1960) has argued that the accuracy curve in the pure blanks case (*Vexierversuch*) undergoes considerable transformation when a stimulus is presented. In the Theory of Signal Detection, it will be recalled, when $SN = N$, (pure blanks), the R.O.C. curve is a straight line. Where, however, $d' > O$, a curvilinear R.O.C. curve is produced.

Should response biases present when no signal is presented ($SN = N$) necessarily be invariant when a stimulus presentation is made? The role of partial recognition has received some attention (e.g., Bricker and Chapanis, 1953; Eriksen and Browne, 1956; Goldberg and Fiss, 1959); the author (Goldiamond, 1960c) explicitly manipulated this variable. Three-letter nonsense syllables were constructed, and were available with different frequencies. When blanks alone were presented, differential frequency alone governed hits. For partial recognition, where recognition must be inferred from accuracy, partial presentation was substituted, that is, a single letter was explicitly flashed on the screen. Response alternatives were immediately restricted to those containing that letter, and, within this set, word frequency governed accuracy. Similar results were obtained when two letters were flashed; when three letters were flashed, the set was restricted to the word exclusively in that set. The function of the stimulus presenta tion was to restrict response alternatives, but within the restricted set, response bias operated, with the curve transformed relative to the relation of such restriction to accuracy. The relationship of restriction of alternatives and accuracy is currently being investigated in reference to the Constant-Ratio rule (e.g. Clarke, 1957; Anderson, 1959).

Response bias

Although differential word frequency was the independent variable in the experiments discussed, it should be stressed that it is but one way of producing response bias. Results analogous to the partial presentation experiments discussed could have been produced through differential reinforcement or punishment (Zeitlin, 1954) of the nonsense syllable responses. Presentation of one letter would have restricted responses to those occasioned by that S^D, with those having a higher probability through greater reinforcement history scoring more hits, and so on. The author (1960c), in a series of *Vexierversuche*, gave a variety of instructions to his subjects. When the stimulus was allegedly a letter of the alphabet, and the response was a letter, *A, B, C* were the easiest to "recognize"; when the accurate response was a word containing that letter, *E* was the easiest to "recognize," in accord with the Dewey (1923) count of linguistic letter frequency; when a color word was allegedly presented, Thorndike-Lorge list (1944) frequency was related to response bias. A student about to be drafted gave a high frequency of "olive drab" responses, presumably indicating the effects of needs upon perception. Restriction of response alternatives influenced accuracy: the smaller the set, the greater the accuracy. Where nonsense syllables were presented with equal frequency, but were differentially reinforced, "speed of recognition" became a function of such reinforcement in the recognition session which followed such training. It proved possible to transpose results between auditory and visual modalities, and between such psychophysical methods as the ascending Method of Limits and a Constant Method. Similar results reported in the literature (Goldiamond, 1958) have been interpreted as indicating determinants of perception; the results reported were obtained with blanks.

In the ascending Method of Limits, accuracy terminates a series. Such notification of accuracy was found markedly to shift consequent response probabilities, in a manner similar to the effects of reinforcement in a fixed interval schedule (Ferster and Skinner, 1957), where response rate drops immediately after presentation of S^r.

Accordingly, the S^D in a perception or recognition experiment may occasion a variety of responses, depending upon contingencies attached to such responses in the past, state variables, constant stimuli, or upon other experimental or cultural variables producing differential frequency or restriction of alternatives. Since response biases shift as the stimulus presentation is increased—that is, they differ from one level to the other—and since they also shift as a function of reinforcement variables operating during the experiment, the use of partial presentation procedures for the study of perception seems to raise questions far more complex than the procedures currently in vogue seem capable of answering (cf. Gibson, 1950, pp. 210–211; Bartley, 1958, pp. 387–388). In such cases, the residual between a blank and a presentation can not readily be assigned to perception since there is shifting interaction between presentation and sources of response bias.

A recognition experiment is a forced-choice experiment which can be related to Signal Detection research (Tanner, 1956; Egan, 1958; Green, 1958); such research depicts R.O.C. curves as functions of explicitly stated variables and parameters under specified conditions. Signal detection or perception is not defined by the use of responses with semantic reference to perceptual experience. These responses can be manipulated independently of such reference. If Tanner gives subjects instructions to state "I am in Phoenix" when SN, and "I am in Tucson" when N, the results will be auditory R.O.C. curves, rather than curves of apparent travel between the two metropoles of Arizona. *Credence in the veracity of the verbal response is not among the operations which define perception or recognition.* Use of instructions or responses which have semantic reference to experience may be a convenient procedure for the experimenter, but does not define the experiment as a perceptual one. Such definition arises from the other procedures used.

Response classes and stimulus classes

A stimulus class is defined as a set of stimuli in the presence of which similar responses may occur, and discrimination training procedures were mentioned as one way of establishing such classes. Similarly, response classes can be established through the application to different responses of similar contingencies in the presence of similar discriminative and constant stimuli. An obvious example is verbal synonyms. Once a class is established, contingencies applied to one member of a class will tend to affect other members of that class. For example, a child slapped for saying "shit" in company, will tend thereafter not to use other words of that class in company. Or in the case of a psychotic who was mute for 19 years, reinstatement of one verbal response through conditioning procedures reinstated verbal behavior in general (Isaacs, Thomas, and Goldiamond, 1960).

Consideration of such response variables is necessary for an analysis of perceptual responses. As an example, a situation will be considered where a light is flashed on a screen, at fixed intervals, for a fixed duration. Its intensity may be the independent variable. The following operant responses may then be related to the presentations:

1. Frequency of pressing button when light appears; frequency of saying Yes when it appears.

2. Frequency of pressing button when both light and tone go on, compared with such frequency when tone alone goes on; frequency of signal detections and false alarms.

3. Frequency of pressing one of n buttons when a corresponding one of n lights in a display goes on; frequency of correct Up, Down, Left, Right responses under similar conditions.

4. Frequency of pressing buttons arranged in a scale; frequency of scaling presentation as 7, 6, 5, 4. . . .; or Bright, Dim, Off; or Certain, Doubtful, Guess. Degree of rotation of handle on a vernier.

5. Frequency of pressing button which turns light off, or attenuates or increases it a fixed amount each step.

6. Frequency of pressing button when another light is presented; frequency of saying Brighter, Dimmer.

7. Reading of a meter attached to another light when subject adjusts it to match the stimulus presentation.

To this list can be added other responses such as verbal description of the light, reading rate when the light is presented (if this is the source of illumination), and so on. Each of these may require somewhat different procedures to establish and maintain them; each may have a different conditioning history.

Respondents such as a GSR, conditioned finger withdrawal, or eyelid closure may also be elicited by the presentation.

The existence of such differing indicators raises a problem for those who would infer perception from the response, namely, which response indicates perception? The subliminal perception effect is based mainly on discrepant curves obtained between procedures analogous to 1 and 3; the subception effect is based on discrepancies between accurate recognition and a GSR. When different responses are required to the same stimulus presentation, for example, scaling from 1–11 and rotating a handle, as in Procedure 4 (Eriksen, 1957), high correlations as well as significant differences are obtained between them. These concurrent operant responses (Garner, Hake, and Eriksen, 1956) are in the same response class, which can also include the respondent GSR. (Eriksen, 1958). Yet, like the synonyms "nice" and "sweet," they can also simultaneously be members of different response classes. Stated otherwise, similarities between the responses (functional relations with stimulus intensity) may be related to similarities in conditioning history and to differences in maintaining stimuli, while differences between them (misses in signal detection during forced-choice accuracy, for example) may be related to differences in conditioning history (equation of false alarms with hallucination; no such consequences for forced-choice misses) or maintaining stimuli (utility differences).

Consideration of these responses in terms of response classes poses further problems. In their discussion of operational definitions, Garner, Hake, and Eriksen (1956) state that one operation does not define a concept. For example, during a training session, a subject is punished for naming a figure presented in the left, and when it is presented for recognition, does not name it. By a narrow operational definition, perception was suppressed, but it can be argued that the response was suppressed. Accordingly, *converging* operations are needed —that is, at least another operation. "Ideally, converging operations would be orthogonal (completely independent), since such operations are the most efficient" (p. 151), but this is not always possible. Parallel operations, which "select among alternative hypotheses along the same dimension, and thus cannot converge to a single concept," are operations which "can be excluded entirely from consideration" (p. 151). Indicators in the same response class are not independent but parallel operations. In the experiment presented as an example, the subject might also be told to *point* to the side containing the figure. This response may also be suppressed, since naming a figure on the left and pointing to the left may be in the same response class ("Don't point; tell"), and attenuation of one may attenuate the other. The responses may be not converging operations, but possibly the same operation repeated (parallel operations), and therefore the additional response may be of no help in choosing between the alternative hypotheses of perceptual suppression or response suppression.

DEFINITIONS OF PERCEPTION

Perceptual experiments are often defined in terms of the schema presented below (Garner, Hake, and Eriksen, 1956), and at least two independent operations are required to establish the term which inter-

$$
\text{Stimulus system} \rightarrow \text{Perception system} \rightarrow \text{Response system}
$$

venes between stimulus and response. This schema and the logic of the establishment of the intervening term holds whether the intervening term is considered a hypothetical construct referring to physiological or subjective events, an intervening variable which serves purely to coordinate stimulus and response conceptually, or a mediated response.

On the other hand, there is Graham's (1950) statement that

$$
R = f\ (a, b, c, d, \ldots n, \ldots t, \ldots x, y, z).
$$

in which the independent variable is among the stimulus variables, $a, b, c, d. \ldots$ This general schema will be referred to as the *procedural* statement to contrast it with the statement containing the intervening term, which will be referred to as the *conceptual* statement. The procedural definition states that the perceptual response is a function of certain stimuli (variables and parameters) under certain conditions.

One reason for the use of conceptual definitions is that the functional relation between S and R is often not a simple one. Accordingly, a black box may be inserted between S and R, with the complexity a function of different "routings." The box may contain hypothetical constructs which may be physiological or experiential. Often the only observables in this internal job analysis are other stimuli and behaviors. The black box may contain intervening variables, as well, which may have specific references to other operations. Argument concerning the pros and cons of hypothetical constructs and intervening variables has a long history (*cf.* Rozeboom, 1956) and will not be materially extended here.

Mediated responses and stimuli

More recently, there has been expression of perception as a mediated response. Skinner (1953) for example, states that the "dinner bell not only makes our mouth water, it makes us see food. In the Pavlovian formula we simply substitute 'seeing food' for 'salivating'" (p. 266). Further, the "verbal stimulus 'heart' is likely to evoke seeing red as well as seeing a heart. It has been shown experimentally that if . . . [a playing card contains] a heart printed in black ink, the heart is sometimes seen as red or as a mixture of red and black, perhaps reported as purple" (p. 267). Although Skinner is not explicitly stating that the subjective response then controls the observable response of verbal report, the inference of such control can be drawn. For example, in a paired-associates task, syllable a is presented and the subject is to respond with syllable b. Presentation of syllable b is now paired with shock. When a is presented, the conditioned GSR occurs, and the "unsaid b" is considered as a mediated but unobservable response occasioned by a, which acts as a stimulus eliciting the GSR (Staats, Staats, and Crawford, 1961). A response which acts as both a stimulus and a response occurs in certain "chaining" experiments in operant conditioning (Keller and Schoenfeld, 1950). Muscle responses which produce proprioceptive stimuli are often the unobservables which are posited as mediating observable S-R relations. Stimuli produced by eye movements and orienting responses, for example, have been considered as affecting visual perception (*cf.* Solley & Murphy, 1960). The effects of mediating responses upon cognitive processes are discussed by Mowrer (1960).

In sensory preconditioning (Brogden, 1939; Seidel, 1959) two stimuli, a and b are initially paired. Stimulus b is now paired with shock. When stimulus a is presented, the conditioned response may occur. The situation is analogous to the prior one, except that stimuli rather than responses are paired, and the term, preconditioning, stems from a relationship between a and b established prior to conditioning. One interpretation is that the conditioned stimulus now mediates between the response and the new stimulus, and since no response is involved in this S-S relationship, S-R approaches are considered embarrassed.

Can perception be considered a mediated response? These mediation experiments do not break the current bounds of behavioral formulations if they are considered in terms of stimulus classes, response classes, and response units. Response units are established in terms of the discriminative and reinforcing stimuli which bracket them. Thus, the pledge of allegiance is a response unit since the reinforcement does not occur until the final "all" is said. Each of its constituent words may have been response units at one time, and may still be so with reference to other controlling stimuli. Experiments in the use of delayed auditory feedback in the analysis of variables maintaining ongoing verbal behavior (Goldiamond, 1961) suggest that in continual verbal behavior, such as reading aloud, the auditory presentation of a word (through the speaker's verbal response) normally controls his next verbal response, which becomes an auditory presentation to control the next, and so on. The chapter assignment may be a response unit by the teacher's stimuli, but each word may be a unit by the speaker-produced stimuli. In a paired associates learning task, the experimenter response unit created is two words (in the pledge it is 31), but auditory presentation of one word controls the verbal response which is the next. The experiment cited by Staats, Staats, and Crawford (1961) suggests that, through respondent conditioning procedures applied to the second word, auditory presentation of the first word can elicit a respondent instead of (or as well as) controlling the operant second word response, as in ordinary speech. The experiment has interesting implications for the effects of verbal behavior on other behavior, and is ingenious, but can be considered without reference to mediated responses. Sensory preconditioning experiments may be related to the discussion on mediated responses, to generalization, or may be interpreted as suggesting experimental procedures for the creation of stimulus classes by contiguity (Guthrie, 1952). Stimulus classes may be created by respondent as well as operant procedures. Like response classes (consensual pupillary reflex), they may also be anatomically related, or possibly innate (Hartley, 1950). The efficacy of the procedures suggested by presensory conditioning and their interpretation must await further investigation.

The procedural definition of perception

The degree to which any experimental findings can be related to perception will depend upon the adequacy of the procedures utilized. Perception experiments are distinguished from other behavioral experiments by the equipment used, the questions such equipment helps answer, the variables and problems investigated in detail. Exposition of these properly belongs in a laboratory.

Definition of perception as an intervening variable depends for its adequacy upon the procedures employed. The use of converging operations properly calls for the explicit statement of the operations involved, *and of the conditions held constant,* since the same converging operations under slightly different conditions (with each set constant), may produce entirely different theoretical formulations, when the answer lies in looking to the conditions. Different results (and therefore different theoretical interpretations) may also ensue when different converging operations are used. A sampling of responses to a light was presented in the section on response classes, any of which could define empirically the dependent variable. The same independent variable may also be defined empirically by different procedures. Brightness, for example, may be varied by altering resistance, voltage, distance of light source, focus, monochromatic filters, hue, angle of incidence, angle of polarization, and so on. Further, differing procedures can be used to maintain the same discriminative response (for example, schedules of contingencies). Two experiments using proper converging operations may accordingly read like similar experiments pertaining to the same logical perceptual problem, and may empirically employ such critical differences in procedures to as make the results incapable of either support or contradiction. They may simply be irrelevant to each other or to the logical problem that dictated them, since they may properly relate to other problems (*cf.* Goldiamond, 1958).

These considerations also hold when the conceptual definition of perception includes the hypothetical construct of subjective experience. To define visual or auditory perception with reference to subjective seeing or hearing may be common sense, but may contribute very little that is not already known to the conduct of adequate scientific investigation. Introspection may help to define a problem, but the scientific resolution of the problem requires different procedures.

Although the complexity of stimulus-response relations may contribute to the use of conceptual definitions of perception, it should be noted that procedural definitions can handle this complexity by resort to variables and parameters anchored in procedures which are explicitly defined. The Theory of Signal Detection deals with extremely complex stimulus-response relations, but has managed to achieve considerable predictability and generality made in terms of explicitly defined variables, parameters, and conditions. *Perception is not defined, but the procedures and conditions employed define a signal detection experiment.* Similarly, there is considerable generality and generalizability in operant conditioning research in this area, but the procedures and conditions are also explicitly defined.

Defining perception in intuitive experiential terms may relate to a historical concern of psychologists that their investigations be applicable and relevant to these important phenomena. A procedural definition includes explicitly specified (and therefore restricted) conditions. It seems to be considerably removed from experiences which are pervasive under a wide variety of conditions. Yet, paradoxically, operant conditioning research, defined by restricted procedures, is proving of tremendous applicability in a variety of areas. There is also arising a technology related to explicitly defined communication systems research, exemplified by the Theory of Signal Detection. Psychological systems which have operated in general terms may turn out to have little generality (in the sense of being applicable to produce alterations under a wide variety of conditions), and some of those which have operated in restricted terms may turn out to have such generality. As the British philosopher, Dingle (1960), remarks, science has been characterized by self-imposed limits on its observations. He considers it paradoxical that disciplines so limited should have had such tremendous application in the unlimited world outside the laboratory. Perhaps the answer to this puzzle is that the subject matter of science is representations (of which statements are one example) denoting the scientist's experience, and that *all* representations, *including nonscientific representations,* in the unlimited world are also limitations. Between an explicitly defined and expressible limitation and an ill-defined and inexpressible limitation, the race is possibly to the explicit.

INTROSPECTION REAFFIRMED: THE
VALID USE OF SUBJECTIVE EXPERIENCE

Although introspection as a method of scientific research has been questioned by some psychologists, "introspection is still with us," as Boring (1953) remarks, "doing its business under various aliases, of which *verbal report* is one," (p. 169). The verbal statements of an untrained observer, which are assumed to be his introspections, are being substituted for the trained observers of Titchener's time, and one can wonder if there has been a net gain. Furthermore, the subject's operant responses are under the control of nonperceptual variables of the ex-

310 LEARNING AND COMMUNICATION

perimental situation, as well as being functions of restrictions in the linguistic representational system used (Whorf, 1956).

Subjective experience can also be considered as a response to stimulation. As the light goes on and off, the room is seen and not seen.

Subjective perception as a guide to research

If subjective perception is considered a response, then, under proper conditions, changes in subjective perception may be attributed to changes in the stimulus conditions. In this case, the experimenter, experiencing a change, may first undertake the task of isolating the stimuli which produced it. He may then assign himself the task of making its control of a response public—that is, relating a subject's behavior to the stimulus. In so doing, the experimenter is not dealing with intuitive perception, but has used his experiences as a guide for perceptual research—that is, to delineate the problem. Thus used, experience has been a fruitful source of research. Statements by others can be used as guides in a similar manner.

Research thus initiated is common in many areas of science. *How* the author obtained his research leads, and what made him attack a particular problem is seldom published in scientific journals. Such absence may stem from the fact that it is irrelevant to the procedural adequacy of the research. Possibly, ascribing research origins to theoretical deductions is reinforced. The intuitive use of perception becomes questionable only when such intuitive definition is substituted for the procedural definition. The procedural definition of perception is not exhausted by the use of a tachistoscope, a psychophysical method, instructions to report what is flashed, the assumption that the subject is honest, and deductions logically made from theory.

It seems to the author that in too many quarters ability to integrate concepts and data has substituted for procedural adequacy. Simultaneously, the intuitive use of perception has become generally questioned. Scientific scholarship requires an evaluation of results in terms of the empirical procedures relevant to their validity; this must precede any evaluation based on theoretical relevance. Further, the significance of an experiment can also reside in the procedures, the variables, or the phenomena discovered. To deny use of subjective experiences of an investigator as clues for properly conducted investigation is to impose restraints not found in other areas of science. The adequacy of the empirical procedures governs the adequacy of the experiment and minimally demonstrates the competence of the scientist. He may apply these procedures to solve a problem created by a theoretical issue, by a procedural issue, by his own subjective experience, by accident, by mistake, by serendipity, or in some other way. To limit the source of problems to any one of these, or to exclude any of them as sources on

the grounds of lack of rigor, lack of relevance to theory or to well-artic-
ulated systems, would seem to confuse the issue of problem source,
where such objections are invalid, with the issue of procedural adequacy, where such objections may be valid. On a parallel philosophical level, it may confuse what Reichenbach (1951) has called the
context of discovery and the *context of justification.*[*]

There is a class of perceptual phenomena which seems to exclude
such explicit experimenter control of the responses involved. Examples
of such phenomena appear to be reversible figures (e.g., Ulrich and
Ammons, 1959; Ammons, Ulrich, and Ammons, 1959) and spirals (e.g.,
Eysenck, 1957; Spivak and Levine, 1957) and after-images. The changing verbal responses are considered to reflect a changing subjective
state. Since the responses change while the stimulus is constant, specification of the variables involved poses difficulties. Negative and positive after-images to color can be made as objective as any standard
color presentation. Bidwell (1895) rotated a segmented episcotister
to present color, white, black, color, white, black, and so on. Under
proper conditions the color that is inserted is immediately presented
as the complement (negative after-image) without prior exposure to
the color itself, and its duration is completely under experimenter

---

[*] The justification discussed, it should be reiterated, is to a considerable extent
in terms of adequacy of the *empirical* procedures. Logical analysis of a problem
may dictate what variables are to be employed, but is no sure guide of the extent
to which the empirical procedures employed may adequately resolve the problem. As is discussed elsewhere in this chapter, there is a myriad of operations
to choose from, each of which may be "coordinated" with equal logical validity
with the constructs employed. These may produce different results or even artifacts.

This qualification can not be reiterated too often in current psychology, at
least. Psychological conventions have announced that methodological papers
will not be accepted for reading. Dissertations and theses are often required to
have postulational systems and hypotheses and to state theoretical relevance.
The complete design and what it is that will be done must often be stated in
advance of the investigation. Students are often required to attend classes in
"research methods," and the analyses presented come from readings. The truism
that the results obtained depend upon the procedures employed is given lip-
service, but is violated by having problems formulated before there has been
training relating empirical nuances to results. The seminar is often headed by
a faculty member with statistical training or bent toward philosophy of science.
"Research methodology" is equated with these disciplines. Since these formal
approaches are neutral with regard to discipline, the lament of the graduate
student that he came to study psychology becomes understandable, and (to the
author, at least) is often justified.

The author is not stating that these approaches do not have merit, but is
questioning the exclusive equation of these areas with research methodology.
The confusion discussed (between problem source and procedural adequacy)
may be related to such identification of methodology with these formal approaches. The empirical (rather than the formal) procedures may define a
discipline, and since the results obtained *do* depend on the procedures employed,
study of these would seem to be an important part of research methodology and
analysis.

control. Thus, the transient and subjective nature of after-images, which has been regarded as characteristic of the phenomenon itself, is a function of the stare-look-away procedure typically used. Further developments with this procedure are reported by Lehmann (1950), Kaplan (1957), Sperling (1960) who substituted light flashes for the episcotister, and Goldiamond and Malpass (1961) who report experimenter control over positive as well as negative after-images. Revesz (1924) reinforced chick responses to the smaller of pairs of varying geometric figures and then presented Jastrow figures and obtained the illusion, hitherto reserved to humans. The Müller-Lyer and Titchener Circles illusions are currently investigated using standard psychophysical procedures involving stimulus variation. The after-image and illusion experiments suggest that even this class of perceptual phenomena may, with perspicacity, be brought under explicit experimental control and definition. This would seem to be the most immediate experimental task in this area (cf. Graham, 1951).

Stimulus-producing responses

The role played by responses which become stimuli which then control other responses has been mentioned in the section on mediated responses. Reference to such responses has wide use. Orienting and ocular responses in vision, proprioceptive stimulation, and chaining are examples of such responses. Systems in which the output governs further output by changing the input are characterized as feedback systems, and analogies from self-regulatory systems constructed to function in this manner have been extended to human behavior, using homeostatic models (Ashby, 1952).

The response is the dependent variable of psychological research, and the stimulus is an independent variable. In the formulations discussed, the dependent variable controls the independent variable, which thereby loses independence. The experimenter's independent variable is, so to speak, at the subject's mercy, making both analysis and control difficult.

The most direct approach to eliminating the problem of the confounding discussed would seem to involve explicit separation of the two variables. In physiological research where complex cycles have been discovered, the physiologist attempts empirically to isolate the various units. There is a distinction between isolating the proprioceptive stimulus which controls a response, by demonstrating such control, and positing the existence of an unisolated proprioceptive stimulus in the explanation of behavior. Since the only referent to proprioception in the latter case is a complicated stimulus-response relation, the latter statement provides no greater control than its omission.

Statement of proprioception as a research problem to be explicitly investigated, rather than as an explanation, is a different story.

Whether or not a visual S^D will control behavior is dependent upon the subject's head and eye orientation, and in intuitive terms, perception and attention are related (cf. Munn, 1961). Experimentally the relationship is the stimulus-producing response under consideration. Experiments in which an *explicit* response produces an S^D, in the presence of which a response may now be reinforced, are reported by Wycoff (1952) and Kelleher (1958) who concluded that the "present objective technique might enable us to make a useful distinction" (p. 102) between "attention" and discrimination. Ferster (1960) and Ferster and Appel (1961) conditioned matching behavior in pigeons: pecking on the illuminated one of three disks turns it off, and the two surrounding ones light up. One is the color of the preceding presentation (the match). Objective definition of observing responses and vigilance is described by Holland (1957, 1958) whose subjects were required to monitor and correct deflections in a voltmeter (for which they were reinforced). The meter was briefly illuminated by pressing a button. These observing responses came under the control of the reinforcement schedule (cf. Laties and Weiss, 1960).*

In chaining, a response also produces a stimulus, an example being verbal behavior, where each word becomes an auditory presentation which may then exercise some control over the next verbal response, which becomes an auditory presentation, and so on. This relationship can be made explicit through the use of delayed auditory feedback. The subject's voice is presented to him through earphones, and is recorded in one head of a recording unit. The playback is from a different head. By controlling the distance between recording and playback heads, the experimenter can control how soon after the response the stimulus it has produced is presented to the subject. He can thus explicitly control the stimulus presentation and make it an independent variable, separating it from the response. The use of delayed visual feedback in a similar manner to separate writing behavior from the visual stimuli (letters) it produces, and which control further writing behavior, has also been reported (Van Bereijk & David, 1959; Smith, McCrary, and Smith, 1960). The visual studies and studies in auditory delay (Black, 1955) report behavioral disruption. However, Goldiamond (1960b, 1962) and Goldiamond, Atkinson, and Bilger (1962) suggest that the disruption ascribed may be related to the limited periods run, since they obtained recovery from disruption when subjects were run for more extended periods. The procedure was used to analyze the stimuli maintaining ongoing verbal behavior (Goldiamond,

---

* This rationale has recently been extended by the author (1961) to the control of responses in ongoing oral and *silent* reading.

1962); new patterns of verbal behavior emerged (of interest in stuttering control) which had the effect of returning verbal behavior to the control of stimuli in the presence of which it had been conditioned.

By controlling the stimulus, the experimenter can control the response it controls, the stimulus produced, and so on. This reverses the conditions prevailing when the subject controls the stimulus through his response, as is the case with stimulus-producing responses. Such control is facilitated by commitment to a procedural analysis. It may also develop from a conceptual analysis, but such analyses often carry with them the temptations to rest after conceptual exposition of the intervening terms, to defend and elaborate these terms, or to devise new indirect indications, rather than to assume direct control and explicit isolation of the stimuli involved.

The experiments cited suggest that even where the stimulus is under response control, or where the response is as subjective as after-images, explicitness and control can be achieved. Much of the future of perceptual research lies in the establishment and extension of procedures which make the stimuli and responses explicit and manipulable. Such control may immeasurably increase investigative possibilities or, on the other hand, may expose the problem as trivial.

SOME IMPLICATIONS AND APPLICATIONS

The present section will consider some implications of the formulation presented for selected areas of perceptual research. Space considerations dictate only a sampling, chosen for relevance to clinical psychology, special education, and other applied areas.

Hypnotic perception

The control of sensation by means of hypnotic instructions has been reported to be extensive, ranging from the extreme of sensation in the absence of normally appropriate stimuli (hallucination), to the extreme of absence of sensation in the presence of normally appropriate stimuli (anesthesia, blindness, deafness). There is dispute as to whether the locus of such response change lies in sensory or in response variables. The sensory interpretation raises questions which seem to justify serious scrutiny of this area. If hypnosis represents heightened suggestibility (Hull, 1933), to what extent are data normally collected influenced by lesser suggestions, implicit or explicit? Further, one can question both the adequacy of theories based on such possibly contaminated data and the generality of theories which do not account for the hypnotic data. Finally, the application of hypnotic procedures (for example, as a surgical anesthetic) has made the question of locus of hypnotic change more than an academic one.

There are few areas in perception in which credence in the subject's response plays as important a role in the definition of perception as it does here. A subject who is told he is blind has "a strong unpleasant affective reaction" (Erickson, 1939, p. 81) and exhibits tremendous relief when told his vision is partially restored; similar data are cited to lend credence to the experimenter's conclusions that "visual perceptions, ordinarily possible only to the color blind and demonstrated as impossible under ordinary conditions to the subjects, were elicited repeatedly" (p. 84). Credence in the subject's response does not define perception. Verbal statements of feeling of relief can be occasioned by variables other than the restoration of sight. Where it is possible to choose between sensory and response loci, the evidence has supported a response locus.

Pattie (1937), for example, utilized the Japanese hand illusion, in which fingers are intertwined in reversed hands so that subjects cannot differentiate left and right hands. He gave hypnotic instructions for skin anesthesia of one arm, had subjects Japanese-clasp their hands, and asked them to count taps felt. *Both* hands were tapped, and about half the taps were reported. But the taps reported were taps to *both* hands. Pattie (1936) induced uniocular blindness which worked in a variety of visual tasks clearly involving that eye, but when procedures were introduced where the subject could not tell which eye was being stimulated, "there was no evidence that the 'blind' eye's functions had been impaired to the slightest degree. The results of all former tests were thus invalidated" (p. 237). Erickson (1939) told hypnotized subjects they were color blind; they reported inability to read the appropriate numbers in the plates. Grether (1940), however, pointed out that the subjects discriminated colors other than those specified by instructions, but which color blind subjects fail to make; the "statement that the hypnotically induced color vision deficiencies were comparable in degree and character with actual color blindness is extremely doubtful" (p. 210). Similarly, Harriman (1942) obtained absence of discriminatory responses for specified color blindnesses, but "no subject made the positive type of responses which are characteristic of the color blind" (p. 90)—Grether's point. Weitzenhofer (1953), in reviewing the literature, concludes that hypnosis can attenuate sensation, but not improve it. The author would find it difficult to do better than 20/400 without his glasses; he can, however, report doing worse, without benefit of hypnosis. Hariu (1961) reports effects of suggestion (without hypnosis) on size judgments.

A series of investigations deals with the problem of negative afterimages to hallucinated color. Erickson and Erickson (1938) used sheets of white typing paper and hypnotically instructed subjects that the sheets were colored. When the white sheet at which they were staring was withdrawn, the subjects exhibited "spontaneous and in-variable hallucination of complementary colors" (p. 588)—that is, re-ported such names. Hibler (1940) ascertained expectations of after-images to designated colors, and obtained "hallucinations" in accord with such expectations, rather than with the after-images expected from color theory. Erickson (1941) asserted that asking the subjects for their expectations may have supplied directions; the controversy has continued (Hibler, 1941; Rosenthal and Mele, 1952). Goldiamond and Malpass (1961) modified the Bidwell apparatus discussed in a preceding section. This apparatus is comparatively unknown and also provides for *presentation* of negative and positive after-images which are under the experimenter's control. Hypnotized subjects were told that specified color chips would be used. When they were used, com-plements were reported, but when grey was used, they were not. Train-ing on negative after-images produced complementary responses for gray or color even when rotation produced positive after-images.

When stimuli outside the subject's range of experience are presented, the effects produced are contrary to the hypnotic sensation position; it can, of course, be argued that hypnotic perception is not governable by the usual rules of perception. In this connection, stationary hypnotized subjects told that they were being rotated were not unbalanced when asked to sit up suddenly. Such imbalance was then demonstrated, us-ing actual rotation with other subjects. Repetition of the first session then produced imbalance, but the direction of fall was contrary to the laws of inertia, since it was in the same direction as the demonstration subjects, while the rotational instructions had been in the opposite direction (Dorcus, 1937)! If consistency is to be followed, then either (1) hypnotic perception and hypnotic body motion are amenable to the same analyses which govern perception and motion under other circumstances, or (2) they are not. If the former alternative is ac-cepted, the evidence for hypnotic alteration of perception is currently not of a nature bearing on perception. If the latter alternative is ac-cepted, then perhaps this is the message of the search for Bridey Murphy (Bernstein, 1956).

Orne (1959) suggests that the trance behavior itself may be related to the "demand characteristics" of hypnosis. Stated otherwise, hypnotic behavior is operant behavior under the control of the hypnotist. Stimu-lus control over operant perceptual responses is established through contingencies supplied by an audience when certain discriminative stimuli and behaviors are paired. In hypnotic perception, the hypnotist is the audience, and the pairings differ, in accord with the experi-menter's instructions. The dissociation of the usual responses from the stimuli with which they are usually paired might profitably be examined in terms of comparative utility, or in terms of the comparative audience control of the subject's responses by the normal audience and the hypnotic audience. This involves reinforcement history and the state variables (motivation) which make a particular reinforcement effective.

Told he will feel no pain, the subject may not flinch, grimace, or in any manner exhibit those operant behaviors normally occasioned in our culture by pain stimuli, nor exhibit the respondents under operant control (cf. Mandler and Kahn, 1960). He may also "forget" about the pain, in the same sense that witnesses to gangster activities have also exhibited memory losses on the witness stand. Pain behaviors disturb the surgeon and may, through muscular tensions, produce other pain (cf. Read, 1944).

Psychotic hallucination and hysterical anesthesia

The data on hypnosis may bear upon the hallucinatory phenomena of psychosis; schizophrenia is defined by such phenomena, or rather by credence in the psychotic's response. The extent to which hallucination represents the same lack of normal stimulus control which characterizes other psychotic behaviors or the extent to which this represents behavior reinforced by hospital contingencies, would appear to be a fertile area for investigation. Certainly, schizophrenics do discriminate between up and down staircases—suggesting that where normal contingencies exist, normal discriminative behaviors exist. It will be recalled that conceptualization and discrimination refer to the same procedures. Accordingly, the simultaneous presence of normal discriminative behaviors and of abnormal discriminative behaviors, and the absence of other normal discriminative behaviors (conceptualization), suggest that the alteration of the abnormalities may involve control of the contingencies involved, rather than relate to a perceptual-cognitive deficit. Brady and Lind (1961) report elimination of hysterical blindness through contingency control; "He states he can see nothing, yet is able to avoid large obstacles in walking, handle eating utensils, reach accurately for small objects, etc." (p. 333).

Unconscious perception

The recent near-hysteria over the possibility that subliminal perception could be used by unscrupulous politicians and advertisers to produce behaviors against the subject's will can be considered an example of what can happen when logical analysis does not keep pace with procedural advances. The unconscious effect in perception is inferred from experiments in which subjects report inability (or are so considered) to perceive a stimulus which is exercising stimulus control over other responses. The control is accordingly presumed to be unconscious. This presumption is based upon definition through credence in the subject's response. In terms of stimulus control, a faint stimulus which exercises no stimulus control over a Yes response (or a recognition response) does exert some control over another response. The experimenter's explanation may be that different variables are involved for these responses (see, for example, the section on decision theory, with reference to Yes-No and forced-choice experiments, or the training procedures involved in conditioning the Yes response, or the relationship between partial presentation and accuracy); the subject's stated explanation for the discrepancy may be otherwise. The author has shown subjects their curves and has obtained explanations ranging from no explanation, to extrasensory perception, to impulses, to statements such as "I often thought I saw it, but was playing it safe." Regardless of the subject's explanation, the experimenter, using *his* generalizations, can predict and produce a whole range of discrepancies.

Discrepant explanations enter into definition of the Unconscious. Where the patient offers an explanation of his own behavior, and the therapist agrees, the patient is considered to be "aware of" or "conscious of" the causes of his own behavior. Where, however, the explanations differ, the patient may be considered "unaware" of the "true" (the therapist's) causes of his own behavior, which are *Unbewusst* to him, and the Unconscious or subconscious may be invoked in explanation.

Where two scientific generalizations about phenomena are in conflict, there are scientific criteria for selecting between them; these include prediction and control. These criteria can also be applied when the discrepancy is between a scientific explanation of the subject's behavior and the subject's own explanation. As the science of behavior expands, and as increasingly complex training in procedures and concepts is required for investigation, there will obviously be an increasing number of cases where the subject's explanations differ from the scientist's. No special constructs are required for the discrepancy in explanations involved when a physicist makes better predictions and has better control over a rocket to the moon than a layman, nor when a physiologist makes better predictions and has better control over the layman's internal organs than does the layman himself, and it is suggested that no special constructs are required when a psychologist makes better predictions and has better control over the subject's behavior than does the subject. Consideration of human behavior as amenable to scientific analysis and control renders the issue of discrepant explanations a trivial one. It should also be recalled that the subject's explanation of his own behavior is verbal behavior, and that verbal behaviors are operants with a considerable history of control by environmental contingencies, even when they semantically denote experiences of the subject. The author would suggest a moratorium on experiments which demonstrate that a stimulus can control one type of behavior while not controlling another. This is a truism in terms of the discussion presented, and also because behaviors occurring simultaneously may be under differing multiple stimulus control (for example, talking while tying one's shoes). The experimental task is to specify the conditions involved.

The author has recently reviewed research in this area, and has concluded that the methodology is inadequate to support conclusions relating it to perceptual variables (Goldiamond, 1958). With regard to the application of subliminal projection to the control of human behavior, "one may question its effectiveness, rather than its ethics" (Goldiamond, 1959a, p. xii). The major discrepancies in such research will be presented. For the stimuli governing the discrepant responses, the original discussion (1958) and appropriate sections of this chapter should be consulted. Subliminal perception experiments typically refer to absence of stimulus control over Yes (signal detection) responses, and presence of some stimulus control over forced-choice responses (signal is reported unperceived but is accurately located or identified) or over other recognition responses. Subception experiments typically refer to absence of stimulus control over a recognition response while that stimulus is exerting control over a response such as the galvanic skin response (word is reported unrecognized, but there is the expected emotional response). Perceptual defense and sensitization refer to differential stimulus control over recognition responses where the stimuli may be words of different classes or different classes of subjects (using one class of words or subjects, more hits [sensitization] or less hits [defense] are scored on the recognition score sheet than are scored using another class). It should be reiterated (see section on response bias) that increasing the stimulus presentation may increase control of the response by the stimulus class of which it is a member—that is, will tend to restrict response alternatives to that class. As energy is altered, the response biases may shift. Research on the constant ratio rule and on restriction of alternatives may increase control over such investigations; but, in all events, a procedural analysis suggests that the recognition experiment is far more complex than is suggested by the simple controls employed in the perceptual defense, sensitization, and subception experiments.

Some Gestalt phenomena

What may be the definitive statement of certain Gestalt phenomena in perception is the second edition of Metzger's classic, *Gesetze des Sehens* (1953). The phenomena presented seem to be of special interest since the compelling nature of many of them suggests that they are not trivial. Subjective experience can be used as a guide to research, the critical experimental task in this case being to bring these compelling stimuli under explicit experimenter control (a task not ignored by Gestalt) and to establish functional relations between these and behavior. Gestalt research has contributed experimental problems, procedures, and subject matter (e.g., Köhler & Wallach, 1944; Spitz, 1958) to perception, and has been characterized by an ingenuity which is often a welcome relief. The present discussion will not be concerned with the laboratory perception data of Gestalt psychology, which merits, in the opinion of the author, more attention than it has currently been receiving, but rather with certain extensions and extrapolations made from such data, especially as they apply to clinical psychology.

The notion of the perceptual primacy of wholes and other organizing principles have been applied not only theoretically to learning (Koffka, 1935) and clinical formulations (Goldstein, 1948) but also to educational training procedures (Broudy and Freel, 1956; Flesch, 1955), among other areas. One source of this organizing principle has been the laboratory demonstration that a broken circle is "perceived" as a circle, that is, is reported as such. Consideration of these results in terms of the earlier discussion of the effects of partial presentation may provide an alternative explanation. Partial presentation of a word will limit response alternatives to a group of words, with the differential probability of these being governed by differing histories of reinforcement of these word responses and by other word variables. The presentation of a partial *figure* may limit response alternatives to a definable set of words (figure names), the differential probabilities of which should be governed by variables affecting operants. Presentation, for example, of ◌, may limit the response alternatives to Q, O, S, G, C, with differential probabilities, or to Rockers, Arcs, depending upon other experimental variables. The whole-part data may simply suggest that, given the conditions of the experiments in which they were obtained, *circle* is a more probable response than *brokencircle* or *arc*, and *triangle* is a more probable response than *brokentriangle*. They are certainly more frequent in the Thorndike-Lorge lists.

Vocabulary shifts in aphasia have been interpreted as Gestalt disturbances: aphasics can name whole objects better than parts of objects; they become concrete and lose abstractions and the like. Howes and Geschwind (Geschwind, 1960) have done word-frequency distributions in aphasics. Low frequency words are much fewer in numbers. This is not a total loss of rare words but a shift of the vocabulary distribution to higher frequencies. Since concrete words tend to be more frequent than abstract words and "whole" words more frequent than "part" words (e.g., fork and tine, axe and haft, shoe and sole), one need not assume a Gestalt explanation but assume merely that the effects are due to word frequency. In fact, where the name for a part of the object is more common than the name for the whole object, one finds that frequency, not the Gestalt explanation, determines word finding. The extent to which such effects on operant behaviors account for the assignment of perceptual differences in other types of brain damage and in mental illness may be considered an open question. Since complex behaviors are usually learned *after* simple behaviors, they have a lesser history of reinforcement, and are controlled by fewer stimuli (generalization). Accordingly, in the stimulus change of trauma, they should go first. Trauma may disrupt those simple tasks which are derived from complex tasks and which are learned later.

The notion of the perceptual primacy of wholes has contributed to the use of the current word-recognition procedures in reading training. Whether or not this is a misunderstanding of Gestalt, as Flesch (1955) asserts, it is most certainly *not* an application of conditioning procedures, as the same author also asserts. Reading training is recognition training, and recognition training is discrimination training, and the problem becomes not one of wholes versus parts, but of the optimal units for the differential responding which defines discrimination. Recognition accuracy is defined by response congruence with score-sheet entries. In reading, the child's responses are occasioned by printed (or textual) stimuli, and the listener (teacher) provides the score sheet. A not-so-hypothetical experiment will be considered which compares word-recognition procedures with phonetic or phonemic procedures. The children taught to read whole words are trained on, say, 200 words which form the test. Their response alternatives will be restricted by this limitation on reading vocabulary in interaction with the restriction of alternatives controlled by discriminative stimuli in the words themselves. Since restriction of alternatives increases score-sheet hits, they should do better than children trained phonetically, who do not have the double restriction working in their favor. What the actual discriminative stimuli are in the word-recognition case can not be easily ascertained (they may be word contours), but are not likely to be the letters, since differential consequences have not been attached to them. That eye-spans of accomplished readers take in whole words and groups of words may be of value in identifying the goal of training, but the process by which this is acquired may involve other considerations. The accomplished pigeon may peck at the disk in a manner different from the tyro, but the process of shaping him to peck in this manner invariably involves behaviors which are essential to shaping, but which are no longer present. What the proper discriminative stimulus units are may require further investigation. Data from the Haskins laboratories (Liberman, Delattre, and Cooper, 1952; Delattre, Cooper, Liberman, and Gerstman, 1956; O'Connor, Gerstman, Liberman, Delattre, and Cooper, 1957) suggest that the relationship between recognition of *vocal* speech and alphabet units may not be simple; the vowel which *follows* a consonant may be critical in recognition of the *prior* consonant (1952). Research by Moore (1959) involves the simultaneous training of reading and writing; proper fingering of an electric typewriter is shaped by the teacher turning off the current when the improper key is hit. Hofsteater's (1959) pertinent report, involving alphabet training, is discussed in the next section. The operant programing of progressions of responses for reading is being investigated by Staats, Staats, and Schutz (1960).

A possible interpretation for the perceptual primacy of relations rather than of absolute stimulus values, for transposition experiments, at least, was offered in the discussion of S^D-S^Δ continua. This was presented in the section on operant discrimination and generalization.

Special education and other child research

The use of language is among the major means of establishing stimulus classes in human cultures, and different cultures establish different classes. Where such stimuli are verbal, the deaf child is handicapped in conceptualization. That such retarded discrimination may be a product of absence of differential contingencies is suggested by Hofsteater (1959), who became unresponsive to sounds during his first year and whose deaf parents raised him as if he "were a normal hearing baby with the sole exception of using the manual alphabet instead of speech" (p. 11)—that is, contingencies attached to speech by the audience, and which underlie its development, were attached to finger spelling: "You reached for the bottle and at the same time spelled 'm-k' several times, just as spontaneously and naturally as a hearing baby of the same age would have attempted to say 'milk,' and perhaps have said 'mik,'" (p. 11). Other word developments, considered characteristic of child *speech*, are reported, such as *puddy* for pudding, *b-n* for banana, and "lisping." At the age of four and a half, Hofsteater reports reading—that is, textual material controlled the appropriate finger spellings.

It has been suggested that differential application of contingencies shapes the child's perceptual responses (*cf.* Graham, 1959). The longer one is exposed to these contingencies, the more effective they should become, producing a developmental curve. That absence of such contingencies attached to mentally retarded behavior (through notions of "acceptance") may account for the overestimative (global) perceptual behavior of mentally retarded children was suggested by the author (Goldiamond, 1959b) in a study comparing chidren of varying ages and I.Q.'s. Retarded children reported triangles as larger (size constancy), gave more false alarms (signal detection, forced-choice and accuracy), assigned more assertive numbers to their reports than did normal children "who performed in a similar manner at early ages, but gradually dropped these behaviors as a function of age" (p. 147). Where "response variables such as effects of consequences, reaction time, serial effect" did not differentiate the subjects, there was an "essential similarity . . . in curves" (p. 148). The procedures used were standard psychophysical and perceptual procedures; Meyerson and Michael (1960) report an adaptation of the Blough procedures for audiometry with such subjects, and Atkinson (1959a, b), reports the use of operant conditioning of the eyelid blink rather than respondent conditioning for audiometry with the mentally retarded. Bijou and Orlando (1961) and Orlando (1961) report use of operant procedures for further analysis of responses of such children.

Perceptual development, a focus of the empiricist-nativist controversy, has been regarded as a function of learning by Hebb (1949), who cites Senden (1960). The development of children's concepts, size constancy, and related phenomena have also been cited in evidence against Gestalt positions and to support positions which can be summarized as "learning to perceive." The argument may not be this one-sided, and the question may be considered open, since the development of perceptual and conceptual (discriminative) behaviors may also be functions of increased exposure to audience contingencies. A further point which might be considered is the extent to which the experimenter's *instructions*, through similar conditioning, comes to control behavior which increasingly approximates adult response to such instructions. Stated intuitively, what may be changing is the child's interpretation of what the proper response (demand characteristics) is, when he is asked how *big* a triangle is or is told to make two triangles *equal* in size. The words italicized have differing meanings (control different responses). The notion of "naïve" subjects—that is, subjects without a history of exposure to environmental contingencies—requires some re-examination.

Factor analysis

Thurstone (1941) in his classical factorial study of perception, obtained twelve primary factors, which he attempted to identify by introspection and which he applied to ascertain the factor loadings of different perceptual tasks—that is, to describe the tests in terms of the dimensions isolated.

The criticism of factor analysis, that one gets out of a factor analysis only the dimensions of the material chosen for study, is actually its strength, since where the dimensions are unknown before one starts, factor analysis can be quite useful in ascertaining them.

Like other formal analyses, the adequacy of a factor analysis is considerably independent of the experimental procedures utilized. Two sets of multiple converging operations can be used to define perception, and the dimensions obtained from equally adequate factor analyses may differ according to differences in the dimensions of the sets of operations chosen. Even for the same task, different procedures will produce different results. For example, Thurstone's use of the Müller-Lyer illusion involved serial order, with the subject stating where equality occurred. The author (1959b) repeated this procedure, and also presented cards in a scrambled and serial order, with the subject stating which side was larger. The results obtained differed considerably, with the serial-equality procedure producing the greatest differences between ascending and descending procedures. Repetition and variation in other tasks also produced differing results.

Accordingly, while a factor analysis may be useful in suggesting the dimensions of *a given set of tasks,* the task results obtained, and therefore the derived factors, will be functions of the specific procedures used to obtain the task scores. Variations in procedures used, for the *same* task, will produce different factors and factor loadings; variations in tasks will produce different factors and factor loadings in the definition of perception upon which the tasks converge. Procedural analysis and adequacy in this area is as critical as it is in any other area.

Communication, recognition, and perception

The relationship between communication and discrimination training was discussed in a previous section, in the context of the procedures used to shape the organism's stimulus classes into the experimenter's discriminative stimuli. When this has occurred, the organism can be said to have "caught on," to "understand" the task—or, "communication" exists. Many other commonsense terms turn out to refer to the same or very similar procedures. To the extent that behavioral responses are involved, "no basis for differentiation exists in the psychological functions obtained" (Graham, 1951, p. 870b) between sensation and perception.

Table 1 is intended to exemplify, rather than to exhaust, these commonalities.

It will be noted from the table that intelligibility and recognition (Row 4) refer to identical situations, but have a stimulus or a subject reference. Similarly, other paired terms, for example, stimulus-control and discrimination (Row 2), refer to identical situations.

Congruence with the score sheet of the behaviors obtained (or lack

TABLE 1

| | EXPERIMENTAL SITUATION | | | TERMINOLOGY | | |
| | | | | REFERENT | | |
PRESENTATION	PRESENTATION	BEHAVIOR	SCORE SHEET	PRESENTATION	SUBJECT	OTHER TERM:
1a.	S/N (tone)	Verbal	S/N, N entries	Audibility	Audition	Detection
1b.	S/N (light)	Verbal	S/N, N entries	Visibility	Vision	} Generalization Perception
2a.	S^D	R	S^D, $S^\Delta = R$	S^D	R	} Recognition
2b.	S^D	R	$S^D = R$, $S^\Delta = O$	Stimulus control	Discrimination	Sensation
3a., b.	S^D_1, S^D_2, S^D_3	R	As above	Commonality, concept	Abstraction, Conceptualization	} Insight Understanding Learning
4.	Word	Word	Word	Intelligibility	Recognition	} Most of foregoing
5a.	Figure	Word	Word	Recognizability	Recognition	Identification
5b.	Figure	Word	Open	Varied	Perception	} Legibility, etc.
6a.	Sentence, paragraph	Words	Words	Message Intelligibility	Reception	} Most of foregoing
6b.	Sentence, paragraph	Other behavior	Statement of behavior	Communicability, Information content	Reception	Understanding

of congruence) defines the terms applied. For example, color blindness (absence of color vision), one of the many omissions in the table, is defined by noncongruencies with the score sheet when certain plates (Hardy, Rand, and Rittler, 1957) are presented or other tests are made. Specified types of color blindness are defined by specified patterns of congruence or noncongruence. In Row 5b, where the score sheet has no specific entry, the experimenter may be attempting to establish such entries for future research, which will involve classification according to patterns of congruences. In Row 6b, the message may be "One if by land, and two if by sea," and communication is defined by allocation of forces congruent with the message sender's score sheet.

In view of the formal relatedness of the various areas presented, it should be apparent why attempts have been made to formalize them in common terms. Form discrimination (Row 5a and 5b) is under study utilizing mathematical procedures relating to communication theory (Wulfeck and Taylor, 1957); Cherry's *On Human Communication* (1957) considers a field ranging from signal detection and physical analysis of tones to complex messages and the identification of a particular speaker above the hubbub of a cocktail party. Information theory (*The Mathematical Theory of Communication,* Shannon and Weaver, 1949) attempts to supply a metric for information and complexity in a message which can be behaviorally defined. The Theory of Signal Detection explicitly considers the utility of communicative behaviors by the subject.

A perception experiment can be formally considered an experiment in communication, as can a conditioning experiment. Subject and experimenter communicate with each other by means of perceptual or conditioning apparatus, as well as through the mediating air during verbal instructions or responses. Verbal instructions, a form of verbal conversation, seem to be quite direct and simple, but inspection of the table suggests that whether or not the instructions are "communicated" by the experimenter, or "understood" by the subject may be definable in terms of the procedures utilized in the communication investigations of Row 6b.

The interrelatedness of these areas suggests that a communication experiment can also be formally considered an operant conditioning experiment. Indeed, the space chimpanzee, Ham, was trained by operant conditioning procedures, and the maintenance of behavioral communication between Ham and scientists on earth as well as other data presented, suggest the value of such procedures in the analysis and control of communicative behavior.

Finally, it might be stated that communication and conditioning can be formally considered in perceptual terms. To the extent that a definition of perception substitutes experiential or other terms for procedural definition, its contribution to the science of psychology may be attenuated. As was stated earlier, such definitions may help to define the problem, but the scientific resolution of the problem must rest on its procedural adequacy. The point of this chapter has been that perceptual experiments are behavioral experiments, and accordingly share variables with other branches of behavioral research. Accordingly, procedural advance in perception, and advance in generalizations which functionally relate behavior to the stimuli, parameters, and conditions studied cannot fail to contribute materially to advances in other areas of scientific behavioral research and application.

At this point, a note of caution should be inserted. The chart presented indicates *formal* similarities, which have suggested formal restatement of the subsections in terms of one approach or another, This may have intellectual appeal. However, from a procedural view, the areas are considerably different. Their formal similarity provides no guarantee that the investigative procedures used are similar. The procedures and language of behavioral investigations in journals of the Acoustical Society of America, the Optical Society of America, and the Society for the Experimental Analysis of Behavior, are quite different, and require different skills and training.* The unity of science is properly a philosophic undertaking; the diversity of science is the obverse side of the unity coin, and is governed to a considerable extent by the different investigative procedures utilized, proficiency in any one set of which constitutes a major part of the training of a scientist. Of what scientific value, then, are behavioral investigations utilizing one procedure for investigations using another? In perception, at least, the discovery (from different behavioral areas) that different variables control the response suggests that they should be explicitly given experimental treatment in a perceptual investigation. If such a "nonperceptual" variable is explicitly held constant, the curve will be limited to that value and will not be a general perceptual curve. Varying that variable may convert the independent variable into a parameter—that is, a family of curves will be drawn which relate the variables with behavior. Since the response is under multiple stimulus control, other variables must be held constant during this procedure, and the families will not be general perceptual curves but will be restricted to the limiting conditions. The various

* The quest for a theory which unifies the sundered disciplines of perception and learning may, according to this orientation, translate into a quest for a unified investigative procedure. This would appear to be a difficult undertaking, for the present, at least.

behavioral areas accordingly impinge on each other and on perceptual research, and serve to suggest what limitations exist to the generalities obtained with a given procedure; they may also indicate artifacts. Since they define (dictionary: "set the limits of") the conditions under which a functional relation holds, they provide a necessary ingredient for prediction and control. A restatement of Graham's procedural equation is:

$$R = f (S), \text{ under empirical conditions } e.^{*}$$

Where e is definable, the generality of the functional relation ($=$ theory) may be tested by establishing e, setting S at a new value, S_n and *predicting* the value of R_n from $f(S_n)$. Similarly, the generality can be tested by establishing e, setting S at a value, S_c, calculated to get a R_c (and for this purpose) expected from $f(S_c)$. This is *control*. In a well-formulated system, it is difficult to differentiate theory, prediction, and control, and specification of e is necessary for all three, a constraint often forgotten in perceptual and other psychological research, where "theory-construction" is often independent of conditions, or arises from data obtained under markedly different conditions—which may be saying the same thing. If $R = f(S)$ under e, it may be $g(S)$ under h, some other set of conditions. The same commonsense term for both, perception, may be their only commonality. Unfortunately, failure to state or control the relevant conditions often makes post-hoc reconciliation difficult if not impossible. A procedural analysis of perception as a behavioral inquiry is recommended as an antidote, or rather, a preventive.

SOME PROCEDURAL COMMONALITIES AND IMPLICATIONS

The author recently described an area of psychology as follows:

Research in this area typically involves a single organism, placed in a highly contricted and controlled environment, or box, depending on size. The same organism is run for hundreds of sessions, and thousands of responses are collected over extended periods of time. Functional relations are drawn, usually without intervening variables. A discovery made is often incorporated into new research, so that each investigation repeats preceding experiments, and knowledge thereby accumulates. Stringent laboratory control and meticulous attention to equipmentation (which then comes to identify the area) substitute for statistical controls.

* The statement of the functional relation is in its simplest and most general form. A functional relation including parameters or functions of functions or other complexities can be substituted. The limiting conditions would still hold, of course.

What is being discussed? The Skinner box and operant conditioning? Or a psychophysical booth, $S = k \log R$, brass instrument psychology, and its descendants? Work on the giant nerve of a squid?

One consequence of long-term research may be characterized by the difference between transient and steady-state phenomena. If the initial functional relations when the organism is introduced to new conditions are transient—that is, are not the same as the steady-state relation which may emerge over time—they obviously cannot be used to describe it. Further, the transient relations may represent lack of current stimulus control, and may be the results of stimulus histories prior to the experiment. Differences or regularities obtained may merely reflect haphazard or experimentally uncontrolled systematic effects. If one is interested in the effects of a variable, it would seem that steady-state behavior against which to assay the variable might be desirable as a baseline from which to conduct experimental analysis. Wundt, for example, did not collect data from his subject until he had first obtained 10,000 responses, and Egan in his Indiana University communication laboratory may run a subject for seven weeks before collecting data for analysis. By virtue of the controlled conditions and consequent response regularities obtained, an alteration in response can be related to a stimulus change; this can be tested and retested by observing response change and recovery as the stimulus is reintroduced and eliminated. A large population of subjects is not necessary to draw valid conclusions. Stated statistically, the standard error of the mean is directly proportional to the variance, inversely proportional to the population. The standard error can be decreased by increasing N or by decreasing the variance. With proper laboratory controls the variance can be so diminished, that is, behavior can be made so regular that valid conclusions can be drawn from slight deviations with a very small N, for example, four nerve fibers, two pigeons, WW (Wilhelm Wundt) and EBT (E. B. Titchener) or GJT (Garth J. Thomas). Laboratory control has been substituted for statistical control. Laws or functional relations obtained thereby are not restricted to the individual case; Graham and Hsia (1958; Berger, Graham, and Hsia, 1958) need only one subject to investigate color vision if that subject has uniocular color blindness.

In the experimental analysis of behavior, the analytic adequacy of the procedures utilized is often contingent upon their degree of control over the behavior being studied—that is, the role of a stimulus may be assessed by its control over behavior as it is being manipulated. Accordingly, these procedures may lend themselves not only to analysis but also to practical application where controlled alteration of behavior is desired. The only difference that often exists between applied and basic research in these areas is the emphasis placed during the report of the investigation. The rapidly developing technology associated with these procedures is partly related to this.

It would seem that this approach has implications for clinical psychology. The clinical alteration of behavior involves long-term work with individual subjects, under conditions which are similar from one session to the next; the therapist's assessment of what course to follow is contingent upon the patient's behavior; there is an initial period of stabilization. Diagnosis and therapy are supposedly relatable.

The procedural analysis of perceptual behavior regards the response as an operant under environmental control, which includes the audience control by the experimenter. The diagnostic session involves verbal and other operant behaviors under the audience control of the examiner. It may reflect personality as invalidly as a response threshold reflects underlying perceptual processes. Like perceptual research, the instructions may restrict response alternatives in a manner unknown to the tester. The tests are usually given in an initial session and may represent transient responses. The author is not trying to state that the clinical task is impossible. The same problems beset the perceptual investigator who tries to define perception independently of the procedures used. Experimental analysis of perception of the type discussed may resolve these problems, partly through the utilization of explicit procedures, partly through restating its problems (procedural definition involving variables and parameters, rather than subjective or sensory processes), and partly by other means discussed in this chapter. The problems facing current clinical practice may have accompanied their diagnostic inheritance from perception. Current perceptual formulations which resolve these problems may have some implications for clinical psychology. Further, the perceptual practices appear in a framework which utilizes alteration of behavior as a method for investigation; diagnosis and therapy *are* intertwined. Clinical investigation, like perceptual research and conditioning research, is behavioral research, and similar variables apply. Like perception and conditioning, its existence as a separate behavioral discipline is contingent on the explicitness of the procedures which define it and on the explicitness of the functional relations obtained and the conditions under which they hold.

Machine definition and the shaping of the scientist

Much current research in communication, perception, and conditioning utilizes machine definition of the response (for example, a switch closes when a lever is pressed), its scoring, and machine scheduling and presentation of the stimulus. Procedurally, machine scheduling can not only eliminate human error and variability but also provide for the immediate application of contingencies, since the same switch can also activate consequences. The human scientist is also freed from drudgery and enabled to scheduled complex combinations beyond his behavioral limits. A permanent record can be made in a form capable of ready analysis, and free from contamination by observer bias. Perhaps the greatest advantage of machine definition is conceptual. Explicit definition of the responses being investigated is required. Open sets or fuzzy or undefinable response classes will result in either divergent response by the machine or none. As with the pigeon, eventually coincidence between stimulus classes will ensue, with the experimenter becoming explicit and using well-defined sets —if he continues in the environment and doesn't time-out (Azrin, 1961). Human scientific behaviors are shaped by the differential reinforcements (working and not working) supplied by the machine, constructed to function according to explicit criteria.

A cartoon shows a rat bragging that he has the experimenter under control: when he presses a lever, the experimenter gives a conditioned pellet response (Skinner, 1958). This exemplifies reciprocal control between subject and audience. Lest it be hastily concluded that scientists working with machines become mechanical (actually, like the *human* designers of the machine, they become explicit), it can be said that the machines (or their designers) may become humanized. It was noted that stimulus classes are not stimulus properties, but are defined by responses of the organism. In the training of a pigeon to discriminate good and bad vitamin capsules, analysis of the discrete "perceptual elements" of the pills is unnecessary. Differential reinforcement is paired with pill classes. In current design of machine systems for perceptual tasks, stimulus elements in a display are analyzed, and a machine system is constructed to respond to them analytically. Operant conditioning research suggests that such mediating analysis into stimulus elements (a point made earlier and in a different context by Gestalt) may not be necessary for differential behavior in organisms, at least, and the possibility exists that such may also be unnecessary for machine systems as well.

Making responses amenable to machine definition permits our advancing technology to bear upon behavioral research. Muscle responses in vision serve to control experiential seeing. Experimental analysis of such minute muscle responses (*cf.* Hefferline, Keenan, and Harford, 1959) may delineate the conditions maintaining ongoing seeing. The riddle of subjective perceptual experience has provoked considerable analysis. Paradoxically, a procedural definition of perception, rather than a subjective one couched in the language of the riddle, may yet help solve the riddle which initiated the quest.

Machine definition is presented as one way to insure explicitness. Needless to say, our current state of knowledge is not such as to make this the only way to be explicit in all areas. There is still room for significant contribution using simpler procedures.

In conclusion, much of classical perception refers to alteration in behavior which can be related to the stimulus changes of signal-noise ratios, of discriminative stimuli, or of those produced by hearing devices and aids, lenses, and the like. This relationship obtains using explicit procedures which distinguish perceptual research from other behavioral research, although it shares commonalities with it. Among the procedures involved is the establishment of the conditions under which the functional relations obtained will hold. The Theory of Signal Detection indicates that pay-offs and a priori probabilities, among others, can alter the SN-response relationship which defines perception. Operant conditioning research indicates that constant stimuli, response contingencies, and state variables serve to maintain discriminative behaviors and can thereby alter them. Perceptual responses typically involve verbal behavior, and the stimuli which control verbal behavior must be considered in analyzing the verbal perceptual operant, or other operant perceptual responses. Differential word frequency and restriction of alternatives, which can be produced in a variety of ways, also enter into the functional relations, as do score-sheet construction and the number of responses allowed before congruence, which defines a hit.

To establish the discriminative behaviors, training procedures are involved which are telescoped by instructions. Stimulus control in the former case may be explicit, whereas in the latter case the condensation may make it difficult to analyze or ascertain.

These variables may interact and covary with the classical stimulus changes of perception. Where such multiple and interactive control exists, assigning response change to perception because such changes are functionally related to these stimulus changes would seem to require considerable attention to procedural details. The relations will be restricted to a range of specific conditions, change in which will change the relations.

Perception may be defined either procedurally or as a schema intervening between stimulus and response class. The schema may involve intervening variables or hypothetical constructs, with the latter including subjective experience. In either case, converging operations establish the mediating term. There exists a tremendous array of possible converging operations, of stimulus presentation methods, of perceptual behaviors, and of limiting conditions which it is possible to utilize. Any schema obtained will be a property of the arbitrary limits imposed on these arrays. Where arbitrary differences exist, the differing schemata may reflect such differences rather than theoretical issues. These issues can not be reconciled where the differing procedures have not been explicitly defined. Accordingly, a procedural definition of perception not only is scientifically basic to other definitions, but may also facilitate evaluation and cross-experimental comparisons. It may help focus on genuine differences, rather than differences which may be artifacts of unstated procedural differences.

Where transient and steady-state phenomena may differ, the experimental analysis of perceptual behavior involves stabilization of behavior and analysis of the role of a stimulus through its functional relation with behavior as it is altered and realtered. Such procedures may lend themselves to application for the correction of undesired behaviors. For example, where signal detection is poor, it can be increased by altering a priori probabilities, pay-offs, and signal-noise ratios, and similar considerations hold for the other variables discussed. Assignment of causality to perception implies that changes in the classical stimulus variables is the exclusive determinant. Hypnotic data and some other clinical perceptual data have been examined. The analysis suggests that including consideration of the other sources of stimulus control as well as perceptual stimuli, may not only account for the data but also suggest research problems which may prove fruitful in advancing knowledge in these areas. It would be of interest to re-examine perceptual conclusions drawn from perceptual response differences in populations ranging from aphasics, brain-damaged, children, drug cases, through Zuni Indians, or with stimulus materials ranging from aircraft, (mammalian) baby forms, circles, through words and zigzags. Since the experimental analysis discussed provides procedures for alteration, such analysis may be of interest to clinical and other applied psychologists, not necessarily because perceptual change is critical for behavioral change, but because the same variables which govern perceptual behaviors also govern other behaviors. This implies not only that procedures developed in behavioral areas other than perception are useful in the experimental analysis of perception but also that procedures developed in perception may be useful in the experimental analysis of other behavioral areas including clinical psychology; the first laboratory of experimental psychology was founded by Wundt.

The perceptual responses are typically verbal operants, like many of the responses observed and modified in clinical psychology. The verbal response may be in the same class as a nonverbal behavior of concern (and also in the same response class as the experiential response; the subjective psychologist and sociologist assume it governs the other responses), and alteration of one may affect the other (and possibly the experiential response). Verbal responses often have semantic reference to subjective experience, and the method of solution of the ensuing problems in perceptual analysis and control may have relevance for clinical analysis and control. Perception is not defined by credence in the verbal response, nor is clinical psychology. The procedures of both define their areas, and both may involve the utilization of what may be the free operant defining human organisms (the verbal response). Acquaintance with the procedures whereby perceptual behaviors are analyzed, and undesired behaviors are changed, may prove useful in the alteration of those behaviors which confront the clinical psychologist, and the redress of which grievous behaviors is the social justification of his discipline.

REFERENCES

Ammons, R. B., Ulrich, P., & Ammons, C. H. Voluntary control of perception of depth in a two-dimensional drawing. *Proc. Montana Acad. Sci.,* 1959, *19,* 160–168.

Anderson, C. D. The constant-ratio rule as a predictor of confusions among visual stimuli of brief exposure duration. *AFCRC-TN*-58-60, 1958.

Appel, J. B. The aversive control of an operant discrimination. *J. exper. Anal. Behavior,* 1960, *3,* 35–47.

Ashby, W. R. *Design for a brain.* New York: Wiley, 1952.

Atkinson, C. J. The use of the eyelid reflex as an operant in audiometric testing. *J. exper. Anal. Behavior,* 1959a, *2,* 212.

Atkinson, C. J. Perceptual and response abilities of mentally retarded children as measured by several auditory threshold tests. Final Report, U.S. Dept., H.E.W., Cooperative Res. Proj. No. 176(6471), 1959b.

Azrin, N. H. Some effects of noise on human behavior. *J. exper. Anal. Behavior,* 1958, *1,* 183–200.

Azrin, N. H. Time-out from positive reinforcement. *Science,* 1961, *133,* 382–383.

Azrin, N. H., Holz, W., Goldiamond, I. Response bias in questionnaire reports. *J. consult. Psychol.,* 1961, *25,* 324–326.

Azrin, N. H., Holz, W., Ulrich, R., & Goldiamond, I. The control of the content of behavior through reinforcement. *J. exper. Anal. Behavior,* 1961, *4,* 25–30.

Bartley, S. H. *Principles of perception.* New York: Harper, 1958.

Békèsy, G. V. A new audiometer. *Acta Oto-laryngologica,* 1947, *35,* 411–422.

Berger, E., Graham, C. H., & Hsia, Y. Some visual functions of a unilaterally color-blind person. I. Critical fusion frequency in various spectral regions. *J. Opt. Soc. Amer.,* 1958a, *48,* 614–622.

Berger, E., Graham, C. H., & Hsia, Y. Some visual functions of a unilaterally color-blind person. II. Binocular brightness matches in various spectral regions. *J. Opt. Soc. Amer.,* 1958b, *48,* 622–627.

Bernstein, M. *The search for Bridey Murphy.* Garden City, N.Y.: Doubleday, 1956.

Bidwell, S. On negative after-images following brief retinal excitation. *Proc. Roy. Soc.,* 1897, *61,* 263–271.

Bijou, S. W., & Orlando, R. Rapid development of multiple-schedule performances with retarded children. *J. exper. Anal. Behavior,* 1961, *4,* 7–16.

Bilger, R. C., & Speaks, C. E. Operant control of non-fluent speech in normal talkers. *Asha,* 1959, *1,* 97 (abstract).

Black, J. W. The persistence of effects of delayed side-tone. *J. Speech*

& Hearing Disorders, 1955, *20*, 65–68.

Blackwell, H. R. The influence of data collection procedures upon psychophysical measurement of two sensory functions. *J. exper. Psychol.*, 1952a, *44*, 306–315.

Blackwell, H. R. Studies of psychophysical methods for measuring visual thresholds. *J. Opt. Soc. Amer.*, 1952b, *42*, 606–616.

Blackwell, H. R. Psychophysical thresholds: experimental studies of methods of measurement. *Eng. Res. Bull.* No. 36, University of Michigan, 1953.

Blough, D. S. Spectral sensitivity in the pigeon. *J. Opt. Soc. Amer.*, 1957, *47*, 827–833.

Blough, D. S. A method for obtaining psychophysical thresholds from the pigeon, *J. exper. Anal. Behavior*, 1958, *1*, 31–43.

Blough, D. S. Generalization and preference on a stimulus-intensity continuum. *J. exp. Anal. Behavior*, 1959, *2*, 307–316.

Blough, D. S. The shape of some wavelength generalization gradients. *J. exp. Anal. Behavior*, 1961, *4*, 31–40.

Boring, E. G. *Sensation and perception in the history of experimental psychology.* New York: Appleton-Century-Crofts, 1942.

Boring, E. G. A history of introspection. *Psychol. Bull.*, 1953, *50*, 169–189.

Brady, J. P., & Lind, D. L. Experimental analysis of hysterical blindness. *A.M.A. Arch. gen. Psychiatry*, 1961, *4*, 331–339.

Bricker, P. D., & Chapanis, A. Do incorrectly-perceived tachistoscopic stimuli convey information? *Psychol. Rev.*, 1953, *60*, 181–188.

Brogden, W. J. Sensory pre-conditioning. *J. exper. Psychol.*, 1939, *25*, 323–332.

Broudy, H. S., & Freel, E. L. *Psychology for general education.* New York: Longmans, Green, 1956.

Brown, C. R., & Rubenstein, H. Test of response bias explanation of the word-frequency effect. *Science*, 1961, *133*, 280–281.

Cherry, C. *On human communication.* New York: Wiley, 1957.

Clarke, F. R. Constant-ratio rule for confusion matrices in speech communication. *J. Acous. Soc. Amer.*, 1957, *29*, 715–720.

Creelman, C. D. *Bibliography on signal detectability.* Mimeo, 1960.

Delattre, P., Cooper, F. S., Liberman, A. M., Gerstman, L. J. Speech synthesis as a research technique. *Proc. VII Internat. Cong. Linguistics* (*1952*), London, 1956, 545–561.

Dewey, G. *Relative frequency of English speech sounds.* Cambridge, Mass.: Harvard Univ. Press, 1923.

Dingle, Review of H. C. W. Churchman & P. Ratoosh (Eds.), Measurement: definitions and theories. *Scientific Amer.*, 1960, *203*, No. 6, 189.

Dollard, J., & Miller, N. E. *Personality and psychotherapy.* New York: McGraw-Hill, 1950.

Dorcus, R. M. Modification by suggestion of some vestibular and visual responses. *Amer. J. Psychol.*, 1937, *49*, 82–87.

Egan, J. P. Message repetition, operating characteristics, and confusion matrices in speech communication. *AFCRC-TR-57-50*, 1957a.

Egan, J. P. Monitoring task in speech communication. *J. Acous. Soc. Amer.*, 1957b, *29*, 482–489.

Egan, J. P. Recognition memory and the operating characteristic. *AFCRC-TN-58-51*, 1958.

Egan, J. P., Schulman, A. I., & Greenberg, G. Z. Operating characteristics determined by binary decisions and by ratings. *J. Acous. Soc. Amer.*, 1959, *31*, 768–773.

Erickson, E. M., Critical comments on Hibler's presentation of his work on negative after-images of hypnotically induced hallucinated colors. *J. exper. Psychol.*, 1941, *29*, 164–170.

Erickson, M. H. The induction of color

blindness by a technique of hypnotic suggestion. *J. genet. Psychol.*, 1939, *20*, 61–89.

Erickson, M. H., & Erickson, E. M. The hypnotic induction of hallucinatory color vision following by pseudo negative after-images. *J. exper. Psychol.*, 1938, *22*, 581–588.

Eriksen, C. W. Prediction from and interaction among multiple concurrent discriminative responses. *J. exp. Psychol.*, 1957, *5*, 353–359.

Eriksen, C. W. Unconscious processes. *Nebraska symposium on motivation.* Lincoln, Neb.: Univ. Nebraska Press, 1958.

Eriksen, C. W., & Browne, C. T. An experimental and theoretical analysis of perceptual defense. *J. abnor. soc. Psychol.*, 1956, *52*, 224–230.

Evans, R. M. *An Introduction to color.* New York: Wiley, 1948.

Eysenck, H. J. *The dynamics of anxiety and hysteria.* London: Routledge & Kegan Paul, 1957.

Eysenck, H. J., Granger, G. W., & Brengelmann, J. C. *Perceptual processes and mental illness.* London: Chapman & Hall, 1957.

Ferster, C. B. Intermittent reinforcement of matching to sample in the pigeon. *J. exper. Anal. Behavior,* 1960, *3*, 259–272.

Ferster, C. B., & Appel, J. B. Punishment of S△ responding in matching to sample by time out from positive reinforcement. *J. exper. Anal. Behavior,* 1961, *4*, 45–56.

Ferster, C. B., & Skinner, B. F. *Schedules of reinforcement.* New York: Appleton-Century-Crofts, 1957.

Flanagan, B., Goldiamond, I., & Azrin, N. Operant stuttering: the control of stuttering through response-contingent consequences. *J. exper. Anal. Behavior,* 1958, *1*, 173–177.

Flanagan, B., Goldiamond, I., & Azrin, N. H. Instatement of stuttering in normally fluent individuals through operant procedures. *Science,* 1959, *130*, 979–981.

Flesch, R. *Why Johnny can't read.* New York: Harper, 1955.

Garner, W. R., Hake, H. W., & Eriksen, C. W. Operationism and the concept of perception. *Psychol. Rev.,* 1956, *63*, 149–159.

Geschwind, N. Word frequency distribution in aphasics. *Amer. Psychologist,* 1960, *7*, 492.

Gibson, J. J. *The perception of the visual world.* Boston: Houghton Mifflin, 1950.

Goldberg, F. H., & Fiss, H. Partial cues and the phenomenon of 'discrimination without awareness.' *Percept. Motor Skills,* 1959, *9*, 243–251.

Goldiamond, I. The relationship of subliminal perception to forced choice and psychophysical judgments, simultaneously obtained. *Amer. Psychologist,* 1954, *9*, 378–379 (abstract).

Goldiamond, I. Indicators of perception: I. Subliminal perception, subception, unconscious perception: an analysis in terms of psychophysical indicator methodology. *Psychol. Bull.,* 1958, *55*, 373–411.

Goldiamond, I. Statement to the New Jersey Commission to Study Subliminal Projection. Trenton: State Supt. Public Documents, *Final Report, Comm. Study Subl. Proj.,* May, 1959a, viii–xii.

Goldiamond, I. Visual signal detection, perception, and response variables as functions of development and mental retardation. Final Report, U.S. Office H. E. W., Cooperative Research Prog., Proj. No. 176(6471), 1959b.

Goldiamond, I. Blocked speech communication and delayed feed-back: an experimental analysis. *AFCCDD-TR-60-37,* 1960a.

Goldiamond, I. The temporal development of fluent and blocked speech communication. *AFCCDD-TR-60-38,* 1960b.

Goldiamond, I. Word frequency, accuracy of recognition, and conditioning. *Amer. Psychologist,* 1960c, *7,* 492.

Goldiamond, I. Ongoing visual monitoring: procedures for experimental analysis. *ESD-TR-61–22*, 1961.

Goldiamond, I. Maintenance of ongoing fluent speech and stuttering. *J. Mathematics*, 1962. In press.

Goldiamond, I., Atkinson, C. J., & Bilger, R. C. Stabilization of behavior during prolonged exposure to delayed auditory feedback. *Science*, 1962. In press.

Goldiamond, I., & Hawkins, W. F. Vexierversuch: the log relationship between word-frequency and recognition obtained in the absence of stimulus words. *J. exper. Psychol.*, 1958, *56*, 457–463.

Goldiamond, I., & Malpass, L. F. Locus of hypnotically induced color changes in color vision responses. *J. Opt. Soc. Amer.*, 1961, *51*, 1117–1121.

Goldstein, K. *Language and language disturbances.* New York: Grune & Stratton, 1948.

Gourevitch, G., Hack, M. H., & Hawkins, J. E., Jr. Auditory thresholds in the rat measured by an operant technique. *Science*, 1960, *131*, 1046–1047.

Graham, C. H. Behavior, perception, and the psychophysical methods. *Psychol. Rev.*, 1950, *57*, 108–118.

Graham, C. H. Visual perception. In S. S. Stevens, *Handbook of experimental psychology.* New York: Wiley, 1951, 868–920.

Graham, C. H. Behavior and the psychophysical methods: an analysis of some recent experiments. *Psychol. Rev.*, 1952, *59*, 62–70.

Graham, C. H. Color theory. In S. Koch, *Psychology: a study of a science. Vol. 1. Sensory, perceptual, and physiological formulations.* New York: McGraw-Hill, 1959, 145–287.

Graham, C. H., & Hsia, Y. Color defect and color theory. *Science*, 1958, *127*, 675.

Green, D. M. Effect of vocabulary size on articulation score. Elec. Def. Gp., University of Michigan, *T.R. 81*, 1958.

Grether, W. F. A comment on "The induction of color blindness by a technique of hypnotic suggestion." *J. genet. Psychol.*, 1940, *23*, 207–210.

Guilford, J. P. *Psychometric methods.* New York: McGraw-Hill, 1954. (2nd ed.)

Guthrie, E. R. *The psychology of learning.* New York: Harper, 1952. (Rev. ed.)

Guttman, N., & Kalish, H. I. Discriminability and stimulus generalization. *J. exper. Psychol.*, 1956, *51*, 79–88.

Hardy, L. H., Rand, G., & Rittler, M. C. *A-O H-R-R-Pseudoisochromatic Plates.* Amer. Optical Co., 1957.

Hariu, T. Suggestion as a determinant factor of apparent size. *Tohoku Psychol. Folia*, 1961, *19*, 103–108.

Harriman, P. L. Hypnotic induction of color vision anomalies: I. The use of the Ishihara and the Jensen tests to verify the acceptance of suggested color blindness. *J. genet. Psychol.*, 1942a, *26*, 289–298.

Harriman, P. L. Hypnotic induction of color vision anomalies: II. Results on two other tests of color blindness. *J. genet. Psychol.*, 1942b, *27*, 81–92.

Hartley, P. H. T. An experimental analysis of interspecific recognition. In *S.E.B. Symposium IV, Physiological mechanisms in animal behaviour.* New York: Academic, 1950, 313–336.

Hebb, D. O. *The organization of behavior.* New York: Wiley, 1949.

Hefferline, R. F., Keenan, B., & Harford, R. A. Escape and avoidance conditioning in human subjects without their observation of the response. *Science*, 1959, *130*, 1338–1339.

Hibler, F. W. An experimental investigation of negative after-images of hallucinated colors in hypnosis. *J. exper. Psychol.*, 1940, *27*, 45–57.

Hibler, F. W. Note on Mrs. Erickson's comments on Hibler's work on negative after-images of hypnotically induced colors. *J. exper. Psychol.*, 1941, *29*, 170–172.

Hilgard, E. R. *Theories of learning.* New York: Appleton-Century-Crofts, 1948.

Hofsteater, H. T. An experiment in preschool education. Washington: *Gallaudet College Bull.,* 1959, 8, No. 3, 1–17.

Holland, J. G. Techniques of behavioral analysis of human observing. *Science,* 1957, *125,* 348–305.

Holland, J. G. Human vigilance. *Science,* 1958, *128,* 61–67.

Howes, D. The nature of the word-frequency variable in perception and association. *Amer. Psychologist,* 1960, 7, 492.

Hull, C. L. *Hypnosis and suggestibility.* New York: Appleton-Century-Crofts, 1933.

Hull, C. L. *Essentials of behavior.* New Haven, Conn.: Yale Univ. Press, 1951.

Isaacs, W., Thomas, J., & Goldiamond, I. Application of operant conditioning to reinstate verbal behavior in psychoptics. *J. Speech & Hearing Disorders,* 1960, 25, 8–12.

Ittelson, W. H. *Visual space perception.* New York: Springer, 1960.

Kaplan, S. Factors influencing perception of afterimages. Paper read at Regional Research Confer., Amer. Psychiat. Assn., University of Oklahoma, School of Med., April, 1957.

Kelleher, R. T. Stimulus-producing responses and attention in the chimpanzee. *J. exper. Anal. Behavior,* 1958a, *1,* 69–72.

Kelleher, R. T. Concept formation in chimpanzees. *Science,* 1958b, *128,* 777–778.

Keller, F. S., & Schoenfeld, W. N. *Principles of psychology.* New York: Appleton-Century-Crofts, 1950.

Koffka, K. *Principles of Gestalt psychology.* New York: Harcourt, Brace, 1935.

Kohler, W., & Wallach, H. Figural after-effects: an investigation of visual processes. *Proc. Amer. Phil. Soc.,* 1944, *88,* 269–357.

Kransner, L. Studies of the conditioning of verbal behavior. *Psychol. Bull.,* 1958, *55,* 148–170.

Lane, H. Control of vocal responding in chickens. *Science,* 1960a, *132,* 37–38.

Lane, H. Temporal and intensive properties of human vocal responding under a schedule of reinforcement. *J. exp. Anal. Behavior,* 1960b, *3,* 183–192.

Laties, V. G., & Weiss, B. Human observing behavior after signal detection. *J. exp. Anal. Behavior,* 1960, *3,* 27–33.

Lehmann, H. Preliminary report on a device for the objective measurement of the negative after-image phenomenon. *Science, 112,* 199–201.

Liberman, A. M., Delattre, P., & Cooper, F. S. The role of selected stimulus-variables in the perception of the unvoiced stop consonants. *Amer. J. Psychol.,* 1952, *65,* 497–516.

Licklider, J. C. R. Three auditory theories. In S. Koch, *Psychology: a study of a science. Vol. 1. Sensory, perceptual, and physiological formulations.* New York: McGraw-Hill, 1959.

Mandler, G., & Kahn, M. Discrimination of changes in heart rate: two unsuccessful attempts. *J. exper. Anal. Behavior.,* 1960, *3,* 21–26.

Metzger, W. *Gesetze des Sehens.* Frankfurt a. M.: Waldemar Kramer, 1953.

Meyer, D. R. Effects of differential probabilities of reinforcement on discrimination learning by monkeys. *J. comp. physiol. Psychol.,* 1960, *53,* 173–175.

Meyerson, L., & Michael, J. L. The measurement of sensory thresholds in exceptional children. *Monographs in somatopsychology,* No. 4. Houston: University of Houston, 1960.

Mowrer, O. H. *Learning theory and the symbolic processes.* New York: Wiley, 1960.

Munn, N. L. *The fundamentals of hu-*

man adjustment. Boston: Houghton Mifflin, 1961.

O'Connor, J. D., Gerstman, L. J., Liberman, A. M., Delattre, P. C., & Cooper, F. S. Acoustic cues for the perception of initial / w, j, r, l / in English. *Word,* 1957, *13,* 24–43.

Orlando, R. The functional role of discriminative stimuli in free operant performance of developmentally retarded children. *Psychol. Record,* 1961, *11,* 153–161.

Orne, M. T. The nature of hypnosis: artifact and essence. *J. abnorm. soc. Psychol.,* 1959, *58,* 277–299.

Pattie, F. A., Jr. A report of attempts to produce uniocular blindness by hypnotic suggestion. *Brit. J. Med. Psychol.,* 1936, *15,* 230–241.

Pattie, F. A., Jr. The genuineness of hypnotically produced anesthesia of the skin. *Amer. J. Psychol.,* 1937, *49,* 435–443.

Pierrel, R., & Sherman, J. G. Generalization of auditory intensity following discrimination training. *J. exper. Anal. Behavior,* 1960, *3,* 313–322.

Read, G. D. *Childbirth without fear.* New York: Harper, 1944.

Reichenbach, H. *The rise of scientific philosophy.* Berkeley, Calif.: Univ. California Press, 1951.

Revesz, G. Experiments on animal space perception. *Proc. VIIth Internatl. Cong. Psychol., Oxford.* Cambridge, 1924, 29–56.

Rosenthal, B. G., & Mele, H. The validity of hypnotically induced color hallucinations. *J. abnorm. soc. Psychol.,* 1952, *47,* 700–704.

Rozeboom, W. K. Mediation variables in scientific theory. *Psychol. Rev.,* 1956, *63,* 249–264.

Salzinger, K. Experimental manipulation of verbal behavior: a review. *J. genet. Psychol.,* 1959, *61,* 65–94.

Seidel, R. A. review of sensory preconditioning. *Psychol. Bull.,* 1959, *56,* 58–73.

Senden, M. von. *Space and sight.* New York: Free Press, 1960.

Shannon, C. E., & Weaver, W. *The mathematical theory of communication.* Urbana, Ill.: Univ. Illinois Press, 1949.

Skinner, B. F. *Science and human behavior.* New York: Macmillan, 1953.

Skinner, B. F. *Verbal behavior.* New York: Appleton-Century-Crofts, 1957.

Skinner, B. F. A case history in scientific method. In S. Koch, *Psychology: a study of a science. Vol. 2. General systematic formulations, learning and special processes.* New York: McGraw-Hill, 1959.

Skinner, B. F. Pigeons in a pelican. *Amer. Psychologist,* 1960, *15,* 28–37.

Smith, W. M., McCrary, J. W., & Smith, K. U. Delayed visual feedback and behavior. *Science,* 1960, *132,* 1013–1014.

Solley, C. M., & Murphy, G. *Development of the perceptual world.* New York: Basic Books, 1960.

Solomon, R. L., & Howes, D. S. Word frequency, personal values, and visual duration thresholds. *Psychol. Rev.,* 1951, *58,* 256–270.

Sperling, G. Negative after-image without prior positive image. *Science,* 1960, *131,* 1613–1614.

Spitz, H. H. The present status of the Köhler-Wallach theory of satiation. *Psychol. Bull.,* 1958, *55,* 1–28.

Spivack, G., & Levine, M. The spiral aftereffect and reversible figures as measures of brain damage and memory, *J. Personality,* 1957, *25,* 767–778.

Staats, A. W., Staats, C. K., & Crawford, H. L. First-order conditioning of meaning and the parallel conditioning of a GSR. *J. genet. Psychol.,* 1961. In press.

Staats, A. W., Staats, C. K., & Schutz, R. E. Development of textual behavior and its function in communication. U.S. Office of Education, Cooperative Research Prog., Contract No. 1048, Sept. 1960.

Stevens, S. S. To honor Fechner and repeal his law. *Science,* 1961, *133,* 80–86.

Swets, J. A. Indices of signal detectability obtained with various psychophysical procedures. *J. Acous. Soc. Amer.*, 1959, *31*, 511–513.

Swets, J. A. Detection theory and psychophysics: a review. *Psychometrika*, 1961a, *26*, 49–63.

Swets, J. A. Is there a sensory threshold? *Science*, 1961b, *134*, 168–177.

Swets, J. A., Tanner, W. P., Jr., & Birdsall, T. G. The evidence for a decision-making theory of signal detection. *Tech. Rep. No. 40*, Electronic Defense Group. Ann Arbor: University of Michigan, 1955.

Swets, J. A., Tanner, W. P., Jr., & Birdsall, T. G. Decision processes in perception. *Psycholog. Rev.*, 1961. *68*, 301–340.

Tanner, W. P., Jr. Theory of recognition. *J. Acous. Soc. Amer.*, 1956, *28*, 882–888.

Tanner, W. P., Jr. Signal detection theory and its application to psychophysics. Tutorial at the University of Arizona, 1959. In press.

Tanner, W. P., Jr., & Birdsall, T. G. Definitions of d' and η as psychophysical measures. *J. Acous. Soc. Amer.*, 1958, *30*, 922–928.

Tanner, W. P., Jr., & Swets, J. A. A decision-making theory of visual detection. *Psychol. Rev.*, 1954, *61*, 401–409.

Thorndike, E. L., & Lorge, I. *The teacher's word book of 30,000 words*. New York: Columbia Univ. Press, 1944.

Thurstone, L. L. *A factorial study of perception*. Chicago: Univ. Chicago Press, 1941.

Ulrich, P., & Ammons, R. B. Voluntary control over perceived dimensionality (perspective) of three-dimensional objects. *Proc. Montana Acad. Sci.*, 1959, *19*, 169–173.

Van Bergeijk, W. A., & David, E. E., Jr. Delayed handwriting. *Percept. Motor Skills*, 1959, *9*, 347–357.

Verhave, T. Recent developments in the experimental analysis behavior. *Proc. Eleventh Research Council, Amer. Meat Institution Foundation*, Chicago, 1959, 113–136.

Verplanck, W. S. The control of the content of conversation: reinforcement of statements of opinion. *J. abnorm. soc. Psychol.*, 1955, *55*, 668–676.

Weitzenhoffer, A. M. *Hypnotism: an objective study in suggestibility.* New York: Wiley, 1953.

Weitzman, E. D., Ross, G. S., Hodos, W., & Galambos, R. Behavioral method for studying pain in the monkey. *Science*, 1961, *133*, 37–38.

Whorf, B. L. *Language, thought, and reality: selected writings.* Cambridge, Mass.: Technology Press, 1956.

Wohlwill, J. F. Developmental studies of perception. *Psychol. Bull.*, 1960, *57*, 249–288.

Wolf, M. Some effects of combined S^D's. Unpublished master's thesis, Arizona State University, 1961.

Woodworth, R. S., & Schlosberg, H. *Experimental psychology.* New York: Holt, 1954. (Rev. Ed.)

Wulfeck, J. W., & Taylor, J. H. (Eds.). Form discrimination as related to military problems. *Natl. Acad. Sci.-Natl. Res. Coun. Publication 561*, 1957.

Wycoff, L. B., Jr. The role of observing responses in discrimination behavior. *Psychol. Rev.*, 1952, *59*, 437–442.

Zeitlin, L. R. A response oriented analysis of the concepts of autism and perceptual sensitization. Unpublished doctoral dissertation, Northwestern University, 1954.

PART THREE

Psychophysiology

10

Psychophysiology of Emotional Behavior

JOSEPH V. BRADY

While interest in the relationships between organismic-environmental interactions described as "emotional" and the internal events of an organism's physiology has long been high, understanding has evolved slowly and somewhat haltingly amidst a host of psychological and biological complexities. At both the clinical and experimental levels, emphasis upon the phenomenological or "feeling" aspect of emotional processes has been prominent in the development of many highly speculative theories. Experimental bulwarks presently available to the clinical practitioner in this area, or likely to develop in the future, however, seem to depend upon the analysis of objectively observable and measureable behavioral events. Not only does it seem necessary objectively to identify relevant emotional processes in terms of their operationally defined behavioral characteristics; it is also clear that such behavioral descriptions must be derived independently of the physiological events to which they will ultimately be related in the course of a psychophysiological analysis. Only under these conditions of independently identifiable and measureable psychological and physiological observations does it seem reasonable to expect that an experimental analysis of the psychophysiology of emotional behavior can provide a sound foundation for clinical practice.

Unfortunately, neither clinical nor experimental accounts of the psychophysiology of emotional behavior have provided such a sound basis for applied efforts in this area. Although extensive descriptions of peripheral bodily changes presumably related to affective processes are available, the objective and measureable definition of the behavioral events critically involved in such interactions have been inadequate. And only recently has the direct analysis of the central neurological factors in emotional behavior segments begun to take firm anatomical and physiological form.

In this discussion of the physiological correlates of emotional behavior, emphasis will focus upon recent experimental developments which seem to relate fundamentally to current clinical problems in this area. Necessarily, however, some brief consideration will first be given to problems of definition, primarily as these relate to the problems of translation between the clinical and experimental realms. We can then proceed to examine some historical experiments which appear to have set the stage for more recent efforts. We will consider primarily the central nervous system research and its implications for the problem under discussion, although the direction of experiments dealing with more peripheral physiological changes will be briefly noted. Against this background, some of the more recent experimental developments in the psychophysiology of emotional behavior can be explored with a view to elaborating observed relationships and assessing the present status and future outlook for this general area.

SOME PROBLEMS OF DEFINITION

In probably no other domain of psychological science has so little empirical data occasioned so much theoretical speculation as in the general area of the "emotions." The voluminous literature on this topic reveals a phenomenological emphasis upon the "affective" or "feeling" aspects of the problem and upon the wide range of digestive, respiratory, secretory, and cardiovascular changes presumably related to emotional experience. The classical James-Lange formulation (Dunlap, 1922; James, 1884; Lange, 1887) and even Cannon's "neural organization" theory of emotion (Cannon, 1927, 1931) can be seen to share this experiential emphasis. And of course the ever-popular Freudian view of emotional processes as "mental states" or "psychic phenomena" (Freud, 1924) continues to pervade even the most sophisticated treatments of the topic.

The history of psychological speculation, however, has not altogether lacked attempts to deal with the emotions behavioristically, if at times somewhat introspectively. The roots of such attempts are to be found as far back as Darwin's early attention to the facial musculature in his consideration of the evolutionary aspects of emotional expression (Darwin, 1872) and Wundt's emphasis upon the emotions as "conscious contents" (Wundt, 1902). Furthermore, Watson's classical treatment of the emotions as conditioned phenomena emphasized interactions between the organism and its environment as the basis for his behavioristic views (Watson, 1914, 1919). More recently, Skinner's analysis of emotion in terms of the probability or predisposition to change of a more or less broad range of behavioral response patterns has continued this descriptive behavioristic tradition (Skinner, 1953a), as has the related view of Keller and Schoenfeld (1950) that emotional behavior represents widespread changes in "reflex strength" as a function of specific environmental contingencies. Many other more or less extreme theoretical views have characterized psychological speculation in this area, and the influence of both clinical and experimental contributions is readily apparent in most of these efforts (Arnold, 1950; Brady, 1957b; Brady and Hunt, 1955; Duffy, 1941; Hunt, 1948; Lashley, 1938; Leeper, 1948; Liddell, 1956; Lindsley, 1951; McDougall, 1926; Miller, 1951; Mowrer, 1950; Papez, 1937; Ruckmick, 1936; Schlosberg, 1954; Young, 1943).

Experimentally, attempts to define emotional behavior for laboratory investigation have focused upon both the antecedent stimulus events which appear to produce or provide the occasion for a given response pattern and the characteristics of the response pattern per se. Typically, for example, both conditioned and unconditioned reactions to aversive stimuli have been regarded as "emotional," and a broad range of internal changes (e.g., through epinephrine administration) and external environmental changes (e.g., electric shock) have been labeled the antecedents of such behavioral events (Brady and Hunt, 1955; Landis and Hunt, 1932). More frequently, however, the properties of a given response pattern appear themselves to serve as the basis for classifying behavior as "emotional." Certain characteristics of an organism's muscular activity (e.g., autonomic changes) are often considered as "indicators" of "emotional" participation in a behavioral situation. Despite extensive research in this direction (Cannon, 1929; Dunbar, 1954), however, it has not been possible to distinguish reliably between emotional activities either on the basis of specific antecedent stimulus events or observable muscular and autonomic response patterns. Even the identification of general emotional behavior by these criteria has presented problems, since such stimulus and response events frequently occur in circumstances not conventionally associated with emotion, such as temperature changes or heavy exercise.

Faced with such difficulties, many psychological studies have been limited to the consequences of emotional situations for a broad spectrum of behavioral processes, in an attempt to define emotion. Commonly, both clinical and experimental emphasis is directed at the disruptive or suppressing effects of emotional disturbance upon ongoing activity (Brady, 1957b; Estes and Skinner, 1941; Lichtenstein,

1950; Masserman, 1943; Schoenfeld, 1950; Young, 1943). The defining properties of emotional behavior segments, however, may as often involve an increased frequency or probability of adaptive response patterns, particularly when the contingencies of the situation require avoidance of aversive stimuli (Miller, 1951; Sidman, Herrnstein, and Conrad, 1957) or emergence of appetitive consequences (Brady, 1961; Herrnstein and Morse, 1957).

In the absence of a satisfactory theoretical or empirical formulation of emotional behavior, the task of defining and delimiting the psychological subject matter for such a psychophysiological analysis presents many difficulties. There are neither adequate conventional criteria for identifying emotional activities nor a definitive analysis on which to base the classification of emotions or the differentiation of subtle "strength" phenomena (from the "milder affects" to the "violent emotions"). The choice of material for this chapter will, of necessity, sometimes seem arbitrary, and the reader may legitimately question the appropriateness of much that has been included as well as much that has been omitted. But since our present level of psychological sophistication hardly justifies a more restrictive or provincial approach, conventional or traditional usage will determine the behavioral coverage. The results of future research efforts will no doubt require extensive modification and reorientation of past and present thinking in this area. But the somewhat descriptive behavioristic framework within which much of the laboratory work on emotional behavior has proceeded should permit some realistic assessment of the past history, present status, and future perspectives of a most complex psychophysiological problem.

SOME HISTORICAL AND METHODOLOGICAL CONSIDERATIONS

The predominant focus of the voluminous clinical and experimental literature devoted to the psychophysiology of emotional behavior over the past two or three decades has been the measurement and analysis of bodily changes in relation to peripheral response mechanisms integrated by the autonomic nervous system, the cerebrospinal system, and the endocrine system. Dunbar's recent revision of her volume *Emotions and Bodily Changes* (1954) carries an exhaustive classified bibliography in this area. Several other authors have also described techniques for recording such peripheral changes and have presented detailed experimental analyses of the characteristic physiological processes associated with more or less broadly defined affective phenomena (Cannon, 1929; Darrow, 1943; Davis, 1948; Gellhorn, 1943; Hunt and Landis, 1936; Lacey, 1956; Landis, 1934; Liddell, 1956;

Lindsley, 1951; Mahl, 1953; Malmo, 1956; Ruckmick, 1936; Wenger and Ellington, 1943; Young, 1943, 1948). Generally, such studies have emphasized the relationship of the emotions to such peripheral phenomena as the electrical response of the skin (Darrow, 1936; Welch and Kubis, 1947a, 1947b), arterial pressure and blood volume (Darrow, 1936; Reiser, Reeves, and Armington, 1955), electrocardiogram and heart rate (Notterman, Schoenfeld, and Bersh, 1952; Reiser, Reeves, and Armington, 1955), respiration (Finesinger, 1944), skin temperature (Mittelmann and Wolfe, 1943), pupillary changes (Lowenstein and Friedman, 1942), salivary secretion (Winsor and Korchin, 1938, 1940), pilomotor effects (Lindsley and Sassaman, 1938), dermographia (Wenger and Ellington, 1943) skin sweating (Wenger and Gilchrist, 1948), changes in the chemical composition of blood, saliva, and urine (Diethelm, Doty, and Milhorat, 1945; Gaskill, 1933; Gellhorn, 1943; Mahl, 1952; Winsor and Korchin, 1938), gastrointestinal activity (Cannon, 1929 ; Mahl, 1952), metabolic rate (Lindsley, 1951), muscle tension (Brothers, 1956; Davis, 1938; Ruesch and Finesinger, 1943), tremor (Berrien, 1939), and even eye blink and eye movements (Lindsley and Hunter, 1939). In addition, of course, autonomic, endocrine, and neurohumoral relationships have been extensively and somewhat more directly analyzed in the quest for a better understanding of emotional processes (Cannon, 1927, 1930, 1931; Cannon and Britton, 1925; Gellhorn, 1943, 1950). And certainly a comprehensive view of the psychophysiology of emotional behavior must include such peripheral physiological response mechanisms, although both historical and logical precedence would seem to warrant attention upon the more central neural participants in this process.

For many centuries, of course, both medical and literary sources have included more or less informal accounts of clinical changes in emotional behavior associated with pathological involvement of central nervous system function (e.g., epilepsy). It was not until the latter half of the nineteenth century, however, that Hughlings Jackson and men like Ferrier and Sherrington began to provide the foundations for systematic analysis of neurological mechanisms in emotional behavior and for subsequent emphasis upon the development of the more experimental approaches. Since that time, clinical literature on the psychological consequences of brain damage and related neurological disorders has contributed both directly and indirectly to our understanding of central nervous system participation in emotional behavior (Cobb, 1944; Fulton, 1948; Klebanoff, Singer, and Wilensky, 1954; MacLean,, 1949; Mettler, 1949). Necessarily, coverage of this clinical material will be highly selective here.

Historically, the earliest laboratory approaches to the experimental analysis of neural mechanisms in emotional behavior used ablation techniques. In the course of their more broadly conceived neurophysiological inquiries into cortical function, for example, Brown and Schafer, reporting in the *Philosophical Transactions* as early as 1888, described the "emotional" changes in rhesus monkeys after temporal lobe lesions involving relatively selective subcortical structures. Goltz's early observations toward the close of the last century (1892) on "emotional" responses to mere handling in the decerebrate dog provided the experimental beginnings for a laboratory analysis of neurological mechanisms in affective expression. With the turn of the century, ablation studies primarily concerned with only indirectly related neurophysiological problems continued to point up the ill-defined role of central neural processes in the organization of emotional behavior. In 1904, an investigation by Woodworth and Sherrington of the spinal pathways related to pain revealed what they described as "pseudo-affective" behavioral changes in the decerebrate cat. Within the first two decades of the century, Dusser de Barenne's observations (1920) following acute decortication in the cat had begun to focus more directly upon emotional behavior changes associated with experimental manipulation of the nervous system.

Starting in the early 1920's, a rapid succession of experimental observations by Bazett and Penfield (1922) and Rothmann (1923), and the now classic investigations of the decorticate preparation's "sham rage" response by Cannon and Britton (1925) further elaborated the specific character of central nervous system involvement in emotional expression. These early studies effectively set the stage for a host of experimental and theoretical efforts over the next three decades or more. Until well into the 1930's, however, ablation techniques combined with gross observation of expressive phenomena in the experimental animal were virtually the only laboratory methods available to the investigator of central participation in emotional behavior. Indeed, Berger's pioneering work on the electrical activity of the nervous system (1929) and even that of Hess (1928) on direct electrical stimulation methods had their origins at a somewhat earlier date. The striking changes in electrical activity of the brain which were observed, even by Berger, to accompany "attention" or "anticipatory responsiveness" to sensory stimulation, early suggested the probable role of electrical recording methods in the elaboration of neural events associated with affective states. It was not until the later work of Lindsley (1950), Darrow (1950b), and others (Hoagland, Cameron, and Rubin, 1938; Walter, 1950), however, that these methods were more directly applied to the problem of emotion. The studies of emotional behavior changes following direct stimulation of selective brain structures by Ranson and Magoun (1939), Masserman (1941,

1943), and others, Brady, 1958b; Delgado, 1955; Delgado, Roberts, and Miller, 1954), which were to follow Hess's fruitful lead (1932, 1954), did not appear in definitive form until the early 1940's.

Clearly, however, the "modern era" in laboratory brain-behavior research on the problem of emotions and the central nervous system can be said to date from Klüver and Bucy's now classic presentation to the 1937 meetings of the American Physiological Society. They reported dramatic emotional behavioral alterations produced by rather extensive temporal neocortical and paleocortical lesions in the rhesus monkey. A few months later Papez' speculative paper, "A Proposed Mechanism of Emotion" (1937), emphasized paleocortical, juxtallo-cortical, and related subcortical structures; in the following two decades, numerous anatomical, neurophysiological, and behavioral studies have underlined the remarkable perspicacity of these early efforts. This enduring interest in the neural substrata of emotional behavior has had the considerable advantage of important technical and investigative advances in neuroanatomy (Nauta, 1956; Nauta and Gygax, 1954) and neurophysiology (Galambos, Sheatz, and Vernier, 1956; MacLean, 1955a; Moruzzi and Magoun, 1949) over the past decade or more, not to mention the many more recent developments in behavioral control techniques (Ferster, 1953; Ferster and Skinner, 1957; Skinner, 1953b). Such combined methodological skills have been profitably applied to the experimental analysis of affective processes (Brady, 1957b, 1958a, 1961; Brady and Hunt, 1955; Brady and Nauta, 1955; Sidman, Brady, Boren, Conrad, Schulman, 1955). Indeed, several recent reviews directly related to the subject (Fulton, 1951; Klüver, 1952; MacLean, 1949; Pribram and Kruger, 1954) reflect the degree and direction of the progress in this interdisciplinary approach.

CENTRAL NERVOUS SYSTEM RESEARCH

Goltz (1892) and Woodworth and Sherrington (1904), in their analysis of the so-called pseudo-affective reactions observed to follow transection of the brain stem at the intercollicular level in laboratory carnivores, were probably the first to attempt systematically to analyze the role of selective central nervous system components in the elaboration of emotional behavior. In the subsequent half-century or more of experimental inquiry, virtually every major portion of the brain stem and forebrain has been implicated in the elaboration of behavioral interactions described rather grossly as "emotional." Many later observations (Bazett and Penfield, 1922; Keller, 1932; Rothmann, 1923; Schaltenbrand and Cobb, 1930) have confirmed the suggestion of the Goltz and Sherrington experiments that the midbrain reticular formation participates importantly in the mediation of at least some fundamental aspects of emotional expression. Certainly, more recent experimental reports (Bard and Mountcastle, 1948; French and Magoun, 1952; Lindsley, Schreiner, Knowles, and Magoun, 1950) continued to draw attention to reticular influences in many basic features of emotional behavior patterns and in the maintenance of "aroused affective states." And Lindsley (1951) has recently proposed an "activation theory of emotion" which assigns critical executive functions to the reticular formation of the brain stem.

Traditionally however, neurological theorizing relating emotional behavior and the nervous system has focused upon thalamic and hypothalamic mechanisms and more rostral forebrain interactions. The early experiments of Dusser de Barenne (1920) and Cannon and Britton (1925), using decorticate preparations to induce the now famous "sham-rage" phenomena, provided the initial impetus for this continuing emphasis upon forebrain participation in emotional expression. Perhaps the clearest indication of the critical role played by the hypothalamus in such emotional activities, however, is to be found in later reports (Bard, 1928, 1934a, 1934b, 1939, 1940; Bard and Mountcastle, 1948; Bard and Rioch, 1937; Rioch, 1938). These clearly demonstrated that such "sham-rage" behavior can still be elicited after removal of all cerebral tissue rostral, dorsal, and lateral to the hypothalamus, but disappears following truncation of the brain stem at any level below the caudal hypothalamus. These authors also describe a somewhat broader range of affective expression including "fear" and "sexual excitement" in such hypothalamic preparations, and Bromiley (1948) more recently reported the long-term maintenance of the capacity for affective expression in such operated animals for periods of three years or more.

The emphasis on hypothalamic mechanisms in the development of psychophysiological approaches to the experimental analysis of emotional behavior has not lessened over the several decades since these early explorations. Later efforts have provided convincing evidence of the central but somewhat complicated role played by hypothalamic portions of the forebrain in the elaboration of affective phenomena. Hess and his collaborators (Gloor, 1954, 1956; Hess, 1949, 1954; Hess and Akert, 1955) have demonstrated the broad range of emotional response patterns which can be selectively elicited from discretely localized electrical stimulation of carefully mapped diencephalic regions. The behavior changes observed following such direct stimulation of the hypothalamus have been compared to the alterations seen in emotional responses of normal animals conventionally associated with "fear," "anger," and "pleasure," as well as with such phenomena as "exploratory tendencies, feeding tendencies, cleaning tendencies, and continuous restlessness." In general, these studies have indicated that more anterior and lateral portions of the diencephalon may be associated with hostile and aggressive "rage" responses—or "affective defense reactions," as Hess prefers to call them. As stimulation is carried more posteriorly, changes in oral behavior, increased restlessness, and escape responses appear, although no clear-cut topographical arrangement of hypothalamic nuclei with specific functional significance for affective processes has yet been discerned. Ranson and Magoun (1939b), Ingram (1952), Ingram, Barris, and Ransom (1936), Masserman (1941, 1942, 1943), and others (Hinsey, 1940; Karplus, 1937) have also demonstrated the emotionally exciting affects ("fear" and "rage" responses with multiple sympathetic manifestations) of direct hypothalamic stimulation in cats and monkeys, and White (1940) has obtained at least some partial confirmation of hypothalamic involvement in emotional activities with electrical stimulation methods in conscious human patients under local anesthesia. Grinker (1939) also recorded selective electrical activity from deep-lying hypothalamic electrodes in man in response to "emotional probing." And, of course, the recent emergence of experimental emphasis upon results obtained with intracranial self-stimulation techniques, following the interesting demonstration by Olds and Milner (1954) of the rewarding effects associated with direct electrical stimulation of selective forebrain structures, has suggested the intimate participation of hypothalamic influences, among others, in the presumably affective components of this phenomenon in a wide variety of species (Brady, 1961; Olds, 1955, 1956).

Practically all the behavioral alterations observed to follow ablation and stimulation of the hypothalamus in experimental animals have also been reported in man after trauma, operative manipulation, tumor, vascular lesions, and infections of the hypothalamus. Although precise anatomical localization of specific diencephalic regions tends to be far from satisfactory under such conditions, various manifestations of affective changes, including "terror," "rage," "anxiety," and even some of the more "pleasant moods" ("witty," "jocular," "obscene"), have been reported following hypothalamic involvement in the human (Clark, Beattie, Riddock, and Dott, 1938; Cushing, 1932; Foerster and Gagel, 1933; White, 1940). And indeed, both experimental and clinical observations over the past three decades have clearly indicated that many other important biological motivations intimately related to emotional expression, including hunger, thirst, sleep, sex, and activity, bear a critical dependence upon the functional integrity of relatively specific hypothalamic components (Anand and Brobeck, 1951; Bard, 1940; Brobeck, Tepperman, and Long, 1943; Brookhart and Dey, 1941; Brookhart, Dey, and Ranson, 1941; Brooks, 1947; Nauta, 1946; Ranson, 1939). Stellar's (1954) "physiological theory of motivated behavior," which places a heavy explanatory burden upon hypothalamic excitation in accounting for a wide range of motivational-emotional behavior patterns, is a most recent expression of this diencephalic emphasis.

The weight of available evidence, then, seems to indicate that at least some primitively organized, relatively undifferentiated patterns of emotional behavior may be elaborated within limited reticular and hypothalamic levels of neural organization. The emergence of homeostatic and adaptive autonomic functions, as well as important somatomotor activities basic to such affective processes, would seem to depend critically upon the unique and direct integration of such brain-stem components with peripheral effector mechanisms. But the functional limitations of such gross reaction patterns contrast sharply with the more delicately balanced and restrained discriminative emotional behavior of which the normal organism is capable. Quite obviously, important influences from more advanced forebrain levels of integration contribute significantly to the elaboration and refinement of complexly organized and finely differentiated emotional response repertories. Head's early writings (1920) and Cannon's subsequent theoretical formulations (1927, 1931) suggested an important role for the more rostral thalamic nuclei in the elaboration of these affective processes, and several clinical and experimental inquiries over the past two decades have clearly justified this speculative focus.

Spiegel and his collaborators (Spiegel and Wycis, 1949; Spiegel, Wycis, Freed, and Archinik, 1951), for example, have reported changes in emotional behavior in both experimental animals and human patients following various thalamic lesions, involving principally the dorsomedial nuclei. Such ablations appear to reduce "anxiety," "tension," "agitation," and "aggressive or assaultive behavior" in psychiatric patients, and at least a transitory reduction in emotional reactivity was presumably observed in similarly operated animals. The anterior nuclei, however, invite special attention in the experimental quest for thalamic participants in emotional behavior. For the most part, lesions in this region of the thalamus in the cat are reported to produce marked reductions in emotional responsiveness (Baird, Gudetti, Reyes, Wycis, and Spiegel, 1951; Schreiner, Rioch, Petchtel, and Masserman, 1953), while the effects of direct electrical stimulation in the anterior thalamus appear to be at least "alerting" in the cat (Baird, Gudetti, Reyes, Wycis, and Spiegel, 1951) and highly rewarding in the rat (Olds, 1956). The range of these emotional changes following thalamic involvement suggests the possibility of a limited modulation of affective processes at this diencephalic level, even though the intimate relationship of these thalamic nuclei with more advanced paleocortical, juxtallocortical, and neocortical systems must provide for the more refined and integrative behavioral expression. The structural and functional interaction between both the mediodorsal thalamus and the frontal neocortex on the one hand, and the anterior thalamus and the cingulate gyrus on the other, would seem to suggest the framework within which this forebrain integrative process in emotional behavior may be best understood. Through the latter of these two systems the anterior nucleus of the thalamus can interact with the "limbic system" circuits which are receiving so much contemporary emphasis in the analysis of emotional behavior (Brady, 1958a; Fulton, 1951, 1953; Gloor, 1956; Klüver, 1952; MacLean, 1949, 1952, 1954, 1955a, 1955b; MacLean and Delgado, 1953; Pribram and Kruger, 1954).

Broca's early reference (1878) to *"le grand lobe limbique"* as a common denominator in all mammalian brains, and Papez' (1937) subsequent theoretical speculations on a possible anatomical "mechanism of emotion," long ago suggested the potential mediating role of the "limbic system" in affective processes. In general terms, Papez' proposal focused on the more medial aspects of the cerebral hemispheres and emphasized the transmittal of the "central emotive process of cortical origin built up in the hippocampal formation" via the fornix to the mammillary bodies. Efferents from this hypothalamic center were then presumed to course both downward to the brainstem and lower effector mechanisms, and upward through the mammillo-thalamic tract to the anterior thalamic nuclei, and onward to the cingulate gyrus, which Papez called the "cortical receptive and association area" for affective behavior.

It was Papez' view that "the hypothalamus, the anterior thalamic nuclei, the gyrus cinguli, the hippocampus, and their connections constitute a harmonious mechanism which may elaborate the functions of central emotion, as well as participate in emotional expression." Certainly, Papez' delimitation of these structures as bearing an important relationship to emotional behavior, and his concomitant prediction of symptomatic changes associated with involvement of this "anatomic circuit," can, in the light of subsequent clinical and experimental developments, be seen to represent a considerable tour de force. The morphological and functional characteristics of this "limbic system" have been more precisely defined and elaborated over the two decades since this original proposal, and a recent semidiagrammatic representation of the more prominent anatomical features of this so-called "emotion brain" is shown in Figure 1. Several systematic attempts have been made to order the obviously complex interrelationships between these structures and other nervous system components according to both anatomico-physiological and behavioral principles (Brady, 1958a; Gloor, 1956; Grunthal, 1947; Herrick, 1933; Kleist,

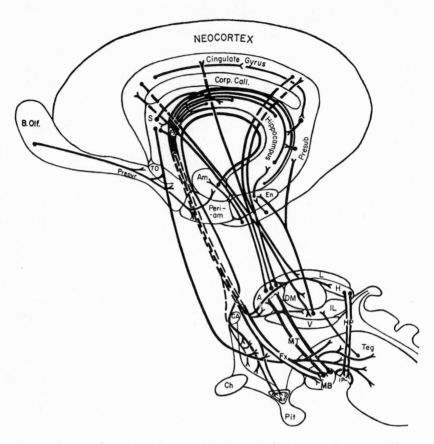

Figure 1. Semidiagrammatic representation of the principal anatomical relationships between the "paleocortex," the "juxtallocortex," and the several
"subcortical structures" considered in the present treatment of the "limbic
system." The brain stem portions of the system have been schematically displaced from the hilus of the hemisphere and represented in the lower half
of the figure to facilitate visualization of the numerous anatomical interconnections involving these structures. Abbreviations: A, Anterior nucleus
of the thalamus; Am, Amygdaloid complex; Ar, Arcuate nucleus; B. Olf.,
Olfactory bulb; CA, Anterior commissure; Ch, Optic chiasm; Corp.
Call., Corpus callosum; DM, Dorsomedial nucleus of the thalamus; En,
Entorhinal area; Fx, Fornix; H, Habenular complex; HP, Habenulo-inter-
peduncular tract; IL, Intralaminar thalamic nuclei; IP, Interpeduncular
nucleus; L, Lateral thalamic nucleus; MB, Mammillary bodies; MT, Mam-
milo-thalamic tract; Periam, Periamygdaloid cortex; Pit, Pituitary; Prepyr,
Prepyriform cortex; Presub, Presubiculum; S, Septal region; Teg, Midbrain
tegmentum; TO, Olfactory tubercle; V, Ventral nucleus of the thalamus.
[From Brady, in Harlow and Woolsey, 1958, courtesy of University of
Wisconsin Press.]

1934; Klüver, 1952; MacLean, 1949, 1955a, 1955b; Olds, 1955; Pribram and Kruger, 1954).

Almost simultaneously with the 1937 publication of Papez' theoretical effort, Klüver and Bucy reported their most striking demonstration of the important participant role which rather extensive "limbic system" components could be expected to play in the balancing, integration, and elaboration of critically profound motivational-emotional behavior patterns. These experiments (Klüver and Bucy, 1937 1938, 1939), defining dramatic behavioral changes in monkeys following temporal neocortical and paleocortical lesions involving the frontotemporal cortex, pyriform lobe, amygdaloid complex, presubiculum and hippocampus, are now too well known to require detailed review. The broad range of behavioral alterations observed in these preparations, however, bears directly on the central problem of nervous system participation in affective processes. After this extensive involvement of the limbic system, the formerly wild and intractable rhesus macaques used in these experiments became tame and docile, showing signs of neither fear nor anger. They would not fight nor retaliate when abused by other monkeys, and also displayed what the authors refer to as "psychic blindness," oral tendencies, and hypermetamorphosis, a kind of compulsive behavior. They behaved as if they could no longer discriminate between objects that were potentially either dangerous or useful to them. As if by compulsion, they would smell and mouth everything (dirt, feces, nails, food) that captured their attention. Unless the object were edible, it was immediately dropped. If presented with a nail 100 times in succession, these animals would smell and mouth it each time as though they had not examined it before. Finally, they showed striking changes in sexual behavior; they appeared hypersexed, masturbated excessively, sought partnership with male or female indiscriminately, and manifested bizarre oral sexual behavior. Of particular interest, too, was the fact that when unilateral excision of only one lobe was accomplished, or when bilateral lesions were restricted to the temporal neocortex and spared the limbic system structures, the animals failed to show any of these dramatic changes in behavior.

Against the background of these early experimental and theoretical efforts, a host of important subsequent neurophysiological and psychophysiological developments have continued to broaden the base for a more thorough understanding of extensive limbic system components involved in the mediation of emotional behavior. Within a few short months of these first reports, Spiegel and his coworkers (Spiegel, Miller, and Oppenheimer, 1940) demonstrated the dramatic participation of the more rostral portions of the limbic system (including the olfactory tubercle and septal region) in rather complicated motivational-emotional behavior patterns. These authors observed "sham-rage" reactions in both cats and dogs, following bilateral lesions confined to the olfactory tubercle and septal region, while similar effects resulted from involvement of the anterior amygdaloid nuclei, parts of the hippocampus, and the fornix. More recent reports by Brady and Nauta (1953, 1955) confirm these findings in the rat; the dramatic demonstrations of rewarding effects consequent upon direct electrical stimulation of these same anteriorly placed limbic structures (Brady, 1961; Olds, 1956; Olds and Milner, 1954; Sidman, Brady, Boren, Conrad, and Schulman, 1955) firmly establish their involvement in affective processes.

The extensive and systematic research program initiated by Bard and Mountcastle (1948) within the decade following the report by Klüver and Bucy represents an important landmark in the further experimental analysis of limbic system relationship and emotional behavior. Concerned primarily with the role of forebrain mechanisms in the expression of "rage" and "angry behavior," their initial experiments with cats showed that removal of all neocortex, while sparing the paleocortical, juxtallocortical, and related subcortical components of the limbic system, produced a markedly placid and emotionally unresponsive animal. In the authors' view, these results indicated that portions of the limbic system, either singly or in concert, could exert a restraining influence upon lower brain mechanisms of demonstrated prepotence in the mediation of gross affective expression. Moreover, subsequent experiments in this same series strongly suggested that the amygdaloid complex, or cingulate gyrus, or both, might be specifically involved in the mediation of this restraining influence in the absence of the neocortex, since rather striking increases in emotional reactivity followed removal of these subcortical and juxtallocortical structures in the previously neodecorticate preparation. Undoubtedly, however, what has come to be known as the "Klüver-Bucy syndrome" (Terzian and Ore, 1955) suggested the most stimulating lead for a host of subsequent research efforts to unravel the complex role of limbic system components in the elaboration of emotional behavior.

However, the clinical and experimental observations which continue to emerge from more recent psychological and physiological analyses of affective processes seem to reflect a considerably broader conception of limbic system participation in emotional behavior. Not only has the conditioned behavior of the individual animal with limbic system involvement come under careful scrutiny in specifically controlled testing situations but even the integration of social behavior and its dependence upon these neural systems has now been explored. Rosvold, Mirsky, and Pribram (1954) observed that the effects of amygdalectomy in eight male rhesus monkeys generally changed their hierarchical position in a group-cage situation from dominant to submissive, even though they appeared somewhat more "aggressive" when in individual cages. And, indeed, clinical reports of observations following temporal lobe and amygdaloid lesions in man by Terzian and Ore (1955) and Sawa, Ueki, Arita, and Harada (1954) have emphasized this same diminution of "social aggressiveness." Gastaut, Morin, and Leseure (1955) have also pointed out that discharging lesions in these limbic system structures, as seen in psychomotor epilepsy, apparently produce a lowered "rage" threshold, since these patients frequently show violent temper outbursts in social situations. It may also be significant that Gastaut and Collomb (1956) have observed a decrease in sexual behavior in patients with irritative lesions of the temporal lobe-amygdala regions, while Gastaut and Mileto (1955) have further elaborated upon the disturbances in sexual behavior which follow involvement of the hippocampus in both human and animal cases of rabies.

Many physiological studies (Cadilhac, 1955; Fulton, 1951; Gastaut, 1952; Kaada, 1951; Kaada, Andersen, and Jansen, 1953, 1954; Koikegami and Fuse, 1952a, 1952b; Koikegami and Yoshida, 1952; MacLean, 1954; MacLean and Delgado, 1953; Pool, 1954; Pribram and Kruger, 1954; Ward, 1948) in both animals and man, using chemical and electrical stimulation as well as electrical recording methods, have also demonstrated limbic system involvement in a wide variety of somatic and autonomic phenomena closely related to the broad range of behavioral activities conventionally associated with emotional expression.

Significantly, it has been difficult to discern any clear-cut topographical organization for specific behavioral components, even though the observations of Kaada, et al. (Kaada, Andersen, and Jansen, 1954) would seem to suggest that such delineation may be possible. For the most part, however, the striking features of such correlative data seem to be the extensive overlap of all sorts of behavioral responses in their representation at this limbic system level (Kaada, Andersen, and Jansen, 1954; Koikegami and Fuse, 1952a, 1952b; Koikegami and Yoshida, 1952), and the remarkably broad spectrum of psychological activities in which these structures seem to participate (Fulton, 1951; Gastaut, 1952; Kaada, 1951; MacLean, 1954, Pribram and Kruger, 1954). The intimate relationship of these limbic structures (particularly the amygdala) to the mechanisms of neuroendocrine integration has been convincingly demonstrated by both stimulation and ablation studies (Harris, 1952; Hume and Wittenstein, 1950; Mason, 1956; Porter, 1953; Sawyer, 1955; Schreiner and Kling, 1953a, 1953b, 1954). Finally, electrophysiological methods have continued to define the characteristic functional interrelationships within the limbic system and subcortical regions basically involved in the elaboration of emotional behavior (Cadilhac, 1955; Faure and Portmann, 1955; Feindel and Gloor, 1954; Gloor, 1955a, 1955b, 1956; Green and Arduini, 1954; Liberson and Akert, 1955; Liberson and Cadilhac, 1954). Of particular importance in this respect are the extensive studies of MacLean and his collaborators (MacLean, 1949, 1952, 1954, 1955a, 1955b; MacLean and Delgado, 1953), and of Gloor (1955a, 1956), carefully delineating the limbic system role in affective processes.

Even with this host of clinical and experimental observations and the rapidly accumulating body of anatomical, physiological, and psychological information, however, no completely satisfactory integration of the limbic system with the necessarily broad range of central neural participants in emotional behavior has as yet emerged. There has never been any shortage of speculative efforts assigning specific functional roles to the various components of this anatomical complex, however, and a significant thread of similarity is discernible among the many neurological hypotheses which have characterized the multidisciplinary theorizing in this area. Almost 30 years ago, for example, Herrick (1933), on a comparative anatomical basis, suggested that the limbic system may serve as a nonspecific activator for all cortical activities, influencing "the internal apparatus of general bodily attitude, disposition, and affective tone." Even Kleist's (1934) speculations of the same era about the "inner brain," as he referred to the more medial aspects of the hemisphere, emphasize the fact that these limbic structures were not only basic for "emotional behavior," "attitudes," and "drives," but were also instrumental in correlating "visceral receptions" from the oral, anal, and genital regions as well as the intestines, thus subserving functions related to the search for food and sexual objects. And clinical observations of human patients with limbic system involvement led Grunthal (1947) to propose that the hippocampus, as the virtual "hub" of the limbic system, may represent a "catalytic activator" which, although not necessarily participating in specialized functions itself, is nevertheless basic for the proper functioning of affective and neocortical activity.

More recently, MacLean (1949) reviewed and elaborated Papez' (1937) earlier theoretical views on emotional behavior and limbic system mechanisms (or "visceral brain," in MacLean's reference), suggesting the basic importance of these forebrain structures not only for affective processes but also for correlating "oral and visceral sensations" as well as "impressions from the sex organs, body wall, eye, and ear." Even Pribram and Kruger (1954), in their comprehensive review of the "olfactory brain," have speculatively assigned "olfactory-gustatory," "metabolic," and "socioemotional" functions to the various "limbic" components comprising their three "systems." And Gloor's (1956) recent analysis of telencephalic influences upon the hypothalamus has assigned to the limbic system the role of "modulator of functional patterns integrated at the level of the hypothalamus and the brain stem tegmentum," even though, in his view, "the limbic system does not fundamentally integrate the functions it is capable of influencing by its activity." The weight of available anatomical, physiological, and psychological evidence seems to support at least some generally similar concept of the "intermediary" role of the limbic system in the integration of brain stem and neocortical participation in emotional behavior.

Despite this recent experimental and theoretical emphasis upon limbic system relationships, however, the quest for "localized functions" at the level of the neocortex continues to exert important influences upon both clinical and laboratory investigations of the psychophysiology of emotional behavior. For the most part, attention has focused on the frontal lobes, with specific references to affective processes (Cobb, 1944; Evarts and Nissen, 1953; Fulton, 1948, 1951; Hebb, 1945; Jacobsen, 1936; Landis, 1952; Landis, Zubin, and Mettler, 1950; Mettler, 1949, 1952; Waterhouse, 1957), although some additional concern with the participant role of more extensive neocortical regions has recently been in evidence (Critchley, 1953; Milner, 1954; Mulder and Daly, 1952; Penfield and Jasper, 1954; Pribram and Weiskrantz, 1957). Understandably, clinical observations comprise the lion's share of the available literature in this area, although the laboratory analysis of ablation consequences and selective changes in electrically recorded potentials from the neocortex has more recently suggested important neural-behavioral relationships. Long before systematic treatment of such problems was fashionable, observations on the behavioral consequences of the "sacred disease"—epilepsy—included both literary and professional descriptions of affective changes presumably related to neocortical involvement. In 1875, David Ferrier gave a provocative description of behavioral changes closely related to emotional phenomena in monkeys following experimental frontal ablations. Somewhat later, Bianchi (1922) made similar observations, and the story of the classic report by Fulton and Jacobsen before the London meetings of the Second International Neurological Congress in 1935 and the subsequent adoption of frontal ablations as a therapeutic procedure by Moniz (1936) is now too well known to require detailed repetition.

Significantly, the presumed therapeutic emotional changes observed to follow such prefrontal lesions have frequently been rationalized in terms of the intimate anatomical and functional relationship of these more or less specific portions of the cerebral mantle with the affective integrative mechanisms of the diencephalon (via principally the dorsomedial thalamus). It is now clear, however, that extensive limbic system influences exert important mediating effects on such diencephalic-neocortical interactions, and that the assessment of emotional changes arising from neocortical involvement must be considered within this integrative relational framework. Indeed, the wide variety of behavioral changes which follow such frontal neocortical ablations seem comprehensible only within the broad framework of such an integrative analysis. For the most part, the consequences of frontal lobe lesions appear to involve changes in the direction of diminished "emotional responsiveness." Both clinical and laboratory reports, however, have also confirmed the frequent appearance of increased "emotional lability" in man and animal following at least some therapeutic and investigative efforts to alter affective behavior patterns with frontal neocortical ablation. We are a long way from a satisfactory understanding of the participant role of such specific neocortical regions in the elaboration of emotional processes, although the evidence for such involvement seems unequivocal.

An important recent emphasis on electroencephalographic studies in relation to "affective states" also seems to hold considerable promise for a more thorough understanding of neocortical functions in emotional behavior. Only within the past decade have the first systematic treatments of this neurophysiological approach begun to appear (Lindsley, 1950; Darrow, 1950b), although, as we have already seen, even earlier explorations of EEG phenomena had suggested their relationship to the "emotions." Characteristically, changes in the EEG pattern "under conditions involving some degree of emotional arousal, as in apprehension, unexpected sensory stimulation, and anxiety states," as summarized by Lindsley in his review, can be reflected in "a reduction or suppression of alpha rhythm and an increase in the amount of beta-like fast activity." Although the observations which provided the basis for these general conclusions did not focus upon any selective neocortical regions in particular, they can be seen to form at least part of the foundation for Lindsley's "activation theory of emotion" (1951) with its emphasis upon neocortical arousal in affective processes. Subsequent reports by Ulett, et al. (Ulett and Gleser, 1953; Ulett, Gleser, Lawler, and Winokur, 1952; Ulett, Gleser, Starr, Haddock, Lingley, and Lawler, 1953) and others (Barker, Burgwin, and Simons, 1950; Darrow, 1950a, 1953; Ellingson, 1956; Knott and Correll, 1954), however, have suggested involvement of more specific cortical areas, and Walter (1950) has even reported that emotional disturbances arising during flicker stimulation experiments can be associated with rather selective EEG changes in the temporal neocortex. Certainly the close anatomical and functional association of the temporal lobes with limbic system structures intimately involved with the elaboration of emotional behavior would seem to fit well with such a suggested delineation of neocortical participation in affective processes.

RECENT RESEARCH DEVELOPMENTS

Probably the most striking feature of the enduring neurophysiological interest in the problem of emotion has been the slowness of the development of experimental analysis of the critical behavioral phenomena. This failure of psychological science to keep abreast of anatomical and physiological developments is reflected in the primitive, phenomenological, and conspicuously prescientific descriptions and definitions of emotional behavior which characterize most of the research in this area—and brings into question the scientific economy of elaborate speculative efforts to develop a comprehensive psychophysiological theory of emotion in the absence of a sound behavioristic account of those presumably affective interaction processes between organism and environment. The analysis of these relationships at a descriptive behaviorist level must provide the foundation for any adequate treatment of psychophysiological participation in "emotional" events.

The experimental analysis of emotional behavior

Within recent years, however, the emerging outlines of an objective psychological science have begun to provide precise and reliable techniques for controlling the behavior of the individual subject as a basis for interdisciplinary psychophysiological analysis. For the most part, the dedication of B. F. Skinner, his coworkers, and others to the experimental analysis of behavior in its own right has been responsible for the development of these methods in a variety of applications and for their recent extension to the investigation of the problem which provides the subject matter for this chapter (Brady, 1951, 1956, 1957a, 1957b, 1958a, 1958b; Brady, Boren, Conrad, and Sidman, 1957; Brady and Hunt, 1955; Brady and Nauta, 1953, 1955; Estes and Skinner, 1941; Ferster, 1953; Ferster and Skinner, 1957; Hunt and Brady, 1951; Mason and Brady, 1956; Mason, Brady, and Sidman, 1957; Morse and Herrnstein, 1956; Sidman, 1953, 1956, 1959; Sidman, Brady, Boren, Conrad, and Schulman, 1955; Skinner, 1938, 1953a, 1953b, 1959; Wilson and Keller, 1953; Brady, Porter, Conrad, and Mason, 1958; Findley, 1958; Skinner and Morse, 1958; Porter, Conrad, and Brady, 1959; Weiss and Laties, 1959; Azrin, 1959; Ferster, 1960; Boren, 1960; Hefferline and Keenan, 1961; Ferster and Appel, 1961). Other relevant applications of these so-called operant conditioning techniques to the analysis of both behavioral and psychophysiological problems basic to clinical practice have been covered in related chapters of this volume. (See chapters 4, 5, 6, 9, 11, 13, 15.)

Estes and Skinner (1941) first suggested an approach to at least one aspect of the "emotion" problem within the framework of this developing behavior science. Several recent extensions of these methods to both the psychological and psychophysiological analysis of affective processes justify their enthusiastic acceptance by a broad interdisciplinary audience (Brady, 1956, 1957a, 1957b, 1958a, 1958b, 1961; Brady and Conrad, 1960a; Brady and Hunt, 1955; Brady and Nauta, 1953, 1955; Hunt and Brady, 1951; Mason and Brady, 1956; Mason, Brady, and Sidman, 1957; Morse and Herrnstein, 1956; Sidman, 1953, 1956). Much of this work is based upon the rather common clinical and experimental observation that "emotional" disturbance can, as one of several possible effects, disrupt or interfere with an organism's ongoing behavior. Experimentally, the fundamental empirical fact for such an approach to the problem of emotion is the suppressing effect of anticipated pain upon an animal's ongoing lever-pressing behavior. This conditioned suppression phenomenon is readily produced by pairing some previously neutral stimulus with pain shock. The typical consequences of such a procedure in the rat, involving repeated presentations of a clicking noise for five minutes followed by pain shock to the feet during a lever-pressing session for water reward, are shown in Figure 2. The clicking noise is introduced at point C on the cumulative lever-pressing curves, continues for five minutes, and is terminated contiguously with shock at point S. Within a few trials, the anticipatory "emotional" response to the clicker begins to appear as a perturbation in the lever-pressing curve, accompanied by crouching, immobility, and usually defecation.

This emphasis upon a rather primitive and somewhat molecular psychological phenomenon as the starting point for an experimental analysis of emotional behavior has several clear-cut advantages from the standpoint of a psychophysiological analysis. First, direct focus upon this conditioned suppression response per se eliminates a major source of error attributable to variables that affect the instrumental behavior from which "emotional" effects are usually inferred in the more conventional observational or even "escape-avoidance" learning approach to this problem. Secondly, this simple, relatively uncomplicated response is elicitable under a wide range of conditions and appears in quite consistent form or topography in all animals. Thirdly, this response is remarkably stable over time, surviving without apparent diminution in the absence of exercise or further reinforcement virtually throughout the entire lifespan of the organism. Finally, and probably most importantly from the standpoint of a relational psychophysiological analysis, the technique of superimposing the emotional response upon a well-established stable lever-pressing habit makes it possible to approximate an objectively quantifiable definition of the behavior in terms of changes in output during various segments of the lever-pressing curve.

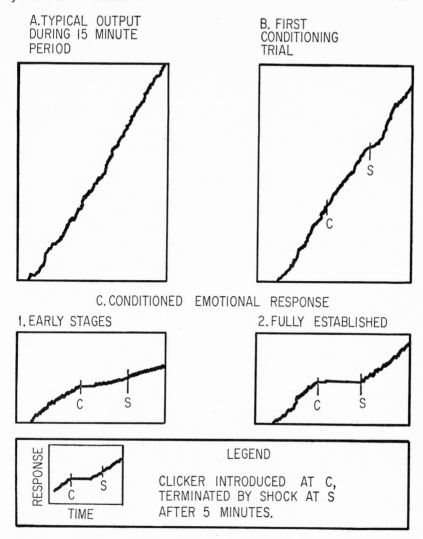

Figure 2. The conditioned emotional response in the rat, as it appears typically in the cumulative response curve. [From Hunt and Brady, 1951, courtesy of *Journal of Comparative and Physiological Psychology*.]

In many respects, this rather restricted behavior sample seems prototypical of the most primitive aspects of an organism's emotional repertoire. The investigation of its vicissitudes—the conditions which determine its increases and decreases in strength, etc.—has already contributed significantly to the differential experimental analysis of both the physiological and psychological variables upon which the organization of emotional behavior depends.

Emotional behavior and the nervous system

The potential implications for a psychophysiological analysis of emotional behavior within this rather broad operant-conditioning framework first became apparent after a series of studies on the effects of electroconvulsive shock (Brady and Hunt, 1955). These experiments showed that it was possible to separate and measure selectively the effects of such physiological manipulations upon the "emotional" components of a behavior segment independently of any gross effects upon the simple repetitive lever-pressing habit which provided the control baseline. Subsequent applications of this approach to the analysis of more direct neurophysiological participation in affective processes have made it possible to show, for example, that the elaboration of even such basic aspects of emotional behavior depends heavily upon the integrity of quite specific portions of the forebrain and brain stem, notably the limbic system. Although large neocortical lesions were found to produce little or no effect upon the acquisition, retention, or extinction of the conditioned suppression pattern, lesions in the septal region and hippocampus produced significant decrements in the maintenance of such behavior and most dramatic changes in gross affective expression (Brady and Nauta, 1953, 1955). In addition, lesions of the habenular complex of the thalamus appear to reduce resistance to extinction of the conditioned suppression response, although cingulate lesions have no apparent effect on such behavior (Brady and Nauta, 1955).

More recently, this approach to the psychophysiological analysis of emotional behavior has been applied dramatically to the exploration of reinforcement or "reward" effects produced by intracranial electrical self-stimulation of the nervous system. Olds and Milner (1954) first reported that rats, stimulating themselves electrically in various portions of the limbic system by pressing a bar, would maintain high lever-pressing rates over long periods of time without any other reward. This same phenomenon has been systematically reproduced and analyzed in many other species, including man (Brady, 1960; Sem-Jacobsen and Torkildsen, 1960), and investigations have begun to delimit some of the critical variables in this area. The specific anatomical locus of the stimulating electrodes, the schedules of intracranial electrical stimulation reinforcement, food and water deprivation, stimulus intensity, temporal factors, and the like have all been shown to constitute critical determinants of this effect (Brady, 1958a, 1958b, 1961; Brady, Boren, Conrad, and Sidman, 1957; Olds, 1955, 1956; Sidman, Brady, Boren, Conrad, and Schulman, 1955; Brady and Conrad, 1960b; Porter, Conrad, and Brady, 1959; Hodos and Valenstein, 1960; Beer and Valenstein, 1960).

Of particular interest from the standpoint of a primary concern with psychophysiological relationships and emotional behavior, however, is the recent demonstration of interaction effects between the conditioned suppression response illustrated in Figure 2 and this intracranial self-stimulation phenomenon (Brady, 1958a, 1958b, 1960, 1961; Brady and Conrad, 1960b). The consequences of repeated pairing of the application to the animal of clicker and shock according to this conditioning procedure have been consistently reported to include suppression of the lever-pressing rate, crouching, immobility, and usually defecation in response to presentation of the auditory stimulus (clicker). This relatively stable conditioned "fear" pattern was readily elicited by presentation of the clicker when both rats and monkeys were pressing a lever for food or water reward; but substitution of brain stimulation through chronically implanted limbic system electrodes (septal region, medial forebrain bundle) for the food or water on the same reinforcement schedule resulted in failure of the auditory stimulus to elicit the emotional suppression of lever-pressing behavior. Figure 3 shows the development of the conditioned "fear" response in a rat with repeated pairings of clicker and shock superimposed upon the water-reinforced lever-pressing curve. This illustrates the striking failure of the suppression behavior to appear in the same animal with the same clicker and

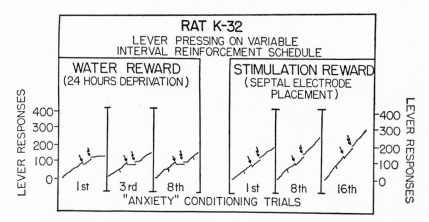

Figure 3. Sample cumulative response curves showing acquisition trials for the conditioned "anxiety" response superimposed upon lever pressing for variable interval (mean of 16 seconds) water and intracranial electrical stimulation reward. The oblique solid arrows indicate the onset of the conditioned auditory stimulus, and the oblique broken arrows indicate the termination of the conditioned stimulus contiguously with the brief unconditioned grid-shock stimulus to the feet during each trial. [from Brady and Conrad, 1960, courtesy of *Journal of Comparative and Physiological Psychology*.]

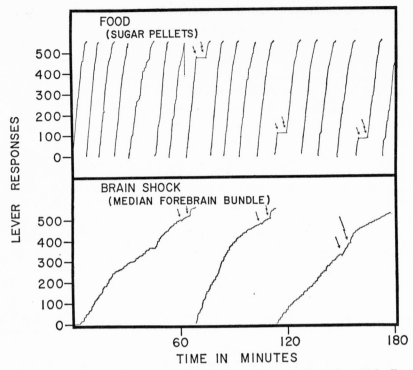

Figure 4. Sample cumulative response curve showing the differential effect of the CER procedure during a continuous six-hour experimental session, the first three hours using sugar-pellet reinforcement and the last three hours using brain-shock reward. The oblique solid arrows indicate the onset of the conditioned auditory stimulus, and the oblique broken arrows indicate the termination of the conditioned stimulus contiguously with the brief unconditioned grid-shock stimulus to the feet during each of the two periods. [From Brady and Conrad, 1960, courtesy of *Journal of Comparative and Physiological Psychology*.]

shock when lever pressing is rewarded with brain stimulation in the septal region rather than water. With the monkey, this same phenomenon has been demonstrated (Figure 4) with the self-stimulation electrodes in the anterior forebrain portions of the limbic system (medial forebrain bundle), although rewarding electrode placements in other brain areas (anterior thalamus) with the same animal do not show this interaction effect with the conditioned emotional response.

Some psychophysiological relationships

Of most recent experimental interest have been the peripheral autonomic and endocrinological pathways through which central nervous system participation in emotional events so frequently finds visceral and somatic expression. Here too objective psychological science has begun to open new vistas in the experimental analysis of psychophysiological relationships by providing stable and reproducible emotional behavior baselines against which such autonomic and endocrinological processes can be evaluated. Of particular value in this connection has been an approach to the establishment, maintenance, and analysis of avoidance behavior developed by Sidman (1953, 1960) and utilized most extensively in recent experimental efforts to approximate laboratory models for various psychosomatic conditions (Mason, Brady, and Sidman, 1957; Porter, Brady, Conrad, Mason, Galambos, and Rioch, 1958; Brady, Porter, Conrad, and Mason, 1958; Brady and Polish, 1960; Clark and Polish, 1960). Briefly, this avoidance procedure involves having the animal press a lever to postpone electric shocks to the feet. The shock is delivered every 20 seconds unless a lever response occurs within that 20-second interval to delay the shock another 20 seconds. Although no exteroceptive warning stimulus signals the approaching shock, monkey subjects rapidly learn to press the lever at a rate far higher than once every 20 seconds. They continue to perform in this manner for many hours without receiving a single shock. In this way, then, it is possible to develop a stable behavioral baseline presumably involving many critical properties common to anticipatory emotional stress situations without the contaminating effects of frequent and physically painful electric shocks.

In an early attempt to assess the peripheral psychophysiological consequences of exposure to such emotionally stressful behavior conditions, a series of experiments was undertaken involving evaluation of plasma 17-hydroxycorticosteroid levels in rhesus monkeys performing in avoidance situations (Mason, Brady, and Sidman, 1957). Extensive exposure to performance requirements involving ratio and interval schedules for food reward produced no significant changes in this steroid measure of adrenal cortical activity. However, marked elevations of plasma 17-hydroxycorticosteroid levels invariably appeared in response to the Sidman avoidance condition. The rate of rise (approximately 20 μg %/hr.) of the steroids observed during a two-hour exposure to this avoidance procedure is comparable to that recorded after single intravenous injections of 16 mg/kg ACTH, which appears to define the maximal rate of rise of which the system is capable. Further explorations of both the environmental and temporal parameters of this relationship between the corticosteroids and avoidance behavior have been conducted to learn the conditions under which warning stimuli, variations in the inverval between avoidance response and shock, and even undeserved shocks alter the adrenal cortical response to avoidance (Sidman, Mason, Brady, and Thach, in press).

In the course of determining some of the endocrinological and autonomic consequences of more protracted but intermittent exposure to
such emotionally stressful avoidance performance in monkeys, a procedural variation was introduced. This required the animal to work
continuously at the avoidance task for periods of six hours alternating
with six-hour periods of nonavoidance or rest (Brady, Porter, Conrad,
and Mason, 1958). Each avoidance animal was paired with an untrained control monkey; they were gently restrained in primate chairs.
In this situation, the experimental monkey of each pair could successfully prevent shocks for both himself and his control partner by pressing the available lever at least once every 20 seconds during the six-
hour avoidance periods. The lever provided for the control monkey
was inactivated, but both monkeys were shocked when the avoidance
animal failed to respond within the required 20-second interval. Under
these conditions, both experimental and control animals received the
same number and distribution of shocks ("physical trauma") although
only the experimental monkeys were required to perform on the avoidance task. In this way, the autonomic and endocrinological effects of
such prolonged avoidance exposure could be assessed while providing
some control for the independent effects of repeated electric shock and
chair restraint per se.

Each pair of monkeys on this procedure received six-hour "avoidance" sessions, during which a red light was illuminated in plain view
of both animals. These sessions alternated with six-hour "rest" periods
(red light off, no shocks) 24 hours each day for periods up to six
weeks. During this time urine of all animals was collected continuously in 24- or 48-hour samples for 17-hydroxycorticosteroid determinations. Lever-pressing response rates recorded during the entire period
reflected the early development of a stable avoidance performance by
the experimental animals of each pair (approximating 20 responses
per minute). These rates showed little change throughout the experiment (Figure 5). Responses during the six-hour "rest" periods typically remained at a low level.

The first four pairs of monkeys observed in this series of experiments
provided only a minimal amount of additional information specific to
adrenal cortical responses in emotional stress situations of this avoidance variety (Brady, Porter, Conrad, and Mason, 1958). The dramatic
fashion in which all four experiments were terminated by the death of
the avoidance monkey in each pair, however, provided a fruitful sequel
to these early attempts at an experimental analysis of psychosomatic
relationships. With the first pair of monkeys, the death of the avoidance animal after 23 days terminated the experiment during one of the
six-hour avoidance periods. The avoidance monkey of the second pair
also expired during one of the six-hour "on-periods," this time 25 days

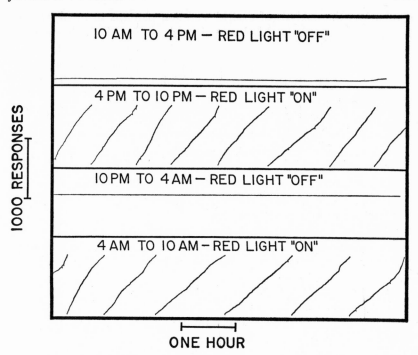

Figure 5. A sample cumulative response curve showing one 24-hour period alternating six-hour "on-off" cycles for experimental "avoidance" monkey M-67 on day no. 18. The oblique "pips" on the record indicate shocks. [From Brady, Porter, Conrad, and Mason, 1958, courtesy of *Journal of the Experimental Analysis of Behavior.*]

after the start of the experiment. With the third pair in this series, the death of the experimental animal again terminated the experiment during one of the avoidance cycles, this time after only nine days. And the experimental animal in the fourth pair of monkeys was sacrificed in a moribund condition after 48 days on the avoidance procedure. In all instances, gross and microscopic analysis revealed extensive gastrointestinal lesions with ulceration as a prominent feature of the pathology of the experimental animals. However, none of the control animals which were sacrificed for comparison with their experimental partners and subjected to complete post-mortem examination, showed any indications of such gastrointestinal complications.

The results of these experiments, while consistent with previous reports of experimentally produced "psychosomatic" conditions (Sawrey, Conger, and Turrell, 1956), still require considerable systematic replication and analysis in order to elucidate some of the critical psychophysiological relationships involved. One series of efforts in this area emphasizes the analysis of gastric secretion patterns in monkeys subjected to such prolonged behavioral stress. A modified Thomas cannula with an animal in the primate restraining chair is used to secure samples of the gastric contents during various phases of these avoidance experiments. Early observations (Polish, Brady, and Thach, in press) with this procedure in an experiment involving twelve hourly samples taken throughout a six-hour avoidance session and the following six-hour "rest" period revealed a marked suppression of the total gastric acid during the actual avoidance period as compared to pre-avoidance baseline levels. During the six-hour post-avoidance rest period, however, dramatic elevations in gastric acid, significantly above basal levels, were recorded.

This observation has since been verified in several acute experiments with monkeys and extended by the analysis of gastric secretory changes in a series of nine animals exposed to the more chronic six-hour "on," six-hour "off" avoidance procedure for a period of 28 days (Polish, Brady, Mason, Thach, and Niemeck, in press). In all cases, the average daily concentration of free acid showed a consistent increase during the first ten days to two weeks of the experiment, with some animals maintaining elevated levels throughout the entire 28-day exposure and others showing a decline during the terminal two weeks. Marked differences in initial control levels of free acid were also observed for the nine monkeys in this series. It may be significant that the two animals found to have developed peptic ulcers by the end of this 28-day period had the highest initial levels, showed a general increase in these levels during the first two weeks of avoidance, and maintained high levels throughout the entire four weeks of the experiment (Polish, Brady, Mason, Thach, and Niemeck, in press). These same two monkeys showed a progressive increase in their avoidance response rates throughout the four-week experiment (Brady and Polish, 1960).

A second direction in which this analysis of the psychophysiology of emotional stress has been extended involves the concurrent measurement of 17-hydroxycorticosteroid and pepsinogen levels in animals exposed to continuous periods of avoidance for as long as 72 hours (Mason and Brady, in press). Under these rather extreme conditions, there is a not unexpected increase in adrenal cortical activity throughout the three-day avoidance period, with maximum steroid levels attained during the last 24 hours of the 72-hour session. (see Figure 6). Following the 72-hour avoidance session there is a rebound suppression of steroid levels within the first 24 post-avoidance hours, with a return to baseline observed within 48 to 72 hours. In marked contrast however, plasma pepsinogen remained consistently below baseline levels throughout all but the first two hours of the 72-hour avoidance

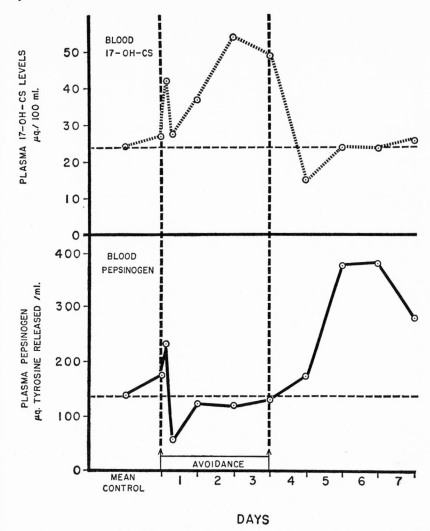

Figure 6. Plasma 17-OH-CS and pepsinogen levels before, during, and after 72-hour exposure to continuous avoidance. [From Mason, Brady, Polish, Bauer, Robinson, Rose, and Taylor, 1961, courtesy of *Science*.]

period. Then, a marked, prolonged elevation in plasma pepsinogen levels developed rather slowly during the first 24 post-avoidance hours, reaching its peak between 48 and 72 hours following termination of the avoidance performance. Even 5 days after the avoidance period, however, plasma pepsinogen levels remained appreciably above pre-experimental baseline determinations.

If these data genuinely indicate that increased pepsinogen production occurs not during but in the aftermath of at least some types of emotional stress, a number of interesting implications are suggested. It may be that the development of peptic ulceration, either in natural life situations or in the laboratory, is at least partly dependent on certain critical aspects of the temporal patterning of alternating stress and rest periods. It would seem that intervening rest periods must be of sufficient duration for the full development of this delayed and prolonged gastric after-effect. It may be pertinent that we have, in current studies, found avoidance programs involving continuously alternating 30-minute periods of avoidance and rest to be ineffective in producing gastro-duodenal ulceration, while programs involving continuously alternating six-hour periods of avoidance and rest have resulted in an increased incidence of gastrointestinal lesions.

In a related series of experiments (Clark and Polish, 1960), the effects of prolonged exposure to relatively short alternating cycles of avoidance and rest (one hour "on," one hour "off") have been explored in relation to alcohol consumption levels with monkeys in a self-selection situation. Intake levels of water and a 20 per cent alcohol solution were determined before (six weeks), during (eight weeks), and after (eight weeks) exposure to the alternating one hour "on," one hour "off" avoidance procedure with two rhesus monkeys gently restrained in primate chairs. During the avoidance phase of the experiment, alcohol intake levels were significantly elevated for both monkeys by comparison with their pre-avoidance control levels (see Figure 7). In addition, Figure 7 shows that termination of the avoidance requirement and extinction of the lever-pressing response had little if any effect upon the elevated alcohol intake levels for at least several weeks. With one monkey (Monkey I, Figure 7), alcohol intake levels were actually observed to increase slightly during the first four weeks after termination of avoidance, and even two months after the avoidance requirement had been removed, alcohol intake levels remained three times higher than the pre-avoidance baseline. These same general relationships are discernable in the data recorded for Monkey II (Figure 7), although the magnitude and duration of the effects are not as great in this second animal. It may also be significant that neither of the monkeys showed any appreciable change in their rate or pattern of lever pressing during the alcohol-avoidance phase of the experiment.

Most recently, attention has focused upon the evaluation of integrated physiological response patterns in laboratory investigations of the psychophysiology of emotional behavior. Of particular interest in this regard have been a series of experiments (Mason, Brady, Robinson, Taylor, Tolson, and Mongey, in press) concerned with defining

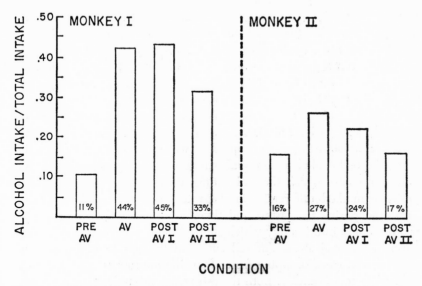

Figure 7. Alcohol intake before, during, and after exposure to alternating one-hour cycles of avoidance and rest.

the relationships between centrally integrated patterns of endocrine responses and emotional stress in laboratory monkeys. In these experiments the emotional stress conditions were produced by exposure of the animals, restrained in chairs, to the "72 continuous hours of avoidance" procedure described above. Measures of thyroid, gonadal, and adrenal hormone secretion patterns were taken before, during, and after the 72-hour avoidance session. Under these conditions, 17-hydroxycorticosteroid, epinephrine, and norepinephrine levels showed an increase to at least twice the baseline control values during the 72-hour avoidance period, with a return to normal levels within two to six days following termination of the session. In contrast, levels of androsterone, a major androgen metabolite, and estrone, a major estrogen metabolite, dropped to below half their baseline values during the 72-hour avoidance session, but showed substantial rebound increases above basal levels during the three to six days following termination of avoidance. Thyroid hormones, as indicated by butanal-extractable iodine (BEI) measurements, showed an increased output to almost twice basal levels. The increase developed slowly but consistently throughout the 72-hour avoidance session, and the output did not return to baseline for at least three weeks following termination of the avoidance exposure. Finally, levels of plasma pepsinogen were observed to remain generally at or below basal values during the avoidance period with gradual rise commencing within 48 to 72 hours after the session and continuing to peak at better than twice basal levels almost ten days after the avoidance requirement had been terminated.

Thus even these preliminary explorations of the psychophysiology of prolonged emotional stress indicate quite clearly that the endocrine response curves of different systems show characteristic topographic and temporal patterns. All the hormones measured in these experiments—thyroidal, gonadal, adrenal—show marked changes in response to such emotional stress. Each hormone, however, appears to have a characteristic response pattern which is defined not only in terms of directional changes but also in terms of its temporal properties. Those hormones which show elevations during such emotional stress evidence marked differences in the rate and duration of elevation, with epinephrine the fastest and thyroid hormones the slowest. The two hormones in this study which showed definite decreases in output during emotional stress differed substantially in rate of depression, with the estrogens dropping faster than the androgens and returning to baseline more quickly. Both the estrogens and androgens, however, show substantial rebound elevations above normal in the aftermath of emotional stress. A tempting synthesis of even these preliminary observations suggests that those hormones which are known to have predominantly catabolic effects on organic metabolism—at least in terms of mobilization of energy resources—are elevated during the emotional stress period, while those with antagonistic or anabolic characteristics are simultaneously depressed. In the recovery period after emotional stress, however, these relationships appear to be reversed, with the anabolic hormones showing predominant activity.

The biological appropriateness of such psychophysiological regulatory mechanisms participating in emotional behavior segments seems obvious, although the validation of such interpretive efforts must necessarily await further confirmatory experimental data. Current efforts are being directed toward the development of physiological assessment methods for insulin and growth hormones and toward the measurement of such multiple psychophysiological response patterns in more chronic emotional stress situation of weeks or months in duration. It seems clear, however, that such an experimental analysis of the dynamic characteristics of endocrine and autonomic participation in behavioral processes may hold considerable promise for new insights and understanding—and the possibility of more sophisticated clinical control in the study of the psychophysiology of emotional behavior.

References

Anand, B. K., & Brobeck, J. R. Hypothalamic control of food intake in rats and cats. *Yale J. Biol. & Med.*, 1951, *24*, 132–140.

Arnold, M. B. An excitatory theory of emotion. In M. L. Reymert (Ed.), *Feelings and emotions*. New York: McGraw-Hill, 1950, 11–33.

Azrin, N. H. Punishment ad recovery during fixed-ratio performance. *J. exp. anal. Behav.*, 1959, *2*, 301–306.

Baird, H. N., Gudetti, B., Reyes, V., Wycis, H. T., & Spiegel, E. G. Stimulation and elimination of anterior thalamic nuclei in man and cat. *Fed. Proc.*, 1951, *10*, 8–9.

Bard, P. A diencephalic mechanism for the expression of rage with special reference to the sympathetic nervous system, *Amer. J. Physiol.*, 1928, *84*, 490–515.

Bard, P. The neuro-humoral basis of emotional reactions. In C. Murchison (Ed.), *Handbook of general experimental psychology*, Worcester, Mass.: Clark Univ. Press, 1934a, 264–311.

Bard, P. On emotional expression after decortication with some remarks on certain theoretical views. Parts I and II. *Psychol. Rev.*, 1934b, *41*, 309–329; 424–449.

Bard, P. Central nervous mechanisms for emotional behavior patterns in animals. In A. Frantz (Ed.), *The inter-relationship of mind and body*. Baltimore: Williams & Wilkins, 1939, 190–218.

Bard, P. The hypothalamus and sexual behavior. In J. Fulton (Ed.), *The hypothalamus and central levels of autonomic function*. Baltimore: Williams & Wilkins, 1940, 551–579.

Bard, P., & Rioch, D. M. A study of four cats deprived of neocortex and additional portions of the forebrain. *Bull. Johns Hopkins Hosp.*, 1937, *60*, 73–147.

Bard, P., & Mountcastle, V. B. Some forebrain mechanisms involved in expression of rage with special reference to suppression of angry behavior. In J. Fulton (Ed.), *The Frontal Lobes*. Baltimore: Williams & Wilkins, 1948, 362–404.

Barker, W., Burgwin, S., & Simons, D. J. Studies in epilepsy; significance of "spontaneous" abnormalities in brain wave patterns as observed during interview with epileptic patients. *J. nerv. ment. Dis.*, 1950, *112*, 187–205.

Bazett, H. C., & Penfield, W. G. A study of the Sherrington decerebrate animal in the chronic as well as the acute condition. *Brain*, 1922, *45*, 185–265.

Beer, B., & Valenstein, E. S. Discrimination of tones during reinforcing brain stimulation. *Science*, 1960, *132*, 297–298.

Berger, H. Uber das Elektrenkephalogramm des Menschen. *Arch. Psychiat.*, 1929, *87*, 527–570.

Berrien, F. K. Finger oscillations as indices of emotion. I. Preliminary validation. *J. Exper. Psychol.*, 1939, *24*, 485–498.

Bianchi, L. The mechanism of the function of the frontal lobes. Translated by J. H. MacDonald. New York: Wood, 1922.

Boren, J. J. Decrement in performance during prolonged avoidance sessions. *J. exper. anal. Behav.*, 1960, *3*, 201–206.

Brady, J. V. The effect of electro-convulsive shock on a conditioned emotional response: The permanence of the effect. *J. comp. physiol. Psychol.*, 1951, *44*, 507–511.

Brady, J. V. A comparative approach to the evaluation of drug effects upon effective behavior. *Ann. N.Y. Acad. Sci.*, 1956, *64*, 632–643.

Brady, J. V. A comparative approach to the evaluation of drug effects on behavior. In W. S. Fields (Ed.), *Brain Mechanisms and Drug Action*. Springfield, Ill.: Charles C Thomas, 1957a, 111.

Brady, J. V. A comparative approach to the experimental analysis of emotional behavior. In P. Hoch & J. Zubin (Eds.), *Experimental psychopathology*. New York: Grune and Stratton, 1957b, 20–33.

Brady, J. V. The paleocortex and behavioral motivation. In H. F. Harlow & C. N. Woolsey (Eds.), *Biological and biochemical bases of behavior*. Madison, Wisc.: Univ. Wisconsin Press, 1958a, 193–235.

Brady, J. V. Temporal and emotional factors related to electrical self-stimulation of the limbic system. In H. H. Jasper, D. L. Proctor, R. S. Knighton, W. C. Noshay, & R. T. Costello. *Reticular formation of the brain*. Boston: Little, Brown, 1958b, 689–703.

Brady, J. V. Temporal and emotional effects related to intracranial electrical stimulation. In E. R. Ramey and D. S. O'Doherty (Eds.), *Electrical studies on the unanesthetized brain*. New York: Hoeber, 1960.

Brady, J. V. Motivational-emotional factors and intra-cranial self-stimulation. In D. Sheer and D. C. Kroeger (Eds.), *Symposium on brain stimulation subcortical integrative system*. Austin, Tex.: Univ. Texas Press, 1961. In Press.

Brady, J. V., Boren, J., Conrad, D., & Sidman, M. The effect of food and water deprivation upon intracranial self-stimulation. *J. comp. physiol. Psychol.*, 1957, *50*, 134–137.

Brady, J. V., & Conrad, D. G. Some effects of brain stimulation on timing behavior. *J. exper. anal. Behav.*, 1960a, *3*, 93–106.

Brady. J. V., & Conrad, D. G. Some effects of limbic-system self-stimulation upon conditioned emotional behavior. *J. comp. physiol. Psychol.*, 1960b, *53*, 128–137.

Brady, J. V., & Hunt, H. F. An experimental approach to the analyses of emotional behavior. *J. Psychol.*, 1955, *40*, 313–324.

Brady, J. V., & Nauta, W. J. H. Subcortical mechanisms in emotional behavior: affective changes following septal forebrain lesions in the albino rat. *J. comp. physiol. Psychol.*, 1953, *46*, 339–346.

Brady, J. V., & Nauta, W. J. H. Subcortical mechanisms in emotional behavior: the duration of affective changes following septal and habenular lesions in the albino rat. *J. comp. physiol. Psychol.*, 1955, *48*, 412–420.

Brady, J. V., & Polish, E. Performance changes during prolonged avoidance. *Psych. Repts.*, 1960, *7*, 554.

Brady, J. V., Porter, R. W., Conrad, D. G., & Mason, J. W. Avoidance behavior and the development of gastrointestinal ulcers. *J. exper. anal. Behav.*, 1958, *1*, 69–72.

Brobeck, J. R., Tepperman, J., & Long, C. N. Experimental hypothalamic hyperplagia in the albino rat. *Yale J. Biol. & Med.*, 1943, *15*, 831–853.

Broca, P. Anatomie comparée des circonvolutions cérébrales. Le grande lobe lombique et la scissure limbique dans la series des mammifères. *Rev. Anthropol.*, 1878, *1*, 385–498.

Bromiley, R. B. Conditioned responses in a dog after removal of neocortex. *J. comp. physiol. Psychol.*, 1948, *41*, 102–110.

Brookhart, J. M., & Dey, F. L. Reduction of sexual behavior in male guinea pigs by hypothalamic lesions. *Amer. J. Physiol.*, 1941, *133*, 551–554.

Brookhart, J. M., Dey, F. L., & Ranson, S. W. The abolition of mating behavior by hypothalamic lesions in guinea pigs. *Endocrinology*, 1941, *28*, 561–565.

Brooks, C. M. Appetite and obesity. *New Zealand M. J.*, 1947, *46*, 243–254.

Brothers, J. D. An investigation of avoidance, anxiety, and escape behavior in human subjects as measured by action potentials in muscles. *Genet. Psychol. Monogr.*, 1956, *53*, 75–118.

Brown, S., & Schafer, E. A. An investigation into the functions of the occipital and temporal lobes of the monkey's brain. *Phil. Trans. B.*, 1888, *179*, 303–327.

Cadilhac, J. *Hippocampe et Epilepsie*. Montepellier: Dehan, 1955.

Cannon, W. B. The James-Lange theory of emotion. *Amer. J. Psychol.*, 1927, *39*, 106–124.

Cannon, W. B. *Bodily changes in pain, hunger, fear and rage*. New York: Appleton, 1929.

Cannon, W. B. The autonomic nervous system: an interpretation. *Lancet*, 1930, *218*, 1109–1115.

Cannon, W. B. Again the James-Lange and the thalamic theories of emotion. *Psychol. Rev.*, 1931, *38*, 281–295.

Cannon, W. B., & Britton, S. W. Studies on the conditions of activity in endocrine glands. XV. Pseudaffective medulliadienal secretion. *Amer. J. Physiol.*, 1925, *72*, 283–294.

Clark, R., & Polish, E. Avoidance conditioning and alcohol consumption in Rhesus monkeys. *Science*, 1960, *132*, 223–224.

Clark, W. E. L., Beattie, J., Riddoch, G., & Dott, N. M. *The hypothalamus: morphological, functional, clinical and surgical aspects*. Edinburgh: Oliver, 1938.

Cobb, S. Personality and the behavioral disorders. In J. Hunt (Ed.), *Personality and the behavior disorders*. New York: Ronald, 1944, 550–581.

Critchley, M. *The parietal lobes*. Baltimore: Williams & Wilkins, 1953.

Cushing, H. *Papers relating to the pituitary body, hypothalamus and parasympathetic nervous system*. Springfield, Ill.: Charles C Thomas, 1932.

Darrow, C. W. The galvanic skin reflex (sweating) and blood-pressure as preparatory and facilitative functions. *Psychol. Bull.*, 1936, *33* 73–94.

Darrow, C. W. Physiological and clinical tests of autonomic function and autonomic balance. *Physiol. Rev.*, 1943, *23*, 1–36.

Darrow, C. W. A mechanism for "functional" effects of emotion on the brain. In W. C. Halstead (Ed.), *Brain and behavior. A symposium. Comp. Psychol. Monogr.* 1950a, *20*, 51–60.

Darrow, C. W. A new frontier: neurophysiological effects of emotion on the brain. In M. L. Reymert (Ed.), *Feelings and emotions*. New York: McGraw-Hill, 1950b, 247–260.

Darrow, C. W. The relation of cerebral to autonomic activity in the conditional emotional reactions of children. *Ann. N.Y. Acad. Sci.*, 1953, *56*, 289–301.

Darwin, C. *The expression of the emotions in man and animals*. London: John Murray. 1872.

Davis, R. C. The relation of muscle action potentials to difficulty and frustration. *J. exper. Psychol.*, 1938, *23*, 141–158.

Davis, R. C. Methods of measuring and recording action. In T. G. Andrews (Ed.), *Methods of psychology*. New York: Wiley, 1948, 391–416.

Delgado, J. M. R. Cerebral structures involved in transmission and elaboration of noxious stimulation. *J. Neurophysiol.*, 1955, *18*, 261–275.

Delgado, J. M. R., Roberts, W. W., & Miller, N. E. Learning motivated by electrical stimulation of the brain. *Am. J. Physiol.*, 1954, *179*, 587–593.

Diethelm, O., Doty, E. J., & Milhorat, A. T. Emotions and adrenergic and cholinergic changes in the blood. *A.M.A. Arch. Neurol. Psychiat.*, 1945, *54*, 110–115.

Duffy, E. An explanation of "emotional" phenomena without the use of the concept "emotion." *J. genet. Psychol.*, 1941, *25*, 283–293.

Dunbar, H. F. *Emotions and bodily changes* (4th Ed.). New York: Columbia Univ. Press, 1954.

Dunlap, K. (Ed.). *The emotions*. Baltimore: Williams and Wilkins, 1922.

Dusser De Barenne, H. G. Recherches expérimentales sur les fonctions du système nerveux central, faites en particulier sur deux chats dont le neopallium avait été enlevé. *Arch. Neerl. Physiol.*, 1920, *4*, 31–123.

Ellingson, R. J. Brain waves and problems of psychology. *Psychol. Bull.*, 1956, *53*, 1–34.

Estes, W. K., & Skinner, B. F. Some quantitative properties of anxiety. *J. exper. Psychol.*, 1941, *29*, 390–400.

Evarts, E. V., & Nissen, H. W. Test of "the Abstract Attitude" in chimpanzees following ablation of prefrontal cortex. *A.M.A. Arch. Neurol. Psychiat.*, 1953, *69*, 323–331.

Faure, M. J., & Portmann, M. Résponse, chez le chien éveillé, de l'aire corticale auditive antérieure et de l'hippocampe à des stimulations sensorielles spéciales. *Rev. Laryng.*, 1955, *76*, 168–178.

Feindel, W., & Gloor, P. Comparison of electrographic effects of stimulation of the amygdala and brain stem reticular formation in cats. *Electroencephalog. & clin. Neurophysiol.* 1954, *6*, 389–402.

Ferrier, D. The croonian lecture. Experiments on the brain of monkeys. (Second series.) *Phil. Trans.*, 1875, *165*, 433–488.

Ferster, C. B. The use of the free operant in the analysis of behavior. *Psychol. Bull.*, 1953, *50*, 264–274.

Ferster, C. B. Suppression of a performance under differential reinforcement of low rates by a pre-time-out stimulus. *J. exper. anal. Behav.*, 1960, *3*, 143–154.

Ferster, C. B., & Appel, J. B. Punishment of S^Δ responding in matching to sample by time out from positive reinforcement. *J. exper. anal. Behav.*, 1961, *4*, 45–56.

Ferster, C. B., & Skinner, B. F. *Schedules of reinforcement.* New York: Appleton-Century-Crofts, 1957.

Findley, J. D. Preference and switching under concurrent scheduling. *J. exper. anal. Behav.*, 1958, *1*, 123–144.

Finesinger, J. E. The effect of pleasant and unpleasant ideas on the respiratory pattern (spirogram) in psychoneurotic patients. *Amer. J. Psychiat.*, 1944, *100*, 659–667.

Foerster, O., & Gagel, O. Ein Fall von ependymcyste des III. Ventrikels. Ein Beitrag zur Frage der Beziehungen psychischer Storungen zum Hirnstamm. *Ztschr. ges. Neurol. Psychiat.*, 1933, *149*, 312–344.

French, J. D., & Magoun, H. W. Effects of chronic lesions in central cephalic brain stem of monkeys. *A.M.A. Arch. Neurol. Psychiat.*, 1952, *68*, 591–604.

Freud, S. *Collected papers.* London: Hogarth, 1924.

Fulton, J. F. A study of the visceral brain in primates and man. *Yale J. Biol. & Med.*, 1953, *26*, 107–118.

Fulton, J. F. *Frontal lobotomy and affective behavior.* New York: Norton, 1951.

Fulton, J. F. *The frontal lobes.* Baltimore: Williams & Wilkins, 1948.

Fulton, J. F., & Jacobsen, C. F. Advances Mod. Biol. (U.S.S.R.), 1935, *4*, 113–126.

Galambos. R., Sheatz, G., & Vernier, V. G. *Science,* 1956, *123*, 376–377.

Gaskill, H. V. The objective measurement of emotional reactions. *Genet. Psychol. Monogr.*, 1933, *14*, 177–280.

Gastaut, H. Corrélations entre le système nerveux végétatif et le système de la vie de relation dans le rhinencéphale. *J. Physiol.*, 1952, Paris, *44*, 431–470.

Gastaut, H., & Collomb, H. A study of the sexual behaviour of epileptics of the psychomotor type. *Ann. Med.-psychol.*, 1956, *2*, 357–364.

Gastaut, H., & Mileto, G. Interprétation physiopathogénique des symptômes de la rage furieuse. *Rev. neurol.*, 1955, *92*, 5–25.

Gastaut, H., Morin, G., & Leseure, N. Etude du comportement des épileptiques psychomoteurs dans l'intervalle de leurs crises. Les troubles de l'activité globale et de la sociabilité. *Ann. Med.-psychol.*, 1955, *1*, 1–27.

Gellhorn, E. *Autonomic regulations.* New York: Interscience, 1943.

Gellhorn, E. Recent investigations of the physiological basis of emotions. In P. Hoch & J. Zubin (Eds.), *Anxiety.* New York: Grune and Stratton, 1950, 205–217.

Gloor, P. Autonomic functions of the diencephalon. *A.M.A. Neurol. Psychiat.,* 1954, *71,* 773–790.

Gloor, P. Electrophysiological studies on the connections of the amygdaloid nucleus in the cat. *Electroencephalog. & clin. Neurophysiol.,* 1955a, *7,* 223–264.

Gloor, P. Electrophysiological studies on the connections of the amygdaloid nucleus in the cat. *Electroencephalog. & clin. Neurophysiol.,* 1955b, *7,* 243–264.

Gloor, P. Telencephalic influences upon the hypothalamus. In W. S. Fields (Ed.), *Hypothalamic-hypophysical Interrelationship.* Springfield, Ill.: Charles C Thomas, 1956.

Goltz, F. Der Hund ohne Grosshirn. *Arch. ges. Physiol.,* 1892, *51,* 570–614.

Green, J. D., & Arduini, A. A. Hippocampal electrical activity in arousal. *J. Neurophysiol.,* 1954, *17,* 533–557.

Grinker, R. R. Hypothalamic functions in psychosomatic interrelations. *Psychosom. Med.,* 1939, *1,* 91–47.

Grunthal, E. Uber das klinische Bild nach unischriebenem beiderseitigem Ausfall der Ammonshornrinde Ein Beitrag zur Kenntnis der Function des Ammonshornes. *Monatsschr. Psychiat. u. Neurol.,* 1947, *113,* 1–16.

Harris, G. W. *Adrenal cortex, transactions of the third conference.* New York: Macy, 1952, 54–88.

Head, H. *Studies in neurology.* London: Frawde, Hodder & Staughton, 1920.

Hebb, D. O. Man's frontal lobes. A critical review. *A.M.A. Arch. Neurol. Psychiat.,* 1945, *54,* 10–24.

Hefferline, R. F., & Keenan, B. Amplitude-induction gradient of a small human operant in an escape-avoidance situation. *J. exper. anal. Behav.,* 1961, *4,* 41–44.

Herrick, C. J. The functions of the olfactory parts of the cerebral cortex. *Proc. Nat. Acad. Sc.,* Washington, D.C., 1933, *19,* 7–14.

Herrnstein, R. J., & Morse, W. H. Some effects of response-independent positive reinforcement on maintained operant behavior. *J. comp. physiol. Psychol.,* 1957, *50,* 461–467.

Hess, W. R. Stammganglien-Reizversuche. 10. Tagung der Deutschen Physiol. Ges., Frankfurt a. M. 1927. *Ber. ges. Physiol.,* 1928, *42,* 554–572.

Hess, W. R. *Die Methodik der lokaliseerten Reizung und Ausschaltung Subkortikaler Hirnabschnitte.* Leipzig: Thieme, 1932.

Hess, W. R. *Das Zwischenhirn: Syndrome, Lokalisationen, Funktionen.* Basel: Schwabe, 1949.

Hess, W. R. *Diencephalon: autonomic and extrapyramidal functions.* New York: Grune and Stratton, 1954.

Hess, W. R., & Akert, K. Experimental data on role of hypothalamus in mechanism of emotional behavior. *A.M.A. Arch. Neurol. Psychiat.,* 1955, *73,* 127–129.

Hinsey, J. C. The hypothalamus and somatic responses. In J. Fulton (Ed.), *The hypothalamus and central levels of autonomic function.* Baltimore: Williams & Wilkins, 1940, 657–688.

Hoagland, H., Cameron, D. E., & Rubin, M. A. Emotion in man as tested by the delta index of the electroencephalogram. *J. genet. Psychol.,* 1938, *19,* 227–245.

Hodos, W., & Valenstein, E. S. Motivational variables affecting the rate of behavior maintained by intracranial stimulation. *J. comp. physiol. Psychol.,* 1960, *53,* 502–508.

Hume, D. M., & Wittenstein, G. J. The relationship of the hypothalamus to pituitary-adrenocortical functions. *Proceedings of the first ACTH con-*

ference. Philadelphia: Blakiston, 1950, 134–147.

Hunt, A., & Landis, C. The overt behavior pattern in startle. *J. Exper. Psychol.,* 1936, *19,* 309–315.

Hunt, H. F., & Brady, J. V. Some effects of electro-convulsive shock on a conditioned emotional response ("anxiety"). *J. comp. physiol. Psychol.,* 1951, *44,* 88–98.

Hunt, W. A. Feeling and emotion. In E. G. Boring, J. S. Tangfeld, & H. P. Weld (Eds.), *Foundations of psychology.* New York: Wiley, 1948, 90–111.

Ingram, W. R. Brain stem mechanisms in behavior. *Electroencephalog. & clin. Neurophysiol.,* 1952, *4,* 397–406.

Ingram, W. R., Barris, R. W., & Ranson, S. W. Catalepsy: an experimental study. *A.M.A. Arch. Neurol. Psychiat.,* 1936, *35,* 1175–1197.

Jacobsen, C. F. Studies of cerebral function in primates. I. The function of the frontal association areas in monkeys. *Comp. Psychol. Monogr.,* 1936, *13,* No. 63, 1–60.

James, W. What is emotion? *Mind,* 1884, *9,* 188–205.

Kaada, B. R. Somato-motor, autonomic and electrocorticographic responses to electrical stimulation of "rhenencephalic" and other structures in primates, cat and dog. *Acta physiol. scandinav.,* 1951, *24,* Suppl. 83, 1–285.

Kaada, B. R., Andersen, P., & Jansen, J. Stimulation of the amygdaloid nuclear complex in unanesthetized cats. *Neurology,* 1954, *4,* 48–64.

Kaada, B. R., Jansen, J., & Andersen, P. Stimulation of hippocampus and medial cortical areas in unanesthetized cats. *Neurology,* 1953, *3,* 844–857.

Karplus, J. P. Die Physiologie der vegetativen Zentren. In O. Bumke & O. Foerster (Eds.), *Handbuch der Neurologie.* Berlin, Springer, 1937, 402–439.

Keller, A. D. Autonomic discharges elicited by physiological stimuli in

midbrain preparations. *Amer. J. Physiol.,* 1932, *100,* 576–586.

Keller, F. S., & Schoenfeld, W. N. *Principles of psychology.* New York: Appleton-Century-Crofts, 1950.

Klebanoff, S. G., Singer, J. L., & Wilensky, H. Psychological consequences of brain lesions and ablations. *Psychol. Bull.,* 1954, *51,* 1–41.

Kleist, L. *Gehirnpathologie.* Leipzig: Barth, 1934.

Klüver, H. Brain mechanisms and behavior with special reference to the rhinencephalon. *Journal-Lancet,* 1952, *72,* 567–574.

Klüver, H., & Bucy, P. C. "Psychic blindness" and other symptoms following bilateral temporal lobectomy in rhesus monkeys. *Amer. J. Physiol.,* 1937, *119,* 352–353.

Klüver, H., & Bucy, P. C. An analysis of certain effects of bilateral temporal lobectomy in the rhesus monkey with special reference to "psychic blindness." *J. Psychol.,* 1938, *5,* 33–54.

Klüver, H., & Bucy, P. Preliminary analysis of functions of the temporal lobes in monkeys. *A.M.A. Arch. Neurol. Psychiat.,* 1939, *42,* 979–1000.

Knott, J. R., & Correll, R. E. Photic driving in stutterers. *Electroencephalog. & clin. Neurophysiol.,* 1954, *6,* 158–158.

Koikegami, H., & Fuse, S. Studies on the functions and fiber connections of the amygdaloid nuclei and peri-amygdaloid cortex. Experiment on the respiratory movements. (1). *Folia psychiat. neurol. Japonica,* 1952a, *5,* 188–196.

Koikegami, H., & Fuse, S. Studies on the functions and fiber connections of the amygdaloid nuclei and peri-omygdaloid cortex. Experiment on the respiratory movements. (2). *Folia psychiat. neurol. Japonica,* 1952b, *6,* 94–103.

Koikegami, H., & Yoshida, V. Pupillary dilatation induced by stimulation of amygdaloid nuclei. *Folia psychiat. neurol. Japonica,* 1952, *7,* 109–125.

Lacey, J. I. The evaluation of autonomic responses: toward a general solution. *Ann. N.Y. Acad. Sci.*, 1956, *67*, 123–163.

Landis, C. Emotion. II. The expressions of emotion. In C. Murchison (Ed.), *Handbook of general experimental psychology.* Worcester, Mass.: Clark Univ. Press., 1934, 312–341.

Landis, C. J. The frontal lobes and anguish: A new formulation of an old problem. *J. nerv. ment. Dis.*, 1952, *115*, 203–214.

Landis, C., & Hunt, W. A. Adrenalin and emotion. *Psychol. Rev.*, 1932, *34*, 467–473.

Landis, C., Zubin, J., & Mettler, F. The functions of the human frontal lobe. *J. Psychol.*, 1950, *30*, 123–138.

Lange, C. G. *Om Sindsbevegelser.* Leipzig: Theador Thomas, 1887.

Lashley, V. S. The thalamus and emotion. *Psychol. Rev.*, 1938, *45*, 42–61.

Leeper, R. W. A motivational theory of emotion to replace "emotion as disorganized response." *Psychol. Rev.*, 1948, *55*, 5–21.

Liberson, W. T., & Cadilhac, J. Hippocampal responses to sensory stimulation in the guinea pig. *Electroencephalog. & clin. Neurophysiol.*, 1954, *6*, 710–711.

Liberson, W. T., & Akert, K. Hippocampal seizure in guinea pig. *Electroencephalog. & clin. Neurophysiol.*, 1955, *7*, 211–222.

Lichtenstein, P. E. Studies of anxiety: I. The production of a feeding inhibition in dogs. *J. comp. physiol. Psychol.*, 1950, *43*, 16–29.

Liddell, H. S. *Emotional hazards in animals and man.* Springfield, Ill.: Charles C Thomas, 1956.

Lindsley, D. B. Emotions and the electroencephalogram. In M. L. Reymert (Ed.), *Feelings and emotions.* New York: McGraw-Hill, 1950, 238–246.

Lindsley, D. B. Emotion. In S. S. Stevens (Ed.), *Handbook of experimental psychology.* New York: Wiley, 1951, 473–516.

Lindsley, D. B., & Hunter, W. S. A note on polarity potentials from the human eye. *Proc. Nat. Acad. Sci.*, Washington, D.C., 1939, *25*, 180–183.

Lindsley, D. B., & Sassaman, W. H. Autonomic activity and brain potentials associated with "voluntary" control of the pilomotors. (MM. arrectores pilorum). *J. Neurophysiol.*, 1938, *1*, 342–349.

Lindsley, D. B., Knowles, W. B., Schreiner, L. H., & Magoun, H. W. Behavioral and EEG changes following chronic brain stem lesions in the cat. *Electroencephalog. & clin. Neurophysiol.*, 1950, *2*, 483–498.

Lowenstein, O., & Friedman, E. D. Pupillographic studies. I. Present state of pupillography: its method and diagnostic significance. *A.M.A. Arch. Ophth.*, 1942, *27*, 969–993.

MacLean, P. D. Psychosomatic disease and the "visceral brain": Recent developments bearing on the Papez theory of emotion. *Psychosom. Med.*, 1949, *11*, 338–353.

MacLean, P. D. Some psychiatric implications of physiological studies on frontotemporal portion of limbic system (visceral brain). *Electroencephalog. & clin. Neurophysiol.*, 1952, *4*, 407–418.

MacLean, P. D. The limbic system and its hippocampal formation. *J. Neurosurg.*, 1954, *11*, 29–44.

MacLean, P. D. The limbic system "Visceral Brain" and emotional behavior. *A.M.A. Arch. Neurol. Psychiat.*, 1955a, *73*, 130–134.

MacLean, P. D. The limbic system "visceral brain" in relation to central gray and reticulum of the brain stem. *Psychosom. Med.*, 1955b, *17*, 355–366.

MacLean, P. D., & Delgado, J. M. R. Electrical and chemical stimulation of fronto-temporal portion of limbic system in the waking animal. *Electroencephalog. & clin. Neurophysiol.*, 1953, *5*, 91–100.

Mahl, G. F. Relationship between acute

and chronic fear and the gastric acidity and blood sugar levels in in mecaca mulatta monkeys. *Psychosom. Med.*, 1952, *14*, 182–199.

Mahl, G. F. Physiological changes during chronic fear. *Ann. N.Y. Acad. Sci.*, 1953, *56*, 240–249.

Mason, J. W. Some aspects of the central nervous system regulation of ACTH secretion. *J. clin. Endocrinol.*, 1956, *16*, 914.

Mason, J. W., & Brady, J. V. Plasma 17-hydroxycorticosteroid changes related to reserpine effects on emotional behavior. *Science*, 1956, *124*, 983–984.

Mason, J. W., Brady, J. V., Polish, E., Bauer, J., Robinson, J., Rose, R., and Taylor, E. Patterns of corticosteroid and pepsinogen change related to emotional stress in the monkey. *Science*, 1961, *133*, 1596–1598.

Mason, J. W., Brady, J. V., Robinson, J. A., Taylor, E. D., Tolson, W. N., & Maugey, E. Patterns of thyroid, gonadal, and adrenal hormone secretion related to psychological stress in the monkey. *Psychosom. Med.* In press.

Mason, J. W., Brady, J. V., & Sidman, M. Plasma 17-hydroxycorticosteroid levels and conditioned behavior in the rhesus monkey. *Endocrinology*, 1957, *60*, 741–752.

Masserman, J. H. Is the hypothalamus a center of emotion? *Psychosom. Med.*, 1941, *3*, 3–25.

Masserman, J. H. The hypothalamus and psychiatry. *Amer. J. Psychiat.*, 1942, *5*, 341.

Masserman, J. H. *Behavior and neurosis.* Chicago: Chicago Univ. Press, 1943.

McDougall, W. *An introduction to social psychology.* (2nd Ed.) Boston: Tuce, 1926.

Mettler, F. A. *Selective partial ablation of the frontal cortex.* New York: Hoeber, 1949.

Mettler, F. A. (Ed.). *Psychosurgical problems.* New York: Blakiston, 1952.

Miller, N. E. Learnable drives and re-

wards. In S. S. Stevens (Ed.), *Handbook of experimental psychology.* New York: Wiley, 1951, 435–479.

Milner, B. Intellectual function of the temporal lobes. *Psychol. Bull.*, 1954, *51*, 42–62.

Mittelmann, B., Wolfe, H. G. Emotions and skin temperature: observations on patients during psychotherapeutic (psychoanalytic) interviews. *Psychosom. Med.*, 1943, *5*, 211–231.

Moniz, E. *Tentatives operatories dans le traitment de certaines psychoses.* Paris: Masson, 1936.

Morse, W. H., & Herrnstein, R. J. The maintenance of avoidance behavior using the removal of a conditioned positive reinforcer as the aversive stimulus. *Amer. Psychologist*, 1956, *11*, 430.

Moruzzi, G., & Magoun, H. W. Brain stem reticular formation and activation of the EEG. *Electroencephalog. & clin. Neurophysiol.*, 1949, *1*, 455–473.

Mowrer, O. H. *Learning theory and personality dynamics.* New York: Ronald, 1950.

Mulder, D. W., & Daly, D. Psychiatric symptoms associated with lesions of temporal lobe. *J.A.M.A.*, 1952, *150*, 173–176.

Nauta, W. J. H. Hypothalamic regulation of sleep in rats: an experimental study. *J. Neurophysiol.*, 1946, *9*, 285–316.

Nauta, W. J. H. An experimental study of the fornix system in the rat. *J. comp. Neurol.*, 1956, *104*, 247–271.

Nauta, W. J. H., & Gygax, P. A. Silver impregnation of degenerating axons in the central nervous system: a modified technique. *Stain Technol.*, 1954, *29*, 91–93.

Notterman, J. M., Schoenfeld, W. N., & Bersh, P. J. Conditioned heart rate response in human beings during experimental anxiety. *J. comp. physiol. Psychol.*, 1952, *45*, 1–8.

Olds, J. Physiological mechanisms of reward. In M. R. Jones (Ed.),

Nebraska symposium on motivation. Lincoln: Univ. Nebraska Press, 1955.

Olds, J. A preliminary mapping of electrical reinforcing effects in the rat brain. *J. comp. physiol. Psychol.,* 1956, *49,* 281–285.

Olds, J., & Milner, P. Positive reinforcement produced by electrical stimulation of septal area and other regions of rat brain. *J. comp. physiol. Psychol.,* 1954, *47,* 419–427.

Papez, J. W. A proposed mechanism of emotion. *A.M.A. Arch. Neurol. Psychiat.,* 1937, *38,* 725–743.

Penfield, W., & Jasper, H. *Epilepsy and the functional anatomy of the human brain.* Boston: Little, Brown, 1954.

Polish, E., Brady, J. V., Mason, J. W., Thach, J., & Niemeck, W. Gastric contents and avoidance behavior in the rhesus monkey. II. Relationships under chronic experimental conditions. *Gastroenterology.* In press.

Polish, E., Brady, J. V. & Thach, J. Gastric contents and avoidance behavior in the rhesus monkey. I. Relationships under acute experimental conditions. *Gastroenterology.* In press.

Pool, J. L. Neurophysiological symposium; visceral brain in man. *J. Neurosurg.,* 1954, *11,* 45–63.

Porter, R. W. Hypothalamic involvement in the pituitary-adreno-cortical response to stress stimuli. *Amer. J. Physiol.,* 1953, *172,* 515–519.

Porter, R. W., Brady, J. V., Conrad, D. G., Mason, J. W., Galambos, R., & Rioch, D. Some experimental observations on gastrointestinal lesions in behaviorally conditioned monkeys. *Psychosom. Med.,* 1958, *20,* 379–394.

Porter, R. W., Conrad, D. G., & Brady, J. V. Some neural and behavioral correlates of electrical self-stimulation of the limbic system. *J. exper. anal. Behav.,* 1959, *2,* 43–55.

Pribram, K. H., & Kruger, L. Functions of the "olfactory brain." *Ann. N.Y. Acad. Sci.,* 1954, *58,* 109–138.

Pribram, K. H., & Weiskrantz, L. A comparison of the effects of medial and lateral cerebral resections on conditioned avoidance behavior of monkeys. *J. comp. physiol. Psychol.,* 1957, *50,* 74.

Ranson, S. W. Somnolence caused by hypothalamic lesions in the monkey. *A.M.A. Arch. Neurol. Psychiat.,* 1939, *41,* 1–23.

Ranson, S. W., & Magoun, H. W. The hypothalamus. *Ergebn. Physiol.,* 1939, *41,* 56–163.

Reiser, M. F., Reeves, R. B., & Armington, J. Effect of variations in labratory procedure and experimenter upon the ballistocardiogram, blood pressure, and heart rate in healthy young men. *Psychosom. Med.,* 1955, *17,* 185–199.

Rioch, D. Mck. Certain aspects of the behavior of decorticate cats. *Psychiatry,* 1938, *1,* 339–345.

Rosvold, H. E., Mirsky, A. F., & Pribram, K. H. Influence of amygdalectomy on social behavior in monkeys. *J. comp. physiol. Psychol.,* 1954, *47,* 173–178.

Rothmann, H. Zusammenfassender Bericht uber den Rothmannschen grosshirnloser Hund nach klinischer und anotomischer Untersuchung. *Ztschr. ges. Neurol. Psychiat.,* 1923, *87,* 247–313.

Ruckmick, C. A. *The psychology of feeling and emotion.* New York: McGraw-Hill, 1936.

Ruesch, J., Finesinger, J. E. Muscular tension in psychiatric patients. Pressure methods on handwriting as an indicator. *A.M.A. Arch. Neurol. Psychiat.,* 1943, *50,* 439–449.

Sawa, M., Ueki, Y., Arita, M., & Harada, T. Preliminary report on the amygdaloidectomy on the psychotic patients, with interpretation of oral-emotional manifestation in schizophrenics. *Folia psychiat. neurol. Japonica,* 1954, *7,* 309–329.

Sawrey, W. L., Conger, J. J., & Turrell, E. S. An experimental investigation of the role of psychological factors in the production of gastric ulcers in rats. *J. comp. physiol. Psychol.*, 1956, *49*, 457–461.

Sawyer, C. H. Rhinencephalic involvement in pituitary activation by intracentricular histamini in the rabbit under nembutal anesthesia. *Amer. J. Physiol.*, 1955, *180*, 37–46.

Schaltenbrand, G., & Cobb, S., Clinical and anatomical studies on two cats with neocortex. *Brain*, 1930, *53*, 449–488.

Schlosberg, H. Three dimensions of emotion. *Psychol. Rev.*, 1954, *61*, 81–88.

Schoenfeld, W. N. An experimental approach to anxiety, escape, and avoidance behavior. In P. Hoch & J. Zubin (Eds.), *Anxiety.* New York: Grune and Stratton, 1950, 70–89.

Schreiner, L., & Kling, A. Behavioral changes following paleocortical injury in rodents, carnivores, and primates. *Medical Film, U.S. Army*, 1953a, 8–7935.

Schreiner, L., & Kling, A. Behavioral changes following rhinencephalic injury in cat. *J. Neurophysiol.*, 1953b, *16*, 643–659.

Schreiner, L., & Kling, A. Effects of castration on hypersexual behavior induced by rhinencephalic injury in cat. *A.M.A. Arch. Neurol. Psychiat.*, 1954, *72*, 180–186.

Schreiner, L., Rioch, D., Pechtel, C., & Masserman, J. Behavioral changes following thalamic injury in cat. *J. Neurophysiol.*, 1953, *16*, 234–246.

Sem-Jacobsen, C. W., & Torkildsen, A. Depth recording and electrical stimulation in the human brain. In E. R. Ramey & D. S. O'Doherty (Eds.), *Electrical studies on the unanesthetized brain.* New York: Paul B. Hoeber, Inc., 1960.

Sidman, M. Avoidance conditioning with brief shock and no exteroceptive warning signal. *Science*, 1953, *118*, 157–158.

Sidman, M. Drug-behavior interaction. *Ann. N.Y. Acad. Sci.*, 1956, *65*, 282–302.

Sidman, M. Behavior pharmacology.

Psychopharmacologia, 1959, *1*, 1–19.

Sidman, M. Normal sources of pathological behavior. *Science*, 1960, *132*, 61–68.

Sidman, M., Brady, J. V., Boren, J., Conrad, D., & Schulman, A. Reward schedules and behavior maintained by intra-cranial self stimulation. *Science*, 1955, *122*, 830–831.

Sidman, M., Herrnstein, R. J., & Conrad, D. Maintenance of avoidance behavior by unavoidable shocks. *J. comp. physiol. Psychol.*, 1957, *50*, 553–557.

Sidman, M., Mason, J. W., Brady, J. V., & Thach, J., Jr., *Quantitative relations between operant behavior and pituitary-adrenal cortical activity in rhesus monkeys.* In press.

Skinner, B. F. *Science and human behavior.* New York: Macmillan, 1953a.

Skinner, B. F. Some contributions of an experimental analysis of behavior to psychology as a whole. *Amer. Psychologist*, 1953b, *8*, 69–78.

Skinner, B. F. *The behavior of organisms: an experimental analysis.* New York: Appleton-Century-Crofts, 1938.

Skinner, B. F. An experimental analysis of certain emotions. *J. exper. anal. Behav.*, 1959, *2*, 264.

Skinner, B. F., & Morse, W. H. Morse, Sustained performance during very long experimental sessions. *J. exper. anal. Behav.*, 1958, *1*, 235–244.

Spiegel, E. A., & Wycis, H. T. Physiological and psychological results of thalamontomy. *Proc. Roy. Soc. Med..* 1949, Supp. *42*, 1–9.

Spiegel, E. A., Miller, H. R., & Oppenheimer, M. J. Forebrain and rage reactions. *J. Neurophysiol.*, 1940, *3*, 538–548.

Spiegel, E. A., Wycis, H. T., Freed, H., & Archinik, C. The central mechanism of the emotions. *Amer. J. Psychiat.* 1951, *108*, 426–431.

Stellar, E. The physiology of motivation. *Psychol. Rev.*, 1954, *61*, 5–22.

Ulett, G. A., & Gleser, G. Psychiatric screening of flying personnel: the development of empirical scales for the prediction of anxiety-proneness from the EEG and reaction to intermittent photic stimulation. *School of Aviation Medicine Report.* USAF Proj. No. 21-020-0007, No. *4*, 1953.

Ulett, G. A., Gleser, G., Lawler, A. & Winokur, G. Psychiatric screening of flying personnel: IV. An experimental investigation of development of an EEG index of anxiety tolerance by means of photic stimulation, its validation by psychological and psychiatric criteria. *School of Aviation Medicine Report.* USAF Proj. No. 21-37-002 No. *4*, 1952. 39 pp.

Ulett, G. A.. Gleser, G., Starr, P., Haddock, J., Lingley, L., & Lawler, A. Psychiatric screening of flying personnel: further studies toward the development of an electroencephalographic screening technic. *School of Aviation Medicine Report.* USAF Project No. 21-0202-0007, No. *5*, 1953, 9 pp.

Walter, W. G. The twenty-fourth Maudsley lecture: the functions of the electrical rhythms in the brain. *J. Ment. Sci.,* 1950, *96*, 1–31.

Ward, A. A., Jr. The cingular gyrus: Area 24. *J. Neurophysiol.* 1948, *11*, 13–23.

Waterhouse, I. K. The effects of prefrontal lobotomy on conditioned fear and food responses in monkeys. *J. comp. physiol. Psychol.,* 1957, *50*, 81–88.

Watson, J. B. *Behavior, an introduction to comparative psychology.* New York: Holt, 1914.

Watson, J. B. *Psychology from the standpoint of a behaviorist.* Philadelphia: Lippincott, 1919.

Weiss, B., & Laties, V. G. Titration behavior on various fractional escape programs. *J. exper. anal. Behav.,* 1959, *2*, 227–248.

Welch, L., & Kubis, J. Conditioned PGR (psychogalvanic response) in states of pathological anxiety. *J. nerv. ment. Dis.,* 1947a, *105*, 372–381.

Welch, L., & Kubis, J. The effect of anxiety on the conditioning rate and stability of the PGR. *J. Psychol.,* 1947b, *23*, 83–91.

Wenger, M. A., & Ellington, M. The measurement of autonomic balance in children. *Psychosom. Med.,* 1943, *5*, 241–253.

Wenger, M. A., Gilchrist, J. C. A comparison of two indices of palmar sweating. *J. exper. Psychol.,* 1948, *38*, 757–761.

White, J. C. Autonomic discharge from stimulation of the hypothalamus in man. In J. Fulton (Ed.), *The hypothalamus and central levels of autonomic function.* Baltimore: Williams & Wilkins, 1940, 854–863.

Wilson, M. P., & Keller, F. S. On the selective reinforcement of spaced responses. *J. comp. physiol. Psychol.,* 1953, *46*, 190–193.

Winsor, A. L., & Korchin, B. The effect of different types of stimulation upon the pH of human parotid secretion. *J. exper. Psychol.,* 1938, *23*, 62–79.

Winsor, A. L., & Korchin, B. Some observations on the effect of mental activity upon parotid secretion. *J. genet. Psychol.,* 1940, *22*, 25–32.

Woodworth, R. S., & Sherrington, C. S. A pseudaffective reflex and its spinal path. *J. Physiol.,* 1904, *31*, 234–243.

Wundt, W. *Outlines of psychology* (2nd Ed.), Translated by C. Judd. Leipzig: Englemann, 1902.

Young, P. T. *Emotion in man and animal.* New York: Wiley, 1943.

Young, P. T. Motivation, feeling and emotion. In T. G. Andrews (Ed.), *Methods of psychology.* New York: Wiley, 1948, 348.

11

Activation

ROBERT B. MALMO

Clinical psychology as an applied science must rest on the foundation of experimental psychology. This I assume is the implication of this volume's title. What this really means is that any major breakthrough in the basic science of psychology will eventually have its impact on clinical psychology. The diversification of interests represented by the contributors to this volume reflects a searching of all areas, including animal psychology, for promising leads. With these thoughts in mind as I was writing, I did not restrict myself to experiments in which the subjects were psychiatric patients or in which some clinical phenomenon was directly involved. But I hope nonetheless that my clinical observations considered in the context of the experiments on activation may provide yet one more example of how clinical understanding and behavioral science may progress together in a mutually reinforcing way.

I shall not attempt a detailed definition of activation until later in the chapter, but I believe a few brief explanatory remarks are required at the outset. In using the term "activation" I am referring to an intensive dimension. "Arousal" is often used interchangeably with activa-

Support for some of the research reported herein has come from the following sources: National Institute of Mental Health, National Institutes of Health, United States Public Health Service: Grant Number M-1475; Medical Research and Development Division, Office of the Surgeon General, Department of the United States Army: Contract Number DA-49-007-MD-626; Defence Research Board, Department of National Defence, Canada: Grant Number 9425-04; National Research Council of Canada: Grant Number A.P. 29, and by Grant Number 604-5-69 from the Department of National Health and Welfare (Canada). Grateful acknowledgment is made to A. Amsel, R. C. Davis, S. M. Feldman, P. Milner, M. M. Schnore, R. G. Stennett, D. J. Ehrlich and L. R. Pinneo for constructive criticism of the first manuscript.

tion; and level of drive (Hull's D) is a very similar concept. For instance, a drowsy subject is low, an alert subject is high in activation. How is activation related to anxiety? It is difficult to answer this question because the word "anxiety" has been used in so many different ways. "Manifest anxiety" as indicated by the MAS (Taylor, 1953) is a term with purely operational meaning and it has been used to distinguish high-drive (D) from low-D subjects. In short, no distinction between anxiety and activation seems required as far as the MAS is concerned. In the animal literature, when the word "anxiety" is used it merely means fear, and the latter term seems preferable. In clinical writings one frequently encounters reference to anxiety when fear (or merely increased vigilance) is all that is really meant. Nor in the light of Hebb's discussion of fear does it appear reasonable to maintain that anxiety and not fear is instigated by irrational or unconscious means (Hebb, 1958, p. 162 ff.). I have argued that the term anxiety should be reserved for a pathological state that seems to be produced in consequence of long continued states of high activation (Malmo, 1957).

There have been three main lines of approach to the problem of activation: (1) through electroencephalography and neurophysiology, (2) through physiological studies of "behavioral energetics," and (3) through the learning theorists' search for a satisfactory measure of drive. Before attempting a formal definition of activation, I shall briefly describe these three different approaches to the concept.

NEUROPHYSIOLOGICAL APPROACH: LINDSLEY'S ACTIVATION THEORY *

The neurophysiological approach to activation had its origin in electroencephalography (EEG). Early workers in the EEG field soon discovered that there were distinctive wave patterns characterizing the main levels of psychological functioning in the progression from deep sleep to highly alerted states of activity (Jasper, 1941). In deep sleep large low-frequency waves predominate. In light sleep and drowsy states the frequencies are not as low as in deep sleep, but there are more low-frequency waves than in the wakeful states. In relaxed wakefulness there is a predominance of waves in the alpha (8–12 c.p.s.) range that gives way to beta frequencies (approximately 18–30 c.p.s.) when the subject is moderately alert. Under highly alerting and excit-

---

* I am using neuropsychology in a rather broad sense, meaning to include the work often referred to by the term "psychophysiology." This usage implies that the chief problems being studied are psychological ones, and it also stresses the importance of neurophysiological techniques. It is true that, strictly speaking, many of the physiological techniques in use are not neurophysiological ones; yet our main interest lies in the central neural control of the physiological functions under study rather than in the peripheral events themselves.

ing conditions beta waves predominate. In addition to the increased
frequency of the waves under these conditions of heightened alertness there is also a change from a regular synchronized appearance of
the tracing to an irregular desynchronized tracing, usually of reduced
amplitude.

For Lindsley's theory, desynchronization (called "activation pattern") became the single most important EEG phenomenon. My use
of the term "desynchronization" is purely descriptive. Desynchronization or "flattening" in the EEG tracing was consistently found associated with increased alertness in a large variety of experiments with
animal and human subjects. The consistency and generality of this
phenomenon suggested the existence of mechanisms in the brain mediating behavioral functions having to do with levels of alertness, although at the time that the original observations were made it was
not at all clear what these neural mechanisms were.

With the discovery of the ascending reticular activating system
(ARAS), however, there was rapid and very significant advance in
theory and experimentation. Some of the most important general findings have been as follows: (1) Lesions in the ARAS abolished "activation" of the EEG and produced a behavioral picture of lethargy and
somnolence (Lindsley, 1957). (2) The "activation pattern" in the EEG
was reproduced by electrical stimulation of the ARAS. Furthermore,
in the monkey, Fuster (1958) recently found that concurrent ARAS
stimulation of moderate intensity improved accuracy and speed of
visual discrimination reaction. He also found that higher intensities
had the opposite effect, producing diminution of correct responses and
increase of reaction times. Interpretation of these latter findings is
complicated by the fact that they were obtained with stimulation intensities higher than the threshold for the elicitation of observable
motor effects such as generalized muscular jerks. It is not stated
whether intensity of stimulation was systematically studied. In any
event, these observations of deleterious effect from high intensity
stimulation are of considerable interest because they are what might
be expected according to the activation theory.

The activation theory as first stated by Lindsley (1951)—although
introduced in a handbook chapter on emotion—was, from the outset,
conceived by him to be broader than an explanatory concept for emotional behavior. The theory was elaborated by Hebb (1955) in an
attempt to solve the problem of drives. With the continuous flow of
new experimental data on the ARAS (Lindsley, 1957), this area of
neuropsychological investigation appears to be heading toward an
important breakthrough. I shall attempt to state very briefly the main
points of the current theory, drawing upon the ideas of several authors.
According to this theory, the continuum extending from deep sleep at

the low activation end to "excited states"* at the high activation end
is very largely a function of cortical bombardment by the ARAS, such
that the greater the cortical bombardment, the higher the activation.
Further, the relation between activation and behavioral efficiency (cue
function or level of performance) is described by an inverted U curve.
That is, from low activation up to a point that is optimal for a given
function, level of performance rises monotonically with increasing
activation level, but beyond this optimal point the relation becomes
nonmonotonic: further increase in activation beyond this point produces a fall in performance level, this fall being directly related to the
amount of the increase in level of activation.

Principles of neural action that could account for the reversal in the
effects of nonspecific neural bombardment of the cortex by the ARAS
have long been known (Lorente de Nó, 1939, p. 428). Circulation of
neural impulses in a closed chain of neurons (or "cell assembly" to use
Hebb's [1949] term) may be facilitated by impulses arriving outside
the chain (e.g. from the ARAS). According to Lorente de Nó's schema,
such extraneous impulses have the effect of stimulating certain neurons
subliminally thus making it possible for an impulse from within the
chain to finish the job, that is, make it fire at the appropriate time in
the sequence, when alone, without the prior hit, it would have failed to
fire it.

Again, according to the same account by Lorente de Nó (1939, p.
428), the deleterious effects of overstimulation from impulses outside
the chain can be explained. A neuron in the chain may fail to respond
to stimulation if, owing to repeated activity, it acquires a high threshold, and this failure to transmit the circulating impulses would mean
cessation of activity in a cell assembly. I proposed this kind of explanation previously (1958) to account for the downturn in the inverted U curve as an alternative to Hebb's suggestion that "the greater
bombardment may interfere with the delicate adjustments involved
in cue function, perhaps by facilitating irrelevant responses (a high
D arouses conflicting $_sH_r$'s?)" (Hebb, 1955, p. 250).

It seems reasonable to suppose that as diffuse bombardment from
the ARAS greatly exceeds an amount that is optimal for some simple
psychological function being mediated by a particular cell assembly,
the operation of that cell assembly will be impaired, and the performance being mediated by it will suffer accordingly. This line of reasoning suggests that the inverted-U relation should be found in quite

* The expression "excited states" is frequently used to refer to the upper end
of the activation continuum. In using this term I do not wish to imply increased
overt activity. In fact, overt activity may be reduced to a very low level at the
high end of the continuum, when—for example—a person is immobilized by
terror.

simple psychological functions. Present evidence appears to support this suggestion. A recent (unpublished) experiment by Bélanger and Feldman, which I shall describe later in this paper, indicates that in rats the inverted-U relation is found with simple bar-pressing performance, and an experiment by Finch (1938) suggests that even such a simple response as the unconditioned salivary response yields the inverted-U curve when plotted against activation level.

It may be noted that according to a response competition hypothesis, the inverted-U relation should appear most prominently in complex functions where opportunities for habit interference are greater than they are in the case of simple functions. According to the response competition hypothesis, in the limiting case where response is so simple that habit interference is negligible, the relation between response strength and activation level should be monotonic. Therefore, finding the nonmonotonic relation in such simple responses as bar pressing and salivation raises strong doubts that the habit interference explanation can account for the seemingly pervasive phenomenon of the inverted-U curve.

Principle of activation growing out of work on behavioral intensity

Even before the EEG work on desynchronization, the behavioral evidence had suggested the existence of some brain mechanism like the ARAS. The writings of Duffy (1951, 1957), Freeman (1948), and others of the "energetics" group have long stressed the importance of an intensity dimension in behavior.

In an attempt to obtain a measure of this intensity variable, Duffy relied mainly on records of muscular tension (1932) while Freeman's favorite indicator was palmar conductance (1948). These workers concluded from their experiments that there was a lawful relationship between a state of the organism, called "arousal," "energy mobilization," "activation," or simply "intensity" and level of performance. Moreover, they suggested that the relationship might be described by an inverted-U curve (Duffy, 1957). This suggestion has proved heuristic as indicated by the current experimental attack on the inverted-U hypothesis (Stennett, 1957a; Bindra, 1959; Cofer, 1959; Kendler, 1959).

The inverted U-shaped curve has been shown to hold in numerous learning and performance situations where the amount of induced muscle tension was varied systematically (Courts, 1942). These findings and those of Freeman (1948, p. 71) suggested that tension induction might be one of the many ways to increase activation level, but not until Pinneo's experiment (1961) was there sufficient direct evidence to draw this conclusion with confidence.

In Pinneo's experiment, 38 male college students were trained in an auditory tracking task. Physiological indicants of activation included

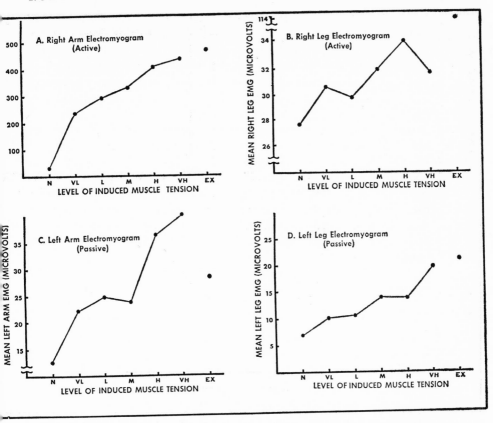

Figure 1. Muscle tension of active limbs (used in tracking or in squeezing on the dynamometer) and passive limbs (not used in any way, merely resting) as a function of induced muscle tension. Baseline intervals are as follows: No tension (N), very light tension (VL), light tension (L), heavy tension (H), very heavy tension (VH). The last unconnected point on each curve is for the "exertion" condition in which the majority of subjects exerted their maximum pull on the dynamometer during a period at the end of the experiment when they were not tracking. [Data from Pinneo, 1961, courtesy of the *Journal of Experimental Psychology*.]

heart rate, respiration rate, palmar conductance, frontal and occipital EEG, and EMG's from active and passive limbs. Following learning trials, the subjects were required to track while squeezing a hand dynamometer in order to maintain one of five predetermined levels of muscle tension.

Figures 1, 2, and 3 clearly show close agreement between amount of tension induced and level of activation as reflected in somatic, autonomic, and EEG indicants. One possible explanation of these results,

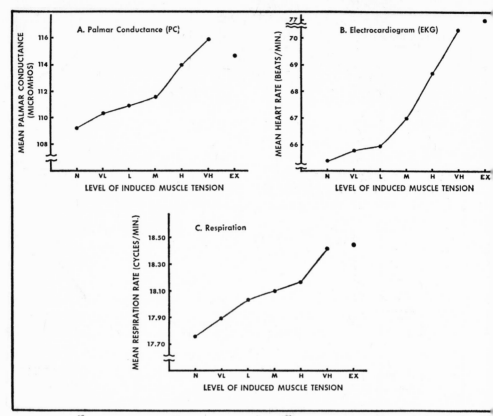

Figure 2. Relations between amount of induced muscle tension and peripheral indicants of autonomic nervous system activity. For key to abbreviations, see legend for Figure 1. [Data from Pinneo, 1961, courtesy of the *Journal of Experimental Psychology*.]

as Pinneo suggests, is that the proprioceptive return from the induced muscle tension produces generalized behavioral and physiological effects indirectly by increasing activity in the ARAS.

Drive and activation

A third approach to the activation principle was made by learning theorists, especially those of the Hull school. I have argued elsewhere (Malmo, 1958) that general drive (D), without the steering component, became identical in principle with activation or arousal. Set aside for the moment the attractive possibility of using ARAS as a neural model for mediation of D, and consider only the methodological advantages of physiological measures in the quantification of D. It seems that none of the other attempts to measure D have been really satisfactory, and that physiological indicants where applied have been

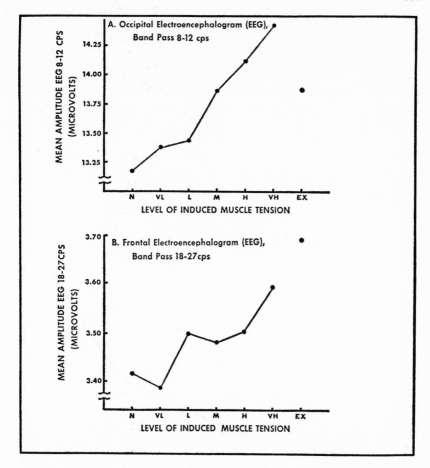

Figure 3. Relations between amount of induced muscle tension and EEG amplitudes. For key to abbreviations, see legend for Figure 1. [Data from Pinneo, 1961, courtesy of the *Journal of Experimental Psychology*.]

surprisingly effective. Learning theorists up to the present time have made only very occasional use of physiological measures. For instance, in arguing that a previously painful stimulus had lost its drive properties, Brown (1955) cited the absence of physiological reaction when the stimulus was applied. More recently, Spence (1958) has reported some success with physiological measures in his studies of "emotionally based" drive.

In keeping with traditional views concerning the place of physiological measures in psychology, on those few occasions that they were employed at all they were applied to aversive or emotionally based drive. According to the activation principle, however, it should be possible to use physiological measures to gauge appetitionally based as well as aversively based drive. This means, for instance, that in a water deprivation experiment there should be close correspondence between number of hours of deprivation and physiological level. That is, heart rate, for example, should be higher in an animal performing in a Skinner box after 36 hours of deprivation than after 24, higher still after 48 hours of deprivation and so on. In my Nebraska Symposium paper I stated that, as far as I was aware, this kind of experiment had not been reported (Malmo, 1958, p. 236).

Bélanger and Feldman in Montreal have recently completed such an experiment, and, as can be seen by inspecting Fig. 4 the results

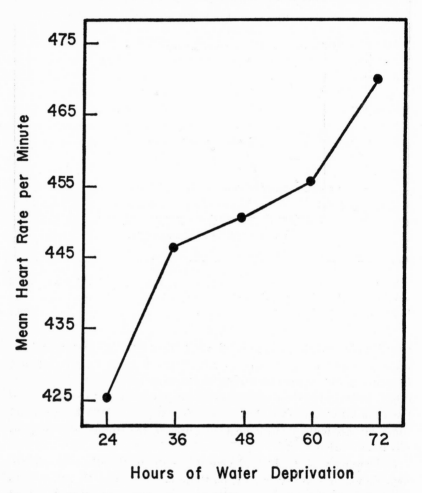

Figure 4. Data from Bélanger and Feldman showing relation between water deprivation and heart rate in rats (N=7). See text for explanation.

were as predicted by the activation hypothesis. Heart rate in rats showed progressive change corresponding with increasing hours of water deprivation. Although there were only seven rats in the group, this change in heart rate was highly significant. Deprivations were carried out serially on the same group of animals, commencing at 12 hours and proceeding to 24, 48 hours and so on with sufficient hydration (four to seven days) between deprivation periods to prevent any cumulative effects from affecting the experiments. Heart rate was picked up by means of wire electrodes inserted in the skin of the animals and was amplified and registered graphically by means of a Sanborn electrocardiograph. Particular care was taken to record heart rate under nearly the same conditions of stimulation each time, that is, when the animal was pressing on the lever in the Skinner box or drinking from the dispenser immediately after pressing. Under these conditions it was not possible to obtain sufficient heart-rate data at the 12-hour deprivation interval. Testing the animal under constant stimulating conditions is a very important methodological consideration. Some exploratory observations indicated that heart-rate measurements taken in a restraining compartment did not agree with those taken under the carefully controlled stimulus conditions provided by the Skinner box. I shall return to this finding later on because, aside from its methodological importance, I believe that it has considerable theoretical significance as well.

Figure 5 presents the behavioral data which are again in remarkably good agreement with prediction from the activation hypothesis. Up to the 48-hour deprivation interval there is an increasing monotonic relationship between number of bar presses and hours of deprivation which is strictly in accordance with Hullian theory. The accompanying rise in heart rate suggests that for this part of the curve, hours of deprivation and the physiological indicant are roughly equivalent as measures of drive. But after the 48-hour point on the curves, the combined heart rate and behavioral data support predictions previously made from activation theory (Malmo, 1958) and suggest that the Hullian position requires revision. This kind of downward turn in the response curve has usually been attributed to a physical weakening of the animal due to the deprivation of food or water. In the absence of physiological data such an assumption appeared reasonable in many cases, although it did not account for response decrement in certain experiments where physical weakening seemed to be ruled out (Finan, 1940; Freeman, 1940; Fuster, 1958; Kaplan, 1952; Stennett, 1957a). Attack on this problem with physiological methods should soon provide a definitive answer concerning the main determinants of this response decrement. The present experiment represents an important first step in a program of animal studies that should go a

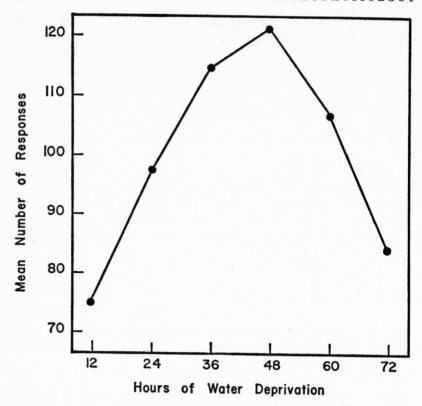

Figure 5. Data from Bélanger and Feldman showing relation between water deprivation and Skinner Box performance in rats (N=7). See text for explanation.

long way toward solving this problem. It is not claimed that this one experiment demolishes the inanition hypothesis, but it does seem that the results are opposed to it. Heart rate in the Minnesota starvation experiments was found lowered in the weakened individuals (Malmo, 1958, p. 252) whereas heart rate in the present experiment was markedly increased during the period when number of responses was declining. Moreover, Bélanger was careful to record the weights of the animals all through the experiments, and he observed only very slight changes in weight, even at the 72-hour deprivation interval. Again, it should be stressed that all through the experiment the animals received four to seven days of hydration between conditions. Furthermore, it is interesting to note that the animals continued to press the bar at fairly regular intervals in the high deprivation conditions (with response decrement). That is, their behavior did not appear as though they had "given up." The acts of pressing continued to occur regularly, only they were separated by longer temporal intervals than under more optimal conditions of deprivation.

The increasing monotonic curve for heart rate did not seem to be due simply to the physical conditions of exertion associated with the act of bar pressing. It is true that up to the peak of the performance curve increasing heart rate was accompanied by increasing frequency of bar pressing, but past this point, heart rate continued to show rise despite the decline in exertion due to bar pressing. One might conjecture that exercise may have had greater effect on heart rate under extreme deprivation, but this would be counterbalanced—to some extent, at least—by the reduced number of presses.

To control for possible serial effects in this experiment there were two checks. First, they obtained similar findings from a second group of rats in which the order of deprivation conditions was reversed, commencing with the 72-hour deprivation condition, and finishing with the 12-hour condition. Second, the group of rats that had the ascending order of deprivation intervals was tested one week after the end of the experiment under the 60-hour deprivation condition. Mean number of responses was 96.7 and mean heart rate was 458.9 beats per minute, thus providing good agreement with the results that were obtained in the main experiment.

Finally, it is possible to speculate along various lines about how the heart-rate data could be accounted for without involving the concept of activation. Obviously, further experimentation is needed, but it is encouraging, nonetheless, that the first animal experimentation specifically designed to explore the relation between appetitional drive and activation turned out according to prediction.

I have related findings (Malmo, 1961) to report from an experiment on heart-rate change in septal self-stimulation. The discovery by Olds and Milner (1954) that electrical stimulation of the septal area and other regions of the rat brain is reinforcing has been followed by a considerable amount of experimental work (Olds, 1955; 1959). But so far as I know, such experimentation has not resulted in any reports on the important question concerning the autonomic effects that are actually produced by the stimulating currents. I have not been able to find any study in which physiological recordings from the autonomic nervous system were taken simultaneously with intracranial self-stimulation.

It is of considerable importance for current theories of learning and reinforcement to determine, for instance, whether there is a significant measurable effect of such stimulation on autonomic functions, and if so whether the effect is predominantly sympathetic or parasympathetic, that is, mainly excitatory or inhibitory. My study was aimed at securing a preliminary answer to such questions.

Heart rate recording was chosen as a first step in the physiological investigation of intracranial self-stimulation (1) because of the clear way in which it reflects the balance between sympathetic and parasympathetic influences, (2) because a method for heart-rate recording in the free-roving rat was available, and (3) because Hess's previous septal stimulation studies in the cat had revealed heart-rate slowing (1957, p. 7).

Electrodes were implanted in the brains of seven 225-gram male hooded rats by the method previously described by Olds and Milner (1954). EKG electrodes were Michel wound clips with soldered bus wire attachments. A recovery period of at least three days was allowed after operation before commencing the two habituation sessions and the five subsequent 20-minute experimental sessions in the testing apparatus (Skinner box) all on consecutive days. A Hunter timer was used in the circuit to cut the current off after a period of 0.5 seconds if the rat continued to hold the lever down. During the initial stage, in teaching the animal to self-stimulate, the experimenter stimulated the animal by activating the bar-depression mechanism from outside the test box. In the latter half of the fifth experimental session the current was turned off so that when the animal pressed the bar there was no electrical stimulation; this was the extinction procedure.

During experimental sessions, continuous tracings of EKG and bar presses were taken on a polygraph.

Figure 6 is a semidiagrammatic representation illustrating part of the electrode track as seen in a brain section from Rat No. 5. This electrode placement appeared favorable for producing high frequency of self-stimulation and marked and consistent heart-rate slowing. The upper part of Figure 7 is a photograph of the EKG tracing from the first part of the fifth session. Note the slowing of heart rate associated with self-stimulation (6 volts), and also the increased amplitude of the R wave. Both phenomena were typical of the rather gross EKG changes regularly observed following self-stimulation in this animal. Systematic quantitative analysis of the heart-rate data for this animal showed that mean heart rate for periods with self-stimulation was 389.4 beats per minute compared with 442.2 beats per minute for preceding periods without intracranial stimulation. Corresponding mean values for subjects 6 and 10 that also had the five full training sessions were 442.8 and 451.2 for subject 6, and 400.8 and 428.4 for subject 10. All of these differences were highly significant statistically ($P < 0.001$).

The lower part of Figure 7 shows the heart rate deceleration produced in Rat No. 7 by the experimenter's presentation of a 7.5-volt stimulation to the septal area. Note the skipped beat. This marked slowing with skipped beat was a reproducible phenomenon in this

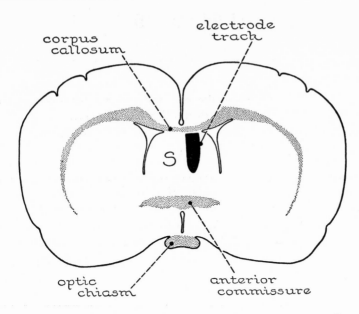

Figure 6. Semidiagrammatic representation of the rat forebrain illustrating part of the electrode track as seen in a brain section from subject 5. The track made by the stimulating tip of the electrode was in the septal area (see S in the diagram).

animal as it also was in Rat No. 8. Heart-rate slowing produced in Rats 7 and 8 by the experimenter or by their own self-stimulation was highly consistent and very reliable statistically.

For the three animals carried through to extinction, per cent bar pressing (computed by the method of Olds and Milner [1954, p. 421]) was from three to five times less than the per cent during reinforcement. No statistically significant heart-rate change was observed during extinction in any of the animals. The animals showed no habituation of the heart-rate slowing response to stimulation. Histological findings for Rat No. 3, dropped from the experiment after one session for lack of promise, showed failure of the electrode to penetrate through the *corpus callosum* into the septal area.

In summary, all six animals with positive histological findings (i.e., electrode track in the septal area) showed significant heart-rate slowing upon stimulation. Results clearly showed that septal stimulation, whether self-produced or presented by the experimenter, had the very consistent effect of slowing the rate at which the heart was beating. As far as heart rate is concerned, therefore, septal stimulation produced a parasympathetic or quieting effect with reinforcing properties. This finding is of interest in relation to the results of the study by

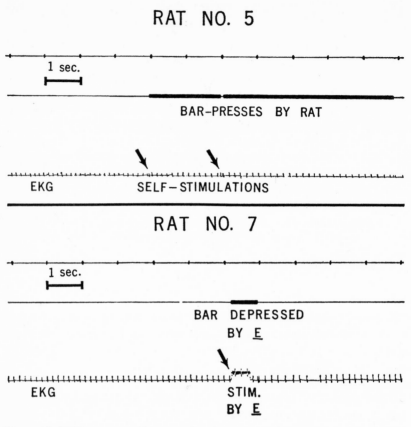

Figure 7. EKG tracings showing deceleration of heart rate produced by septal self-stimulation in animal No. 5, and by septal experimenter-produced stimulation in the brain of animal No. 7. Arrows indicate the onset of stimulation, and duration of stimulation may be seen in the artifact in the EKG tracing. Other switching artifacts in the EKG tracing occurred with onset and termination of bar pressing. Top line is time marker.

Brady and Nauta (1953) which, as Olds and Milner noted, "suggests that the septal area is a quieting system, for its surgical removal produced an extremely active animal" (1954, p. 426).

The fact that a consistent, objectively recordable physiological change of this kind occurs in association with the act of septal self-stimulation is encouraging with respect to further experimental inquiries into the nature of reinforcement produced by intracranial stimulation, and into the problem of reinforcement generally.

Putting these findings together with some previous findings of Olds suggests a specific line of attack on one major aspect of the reinforcement problem, that of the molecular (neural) events underlying the behaviorally observed (molar) phenomena of reinforcement. Olds' findings are summarized in his own words as follows: "if we implant electrodes in the medial lemniscus which is believed to fire the reticular formation, we produce zero percentage scores during acquisition time" (1955 p. 95). As Olds explains, zero percentage scores indicate that the stimulating currents are having punishing effects on the animals, and it thus appears that under the conditions employed by Olds increased activity in the ARAS had aversive effects. That is, it appeared that *reticular* stimulation (overstimulation?) had punishing effects. Conversely, the question is does *septal* stimulation have its rewarding effects by virtue of *reducing* the level of activity in the ARAS, and is the drop in heart rate that I observed merely *one* of the consequences of a much more general change initiating in the ARAS? With septal stimulation and electrographic recording of activity in the ARAS, it should be possible to launch an experimental attack on this problem.

CHARACTERISTICS OF ACTIVATION

The three approaches described in the previous section appear to lead to the same fundamental concept of activation. It will, of course, be difficult to state a precise definition of activation that will satisfy everyone. Neurophysiologically oriented workers will maintain a healthy scepticism concerning the so-called "peripheral" indicants of activation. The "energetics" group while welcoming the extended use of what is essentially their own methodology will, in company with some learning theorists, look askance at theoretical models that verge on neurologizing. Despite differences in point of view, however, it seems worth while to attempt to deal with certain major characteristics of activation on which we may expect a large measure of agreement.

Activation level a product of multiple factors

When a man is deprived of sleep for some 60 hours his activation level appears higher than it was before he had suffered sleep loss. Physiological indicants reveal an upward shift in activation level that is gradual and progressive throughout the vigil (Malmo and Surwillo, 1960). Having once demonstrated these physiological changes it is tempting to dispense with physiological recording in further work, assuming that 60 hours of deprivation will invariably produce a heightened state of activation. Such an assumption, however, cannot be made. An example will make clear why this assumption is untenable. A sleep-deprived subject requires constant stimulation to prevent him from going to sleep. It is a general finding in such studies that despite the best intentions of the subject to remain awake he will "catnap" if left alone. When he is working at a task trying to keep his efficiency from falling, the effect of major sleep loss is to produce a large increase in activation level. The important point to see here, however, is that the higher activation level is a combined product of the stimuli and their demands on him plus the condition of sleep loss. Without such stimulation, the subject would surely fall asleep and we know from our studies of sleep that physiological levels drop very rapidly as one drifts into sleep. It is obvious, therefore, that in the absence of the task, physiological indicants at 60 hours' deprivation would show lower, not higher, activation in comparison with the rested condition.

That the "drive state" is in large part determined by environmental stimulating factors is indicated also by the observations of Bélanger and Feldman in their water deprivation experiments. Incidental observations suggested that, in addition to being more variable, heart rates recorded from the animal in a restraining compartment seemed to be consistently lower than those that were recorded when the animal was pressing the lever or drinking. In the restraining compartment the animal could view the lever through glass so that apparently mere sight of the lever was insufficient stimulation to produce the full effect upon heart rate that was produced by the acts of pressing on the lever and drinking. It thus appeared that, with deprivation time approximately the same, activation level differed appreciably depending upon the conditions of external stimulation. These observations were merely incidental ones in this experiment, and they should be repeated; but they encourage the point of view that activation level is in large part a function of environmental stimulating conditions. The experiments of Campbell and Sheffield (1953) seem to point in the same direction. In the absence of sufficient environmental stimulation, food-deprived rats are no more active than satiated ones, but with stimulation they are much more active than the satiated controls.

The same kind of interaction effect appeared in Rust's (1960) study of sleep deprivation in rats. Rats trained to bar press for food were sleep deprived in increasing 12-hour periods up to 48 hours. Figure 8 presents the data relevant to this point. Compare bars E and F. High-rate bar pressing was defined as two or more bar presses in a 10-second period, low-rate bar pressing as one bar press in 10 seconds. Note the significantly faster heart beat for the high press-rate condition in the 48-hour sleep-deprived rats (20 rats in a self-control design). That this difference in heart rate was not simply an artifact of greater exertion in the high press-rate condition is indicated by the absence of a significant difference between these conditions under control conditions (without sleep deprivation). It is of interest that

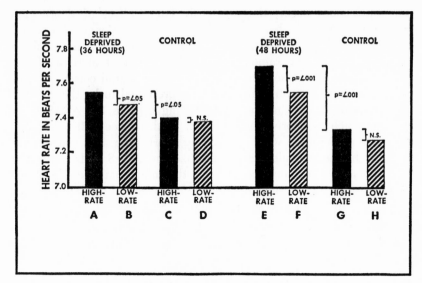

Figure 8. Heart rate differences between high- and low-rate bar-pressing performance. Levels of significance are indicated in brackets. See text for explanation. [Data from Rust, 1960.]

there was a significant difference in the same direction for the 36-hour condition (compare bars A and B), though not so large nor so significant a difference as for the 48-hour condition. The accelerated heart beats under conditions of high-rate bar pressing (in sleep-deprived rats) thus appeared to reflect an interaction between cue stimulation and the internal deprivation effects. Stated in another way, under the high press-rate condition the cues were more effective in controlling behavior, and heart rate was higher than under conditions (low-rate pressing) when cues were less effective. These results were interpreted as direct evidence of interaction between cue stimulation and internal deprivation effects.

Taking the example of a deprived rat in the Skinner box, the two major factors determining the level of activation in that situation are (1) the internal conditions produced by deprivation and (2) the environmental stimulating conditions. To restate a point previously made, level of activation does not seem to be simply determined by the condition of deprivation alone. This would mean that depriving an animal of water per se could not produce some direct effect on motor mechanisms such as a simple discharge into the cardiac accelerating mechanism, leading to increased heart rate. Instead of some direct effect of this kind leading immediately over to some observable effector action, deprivation appears to have a sensitizing effect that is undetectable (or latent). According to this view, when appropriate stimulation does occur, the previously latent effect of deprivation will show itself in the heart rate: within limits, the longer the period of deprivation the higher the heart rate. Furthermore, according to activation theory, the same central mechanism that increases heart rate also acts to increase bombardment of the cerebral cortex. As previously stated, this central mechanism is presumed to be the ARAS.*

What could be the means of sensitizing cells in the ARAS by a condition such as deprivation of water, food, or sleep? If some hormone like epinephrine were released by deprivation, it is conceivable that this hormone could act to sensitize the ARAS cells in degree proportional to the amount of time that the animal had been deprived. As a matter of fact, hormonal sensitization of neural mechanisms is a currently active area of research (Saffran, Schally, and Benfey, 1955; Dell, 1958).

There are some real difficulties in defending the position that the ARAS is a unitary intensity-mediating mechanism, because the ARAS does not appear to be a homogeneous anatomical system. Indeed, as Olszewski (1954) has shown, these central brain-stem structures appear very complex and highly differentiated. This unreassuring fact must not be forgotten, but neither should it be accepted as precluding the unitary function. As Lashley points out in the discussion of Olszewski's paper, structural differences are not reliable indices of function when unsupported by other evidence.

As a matter of fact, there is some important functional evidence which encourages the unitary view despite the structural complexity of the ARAS. Dell (1958) has found that: "Epinephrine does not activate selectively mammillothalamocingular systems, . . . but instead activates the ascending reticular system *en masse*, thus leading to a generalized cortical arousal" (p. 370). Control experiments showed that the activation effect was due to a direct action of the epinephrine at the reticular level and not to an effect on the cerebral cortex. Similar results have been obtained by Rothballer (1956).

Another kind of difficulty for the quantitative view would be posed by showing that patterned discharge from the ARAS to the cortex (not merely total quantity of discharge) was the crucial factor in supporting some behavioral action. Don't the effector patterns of standing, walking, and righting pose just such a difficulty? The relation of midbrain mechanisms to posture seems to be clearly one in which patterns of discharge from the midbrain are important. But the decorticate mammal (guinea pig, rabbit, cat, dog) in which the cortex of both hemispheres has been removed shows approximately

---

* It is very likely that the descending reticular activating system is involved here too, but, at the present stage of knowledge in this field, it does not seem wise to introduce further complications into the neuropsychological model.

normal postural and progressional activities (Dusser de Barenne, 1934, p. 229). Since the activation concept under review deals with bombardment of the cerebral cortex, it appears that these noncortically mediated response patterns fall outside of phenomena under present consideration.

I should add, finally, that my admittedly speculative suggestion concerning hormonal sensitization is by no means essential to the main point—which is that the behavioral evidence clearly shows the effects of deprivation to be latent (i.e., unobservable) under certain conditions. Moreover, this stress placed on the latent effects of deprivation is not mere hairsplitting. In addition to being required for an explanation of the Montreal experiments, this concept of latent deprivation effects appears to account in large measure for the findings of Campbell and Sheffield (1953), and more generally for the failure of random activity to adequately serve as a measure of drive or activation (Malmo, 1958).

Activation and the S-R framework

As the product of interaction between internal (perhaps hormonal) conditions and external stimulating ones, activation cannot be very reasonably classified as either stimulus or response. This means that the physiological measurements that are used to gauge level of activation do not fit very well into the S-R formula. It is perhaps useful to think of these physiological conditions as part of O in the S-O-R formula (Woodworth and Schlosberg, 1954, p. 2).

The momentary physiological reaction to a discrete stimulus like the sudden rise in palmar conductance accompanying pin-prick is not of primary concern to us in our study of activation. This kind of S-R reaction, important as it undoubtedly is for investigating other problems, is of little relevance for the study of activation, compared with the longer lasting changes. As Schlosberg has put it to me in personal communication, in employing skin conductance to gauge level of activation, one observes the "tides" and not the "ripples." I do not mean to disparage studies that use physiological reactions as R terms in the strict S-R sense. It is just that in this chapter I am concerned with physiological functions only insofar as they are related to activation.

It may be queried whether we are dealing with a needless and hairsplitting distinction by saying that activation is not a response. However, the kind of difference I have in mind appears quite distinct and useful to keep in mind, though it should not be stressed unduly. Basically, it is the same distinction which Woodworth and Schlosberg (1956) make when they draw particular attention to the difference between slow and rapid changes in skin conductance. As examples of rapid changes in skin conductance, there are the "GSRs" as R terms in conditioned responses and in free association tests. Examples of slow skin-conductance changes, on the other hand, are the gradual downward drifts that occur over hours during sleep (see Fig. 10), the slow downward changes in skin conductance in subjects as they become gradually habituated to an experimental situation (Davis, 1934; Duffy and Lacey, 1946), and (going up the activation scale) the progressive upward changes in conductance during a vigil (Malmo, 1958).

I would not deny that there are stimuli and responses going on in the physiological systems, but at the present time I see no way of identifying and handling them. It should be added, however, that this does not give one license to disregard completely the antecedents of physiological changes. For instance, if the hand of a sleeping subject becomes hot by being covered with heavy bedclothing, the local thermal sweating induced thereby will bring about a sudden rise in palmar conductance which has nothing to do with activation. Or sleep may be induced by certain drugs which have a specific stimulating effect on respiration, such that respiration rate will not fall during sleep as it usually does (see Fig. 11 for curve obtained under nondrug conditions). Furthermore, artifacts due to movement and postural shifts may prevent muscle potentials from serving as reliable indicants of activation level. I would stress that in working experimentally with activation, it is essential *not* to work with uncontrolled conditions of cue stimulation and without regard to the subject's behavior (especially his motor activity).

Limitations of the activation concept

I am not attempting to solve the problem of selection, i.e., the problem of finding the neurophysiological mechanisms that determine which cues in the animal's environment are prepotent in the sense of winning out over other cues in triggering off a pattern of effector action. This point seems clear enough, especially when it is stressed that activation has no steering function; and yet there is still the risk that some critics may misunderstand and state as one shortcoming of this theory that it does not adequately handle the problem of selection. The theory may be open to criticism on the grounds that it is limited, but it should not be criticized for failing to do something which it was not intended to do.

It will be noted that in general an attempt is made to raise theoretical questions that stand a good chance of being answered by available experimental techniques. Schematically, the experimental paradigm is as follows:

Activation level:	Low	Moderate	High
Expected performance level:	Low	Optimal	Low

It is important to stress that the measure denoted by "moderate activation level" has meaning only in relative (not in absolute) terms. That is, the level is "moderate" because it is higher than that of the low activation condition, and lower than the level of the high activation condition. To the best of my knowledge, comparisons yielding the inverted-U function have invariably been of the within-individual, within-task kind, which means that the level of activation which was found to be optimal for one individual and one task was not presumed to be the optimal level of activation for another individual, or for another task.

To repeat, there is little doubt that for the study of activation phenomena per se the within-individual design is far more powerful than any between-individual design. But if the investigator's main interest happens to be individual differences he is, of course, forced to employ a between-individual design. In these circumstances, as in the case of many clinically oriented experiments, some precision is sacrificed for an important purpose. In some earlier studies from our laboratory motor control was found to be inferior to that of normals in a group of psychoneurotics whose activation level, as gauged by heart rate and blood pressure, appeared abnormally high (Malmo, Shagass, Bélanger and Smith, 1951, p. 543; Malmo, Shagass, and Smith, 1951, p. 368; Malmo and Shagass, 1952, p. 89). Martin has recently reviewed the literature in this field, noting Eysenck's suggestion that "neurotics as a group demonstrate overreactivity of the sympathetic division of the A.N.S. in response to stressful stimuli" (1961, p. 450).

It should perhaps be explicitly stated that performance decrement (or increment) is by no means wholly dependent upon activation conditions. Results from a recent unpublished experiment of mine provides a good example of this point. On alternate trials, subjects performed a manual tracking task with divided, and unified set. That is, under the condition of unified set they tracked to an auditory cue, knowing that was all they would have to do during that trial. Under the condition of divided set, they carried out exactly the same task but they expected at any moment to receive a vibratory stimulus that would start them on a double-tracking task involving operation of a foot pedal to track to the vibratory cue, in addition to continued manual tracking to the auditory cue. Although, as mentioned, the physical demands of the tracking task were exactly the same under both conditions, the tracking score was significantly worse under the condition of divided set. But this performance decrement appeared to be entirely independent of any change in activation, because comparison

of the two conditions with an extensive battery of physiological indicants failed to show a single reliable difference.

Again, the theoretical formulations may be criticized for being too
narrow. But it must be kept in mind that their narrowness is due to
the close nexus between theory and experiment in this program.
These formulations may also be criticized for an unjustifiable assumption in the postulation of a communal drive mechanism. One may well
ask where the evidence is that proves the existence of a state of
general drive. In dealing with this kind of question, it is essential to
refer back to the outline of the experimental paradigm. The experimental induction of the three discriminable activation levels referred
to in the outline depends on the controlled variation of certain conditions in the subject's environment. The fact that by varying conditions as dissimilar as appetitional deprivations and verbal incentives
it is possible to produce similar shifts in physiological indicants provides
a sound basis for introducing the operationally defined concept of
activation level that cuts across traditional demarcation lines of specific
drives. All this, of course, does not constitute final proof for a communal drive mechanism. Certainly further data are required before it is
even safe to conclude equivalence of drive conditions in the alteration
of physiological levels, to say nothing of proving the existence of a
communal drive mechanism.

INTERRELATIONS BETWEEN PHYSIO-
LOGICAL INDICANTS OF ACTIVATION

Criticism directed against physiological measures as indicants of activation usually involves one or both of the following points. The first
objection is that intercorrelations between physiological measures are
so low that it is unreasonable to consider their use for gauging a single
dimension of behavior. A second objection is that activation properly
refers to events in the brain and that the correspondence between
these central events and what may be observed in such peripheral
functions as heart rate, respiration, muscle tension, and the like is not
close enough to permit valid inferences from the peripheral events
to the central ones. In the following section, I shall attempt to answer
these criticisms.

Intra- and interindividual correlations among physiological indicants
of activation

In an unpublished paper, Schnore and I have discussed certain mis-
conceptions that have confused some critics of physiological methods.
The most serious misunderstanding concerns correlations among physiological measures. It is true that *inter*individual correlations are low,

but this fact is actually irrelevant insofar as using these measures to gauge activation is concerned. The important question is whether significant *intra*individual correlations are found in a sufficiently high proportion of individuals, and the answer appears to be yes (Schnore, 1959).

What the low *inter*individual correlations mean, of course, is that an individual in any given situation may have a heart rate that is high relative to the mean heart rate for the group, and at the same time have a respiration rate or a blood pressure that is low relative to the group mean. These findings are in line with the principle of physiological specificity that is now supported by several lines of evidence.* Physiological specificity is a separate problem that is in no way crucial for the activation hypothesis. An illustration will make this clear. Take a rather extreme example of an individual with very *high* heart rate (say 95 when the mean for his group under specified conditions is 75) and very *low* palmar conductance (50 micromhos when the group mean is 100). In an experiment with varied incentive, in going from a low incentive to a high incentive condition this subject will likely show an increase in heart rate from 95 to say 110 and an increase in palmar conductance from 50 to say 60 micromhos. The main point is that even though the subject's heart rate is already high compared with the mean for his group, it goes still higher (concordantly with palmar conductance) when the stimulating situation increases the level of activation. This is the kind of intraindividual correlation between physiological measures† that is required for gauging the dimension of activation and, to repeat, the evidence strongly indicates that the intraindividual correlations are sufficiently high for this purpose.

RELATIONS BETWEEN CENTRAL AND PERIPHERAL INDICANTS OF ACTIVATION

As previously noted, the pioneer EEG workers observed definite changes in EEG pattern accompanying major shifts in the conscious state of the subject. Moreover, they recognized a continuum of in-

---

* The general principle of physiological specificity states that under significantly different conditions of stimulation individuals exhibit idiosyncratic but highly stereotyped patterns of autonomic and somatic activation. I use the term *physiological specificity* as a generic reference to autonomic-response stereotypy (Lacey and Lacey, 1958) to symptom specificity (Malmo and Shagass, 1949), and to stereotypy of somatic and autonomic activation patterns (Schnore, 1959).

† It is not claimed, however, that all physiological measures are equally useful for the purpose of gauging activation level. On the contrary, as Schnore's experiments have suggested, some measures appear superior to others, and eventually we may be able to select the most discriminating ones and thus improve our measurement (Schnore, 1959).

creasing activation usually referred to as the sleep-waking-excitement continuum, just as other workers like Freeman (1948) and Duffy (1957) employing peripheral measures of palmar sweating and muscular tension recognized it. Among the early workers in this field, Darrow (1947) studied EEG and other measures simultaneously, but only very recently have techniques been made available that can provide the kind of quantitative EEG measurements required for critical comparisons along the activation continuum. That is, from simple inspection of the raw EEG tracing it is possible to see gross differences between sleeping and waking, or between a drowsy, relaxed state and one of extreme alertness. But for experiments on activation it is necessary to have an instrument that will reveal measurable differences for "points" lying closer to each other on the activation continuum. For example, it is essential to have a measure that will discriminate reliably between a moderately alert and a highly alert state. For such discriminations the method of inspection will not do, and a device is required for objective quantification of the wave forms.

Because of its complexity the EEG tracing has been difficult to quantify, and although gross differences in activation level could be detected by simple inspection of the tracing, this method was too crude for more detailed work. However, with the advent of EEG frequency analyzers, quantification of the EEG looked promising because these analyzers were designed to provide quantified EEG data for each of many different narrow frequency bands. Unfortunately, these instruments have not proved useful because of insufficient stability. In our laboratory we have been trying band-pass filters to provide stable quantification of various selected frequency bands in which we are primarily interested (Ross and Davis, 1958). Results thus far appear highly encouraging.

Data indicating relationships between EEG and other physiological functions

In a recent sleep-deprivation experiment, we found that palmar conductance and respiration showed progressive rise during the vigil, indicating increasing activation with deprivation of sleep. In the same experiment we recorded EEG and, by means of a band-pass filter, obtained a quantified write-out of frequencies from 8–12 per second, in the alpha range. It will be recalled that the classical picture of activation is reduction in the amount of alpha activity. Therefore, what we might expect to find in this experiment is progressive decrease in the amount of alpha activity. As a matter of fact, this is exactly what was found (Malmo and Surwillo, 1960).

As Stennett (1957b) has shown, however, the relationship between

EEG alpha activity and other physiological variables is sometimes curvilinear. In the sleep-deprivation experiments physiological measurements were taken under highly activating conditions and at this high end of the continuum further increase in activation seems invariably to decrease the amount of alpha activity. But at the lower end of the continuum with the subject in a drowsy state, increased activation has the opposite effect on alpha activity. An alerting stimulus, instead of producing a flattening of the EEG tracing, will actually produce an augmentation of the alpha activity. This has sometimes been referred to as a "paradoxical" reaction, although it seems paradoxical only when it is assumed that the relation between activation level and alpha amplitude is a decreasing monotonic one throughout the entire activation continuum. But Stennett (1957b) has shown that the relationship is not monotonic. From his data he plotted a curve which has the shape of an inverted U. From this curve it would be predicted that with a drowsy subject, stimulation should *increase* alpha amplitude. From the same inverted-U curve it would also be predicted that a subject whose activation level was sufficiently high (past the peak of the curve) before stimulation would show a *decrease* in alpha amplitude. Actually, some experiments on startle by Bartoshuk (1959) fit these predictions very well.

Recent data indicate the usefulness of a 2–4 cycles per second bandpass filter in experiments on sleep. The data in the figures that follow represent mean values from three men who slept all night in our laboratory after serving as subjects in our sleep deprivation experiments.

Bipolar sponge electrodes, soaked in electrode jelly and attached to the subject by Lastonet bands, were used for the parietal EEG placement (two thirds of the distance from nasion to inion, and 3 cm. from the midline on each side). The primary tracing was recorded by an Edin electroencephalograph, and the two secondary tracings were integrations of the EEG potentials that were passed through band-pass filters for selective amplification of signals in the 2–4 and 8–12 cycles per second frequency bands. Measurements on the secondary tracings were carried out with special rulers, and these measurements were converted to microvolt values by reference to calibration standards.

Method of recording and measuring palmar conductance was similar to that described by Stennett (1957a).

Electrocardiograms were picked up from electrodes placed on contralateral limbs, and heart rates were determined from measurements of electrocardiotachometric tracings. Respiration rates were obtained by means of a Phipps and Bird pneumograph.

All three subjects slept well throughout the night (approximately from 10 P.M. to 9 A.M. after some 60 hours without sleep). Phys-

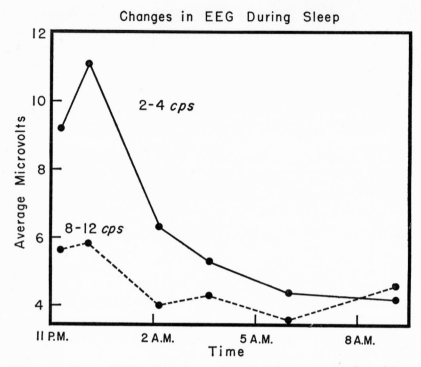

Figure 9. Mean EEG values from three healthy young male subjects during a night's sleep. Subjects had been sleep-deprived. Band-pass filters were used in connection with electronic integrators to provide quantitative data in the two different frequency bands.

iological recordings were carried out continuously during the whole period of sleep in each case, and except for occasional attention to electrodes (e.g., application of electrode jelly and saline to electrodes) the subjects were undisturbed.

Four pairs of cellulose sponge electrodes were attached to the four limbs (to the pronator teres muscles of the arms and the peroneal muscles of the legs) for the purpose of recording muscle potentials. Primary muscle-potential tracings were recorded on the chart of a custom built Edin electromyograph (EMG). Electronic integrators (employing the condenser charge-discharge principle, like those used for the secondary EEG tracings), attached in parallel across the galvanometers of this EMG unit, integrated the muscle potentials over successive four-second periods.

These muscle-potential tracings were used to record movements and periods of restlessness during sleep. Five-minute periods free from muscle-potential activity and preceded by at least five minutes of movement-free tracings were chosen for measurement in order to pro-

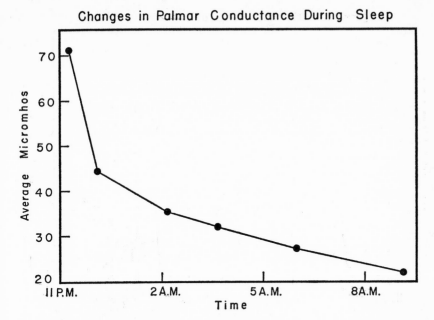

Figure 10. Mean palmar conductant values from the same subjects at the same time during sleep as in Figure 9.

vide the values plotted in Figures 9–11. The actual times plotted on the baseline represent the medians for the three subjects. In each instance the three times were close to one another.

In Figure 9 observe that, following a brief rise early in sleep, the upper curve for 2–4 cycles per second falls continuously during the entire period of sleep. This curve is consistent with published accounts of changes in EEG during sleep noted by inspection of the raw tracings (Lindsley, 1957, p. 68). Early in sleep there is an increase in slow waves around 2–4 cycles per second, but as sleep continues these waves are replaced by even slower ones. As far as I am aware, the data in Figure 9 represent the first use of a 2–4 band-pass filter to quantify the EEG. The curve for 8–12 cycles per second EEG also shows some fall, and the voltage is low in accordance with the well-known disappearance of alpha waves from the raw tracings during sleep.

Figures 10 and 11 show data for palmar conductance, heart rate, and respiration, that were recorded at the same time as the EEG data. From the second plotted point on, there is rather close resemblance between these curves and the one for 2–4 cycles per second EEG. It seems likely that a band-pass filter for fast frequencies in the beta range might yield a continuously falling curve commencing with

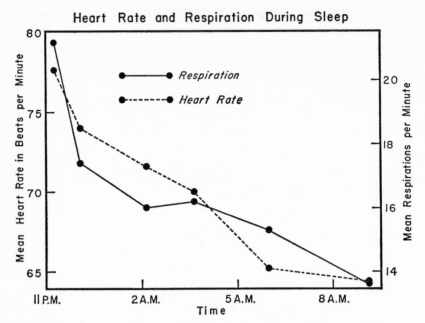

Figure 11. Mean values for heart rate and respiration from the same subjects at the same times during sleep as in Figures 9 and 10.

drowsiness and continuing through the onset and early stages of sleep. There are serious technical difficulties in quantifying the next step of frequencies above the alpha band, but we are hopeful that a band-pass filter that has recently been constructed in our laboratory will overcome these difficulties.

Direct alteration of ARAS activity by means of electrical stimulation and related animal experimentation

The most relevant experiment on direct stimulation of the ARAS is, as far as I know, the one by Fuster (1958) that was mentioned earlier. By stimulating in the same part of the ARAS that produces the EEG picture of activation, Fuster was able to produce improved discrimination performance in the monkey. Presumably this effect was achieved by causing a larger number of impulses from the ARAS to bombard the cortex. The assumption would be that before the onset of electrical stimulation the cortex was not receiving sufficient bombardment for optimal performance (Hebb, 1955) and that ARAS stimulation brought total bombardment in the cortex closer to the optimal value. The situation may not be as simple as this, but the success of the Fuster experiment encourages further experimentation along these same lines. Finding that level of performance can be altered by electrical stimulation of the ARAS opens up the exciting possibility that if amount of neural activity in the ARAS can be measured, we might find a direct correlation between a central measure of activation and level of performance. For instance, the Bélanger and Feldman experiment described earlier might be repeated with the addition of recordings from the ARAS. The aim of such an experiment would be to determine whether the continuous rise in the heart-rate curve with increasing deprivation times could be matched by a similar rise in amplitude of deflections from recording in the ARAS with implanted electrodes. Recent neurophysiological experiments appear encouraging with respect to the feasibility of such an approach (Li and Jasper, 1953, pp. 124–125; Magoun, 1958, p. 68).

EFFECTS OF INCREASED ACTIVATION ON LOCALIZED SKELETAL-MUSCLE TENSION IN PSYCHIATRIC PATIENTS

The implication of activation theory for various clinical phenomena might very well be the topic of a separate paper. Certainly there is not space to deal at length with the topic here. I have chosen, therefore, to present a few recent observations, chiefly in order to suggest how level of activation may be studied in relation to a clinical phenomenon.

The graph in Figure 12 illustrates what appears to be a general finding in patients complaining of tensional discomfort in a localized muscular site. The data for the curves plotted in the figure were obtained from a psychiatric patient, a 42-year old woman who complained of muscular discomfort localized in the left thigh. In the session when these data were taken electromyograms (EMGs) were recorded from various muscles over the body; those from the left and right thighs are shown in the figure. The patient was engaged in pursuit tracking using an apparatus similar to the one employed by Surwillo (1955, 1956). Figure 12 shows that when a loud distracting noise, of the kind described by Schnore (1959) was presented during tracking, the tension in the left thigh was very much higher than that of the right thigh. When tracking was carried out under distraction-free conditions this tensional difference between thighs was not observed.

Interpretation of these data seems quite straightforward. When level of activation was increased by presenting a loud distracting noise the effect was shown entirely in one muscle group, the left thigh, which was the symptom area in this patient. Simultaneous recordings of tension from other parts of the body showed that the tension was

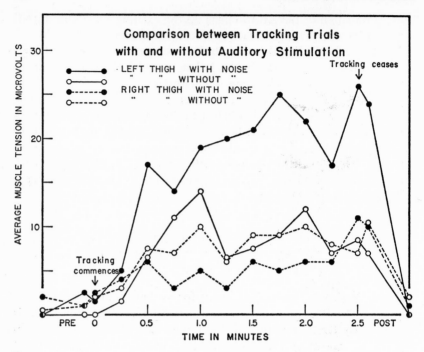

Figure 12. Mean muscle tension from left thigh and right thigh from patient with complaint of tensional discomfort in the left thigh. Note that when patient was performing the tracking task under distraction (loud noise), tension rose in the left thigh but not in the right. See text for explanation.

specific to the left thigh and was not merely increased on the whole left side of the body.

The specificity of the left thigh in indicating the higher activation is quite clear. Observe that tension in the thigh muscles on the opposite side of the body actually fell slightly under the activating condition.

The same procedure was carried out with a second patient, a young girl of 28, who complained of a distressing feeling of tightness in the neck on the right side. Results were similar to the ones obtained in the previous case, with activation again showing its effect specifically in the symptom area. When the loud distracting noise was turned on during tracking, tension in this area showed marked increase, whereas tension in the muscles on the left side of the neck showed no rise whatever.

Very similar results were obtained from two additional patients whose areas of tensional discomfort were localized in still different parts of the body. One woman with complaint of tension on the left side of her neck served as a useful control for the patient previously described with tension localized in the opposite side of the neck. No tracking experiment was carried out with this patient. Apparently the sight of the EMG recording room for the first time was itself sufficient to increase the amplitude of muscle potentials from the symptom area so that they became appreciably higher than those on the opposite side of her neck. The other woman (fourth patient in this series) complained of tensional discomfort that appeared to originate in the left shoulder. EMGs were recorded from the left and right shoulders of this patient while she lay in bed listening to the playback of a recorded interview. During the first part of the playback, tension was about the same on the two sides of the body. But when the topic of her dead sister commenced to come over the speaker, tension in the left shoulder became much greater than that in the right.

As far as could be determined, the EMG data from all these patients were consistent in suggesting that for skeletal-muscle tension in patients with well-developed tensional symptoms, increasing the activation level up to a certain point has the effect of raising muscle tension in one localized muscle group, the one in which the patient complained of tensional discomfort. It was not necessary for the patient actually to feel the discomfort during the experimental session for this differential result to appear. I have been using the term "symptom area" to refer to the muscle group where the discomfort was localized when present.

Interesting findings that appear to parallel those from the patients were obtained from three young male nonpatient subjects in our recent investigation of sleep deprivation. As previously mentioned, evidence from EEG, palmar conductance, and respiration indicated that activation during tracking increased progressively with hours of sleep deprivation. In addition to these other physiological tracings, EMGs from various areas over the body were also recorded. One muscle area, a different one for each subject, showed significant rise in tension over the vigil. It was the neck muscles in one subject, the forehead in another, and the biceps muscle of the right arm in the third. In each case the one muscle showed statistically significant rise in tension, and in none of the subjects was there significant tensional rise in any other muscle. In fact, there was regularly progressive and very significant fall in the tension of the left forearm in all three subjects. As far as I know, none of the men actually complained of tensional discomfort in the areas showing rise in tension during the vigil.

Where high-level activation is long continued, as in a vigil or in certain psychoneurotic patients, it appears that skeletal tension may become localized to a single muscle group. The discomfort associated with this tension in some patients can become extremely severe. It should be noted that in one-session experiments, where rise in activation was for relatively short intervals of time, tensional rise occurred in more than one muscle group (Surwillo, 1956; Stennett, 1957a).

Methodologically, these results are important because they reveal a difference between EMGs and some other physiological measures with respect to gauging activation. Unlike heart rate or respiration rate that invariably yields one measure no matter how it is recorded, there are as many measures of muscle tension as there are muscles that can be recorded from. It appears that when sufficient care is taken, EMGs may be very valuable in helping to gauge activation, but that considerable caution is required in the interpretation of results, and especially in the interpretation of negative results.

From the clinical point of view it seems an interesting speculation that the patient's localized muscle tension may itself actually increase the general activation level. If, as seems reasonable, the area of localized muscle tension in the patient acts like tension that is induced, for example, by having a subject squeeze on a dynamometer, then, from the results of Pinneo's experiment (1961), as the patient's muscle tension increased, general activation level would rise with it. The results of two more recent experiments are also in line with this general notion. Meyer and Noble (1958) found that induced tension interacted with "anxiety" in verbal-maze learning ("anxiety" measured by means of the MAS [Taylor, 1953]), while Kuethe and Eriksen (1957) in a study of stereotypy likewise reported a significant interaction between these two variables when "anxiety" was experimentally produced by means of electric shocks. The MAS appears to select individuals who are significantly above the mean in activation, and from the results of Schnore (1959) and Feldman (1961) it seems safe to conclude that anticipation of shock also leads to increased levels of physiological activity. In short, generalizing from the induced tension experiments, it seems reasonable to suppose that a patient's muscular tension in a small focal area might have the general effect of increasing activation. If such is the case symptomatic treatment might have significant general as well as specific effects. Although based on only one patient, Yates' (1958) results from symptomatic treatment of tics seems encouraging with respect to the feasibility of research in this general area.

SUMMARY

The neuropsychological dimension of activation may be briefly described as follows. The continuum extending from deep sleep at the low activation end to "excited" states at the high activation end is a function of the amount of cortical bombardment by the ARAS, such that the greater the cortical bombardment the higher the activation. The shape of the curve relating level of performance to level of activation is that of an inverted U: from low activation up to a point that is optimal for a given performance or function, level of performance rises monotonically with increasing activation level; but past this optimal point the relation becomes nonmonotonic: further increase in activation beyond this point produces fall in performance level, this fall being directly related to the amount of the increase in level of activation.

Long before the discovery of the ARAS the behavioral evidence of Duffy, Freeman, and others of the "energetics" group had suggested the existence of some such brain mechanism. Moreover, learning theorists of the Hull school have in their concept of the general drive state come very close to the activation principle. Up to the present time they have employed physiological measures only sparingly and have restricted their use to the aversive aspects of drive. But with evidence that such measures may also be applied to nonaversive (appetitional) drive, it seems likely that the present rather unsatisfactory measures of drive may eventually be replaced by physiological indicants.

Activation has a number of main characteristics that may be listed as follows: (1) Activation has no steering function in behavior. (2) It is considerably broader than emotion. (3) Activation is not a state that can be inferred from knowledge of antecedent conditions alone, because it is the product of an interaction between internal conditions such as hunger or thirst and external cues. (4) Activation does not fit very well into the S-R formula. It is a phenomenon of slow changes, of drifts in level with a time order of minutes (even hours), not of seconds or fractions thereof. (5) Activation is a quantifiable dimension and the evidence indicates that physiological measures show a sufficiently high intraindividual concordance for quantifying this dimension.

It is suggested that activation is mediated chiefly through the ARAS which seems, in the main, to be an intensity system. Neurophysiological findings strongly suggest that it may be possible to achieve more precise measurement of activation through a direct recording of discharge by the ARAS into the cerebral cortex. Research on this problem is urgently needed.

The concept of activation appears to have wide application to phenomena in the field of clinical psychology. As one illustration, in this paper, activation was applied to clinical phenomena of tensional symptoms.

References

Bartoshuk, A. K. Electromyographic reactions to strong auditory stimulation as a function of alpha amplitude. *J. comp. physiol., Psychol.*, 1959, 52, 540–545.

Bindra, D. *Motivation. A systematic reinterpretation.* New York: Ronald, 1959.

Brady, J. V., & Nauta, W. J. H. Subcortical mechanisms in emotional behavior: affective changes following septal forebrain lesions in the albino rat. *J. comp. physiol. Psychol.*, 1953, 46, 339–346.

Brown, J. S. Pleasure-seeking behavior and the drive-reduction hypothesis. *Psychol. Rev.*, 1955, 62, 169–179.

Campbell, B. A., & Sheffield, F. D. Relation of random activity to food deprivation. *J. comp. physiol. Psychol.*, 1953, 46, 320–326.

Cofer, C. N. Motivation. *Ann. Rev. Psychol.*, 1959, 10, 173–202.

Courts, F. A. Relations between muscular tension and performance. *Psychol. Bull.*, 1942, 39, 347–367.

Darrow, C. W. Psychological and psychophysiological significance of the electroencephalogram. *Psychol. Rev.*, 1947, 54, 157–168.

Davis, R. C. Modification of the galvanic reflex by daily repetition of a stimulus. *J. exper. Psychol.*, 1934, 17, 504–535.

Dell, P. C. Humoral effects on the brain stem reticular formations. In H. H. Jasper, L. D. Proctor, R. S. Knighton, W. C. Noshay, & R. T. Costello (Eds.), *Reticular formation of the brain.* Toronto: Little, Brown, 1958, 365–379.

Duffy, Elizabeth. The measurement of muscular tension as a technique for the study of emotional tendencies. *Amer. J. Psychol.*, 1932, 44, 146–162.

Duffy, Elizabeth. The concept of energy mobilization. *Psychol. Rev.*, 1951, 58, 30–40.

Duffy, Elizabeth. The psychological significance of the concept of "arousal" or "activation." *Psychol. Rev.*, 1957, 64, 265–275.

Duffy, Elizabeth, & Lacey, O. L. Adaptation in energy mobilization: changes in general level of palmar skin conductance. *J. exper. Psychol.*, 1946, 36, 437–452.

Dusser de Barenne, J. G. The labyrinthine and postural mechanisms. In C. Murchison (Ed.), *A handbook of general experimental psychology.* Worcester, Mass: Clark Univ. Press, 1934, 204–246.

Feldman, S. M. Differential effects of shock in human maze learning. *J. exper. Psychol.*, 1961, 62, 171–178.

Finan, J. L. Quantitative studies of motivation. I. Strength of conditioning in rats under varying degrees of hunger. *J. comp. Psychol.*, 1940, 29, 119–134.

Finch, G. Hunger as a determinant of conditional and unconditional salivary response magnitude. *Amer. J. Physiol.*, 1938, 123, 379–382.

Freeman, G. L. The relationship between performance level and bodily activity level. *J. exper. Psychol.*, 1940, 26, 602–608.

Freeman, G. L. *The energetics of human behavior.* Ithaca, N.Y.: Cornell Univer. Press, 1948.

Fuster, J. M. Effects of stimulation of brain stem on tachistoscopic perception. *Science*, 1958, 127, 150.

Hebb, D. O. *The organization of behavior.* New York: Wiley, 1949.

Hebb, D. O. Drives and the C.N.S. (conceptual nervous system). *Psychol. Rev.*, 1955, 62, 243–254.

Hebb, D. O. *A textbook of psychology.* Philadelphia: Saunders, 1958.

Hess, W. R. *The functional organization of the diencephalon.* New York: Grune & Stratton, 1957.

Jasper, H. H. Electroencephalography. In W. Penfield & T. C. Erickson

(Eds.), *Epilepsy and cerebral locali-zation*. Springfield, Ill.: Charles C Thomas, 1941, 380–454.

Kaplan, M. The effects of noxious stim-ulus intensity and duration during intermittent reinforcement of escape behavior. *J. comp. physiol. Psychol.*, 1952, *45*, 538–549.

Kendler, H. H. Learning. *Ann. Rev. Psychol.*, 1959, *10*, 43–88.

Kuethe, J. L., & Eriksen, C. W. Person-ality, anxiety, and muscle tension as determinants of response stereotypy. *J. abnorm. soc. Psychol.*, 1957, *54*, 400–404.

Lacey, J. I., & Lacey, Beatrice C. Verification and extension of the principle of autonomic response-stereotypy. *Amer. J. Psychol.*, 1958, *71*, 50–73.

Li, C. L., & Jasper, H. H. Microelec-trode studies of the electrical activity of the cerebral cortex in the cat. *J. Physiol.*, 1953, *121*, 117–140.

Lindsley, D. B. Emotion. In S. S. Stevens (Ed.), *Handbook of experi-mental psychology*. New York: Wiley, 1951, 473–516.

Lindsley, D. B. Psychophysiology and motivation. In M. R. Jones (Ed.), *Nebraska symposium on motivation 1957*. Lincoln Neb.: Univ. Nebr. Press, 1957, 44–105.

Lorente de Nó, R. Transmission of im-pulses through cranial motor nuclei. *J. Neurophysiol.*, 1939, *2*, 402–464.

Magoun, H. W. *The waking brain*. Springfield, Ill.: Charles C Thomas, 1958.

Malmo, R. B. Anxiety and behavioral arousal. *Psychol. Rev.*, 1957, *64*, 276–287.

Malmo, R. B. Measurement of drive: An unsolved problem in psychology. In M. R. Jones (Ed.), *Nebraska symposium on motivation 1958*. Lincoln: Univ. Nebr. Press, 1958, 229–265.

Malmo, R. B. Slowing of heart rate following septal self-stimulation in rats. *Science*, 1961, *133*, 1128–1130.

Malmo, R. B., & Shagass, C. Physiologic study of symptom mechanisms in psychiatric patients under stress. *Psy-chosom. Med.*, 1949, *11*, 25–29.

Malmo, R. B., & Shagass, C. Studies of blood pressure in psychiatric pa-tients under stress. *Psychosom. Med.*, 1952, *14*, 82–93.

Malmo, R. B., Shagass, C., Bélanger, D. J., & Smith, A. A. Motor control in psychiatric patients under experi-mental stress. *J. abnorm. soc. Psy-chol.*, 1951, *46*, 539–547.

Malmo, R. B., Shagass, C., & Smith, A. A. Responsiveness in chronic schizophrenia. *J. Pers.*, 1951, *19*, 359–375.

Malmo, R. B., & Surwillo, W. W. Sleep deprivation: changes in performance and physiological indicants of acti-vation. *Psychol. Monogr.*, 1960, *74* (15, Whole No. 502).

Martin, Irene. Somatic reactivity. In H. J. Eysenck (Ed.), *Handbook of abnormal psychology*. New York: Basic Books, 1961, 417–456.

Meyer, D. R., & Noble, M. E. Summa-tion of manifest anxiety and muscu-lar tension. *J. exper. Psychol.*, 1958, *55*, 599–602.

Olds, J. Physiological mechanisms of reward. In M. R. Jones (Ed.), *Ne-braska symposium on motivation 1955*. Lincoln, Neb.: Univ. Nebr. Press, 1955, 73–139.

Olds, J. High functions of the nervous system. *Ann. Rev. Physiol.*, 1959, *21*, 381–402.

Olds, J., & Milner, P. Positive rein-forcement produced by electrical stimulation of septal area and other regions of rat brain. *J. comp. physiol. Psychol.*, 1954, *47*, 419–427.

Olszewski, J. The cytoarchitecture of the human reticular formation. In J. F. Delafresnaye (Ed.), *Brain mech-anisms and consciousness*. Spring-field, Ill.: Charles C Thomas, 1954, 54–76.

Pinneo, L. R. The effects of induced muscle tension during tracking on level of activation and on performance. *J. exper. Psychol.*, 1961, *62*, 523–531.

Ross, W. R. D., & Davis, J. F. Stable band-pass filters for electroencephalography. *IRE Canad. Convention Rec. 1958*, Paper No. 860, 202–206.

Rothballer, A. B. Studies on the adrenaline-sensitive component of the reticular activating system. *EEG Clin. Neurophysiol.*, 1956, *8*, 603–621.

Rust, L. D. Changes in bar-pressing performance and heart rate in the sleep deprived rat. Unpublished master's thesis, McGill Univer., 1960.

Saffran, M., Schally, A. V., & Benfey, B. G. Stimulation of the release of corticotropin from the adenohypophysis by a neurohypophysial factor. *Endocrinology*, 1955, *57*, 439–444.

Schnore, M. M. Individual patterns of physiological activity as a function of task differences and degree of arousal. *J. exper. Psychol.*, 1959, *58*, 117–128.

Spence, K. W. Theory of emotionally based drive (D) and its relation to performance in simple learning situations. *Amer. Psychologist*, 1958, *13*, 131–141.

Stennett, R. G. The relationship of performance level to level of arousal. *J. exper. Psychol.*, 1957a, *54*, 54–61.

Stennett, R. G. The relationship of alpha amplitude to the level of palmar conductance. *EEG Clin. Neurophysiol.*, 1957b, *9*, 131–138.

Surwillo, W. A. A device for recording variations in pressure of grip during tracking. *Amer. J. Psychol.*, 1955, *68*, 669–670.

Surwillo, W. W. Psychological factors in muscle-action potentials: EMG gradients. *J. exper. Psychol.*, 1956, *52*, 263–272.

Taylor, Janet A. A personality scale of manifest anxiety. *J abnorm. soc. Psychol.*, 1953, *48*, 285–290.

Woodworth, R. S., & Schlosberg, H. *Experimental psychology.* New York: Holt, 1954.

Yates, A. J. The application of learning theory to the treatment of tics. *J. abnorm. soc. Psychol.*, 1958, *56*, 175–182.

12

Psychopharmacology

P. B. DEWS

A coherent account of psychopharmacology has not yet been resolutely attempted, nor is this short essay the right occasion for that attempt. Its aims are more modest. They will have been achieved if a few experimental psychologists are spared the labor of conducting otherwise good experiments that are invalidated by pharmacological misapprehensions or errors, and if clinical psychologists are enabled to recognize flaws in some papers on behavioral pharmacology and are thereby prevented from putting too much confidence in dubious conclusions. Since most of the difficulties to be discussed have been overlooked by numerous authors, it would be invidious to cite particular papers as illustrative of particular errors, and useless to catalogue all errors. References therefore will not be given.

The general principles of psychopharmacology are only now beginning to emerge. The writer hopes that authors who recognize errors in their past ways—as does the writer—will not be personally disturbed. The important thing is to do better in the future. It will be assumed that the reader, unlike the writer, is interested in drugs primarily to help understand behavior, rather than in pharmacology per se.

The discussion will be limited to the basic science aspects of psychopharmacology; that is, to the objectively assessed behavioral effects of drugs. This is in conformity with the title of this volume. It does not

Research reported herein was supported by the Eugene Higgins Trust and the National Institute of Mental Health (M 2094). The author would like to express his gratitude to his colleague, W. H. Morse, without whose help this chapter would have had many fewer ideas and more errors.

imply that only scientifically established information should be used by clinical workers. It is in the nature of their work that the clinical psychologist and the psychiatrist are obliged constantly to make decisions as to the disposition of their patients—decisions that usually cannot be made solely or even primarily on the basis of available scientific evidence. It is the clear duty of the clinician to make his decision on the basis of all available information. It is the equally clear duty of the basic scientist *not* to come to a decision until the scientific evidence justifies it. This difference in the social obligations of the clinician and the basic scientist seems to be the basis of the frequent lack of sympathy between the two groups. It leads to the clinician's accusation of the scientist as too vague and noncommittal to be helpful, and the scientist's counteraccusation that the clinician does not understand the nature of science, since he so frequently comes to decisions not scientifically defensible. It should be added, however, that in dealing with the natural phenomena of disease—with aberrations of behavior as well as with disorders of intrabodily systems—scientific evidence is of vastly greater value than other kinds. And it is the only kind that systematically increases with time.

The effects of drugs on behavior has been a subject of fascination since the ancient times when men first imbibed the products of alcoholic fermentations or consumed the exudates of the opium poppy or the Indian hemp plant. The idea of using drugs as instruments of exploration into the complexities of behavior is, however, of very recent origin and has led, so far, more to promises than to substantive contributions. Hope for the future arises largely by analogy to the profound contributions that pharmacological procedures have made in the analysis of physiological phenomena.

SCOPE

This chapter will discuss first the potential contributions of the introduction of pharmacological techniques into experimental psychology; it will then go on to discuss some of the difficulties and limitations of the use of drugs. It should become apparent that while the use of drugs may indicate the existence of hitherto unsuspected types of phenomena, and may give leads as to which one of a number of possible explanations for a phenomenon is most likely to be true, it is usually difficult to achieve final proof of an interpretation solely by the use of pharmacological techniques. Further, interpretations of psychological phenomena derived from drug studies based on incomplete or erroneous information about the drugs are likely to be not merely unsound but actually highly misleading and wasteful.

Advantages of Pharmacological
Techniques in Psychology

There are both practical and theoretical reasons for the appeal of drugs as means of analyzing psychological phenomena. The practical reasons arise from the relatively short period of persistence of most drugs in active concentrations in the organism. This makes possible, in most instances, repeated observations in a single individual. The range of effects of various doses of a drug can be explored with more ease and speed than can be attained with most independent variables in psychology. Such variables as, for example, changes in training procedure, in motivational factors, or in schedule parameters almost always necessitate much more laborious and time consuming studies. This is not a trivial advantage. There appears to be a minimum critical mass of empirical information necessary before a body of information on natural phenomena can cohere into genuine science. It may be doubted whether the information about behavior has attained this happy state of coherence; the subject can hardly compare yet, as a systematic science, with chemistry or even physiology. In a field as complex and difficult as behavioral science, and one so little charted, speed and efficiency in mapping is of great importance, not merely in conserving the energies of investigators but in making even possible the accumulation of a sufficient body of knowledge for coherence.

Theoretical reasons for the appeal of drugs arise from the relations of psychology to biology. To an impartial observer, the systems of behavior that have been proposed by such authorities as Tolman, Hull, and Spence have by their nature an arbitrariness that sets them apart from the theories of other sciences. This is recognized by their proponents; indeed, many authors seek as an ideal an axiomatic-deductive type of system comparable to that of mathematics. Such a nature would certainly distinguish psychology from the sciences. An alternative ideal is a science of behavior that will be compatible and indeed contiguous with the science of physical biology.* If this ideal is accepted, then the arbitrariness in selection of systems must disappear; the theoretical framework for behavioral science must be chosen to accord with physical biology. This is not to anticipate simple isomorphism between behavioral phenomena and, for example, neurophysiological phenomena, but rather to emphasize that insofar as identical variables are involved in behavioral science and in physical biology, the systems of reference and the nomenclature in the two universes must be congruent with respect to those variables. This view gives

---

* Since the science of "biology" may be reasonably supposed to include the science of behavior, the term "physical biology" will be used to designate all of biology except psychology.

peculiar importance to such common variables, of which relatively few are known, if we are to make judicious choice of systems of references in behavioral science. One such common variable is real time; another is drug action.

Both behavioral and physiological phenomena occur in the same progression of real time. The frames of reference and nomenclature of these two disciplines must therefore be congruent in this dimension. For example, terms such as *memory* and *learning* have come to refer, in psychology, to phenomena that are only slowly, if at all, reversible in time. It would be improper, therefore, for these terms to be applied to neurophysiological phenomena that persist only seconds or less.

Because of the great diversity of their effects, drugs comprise a whole family of variables that, properly utilized, should be of inestimable value in helping to choose a theoretical system of behavior that will have continued compatibility with physical biology. The impact of the drug has measurable consequences in both the biological and psychological frames of reference; the strength of the impact can be varied easily by varying the dose of drug. Biological and psychological phenomena that do not covary in the presence of different concentrations of drug cannot be immediately causally related to any major extent. For example, a certain pattern of relatively "high voltage slow wave" electrical activity recorded from the brain has been associated with a sleeping (or nonalert) behavioral state. Under the influence of atropine, the electrical activity characteristic of "sleep" is seen, but the behavioral state remains one of alertness. The "high voltage slow wave" electrical activity is therefore not a sufficient condition for establishing the behavioral state of sleep.

Drugs can help to maintain contact with the realm of biology even in studies conducted entirely in the behavioral universe of discourse. In general, drugs exert their effects through interactions between molecules of the drug and cells. The modifications wrought by the drug in the functioning of the cells, and consequently in the functioning of organs and systems, must be along physiologically meaningful lines. In other words, the organization of function must "make sense" in the presence of the drug just as in its absence. By the principle of congruence, the modifications in behavior by a drug also "make sense." From this it would follow that if the pattern of a drug effect on behavior does not fit naturally into a theoretical system of behavior, then the elements and operations in the behavior system cannot bear any simple relationship to the physiological substrata of behavior. Note that the converse is not true; that a drug disrupts behavior along lines conforming to the framework of a descriptive system of behavior does not mean, unfortunately, that that framework of behavioral science can be taken to have physiological correspondents.

These suggestions arise by analogy to the situations obtaining in other areas of pharmacology, and there is little direct evidence of their applicability to the central nervous system and behavior. Indeed, these principles should be taken to apply in broad outline rather than in specific detail, and anomalies are to be expected. Consider the current thinking on the nature of drug effects upon the central nervous system. The most important functional element of the central nervous system is taken to be the neurone. Neurones influence other neurones primarily through making synaptic connections, and the influence is transmitted from the presynaptic cell to the postsynaptic cell, at least in the majority of instances, through the release of a chemical substance by the former. It has been postulated that there are several different neurohumoral transmitters in the brain with differing effects on the postsynaptic membrane. It has been further postulated that the primary site of action of exogenous drugs in the brain, as in the peripheral nervous system, is at synapses. If drugs affecting the brain were to have differential effects which depended upon the chemical nature of the synapse and perhaps also upon the anatomical characteristics of the synapse, then a relatively small number of transmitters and anatomical types of synapses could account, by combinations of varying complexity, for the wide variety of drug effects on the central nervous system. If this general picture be reasonably correct—and it should be emphasized that it is no more than vaguely conceived at present—then the modification of function by drugs should correspond to different classes of synapses. It may be anticipated that particular types of synapses will generally assume some relatively homogeneous type of function, but there is no evolutionary reason why this should be true in detail. Analogy to the autonomic nervous system* underlines these considerations. Cholinergic postganglionic neurones generally modulate functions over which relatively rapid control is functionally desirable, such as accommodation of the eye; but the postganglionic sympathetic neurones innervating the sweat glands in man also are cholinergic. There is no obvious functional advantage to rapid discrete control of sweat gland function. This is anomalous also because postganglionic cholinergic neurones are otherwise generally confined to the parasympathetic division of the autonomic nervous system. The effects of drugs such as atropine are related to the chemical nature of the synapse rather than to the functional significance of pathway; they therefore reflect the anomaly of the sweat glands, and to this extent their effects do not "make sense." It is to be feared that there will be many, many examples of this sort in the pharmacology of the central nervous system.

* The autonomic nervous system was defined by Langley as a peripheral, efferent system. It is in this sense that the term is used here.

Multiplicity of drug action

Probably all drugs have more than one type of action. This is especially true of drugs affecting the central nervous system. The task of giving a coherent account of the effect of a drug thus involves the perilous passage between the Scylla of ad hoc theories to "explain" every individual experimental result and the Charybdis of unified theories fatally weakened to accommodate facts which should not be subsumed by the theory. The prudent pharmacologist follows the dictum of Occam in his professional life, but always with the reservation that facts anomalous to the accepted mode of action of a drug may presage additional modes of action rather than demonstrate the fallacy of the already accepted mode. This difficulty is frequently met in aggravated form in pharmacology, since a well-known mode of action of a drug may be able to give a plausible explanation for the observed facts; the facts therefore do not immediately appear as anomalous, yet the explanation may be wrong.

A concrete example may serve to clarify this problem. Consider the drug *d*-tubocurarine chloride, which has had considerable use as a tool in behavioral studies. When given intravenously, this drug causes a reversible paralysis of skeletal muscle and, in most species, a fall in blood pressure. The paralysis of skeletal muscle was shown by Claude Bernard to be due, not to an action on skeletal muscle fibers or nerve fibers or any preceding neural link, but to an effect on the junctional region between motor nerve and muscle fiber. The motor end plate of the muscle is rendered insensitive to the normal depolarizing action of acetylcholine liberated when impulses arrive at the terminals of the motor nerve.

Can we explain the fall in arterial blood pressure following intravenous *d*-tubocurarine by the antagonism of a depolarizing action of acetylcholine? The transmission of tonic sympathetic vasoconstrictor impulses through autonomic ganglia is mediated by acetylcholine, and *d*-tubocurarine might interfere with this transmission—and, in fact, *d*-tubocurarine has been shown to have such an effect.

Second, the importance of skeletal muscle movements in returning blood to the heart is well established; paralyzed muscles will not perform this function; this leads to diminished venous return, fall in cardiac output, and, other things being equal, a tendency for blood pressure to fall. Thus the fall in blood pressure following intravenous *d*-tubocurarine can be plausibly accounted for in terms of a unitary hypothesis as to the mode of action of the drug, viz., an antagonism of acetylcholine. Yet despite its plausibility, this account is substantially wrong. In fact, a major part of the fall in arterial blood pressure following intravenous d-tubocurarine is due to the ability of d-tubocurarine to liberate histamine from a variety of tissues; the free histamine then causes a fall in arterial blood pressure in most species.

Should an attempt be made to relate this action of d-tubocurarine to its effect on motor end plates? Two sets of observations make the answer to this query almost certainly no. First, the drug flaxedil has a similar effect on motor end plates, but does not cause liberation of histamine. Second, a variety of substances have actions similar to d-tubocurarine in liberating histamine, but have no effect on motor end plates. What we must suppose, then, is that the molecular configuration necessary to antagonize acetylcholine at certain sites and the configuration necessary to liberate histamine are "accidentally" both represented in the molecule of d-tubocurarine.

This story has a number of lessons for psychopharmacology. The limitation in specificity of drug actions weakens the inferences that can be made from the observed behavioral effects of a drug—even a drug with a well-established type of action. It has been shown that morphine can liberate histamine, in a way similar to d-tubocurarine. No one appears to have suggested that the analgesic effects of morphine are dependent upon its histamine liberating properties. Yet when reserpine was shown to liberate 5–HT* a few years ago, the suggestion was quickly made that the behavioral effects of reserpine were dependent on its ability to liberate 5–HT. There was, of course, ancillary evidence supporting the suggestion, but nevertheless the demonstration that reserpine also liberates catecholamines and other amines indicated the incompleteness of the evidence. Moreover, this emphasizes the gap between a plausible account and an established account. The plausible account of the genesis of the hypotension following intravenous d-tuborcurarine turned out to be misleading. It is plausible that reserpine should mediate its effects on the brain through liberation of one or more amines (just as it is plausible that some of the behavioral effects of atropine should be due to antagonism of acetylcholine and some of those of LSD† to antagonism of 5–HT or other amines, and so on). It is reasonable that the hypothesis of the mode of action of reserpine should have been stated. It is an indication of the value of the pharmacological approach that these hypotheses were able to be made, because it is inconceivable that they could have been formulated at the present time except as a result of the leads started by drug studies, particularly those instigated by the discovery of reserpine and LSD. It is, at the same time, essential that

* 5-hydroxytryptamine.
† d-lysergic acid diethylamide.

the hypothetical nature of these relationships be kept constantly in mind; constant reiteration of a mere hypothesis should not be allowed to canonize it into a theory nor lead to its acceptance into the established body of scientific knowledge. It would be sad if the avenues of exploration opened by these pharmacological studies were to be closed by spuriously established theories.

Finally, that drugs may have two or more types of action does not necessarily mean that their effects are therefore so complex and uncertain that they should not be used as tools. Although d-tubocurarine has very many, apparently heterogeneous, actions that can be demonstrated, the vast majority of those seen at reasonable concentrations can be attributed either to antagonism of specific actions of acetylcholine or to liberation of histamine. But it is important that the user of the drugs be aware of the situation.

In summary: (1) Since probably all drugs have more than one type of action, inferences from drug studies based on assumption of specificity of the drug effect must always carefully consider the possibility that other actions of the drug are involved. (2) A plausible explanation for a drug action must never be mistaken for an established explanation. When mere possibilities are compounded, the probability that the final statement will be true is so small as to be unworthy of consideration.

Direct and indirect action of drugs

When a constraint is applied to an animal or man, there is frequently a change in the organism that tends to reduce the consequences of the constraint. Animals tend to react physiologically in such a way as to maintain the constancy of their *milieu interieur*. Similarly, behavior patterns undergo modification to minimize the effect of applied constraints. Drugs may function in this sense as constraints on the operations of animals, and, in consequence, tend to evoke compensatory reactions. Some physiological compensations to pharmacologically induced changes are reasonably well understood—for example, the mechanisms of restoration of blood pressure toward normal levels following injection of a depressor agent. Some of the psychological adaptions are also understood—for example, the development in the chronic alcohol imbiber of slow speech and of gait with feet wide apart can be looked on as a consequence of differential reinforcement of more effective patterns of behavior. However, the mechanisms of the more purely pharmacological compensations, such as those involved in tachyphylaxis and in acute and chronic tolerance, are in most cases completely obscure.

It frequently happens that the compensatory reactions to a drug are more obvious than the direct effects. An injection of norepinephrine frequently leads to a fall in heart rate, despite the powerful positive chronotropic effects of the drug, because the compensatory mechanisms activated by the rise in blood pressure are even more powerful. This can obviously lead to very mistaken ideas about the nature of the drug action. The traditional pharmacological procedures for distinguishing direct from indirect effects of a drug is to analyze the relevant system and to study its component parts in functional isolation. Functional isolation is achieved by anatomical isolation, either by complete removal from the body—as when a heart or piece of intestine is studied outside the body—or *in situ*, by interruption of compensatory influences on the organ or tissue under study. Anatomical isolation is not possible in behavioral situations, but an analogous procedure can be used. A behavioral situation can be analyzed into its simplest components by identifying the smallest fragments of behavior that function as units. If the nature of the modification by a drug of the emission of such units of behavior is relatively unaffected by environmental and behavioral changes (compatible with emission of the behavior), then that behavioral effect of the drug may be considered to be direct. For example, if a drug were found to increase the probability of a particular type of behavior in a variety of situations, or to attenuate discriminative control by a specific sensory modality—again, more or less regardless of the other components of the situation— then these types of drug effects could be defined, by analogy, as "direct" effects of the drug on the respective elements in the behavioral complex. This procedure has not been fully utilized to date, so it is not known whether "direct" and "indirect" behavioral effects of drugs can be pragmatically differentiated. It can be stated with some assurance, however, that no information on the validity of the concept of direct and indirect behavioral effects of drugs will ever be possible from studies confined to complex situations; analytical procedures, such as operant conditioning procedures, will be necessary.

Another aspect of the problem of direct and indirect effects of drugs is their anatomical locus of action. A drug may affect the functioning of a system even though it has no effect on, or may not even come into contact with, that system at all. Awareness of this possibility is almost universal, and its more obvious aspects would hardly lead even the pharmacologically naive investigator astray, even in behavioral pharmacology, where this type of mechanism is particularly common and potent. Almost any profound change in any physiological system can lead to behavioral changes. Violent diarrhea in a cat due to administration of reserpine must be expected to have effects on the behavior of the animal that will be compounded with other effects of reserpine. This much is obvious. In this case, procedures such as production of similar diarrhea by drugs that are not absorbed from the gastrointestinal lumen may help to assess the contribution of the diarrhea itself to the behavioral effects of reserpine.

Another example, presenting greater problems in sorting out direct and indirect effects, is LSD, a drug known to have actions on many effectors of the autonomic nervous system. LSD has also "psychological" effects. Conditioned autonomic responses to discriminative stimuli are well known. If LSD occasions somatic behavioral responses appropriate to nonexisting discriminative stimuli—for example, verbal descriptions of frightening hallucinations—may it not also occasion the autonomic response to these same "stimuli"? In other words, to what extent are the autonomic changes seen in LSD intoxication due to direct effects on the "central origins" of the autonomic nervous system impulses, and to what extent are they "consequences" of the hallucinations?

This leads to a particular problem of anatomical localization of drug action. How can the distinction be made between (1) those effects of drugs exerted directly on the effectors, (2) those effects due to peripheral effects of the drug, which lead to changes in afferent input to the central nervous system, and (3) those effects on behavior due to direct action of the drug on the central nervous system (so-called centrally acting drugs)? Curare is a drug that modifies behavioral capabilities through an effect on effectors. Drugs producing behavioral effects exclusively through change in afferent input are less well authenticated, but whenever the injection of a drug leads to stimulation of nerve endings subserving pain, the possibility of this having behavioral consequences must always be considered; for example, intraperitoneal injection into rats of "irritant" substances such as alcohol, or buffered substances of high or low pH, may have considerable behavioral effects through this mechanism.

In general, psychopharmacologists have been mainly concerned with effects of drugs directly on the central nervous system. Peripheral effects of the drugs tend to be regarded as a nuisance, since they necessitate additional controls. This predilection is not logically defensible; it results, no doubt, from the tendency in contemporary society to look upon behavior as the manifestation of activity of the brain rather than as the activity of the organism as a whole, as it properly should be. It is reasonable enough in practice since the specificities and subtleties of drug effects on behavior are in most instances due to direct effects of drugs on the brain. It should be noted that, to identify a drug effect as being directly on the brain, the mere fact that the author cannot think of any other mechanism for it is not sufficient evidence.

Argument by exclusion is inherently weak in biology. Unfortunately, it is surprisingly difficult to obtain positive evidence that an observed behavioral effect is due to a direct effect on the brain, and direct evidence is almost entirely lacking even for some of the favorite drugs of psychopharmacology. Some authors seem to argue that because a drug has effects on behavior it must have direct effects on brain, and may even infer on the basis of behavioral evidence alone what parts of the brain are affected. Probably the best attitude to adopt at the present time is tentatively to ascribe to direct effects on brain the effects on behavior of those drugs that (1) have not been shown, in spite of extensive study, to have substantial peripheral effects in reasonable doses (for example, barbiturates) or (2) in which the peripheral effects per se have been shown to have very different consequences on behavior (for example, amphetamines). In view of the tentative nature of the attribution of the drug actions to a direct effect on brain, it is probably fruitless to guess as to site of action within brain on the basis of behavioral data. Localization of action within brain is a job for neuropharmacologists.

COMMENTS ON COMMON PRACTICES

Individual differences

That the effect of a given dose of a drug differs in comparable animals has been a matter of common observation since the beginning of pharmacology, and variability from animal to animal is considered by many to be a fundamental law of biology It is generally assumed that a major part of biological variability is genetically determined. The variation in the behavioral response to a drug is, in general, considerably greater from animal to animal than is the variation in response to most other types of drug action. It is inconceivable that some part of this variation should not be genetically determined.

The behavioral effects of a drug, however, are demonstrably profoundly influenced by the past history of the organism, so differing histories from animal to animal will lead to great individual variation in the effects of the drug. The mere existence of individual differences in the behavioral effects of a drug is quite insufficient evidence to infer a genetic basis for the differences. As before, argument by exclusion is weak. Differences between individuals—and even between representatives of different species—in their behavioral response to a drug should be accepted as genetically based only when positive evidence for such a basis is presented, and this, of necessity, involves genetic studies.

Further remarks on anatomical localization of drug effects

When a substance has been shown to exert pharmacological effects on an organism, the first step in the analysis of its pharmacological action is to find out on which organs and tissues the drug acts; in other words, to identify the anatomical sites of action. When a drug has been found to act on the central nervous system, it is natural to attempt to carry the localization one step further and to identify the specific parts of the brain on which the drug acts, so that one might say (as has been said of various drugs) that this drug affects the hypothalamus, this the cerebral cortex, this the brain stem medial reticular formation and so on. Unfortunately, the problem of localization of drug action within the brain has turned out to be an overwhelmingly more difficult problem than the localization of drug actions outside of the central nervous system. Reasons for this include the anatomical and histological complexities of the central nervous system and the very high degree of interdependence of the different parts of the central nervous system. The former difficulty poses formidable technical problems, the latter difficulty adds further to the technical difficulties and also poses epistemological problems. If the electrical activity of one part of the brain is changed by a drug, may this not be due to changed input to this part of the brain from another part or parts of the brain that are the primary sites of action of the drug? If the effect of the drug is profoundly modified by ablation of parts of the brain, again, may this not be due to changed functional activity of the unablated primary sites of action of the drug consequent upon the ablation? None of these problems may be permanently insuperable and modern electronic and computor technologies may overcome them, but most of the statements to be found today in standard reference manuals on intracranial sites of action of drugs are quite unwarrantedly specific and categorical. In spite of much effort, there are few, if any, drugs of which it can be said that the hypothalamus or the thalamus or the cerebral cortex or any other gross subdivision of the brain has been proved to be their primary site of action.

A further reason for the difficulty that is being encountered in specifying the sites of action of drugs in terms of recognizable anatomical parts of the brain may be in the relatively fortuitous and functionally inconsequential nature of the gross anatomy of the brain. Since the vertebrate nervous system retreated into its bony protective casing, the brain, so far as its gross anatomy is concerned, has been relatively free to become distorted and convoluted, without the anatomical aspects of these changes having appreciable consequences for survival. The evolution of progressively more effective behavioral mechanisms apparently necessitated the evolution of a larger and larger brain, but the anatomical progression was exempted from the organizing influence of survival consequences. Hence the exquisite behavioral capabilities of the human organism are dependent on an anachronistic brain that is, so far as its gross anatomy is concerned, a monument to past accidents of evolution. There is no more logical reason why the studies of the arrangements and connections of cells in the cerebral cortex should help us understand anything about behavior than there is that knowledge of the course of the motor part of the seventh cranial nerve round the nucleus of the abducens nerve should help us understand the nature of facial expressions. Of course, when the functions of brain are understood, the anatomical arrangements will be found to be capable of subserving them. But studies of neuroanatomy, even functional neuroanatomy, are much more likely to contribute in the future, as in the past, to our understanding of ontology than to our understanding of behavior.

It may be noted, in passing, that the development of behavioral pharmacology seems to have been delayed because, paradoxically, behavior mechanisms are so appropriate. Apposite behavior is so crucial for survival that there must have been a maximum of evolutionary pressure on perfection of mechanisms for attainment of "appropriateness"; so that the behavior of the organism is continuously adjusted to the exigencies of a changing environment. In higher animals, behavior has become so appropriate that uninformed people have been unable to conceive of these mechanisms as being part of the physical world; they feel impelled to postulate a supranatural "purposiveness," and thus have been discouraged from applying the methods of scientific analysis to problems of behavior in general, including behavioral pharmacology.

The conception of the segregation of the neurological substrata of specific psychological attributes in relatively discrete anatomical regions of the brain, by analogy to the localization of function in different organs of the rest of the body, is generally losing ground, but statements in which this concept is implicit are still encountered. For example, drugs are still posited as modifying "emotional behavior" by acting on the hypothalamus, or modifying "intellectual activities" by acting on the cerebral cortex. In place of the idea of discrete suborgans in brain, the concept is emerging of the brain as a number of systems of neurones acting on one another through the liberation of an unknown number of humoral transmitters, with the different regions of brain differing in the relative concentrations and preponderances of the different types of cells. If this hypothesis more nearly approaches the truth than previous ideas, then it is clear that ablation studies, necessarily of discrete parts of brain, will be a relatively unprofitable approach to understanding of brain function. If we are interested in the trade activities of, say, Western Europe with the rest of the world, we would learn little from studying the effects of ablation of Italy; the place of Fiats in the ships leaving Europe would be rapidly filled by Renaults and Volkswagens and that of chianti by claret. Nor, incidentally, would we learn much more by transfixing occasional inhabitants with large telephone receivers and then listening carefully to what they said in their surviving minutes; talk they might, and they might tell us something about themselves if we understood their language, but it is unlikely they would be informative on world trade.

An approach more appropriate to the "humoral systems" hypothesis of functional organization of brain may be derived from analogy to what has been found fruitful in analysis of the peripheral autonomic system. In this system, drugs have been found that have highly specific effects on the junctional regions between neurones and between neurones and effectors—effects that are highly dependent on the humoral type of the cell. For example, atropine will block the effects of cholinergic neurones on smooth muscle, but it will not, in comparable concentrations, block the effects of adrenergic neurones on the same tissue, or even the effects of preganglionic cholinergic neurones on ganglion cells. If a similar state of affairs as regards site and specificity of drug action obtains within the central nervous system, then clearly drugs promise to be very helpful in sorting out some of the complexities of brain function.

Some words of caution are necessary at this point. The simplicity of this conception of drug action should not be allowed to obscure the fact that prodigious labor will be required to establish drug effects of this kind. The gap between understanding in principle and factual knowledge of the actual state of affairs is indeed great. It took about 50 years of work, and involved the activities of most of the greatest pharmacologists and many of the greatest physiologists during that time, to elucidate the pharmacological relationships in the peripheral autonomic nervous system relationships that today seem almost absurdly simple and straightforward. One is probably safe in assuming that the situation in the central nervous system will be considerably more complex, and that great exertions of great men will be required to unravel the complexities. In the meantime, the casual assumption that drugs have similar actions inside and outside the central nervous system, and sweeping inferences on the basis of fragmentary information as to the specific humoral importance of particular substances, may each have some heuristic value; but if ideas derived from this type of reasoning are widely accepted, then, at the present stage of the subject, a great deal of harm is done. The game of discerning similarities between different molecules and inferring from these an "explanation" of interactions between substances, such as the mimicking or counteraction of putative neurohumors, has almost certainly been overplayed. This is a matter for experts in molecules; guesses of nonexperts and sometimes of experts are likely to be ludicrous.

Dosage considerations

Drug concentration is the central independent variable in pharmacology. The need for exploration along the dosage variable in behavioral studies has been emphasized repeatedly, and the logical impossibility of making any statement as to specificity or as to qualitative differences between drugs on the basis of observation at a single dose level is generally recognized.

Monotonic dose effect curves are the exception. Indeed, they are impossible in situations where a drug at some dose level causes an enhancement of behavioral output, since enough of any drug will abolish behavior, even if this only occurs at lethal doses.

In situations in which a drug causes first an increment and then a decrement in the output of a particular type of behavior, there has been a tendency to make analogies to the situation obtaining, for example, in the action of acetylcholine on autonomic ganglion cells. Acetylcholine in certain concentrations causes repetitive firing of these cells; very much higher concentrations lead to paralysis of the cells so far as excitation by acetylcholine, or preganglionic stimulation, is concerned. These analogies are extremely tenuous. While paralysis of ganglion cells by acetylcholine is undoubtedly a real phenomenon, it is ordinarily difficult to achieve in the intact animal and requires very much larger (by orders of magnitude) doses than those that produce stimulation. This type of phenomenon would seem to bear little relationship to the situation where a "stimulant" action of a drug is converted to a "depressant" action with a two- or threefold increase in dose.

Stimulants and depressants

These terms as nouns, or as simple qualifiers of "drug," have outlived their usefulness. One of the best-established results in the infant science of behavioral pharmacology is that the "stimulant" or "depressant" action of drugs does not occur in equal measure on all aspects of behavior. It has been demonstrated repeatedly that a given dose of a drug in a given organism may cause "stimulation" of some behavioral activities and simultaneous "depression" of others, using the terms "stimulation" and "depression" in the sense of increased and decreased output respectively of the behavior according to the method of measurement in use. It is entirely likely that this could be demonstrated for any drug, given the right combination of dose and behavioral situations. Clearly, then, acceptable statements should take the form "Drug A depresses (or stimulates) the output of behavior in situation B." The blanket statement "A is a depressant (or stimulant) drug" is inadmissible. Actually the former statement would be much better phrased "Drug A decreases (or increases) the output of behavior in situation B."

The terms stimulation and depression are used also by neurophysiologists and neuropharmacologists, usually in the sense of increased or decreased rates of firing of nerve cells. It is obvious that there is no simple universal isomorphic relationship between stimulation and depression in the behavioral and in the neurophysiological senses, and in fact, no necessary direct relationship at all. Stated thus baldly, it is unlikely that anyone would wish to maintain that there were. It is, nevertheless, a fact that the double usage of the terms leads to confusion and it is frequently apparent that in the discussion sections of papers there is implicit the assumption that homonymy implies causal relationship. It would seem better to prevent confusion by the simple expedient of eschewing the terms. They merely seem to say more than they do. Similar remarks apply to excitation, facilitation, inhibition, reflex, learning, memory and so on; in fact, to all terms used according to different definitions by physiologists and psychologists.

Tolerance

It is generally believed that optimum development of tolerance to the physiological effects of a drug necessitates maintenance of significant concentrations of the drug in the organism for a reasonable proportion of the day over a period of time. It is unlikely that much tolerance to nicotine would be developed by an individual who inhaled rapidly only one cigarette per week. It is, however, a matter of common observation in behavioral pharmacology that the behavioral effects of a given dose of drug administered say one week after the initial exhibition are likely to be substantially different on the second occasion than on the first. This has been rather loosely called tolerance, and has been assumed to be related in some way to physiological changes of the same general nature as those occurring, for example, in continuous morphine administration. The temporal relations make it unlikely that the behavioral phenomena resemble in any important way the physiological type of tolerance.

It might appear that the phenomena of tolerance could be avoided in behavioral pharmacology by the simple expedient of giving each animal or subject only one dose of drug. This is probably not a satisfactory solution: The behavioral effects of an initial dose of drug are the resultant of two factors: first, the specific effects of the drug, and second, the nonspecific impact of the novelty of any drug effect. Drugs produce effects that function as discriminative stimuli that modify the subject's behavior. Crudely put, on initial exposure the drug makes the subject "feel" different than he did in any previous experience and upsets his behavior. Thus, if each subject were given a drug only once the specific effects of the drug would be completely confounded with the novelty aspect of the drug effect. There is almost no quantitative information on the development of "tolerance" to the novelty aspect of the action of a drug. The writer has the impression that in most situations it develops extremely rapidly and is complete after two or three doses of drug; and that there is substantially complete "cross tolerance" between most commonly used drugs. When the subject is "used to" one drug, another drug is much less of a novel stimulus.

If an animal or man is put under the influence of a drug repeatedly, or continuously over a prolonged period, patterns of behavior may emerge that tend to minimize the change of behavior caused by the drug. The broad-based gait in acute alcoholic intoxication has already been given as an instance of this type of phenomenon. The drug produces coordination disabilities that lead to swaying and falling down. If the erect posture is essential, frequency of falling down can be reduced by keeping the feet apart. This becomes an avoidance response that is acquired in a way similar to that seen in passengers on a pitching and rolling ship. Apparently it matters little whether the origin of the tendency to sway is inside or outside the individual. To call this adaptation the development of "tolerance" to the knock-down action of alcohol (or the moving ship) is a rather dubious extension by analogy of the term "tolerance" as used in pharmacology, and one with little etymological sanction. New patterns of behavior acquired under the influence of a drug, as would be expected, frequently persist after the drug has been eliminated, just as a tossed mariner may stagger a while after he reaches *terra firma*. This is undoubtedly the main source of "day after" effects produced by drugs that are known to persist in the body in significant concentrations for only a few hours. It must also be the basis of persistence of beneficial therapeutic effects after discontinuance of drug administrations.

The organization of the autonomic nervous system

Many people think of the autonomic nervous system as being organized into two divisions, each innervating most of the body and having opposite actions on the various tissues and organs. The divisions are thought of as operating more or less as unitary wholes, and the general state of the body is held to depend on which division currently has predominance.

These are gross and probably misleading oversimplifications. In the first place, a great many tissues have nerves from one division only. For example, the vast majority of the arterioles of the body receive only sympathetic innervation; those that receive parasympathetic innervation are so few as to have an inappreciable influence on total peripheral resistance, and so the neural control of this exceedingly important factor in cardiovascular homeostasis is effected by the autonomic nervous system solely through modulation of sympathetic vasoconstrictor tone. Even in organs that receive dual and antagonistic types of innervation, one is usually preponderant. For example, usual changes in heart rate are mediated by changes in vagal tone with inconsequential changes in sympathetic influences. Sometimes the two systems do not have antagonist effects; for example, on the salivary glands.

Finally, the divisions of the autonomic nervous system, particularly the parasympathetic division, do not ordinarily discharge as a unitary whole; frequency of impulses in, for example, the ciliary nerves, the vagi and the nervi erigens are not closely related. Accommodation of the eye for reading is not ordinarily accompanied by slowing of the heart; and either can take place without genital erection. Even in the sympathetic system, cardiovascular regulations are carried on more or less independently of sweat gland activity. Fortunately, methods are now available for assessing most autonomic changes, so they can be particularized in an objective and quantitative manner. If specific autonomic changes are postulated to play an important role in a behavioral phenomenon, then these changes must be explicitly demonstrated rather than inferred.

Conclusion

Pharmacological techniques are likely to play an important role in the development of the science of behavior, particularly in helping decide between alternative formulations of accounts of behavior, and in providing clues as to the existence of hitherto unsuspected types of phenomena. Serious difficulty is usually encountered, however, in obtaining definitive proof of the nature of a phenomenon through the exclusive use of pharmacological techniques.

The following principles are suggested that, if violated by putative contributions to psychopharmacology, should lead the nonexpert seriously to question their credibility:

1. The results of studies conducted entirely in the behavioral frame of reference should be described in behavioral, and not neurophysiological, terms. Conversely, the validity of conclusions about behavior drawn from primarily neurophysiological studies are limited by the validity of the behavioral technique used—which in most instances in the past has been poor.

2. Conclusions predicted on the assumption of a high degree of specificity of action of a drug require that that specificity be exhaustively established. Probably all drugs have more than one type of action.

3. Merely plausible theories in behavioral pharmacology have a low probability of being right. If the derivation of a conclusion involves the serial compounding of two or more plausible inferences, then the conclusion has an infinitesimal chance of being right.

4. If the effect of a drug is stated in categorical terms to be on a certain gross anatomical region of brain, the reader would almost always have been right to be skeptical in the past; he will probably continue to be right a very large proportion of the time in the foreseeable future if he maintains the same strategy.

5. Conclusions as to inborn specific individual differences require genetic techniques for their establishment.

6. No valid statement can be made as to specificity or qualitative differences between drugs on the basis of observation at a single dose level.

7. The considerable number of terms used both by psychologists and physiologists almost never have the same meaning in the two universes of discourse. Great care should be taken to find out in which sense a term is being used in a given context.

13

The Neuropsychology of Sigmund Freud

KARL H. PRIBRAM

The experimental foundations of clinical psychology deal, for the most part, with investigations of psychopathology. There is found another, somewhat less prevalent theme, however, characterized by an emphasis on basic, theory-directed questions. Clinical material is used as a caricature of the theoretical problem, and the hope is that better theory will be attained when the clinical phenomenon is related to laboratory experience. There is one branch of clinical endeavor that consistently uses this method: clinical neurology.* Pathological material is used to gain a better understanding not only of the abnormalities in question but also of the fundamental workings of the brain and its regulation of behavior. John Hughlings Jackson, Henry Head, Otto Foerster, Harvey Cushing, Percival Bailey, Wilder Penfield, D. Denny-Brown and F. M. R. Walshe are only a few names that attest to this tradition.

Much of clinical psychology today either takes for granted or makes actual investigations of notions which can be directly traced back to Sigmund Freud. Many of the chapters in this book detail experimental

* As I indicated in a recent paper on the interrelations between psychology and the neurological sciences (1962), clinical neurology is, to a large extent, a neuropsychological discipline; namely, the investigation of neurological processes—normal and pathological—by *behavioral* techniques. Perhaps partly because of the poor prognosis attached to diseases of the central nervous system, and partly because of the difficulties in the mastery of neurological knowledge in the first place, clinical neurologists have invariably used clinical material to pose basic, i.e., theory-directed questions.

analyses of problems discussed extensively in psychoanalytic literature. This is an appropriate place, therefore, to look at one of the earlier of Freud's works from today's vantage.

Forgotten, for the most part, is the fact that Freud was an internationally respected and competent neurologist deeply steeped in his tradition. He coined the term *agnosia* which is used today in the neurological clinic. His work on aphasia is still one of the best statements of the problems encountered when language is disrupted by brain damage. Freud was also an excellent observer in the field of behavioral science, even though behavioral science then was, of course, rudimentary. In his attempt to objectify his observations of behavior, Freud turned first to neurology, as did many others of the period—Sechenov, Bechterev, and Pavlov, for example. Consequently, the results of behavioral observations as well as the inferences drawn from them were often couched in neurological terms. These confusions between the behavioral and neurological levels of discourse made these early attempts so "difficult" that Freud finally abandoned the explicit neuropsychological approach.*

My curiosity was piqued by a reference to the "Project for a Scientific Psychology" in Jones's biography (1953). I fully expected the Project (13) to be of historical interest—but if this were all, there would be little use in preparing a chapter such as this. I found rather, that the Project contains a detailed neurological model which is, by today's standards, sophisticated. The special points of interest center on Freud's conceptions of the neurological processes presumed to underlie "pain," "pleasure," "memory," "motive," "learning," and "thinking," conceptions often considerably different from those current today. These differences can be stated explicitly so that they can be tested in the laboratory. The Project is therefore very much alive and not just of historical significance. An added dividend accrues as definitions, in biologically relevant operational terms, of concepts that are household words in the worlds of clinical psychology, psychiatry, the social sciences, and humanities.

There are important deficiencies in the Project. Some of these were recognized by Freud and probably led to its abandonment before publication. In an attempt to remedy these deficiencies I shall here use the device of referring to neurological data and the inferences made from such data with one set of terms, and to use another set when the notions to be described arise from observations of behavior. This makes exposition (though not content) a bit different from the original, but prevents the escape into psycho-physical dualism to which Freud resorted in later years.

*My thanks to Jerome Bruner, whose enthusiasm for Freud's neuropsychological contribution kindled my curiosity.

THE BEHAVIOR OF ORGANISMS AND
OF NEURONAL AGGREGATES

Inertia

Freud begins with a first postulate. He calls this inertia, which in
many respects is similar to what we today know as homeostasis. Inertia is homeostasis in its baldest form: an organism, when stimulated,
attempts to get rid of that stimulation, i.e., to return to the unstimulated condition. By invoking the principle of inertia, Freud feels that
he can begin to quantify behavioral phenomena. He adduces behavioral evidence to support the postulate: for example, the escape from
injurious excitation results in the cessation of stimulation.

He adds, however, a modification; the postulate does not cover all
circumstances. Whenever an organism is sufficiently complex it can
stimulate itself, as with endogenous physiological substances. From
these, the organism cannot withdraw itself as it does from external
stimuli. Endogenous stimuli cease only when certain definite conditions are realized in the external world. His example—the need for
nourishment. Relief from endogenous stimulation requires an effort
which is independent of this endogenous stimulation. The organism is
consequently obliged to abandon the original trend toward a reduction of its level of excitation to zero. Organisms must, therefore, learn
to tolerate a store of excitation sufficient to meet the demands of the
specific actions necessary to relieve endogenous stimulation. The trend
toward a reduction of excitation persists in modified form in which
there is a tendency to keep the level of tension down and constant.

When the organism reacts so as to maximally reduce excitation, this
is called a *primary process*. When the level of excitation is maintained
relatively constant through a complex set of interactions with the environment (see below) this is called a *secondary process*.

The "excitation" involved in homeostasis is defined in neurophysiological terms. Neural impulses are conceived as measures of "quantities of excitation in flow." In other words, the nerve impulse as
measured electrically is considered an index of the excitatory state
of the neural tissue from which the record is made. But note clearly
that this index defines only *transmitted* excitations.

Neurons

The second postulate Freud proposes is the neuron theory. Freud
develops the neuron theory very briefly in only two paragraphs. This
is essentially a statement of the "modern neurohistology" of 1895
(Waldeyer, 1891) and is in no way as detailed and beautiful a development of neuron theory as that presented by Foster and Sherring-

ton (1897) a few years later or in Sherrington's *Integrative Action of the Nervous System* (1906). Nonetheless, with one exception of emphasis, neuron theory *à la* Freud is very similar to neuron theory as we know it today.

That exception stems from Freud's attempt to relate his first postulate to the facts of neuron theory. The electrical recording of neural potential changes measures *only* "quantities of excitation *in flow*." Freud takes cognizance of the fact known since du Bois-Reymond's *Untersuchungen* of 1845 and Pflüger's (1859) comprehensive work on the subject, that quantity of "electrotonic" excitation may increase or decrease in neural tissue without necessarily initiating transmitted impulses. For Freud, a neuron may "fill"—i.e., become *cathected*—with excitation even though no transmitted activity results. In his words "we arrive at the idea of a cathected neuron filled with a certain quantity, though at other times it may be empty."

This emphasis on cathexis is one of those strokes of luck or genius which in retrospect appears uncanny, for only in the past decade have neurophysiologists recognized the importance of the graded nonimpulsive activities of neural tissue—graded mechanisms such as those of dendritic networks whose functions are considerably different from those of the transmitted impulsive activity of axons (Bullock, 1958; Bishop, 1956; Pribram, 1960).

In other respects, there are many similarities between Sherrington's model and Freud's. Sherrington attributed to the synapse the properties of the reflex that could not be accounted for by the properties of nerve conduction. He inferred that synapses were endowed with a dual set of properties which he named "central inhibitory and central excitatory states." Freud talked of synapses as *contact barriers* (the term synapses was introduced by Foster and Sherrington two years after Freud wrote the Project; the term neuron had become current only a few years earlier through Waldeyer's neuroanatomical contributions). Freud attributed the single property of *resistance* to contact barriers. "Resistance opposes the discharge of excitation from one neuron to another."

ADAPTIVE PROCESSES: NEURAL AND BEHAVIORAL

Freud poses the issue that an organism must remain sensitive to new excitations, yet at the same time develop the stabilities necessary to retain traces of prior stimulation. As those who have tried to stimulate neuronal networks have found out, design of this dual system characteristic is beset with difficulties. If the receptive aspects of such a stimulated network are emphasized, then the behavior of the net is continually modified—i.e., the net is stimulus bound—and it retains little. If, on the other hand, the retentive capacities of the network are overemphasized, "one-trial learning" and inability to allow subsequent modification characterizes the behavior of the system.

Freud examines the retentive process. He abandons the then current and not as yet completely abandoned view, that sensory and memory mechanisms are separable on a gross anatomical basis. He adopts the now well-worn, though still unsupported, idea that receptor excitation repeatedly transmitted through the nervous system lowers synaptic resistance (Gerard, 1949, 1950, 1960). Memory is, according to this notion, a grooving or *bahnung* of transmission pathways in the nervous system.

But even here Freud adds his own peculiar twist. He states that every neuron must in general be presumed to have several paths of connections with other neurons, i.e., several contact barriers. He details explicitly the conditions under which transmission of excitation takes place and under what conditions it does not take place. (For these, see below, under Functional Localization.) Thus he shows that the possibility exists for a choice among paths. This being so, he adduces that the condition of facilitation of each contact barrier *must* be independent of that of all others in the same neuron. Otherwise, transmission would be random. Organisms do not behave as if all paths were equally likely—they are *motivated*, their behavior is directed, often on the basis of prior experience.

Motive, for Freud, does not initiate behavior; motive directs ongoing processes. Motivation is selection and selection is to a large degree a result of experience. In this fashion, Freud calls attention to the inexorable linkage of motive and memory. David Rapaport considers this the third great step in the study of memory processes (1950). According to Rapaport, the first of these steps was the experimental study of rote memory by Ebinghaus, the second was the demonstration by the Gestalt investigators that remembering is lawfully organized, and the third is the notion that motive and memory are so intimately interwoven.

Freud goes on to point out that facilitation cannot be based solely upon the excitation transmitted to a single neuron, nor on the cathexis of excitation that is retained in that neuron, for this would not produce differences of facilitation between contact barriers of the same neuron. Here, again, Freud is ahead of his time in posing the important problem. It is only recently that neurophysiology has attained the techniques to study simultaneously what goes on in different portions of a neuron (Bullock, 1957; Bullock and Terzuolo, 1957, 1958). It has been conclusively demonstrated, at least for the nervous system of lower organisms, that graded response mechanisms in different parts of the neuron can vary independently of one another, and that transmitted activity results only under very special and as yet incompletely understood circumstances. The techniques are now available, therefore, to take into the laboratory the question of how neural impulses are directed through a net, and under what conditions such selective direction leads to an adapted repetition of the neuronal pattern.

In summary of this portion of the Project, comparison with Sherrington's treatment of similar problems in *The Integrative Action of the Nervous System* is profitable. Sherrington takes as his paradigm an idealized spinal reflex. He points out that the known characteristics of the reflex and those of neurotransmission are not in consonance. He therefore turns to the neuron theory and suggests that reflex behavior can be explained in terms of the inferred properties of the synaptic junctions between neurons. Sherrington builds upon the notion of a final common path through which reflex action must discharge: "The resultant singleness of action from moment to moment is a keystone in the construction of the individual whose unity it is the specific office of the nervous system to perfect." In order to account for the phenomena to which he addresses himself, he infers central excitatory and inhibitory states, simultaneous and successive spinal induction and comes to classify integrative action as based on two sorts of interactions among reflexes: antagonistic (differentiative) and allied (combinatorial).

Freud also begins with observed behavior—his paradigm is escape from noxious stimulation. He addresses himself not to the reflex, but to homeostatic aspects of the situation. He also invokes the neuron doctrine to interpret discrepancies between observed behavior and the behavior to be expected if the sole property of nervous tissue were the conducting of excitation. However, Freud places the locus of the resolution of his problem only in part at the synaptic contact between neurons. He makes use as well of the other known graded nonconducted excitations of neural tissue. He calls attention to the fact that transmitted excitations are not the whole story. Excitation can build up within a neuron and this increase need not necessarily lead to conducted impulsive activity.

Sherrington uses the single behavioral conception "reflex" to compose the coordinated behavior of the organism by the addition of a considerable number of neurologically derived constructs. Freud, on the other hand, analyzes a variety of behaviorally derived concepts (such as motive and memory) and attempts to find explanatory reductive correlations among a relatively few well substantiated neuroanatomical and neurophysiological concepts. It is obvious that Freud found his task the more difficult one, since the presentation of the Project is not nearly so well worked out as that in *The Integra-*

tive Action of the Nervous System. Nonetheless, in the long run, Freud's approach may prove to be equally fruitful, since it tackles problems that can only be handled with great difficulty by the building block approach.

FUNCTIONAL LOCALIZATION IN THE CENTRAL NERVOUS SYSTEM

Projection and nuclear systems

For Freud, the problem demands that there be at least two differently organized systems of neurons. Neural tissue has to receive and to discharge excitations both of exogenous and of endogenous origin; also, neural tissue has both to retain receptivity and to remain receptive.

He suggests the hypothesis that there are two neural systems. The first consists of permeable tissues and the latter consists of impermeable ones. "The suspicion now arises that each system may serve two of the four functions under consideration. If that were so, we should not have invented them. We should have discovered them. It would only remain to identify them with what is already known. And, in fact, we know from anatomy that there is a system of neurons which is alone in contact with the external world and a superimposed system which has no direct peripheral contacts, but which is responsible for the progressive development of psychological complexities."

Freud goes on to identify one system as composed of the spinal tracts leading up to the brain, and the other system as the gray nuclear masses of the brain stem and forebrain. The difference between the functions of the two systems is attributed to their permeability, i.e., the permeability of their synapses. But this difference is ascribed not to any intrinsic dissimilarity between the neurons of the two systems, but to a distinction of their connections. The spinal projection system handles the greater quantity of excitation since it is in direct contact with peripheral receptors and therefore is continually stimulated by the environment. The neurons in the nuclear system, in contact with the spinal system and some "internal" neuroreceptors (see below), are reached only by quantities of excitation of the same order of magnitude as the resistances of the synapses. Thus neurons are neurons irrespective of their location; the only distinction is in the milieu to which they happen to be allocated.

"Now, however, we must examine the assumption that the quantities of excitation reaching the neurons from the external periphery of the body are of a higher order than those from the internal periphery." Freud deals with this problem for several pages and brings to bear some "recent" neurohistologic findings, but these are of little use today. Though much work has been done since the turn of the century to prove the existence of osmoreceptors, glucostats, and other neuroreceptors in the midline regions of the brain stem (Pribram, 1960), the quantitative data necessary to support Freud's argument are still unavailable.

Nonetheless, the distinction Freud makes is in many respects similar to that current today between the modally specific projection systems and the nonmodally specific, more diffusely organized core systems of the cephalic portion of the neuraxis. The classical sensory-motor projection systems, with their rapid conduction of neural impulses over long fiber tracts interspersed with few synapses, fulfill the descriptions of Freud's projection system. The nonspecific systems, on the other hand, are made up of many branching neurons usually shorter than those of the projection systems. They received stimulation from the external world only through collaterals from the projection systems. Further, these nonspecific systems lie close to the midline neuroreceptors of the brain stem. Propagation of excitation takes place only under certain, yet to be determined, circumstances in the nonspecific systems. The work of Gloor (1955), for instance, has demonstrated that (in the forebrain portion of these systems) an electrical stimulus in one location will increase the excitation in the dendritic layer of an adjacent structure, but that this increase in graded dendritic potentials fails to be transmitted immediately as impulsive discharge in the tract that leads from this structure. So the notion—oversimplified though it is—that the central nervous system consists of two types of neural systems is at least as tenable today as it was at the turn of the century.

The commonly ignored, nontransmissive, graded response characteristics of neural tissue are conceived by Freud as important properties of the nuclear system. The process of cathexis, i.e., of increase in the nontransmitted "bound" excitation of nervous tissue must take place mainly in this system. So must the differential decrease in synaptic resistance that makes possible motive and memory. Freud spells out his own views in detail:

Each neuron in the system is in contact with many others, not just one; connections are diffuse, not discrete. In fact, a drawing of a neural net appears in the Project and Freud refers to the nuclear system in several places as a network of neurons. Freud postulates that, when in adjoining neurons excitation builds up simultaneously, a temporary facilitation of the synapses between them results and thus modifies the course of any transmitted excitation that might be initiated in peripheral receptors. The build-up of excitation in the system can accrue as a residual excitation from prior stimulation of peripheral receptors; as endogenous stimulation through internal neu-

roreceptors; and, of course, as intrinsic activity of the nervous tissue itself. In today's language, the conception is that of (1) an originally
more or less randomly connected net into which only a few initial constraints are built; (2) these constraints together with momentary
peripheral and endogenous inputs progressively direct the essentially
stochastic processes of propagation of excitation through the net; until
(3) in the motivated adult, neural transmission is no longer random but
selectively directed.

The cortical system

There is another problem, however, which is not handled by the
division of the nervous system into (1) a reception and transmission
system and (2) another that is closely related to the internal environment of the organism and in which excitations build up more or less
gradually before discharge. Freud needs a third system of neurons
because he wants to deal with the problem of the qualities of sensation: "We may ask how qualities originate and where qualities originate. Where do qualities originate? Not in the external world, for
'out there' there are only masses in motion and nothing else. In the
projection system perhaps? This would tally with the fact that the
qualities are connected with sensation but it is contradicted by everything that rightly speaks in favor of the involvement of higher levels
of the nervous system. In the nuclear system then? There is an important objection to this. The nuclear system is primarily involved
in the reproductive processes that underlie memory and motive.
Thus we must summon up enough courage to assume that there is
a third system of neurons, 'perceptual' neurons they might be called,
which are excited along with the others during perception but not
during reproduction, and whose states of excitation give rise to the
different qualities, that is to say, 'conscious sensations.'"

Freud must now reconcile some difficulties. The projection system
is conducting because it has been recurrently subject to large amounts
of excitation. The nuclear system is retentive because these large
amounts of excitation rarely occur. Freud is in trouble if his third
system were to receive its excitations from the projection *through*
the nuclear systems. "Perception is characterized by its immediateness,
mutability, transitoriness, and the easy combination of simultaneously
perceived qualities. All of these characteristics would tally only with
complete permeability of the third system coupled with a full return
to a prior state."

Again, Freud finds an ingenious solution. Hitherto he had regarded
only quantities of neural excitation and their transmission. But excitation has another attribute, a temporal characteristic—frequency.
"Thus I shall assume that the resistance of the contact barriers

applies *only* to the *transmission* of the *quantity* of excitation but that the pattern of its *frequency is transmitted without inhibition in every direction as though it were a process of induction.* Much remains to be done here in the way of neurophysiological clarification. . . . Where do these differences in frequency pattern originate? Everything points to the sense organs where "qualities" of receptor stimulation must be represented by different frequencies. These sense organs operate not only as screens against quantity like every nerve-ending apparatus but as sieves, for they only let through stimuli of a particular frequency. They probably transfer the specific frequencies directly to the projection system and from there to the nuclear system which in turn, after considerable modification—especially in the quantity of excitation that accompanies the process—pass them on to the third system." The transmission of frequency that leads to the perception of "quality" is not durable—it leaves no traces, and therefore cannot be reproduced.

This is not the final solution for Freud of the relation of the third system to the others. The problem continued to plague him. Further along in the Project he states that the third and the nuclear systems "function to some extent like intercommunicating pipes." A year later—in a letter written in January, 1896—he has another view of the matter: "In my new scheme I insert the perceptual neurons between the projection and the nuclear neurons, so that the projection system transfers 'quality,' but merely excites the nuclear system."

This "new scheme" is maintained in Chapter VII of *The Interpretation of Dreams,* and is an unfortunate modification. For, what does "excite" mean other than the transmission of the intensity or frequency of neural activity? By intercalating processes important to "perception" between those that transmit sensory input and those involved in memory and motive, Freud loses a great deal of richness of *interaction* between motive, memory, and percept that the earlier model allows. And all this only to gain a false simplicity that will allow some unitary central process (in the nuclear system) to "parallel" and therefore culminate in the psychic! Dualism has taken its toll; for the later Freud, the black box that is the brain can safely be assumed to give forth the essence that is mind.

But Freud was also driven to his modifications by neuroanatomical fact. The projection systems terminate in the cerebral cortex (albeit after an interrupted passage through the dorsal thalamus). Are these "projection areas" then to be part of the nuclear system—or are they the location of the cells of the third system? Freud vacillates even in the Project. In places he divides the nuclear systems into two components—one of which is pallial (i.e., cortical). Yet, for the most part, the characteristics he ascribes to the nuclear system are unitary and noncortical, while those he ascribes to the third system he identifies with the properties he believes to be cortical.

Here, I shall assume that Freud is correct on all counts (provided there is no conflict). The third system according to this view which is characteristic of the latter part of the Project both receives excitations from the nuclear system and *at the same time* is intercalated between the projection and nuclear systems. Thus, the third, i.e., the cortical, and the nuclear systems are considered related as by "intercommunicating pipes"; the direction of transmission to be dependent on the particular parameters operating on the systems at any moment.

To summarize: There is a direct projection system. This is connected with exteroceptors which act as "sieves that let through" certain quantities of excitation with specific frequency characteristics. Because of repeated bombardment, the synapses between projection system neurons have a low resistance. This system acts essentially as a conduction pathway for the transmission of neural impulses. Both the quantity and the patterns of frequency of excitation are transmitted.

The connections of the projection system are both with a nuclear system and with a cortical system. The nuclear system is directly influenced as well by the internal environment of the organism through centrally located neuroreceptors. This nuclear system, since it is bombarded by smaller quantities of excitation, does not transmit indiscriminately. Synaptic resistance is lowered selectively by convergent excitations from various sources. The selectivity is the basis of memory and motive. Because of the relatively diffuse interconnections of the nuclear system, quantities of excitation are transmitted from the projection to the nuclear system "as from a trunk of a tree to its branches." Thus, what is quantity in the projection system is expressed as complexity in the nuclear system. Quantity of excitation in the projection system can be recorded in the form of neural impulses—in the nuclear system this same neural activity becomes cathected, i.e., bound, nontransmitted excitation, and is recordable as a graded potential change.

Primarily, although not exclusively, only the frequency characteristics of the excitation in the nuclear systems affect the cortical system. Thus the activity in the cortical system is a resultant of exteroceptive excitation transmitted both directly and in modulated form. The modulations are imposed in a matrix of the traces left in the nuclear system by the effects of prior similar excitations. According to this model, perceptions result from an interaction between current external stimulation and the residuals of prior experience with similar situations, an interaction modified by concurrent prior and present endogenous excitations. The now well-known experimental demonstrations by Bruner and Postman (1949) on the attainment of veridical perception are certainly more easily handled by this than by any other neurological model of the perceptual process current today. And what better view of the functions of the central nervous system have we that accounts for Lindsley's (1957) facilitation of tachistoscopically presented discriminations by electrical stimulation of the mesencephalic reticular formation?

PSYCHOLOGICAL DERIVATIVES OF
BASIC NEURAL PROCESSES

The model which Freud presents of the consequences of noxious excitations is thus not a simple one The operation of the model in psychological processes is still more complicated. There is in the Project no assumption similar to the "pain and pleasure centers" of the brain (Olds, 1959). Nor is there any oversimplified notion of some "optimal" level of over-all neural excitation which is rewarding (Hebb, 1955; Lindsley, 1957). Yet Freud's model is explicit and sophisticated, on both the neurological and on the behavioral level. Three sets of concepts are distinguished; each set deals with a different order of the complexity of events. The first refers to the *locus of origin* of the excitations that give rise to the awareness of *pain* and of *strain*. The second set of terms deals with affects—these are based on *memory traces* left in the nervous system when the organism has been subjected to pain or strain: *negative affects* on episodes of pain and strain; *positive affects* on relief from strain. Finally, a third set is used to describe a still more complex set of processes: *defense* and *satisfaction* involve the interactions between the memory traces that underlie affects and current excitations.

Pain, strain, and pleasure

Pain is defined on the basis of attempted escape from intense stimulation. Whenever the organism is subjected to noxious stimulation that originates outside, it attempts to escape. Therefore, pain—the result of excitation of the somatic receptors—is transmitted through the projection systems to the nuclear systems where, "like a stroke of lightning," transmission is facilitated. This facilitation makes it possible for the cortical system to receive in addition to the frequency the quantitative aspects of the stimulus. Another way of stating this is to say that the cathexis in the cortical system is suddenly and dramatically increased. The awareness of pain, for Freud, is a function of this sudden marked increase in cathexis in the cortical system. Pain ceases abruptly when the organism has removed itself from the noxious stimulation, because the "high permeability" of the cortical system allows it to get rid of excitation rapidly through efferent discharge.

Strain results from an entirely different mode of excitation. Strain is

produced when the receptors internal to the nervous system, the neuroreceptors, are stimulated. Here the organism has no simple mode of
removing himself from such excitation. Strain must be handled in a
different fashion, i.e., by changing the physicochemical environment
of these receptors through more complicated actions. The excitation
of the internal neuroreceptors also produces an increase in the cathexis
of the nuclear system which can be transmitted to the cortical system.
The awareness of strain is dependent on this increase of cathexis in
the cortical system; this increase is neither as sudden nor as great as
that which characterizes pain. The awareness of the relief from strain,
i.e., of *pleasure,* is dependent on a diminution, which is also gradual,
of this cortical cathexis.

The affects

The excitations that initiate and relieve pain and strain intimately
involve the nuclear system. Traces of these excitations are left in this
system, and these traces facilitate conduction paths so that on future
occasions they will be selectively activated. As already noted, these
selectively activated neural networks are the basis of memory and
motive. Minimal cathexis of the cortical system derived from the
excitations in these networks of the nuclear system is the neural concomitant of the affects.

Under what conditions, asks Freud, do affects occur, and what are
their components? Negative affects cannot be differentiated on the
basis of whether the irritant was external or internal, for there is in the
nuclear system considerable convergence of the pathways initiated by
the somatic and by the internal neuroreceptors. In fact, Freud points
out that the nuclear system is endowed in its midline portion with
secretory mechanisms and these are activated whenever the quantities
of excitation in the system reach a certain level. This is one reason
why strain cannot be simply relieved: stimulation of the internal
neuroreceptors activates the nuclear system, and when a certain level
of excitation has been reached, the neurosecretory cells are discharged.
This, in turn, results in the production of more of the chemical substances that stimulate the internal receptors. The cycle can be interrupted only through external intervention designed to diminish
abruptly the chemical stimulation, e.g., by feeding or by sexual release. So also, when a noxious external stimulus results in marked
increase in the quantity of excitation in the nuclear system, chances
are that this will activate the neurosecretory elements to pour out the
chemical subsances that stimulate the internal neurorecepors. As an
example, should one burn one's hand and withdraw it ever so quickly,
there is nonetheless a temporary increase in the adrenalin circulation
in the blood. Freud postulates a neurosecretory, i.e., a neurochemical

stimulation of the adrenal rather than (or in addition to) the direct neural stimulation of this gland.

Thus, the neural traces left by stimulation initiated either externally or internally come to include the effects of internal excitation. Negative affects, therefore, are based on more than a one-to-one reproduction of the initiating experience. The neural concomitants of the negative affects, i.e., minimal patterned increases in cortical cathexis, are the results of the interactions of the effects of the initiating experiences with those of the organism's internal reactions to the experience.

Positive affects are based on an additional complication. Whenever stimuli excite the nuclear systems, they activate not only the paths associated with an increase but also those that on prior occasions had led to a decrease in excitation. The effects from these trace excitations are to activate efferent motor discharge and so to minimally diminish cathexis in the cortical system; thus the organism experiences a positive affect. Should circumstances be similar to those that relieved the strain on prior occasions, positive affect accompanies actions that lead to pleasure. Should circumstance have changed significantly, however, then strain will not be relieved by these actions. And here it is necessary to invoke yet a third level of complexity.

Defenses and satisfactions

Prolonged and intense excitation can be initiated by an affect, i.e., by awareness of a memory of pain and strain and the situations that led to their alleviation. Such remembrances can stimulate the neurosecretory cells of the nuclear system—and thus start the accruing strain spiral anew. The normal organism is not continually strained. Freud postulates, therefore, that the individual develops a *defense* against this release of neurosecretions. The defense mechanism is conceived as a lateral distribution of excitation in the neural network of the nuclear system, i.e., a distribution in a direction other than the transmission of excitation to the neurosecretory and cortical cells. The defense consists therefore of a diffusion of excitation that brings into functional contact an increasingly larger pool of neurons in the nuclear system and so delays and often prevents the transmissions of excitation to the neurosecretory and cortical cells. Defense mechanisms so conceived prevent the build-up and maintenance of excessive strain.

The emphasis throughout the Project is on the interpersonal as well as on the neurological bases of the intrapsychic process. Freud therefore takes this opportunity to define as hostile those people whose actions could induce affects that would lead to strain. Defense in this context deals with hostilities. More of this in a moment.

Just as defenses develop to prevent affect from producing prolonged or overly intense strain, so satisfactions develop when affects result in pleasureable actions. The characteristics of satisfactions are rather different from those of defenses. The neural mechanisms of defense involve primarily the nuclear system, the neural mechanisms of satisfactions involve primarily the cortical system. When the organism repeatedly experiences pleasure—that is, the relief of strain—memory traces of the experience are built up in the nuclear system. When these traces are activated for whatever reason, and the excitations are transmitted to the cortical system, the person becomes aware of positive affects.

When the actions he undertakes on the basis of these positive affects are in concordance with the current situation, they lead to an experience of satisfaction. "As we showed in the beginning of the discussion, no discharge can bring about any permanent relief of tension as long as endogenous stimulations continue to be initiated and, in the nuclear system, excitation continues to be reestablished. The removal of these stimulations can only be effected by actions which will more or less stop the release of chemical substances in the interior of the body."

Again the emphasis is on the interpersonal:

> The excitation of the cortical system thus acquires an extremely important secondary function—that of bringing about an understanding with other people. The infant is so constituted that an extraneous helper must carry out specific actions in the external world on its behalf. Only when these are accomplished is the infant in a position by means of reflex contrivances to perform what is necessary in the interior of his body in order to remove the endogenous stimulus. This total series of events constitutes the basis of an experience of satisfaction: persons become a prime source of satisfactory (and unsatisfactory) experience; further, the actions undertaken to obtain satisfaction usually involve other persons—thus moral motives are built up. But these are only some of the momentous consequences in the functional development of the individual.

Before we go on to other momentous consequences, a brief review of this section is in order: At the simplest level Freud differentially defines pain and strain. Pain is consequent upon excitation of somatic receptors, and strain ensues from excitation of the neuroreceptors in the center of the brain. Pain can usually be escaped by removing the receptor from the excitant. Strain cannot be so easily done away with, especially since the neural mechanism into which the excitation feeds (the nuclear system) contains neurosecretory elements whose secretions directly regulate the chemical substances that presumably excited the neuroreceptors in the first place. The vicious spiral of accruing excitation that results in prolonged and excessive strain can be prevented only by the intervention of a complex series of actions undertaken by the organism or by others on his behalf.

The excitations that accompany experiences of pain and strain and their alleviation leave traces in the nuclear system. These traces, when they minimally change cathexis in the cortical system, are the basis of the affects. Affects may be set off by the current situation or they may be internally triggered. Affects are based on experience and they motivate (i.e., give direction to) behavior.

Accumulating excitation that could accompany affects has to be defended against. Neural defense mechanisms are conceived in terms of the development of lateral pathways in the nuclear system which act to diffuse excitation and so prevent, or at least delay, its transmission to neurosecretory and to cortical cells. Thus the organism is relatively protected against the prolonged unremitting strain that would otherwise be initiated by hostility, pain, and the stimulations of neuroreceptors that recur in the ordinary course of events.

Satisfactions are obtained when positive affects are congruent with reality, i.e., when the inputs to the cortical system from the projection and the nuclear systems are comparable, so that actions undertaken on the basis of positive affects lead to the relief from current strain. Pleasure can occur by happenstance; satisfaction depends always on achieving a match between the record of experience and stimulations produced in the current situation.

PSYCHOLOGICAL DERIVATIVES OF ADAPTIVE PROCESSES

Learning

Freud contends that learning results through the experience of satisfaction. When learning takes place, interconnections must be facilitated between trace and new neuronal excitations in the nuclear system; thus, the initial network is functionally extended so that subsequent excitation will cathect this larger network. Freud notes that this conception of the learning process assumes a fundamental "law of association by simultaneity." His mechanism of learning is also a physiological-drive-reduction theory of reinforcement.

There is a difference, however, between Freud's conception and that which characterizes current drive reduction theories. In much of current learning theory, drive reduction is assumed invariably to *initiate* the association of an environmental stimulus with the organism's response to this stimulus. For Freud, drive reduction is achieved as a *consequence* of an association by contiguity between the input from an environmental stimulus and memory traces left by prior drive-reducing experiences. Only when these associations lead to adaptive actions that reduce internal excitation for a fairly prolonged period can learning be said to have taken place. When, on the other hand, the situation has changed, and the actions taken are incongruous to the situation, no learning results. Nonetheless, reinforcement continues to occur by virtue of a temporarily effective discharge of the cathexis of the nuclear system. But this is accomplished only at the price of a rebound of even greater strain. The initially exciting stimulation is not removed and on each subsequent occasion it cathects a larger network of nuclear neurons. Thus there is an increasing likelihood that the defense mechanism will be overrun—unless it is simultaneously strengthened—and the accruing neurosecretory-neuroreceptor spiral of excitation established. In Freud's scheme, therefore, a nonadaptive neural process can be reinforced. Again Freud has anticipated the struggles that learning theorists have had with a problem.

Thinking

Freud now has the basis for making a distinction between two types of thinking: productive (cognitive) and reproductive (wishful). When an affect is modified (because a disparity between a memory and the reality situation is recognized) or, when a new affect replaces the old, productive thinking is taking place. When, on the other hand, such a change in affect does not take place, thinking is purely reproductive.

Reproductive thinking results when the cathexis of the neural networks involved in the positive affect overrides that produced by the current input. Such reproductive or *wishful* thinking carried to the point of hallucination involves a complete expenditure of the lateral cathexis (defense) in the nuclear system and is noted by Freud to be a *primary process*, since excitation is thus completely though temporarily discharged. Moderations of the total discharge of excitation—i.e., the maintenance of some cathexis in the nuclear system—is the *secondary process*. Correct exploitations of the indications of reality are possible only when there is sufficient lateral cathexis (i.e. defense) in the nuclear system to delay or prevent the accruing of excitation through the vicious spiral of neurosecretory-neuroreceptor stimulation. This defense against excessive discharge by dispersal of excitation within the nuclear system Freud calls the organism's ego function.

The case of cognitive thinking is the more puzzling one for Freud from the neurological standpoint. When the thought about a possible external object is initiated by a positive affect, that is, when a *wish* has been initiated and this wish and an external object are perceived to be similar but not identical, a "judgment" is made. There must be some mechanism to compare the similarities and differences between the excitation set up by the memory trace and that initiated by the current input. What that mechanism might be was far beyond the scope of nineteenth century neurology and Freud could not even hazard a guess as to its nature.

But recent work on the habituation of orienting reaction, (Sharpless and Jasper, 1956) has begun to fill the gaps in Freud's model of cognitive thinking. An organism is repeatedly exposed to a stimulus which, on the first occasion, was a novel one; electrical activity is comcomitantly recorded from the brain; gradually, the electrical patterns that are characteristically recorded only during the organism's exposure to novelty drop out. That this "habituation" to the novel stimulus is not due to fatigue of nerve cells has been shown. For instance, dishabituation (re-orientation) occurs immediately when, after habituation to a tone of a certain frequency and intensity has been in effect, the intensity of that tone is suddenly diminished. Dishabituation also occurs when the duration of the tone is shortened. The electrical patterns characteristic of orientation begin only at the moment the tone is turned off and persist for the duration of the "expected" length of the tone. Traces representative of the stimuli aroused by the situation must be built up in the nervous system during habituation so that the input of the moment can be matched against these traces. Response depends on this match or "judgment."

Electrical patterns have also been demonstrated to be characteristic of various phases of problem solution (Adey, 1960; Freeman, 1960). Certain electrical patterns recorded from limbic areas of cats during the early stages of training recur during later stages of training only when the animal makes an error. And two very sophisticated analyses of these electrical records have been interpreted to show that a "comparator" must be located in the regions from which the recordings are made!

In summary: For Freud, learning takes place only when the memory traces of initial pleasureable, i.e., strain relieving, experiences are modified by the current situation. On the other hand, reinforcement occurs whenever excitation in the nuclear system is discharged. A rebound from the discharge results when the actions on the basis of the memory trace are inappropriate to the situation—i.e., when affect is inadequately modified or unmodified by the input of the moment. In such instances the thinking that accompanies the discharge is termed wishful or reproductive. Satisfaction results only when the affect is modified sufficiently to take into account the current situation until it becomes conducive to lasting relief from strain. The thinking that accompanies this type of discharge is productive—cognitive— and entails a judgment or comparison between a wish and the reality of the moment. This comparison leads to the modification of the memory traces that initiated the wish—the modification necessary for learning to take place.

The remainder of the Project is concerned with an amplification of Freud's ideas and observations of normal and clinical behavior, as these are shaped by the neurological model he has developed. But then, the rest of Freud's career was engaged in this spirit. As time went on he tended to leave the neurological model implicit rather than, as in the Project, to detail it explicitly. There was good reason for this. Neurology had gone through a burgeoning period of factual and theoretical growth during the nineteenth century. The first part of the twentieth was involved in settling issues uncovered during the previous ferment and developing new technical tools with which to tackle the nervous system afresh. Freud continued to ferment. From the mid-twentieth century, it sometimes appears as if Freud turned from the "hard" science of the laboratory and the neurological clinic to the "softer" procedures of analysis of verbal behavior. But for Freud, psychological analysis was as rigorously conceived a scientific method as was neurohistological analysis. And in the context of history, Freud's evaluation of his own work may well prove the more accurate. A brief review of the "Zeitgeist" in Vienna around the turn of the century illuminates this view.

Toward the latter part of the last century, empirical analysis of the thought process was the dominant interest that occupied all psychologists. A human subject was given a task, asked to introspect— look inward while he tackled the problem—and to tell the experimenter the steps he took as he went along. Very often, in fact, the experimenter served as his own subject. Though the technique proved to be of limited value due to the differences between people in what their introspections revealed, some unexpected discoveries did result. The most systematic studies were made by a group of investigators at the University of Würzburg in Germany, who pinned down beyond a reasonable doubt the importance of the initial presentation of a task in determining all the subsequent events that take place during problem solution. Provided a problem is adequately accepted, the thought process seems to run itself off automatically when released. Great difficulty was experienced in any attempt to specify the nature of this running off process. Thus, thoughts were distinguished from thinking. Thoughts could be described in detail—and these descriptions were dubbed the "content" of the thought process. Thinking, on the other hand, became the more elusive and therefore the more interesting problem. The activity or act of thinking (Brentano, 1874) demanded an analysis of the antecedents of the content of thought, an analysis which taxed the capabilities of the scientific effort of the time.

As Edwin G. Boring has succinctly summarized (1950): "Act and content were in Europe the two horns of a dilemma. The empiricist who has his attention always on the nature of his own consciousness is burdened to accept activity as the essence of mind. The experimentalist [on the other hand] accepts content because he can work with it. . . . The empiricist accuses the experimentalist of being prejudiced by his method; the experimentalist replies that casual empirical observation has always failed to yield the truth and that science resorts to experiment for this reason."

The dilemma was temporarily resolved within the Würzburg school: both act and content were accepted and fairly rigorous descriptions were given of the laws that govern each. The result was a short-lived bipartite psychology (Külpe, 1893) which fell under the onslaught of the new approaches. As an example of this onslaught, William James (1950), the outstanding American empiricist, held that psychological processes were just that—processes. The stream of thought is his most eloquent example. He rejected analysis of process into content and act: "Though analysis is the necessary scientific method, analytic descriptions of mind fall short. The real mind is more than an aggregate of elements." The dilemma as stated by James is not between content and function, but between descriptive analysis and process. From today's vantage there is, of course, no such dilemma. Data are analyzed, processes are inferred from the analysis. Today data relevant to the study of the thought process are no longer limited to verbal reports of introspections made during problem solving behavior—all sorts of neurological and behavioral responses are admitted as evidence. But we are ahead of the story. James was not completely wrong in his criticism. The analytic approach of the Germans had served only as a beginning, but an excellent beginning it was.

The Viennese, just as the Americans, were especially concerned with the whole thought process. However, they did not reject identification of the central issue as the determination of what goes on during the *activity* of thinking. But they, as had the Würzburgers before them, came to see that superficial examination of the contents of thought did not directly lead to an understanding of process.

It was within this Zeitgeist that Freud began his studies of mental illness. As already mentioned, he had worked in the best neurological clinics and laboratories on the continent where such advanced (even by today's standards) methods as hypnosis were often used. From this background came a new technique: to allow the patient, by letting him say *anything* that came to mind, to reveal the contents of thoughts usually hidden to himself and to others. Freud seized the importance of his discovery: provided this usually hidden thought content is thoroughly explored, the activity of thinking *can* be understood. In essence, the technique reveals a whole series of thought contents, and from this series inferences can be made regarding the total process. Freud noted that the great majority of the contents of thought are not immediately accessible to introspection, and he called these contents preconscious and unconscious. Psychoanalytic theory thus became one important answer to the Würzburg dilemma. Act *can* be derived from content, provided the variety of nonreadily accessible content is adequately unveiled. The criticism of William James is met: exposure of contents of different levels of accessibility provides the continuity that an understanding of process demands.

The writings that describe the findings obtained in the psychoanalytic laboratory are many. For the most part, this body of evidence has little relation to the knowledge that comprises the biological and physical sciences. But a relationship should be discernible if a single scientific universe of discourse is to include both biological and social events. For those interested in the development of such a single universe through the formulation and execution of their research, the Project can prove valuable as a psychobiological Rosetta stone. To this end, and as a summary of this paper, a glossary of the neuropsychological concepts to be found in the Project is appended.

Glossary

AFFECTS: Neurologically, the affects result when cathexis in the cortical system minimally increases (negative affects) or decreases (positive affects). Such minimal changes in cortical cathexis accompany the activation of traces laid down in the nuclear system on prior occasions during episodes of pain and strain (the negative affects) and during experiences of the relief from strain. Affects, therefore, "color" current experience with pigments prepared on the palette of past impressions.

CATHEXIS: The excitation of neural tissue is measured as changes in electrical activity recorded from the tissue. Abrupt potential change —the nerve impulse—is a measure of propagated excitation. Recently the attention of neurophysiologists has again focused (as it had been in the latter half of the nineteenth century) on the nontransmitted electrical activities of neural tissue. The graded, spontaneously waxing and waning mechanisms were characteristically found where synaptic and dendritic fields predominate. These electrotonic manifestations of local neural excitability are measures of the cathexis of the tissue. Cathexis, therefore, refers to the amount of local nonpropagated neural excitation which leads to impulsive, transmitted excitation only under certain special circumstances.

COGNITIVE THINKING: Propagated neural activity has two aspects, a quantitative (number of impulses) and a qualitative (pattern of impulses). The propagation of quantity of excitation results in changes in cathexis; the transmission of quality does not. Perceptions result when patterns of excitation developed in receptors activate the cortex. Thoughts occur when patterns of excitation developed in the nuclear portions of the brain activate the cortex. Cognitive thinking takes place when the patterns of excitation developed in the nuclear systems and those developed in the receptors are matched—i.e., when thought and perception are compared. An incongruity may exist. Thinking is considered productive or cognitive when the incongruity is met by actions that change either the environment directly and thus the percepts, or the experience of the individual in the environment and thus the traces in the nuclear system from which the thoughts take origin. Changes in traces will, of course, also change the cortical cathexis and therefore the affects that accompany the thoughts. Any such change in the direction of congruity between thought and percept is adaptive.

DEFENSE MECHANISM: The nuclear systems have certain characteristics. (1) Their connections from the projection systems are like branches from the trunk of a tree. (2) They contain in their core, midline portion, both chemically sensitive neuroreceptors and neurosecretory cells. These characteristics determine certain consequences. The quantitative aspects of propagated excitation in the projection systems become distributed more or less randomly in the nuclear systems. Because of synaptic resistance propagation is hindered, and transmitted excitation is converted to local graded activation, that is, cathexis. An overwhelming or an oft-repeated excitation can overcome synaptic resistances and in this fashion transmission pathways are established through the nuclear systems. These pathways, though initially random, become structured by a process of selection that occurs at the neuronal level. This selection is the basis of directed behavior—i.e., of motive. The structure of the pathways is the neural memory trace. Excitation can thus be transmitted to the neurosecretory cells and to the cortex. Stimulation of neurosecretory elements results in an increase of the chemical substances to which the neuroreceptors are sensitive. A spiral of accruing excitation within the nuclear system is therefore possible and a mechanism must exist to defend against such accrual. The mechanism of defense is the lateral extension of the nuclear neural network that becomes activated on stimulation. This lateral extension in a direction other than that necessary for transmission of excitation to the neurosecretory cells and to the cortex—serves to disperse the excitation, and thus delays or prevents excessive accrual.

EGO STRUCTURE AND FUNCTION: The manifestations in behavior of the distributions of excitation in the nuclear system constitute an individual's ego characteristics. Ego structure depends on the particular nuclear networks of traces activated; ego function is the defense against a spiral of accruing excess of excitation.

EXCITATION: Organisms are alive, they therefore make transformations on systems of energy. Metabolic processes are one example of such transformations. Behavioral interactions with chemical and physical stimuli (psychological processes) are another. These interactions must be quantifiable. The problem is what to measure. The nervous system is intimately involved in regulating behavior—why not use indices of neural excitation as measures of the transformations of energy involved in the psychological process? And so, the nerve impulse, recorded electrically, is used as a measure of propagated neural activity. That leaves local, nontransmitted excitation. Electrotonic potential changes (and in today's language, other graded response mechanisms of neural tissues such as dendritic and synaptic potential changes) serve as indices of this type of neural activity. Freud uses the term cathexis to denote this localized neural excitation. The transformations of energy involved in the psychological process are therefore to be understood as changes in the neural processing of the interactions between the organism and its physical and chemical environment.

LEARNING: The adaptive behavioral change that accompanies a change in the structure of the neural traces in the nuclear systems. Learning takes place when a relatively durable relief from strain is achieved consequent to actions that minimize the incongruity between thought and percept. Such actions serve both to alter the situation and to provide new experience in the situation. Learning invariably involves some change in the affects that accompany the thought and percept since these affects result from the same neural trace structure that is undergoing change.

MEMORY: Synapses have only one property—they resist the transmission of quantity of excitation through the neural net. (They do not distort the propagation of frequency patterns, however.) Synaptic resistance is usually overcome only when the quantity of excitation on *both* sides of the synaptic junction builds up above some threshold. Resistance can also be overridden by excessive excitation. Repeated lowering of resistance at a particular synapse leads to a permanent conduction path through that synapse. Such permanent facilitation is the basis of memory. In the projection and cortical systems synaptic facilitation is relatively complete due to fairly direct contact with an ever exciting environment—their local patterns of excitation are therefore determined for the most part by the inputs to these systems. The nuclear systems, on the other hand, somewhat more isolated from external stimulation, provide the locus where synaptic facilitation can be selective. Here, therefore, patterns of excitation are dependent as much or more on traces left by previous synaptic facilitations as on those produced by current stimulation. The structure of memory at any moment is thus a function of these nuclear system traces as they are currently activated.

MOTIVE: Each cell within the nuclear system is in multiple contact with its neighbors. If resistance were overcome with equal ease at all of these contacts, transmission would be random. The organism does not behave randomly—his behavior is directed, i.e., motivated. To account for this, the assumption is made that the resistance of the various synaptic contacts of a cell are differentially affected in the nuclear system. All parts of a neuron must therefore not necessarily behave in the same way at any moment. That this is so has been demonstrated conclusively, at least in the invertebrate nervous system. Neurons, therefore, are the selectors of the paths of conduction that build up the memory trace. The function of this selection is to give direction—to motivate—behavior. The pattern of pathways of lowered resistance that are based on the selection form the memory trace.

PAIN: A sudden, dramatic increase in cortical cathexis follows noxious stimulation of somatic receptors. The psychological concomitant of this increase is pain. Not only are the usual frequency patterns of neural impulses transmitted to the cortex through the projection systems but a large quantity of excitation erupts from the nuclear systems because synaptic resistances are overwhelmed. With removal of the stimulus, there is a sudden drop in cortical cathexis, and thus a relief from pain.

PERCEPTION: Propagated neural excitation has two characteristics, quantity, based on the number of impulses, and quality, based on their frequency patterns. Frequency patterns are transmitted throughout the nervous system without modification by synapses. Those cortical frequency patterns that are derived from stimulation of somatic receptors are the basis of percepts. Cortical frequency patterns derived from the nuclear system are the basis of thoughts. There must therefore be in the cortex a mechanism that allows the input from projection and from nuclear systems to be distinguished. In fact, evidence is beginning to accumulate that such a mechanism does exist and that it serves as a comparator that matches the inputs for congruity.

PLEASURE: When the neuroreceptors of the nuclear system are stimulated, cathexis builds up gradually in the system. When this cathexis is transmitted to the cortex, strain is experienced. When stimulation of the neuroreceptors ceases, nuclear and therefore cortical cathexis gradually diminishes. This is felt as pleasure.

REINFORCEMENT: Whenever cathexis is discharged in the nuclear systems, there is lowering of the synaptic resistances involved—thus the particular pathways that are activated become reinforced. *Only* when the discharge (1) extends to new neurons in the network, or when the older pathways are modified, and (2) these changes lead to actions that effectively prevent the excessive accruing of nuclear system excitation, does the reinforcement lead to learning.

RESISTANCE: The property of synapses that counters the propagation of quantity of excitation in a neural net. The transmission of frequency patterns of nerve impulses is not altered by resistance. Synapses have no other property Current neurophysiological knowledge has not been looked at from this viewpoint. The techniques to study the transmission of patterns of frequency are in their infancy.

SATISFACTIONS: Satisfactions result from actions that diminish the incongruity between thought and percept so that further action leads to long lasting relief from strain. Pleasure may come inadvertently; satisfaction involves learning. Both are based on a diminution of cortical cathexis. When pleasure is experienced the nuclear trace systems remain unchanged; therefore the affects of the moment remain unchanged. For example, pleasurable sadomasochistic experiences are thus possible. When satisfactions are obtained, on the other hand, the nuclear trace systems do undergo change because of the experience involved in the attempt to match thought and percept. Thus the affects of the moment may undergo considerable change. The satisfying creative experience is fraught with such changes.

STRAIN: All noxious excitation cannot be escaped: e.g., stimulation of the neuroreceptors in the core of nuclear systems. Such excitation must be held at a minimum by actions on the part of the individual and his environment—for example, actions designed to reduce the amount of the chemical substances that stimulate the neuroreceptors. The gradually increasing cathexis produced by such stimulations, when transmitted to the cortical systems, are experienced as strain.

WISHFUL THINKING: A thought is wishful when the actions initiated by the thought override those that would be initiated by the percept in the situation. Such wishful actions are reinforcing because cathexis is temporarily relieved through efferent discharge. There is danger of rebound, however, since the conditions that led to the thought have remained unchanged and will re-initiate the now-reinforced wish. Should this process get out of hand, hallucinations develop. These are accompanied by the complete breakdown of the defense mechanism in the nuclear system, with the result that a vicious spiral of accruing neurosecretory-neuroreceptor excitation is established. Wishful thinking may occur when a situation changes so suddenly that thought and percept are so disparate that congruity cannot be established. Wishful thinking is apt to take hold in such circumstance when the thought is accompanied by strong affect—that is, when cortical cathexis is high.

References

Adey, W. R. Studies of slow wave activity in the hippocampal system in approach learning, and use of correlation analysis of the wave process. E. N. Sokolov (Ed.)., *Cybernetics and brain mechanisms,* Moscow, 1961.

Bishop, G. Natural history of the nerve impulse. *Physiol. Rev.,* 1956, *36,* 376–399.

Boring, E. *History of experimental psychology.* New York: Appleton-Century-Crofts, 1950.

Brentano, F. *Psychologie von Empirischen Standpunkte,* 1874.

Bruner, J. S., & Postman, L. On the perception of incongruity: a paradigm. *J. Personality,* 1949, *18,* 206–223.

Bullock, T. H. Neuronal integrative mechanisms. In *Recent advances in invertebrate physiology.* Eugene, Ore.: Univ. of Oregon Publications, 1957.

Bullock, T. H. Parameters of integrative action of the nervous system at the neuronal level. *Exper. Cell Research,* 1958, *5,* 323–337.

Bullock, T. H. Neuron doctrine and electrophysiology. *Science,* 1959, *129,* 997–1002.

Bullock, T. H., & Terzuolo, C. A. Diverse forms of activity in the somata of spontaneous and integrating ganglion cells. *J. Physiology,* 1957, *138,* 341–364.

Dubois-Reymond, E. *Untersuchungen,* 1849, Bd. i.

Foster, M., & Sherrington, C. S. The central nervous system. In *A text book of physiology.* (7th ed.) Pt. III, London: Macmillan, 1897, 915–1252.

Freeman, W. J. Correlation of electrical activity of prepyriform cortex and behavior in cat. *J. Neurophysiol.,* 1960, *23,* 111–131.

Freud, S. Project for a scientific psychology. Appendix in *The origins of psycho-analysis. Letters to Wilhelm Fliess, drafts and notes 1887–1902.* New York: Basic Books, 1954a.

Freud, S. Letter 39. In *The origins of psycho-analysis. Letters to Wilhelm Fliess, drafts and notes 1887–1902.* New York: Basic Books, 1954b.

Freud, S. The interpretation of dreams. New York: Basic Books, 1955.

Gerard, R. W. Physiology and psychiatry. *Amer. J. Psychiat.,* 1949, *106,* 161–173.

Gerard, R. W. Some aspects of neural growth, regeneration and function. In Weiss (Ed.), *Genetic neurology.* Chicago: Univ. Chicago Press, 1950, 199–207.

Gerard, R. W. Neurophysiology: an integration (molecules, neurons and behavior). In J. Field (Ed.), *Handbook of physiology, Vol. III.* Washington: American Physiological Society, 1960, 1919–1965.

Gloor, P. Electrophysiological studies on the connections of the amygdaloid nucleus in the cat. Part I; *EEG Clin. Neurophysiol.,* 1955, 7, 223–242. Part II; *EEG Clin. Neurophysiol..* 1955, 7, 243–264.

Hebb, D. O. Drives and the CNS (conceptual nervous system). *Psychol. Rev.,* 1955, *62,* 243–254.

James, W. *Principles of psychology, I.* New York: Dover Publications, 1950, 489–490; 177–179.

Jones, E. *The life and work of Sigmund Freud, Vol. I. The formative years and the great discoveries.* New York: Basic Books, 1953, 365–404.

Külpe, O. *Grundriss der Psychologie,* 1893.

Lindsley, D. B. "Emotion." In *Handbook of experimental psychology.* New York: Wiley 1951, 473–516.

Lindsley, D. B. Psychophysiology and perception. In *University of Pittsburg tenth annual conference on current trends in psychology: The description and analysis of behavior.* Pittsburgh: Univ. Pittsburgh Press, 1957.

Olds, J. Higher functions of the nervous system. In *Annual review of physiology,* Vol. *21.* Palo Alto: Annual Reviews, Inc., 1959, 381–402.

Pflüger. *Electrotonus.* Berlin, 1859.

Pribram, K. H. A review of theory in physiological psychology. In *Annual review of psychology.* Palo Alto: Annual Reviews, Inc., 1960, 1–40.

Pribram, K. H. Interrelations of psychology and the neurological disciplines. In *Psychology: a study of a science,* Vol. *4.* Washington, D.C.: American Psychological Association, 1962.

Rapaport, D. *Emotions and memory.* New York: International Universities Press, 1950.

Sharpless, S., & Jasper, H. Habituation of the arousal reaction. *Brain,* 1956, *79,* 655–658.

Sherrington, C. S. *The integrative action of the nervous system.* (1906) New Haven, Conn.: Yale Univ. Press, 1947 ed.

Sokolov, E. N. In M. A. B. Brazier (Ed.), *The central nervous system and behavior, transactions of the third conference.* New York: Josiah Macy Jr. Foundation, 1960.

Waldeyer-Hartz, W. von. *Deutsche med. Wchnschr.,* Leipzig, 1891.

PART FOUR

Behavior Modification: Experimental Bases of Psychotherapy

14

Prescribed Behavior Therapy: Suggestions from Interview Research

JOSEPH D. MATARAZZO

Psychologists during the past two decades, seem to have concentrated their theoretical and investigative efforts in the main on the study of *intrapsychic* factors in personality development and functioning. Thus, in common with their psychoanalytic and psychodynamically-oriented psychiatric colleagues, they tended during this period to pay less attention to extraindividual, or situational, variables in human behavior. However, this has not been true of all psychologists. Even before the post World War II period of mushrooming interest in projective techniques and the concomitant, almost exclusive assessment of intrapsychic personality dimensions, one psychologist, MacKinnon (1944), after a clear and critical presentation of various approaches to the study of personality, concluded:

> No longer can there be any doubt that there is both specificity and generality of behavior. Both personal consistency and inconsistency must be recognized.
> Proponents of a radical anti-trait theory who deny any generality of behavior or any consistency of personality commit the "situation error," the error of assuming that all behavior is determined solely by the specific situation, physical and social, in which the individual

The studies described in this chapter were supported by research grants (M-735, M-1107, and M-1938) from the National Institute of Mental Health, of the National Institutes of Health, U.S. Public Health Service.

finds himself. On the other hand, supporters of an extreme trait theory who deny any specificity of behavior or any inconsistency of personality commit the "organism error," the error of thinking of behavioral traits as fixed attributes of an *organism* as stable and as unchanging as a finger print or a birth mark (Murphy and Murphy, 1931). A field theory of personality which sees behavior and personality as functions of a total field of which they are subparts is the form of theory which today seems best suited for the conceptual representation of personality. Such a theory is slowly emerging from the work of many investigators . . . (p. 43).

As is well known, the problem of personality assessment has not been the concern of psychologists exclusively. For a number of years, other behavior scientists, notably Moreno (1934), Chapple (1940), H. S. Sullivan (1953), Bales (1951), Lennard and Bernstein (1960) to mention but a few, have concerned themselves with this problem. Although the terms used ("sociometry," "interaction theory," "interpersonal relations," "interaction process analysis," "action system"), differ from those used by psychologists, the problem area is the same. Research on the interview, both by psychologists and other behavior scientists, also has been extensive. To merely list the authors and titles of the thousands of studies on the interview would require numerous pages of the present chapter. An excellent review of many of the best studies on the interview will be found in (1) the *Handbook of Social Psychology*, especially in the chapter on the interview by Maccoby and Maccoby (1954), and also in the chapters by Heyns and Lippitt (1954), and Lindzey and Borgatta (1954); (2) the *Annual Review of Psychology*, volumes I to XII (1950–1961); (3) the book *Interviewing in Social Research* by Hyman, Cobb, Feldman, Hart, and Stember (1954); and (4) the book *How to Interview* by Bingham, Moore, and Gustad (1959). As might be expected, the almost exclusive concern of individuals doing research on the interview has been on the *content* of the interview. That is, investigative effort has been focused on *what* people say, whether the interview was for psychotherapeutic, diagnostic, selection, assessment, industrial, opinion polling, or other purposes.

The present chapter will focus on *non-content* aspects of the interview. That is, not on the *what* but on the *how* of interview behavior. In contrast to the hundreds of content-oriented investigators, to date only a handful of individuals have concerned themselves with non-content dimensions of interview behavior. The work of these few investigators will be reviewed at the end of this chapter. It is hoped that the research presented in this chapter will suggest to the reader that the methods of experimental psychology have much they can offer to clinical psychology.

THE CHAPPLE INTERACTION THEORY
OF PERSONALITY

Almost a decade ago, the present writer and a psychiatrist-colleague, George Saslow (and at various periods other psychologists and physician-colleagues) began a program of research on the interview which attempted to assess both organismic and situational variables in personality functioning and behavior. Our research methodology was heavily influenced by the previous work of Eliot D. Chapple, a Harvard anthropologist who later became a consultant to industry in personnel selection and organizational problems.

During the 1930's and 1940's, Chapple began to develop a technique for the objective measuremeant and description of "personality" based on an analysis in time units of the interaction between an interviewer and an interviewee (see Chapple, references 1939–1954). In one of these papers he stated: ". . . if we want to predict how people *will* act, the way to do it is to watch how they do act and not to infer their behavior from what they say without any means of observational check" (Chapple and Donald, 1946, p. 199).

This approach probably reflected Chapple's (and others') dissatisfaction with attempts to evaluate "personality" characteristics in terms of second and third order inferences from the basic or raw units of observation, such as assessing oral-dependent needs from a patient's free associations, or inferring "passivity" from a patient's use of shading nuances on the Rorschach. Chapple stated further that the "content" of the interview, what the patient says, is a much more difficult variable to quantify than is how he acts while saying it. The latter is an observable event which can be recorded by an observer and the question of "what the patient meant by what he said," i.e., the problem of low interjudge reliability in interpretation of levels of explanation of the content, is avoided. (Since these statements by Chapple, a number of investigators, notably Dollard and Auld [1959], Murray [1956], Strupp [see his chapter, this volume], as well as our own group, Phillips *et al.* [1961] have developed reliable methods of analyzing content.)

The core of Chapple's interaction theory is that the time dimension of one's interpersonal actions provides the major framework for understanding personality. Chapple arrived at his conclusion that time was an important variable for describing human relations after he and his early collaborator, Arensberg, found that their field work as anthropologists was unduly hampered by the lack of precision and communicability of the various "subjective" variables which anthropologists (and other behavior scientists) were then using to describe human relations in the family, tribe, interview situation, etc. Chapple

(1946) has described in everyday terms the importance of the time variable in human interactions.

> When we had come to the conclusion that existing methods of appraising personality were inadequate, we decided to try a different approach. What was needed was an objective yardstick. We began, therefore, by agreeing to limit ourselves to those aspects of a person's behavior which could be directly observed and recorded. From an examination of our previous studies in evaluation of personality, we concluded that one measurable factor that seemed highly significant was time. The question then arose: what traits of personality express themselves in time (Chapple, and Donald, 1946, p. 199).
>
> . . . the class of phenomena with which we are concerned comprises the (timing of) actions and interactions of individuals. It is now necessary to give a more precise definition of what this includes. As a matter of everyday observation, we see individuals coming together, and from the evidence of what we see and hear we unconsciously make certain judgments about their behavior. Such judgments are that one individual started to talk, and that the second individual to whom he was talking replied, and that both accompanied their speech with facial or bodily gestures (Chapple, 1940, pp. 21–22). We all know, as a matter of observation, that people have different rates (timing) of interaction. Some of our friends or acquaintances seem to talk and act very speedily as compared to ourselves; others are slow and deliberate. These characteristics of individuals are something we intuitively recognize, and we often are at variance with the rates at which others act. For example, where there are two persons in interaction, one whose actions are quick and speech voluble, and the other, slow and given to long, well-rounded periods, we are apt to find that the speedy one keeps interrupting the slow one, jumping in when the other pauses, and so on. If the slow individual is persistent, he may finally wear the other down, and our fast individual will subside into silence broken with a few "impatient" or "bored" remarks. Or conversely, the speed at which the fast person acts may so upset the slow individual that it will throw him off his stride and he will later confess that he thought the other person "hard to talk to," "never stuck to the subject," "always interrupted" (Chapple, 1940, pp. 31–32).

As we explained before, we do not infer and then attempt to record "feeling states" or "emotions" because we have no operations to deal with them and because we shall find that the quantitative analysis of interaction will in large measure describe such phenomena. In operations describing the timing of actions and events, we hope the reader will discover a useful and highly supple instrument. If the reader sharpens his powers of observation, he will see that in many cases people whom he does not like or cannot get along with, *say* exactly the things that the people he does like say.

So actors frequently take a short play, play it first as a tragedy and then, using the same words, play it as a comedy. Here the language is seen as unimportant, and the timing is the factor which makes the difference in its effect on the audience" (Chapple, 1940, p. 33).

From observation, we note how different people have different rates at which they originate (initiate) action. We all know cases of "bashful" people who will never speak unless spoken to. If spoken to they very frequently turn out to be very lively interactors. On the other hand, the "glad-hand artist," the "greeter," the man who speaks to everyone is a man with a very high origin (initiative) rate (Chapple, 1940, p. 43).

The above quotations will suffice to give an introduction to Chapple's interaction theory of personality. He early took the position that personality could be assessed without recourse to intrapsychic and other then currently popular psychodynamic formulations, and further that this assessment involves merely the process of observing the time relations in the interaction patterns of people. Accordingly, Chapple indicated that this method, because of its objectivity, could lead to a science of personality. This method, it can be seen, was consistent with MacKinnon's conclusion that the most promising approach to personality assessment would come from a "field theory" which gave sufficient weight both to "organismic" factors (the individual's behavior) and the "situational" or "field" (which involves the other interactees) variables (MacKinnon, 1944, p. 43).

Over the years, in work in both psychiatric and industrial settings (Chapple and Lindemann, 1942; Chapple, 1949, 1953; Chapple and Donald, 1946), Chapple has continued to develop both his theory and the instrument of measurement, the Interaction Chronograph, required to make the necessary observations.

In his early study of interaction patterns during interviews, Chapple placed little restriction upon the interviewer other than that he should use a nondirective interview of the type described by Rogers (1942). Chapple soon discovered, however, that every interviewer was different not only in the way he behaved but in the results that he obtained from the same subject (1949, p. 296; 1953, p. 23; Chapple and Donald, 1946, p. 203). Thus, it became clear not only that different interviewers have different interaction patterns when behaving in their own characteristic manner but that, as a result of these interviewer differences, different interaction patterns were elicited from the same patient when seen by two different interviewers. This was apparently true even though one could perceive no difference in what the interviewers said as judged by stenographic transcripts and even though they were following a supposedly uniform style of interviewing. For this reason

Chapple developed a standardized research interview. The character-istics of this interview are shown in Table 1, and its details will be described in greater length below. A full review of the development of this research interview will be found in two publications (Matar-azzo, Saslow, and Matarazzo, 1956; and Saslow and Matarazzo, 1959), and a description of the method is given in these papers as well as in Chapple's own publication (Chapple, 1953).

PREVIOUS RESEARCH

In a number of previous studies, use of Chapple's research interview (Chapple, 1953; Matarazzo, Saslow and Matarazzo, 1956), similar in all respects to a typical initial interview despite its being standard-ized along certain temporal dimensions, has allowed us to investigate a number of characteristics of the overt interview interaction behavior of patient and normal subjects. As will be described below, stand-ardization of this otherwise typical initial psychiatric interview has been limited to (1) having the interviewer confine each of his com-ments to a uniform duration of approximately five seconds; and (2) having him vary his behavior so that in three periods of the interview he carries out a free give-and-take, nondirective type of interview, and in two other periods he places the patient in a mildly stressful situ-ation. The latter is accomplished, as will be described, by the inter-viewer's remaining silent twelve times during one period of the inter-view (Period 2), and systematically interrupting the patient twelve times during another period (Period 4).

No restrictions of any kind are placed upon the *content* of the inter-view by the slight standardization and thus, as with other initial inter-views, the interviewer typically follows the leads of the patient as to what is discussed in the interview. Our experience with hundreds of different subjects and six different interviewers has made it clear to us that experienced visiting psychiatrists and psychologists watching the interviews through a one-way mirror, when told nothing of the minimal standardization, cannot differentiate these interviews from the typical initial interview. That is, when the research interviewer's 12 silence and 12 interrupting responses occur in their predetermined sequence (see Table 1), uninitiated but experienced therapists are un-aware of the striking planned changes in the interviewer's behavior. Perhaps their unawareness is related to their habitual attention to the content of the interview rather than to the temporal or expressive aspect.

We have found that inexperienced as well as experienced inter-viewers can learn in a moderate number of practice interviews to be-come comfortable and spontaneous, while following reliably such

standardization rules as speaking in utterances of five-seconds duration, falling silent in a predetermined way in the silence period, and
interrupting in a planned way in the interruption period. Our first two
interviewers received 40 practice sessions (Saslow, Matarazzo, & Guze,
1955). We have since learned that fewer practice interviews are sufficient.

Reliability Studies

To date, our results with the partially standardized interview suggest that interviewee interaction behavior has the following characteristics. First, there are wide individual differences in interaction behavior
among subjects. Second, the interviewee interaction behavior for any
given subject is highly stable (reliable and unique for him) across two
different interviewers when the latter standardize their interviewing
behavior along the predefined dimensions of our method. At the same
time, the interviewee behavior is demonstrably and reproducibly
modifiable by planned changes in the intra-interview behavior of either
interviewer (Matarazzo, Saslow, Matarazzo, and Phillips, 1958).
Third, the marked stability and reproducible modifiability of an individual's interaction behavior, found for one sample of subjects (Saslow, Matarazzo, and Guze, 1955), could be crossvalidated in a second
sample (Matarazzo, Saslow, and Guze, 1956). Both these studies
utilized two interviewers, each independently and in counterbalanced
order interviewing the same patients; and employed a test-retest interval of only a few minutes between the first and second interview.
Fourth, the stability and modifiability were equally striking when
only a single interviewer was used and the test-retest interval between
his two interviews with the same patient was extended to seven days
(Saslow, Matarazzo, Phillips, and Matarazzo, 1957); five weeks (Saslow and Matarazzo, 1959); and eight months (Saslow and Matarazzo,
1959).

These various studies also established high reliability for: (1) the
behavior of the *interviewer*, who serves as the independent variable
by conducting the standardized interview (Saslow and Matarazzo,
1959, pp. 135–139); (2) as described above, the reliability of *interviewee* interaction behavior, the dependent variable (pp. 139–148);
(3) the reliability of the *observer*, who observes the interviewer-inter-
viewee interaction and records his observations by pressing separate
keys for each participant (Phillips, Matarazzo, Matarazzo, and Saslow, 1957); and, finally, (4) the reliability of the *scorer* (Saslow, Matarazzo, and Guze, 1955, p. 429), who scores the interaction record
that is made of the interview by use of a specially designed recording
device, the Interaction Chronograph (Chapple, 1949; Matarazzo, Saslow, Matarazzo, 1956).

Validity Studies

Having established unusually high reliabilities for these interview interaction behaviors, we have thus far approached the question of their validity from a number of points of view (Cronbach and Meehl, 1955). The first of these studies was an attempt to establish one aspect of what Cronbach and Meehl (1955, p. 287) call *construct validity*, and involved a factor analysis of twelve of the interview interaction variables (Matarazzo, Saslow, and Hare, 1958). The results revealed that the standardized interview was made up of two stable and independent factors: *silence* behavior and *action* behavior (i.e., the average duration of the interviewee's habitual silence, or latency, before speaking, and the average duration of each of his utterances, or actions). Two weaker factors also emerged: *initiative* behavior and *adjustment* behavior (the frequency with which a subject initiates or starts again with another communication of his own when his partner has not answered him; and the efficiency with which a member of the communicating pair adjusts, or maladjusts, to his partner by waiting too long and by interrupting).

A second construct validity study (Kanfer, Phillips, Matarazzo, and Saslow, 1960) involved an investigation of the effects of an interviewer content variable (interpretations of S's motives, personality, etc.) on S's duration of speech units (S's interview Actions). The results showed a decrease in S's durations of Actions when the interviewer introduced the experimental variable (a change from previously neutral nondirective five-second utterances to more challenging, interpretive five-second utterances), and a subsequent increase in S's duration of Actions when the interviewer returned to the previously more neutral type of interview content. Other types of construct validity studies are currently underway.

Our concurrent validity studies have been of four types. In one we examined by a variety of psychological assessment techniques the same patients whom we also interviewed by this interview method and we found a number of interesting psychological test and organismic correlates of interviewee behavior (Matarazzo, Matarazzo, Saslow, and Phillips, 1958). In a second study we investigated the relationship of some aspects of an interviewee's self-description (as revealed in the content of his interview) and the formal (measured in time units) overt interviewee interaction behavior (Phillips, Matarazzo, Matarazzo, and Saslow, 1961). In this study a number of suggestive relationships were found between self-description (content) and actual interview responses (interaction behavior). A third concurrent validity study involved the simultaneous recording of *Bales Interaction Process* scores and our own interview interaction measures in twenty four interviews, and revealed a number of significant relationships between the two independent sets of interview measures (Hare, Waxler, Saslow, and Matarazzo, 1960). The fourth study involved an analysis of the differences in total interview interaction behavior in five groups of subjects, ranging from hospitalized schizophrenics, through outpatient neurotics, to two groups of normal subjects (Matarazzo and Saslow, 1961). This study revealed that there were a number of striking differences between the total interview behaviors of the various patient and normal groups.

The purpose of the validity study to be described in detail below was to investigate still another aspect of the construct validity of interviewee interaction behavior. More specifically, having found that the over-all interview behavior of different diagnostic groups was demonstrably different, we set out to study whether or not the subjects in the five diagnostic groups were equally amenable to the intra-interview influence of the interviewer's standardized changes in behavior from one interview period to another. (These changes in interviewer behavior are shown in Tables 1 and 3.) In a previous study (Matarazzo, Saslow, Matarazzo, and Phillips, 1958), we had shown that the intra-interview behavior of 60 outpatient psychiatric patients (primarily neurotics) could be modified by the planned changes in an interviewer's behavior. It was the purpose of the study which will now be described to extend this investigation to four additional diagnostic groups.

INTERVIEWER-PRODUCED CHANGES IN INTERVIEWEE INTERACTION BEHAVIOR

The five groups consisted of two normal groups and three patient groups. They were: (1) 17 unselected "normals" who were applicants for sales and sales-supporting jobs (14 female, 3 male, all white) from the Carson-Pirie-Scott Department Store in Chicago; (2) 40 unselected "normals" who were applicants for sales and sales-supporting jobs (20 female, 20 male, all white) from Gilchrist's Department Store in Boston; (3) 60 unselected outpatients, primarily "neurotic" (all white, 32 female, 28 male, ranging in age from 16 to 62, mean of 33) from the Washington University School of Medicine (St. Louis) Department of Psychiatry Outpatient Clinic; (4) 20 unselected mixed acute "psychotic and neurotic" patients* (5 inpatients and 15 outpatients, 12 females and 8 males, all white, mean age of 42, and a range from 15 to 80) from the Massachusetts General Hospital in Boston; and (5) 19

---

* These 20 subjects constituted the total sample of group 1 of two groups of 20 subjects each studied by us in Boston (Matarazzo, Matarazzo, Saslow, and Phillips, 1958).

highly selected, chronic (all hospitalized uninterruptedly for a mean of 8.3 years, range 3 to 18 years), white, male, schizophrenic patients (diagnosis agreed upon by two very experienced psychiatrists in each case), ranging in age from 27 to 42 with a mean of 33, who were interviewed by us at the Research Facility of the Rockland (New York) State Hospital.

The recording of the interview behavior for each of the five groups was by Chapple's Interaction Chronograph (Matarazzo, Saslow and Matarazzo, 1956). This instrument, a large electro-mechanical recording device which is activated by an observer from the other side of a one-way mirror, permits the continuous and simultaneous measurement and recording of such interviewee and interviewer interaction variables as: the number of units of each person's interaction; duration of each of these communicative actions; the duration of each silence; the frequency with which the interviewee takes the initiative during a subperiod in which the interviewer purposely reacts with silence by failing to respond to the interviewee's last utterance; the frequency and duration of each participant's interruptions, the resulting dominances and submissions, and several other variables. Definitions of these variables are given in our previous publications.

Unknown to the interviewee, the standardized interview is divided into five periods, with Periods 1, 3, and 5 as free give-and-take periods (essentially nondirective interviewing), and Period 2 (silence) and Period 4 (interruption) as stress phases of the interview (Chapple, 1953; Matarazzo, et al., 1956). The over-all characteristics of this minimally standardized interview are shown in Table 1, whereas

TABLE 1

Characteristics of the Standardized Interview

PERIOD	TYPE OF INTERVIEWING	DURATION OF PERIOD	
		FIXED DURATION	VARIABLE DURATION
I	Free	10 minutes	
II	Stress (Silence)		12 failures to respond, or 15 minutes, whichever is shorter
III	Free	5 minutes	
IV	Stress (Interruption)		12 interruptions, or 15 minutes, whichever is shorter
V	Free	5 minutes	
Total		20 minutes	plus a maximum of 30 more minutes

TABLE 2

Standardized Interviewer's Behavior: Rules for Interviewer

PERIODS 1 TO 5 (ALL PERIODS)

a. Interviewer introduces each period by a five-second utterance (following his signal to the observer).

b. All interviewing must be *nondirective*. No direct questioning, no probing or depth interviewing. Interviewer can reflect, ask for clarification, ask for more information, introduce a new topic area, etc. In general, interviewer's comments should be nonchallenging and open ended and related to the patient's past comments or to some new, general topic.

c. All interactions must be verbal only, or verbal and gestural at the same time; i.e., interviewer cannot use head nods and other gestures alone. This rule simplifies the observer's task.

d. All of the interviewer's utterances must be approximately five seconds duration.

e. After patient finishes a comment or other interaction, interviewer must respond in less than one second, except as otherwise noted in Period 2.

f. Each time patient interrupts interviewer, the latter must continue to talk for two more seconds. This rule insures more explicit definition of a patient's ascendance submission pattern than would be possible if interviewer "submitted" immediately.

PERIODS 1, 3, AND 5

a. Interviewer must never interrupt patient.

b. If after interviewer makes a comment patient does not respond, interviewer must wait fifteen seconds and then speak again for five seconds.

PERIOD 2 ONLY

a. Interviewer must "fail to respond" to last interaction of patient a total of twelve times (or for 15 minutes, whichever is shorter).

b. After interviewer has been silent for fifteen seconds (and patient has not taken initiative) interviewer makes another five-second comment.

PERIOD 4 ONLY

a. Each time patient acts, interviewer must interrupt patient for five seconds for a total of twelve times.

b. Interviewer's interruption should begin about three seconds after patient has begun his interaction.

c. After having interrupted patient, if the patient continues through the interruption (does not submit), interviewer will not interrupt again until patient has finished his utterance, i.e., interviewer will interrupt patient only once during each utterance of the latter if patient does not "yield."

d. The period is ended after twelve interruptions or fifteen minutes of attempting to obtain these.

the rules guiding the interviewer's intra-interview (period-to-period) behavior are shown in Table 2. Essentially, this standardized interviewing procedure requires the interviewer to (1) increase his own duration of silence before responding to the interviewee from the short one-second (or less) latency he has been following in Period 1 (and Periods 3 and 5) to 15 seconds in Period 2 (Silence Period), and to have no silences at all in Period 4 (Interruption Period) when for 12 of the exchanges of this period the interviewer is interrupting the interviewee; and (2) correspondingly, since he is remaining silent in Period 2, to decrease his own durations of action from five-seconds per each action in Period 1 (and Periods 3, 4, and 5) to zero-second actions (silence) in Period 2. The essentials of the interviewer's modification of his own silence and action behavior are schematized in Table 3.

Within each of the stress periods (Periods 2 and 4) one finds, as shown in Table 3, that the interviewer has two possibilities of silence and of action behavior. Period 2 describes those interviewer interactions in which the interviewee has finished a comment and the interviewer does not answer him (i.e., applies a silence stress to that unit of interviewee action). As appears in Table 1, the standardized procedure requires that the interviewer apply the silence stress 12 times. Some interviewees react to this sudden change in interviewer behavior (from Period 1, interviewer silences of less than one second to Period 2, interviewer silences of 15 seconds) by taking the initiative in less than 15 seconds (Table 3, Period 2a); i.e., by talking again and thereby breaking the silence following their own last utterance. As is shown in Table 3, Period 2a, in these instances in which the interviewee himself speaks again within 0 to 14 seconds following his own last utterance, the interviewer's action (since he has not been speaking) is zero.

Since it is possible (during the interviewer silence) for an interviewee, himself, to fail for an indefinite period to speak after one of his own last utterances, thereby showing no initiative behavior for that

TABLE 3

Duration of Interviewer's Behavior

PERIOD		SILENCE	ACTION		SILENCE	ACTION	
I		1	5				
II	(a)	0–14	0	or	15	5	(b)
III		1	5				
IV	(c)	Interruption	5	or	1	5	(d)
V		1	5				

unit of exchange, an empirically useful upper limit of 15 seconds (Table 3, Period 2b), has been put on the interviewer's silence for each of the interviewer's 12 silence units. Thus, for any given unit, if an interviewee fails to take the initiative for a duration of the full 15 seconds, the interviewer will restimulate him with another five-second utterance for that unit of interaction (Table 3, Period 2b). Following the interviewee's action to this restimulation, the interviewer proceeds with the next unit of silence stress. This is continued until 12 silence responses have been given by the interviewer, or a total of fifteen minutes have elapsed in Period 2 (as shown in Table 1).

Data from a recently completed sample of 40 young Portland normal males (20 policeman and 20 firemen applicants) show that the percentage of responses in which these subjects *do not* take the initiative (i.e., do not respond again following their own last utterance within 15 seconds) is 35.4; while the percentage in which they *do* take the initiative is 64.6. For these 40 subjects the mean duration of interviewer latency in the former case (Table 3, Period 2b), as expected from the standardization rules, was 15.75 seconds (i.e., he waited the full 15 seconds for them to take the initiative during his planned silence); while the mean duration of interviewee* latency in the latter case (Table 3, Period 2a) was 4.48 seconds (i.e., in those 64.6 percentage of instances in which subjects *did* take the initiative during E's planned 15-second silence, they took the initiative in 4.48 seconds, on the average). Thus during 12 planned 15-second interviewer silences, these young, normal subjects took the initiative and talked again in two thirds of the cases, and did so in 4.48 seconds after getting no response from the interviewer. In the remaining one third cases, the subjects waited the full 15 seconds, after which time the interviewer talked.

As shown in Table 3, during the interviewee Period 2 silence behavior (type a), the interviewer's corresponding Action behavior is by definition zero seconds (i.e., he remains silent and thus is not talking until S takes the initiative or the full 15 seconds have elapsed). However, since, in a sizable percentage of the instances in Period 2 (35.4 per cent in our recent sample) the interviewee *does not* show initiative, and himself fails to respond in the 15-second period, E, in fact does do some talking in Period 2. These instances in Period 2 in

---

* Technically this 4.48 seconds is the duration of *interviewer* latency since the interviewee spoke last. It is here called interviewee latency because it is the interviewee who responds again to his own last utterance. To differentiate this interviewee latency measure from interviewee latencies in other periods, Chapple has called these durations of latency to one's own last utterance *quickness*. Quickness is measured only in Period 2, and only in those instances in which the interviewee, himself, responds to his own last utterance during the interviewer's 0–14 seconds of planned silence (i.e., Quickness is scored only in Table 3, Period 2a, situations).

which E must restimulate (after the full 15-second silence stress for each interviewee unit) we have labeled Period 2b situations. As shown in Table 3, E's durations of actions following Period 2b silences, as with all of E's actions, are approximately five seconds in duration.

One type of silence behavior by E during the Period 4 stress cannot be given a duration value in Table 3 (Period 4c), unless, of course, it were labeled as zero seconds (which value is not strictly correct). This follows by definition, since E is interrupting in Period 4 and thus cannot earn any latency or silence score after S has stopped talking. Since E's interruptions are five seconds each, E's corresponding action behavior in Table 3, Period 4c is shown as five seconds. In many instances in Period 4, when E interrupts S with a five-second utterance, S will abruptly (or shortly) terminate his own utterance. In these instances, Chapple considers that the interviewer has "dominated" and the interviewee has "submitted." On the other hand, Table 3, Period 4d situations occur in Period 4 when the interviewee does not submit during one of the interviewer's 12 interruption units but, rather, continues to talk beyond the five-second point at which the interviewer, himself, must terminate his interruption. Following the termination of this "nonsubmission" utterance by S, E waits one second and then, himself, speaks for five seconds (thus manifesting a Period 4d silence and a Period 4d Action as shown in Table 3).

Thus, Table 3 provides a schematic presentation of the intra-interview changes in the interviewer's behavior during a standardized interview. The purpose of the present research was to examine the effects of this planned modification in the interviewer's behavior from Period 1 through Period 5 (Table 3) upon the silence and action behavior of a variety of subjects.

Before presenting the results, a word should be said about two relevant features of our recording device, the Chapple Interaction Chronograph. Although this computer is currently in the process of continuing modernization, the model we used during the five years during which data for the present study were collected had several minor shortcomings. One is that the data are recorded in hundredths of a minute rather than in seconds, since 60-second commercial counters were not considered feasible when Chapple first developed the present model of his recording device. This shortcoming is overcome simply by multiplying the duration figures given by the Interaction Chronograph by .6, thus converting hundredths of a minute to seconds. This should be done for the data in Tables 4 and 5, if the reader wishes to know the values in seconds.

The second shortcoming of the model of the Interaction Chronograph we used in the present research was a little more vexing, although, again, not a major problem. Apparently, in order not to multi-ply indefinitely the number of recording counters required for his purposes, Chapple built into his device a Silence counter which re-corded not only the interviewee's silences as commonly understood (i. e., his latencies or reaction times following the termination of E's last action) but also any and all silences on the part of the inter-viewee. Thus, not only are S's reaction times to E's last action re-corded by this counter, but also recorded by the Silence counter are all those durations in which E is talking (and, of course, S is silent, presumably listening).

Since, by definition, when E does talk he does so for a prescribed duration of approximately five seconds, this potentially contaminating factor in Chapple's Silence variable is a constant and, thus, should not handicap the purposes of the present study. To test this hypothesis, we went through the laborious procedure of doing a unit-by-unit analysis of similarly standardized interviews with our 20 young Portland fire-men applicants. Although tedious, the analysis provided us with indi-vidual duration measures of S's Latency (or S's reaction time follow-ing E's last utterance) and S's Silence (Chapple's contaminated vari-able; i.e., S's duration of latency plus duration of interviewer's Action) for each unit given by S in each of the 20 interviews. The data thus obtained permitted us to correlate the desired S's Latency variable with the machine-given S's Silence variable. For the 20 subjects, a Pearson Product-Moment correlation between these two variables was .83, significant at the .001 level of confidence. Since our hypothesis was confirmed, we have concluded that Chapple's S's Silence variable is an adequate measure of S's Latency to E's last utterance, one of the two variables we were studying in the present research.

From Table 3 and the earlier discussion, it is clear that the inter-viewer changes his own silence behavior in two periods, Periods 2 and 4. In the former period he increases his own silences from their pre-vious Period 1 durations of one second or less to 15 seconds in Period 2, whereas in Period 4 he changes from the previous one-second or less durations of Period 3 to interruptions (i.e., *no* latency at all). In Period 5 the interviewer returns to one-second or less latencies.

Such changes in an interviewer's own latency behavior are reliably learned, and reliability data for this variable are presented in an earlier report (Saslow and Matarazzo, 1959; pp. 137–138) for one E with a sample of the S's of the present study. Comparable data are given in the same reference for the reliably learned five-second utterances by E.

Table 4 presents the results for our five present groups for S's Silence variable during each of the five interview periods. Because of the lack of any published research with these interview interaction variables,

TABLE 4

Changes in Mean Durations of Silences of Patients and Normals
as Interviewer Modifies His Own Durations of Silence During
Five Periods of a Single Interview

		SCHIZ		MIXED GROUP		OUTPATIENT		NOR-MAL	NOR-MAL
		ORIG	REPL	ORIG	REPL	ORIG	REPL	GIL	CARSON
Period	N	19	19	20	20	60	60	40	17
I	M	11*	10	8	8	8	8	11	7
	SD	4	4	2	2	2	2	4	2
II	M	16	16	14	14	14	14	17	13
	SD	11	12	6	6	7	6	6	6
III	M	11	12	9	8	9	9	12	11
	SD	6	6	2	2	4	3	6	11
IV	M	9	8	6	6	6	6	7	6
	SD	7	5	2	2	2	3	4	2
V	M	10	12	8	8	8	8	10	8
	SD	4	6	2	2	2	2	7	2
F-test		4.80	7.95	17.84	19.97	44.70	46.45	18.00	4.34‡
Friedman test		12†	10†	37	35	104	102	75	36
p		.01	.001	.001	.001	.001	.001	.001	.001

* These average silences are expressed in hundredths of a minute. To convert to seconds multiply by 0.6.
† Significant at the .05 level of probability.
‡ Significant at the .01 level of probability.

and for other reliability* researches then underway, we felt it necessary to attempt to crossvalidate our findings. Thus, the outpatient group of 60 subjects was given a second standardized interview (for 40 of these 60 subjects, five minutes later by a second interviewer who had not observed the first interview, and seven days later by the same interviewer for the remaining 20 subjects); the mixed group of 20 subjects was re-interviewed after an average period of eight months; while the 19 chronic schizophrenics were re-interviewed after five weeks. Since it was not possible to replicate the results with our group

* The test-retest reliability coefficients for the silence and action data shown in Tables 4 and 5 are of the order of .77 and .90, respectively (Saslow and Matarazzo, 1959, pp. 141–147).

of 17 Carson-Pirie-Scott normals, we attempted to crossvalidate the findings with this group on a second group of normals (i.e., the 40 Gilchrist normals). Thus Table 4 shows results from an original study and a replication (reliability) study for each of the three patient groups, and, in effect, one normal group with the second normal group serving as its replication group.

The results shown in Table 4 indicate clearly that interviewee silence behavior is influenced by planned changes in the interviewer's own silence behavior (as these are shown in Table 3). Thus, as the interviewer increased his own silences from less than a second in Period 1 to 15 seconds in Period 2 (see Table 3), each of the five groups shown in Table 4 shows a corresponding increase in silence behavior from Period 1 to Period 2: i.e., an increase from 7-13; 11-17; 8-14; and 11-16 hundredths of a minute. This increase in mean interviewee silence duration from Period 1 to Period 2 ranged from 45 to 86 per cent for the original interviews with the five groups. When the interviewer next decreased his own latencies to less than one second in Period 3, each of the five groups, in turn, showed a similar decrease in its Period 3 silences. In Period 4 the interviewer typically has no latencies at all (since mostly he is interrupting); i.e., while Period 3 latencies are one second or less, these interruptions constitute a further decrease in the interviewer's own latency from Period 3 to Period 4. Table 3 schematizes this as a change from one-second latencies in Period 3 to less than zero-second latencies (interruptions) in Period 4. Table 4 shows for the five groups a corresponding decrease in the subjects' own silence behavior from Period 3 to Period 4. In Period 5 the interviewer returns to latencies of one second or less (i.e., an increase in his own latency from Period 4 to Period 5). Table 4 shows a similar increase in silence behavior from Period 4 to Period 5 in each of the five groups.

Since the standard deviations for this silence behavior were quite large, especially in the chronic schizophrenic group, statistical analysis of the silence behavior of each of the diagnostic groups across the five periods was carried out by both F-test and by a nonparametric test. The former was an F-test for correlated means (McNemar, 1955, pp. 288–290), while the latter was the Friedman test (Siegel, 1956, pp. 166–171). Table 4 shows that the results of both statistical analyses clearly indicate that the changes in interviewee silence behavior across the five interview periods are highly significant (typically at the .001 level). In addition since the direction of change (increase in interviewee silence behavior in Period 2, decrease in Period 4) is (1) identical in all groups, (2) crossvalidated through replication studies in the three patient groups, and (3) crossvalidated by use of a second normal group in the Carson-Pirie-Scott normal sample, it is fair to conclude that the finding that interviewee silence behavior is susceptible to interviewer influence is highly reliable.

For each diagnostic group and its replication (eight groups in all), the data in Table 4 were subjected to a t-test analysis of the differences between pairs of means. While an occasional pair of means was significantly different when each of the three nonstress periods (Periods 1, 3, and 5) were compared, one with every other, by far the greatest influence (both in magnitude of the differences and the absolute number of significant t-tests) was contributed by the two stress periods (Periods 2 and 4). Out of 24 t-tests of the possible three nonstress period pairs of means' comparisons (Periods 1, 3, and 5 with each other), five (or 21 per cent) were significant. While, for the two stress period comparisons, comparing Period 2 with Period 4 eight times, eight out of eight (100 per cent) t-tests were significant. Comparing Period 2 with each of the three nonstress periods, and also Period 4 with each of the three nonstress periods resulted in 42 (89 per cent) significant t-tests out of 48 possible. Thus the behavior of the interviewer in the two stress periods contributed the largest effect on the interviewee.

These period by period comparisons and the over-all results shown in Table 4 support the conclusion that experimentally introduced changes in duration of interviewer silence behavior are followed by similar changes in interviewee silence behavior. In addition, for this (silence) interaction dimension at least, normals, neurotics, mixed neurotics and psychotics, and schizophrenics act similarly; i.e., are influenced by the interviewer's behavior in identical directions.

The latter finding is not true for the second interview dimension: duration of interviewee action.

Table 3 shows that the interviewer, in effect, modifies his own action behavior from five-second actions in Period 1, to zero-second actions, for the most part, in Period 2 (a very sizable decrease), to five-second utterances in Period 3, to five-second utterances (and the additional dimension that these are interrupting five-second utterances) in Period 4, to neutral five-second utterances in Period 5.

Table 5 shows the corresponding action behavior data for the interviewees of the five diagnostic groups. While it is clear from the bottom of the table that, statistically speaking, effects of similar magnitude (p of .001) to the silence data were produced in interviewee action behavior, it is also clear that only four of the five diagnostic groups behaved similarly under this standardized interview behavior. The fifth group, the 19 chronic schizophrenics, reacted differently to the Period 2 silence stress.

TABLE 5

Changes in Mean Durations of Actions of Patients and Normals
as Interviewer Modifies His Own Durations of Action
During Five Periods of a Single Interview

		SCHIZ		MIXED GROUP		OUTPATIENT		NOR-MAL	NOR-MAL
		ORIG	REPL	ORIG	REPL	ORIG	REPL	GIL	CARSON
Period	N	19	19	20	20	60	60	40	17
I	M	77*	85	45	44	69	59	120	134
	SD	117	145	50	32	81	40	74	102
II	M	120	108	35	28	52	52	84	67
	SD	234	188	25	10	46	54	50	43
III	M	131	111	39	57	64	66	227	140
	SD	246	179	33	85	60	86	224	113
IV	M	8	12	7	6	10	13	82	75
	SD	8	28	4	2	5	30	207	58
V	M	95	142	42	35	59	50	182	102
	SD	229	271	48	31	78	49	208	81
F-test		2.87†	3.41‡	6.62	5.20‡	13.08	14.98	8.40	4.47‡
Friedman test		38	39	42	46	114	122	78	32
p		.001	.001	.001	.001	.001	.001	.001	.001

* These average actions are expressed in hundredths of a minute. To convert to seconds multiply by 0.6.
† Significant at the .05 level of probability.
‡ Significant at the .01 level of probability.

Thus, as the interviewer decreased his own durations of utterance from five seconds in Period 1 to zero seconds (silence) in Period 2, the two normal and two other patient groups each showed a corresponding decrease in their Period 2 durations of action. The magnitudes of change ranged from 12 to 50 per cent in the four groups.

Interestingly, and unlike each of these four groups, the schizophrenics reacted to the interviewer's Period 2 silence by a sharp increase in their own action behavior. Thus, in the original interviews, they went from a mean duration of action value of 77 hundredths of a minute in Period 1 to 120 hundredths of a minute in Period 2 (a 56 per cent increase). The replication interviews five weeks later with the same schizophrenic subjects show a change from 85 hundredths of a minute to 108 hundredths of a minute (an increase of 27 per cent), crossvalidating, and thereby confirming, this finding. Thus, four groups reacted to the interviewer's Period 2 decrease in action (silence) by decreasing their own durations of actions. The schizophrenic group, on the other hand, reacted to this same decrease in interviewer action (silence) by increasing their own durations of actions.

As the interviewer next increased his actions to five-second durations in Period 3 each of the five groups increased their own average duration of action. Likewise, in Period 4, when the interviewer next continued his durations of action at five seconds each, but introduced the interruption variable, each of the five groups showed a marked decrease* in their own average durations of actions. Similarity of behavior across all five groups is likewise evident in their Period 5 behavior. When in this Period the interviewer continues his five-second actions, but terminates the concomitant interruption stress of Period 4, the average duration of action of each of the five diagnostic groups shows a similar increase from the Period 4 low.

For each of the diagnostic groups and its replication, a t-test analysis of the differences between pairs of period means shown in Table 5 also was carried out. Again the major influence is contributed by the two stress periods. The 24 t-test comparisons of each period with each other (for Periods 1, 3, and 5) yielded one (4 per cent) significant value; whereas six (or 75 per cent) of the eight possible comparisons of Period 2 with 4 were significant; and 29 (60 per cent) out of 48 possible comparisons of each of the two stress periods with each of the three nonstress periods were significant.

The results in Table 5 therefore allow the conclusion that, like the interviewer silence dimension, planned changes in interviewer action behavior are followed by significant, reliable, and for the most part, parallel changes in the interview action behavior of interviewees. In addition, while this change is the same for all five groups under the interviewer action behavior (interruption) of Period 4, it is similar under the conditions of interviewer silence in Period 2 for only four of the five groups: schizophrenics increased their own actions when the interviewer introduced silence, while the other four groups decreased their actions in like manner to the interviewer.

---

* This decrease in interviewee duration of utterance in Period 4 sometimes results from the interviewer terminating an utterance in the middle of a sentence. Surprisingly, however, under interviewer interruption, many interviewees seem also to adjust to this change in interviewer behavior by making their *complete* utterance much shorter. Thus, the Period 4 means shown in Table 5 are not merely artifacts representing incompleted interviewee utterances. Were they merely this latter they, nevertheless, still would represent an interesting reaction to interviewer interrupting behavior.

IMPLICATIONS FOR PRESCRIBED
BEHAVIOR THERAPY

This research has shown that interviewers can utilize a minimally standardized interview (the independent variable being the few prescribed rules governing the interviewer's own behavior) and thus facilitate the study of one aspect of a class of dependent variable long of interest to psychologists and psychiatrists; i.e., suspected differences in the interview behavior of different diagnostic groups. Earlier research by us (Matarazzo and Saslow, 1961) showed that, if one analyzed the total interview as a unit, our five groups could be statistically differentiated by a number of Chapple's 12 Interaction Chronograph variables. The present results indicate that planned intra-interview changes in the interviewer's behavior have a marked, and reproducible, effect on the corresponding intra-interview behavior of interviewees from a variety of crude diagnostic groups. In addition, the results permit one to conclude that, within the framework of the present research interview, chronic schizophrenics are as amenable to influence in the silence dimension as are a mixed psychotic-neurotic group, a neurotic group, and each of two normal groups. However, this is not the case with the duration of action dimension. For this variable, the schizophrenics increase their action when the interviewer decreases his own action with the introduction of silence in Period 2, whereas the four remaining groups decrease their actions.

These findings may be merely an isolated observation. On the other hand, in conjunction with the analogous interviewer-produced changes in the content area suggested by the recent researches on verbal conditioning (Greenspoon's chapter in this volume; Krasner, 1958; Salzinger, 1959), the results of our present study suggest the possibility of beginning investigations of prescribed behavior therapy. That is, if one of the characteristics of some depressed patients is that they speak infrequently, and when they do, do so in utterances of short durations, then one might ask what would be the effect on their duration of utterances of an interviewer, himself, using only long utterances when interviewing them? Would there be a corresponding increase in the patient's own duration of utterance and, thus, along this one dimension, at least, less "depression"? Likewise, with patients who speak in unusually long utterances, e.g., the so-called manic patient, would the effect of an interviewer using unusually brief utterances (e.g., one or two words per communication unit) be to reduce these long patient utterances? Even if such suggested interviewer-produced changes in patient-interviewee behavior could be produced within the interview situation itself, such changes would be merely a beginning, since further research would then need to be undertaken to study whether or not, and with what persistence, such intra-interview-produced interviewee changes do, in fact, generalize to the patient's everyday behavior in a variety of life situations.

Numerous studies suggest themselves here: (1) which dimensions of interview behavior can be modified within the interview (in the study reported here, modification in action and silence behavior was studied—can one also modify, for example, such additional non-content interviewee behaviors as number and duration of interruptions and resulting "dominances" or "submissions"; number of initiative responses when the interviewer remains silent in Period 2 of the standardized interview, and others of Chapple's interaction variables?; (2) which type of patient is most amenable to non-content intra-interview behavior change, and along which interview dimensions?; (3) which intra-interview behavior changes will generalize to noninterview situations, and under which extra-interview conditions?; (4) which interviewer characteristics (age, sex, experience, interaction characteristics, etc.) are related to which interviewee changes, if any?; (5) under which conditions can content and non-content variables be manipulated simultaneously, or in varying combinations, to produce which effects?; etc. It is clear from merely the few research possibilities here suggested, and the results earlier described, that careful study of non-content (as well as content) interaction measures may make it possible for us someday to pair (for psychotherapy) an interviewer, with his own unique interaction characteristics, with a selected patient with whom this interviewer's interaction pattern might best be suited.

Another lead for prescribed behavior therapy comes from the results in Table 5. If, as has been observed clinically, one of the significant features of the chronic schizophrenic is the tendency to disturbed thinking (as reflected in his verbalizations) as he increases the duration of each verbalization, then, the results in Table 5 suggest that an interviewer should not remain silent with this type of patient. Rather, he should verbally interact in an active sense. Clinicians with a number of different theoretical orientations, including psychoanalytic, have long discouraged a silent, passive interviewer role with schizophrenics.

In view of the possibility that one might wish to begin preliminary studies of the feasibility of prescribed behavior therapy as suggested above, we asked ourselves how general were the group results in Table 5 across individuals within each group. Analysis revealed that, of the 156 subjects in the five diagnostic groups, 144 (or 92 per cent) showed the decrease in action from Period 3 to Period 4 and the increase from Period 4 to Period 5. Thus, under interviewer interruption in Period 4, a decrease in interviewee action is almost universal. This finding was crossvalidated in all the replication studies.

The finding was not as universal for the Period 2 decrease in action shown by the four groups (excluding the schizophrenics) in Table 5. The number of individual subjects who followed the group pattern (i.e., the pattern the interviewer followed) of a decrease in action from Period 1 to Period 2 *and* an increase in Period 3, was 8 out of 20 subjects (40 per cent) in the mixed group; 24 (or 40 per cent) out of 60 in the neurotic outpatient group; 30 (or 75 per cent) out of 40 in the Gilchrist normal group; and 17 (or 100 per cent) out of 17 in the Carson-Pirie-Scott normal group. Thus, the individual subjects in the two normal groups showed the group trend in this period in greater percentages than did the individual subjects in the two above patient groups. It is of interest that the "deviates" from this Period 2 group pattern (i.e., the remaining 12 out of 20 in the mixed group, etc.) also were, by and large, deviates in the same direction in the replication interviews. Thus, whether an individual followed the group trend or not, he *himself* was stable in this behavior.

Four (21 per cent) of the 19 schizophrenic subjects also followed the interviewer's pattern of a decrease in action in Period 2 and an increase in Period 3. Of the remaining 15 schizophrenic subjects, four (21 per cent) went down in Period 2 but also went down in action in Period 3. The other 11 subjects (58 per cent) did not follow the interviewer's pattern of decreased action in Period 2 but, rather, *increased* their own action in this period. Thus, the increased schizophrenic mean action in Period 2, shown in Table 5, also is representative of the majority of the *individual* subjects in this group. This finding, of an increase in Period 2, relative to Period 1, was crossvalidated in the replication interview with the 19 schizophrenic subjects, as evidenced by the replication group means shown in Table 5 and the fact that 10 (53 per cent) of the individual subjects showed this increase in the replication interview. (Stability of this "deviate" schizophrenic increase in Period 2, relative to the interviewer's decreased action in Period 2, is seen by the fact that 7 of the same 11 subjects (63 per cent) who showed an increase in action in Period 2 in the first interview also showed an increase in the replication interview.)

The group silence data shown in Table 4 also was analyzed for individual subjects. Of the 156 subjects in the five diagnostic groups, the following numbers showed the Table 4 group mean increase in silence in Period 2 (relative to Periods 1 and 3); 10 out of 19 schizophrenics (53 per cent); 14 out of 20 subjects in the mixed group (70 per cent); 40 out of 60 outpatient neurotic subjects (67 per cent); 30 out of 40 Gilchrist normals (75 per cent); and 15 out of 17 Carson-Pirie-Scott normals (88 per cent). Showing the Period 4 group decrease in silence (relative to Periods 3 and 5) were 13 out of 19 schizophrenics (68 per cent); 16 out of 20 subjects in the mixed group

(80 per cent); 50 out of 60 (83 per cent) outpatients; 32 out of 40 (80 per cent) Gilchrist normals; and 16 out of 17 (94 per cent) Carson-Pirie-Scott normals. Essentially the same percentages were obtained in the replication interviews.

A further research suggestion that someday the behavior of an interviewer with a given patient may be prescribed in advance, depending upon the given patient's unique interactional ("personality") requirements, comes from the work of Goldman-Eisler, a British psychologist (1951, 1952, 1954a, 1954b). Goldman-Eisler, working at Maudsley Hospital in London with an ink-writing version of Chapple's Interaction Chronograph, has added further evidence for the influence of interviewers' behavior on the behavior of interviewees. In her first study (1951), using seven members of the Psychology Department as subjects, she demonstrated that, in free conversation, each had interaction patterns (short and long silences and short and long actions) which were rather stable for any particular individual. She also found that the silence variable (this differs a little from Chapple's) was a somewhat more stable personality characteristic than was action. Her next study (1952) was designed to investigate individual differences between interviewers (three senior psychiatrists) and the effects of these differences on the interaction patterns of patient-interviewees. Each of her interviewers used his own pattern of interviewing, i.e., the latter was nonstandardized and was one of the variables under study. She confirmed Chapple's findings in that the three psychiatrists each had his own individual interaction pattern regardless of the type of patient he was interviewing (depressed versus active patients), although this pattern could be adjusted to the type of patient (within the limits of each interviewer's own pattern) somewhat. Furthermore, her results are striking in their demonstration that these three doctors influenced the interaction patterns (total activity, and ratio of short silences to long silences) of the same ten patients in different ways. Thus, depressed patients talked more with one doctor than with another, while these same doctors had opposite effects on talkative (anxious) patients. Goldman-Eisler notes, "Thus it would seem from the above that the depressed patient responds best to active stimulation, and the one who talks easily gets the best chance with the passive interview technique" (1952). Here, again, is evidence suggesting that planned "behavior therapy" may ultimately be possible.

Our own results, presented above, suggest that the group results for interviewee silence and action behavior, shown in Tables 4 and 5, respectively, are fairly representative of the behavior of individual subjects. The findings suggest the feasibility of preliminary studies of prescribed behavior therapy along one or both of these dimensions for selected individual clinical subjects. If, along with planned experimental manipulation of these two non-content variables, it should become possible to introduce control of the content variable, the study of psychotherapy or other forms of therapeutic intervention would be facilitated. In addition, highly objective data of the type provided by recording devices like the Interaction Chronograph seem to permit measurement of stable dimensions of (unique) individual behavior which may provide considerable aid in the refinement of individual clinical diagnosis, or other individual assessment procedures.

A REVIEW OF OTHER INVESTIGATIONS OF NON-CONTENT ASPECTS OF INTERVIEW BEHAVIOR

As mentioned previously, study of the non-content dimensions of interview behavior, despite their unusually high reliability and promising validity, have been pursued by only a few investigators. The studies of Chapple, Goldman-Eisler, and our own group have been reviewed earlier in this chapter. Two of Chapple's early Massachusetts General Hospital colleagues, Verzeano and Finesinger, also concerned themselves with non-content interaction characteristics of interview behavior. In order to facilitate their recording (microphones replaced Chapple's human observer) and subsequent analysis (Chapple's human scorer is also not needed) of interaction behavior, Verzeano and Finesinger (1949) developed an automatic analyzer of interview verbal behavior. This automatic analyzer was used for the study of frequency distribution characteristics of durations of speech in the free interview behavior of eight normal university students who were interviewed individually by an experienced psychiatrist. The results (Verzeano, 1950, 1951) show that durations of interviewee utterances of speech are skewed, with many short utterances and a tailing off toward the high end, following a Poisson distribution in most cases.

Hargreaves and Starkweather (1959), and Hargreaves (1960) have extended these observations regarding the form of the frequency distribution of speech behavior. Their speech data, automatically recorded, thus doing away with a human observer, were collected in such situations as that of a single person delivering a lecture; a two-person role playing situation; two-person interviews; the Senator McCarthy-Lawyer Welch U.S. Army hearings; a husband and his wife alone and in interaction with another couple; college dormitory roommate pairs in three different situations; etc. Although they were not primarily concerned with interview interaction, a number of interesting findings have emerged from these studies, including the following: (1) as in Verzeano's work (1950, 1951), the shape of the frequency distribution of actions (in either single or two-person behavior) is a direct function of the built-in silence tolerance, or time delay, in automatic analyzers (this is not a problem for investigators using the Interaction Chronograph, since the human observer is guided by the content of the interview in deciding when a momentary pause in a single utterance is the end of that utterance or is, in fact, merely a pause in a continuing unit of speech; see Matarazzo, Saslow, and Matarazzo (1956); and (2) for any given individual, or for groups of individuals, the shape of the distribution of single actions is also a function of the *situation* the person finds himself in. To obtain their data these two investigators have developed automatic recording devices which they call a Speech Rate Meter and a Duration Tabulator. Our own group, after years of experimentation, also is developing an interview Interaction Recording Device. This device is activated by a human observer and, utilizing a paper-tape punch principle, records all of Chapple's 12 Interaction Chronograph variables and many others. To facilitate unit-by-unit scoring of an interview, the punched paper tape is fed into a Burroughs 102 (or other computer), permitting analysis of the complete interview interaction (including sums, means, and standard deviations of these interview variables) in a relatively short time after the interview. Such a device, and those previously described, may increase many times the number of investigators working in the area of non-content aspects of interview behavior.

Another investigator who has investigated non-content (as well as content) dimensions of interview interaction is Mahl. For years he has conducted a program of research aimed at investigating the psychodynamic aspects of on-going psychotherapeutic interaction. Although he has been interested in interview content, e.g., anxiety, speech-disturbance ratios, etc., he also has concerned himself with such non-content measures as durations of patient silence and durations of patient and interviewer talk (Mahl, 1956a, 1956b). In common with Chapple, Goldman-Eisler, and our own group, Mahl has found that interview action and silence are unusually reliable and stable interviewee characteristics. In one of these publications (Mahl, 1956b), he describes an interview interaction recording device which can be constructed economically and simply, and which gives reliability results (for action and silence only) not unlike those obtained with the much more complex recording instruments used by Chapple, Verzeano, Hargreaves and Starkweather, and our own group. Mahl's inexpensive device should be of help to the graduate student wishing to work in this area but who is unable to obtain large scale financial support.

Still another investigator who studied non-content measures during on-going psychotherapy interviews was Lundy (1955, unpublished). By employing two psychotherapists with one patient for 38 interviews (each therapist saw the patient individually for 19 interviews in an odd-even design), Lundy was able to relate Chapple interview Interaction Chronograph variables to certain clinical impressions regarding the progress of psychotherapy as these qualitative data were assessed from the typewritten interview transcripts. In addition to demonstrating some interesting relationships of this type, in a study which utilized "free" psychotherapy interviewing in contrast to the standardized interview used by Chapple and our own group, Lundy reports the results of a factor analysis of the Interaction Chronograph variables. The results of this factor analysis were similar to the previously mentioned factor analysis of Chapple's variables completed by us (Matarazzo, Saslow, and Hare, 1958), and indicate that interview interaction is composed of two very stable factors for any given individual: (1) how long on the average he or she waits or remains silent before communicating, and (2) the number and average duration of each of these communicative interactions. Several weaker factors also emerged in Lundy's analysis (as well as our own), but the amount of variance they accounted for was minimal relative to the silence and action factors.

In 1954 Chapple, Chapple, and Repp presented definitions of twenty-eight personality and temperament characteristics. Many of these are not recorded directly by the Interaction Chronograph, but represent changes in an interviewee's behavior, relative to the first period baseline, as the interviewer proceeds through Chapple's five-period standardized interview. Guze and Mensh (1959) present data which they suggest questions the adequacy of the first ten minutes of Chapple's standardized interview as a baseline for comparison with behavior in other periods. In their study, Guze and Mensh (1959) used the Chapple Interaction Chronograph to study the correlation between the average duration of interviewee action in the first ten minutes of a 30-minute nondirective interview with the average duration of interviewee action in the next ten-minute period; and also the next ten-minute period. Their study yielded correlations of .58 (p of .01) between the first and second ten-minute periods; .49 (p of .05) between the first and third ten-minute periods; and .82 (p of .001) between the second and third ten-minute periods of the 30-minute total interview.

While pointing out that earlier research had established an unusually high degree of reliability for the first ten-minute period when this same *first* ten-minute period was correlated with a similar *first* ten-minute period in a second, or retest interview, Guze and Mensh say: "It is clear that the variation within any single 30-minute interview between successive ten-minute intervals under baseline conditions is too great to justify selecting ten minutes as a baseline for comparison with other intervals during which different events are going on even though comparing the first ten minutes of one interview with the first ten minutes of a second interview with the same patient gives high reliability" (1959). It seems to the writer that Guze and Mensh were unduly pessimistic in the interpretation of their own results for the following reasons. First, examination of the raw data given in their Table 1, and the three previously cited correlations resulting from these raw data (i.e., .58, .49, and .82), and consideration of the notoriously low correlations usually found in interview research, lead the writer to interpret the Guze-Mensh study as showing an encouragingly high relationship in the non-content behavior of a given patient as he moves progressively from one segment of an interview to another segment. Second, and much more to the point, it was difficult for the writer to understand the rationale of the research design of the Guze-Mensh study. In a personal communication (1957) he asked them on what prior basis they believed that behavior (whether it be interview behavior in each of three successive periods; the behavior of a boxer in each of ten rounds; the response over time to a pin prick, with the pin not being withdrawn; free associations to card I of the Rorschach test during each of five successive minutes; etc.) should correlate with itself indefinitely or, more specifically, for a finite time like the 30 minutes they used. In reviewing the Guze-Mensh study for the *Annual Review of Psychology*, Riecken (1960) raises the same question: "What seems to be missing (in the Guze-Mensh study) is some adequate notion of what is meant by stabilized or representative behavior. Surely something like fatigue or boredom with the nondirective interview must appear sooner or later, and there seems to be no rationale for choosing any particular length of time as representative or stable." Granting this fundamental criticism raised by Riecken and myself, the writer is still impressed with the magnitude of correlations the Guze-Mensh research design did yield.

The above critique of the Guze-Mensh study was necessary because they had raised a fundamental question regarding the design of future studies with Chapple's five-period standardized interview. In effect, they asked, if "10 minutes are sufficient to reach a stable pattern of patient communication . . . (then) 10 minutes may be sufficient to use as a baseline when evaluating the effects of drugs, EST, and other stimuli upon such behavior" (1959, p. 269). Since the allegedly unreliable ten-minute Period I baseline was used in our own previously described study (see Tables 4 and 5 this chapter), we offer the results shown in these tables as evidence that with a second, or retest, interview with each subject as part of the research design it is possible to check the adequacy of the first ten minutes as a baseline without raising the difficult philosophical question posed by the Guze-

Mensh design: Is the interviewee in a second ten-minute period which follows *directly after* a prior ten-minute period the same behavioral organism that he was in the first ten minutes, or has some relevant behavioral dimension changed? Put another way: Is the behavior of a boxer in round 3 (or round 10) the same as his behavior in round 1 or round 2? It would appear to us that the methodology employed in gathering the data in Tables 4 and 5 of the present chapter (i.e., comparing the boxer's total behavior as he goes from round 1 to round 2 to round 3, 4, and 5 in one match, to his total behavior as he again proceeds from round 1 to 2 to 3, 4, and 5 in a second fight at a later time) is a more adequate test of the usefulness of Chapple's first period baseline.

The earlier mentioned study by Kanfer, Phillips, Matarazzo, and Saslow (1960) yields evidence that Guze and Mensh could, in fact, have employed their own research design for further studies, provided, of course, that they interpreted their three statistically significant correlations optimistically (as did the writer) rather than pessimistically. Using a 35-minute interview arbitrarily divided as follows: Period I, 15 minutes; Period II, ten minutes; and Period III, ten minutes, Kanfer *et al.*, studied, relative to Periods I and III, the effect of the interviewer's introducing emotionally "loaded" content in Period II on the duration of interviewee actions. As might be expected, and with durations of interviewer actions standardized across the three periods, the change from neutral interviewer content in Period I to "loaded" interviewer content in Period II was a marked decrease in durations of interviewee action. When the interviewer resumed his neutral content in Period III, the durations of interviewee actions increased as expected. In order to test the reliablity of their findings, the authors did not correlate Period I with both Period II and III, and Period II with Period III. Rather, they (1) crossvalidated their findings with the first experimental group of subjects on two additional experimental groups, and (2) studied two control groups; groups in which the interviewer's content was neutral during all three Periods, and in which no significant differences were found in mean duration of interviewee actions across the three Periods.

Thus the use of crossvalidation samples, as well as additional control groups, represent a second and third approach to the solution of the methodological problem posed by the Guze and Mensh research report. Many other research methodological solutions exist.

Focusing on the problem of noncontent dimensions of speech behavior from another point of view Maclay and Osgood (1959) also have studied hesitations and silence behavior in American speech. These investigators analyzed a sample of utterances by 13 male speakers, all professional persons, at a conference held at the University of Illinois. The hesitation variables studied were: False Starts; Repeats; Filled Pauses; and Unfilled Pauses, and they bear a resemblance to some of the variables studied by Mahl (1956a, 1956b). Although the research did not involve interview interaction data, among many other interesting linguistic and psycholinguistic findings reported, Maclay and Osgood again point out the large individual differences in these speech hesitation phenomena, and the unusually high reliability of these phenomena in the speech behavior of any given individual.

The problems of identifying and isolating suitable variables for the evaluation of group psychotherapy are as formidable as those confronting investigators attempting to evaluate the results of individual psychotherapy. In a prior publication (Saslow and Matarazzo, 1959), it has been suggested that non-content interview interaction variables would appear to hold promise for investigators interested in assessing change following individual psychotherapy (or psychosurgery, the effects of drugs, etc.). The same suggestion regarding content-free interaction measures has been made for group psychotherapy by Timmons, Rickard, and Taylor (1960). In a very interesting series of three studies, Timmons *et al.* have *adapted* the five-period standardized interview, shown in Tables 1, 2, and 3 of this chapter, to the group psychotherapy situation. By use of such minimal rules as that the group therapist (1) should speak only in five-second utterances, (2) should address each patient in the group three times in succession, and so on, these investigators have shown that the behavior of individual patients in a group (e.g., how often he speaks, the duration of these comments, etc.), while different from patient to patient, is highly *stable* for any given patient, independent of the group therapist (three different therapists were used, two employing standardized behavior, one using his own, free group therapy behavior). The results of this study may very well open the way for the use of more controlled stimulus conditions, and methods of observation and recording in such complex applied areas as that represented by group psychotherapy.

An earlier application of interactional observational approaches to small patient groups was reported by Roberts and Strodtbeck (1953). These investigators successfully applied Bales (1951) content-oriented technique of Interaction Process Analysis in the study of the differential attributes of the behavior of a small group of paranoid schizophrenic patients and a small group of depressed patients. While demonstrating that the content of the behavior of individuals in each of the two diagnostic groups was somewhat different (e.g., the verbalizations of the depressed patients expressed more positive feelings toward the group leader and other patient-members of the group than did the comments of the paranoid group), the study also revealed that the two groups differed significantly on non-content measures of interaction. For example, (1) relative to the paranoid group, the depressed group directed a higher percentage of their acts to other patients; (2) in 35 minutes the paranoid schizophrenic group originated (this is comparable to Chapple's Units variable) 1155 acts at a rate of 33 acts per minute, while the depressed group originated only 808 acts in 34 minutes, a rate of 23.8 acts per minute. This difference was significantly different statistically. The results of this study strongly suggest the possible superiority of these non-content measures over content measures in identifying differences in the behavior of different diagnostic groups.

For the investigator interested in studying group interactions of the type investigated either by Roberts and Strodtbeck (1953), or Timmons et al. (1960), the inexpensive recording device (a modified Stenograph) developed by Carter, Haythorn, Meirowitz, and Lanzetta (1951) should be of considerable help. Although used by these investigators to record content categories, the moving tape and typewriter keys for shorthand notations regarding interactions clearly constitute an inexpensive Interaction Chronograph (the device can be built for approximately 30 dollars). In many ways the recording principle is the same as the one underlying Chapple's early form of the Interaction Chronograph (Chapple, 1949), except that the device of Carter et al., when adapted to recording non-content variables, should make the scorer's task infinitely less tedious than Chapple's early ink-writing device. The device of Carter et al. permits the recording of many variables, and thus may be more useful than the previously described economical device developed by Mahl (1956b).

An interesting use of non-content measures (interviewer and interviewee actions and silences) in interview behavior was made by Anderson (1960). A sample of 115 employment interviews conducted by six Army personnel officers was examined. Two stop watches were used to measure the durations of time the applicant spoke and the time the interviewer spoke in each interview. The total time was measured by starting a third watch at the beginning of the interview and stopping it at the end. The decisions reached indicated that the applicant was accepted by one of the six interviewers in 70 cases and rejected in 45 cases.

Anderson's analysis (performed independently and later) of the 115 interviews revealed the following findings:

1. the length of the interview is the same in the acceptance cases as in the rejection cases.

2. the amount the applicant talks is the same in the acceptance cases and the rejection cases.

3. the amount of time free of speech (i.e., both persons silent) is less in interviews with applicants who are accepted than in interviews with those who are rejected.

4. the interviewer talks more in interviews with applicants he accepts than in interviews with those he rejects.

A somewhat more complicated social interaction situation has been studied by Cervin (1956; 1957). Using two "informed" and a third "naive" subject working in three-man groups, and a theoretical framework derived from Pavlov and Hull, Cervin (1956) attempted to study the relationship between personality variables (anxiety and neuroticism) and such non-content behavior variables as response latency (silence) and degree of participation (ratio of S's action to total action). Among other things he found a shorter latency of verbal response (silence) in high-anxious subjects than in low-anxious subjects. Anxiety was measured by the Taylor Anxiety Scale. In his next study, Cervin (1957) used a Guttman scale for measuring emotional responsiveness and found that, in a two-person interaction, high-emotional subjects (1) participated more (longer actions) in the discussion and (2) had a shorter latency in giving their opinions. (Among many other personality correlates of non-content interview behavior found by us [R. G. Matarazzo *et al.*, 1958], we, too, found that the higher an individual's Taylor Anxiety score, the shorter were his interview silences.) An interesting additional finding by Cervin in these studies was that, using two independent observers, an individual's latency before speaking as measured by a stop watch correlated .99 with the same variable measured by the Interaction Chronograph (1956). This agrees with our own observer-reliability finding for the silence variable (r of .98) when two independent observers each used a separate Interaction Chronograph (Phillips, Matarazzo, Matarazzo, and Saslow, 1957).

Words spoken per unit of time, or verbal rate, is another non-content interview measure which often has been related to personality characteristics. Goldman-Eisler, whose research was previously described, has been interested in verbal rate as a stable individual characteristic (1951, 1952, 1954a, 1954b). Kanfer (1959), in addition to finding that the variability in one's rate of interview speech is a fairly stable individual characteristic, also has found that verbal rate increases for those topics (content) on which a subject's adjustment was rated poorest (when compared with those topics on which his adjustment was rated as well adjusted). His data were derived from individual interviews with 20 normal college undergraduates. The interviews were standardized so as to cover the same five content areas for each subject. Although word rate for the group of subjects did not differ significantly from topic area to topic area, Kanfer did find a significant interaction (statistical), suggesting that the five different topics had different effects on individual subjects. Also, his poorer-adjusted group of subjects did not have a higher verbal rate than his better-adjusted group. Benton, Hartman, and Sarason (1955), using the Taylor Anxiety Scale rather than a clinical interview measure of adjustment such as Kanfer used, also were unable to find a significantly faster rate of speaking in their high-anxious subjects relative to low-anxious subjects. (However, their anxious subjects used significantly more words and with a significantly shorter latency in the TAT task situation.) Thus, while group interaction behavior may not be sensitive to word rate as a measure, the behavior of any single individual may be. Kanfer (1959) suggests that the lack of significant findings with the group data may be in the inadequacy of the "adjustment" measure used with his homogeneous group of college students, and suggests further that a different adjustment measure, such as psychiatric hospital status versus nonpsychiatric status, may be a more adequate test of the correlation between word rate and adjustment. It can be seen that, as described earlier, this is exactly what Roberts and Strodtbeck (1953) found; i.e., word rate was a highly efficient variable for differentiating a group of paranoid schizophrenic patients from a group of depressed patients. Thus, while some studies (e.g., Lorenz and Cobb, 1954) have shown that the use of such content-derived variables as adjectives, adverbs, pronouns, etc. can differentiate patient groups from normals, and one patient group from other patient groups, these studies would suggest that non-content variables may be equally effective, if not more so, in differentiating both groups and individuals.

As one such test of the diagnostic efficiency of a number of non-content interview interaction measures, Matarazzo and Saslow (1961) compared the interview behavior of four different diagnostic groups. The interview variables were the 12 interaction variables recorded by the Interaction Chronograph, and the patient and normal groups were the same ones as listed in Tables 4 and 5 of this chapter. The results were surprisingly clear, and indicated that despite some overlap in the distributions of the various groups, 11 of the 12 (total interview) variables differentiated the groups at better than the .001 level of confidence. (The results with these same groups, presented in Tables 4 and 5 of the present chapter, also clearly demonstrate that non-content interview interaction measures provide useful data for psychiatric, or individual, assessment purposes.) This efficiency of Interaction Chronograph variables in differentiating the behavior of schizophrenic patients from that of normals was crossvalidated by Chapple, Chapple, Wood, Miklowitz, Kline, and Saunders (1960). Their research involved 23 normal controls and 37 chronic and acute schizophrenic patients. The 37 schizophrenic patients were obtained in 1958 from the same psychiatric hospital as were our 19 chronic schizophrenics a year earlier, but there apparently was no overlap of subjects in the two studies.

One of the most interesting and stimulating studies of interview interaction is contained in a recent book by a sociologist and psychologist, Lennard and Bernstein (1960). Their research addressed itself to a description in quantitative terms of the verbal interaction that takes place in the course of psychotherapy. This was done by recording eight therapies (four therapists with two patients each) for a period of eight months. Over 120 of these sessions were subjected to an intensive analysis that resulted in the classification of more than 40,000 verbal propositions along several dimensions—dimensions dealing with structure and process rather than with psychodynamic content, pathology, and psychotherapeutic change. In the introductory words of the authors, "It seems to us . . . that perhaps researchers in the field of psychotherapy and human relations have been overzealous in their pursuit of the more subtle facets and nuances of the therapeutic relation, without having first taken note of the more obvious and gross features" (pp. 9–10). Thus, Lennard and Bernstein suggest that investigation of psychodynamic material, for example, while rich and tantalizing, may have to await considerable refinement in measurement approaches. In the meantime they suggest as alternatives borrowing from theory and methodology already developed by social scientists (i.e., the concepts of "action system," "role relationships," "patient and therapist expectancies," "systems in equilibrium," etc., and the measurement approaches exemplified by Bales Interaction Process Analysis, and others). Their book represents an application of this theory and methodology to the 40,000 verbal statements included in the 120 psychotherapy sessions.

While most of the approach is content-oriented, Lennard and Bernstein do present some data on non-content measures of psychotherapy interaction. For example, statements of their four therapists' pre-psychotherapy expectations (assessed by questionnaire) of how verbally active each felt he was in psychotherapy correlated very highly with how verbally active he was, in fact, during a number of psychotherapy sessions with two different patients. The three measures of therapist verbal activity were: (1) the absolute number of therapist statements in therapy, (2) the proportion of these therapist verbal statements, i.e., the number of his statements divided by the sum of the therapist and patient statements, and (3) the rate of the therapist's interaction, i.e., how often he speaks.

In addition, when the ratings given by patients regarding the ease with which each therapy session had gone for them were correlated with the volume of the therapist's verbal output, it was found that "the therapists' verbal output during the therapy sessions rated by patients as proceeding 'more easily' was about twice as large as in the sessions rated as proceeding 'about the same' or 'less easily,' while the verbal output of patients was about 25 per cent higher." In addition,

the average number of interactions per session was about 50 per cent greater in the sessions rated "more easily." The ratio of therapist propositions (verbalizations) to patient propositions (ver-balizations) increased on the average from .19 to .29. Evidently, therapeutic communication is rated by patients as proceeding more easily when the therapist's verbal participation reaches a certain level as measured by verbal output and interaction rate. Also, the more symmetrical (perhaps within optimal ratio limits) the quantita-tive distribution of verbal participation between the patient and the therapist, the greater the satisfaction the patient experiences with the communication process. Increased participation in treatment is not uniquely determined by the specific nature of the content of the communications exchanges, but also appears to be a function of certain formal characteristics of the communication process itself (pp. 183–184).

Probably their most stimulating work on non-content measures of interview interaction is contained in the chapter entitled "Equilibrium Processes." In this chapter, Lennard and Bernstein present data which show (1) that there is a definite equilibrium process in psychotherapy such that the relative amounts of therapist and patient speech stabilize at a fixed ratio (which differs for different therapist-patient pairs!) and that this ratio is maintained during the course of many therapy sessions; (2) although therapists differ in the amount of their thera-peutic talk, the amount of talk for any given therapist (i.e., his propor-tion of talk per session) tends toward a steady state by being rela-tively stable from session to session; (3) nevertheless, within these individual therapist limits, therapists compensate for higher patient output by reducing their own output and compensate for lower patient output by increasing their own output; (4) considering the number of silences (greater than ten seconds) per session as an index of "session strain," psychotherapy sessions exhibiting most silences were succeeded by sessions characterized by a higher percentage of therapist evalua-tive acts and therapist acts of high informational specificity (two con-tent measures); (5) low therapist verbal output was associated with post-session patient dissatisfaction with communication during that session; (6) therapists differ in the degree to which they can vary their ratio of verbal activity, with some therapists showing considerable flexibility in their proportion of verbal output from therapy session to therapy session and other therapists showing a constant equilibrium process.

Thus from the humble beginning of measurement of such noncontent interaction variables as frequency and duration of patient and interviewer actions and silences in initial psychiatric interviews, through correlating these individual session recordings with a variety of noninterview measures, as has been done by other investigators and presented earlier, Lennard and Bernstein have succeeded in demonstrating that these same measures may have considerable utility for study of the complexities of psychotherapy.

Summary

The early part of this chapter reviews the work of Chapple and our own research group on the reliability and validity of non-content aspects of interview interaction behavior, and describes in some detail a previously unpublished validity study designed to investigate the effect of planned changes in the interviewer's action and silence behavior upon the corresponding behavior of individuals in five diagnostic groups. The method of interview observation and measurement was the Interaction Chronograph. The results (crossvalidated) show that (1) the effect of an increase in interviewer silence behavior is an increase in interviewee silence behavior in all five groups; (2) the effect of a decrease in interviewer action is a similar decrease in interviewee action in four of these groups, but an *increase* in the action behavior of the schizophrenic subjects; and (3) the effect, in all five groups, of the interviewer's planned interruption of the interviewee was a decrease in the durations of silence behavior (i.e., a quickening of subject's response), and a corresponding decrease of his durations of action under these interruptions.

The results were discussed in relation to possible *planned behavior therapy;* i.e., the formal interview behavior (action and silence) of the interviewer being prescribed individually for each patient, depending upon the latter's own current or long-range interaction requirements.

The last part of the chapter contains a review of the work of other investigators who have studied non-content aspects of interview behavior. This review suggests that the non-content dimensions of interview behavior may hold considerable promise as an area for the application of experimental methods to clinical phenomena.

References

Anderson, C. W. The relation between speaking times and decision in the employment interview. *J. applied Psychol.*, 1960, *44,* 267–268.

Bales, R. F. *Interaction process analysis.* Cambridge, Mass.: Addison-Wesley, 1951.

Benton, A. L., Hartman, C. H., & Sarason, I. G. Some relations between speech behavior and anxiety level.

J. abnorm. soc. Psychol., 1955, *51*, 295–297.

Bingham, W. V., Moore, B. V., & Gustad, J. W. *How to interview* (4th Revised ed.). New York: Harper & Brothers, 1959.

Carter, L., Haythorn, W., Meirowitz, Beatrice, & Lanzetta, J. A note on a new technique of interaction recording. *J. abnorm. soc. Psychol.*, 1951, *46*, 258–260.

Cervin, V. Individual behavior in social situations: its relation to anxiety, neuroticism, and group solidarity. *J. exp. Psychol.*, 1956, *51*, 161–168.

Cervin, V. Relationship of ascendant-submissive behavior in dyadic groups of human subjects to their emotional responsiveness. *J. abnorm. soc. Psychol.*, 1957, *54*, 241–249.

Chapple, E. D. Quantitative analysis of the interaction of individuals. *Proc. Nat. Acad. Sci.*, 1939, *25*, 58–67.

Chapple, E. D. "Personality" differences as described by invariant properties of individuals in interaction. *Proc. Nat. Acad. Sci.*, 1940, *26*, 10–16.

Chapple, E. D. The Interaction Chronograph; its evolution and present application. *Personnel*, 1949, *25*, 295–307.

Chapple, E. D. The standard experimental (stress) interview as used in Interaction Chronograph investigations. *Human Organiz.*, 1953, *12*, 23–32.

Chapple, E. D., with Arensberg, C. M. Measuring human relations: An introduction to the study of the interaction of individuals. *Genet. Psychol. Monogr.*, 1940, *22*, 3–147.

Chapple, E. D., Chapple, Martha F., & Repp, J. A. Behavioral definitions of personality and temperament characteristics. *Human Organiz.*, 1954, *13*, 34–39.

Chapple, E. D., Chapple, Martha F., Wood, Lucie A., Miklowitz, Amy, Kline, N. S., & Saunders, J. C. Interaction Chronograph method for analysis of differences between schizo-

phrenics and controls. *A.M.A. Arch. Gen. Psychiat.*, 1960, *3*, 160–167.

Chapple, E. D., & Donald, G., Jr. A method for evaluating supervisory personnel. *Harvard Bus. Rev.*, 1946, *24*, 197–214.

Chapple, E. D., & Lindemann, E. Clinical implications of measurements of interaction rates in psychiatric interviews. *Appl. Anthrop.*, 1942, *1*, 1–11.

Cronbach, L. J., & Meehl, P. E. Construct validity in psychological tests. *Psychol. Bull.*, 1955, *52*, 281–302.

Dollard, J., & Auld, F. *Scoring human motives: a manual*. New Haven: Yale University Press, 1959.

Goldman-Eisler, Frieda. The measurement of time sequences in conversational behavior. *Brit. J. Psychol.*, 1951, *42*, 355–362.

Goldman-Eisler, Frieda. Individual differences between interviewers and their effect on interviewees' conversational behavior. *J. Ment. Sci.*, 1952, *98*, 660–671.

Goldman-Eisler, Frieda. A study of individual differences and of interaction in the behavior of some aspects of language in interviews. *J. Ment. Sci.*, 1954a, *100*, 177–197.

Goldman-Eisler, Frieda. On the variability of the speed of talking and its relation to the length of utterances in conversations. *Brit. J. Psychol.*, 1954b, *45*, 94–107.

Greenspoon, J. Verbal conditioning and clinical psychology. In A. J. Bachrach (Ed.), *Experimental foundations of clinical psychology*. New York: Basic Books, 1962.

Guze, S. B., & Mensh, I. N. An analysis of some features of the interview with the Interaction Chronograph. *J. abnorm. soc. Psychol.*, 1959, *58*, 269–271.

Hare, A. P., Waxler, Nancy, Saslow, G., & Matarazzo, J. D. Simultaneous recording of Bales and Chapple interaction measures during initial psychiatric interviews. *J. consult. Psychol.*, 1960, *24*, 193.

Hargreaves, W. A. Time patterns in

spontaneous conversation. Unpublished M.A. thesis, Univ. of Chicago, 1955.

Hargreaves, W. A. The duration of utterances. Unpublished doctoral dissertation, Univ. of Chicago, 1959.

Hargreaves, W. A. A model for speech unit duration. *Language and Speech*, 1960, *3*, 164–173.

Hargreaves, W. A., & Starkweather, J. A. Collection of temporal data with the Duration Tabulator. *J. exp. anal. Behav.*, 1959, *2*, 179–183.

Heyns, R. W., & Lippitt, R. Systematic observational techniques. In G. Lindzey (Ed.), *Handbook of social psychology*. Cambridge, Mass.: Addison-Wesley, 1954, 370–404.

Hyman, H. H., Cobb, W. J., Feldman, J. J., Hart, C. W., & Stember, C. H. *Interviewing in social research*. Chicago: Univ. Chicago Press, 1954.

Kanfer, F. H. Verbal rate, content and adjustment ratings in experimentally structured interviews. *J. abnorm. soc. Psychol.*, 1959, *58*, 305–311.

Kanfer, F. H., Phillips, Jeanne S., Matarazzo, J. D., & Saslow, G. Experimental modification of interviewer content in standardized interviews. *J. consult. Psychol.*, 1960, *24*, 528–536.

Krasner, L. Studies of the conditioning of verbal behavior. *Psychol. Bull.*, 1958, *55*, 148–170.

Lennard, H. L., & Bernstein, A. *The anatomy of psychotherapy: systems of communication and expectation*. New York: Columbia Univ. Press, 1960.

Lindzey, G., & Borgatta, E. F. Sociometric measurement. In G. Lindzey (Ed.), *Handbook of social psychology*. Cambridge, Mass.: Addison-Wesley, 1954, 405–448.

Lorenz, Maria, & Cobb, S. Language patterns in psychotic and psychoneurotic subjects. *A.M.A. Arch. Neurol. Psychiat.*, 1954, *72*, 665–673.

Lundy, B. W. Temporal factors of interaction in psychotherapy. Unpublished doctoral dissertation, University of Chicago, 1955.

Maccoby, E. E., & Maccoby, N. The interview: a tool of social science. In G. Lindzey (Ed.), *Handbook of social psychology*. Cambridge, Mass.: Addison-Wesley, 1954, 449–487.

MacKinnon, D. W. The structure of personality. In J. McV. Hunt (Ed.), *Personality and the behavior disorders*. New York: Ronald Press, 1944, *1*, 3–48.

Maclay, H., & Osgood, C. E. Hesitation phenomena in spontaneous English speech. *Word*, 1959, *15*, 19–44.

Mahl, G. F. Disturbances and silences in the patient's speech in psychotherapy. *J. abnorm. soc. Psychol.*, 1956a, *53*, 1–15.

Mahl, G. F. A simple device for obtaining certain verbal activity measures during interviews. *J. abnorm. soc. Psychol.*, 1956b, *53*, 388–390.

Matarazzo, J. D., and Saslow, G. Differences in interview interaction behavior among normal and deviant groups. In I. A. Berg & B. M. Bass (Eds.), *Conformity and deviation*. New York: Harper, 1961, pp. 286–327.

Matarazzo, J. D., Saslow, G., & Guze, S. B. Stability of interaction patterns during interviews: a replication. *J. consult. Psychol.*, 1956, *20*, 267–274.

Matarazzo, J. D., Saslow, G., & Hare, A. P. Factor analysis of interview interaction behavior. *J. consult. Psychol.*, 1958, *22*, 419–429.

Matarazzo, J. D., Saslow, G., & Matarazzo, Ruth G. The Interaction Chronograph as an instrument for objective measurement of interaction patterns during interviews. *J. Psychol.*, 1956, *41*, 347–367.

Matarazzo, J. D., Saslow, G., Matarazzo, Ruth G., & Phillips, Jeanne S. Stability and modifiability of personality patterns during a standardized interview. In P. A. Hoch & J. Zubin (Eds.), *Psychopathology of communication*. New York: Grune and Stratton, 1958, 98–125.

Matarazzo, Ruth G., Matarazzo, J. D., Saslow, G., & Phillips, Jeanne S. Psychological test and organismic correlates of interview interaction behavior. *J. abnorm. soc. Psychol.*, 1958, *56*, 329–338.

McNemar, Q. *Psychological statistics*. New York: Wiley, 1955.

Moreno, J. L. Who shall survive? *Nerv. & Ment. Dis. Monogr.*, Washington, D.C., 1934, No. 58.

Murray, E. J. A content-analysis method for studying psychotherapy. *Psychol. Monogr.*, 1956, *70*, No. 13 (Whole No. 420).

Phillips, Jeanne S., Matarazzo, J. D., Matarazzo, Ruth G., & Saslow, G. Observer reliability of interaction patterns during interviews. *J. consult. Psychol.*, 1957, *21*, 269–275.

Phillips, Jeanne S., Matarazzo, Ruth G., Matarazzo, J. D., Saslow, G. Relationship between descriptive content and interaction behavior in interviews. *J. consult. Psychol.*, 1961, *25*, 260–266.

Riecken, H. W. Social psychology. In P. R. Farnsworth & Q. McNemar (Eds.), *Annual review of psychology*. Palo Alto: Annual Reviews, Inc., 1960, Vol. *11*, 479–510.

Roberts, B. H., & Strodtbeck, F. L. Interaction process differences between groups of paranoid schizophrenic and depressed patients. *International J. Group Psychotherapy*, 1953, *3*, 29–41.

Rogers, C. R. *Counseling and psychotherapy*. Boston: Houghton Mifflin, 1942.

Salzinger, K. Experimental manipulation of verbal behavior: a review. *J. gen. Psychol.*, 1959, *61*, 65–94.

Saslow, G., & Matarazzo, J. D. A technique for studying changes in interview behavior. In E. A. Rubenstein & M. B. Parloff (Eds.), *Research in Psychotherapy*, Washington, D. C.: American Psychological Association, 1959, 125–159.

Saslow, G., Matarazzo, J. D., & Guze, S. B. The stability of Interaction Chronograph patterns in psychiatric interviews. *J. consult. Psychol.*, 1955, *19*, 417–430.

Saslow, G., Matarazzo, J. D., Phillips, Jeanne S., & Matarazzo, Ruth G. Test-retest stability of interaction patterns during interviews conducted one week apart. *J. abnorm. soc. Psychol.*, 1957, *54*, 295–302.

Siegel, S. *Nonparametric statistics for the behavioral sciences*. New York: McGraw-Hill, 1956.

Starkweather, J. A. The communication value of content-free speech. *Amer. J. Psychol.*, 1956, *69*, 121–123.

Starkweather, J. A. Vocal behavior: the duration of speech units. *Language and Speech*, 1959, *2*, 146–153.

Starkweather, J. A. A speech rate meter for vocal behavior analysis. *J. exp. anal. Behav.*, 1960, *3*, 111–114.

Starkweather, J. A. Vocal communication of personality and human feelings. *J. Communication*, 1961. In press.

Strupp, H. J. Patient-doctor relationships: the psychotherapist in the therapeutic process. In A. J. Bachrach (Ed.), *Experimental foundations of clinical psychology*. New York, Basic Books, 1962.

Sullivan, H. S. *The interpersonal theory of psychiatry*. New York: Norton, 1953.

Timmons, E. O., Rickard, H. C., & Taylor, R. E. Reliability of content-free, group verbal behavior. *Psychol. Record*, 1960, *10*, 297–305.

Verzeano, M. Time-patterns of speech in normal subjects. *J. Speech & Hearing Disorders*, 1950, *15*, 197–201.

Verzeano, M. Time-patterns of speech in normal subjects, Part II. *J. Speech & Hearing Disorders*, 1951, *16*, 346–350.

Verzeano, M., & Finesinger, J. E. An automatic analyzer for the study of speech in interaction and in free association. *Science*, 1949, *2845*, 45–46.

15

Verbal Conditioning and Clinical Psychology

JOEL GREENSPOON

The importance of verbal behavior in clinical practices has long been recognized. However, the major emphasis in utilizing verbal behavior has been on the symbolic level. That is, the clinician has tended to interpret the verbal behavior of the patient. This emphasis on the interpretative or symbolic aspects of verbal behavior probably reached its peak within the framework of psychoanalytic therapies. Moreover, the usage of verbal behavior in the clinical setting has not tended to conceptualize verbal behavior within the rubric of learning. This is not intended to imply that psychologists had not investigated verbal behavior in the laboratory. The research literature reveals a plethora of experiments on verbal behavior. The implication here is that these research efforts provided little assistance to the clinician who was working with a patient's verbal behavior. It was primarily through the efforts of B. F. Skinner (1948) that verbal behavior came to be studied and examined in a way that may provide the clinician with some aids in working with the verbal behavior of patients. The essence of the Skinner approach to verbal behavior is the acceptance of the verbal behavior as a response in and of itself. Verbal behavior, as any other kinds of behavior, may be arbitrarily divided into response classes for investigative or clinical purposes. Members of the response class may occur with some ascertainable frequency prior to the introduction of

This review of the literature was supported in part by U.S. Public Health Service Grant M-3216. Some of the unpublished research reported in this review was also supported by this grant.

any specific set or sets of operations by the experimenter. If such conditions prevail, then it should be possible to work with verbal behavior in much the same way that experimenters have worked with the behavior of rats, pigeons, etc. It should also be possible to investigate the same kinds of variables that have been investigated with the nonverbal behavior of humans and infrahumans.

The tremendous interest in verbal conditioning is evidenced by the appearance of two excellent reviews of the literature, one by Krasner (1958a) and one by Salzinger (1959), despite the fact that the phenomenon has a relatively short experimental history. These reviews illustrate that, although verbal behavior may have special significance for the clinician, it is a form of behavior that may also be of great interest to other psychologists. As a matter of fact, it is the writer's opinion that verbal behavior represents an excellent meeting ground for both the experimental and applied psychologist. This opinion has led to the organization of this chapter. The first part will be concerned with basic research in verbal conditioning, using both normal and abnormal subjects. The second section will survey research in verbal conditioning involving testing, and the third section will be concerned with research in verbal conditioning related to interviewing, counseling, and psychotherapy.

BASIC RESEARCH IN VERBAL CONDITIONING

Acquisition in normal subjects

The initial research in the area that has come to be designated verbal conditioning was conducted by Greenspoon (1951, 1954, 1955). This research was designed to create an experimental situation to study verbal behavior that paralleled the operant conditioning conditions with infrahumans. Human subjects, college students, were instructed to say words individually and not to use sentences, phrases, or numbers. The experimental session was 50 minutes long. During the first 25 minutes, the contingent stimuli were introduced, and during the second 25-minute period, the contingent stimuli were omitted.

Four different contingent stimuli were used: the verbal stimuli "mmm-hmm" and "huh-uh," a visual stimulus (a five-watt red light flash), and an auditory stimulus (a 190-cycle tone). Two different response classes were used, a plural noun response class and a response class that included all verbal responses except plural nouns.

There was a different group of subjects for each contingent stimulus and each response class. In addition, there was a control group that responded for 50 minutes without any stimulus introduced throughout the experimental session. All subjects were interviewed on completion of the experiment to determine if the subject verbalized the relationship between the contingent stimulus and the response class.

The effect of the four contingent stimuli on the frequency of plural noun responding was clear cut. The introduction of the verbal stimulus "mmm-hmm," the visual stimulus, and the auditory stimulus resulted in a significant increase in the number of plural noun responses when compared to the control group. The effect of the verbal stimulus "huh-uh" will be reported in a later section of this chapter.

Cohen, Kalish, *et al.* (1954), used the Taffel (1955) procedure in a verbal conditioning experiment. The subjects were instructed to select one of six pronouns and to form a sentence with the verb that was also printed on a white card. They obtained a significant difference in the frequency of selection of the first person pronoun between the group that was reinforced with the verbal stimulus "good" and a control group that received no reinforcement. Wilson and Verplanck (1956) obtained similar results when they followed each emission of a noun, adverb, travel word, or living thing with "mmm-hmm," "good," or writing down the response. Similar results were obtained by Solley and Long (1958) using a perceptual response class, and Salzinger and Pisoni (1960) using an affect response class.

Naumoff and Sidowski (1959) reported an interesting experiment in which they investigated the effect of pacing on the acquisition of plural responses. The subjects in the pacing groups were instructed to emit a response each time a light came on, and the light was cycled to come on every five seconds. Subjects in the nonpacing groups emitted words at their own rates. The contingent stimulus was "good" and the critical response class was plural responses. Acquisition occurred under both conditions. The analysis of the data showed a significant increase in the frequency of plural responses for the Problem and Nonproblem groups of subjects. The rate of conditioning was faster for the Problem groups under both the paced and nonpaced conditions. The Nonproblem groups significantly increased their rate of plural responding only after the first 260 responses under both the paced and nonpaced conditions.

Greenspoon (1951) obtained results that suggested that the magnitude of the response class may be a variable affecting the acquisition of a verbal response. The verbal stimulus "huh-uh" tended to depress the frequency of plural noun responding and to increase the frequency of nonplural noun responding. The plural noun response class included approximately 11 per cent of all responses, and the nonplural noun response class included approximately 89 per cent of all responses. The effectiveness of all of the stimuli used by Greenspoon, "mmm-hmm," "huh-uh," a five-watt red light flash, and a 190-cycle tone, was markedly less when used with the larger response class.

The issue of magnitude of response class was attacked directly by Prutsman (1961) who used several different response classes that varied in magnitude. He obtained results that indicated that a small response class, such as modifiers that represented approximately 4 per cent of the total verbal output, was not as capable of being affected by reinforcement as a larger response, such as plural nouns that represented approximately 12 per cent of the total verbal output. He used a free responding situation in which the subject was instructed to say words individually. His contingent stimulus was "mmm-hmm."

Matarazzo, Saslow, and Pareis (1960) have also investigated the importance of the response class as a variable in verbal conditioning. They found that three different experimenters were unable to demonstrate verbal conditioning of plural nouns, but two different experimenters were successful in producing increases in the frequency of human responses. The same contingent stimuli, "good" or "that's good," were used for both response classes.

The general idea that the response class may be a critical variable in verbal conditioning has received attention from other researchers. Cushing (1957) investigated the effect of the affective component of the response on verbal conditioning. The subjects were instructed to rate a series of pictures on whether they thought they would like or dislike the person whose photograph appeared in the picture. A significant increase was obtained for the "like" response class but not for the "dislike" response class. Friesen and Ekman (1960) did not report getting a difference between the conditionability of like and dislike responses in a similar situation. They found both responses showed the same evidence of conditionability.

Weide (1959) hypothesized that there would be differential amounts of conditioning as a function of the reinforced response class. He used three different response classes, benevolent words, malevolent words, and neutral words. His results showed that all three response classes were capable of being conditioned. There was only slight evidence to support the hypothesis of differential amounts of conditioning as a function of response class. The operant level for malevolent words was significantly lower than the operant levels of benevolent and neutral words.

Everstine and Bendig (1960) found that subjects showed an increase in frequency of both neurotic and nonneurotic phrases. The rate of acquisition was faster for the neurotic response class, but the final level of learning was higher for the nonneurotic response class. However, the operant level of nonneurotic responses was higher than the operant level of neurotic responses.

The successful conditioning of the hostile and aggressive verbal response classes has been reported by O'Donnell (1959), Scott (1958), Zedek (1958), Buss and Durkee (1958), Binder, McConnell, and Sjohelm (1957), Anderson (1958), Ferguson and Buss (1960), and Simkins (1961). The more general response class of affective responses was successfully conditioned by Salzinger and Pesoni (1960).

Most investigators who used the personal pronoun as the to be reinforced response class have followed the pattern of Taffel (1955) and used the first person singular and plural personal pronouns. Grossberg (1956) investigated the effect of two different pronoun response classes in acquisition. He found that the I-We and He-She response classes did not differ significantly in their conditionability.

Acquisition in subjects with behavior disorders

The acquisition of various classes of verbal responses of subjects who had various behavior disorders has been investigated by a number of experimenters. Cohen and Cohen (1960) used hospitalized patients, half of whom were diagnosed as schizophrenic and half of whom were diagnosed as neurotics. They found that the neurotic subjects showed significant evidence of acquisition but the schizophrenic subjects failed to show any evidence of conditioning. The reinforced response was a personal pronoun and the reinforcing stimulus was "good." However, Krasner (1958b) reported an increase in the frequency of "mother" references when reinforced in two schizophrenic patients who were in remission. The fact that the patients were in remission may have been responsible for the differences between the results obtained by Krasner and those obtained by Cohen and Cohen. But this would not appear to be the case in the light of the results reported by Klein (1954). He indicated no difficulty in obtaining conditioning in neuropsychiatric patients. His experimental conditions were similar to Cohen and Cohen in that the reinforced response class was a personal pronoun and the reinforcing stimulus was "good." O'Connor and Rawnsley (1959) reported verbal conditioning in both paranoid schizophrenic patients and nonparanoid schizophrenic patients. However, Hartman (1955) reported difficulty in obtaining verbal conditioning using schizophrenic patients. His reinforced response class was a personal pronoun, and his reinforcing stimuli were "good" and a nod of the head.

The only experiment involving mental defectives was reported by Barnett, Preyer and Ellis (1959). They found significant differences between their defective experimental and control groups. The use of a geriatric population in verbal conditioning research has been reported by Dignam (1960). He used three different contingent stimuli, "mmm-hmm," a head nod, and a smile, singly and in various combinations.

The task involved making up sentences in response to a card that contained one verb and four different subjects, e.g., my parents, some individuals. His results indicated that the verbal behavior of geriatric subjects could be increased using "mmm-hmm," a head nod, "mmm-hmm" and a smile, "mmm-hmm" and a head nod, and all three together.

The failure to obtain conditioning in either the free responding situation or the selection of a response situation was reported by Mandler and Kaplan (1956), Dailey (1953), Caruth (1959), Sullivan and Calvin (1959), and Matarazzo, Saslow and Pareis (1960). Mandler and Kaplan found, however, that subjects who reported that they considered "mmm-hmm" to be encouraging or having positive value did show evidence of conditioning. Subjects who reported that they considered "mmm-hmm" to be discouraging or indicative of disapproval showed a decline in frequency of the devised response class.

Dailey (1953) and Caruth (1959) used a Taffel-type situation in which the subject selected a pronoun and verb from a card and formed a sentence. In both of these experiments, the subject was able to go through the cards at his own rate. Experimenters who have reported successful conditioning in this type of experiment have required the subject to go through the cards at a fixed rate. Sullivan and Calvin (1959) instructed college students to discuss the issue of science, fine arts, and English as the essence of a college education. Subjects were reinforced with "mmm-hmm" for any statements about one of these three areas. They obtained no evidence of conditioning when the process was continued over several days. It is difficult to determine the precise basis for a response to warrant reinforcement in this experiment. The length of the daily session was also not indicated. Verbal conditioning, as any other conditioning, involves discrimination and the basis of discrimination may not be sufficiently defined to enable the discrimination to be made.

Matarazzo, *et al.* (1960) suggested several explanations for their successful conditioning of human responses and their failure to condition plural responses. One explanation revolved around awareness. They found that there was more awareness of the response contingency in the subjects who were reinforced for human responses than plural responses. They also presented the suggestion made by Skinner that involved the concept of the discrimination stimulus, S^D, and the prior reinforcement and conditioning history of the subject. The concept of the S^D, as applied to this situation, requires the prior learning of the class of responses and that the verbal stimulus, "good," is a stimulus in the presence of which the subject has been reinforced for the particular response class in the past. Thus, subjects, i.e., people, have been reinforced for being interested in people but may not have been reinforced for an interest in plural nouns. Human responses have been brought under stimulus control, but plural responses have not. The suggestion that the verbal stimulus served more as an S^D than a reinforcing stimulus was also related to the difficulty of the response class. It may be more difficult to relate plural nouns than it is to relate human responses. A final possible explanation involved the concept of expectancy-set. Since the research was conducted in the laboratories of the psychology-psychiatry service, the subjects may have been set to talk about people but not about plurals.

This summary of the literature on the effect of the response on the acquisition of a verbal response indicates the degree of confusion that prevails in the area of verbal conditioning. Direct contradictory results have been reported, using the same response class and the same experimental procedures. Some experimenters have reported a complete failure to obtain verbal conditioning. Other experimenters have reported no difficulty in obtaining clear-cut evidence of verbal conditioning. Dulaney (1960) has questioned the legitimacy of including verbal conditioning within the framework of operant conditioning. Dulaney argues that in his research plural nouns were not learned. Subjects who showed an increase in plural noun responding were those who demonstrated the transfer of a complex verbal habit and were essentially reinforced for associating. Subjects who did not associate did not show an increase in the frequency of plural noun responding.

The essential issue raised by Dulaney, and a very important issue it is, is what does transpire in the experimental situation called verbal conditioning. It should be readily conceded, even by the most ardent verbal conditioners, that subjects in verbal conditioning experiments do not acquire new verbal responses. All verbal responses made by the subject were acquired before he entered a verbal conditioning experiment.

Even in the experiment by Rechtschaffen and Mednick (1955) in which subjects spelled out words being "made by the movement of a light" in an autokinetic setting, the responses by S had been learned before he came into the experimental setting. The response of bar pressing by a rat had been acquired in some strength prior to being introduced into the experimental apparatus. However, if the operant conditioning paradigm is characterized by a shift in probability of making a predetermined response, then the research of verbal conditioning may be considered within the operant conditioning paradigm. It would appear that Dulaney in accounting for the shift in response probabilities with reinforcement prefers a mediational hypothesis. Other researchers in the area prefer to consider the shift of response probabilities within the framework of operant conditioning. It might be contended by some in the latter group that Dulaney has uncovered an important personality variable that may be a determiner of who will and will not condition. That is, subjects who can associate will condition, but those who don't associate will not condition.

Preconditioning conditions

As the handling of rats prior to experimentation may affect their responsivity and conditionability in the Skinner Box, so may the prior subject-experimenter interactions in verbal conditioning experiments affect the verbal conditionability of the subjects. In the early experiments in verbal conditioning, subjects were reported to have been engaged in casual chit-chat prior to the beginning of the verbal conditioning experiment. However, there was no formal investigation of the pre-experimental interaction of the subject and experimenter to determine their relation to verbal conditionability. Solley and Long (1958) reported that if the experimenter engaged the subject in chit-chat before the beginning of verbal conditioning, there was a higher probability that the subject would condition than if there was no pre-experimental interactions. Moreover, it would require fewer trials to show evidence of conditioning if the subject and experimenter interacted prior to the beginning of conditioning.

Kanfer and Karas (1959) systematically manipulated prior subject-experimenter interactions by administering an initial task to the subject and then criticized, praised, or said nothing to the subjects. All groups of subjects that had prior interaction with the experimenter made a significantly greater number of the reinforced response class than a group of subjects who underwent the verbal conditioning task without any prior interaction with the experimenter.

Gewirtz and Baer (1958) investigated the effect of deprivation of social interaction on the reinforcing values of a verbal contingent stimulus. Children were deprived of social interactions, untreated, or sated with social interactions prior to dropping marbles into one of two holes. The results showed that the socially deprived subjects were more responsive to the verbal contingent stimulus than the sated subjects.

Hall (1958) examined the effect of "set" on verbal conditionability. He found that subjects who were given an ego-oriented set made a significantly greater number of reinforced responses than subjects who were given a task-oriented set or no set at all. Naumoff and Sidowski (1959) found that subjects who were instructed to try to make the experimenter say "good" as frequently as possible learned faster than subjects who were not so instructed.

The results of pre-experiment interactions suggest that this variable may be significantly related to verbal conditionability. However, there is some confusion surrounding this issue as it appears that the nature of the interaction is not important. It is somewhat surprising that

Kanfer and Karas (1959) found that subjects criticized for their pre-experiment performance were slightly superior in the conditioning task to subjects who were praised for their pre-experiment performance. However, Solley and Long (1958) and Timmons (1959) obtained results that suggested that subjects should be treated pleasantly in the pre-experiment interactions.

Experimenter characteristics

Verbal conditioning experiments may be somewhat different from other operant conditioning experiments in that the purveyor of reinforcement—the experimenter—may be a significant variable. In infrahuman experiments the purveyor of reinforcement is usually impersonal since it is a piece of apparatus. However, even the results of infrahuman research have indicated that characteristic sounds of the apparatus may acquire reinforcing properties. In verbal conditioning experiments, the purveyor of reinforcement may have acquired reinforcing properties in much the same way. The appearance of the experimenter, the personality of the experimenter, and possibly other unspecified aspects of the experimenter may affect the reinforcing value of any stimuli that he may use as a contingent stimulus. Verplanck (1955), for example, reported that student-experimenters who were successful in conditioning the verbal behavior of subjects tended to have more prestige than experimenters who were not successful. However, Ekman and Friesen (1960) reported that experimenters who were actually enlisted men in the army or who were dressed as enlisted men were as successful in conditioning hostile responses in enlisted men as experimenters who were officers or dressed as officers. These results may be confounded by many other variables, particularly other responses that may be elicited from enlisted men by officers.

Binder, McConnell, and Sjoholm (1957) used two experimenters who differed markedly in personal appearance. They found that an attractive, petite female experimenter was able to produce verbal conditioning in male and female subjects, but a big, husky male experimenter was not successful in producing verbal conditioning. Krasner, Ullmann, Weiss, and Collins (1960), however, found no significant differences in the verbal conditioning of subjects by three different experimenters, one of whom was a female. In the Binder, *et al.*, experiment the reinforced response required subjects to select a hostile verb with which to make a sentence. There may have been a well-conditioned competing response that tended to mitigate the effects of reinforcement of the male experimenter. The inhibition of hostile responses in the presence of big, husky men is a well-conditioned reaction in most people.

The variables of attractiveness and compatibility of experimenter and subject were investigated by Sapolsky (1960). He created a high and a low attractiveness group and a high and a low compatibility group. Subjects were told that the experimenter was just the kind of person or not the kind of person thay had indicated they found attractive. For the compatibility measure he selected subjects who were compatible or incompatible with the experimenter as measured by the FIRO-B Scale. His results showed conditioning for the high attraction and compatibility groups but not for the low attraction and compatibility groups.

Ferguson and Buss (1960) found that a neutral experimenter tended to be more effective in increasing the frequency of selection of hostile verbs than an aggressive experimenter.

Rosenblum (1959) reported data that showed that the presence of the experimenter did not significantly affect the conditioning of subjects in a free responding situation. The same procedure was followed for two groups of subjects except that in one group the experimenter was present and in the other group the experimenter was absent and the contingent stimulus was introduced over a loud speaker system.

Examiner characteristics and verbal conditioning of neuropsychiatric patients

The most comprehensive research on the relationship between examiner characteristics and verbal conditioning was done by Campbell (1960). He administered a personality inventory to a number of nurses and then ran them through a verbal conditioning experiment. The nurses were then used as experimenters in the verbal conditioning of NP patients. The nurses were divided into high and low hostility groups on the basis of their performance on the personality inventory. Patients were assigned to nurses as subjects on the basis on their diagnosis, hostility and anxiety measures, and the hostility measures of the nurse. In this way, high hostile patients were assigned to both high and low hostile nurses. Low hostile patients were also assigned to both high and low hostile nurses. The hostility level of the nurses and patients did not significantly affect performance in verbal conditioning. There was a differential interaction effect involving the conditionability of the nurses, the kind of reinforcement and trials. The effectiveness of the reinforcement and the conditionability of the nurses depended on the stage of conditioning. The nurses who showed the greatest amount of conditioning when they were subjects and used verbal reinforcement had patients whose critical response level started out at the lowest of all combinations, but at the end of conditioning this group was second highest in frequency of critical responses. The nurses who showed the least effects of conditioning and who used nonverbal reinforcement had subjects whose response rate was lower at the end of conditioning than at the beginning.

Marion (1956) used as subjects students who were coming to the university clinic for counseling. The research was concerned with the effect of the status of the experimenter on the verbal conditionability of the subject. Students in a course in counseling and regular clinic counselors served as experimenters. Each student and regular counselor ran two experimental and two control subjects. The counselor introduced himself as a student in the counseling class or as a regular counselor to each of his subjects. The Taffel-type experimental situation was used and the subject could go through the cards at his own rate. The experimental and control groups did not differ significantly on either the mean criteria score or trend. There was a significant difference between the experimental and control group of subjects run by the regular counselors, though both groups showed a significant trend. The two groups of subjects run by the student counselors failed to show a significant difference or a significant trend. The results also suggested that regular counselors who had been at the clinic longer produced greater changes in both groups than the short-term counselors.

As has been the case with respect to other variables affecting verbal conditionability, the issue of the effect of examiner characteristics is unresolved. The results of the research on this issue indicate that examiner characteristics affect the verbal conditionability of subjects, but the precise nature of this relationship has not been determined. The instruments used to measure examiner characteristics have many deficiencies with respect to their reliability and especially their validity. The specification of the relationship between examiner characteristics and verbal conditionability requires measuring instruments that are both precise and valid. Moreover, there are probably complex interactions between subject and examiner characteristics, plus other unspecified variables that make the specification of this relationship very difficult.

Personality characteristics of subjects

Many investigators in verbal conditioning have been impressed with two consistent observations. One observation is the large variability that consistently occurs in research in verbal conditioning. The other observation is that not all subjects show evidence of conditioning. These two observations are probably interrelated, since the failure of some subjects to show a change in probability of responding with reinforcement increases the within group variability. A number of experiments have been designed to investigate personality differences that may account for some of the variance in verbal conditioning research.

A variable that would appear to be related to verbal conditionability is hypnotizability. Weiss, Ullmann, and Krasner (1960) investigated the relationship between likelihood of being hypnotized and verbal conditionability and obtained a statistically significant positive correlation of .35. The resultant correlation indicates that hypnotizability accounts for a relatively small proportion of the variance of verbal conditionability. Webb (1961) found that subjects who were highly suggestible as measured by the Hull sway test tended to condition better than subjects who were low in suggestibility.

Another variable that would appear to be related to verbal conditionability is need for approval. On a priori grounds it would be hypothesized that subjects with a strong need for approval would show greater effects of reinforcement than subjects with less need for approval. Reidy (1958) investigated this variable and found that subjects who scored high on a Need for Approval Scale did not respond significantly better than subjects who scored low on the same scale.

Various needs as measured by the Edwards Personal Preference schedule were related to verbal conditioning by Kirman (1958). He obtained a statistically significant positive correlation of .33 between deference and verbal conditionability. Autonomy was not correlated with verbal conditionability; however, subjects who were more deferent than autonomous had significantly higher rates of learning than subjects who were more autonomous than deferent. Intraception was positively correlated, but succorance was negatively correlated with verbal conditionability.

O'Donnell (1959) investigated the relationship between manifest hostility, defensiveness, and sex and verbal conditionability under two levels of hostility arousal. Reinforcement was contingent on the selection of a hostile verb in the construction of sentences. The hostility level did not significantly affect rate of learning, but high defensive subjects used more hostile verbs in the high arousal conditions. The reverse was true in the low arousal conditions. There was not a significant difference between the sexes in the use of hostile verbs, but there was an interesting interaction between sex and arousal level. The high arousal males and the low arousal females used significantly more hostile verbs than the low arousal males.

Need for approval, aggressiveness, and fear of punishment were investigated by Anderson (1958). Need for approval did not significantly affect verbal conditionability; however, the high aggressive subjects showed more evidence of conditioning than low aggressive subjects in a situation where the formation of a sentence using the aggressive verb was reinforced. Subjects who had a low fear of punishment also showed more evidence of conditioning in a similar experimental situation.

Rosenberg (1957) also investigated the relationship between dependency and verbal conditioning. He found no relationship between dependency and verbal conditioning in two different verbal conditioning situations. He used a Taffel-type and a Kanfer-type conditioning situation.

Medini (1957) investigated the relationship between obsessiveness and hysteria and verbal conditionability. Subject were selected who were high on the psychasthenia (Pt) and hysteria (Hy) scales of the Minnesota Multiphasic Inventory. The reinforcing stimulus was "good" and the reinforced response class was a personal pronoun. The subjects who were high on the Hy scale tended to condition at a faster rate than the subjects who were high on the Pt scale, but both groups of subjects showed evidence of conditioning.

Buss and Durkee (1958) reported a significant sex difference in the conditioning of hostile responses. However, Ferguson and Buss (1960) found no sex difference in a similar experimental setting.

Campbell (1960) found no significant differences between high and low anxious nurses and high and low hostile nurses on verbal conditionability. The experimental situation involved two pronouns and three verbs that differed on a dimension of hostility. The high hostile nurses had a higher operant level than the low hostile nurses, but both groups gave evidence of conditioning.

Anxiety level was found to be positively related to verbal conditionability by Rosenblum (1959). Subjects who scored high or medium high on the Taylor Manifest Anxiety Scale showed significantly greater effects of the contingent stimulus than subjects who scored low on the same scale.

Everstine and Bendig (1960) reported that subjects who were high or low on the Neuroticism Scale of the Maudsley Personality Inventory gave evidence of greater conditionability than subjects who were in the middle range of the scale.

Personality characteristics of patient-subjects and verbal conditionability

Taffel (1955) used psychotic patients who were differentiated on the basis of scores on the Taylor Manifest Anxiety Scale. The subjects were required to make up sentences using one of six pronouns and a verb. He used a verbal stimulus, "good," and a nonverbal stimulus, a light, as the contingent stimuli. He found that the verbal stimulus increased the frequency of the critical response in the high and medium anxiety groups but not in the low anxiety groups. The light did not increase the frequency of critical responding in any group.

Campbell (1960) investigated the effects of level of hostility and anxiety of neuropsychiatric patients and kind of reinforcement on verbal conditionability. The critical response was the use of the hostile verb in the construction of a sentence. The two kinds of contingent stimuli were a verbal stimulus—good—and a nonverbal stimulus—the flash of a green light. High anxious patients made significantly more hostile responses than low anxious patients. The hostility variable did not appear to have an independent effect. The verbal stimulus had a significantly greater effect than the nonverbal stimulus. Moreover, the effects of verbal reinforcement were greater in the later stages of conditioning.

Sarason (1958) obtained a number of personality measures from tests and therapists' evaluation of 60 neurotic and psychotic patients. The verbal conditioning task consisted of forming sentences. The critical response class was the activity verb, and the contingent stimulus was "mmm-hmm." Patients who were high on measures of test anxiety and lack of protection gave significantly more critical responses than subjects who scored low on these measures. High general anxiety patients tended to give more critical responses than low general anxiety patients, but the difference was not statistically significant. Defensiveness tended to be negatively related to verbal conditionability, but hostility was unrelated to conditionability. Compliance was positively related to conditionability but dependency was unrelated to conditionability.

It is apparent that pin-pointing critical subject characteristics that may be related to verbal conditionability remains to be done. It is probably true that the inadequacy of the measuring instruments contribute to the difficulty of the problem. In addition, there are probably many other variables that interact with the characteristics of the subjects to affect the verbal conditionability of any one subject.

SCHEDULES OF REINFORCEMENT AND ACQUISITION

Schedules of reinforcement have been examined extensively in the case of nonverbal behavior, especially in infrahuman subjects. Much of this research has been oriented toward the effect of various schedules of reinforcement on resistance to extinction. The effect of schedules of reinforcement on the acquisition of a verbal response has been investigated by several experimenters. Kanfer (1954) found that the schedule of reinforcement was a critical variable in the acquisition of a verbal response. Kanfer (1958), in another experiment in which he manipulated the kind of reinforcement schedule, FR, FI, and VI, found that the groups receiving different kinds of schedules of reinforcement did not differ in acquisition. In his first experiment, he investigated the extent of reinforcement, 100 per cent, 67 per cent, 50 per cent and 0 per cent. Rosenberg (1957) reported that 43 out of 71 subjects reached criterion in the Kanfer-type autokinetic situation on a 67 per cent random reinforcement schedule. Grossberg (1956) found no significant difference in acquisition among groups that received 50 per cent, 75 per cent, and 100 per cent reinforcement during acquisition. All three groups showed evidence of conditioning. McNair (1957) used an "FI-15" and an "FI-60" reinforcement schedule in the reinforcement of rate of verbal responding. He found that the higher reinforcement rate produced the highest rate of verbalizations. Solley and Santos (1958) reinforced a perceptual response, a response to a biased Necker cube, on a 70 per cent schedule of reinforcement and increased the frequency of the reinforced percept. Timmons (1959) used a 50 per cent and a 100 per cent reinforcement schedule in which a bell and "right" were the reinforcing stimuli. The continuous reinforcement schedule resulted in faster learning.

The results of the effect of the schedule of reinforcement on the acquisition of a verbal response are generally in agreement with the results obtained from other kinds of responses and organisms.

The issue of awareness

The issue of awareness in learning has received considerable attention from experimenters since the early experimenters in verbal conditioning reported obtaining learning despite the fact that many subjects appeared to be unable to verbalize the relationship between the response class and the contingent stimulus. Numerous experimenters have reported the lack of awareness on the part of their subjects, but the question of awareness tended to be a side issue to the major variables of the experiments. However, there have been research efforts specifically designed to establish a clearer relationship between awareness and learning.

Sidowski (1954) made the first direct attack on the problem of awareness by having one group of subjects who were told that their task was to turn on the light. Another group of subjects also received the light as the contingent stimulus but were told nothing about the function of the light. His results indicated no significant difference in the amount of conditioning between the two groups.

Medini (1957) investigated the relationship between speed of insight and learning without awareness in a Taffel-type experimental situation. At the end of each ten trials subjects were asked when the experimenter said "good." This procedure was followed until the subject verbalized insight or until 200 trials had been completed. Learning was demonstrated by a significant increase in the frequency of the critical response over the frequency in the operant level phase. There was no significant relationship between the speed of insight and the rate of learning. Difference in the point of onset of conditioning and verbalization of insight was significant when computed in terms of blocks of trials. However, when the difference was analyzed in terms of critical responses, the difference was not significant.

Kirman (1958) also investigated the relationship between learning with and without awareness. On completion of the training session, the subjects were interviewed about the experimenter's activities, especially if the experimenter's activities influenced his response. Judges evaluated these interviews and rated the subjects on a three point scale of totally aware, partially aware, and unaware. Out of the 100 subjects, 18 subjects were totally aware, 31 subjects were partially aware, and 51 subjects were unaware. Curves were plotted for frequency of critical responding for each level of awareness. The total aware and partially aware subjects showed a significant increase in frequency of critical responses over the operant level, but the unaware group of subjects did not. The unaware subjects showed a very slight increment over the operant level.

Zedek (1958) divided subjects into aware and unaware groups on the basis of a post-training trials interview. Though awareness was related to anxiety level and measures of interpersonal skills, there was no relationship between degree of awareness and level of conditioning. The degree of awareness was also related to over-all response level. The high degree of awareness subjects gave more aggressive responses than subjects with a low degree of awareness.

The most comprehensive investigation of awareness and verbal conditioning was reported by Levins (1959). He used a Taffel-type experimental condition and reinforced subjects with the verbal stimmulus, "good," for predetermined personal pronouns. On completion of the training session, the subjects were interviewed to determine awareness. He used a sixteen item interview, the first four items were commonly used in tests of awareness by previous investigators. If the subject verbalized correctly, he was asked questions to determine when he first got the correct contingency.

Only three out of the 60 experimental subjects verbalized the correct contingency on the basis of the first four questions. An additional 19 subjects were classified as aware on the basis of the full scale interview. All of the aware subjects indicated awareness of the contingency during the task.

Significant differences were obtained between the control group and the 57 subjects who were unaware on the basis of the first four questions. However, when the 57 subjects were divided into aware and unaware groups on the basis of the full-scale interview, only the aware subjects gave a significantly greater number of critical responses than the control group. The dividing of the unaware subjects into two groups—those aware of the reinforcement but the wrong contingency, and those unaware of the reinforcement—produced an interesting result. The subjects who were unaware of the reinforcement performed like the aware subjects. The subjects who were aware of the reinforcement but verbalized the wrong contingency performed like the control subjects.

Krasner, Weiss, and Ullmann (1959) manipulated awareness in several ways. Their subjects had been exposed to discussion of verbal conditioning and had an exercise in verbal conditioning in which they served as the experimenter. The experiment involved the subjects' telling four-minute stories to Thematic Apperception Test cards in which emotional words were reinforced with the verbal stimulus, "mmm-hmm." There were four major conditioning sessions. In the first session, subjects had one practice trial, two operant level trials, and two conditioning trials. Each story constituted a trial. Differential emotional atmospheres were introduced after the first session. Then a second conditioning session was conducted, following which subjects were interviewed in the usual open-ended interviews to determine awareness. Interviews were rated from no mention of reinforcement to a correct report of the contingency. Then, cues were introduced to produce increased awareness. The experimenter recalled the subject's previous experience with verbal conditioning, including a mention of the use of "mmm-hmm." There was no mention of the actual experiment being conducted. Then two more conditioning trials were given, after which the experimenter stated the nature of the reinforcing contingency and gave definitions plus examples of emotional words. Additional information concerning control of the subject's behavior was also introduced prior to the final two conditioning trials.

During the interviews, 62 per cent of the subjects failed to mention any awareness. The other 38 per cent mentioned some degree of awareness of the reinforcement contingency. There was no relationship between initial responsiveness to verbal conditioning and rated level of spontaneous awareness. There was no relationship between rated level of awareness and number of emotional words emitted on the last two conditioning trials of the first session. The subjects who were given awareness cues showed a decrease in responsivity. The high level awareness subjects who were provided with a hostile environment showed the greatest decline in responsiveness. On the post-experiment interviews, all subjects reported that they had some degree of awareness, but they forgot to mention it.

Matarazzo, Saslow, and Fareis (1960) presented impressive results showing the relationship between awareness and verbal conditioning.

In the case of the plural noun response class, practically none of their subjects was aware, but there was no evidence of conditioning. On the other hand, when the response class was human, the degree of awareness rose markedly and so did the evidence for conditioning of this response class. They investigated awareness through the use of two open-ended questions to which the subjects wrote their answers. The answers were scaled in terms of a four-point scale of awareness.

The results of research specifically designed to gain a clearer picture of the relationship between verbal conditioning awareness leave the relationship still confused. Some of the confusion obviously revolves around the definition of awareness. Most experimenters have operationally defined awareness in terms of a specific set of questions that are asked the subject, usually on completion of the experiment. It appears to the author that an increase in the number of questions or the use of different questions on completion of the experiment may have a profound effect on the number of subjects who are classified as aware. Each question may provide some information about the contingency, and it is even possible that, if enough questions of different kinds are asked all subjects, even those who give no evidence of conditioning will verbalize the contingency. Drennen and Greenspoon (1960), in an unpublished study conducted at Florida State University, told subjects the contingency prior to the beginning of the conditioning trials. They informed the subjects that the experimenter would say" good" every time the subject created a sentence using a predetermined personal pronoun. They found that their subjects tended to fall into three groups. One group of subjects started with the designated critical response and created all sentences using that critical pronoun. Another group of subjects never created a sentence using the critical pronoun, and a third group of subjects showed the increase in frequency of the critical response that has often been reported.

It is probably true that subjects test various hypotheses concerning the contingency during the course of the training trials. However, this testing of hypotheses concerning reinforcement contingency may also contribute to the large variability that is freqently associated with verbal conditioning research. The writer noted in his research (Greenspoon, 1951) that subjects tended to follow through on a class of responses that had a member reinforced. For example, if the subject were reinforced for "potatoes," he may continue saying vegetables until several singular vegetables failed to provide reinforcement. Then the subject would shift to other responses. However, most subjects reported that they had abandoned hypotheses after ten to fifteen minutes of responding, and concentrated on saying words. It is interesting to note that the acquisition curves for these data show a rapid initial increase in frequency of the critical response class often followed by a decrement and a final upsurge in the last five minutes of the acquisition period.

Though some efforts have been expended to query the subjects during the acquisition period, there must be some reservation about awareness that is evaluated after the experiment has been completed. If the subject fails to report awareness, it may mean that the questions used to elicit information indicating awareness were not well constructed. On the other hand, if the subject indicates awareness of the contingency he may have become aware after he had attained a relatively high rate of responding and the discrimination has become more apparent. Thus, it is difficult to determine if the subject conditioned because he was aware, or if he was aware because he conditioned. The verbal conditioner, it would appear, finds himself keeping company with the biologist who has difficulty determining which came first—the chicken or the egg.

Though the issue of awareness is not resolved, there is some question about the importance of the issue. It may have some theoretical import, but there seems to be little empirical import to be attached to the issue. The theoretical importance of the issue cannot be resolved until the definition of awareness is firmly established. To argue the issue using differing definitions of the crucial construct seems to be a fruitless, though probably an interesting, activity.

Extinction of a reinforced verbal response

The results of experimental extinction in verbal conditioning research also present some interesting contradictions. Some investigators (Greenspoon, 1951), Verplanck (1955), Buss and Durkee (1958), Ekman and Friesen (1960), Wilson and Verplanck (1956), Timmons (1959), Cox and Cox (1956), Branson (1959), Hartman (1955), Weiss, Krasner, and Ullman (1960), reported that the omission of reinforcement resulted in a reduction in the frequency of the previously reinforced response. Other investigators, notably Cohen, Kalish *et al.* (1954), have reported that omission of reinforcement did not result in a decrement in responding, or that the decrement in responding was for one kind of response but not for another. Friesen and Ekman (1960) reported that the omission of reinforcement resulted in a decline in frequency of previously reinforced hostile responses, but not in the frequency of previously reinforced friendly responses.

Interesting results in extinction have been obtained in other experimental settings. Weiss, Krasner, and Ullmann (1960) created two degrees of emotional climate prior to extinction. One group had a friendly atmosphere and the other group had a hostile atmosphere created immediately preceding extinction trials. The hostile group that was placed on extinction showed a reduction in the frequency of emotional responses that had previously been reinforced. Sapolsky (1960) reported some very interesting results that related two interpersonal relationships to the effects of extinction. His two interpersonal variables were personal attraction and compatibility. He had high and low degrees of both interpersonal variables. Both the high attraction and high compatibility groups failed to show a decrement in the previously reinforced response class even though extinction was carried out in the absence of the experimenter. The low attraction and compatibility groups, however, had failed to show evidence of conditioning, but when extinction was conducted in the absence of the experimenter both groups showed an increase in the frequency of the previously reinforced response class.

The effects of schedules of reinforcement on resistance to extinction have been investigated by several experimenters. Kanfer (1954) reported that partial reinforcement schedules produced the greatest resistance to extinction. The continuous reinforcement group had the highest initial rate of responding at the beginning of extinction, but its rate dropped very sharply. Fattu and Mech (1955) also found that a partial reinforcement schedule resulted in increased resistance to extinction over a continuously reinforced group. Grossberg (1956) reported similar results when he investigated the effects of partial reinforcement on extinction. Kanfer (1958) found that subjects who had received reinforcement on an FR, FI, or VI schedule did not show signs of extinction, although the FR groups gave the greatest number of responses in the period when reinforcement was omitted. Spivak and Papajohn (1957) also found that a VI schedule of reinforcement resulted in increased resistance to extinction. They reinforced subjects in an autokinetic situation on either a continuous or VI reinforcement schedule. Both groups of subjects received the same number of reinforcements. The response of the continuously reinforced subject was extinguished within the limits of the extinction trials, but the response of the subjects on the VI schedule did not extinguish.

Greenspoon (1951) found that the omission of the contingent stimuli of "mmm-hmm," a five watt red light, and a 190 cycle tone resulted in a decrement in the response rate to the level of the control group. He also found that the group of subjects who received the light as the contingent stimulus showed the greatest resistance to extinction. The light stimulus was the only stimulus that was within the visual field of the subject during extinction. Salzinger and Pisoni (1960) obtained a decrement in frequency of affect responding with omission of reinforcement, but the response rate had not declined to the operant level.

The effect of delay of extinction on resistance to extinction was investigated by Greenspoon and Gersten (1960). They conditioned subjects to a criterion and then conducted extinction 0, 24, 48, 72, or 96 hours later. No significant differences were obtained among the groups when the total response rate was controlled by statistical means. These results are in agreement with those obtained by Skinner (1938) using rats and a bar press response.

Four different extinction procedures were used in an experiment by Timmons (1959). The four procedures were: omitting right following the previously reinforced response; omitting right and adding wrong to the previously reinforced response; omitting right from previously reinforced response and introducing it following the previously un-reinforced response; and omitting right from the previously reinforced response, adding wrong to the previously reinforced response, and add-ing right to the previously unreinforced response. Slowest decrement in extinction was produced by omission of reinforcement. Punishment plus counterconditioning resulted in the fastest decrement in response rate of the previously reinforced response. Counterconditioning re-sulted in the second fastest decrement in responding of the previously reinforced response, and punishment resulted in the second slowest decrement in responding.

Spontaneous recovery of a reinforced verbal response in children was reported by Cox and Cox (1956). Two groups of children who were reinforced with either "good" or "mmm-hmm" showed a reduc-tion of frequency of plural nouns during the first extinction period. During the second extinction period conducted one week later, both experimental groups showed some recovery in response frequency at the end of the first extinction period. The group of subjects who were reinforced with" good" was somewhat superior to the group of subjects who received "mmm-hmm" during the period of reinforcement. How-ever, the group of subjects who received "mmm-hmm" as the rein-forcement showed the greater recovery during the period of spon-taneous recovery.

Extinction in neuropsychiatric patients

Klein (1954) conducted an intensive investigation of three different extinction procedures on the extinction of a reinforced verbal response in hospitalized neuropsychiatric patients. The three extinction pro-cedures were omission of reinforcement, counterconditioning, and punishment of the previously reinforced response. The three different procedures resulted in a significant decrement in the frequency of the critical response, a personal pronoun. The omission of reinforce-ment resulted in significantly greater resistance to decrement of re-sponding than punishment of the previously reinforced response. The differential effects of extinction did not occur until the second block of 20 extinction trials. In a second experiment in which the extinc-

tion procedures were carried out for additional trials, the three extinction procedures resulted in significant differences in resistance
to extinction. The asymptote of the group in which reinforcement was
omitted was at the operant level, but the use of punishment of the
previously reinforced response and counterconditioning resulted in
asymptotes significantly below the operant level.

Krasner (1958) reported that two schizophrenic patients in remission showed a decrement in response during periods when the reinforcing stimulus was omitted. Cohen and Cohen (1960), however, failed
to obtain extinction effects with omission of reinforcement in a group
of hospitalized neurotic patients.

The results of research involving an extinction procedure provide
some very interesting contrasts. Some experimenters report obtaining
a very systematic decrement in response with omission of reinforcement, regardless of whether the subject is a normal person or a
psychiatric patient. Other experimenters have obtained extinction with
psychiatric patients, but not with normals or neurotics. It would appear
from this review of the literature on the extinction of a reinforced
verbal response that a decrement in response strength with omission
of reinforcement is dependent on at least several other variables. The
response class, the characteristics of the examiner and subject, and
the reinforcing stimulus seem to be pertinent variables in extinction.

This problem may be confounded by the fact that verbal conditioning is essentially reclassifying previously learned verbal responses
into new or different classes. No new responses have been added to
the behavioral repertoire of the subject. Under these conditions, it is
possible that variables other than the reinforcing stimulus may affect
the performance of subjects in the extinction period. However, it is
interesting to note that schedules of reinforcement tend to have the
same effect on the extinction of a reinforced verbal response as they
have on reinforced nonverbal responses.

Generalization of a reinforced verbal response

A critical issue in evaluating any conditioning procedures is the
generalization of the reinforced response. The generalization of a
reinforced motor response in human and infrahuman subjects has been
demonstrated in many experiments. The generalization of a reinforced verbal response has also been investigated, but the results have
not been very conclusive.

Sarason (1956) used a Taffel-type experimental situation in an
extensive investigation of generalization of a reinforced verbal response. The reinforced response class consisted of either verbally active
or bodily active verbs selected for usage in the construction of a
sentence. The contingent stimulus was "mmm-hmm." There were two

generalization tasks; one was saying words, and the other consisted of booklets that contained 24 consecutive carbon copies of a past tense verb. There were four sets of booklets, one that contained the verbally active verbs or bodily active verbs that appeared in the conditioning task, a second set that contained words from the reinforced class but had not appeared in the conditioning task, a third set that contained neutral verbs that appeared in the conditioning task, a third set that contained neutral verbs that appeared in the conditioning task, and a fourth set that contained neutral verbs that had not appeared in the conditioning task.

The subjects said words for four minutes and went through the booklets prior to the conditioning task. During the conditioning task the subjects were reinforced for selecting bodily active or verbally active verbs in the construction of sentences.

The groups did not differ significantly on the total number of words emitted after the conditioning task, but subjects who were reinforced gave a significantly greater number of members of the reinforced verb class than subjects who were not reinforced. Moreover, the reinforced subjects gave a significantly greater number of verbs in the nonreinforced class than the unreinforced subjects. There was also a gradient effect in that verbs that appeared in the conditioning task were emitted with the greatest frequency, followed by verbs of the reinforced class not appearing in the conditioning sessions, and then followed by verbs not in the reinforced class. Similar results were obtained with the generalization measure involving the booklets. A similar gradient was also obtained. Thus, Sarason's results suggest that a reinforced verbal response can generalize.

Scott (1958) also reported a generalization effect. His experimental procedure involved the reinforcement of forming socially acceptable or unacceptable aggressive responses from scrambled words. Though his major concern was not generalization, he found that reinforcement of socially acceptable aggressive responses tended to increase the frequency of socially unacceptable aggressive responses. The reinforcement of socially unacceptable aggressive responses did not have a noticeable effect on the frequency of socially acceptable aggressive responses.

Timmons (1959) was also successful in obtaining generalization of a reinforced verbal response. Subjects were reinforced on a random schedule for emitting verbal responses related to buildings. Then they were asked to draw a picture of the first thing they could conceive. Subjects who were reinforced for building responses drew pictures of buildings on their first draw much more frequently than subjects who were not so reinforced.

Results similar to Timmons were obtained by Greenspoon and

Thompson (1959). Subjects who were reinforced for animal responses in a free responding situation gave significantly more animal responses to Card X of the Roscharch than subjects who were not reinforced for animal responses.

Deering (1958) reinforced subjects for angry or egotistical responses in a training situation. Reinforcement consisted of the experimenter's saying "point" for the desired response and "no point" for undesired responses. The subjects were tested for generalization of angry or egotistical responses in a test situation that resembled but differed from the training situation. The training situation consisted of cards that described social situations with several alternative responses from which the subject could select. The alternative responses were graded with respect to degree of anger or egotistical responses, subjects were reinforced for easy versus difficult discriminations and for shouting, or speaking responses quietly. The test situation consisted of cards on which social situations were described, but the subject was required to complete an incomplete sentence which would designate his reaction to the described social situation.

Evidence for generalization was indicated by a significantly greater number of angry responses on the post-test situation by subjects who had been reinforced for angry responses in the training situation. Difficulty of discrimination and the tone of voice reinforced in the training situation did not give evidence of generalization in the post-test situation.

The generalization of words reinforced in a Taffel-type situation was investigated by Weide (1959). Verbs were classified as malevolent, benevolent, or neutral by a set of judges. Subjects were reinforced with "good" for the selection of malevolent, benevolent, or neutral verbs in the construction of sentences. The generalization task consisted of word matching. A set of 15 or 18 adjectives and nouns was presented with a set of five or six objects. The subject's task was to select the word from the set of 15 or 18 that was most appropriate for each of the five or six objects. Words from the set of 15 or 18 could be used more than once. The set of 15 or 18 words had also been classified as malevolent, benevolent, or neutral.

Only subjects who were reinforced for malevolent words showed evidence of generalization by selecting a significantly greater number of malevolent words in the generalization task than the unreinforced control group. An adjunctive generalization problem was indicated by the change in response strength of the nonreinforced responses during the training trials. In the groups in which benevolent and malevolent words were reinforced, there was a significant decline in the frequency of selection of neutral words. In the group reinforced for neutral words there was a significant decline in the frequency of selection of benevolent responses.

An interesting attack on the problem of generalization was attempted by Carpenter (1959). She used words that were four, five, six, seven, and eight letters long, and printed sets of five words on cards. Each card included one four letter word, one five letter word, etc. The words, though they differed in length, were rated as having comparable frequencies of usage by Thorndike and Lorge. Assuming that each word would have equal probability of selection, and that reinforcement for the selection of words of a given length would increase the frequency of selection of the reinforced word length, she hypothesized that the reduction in probability of nonreinforced word length would be related to the proximity of the word length to the reinforced word length.

The results of this research were not too clearcut. Some of the difficulty involved the conditioning of word length. Moreover, though words may have comparable frequencies of usage, they do not necessarily have comparable probabilities of being selected as the basis for forming a sentence. There was a decided tendency for subjects to select the longer words, even though they had great difficulty in pronouncing the words. An examination of the frequency of selection of words suggested that there was some tendency for generalization to be demonstrated. That is, there was a tendency for word lengths farthest removed from the reinforced word length to have the greatest reduction in frequency of selection. Word lengths near the reinforced word tended to show slight increments.

Though there may be some reservations about the results of the Carpenter experiment, the methodological procedures warrant some consideration. Her approach to the problem of generalization permitted generalization effects to be examined during the acquisition phase. Many experiments in generalization use resistance to extinction as a measure of generalization. Moreover, her approach may permit an analysis of verbal conditioning within the framework of probability learning theory.

An experiment by Fadigan (1961) illustrated another facet of the generalization problem. He raised the important problem of whether the reinforcement of one subject will affect the frequency of the critical response of another subject who is present during reinforcement but is never reinforced for the critical response. A Taffel-type situation was used in which a "stooge" formed sentences using the desired personal pronoun according to a pre-arranged schedule so that he received reinforcement for 75 per cent of his critical response. The "stooge" and subject alternated blocks of 20 cards until the subject had made a total of 100 responses. In a control group the same alternative procedure was followed except that the "stooge" never received any reinforcement. The subjects who were present when the "stooge" was reinforced showed a significant increase in frequency of the critical response class over the subjects who were present with a "stooge" who was not reinforced. These results have considerable import for the control and modification of behavior and this particular experiment should be repeated.

Generalization across experimenters and physical conditions was investigated by Greenspoon and Ward (1960). Subjects were reinforced in a Taffel-type situation in one room, but were put through extinction in another room and by another experimenter. The results of this experiment failed to show any differences in resistance to extinction, the measure of generalization used in this experiment, among groups of subjects regardless of the change of rooms and/or experimenter. These results are puzzling to the writer, who believes that the experiment should be repeated. It is interesting to note that all groups of subjects showed evidence of extinction with omission of reinforcement.

The generalization of a reinforced response as a function of the reinforcing stimulus was investigated by Simkins (1961). A Taffel-type situation was used in which the subject chose between a hostile and neutral verb to construct a sentence. All subjects were administered 20 cards to obtain an operant level of selection of hostile verbs and one half of the Rosenzweig Picture Frustration Test prior to the conditioning task. One experimental group of subjects was reinforced for the selection of hostile verbs with the verbal stimuli, "good," or "that's fine," and a second group of subjects was given points which were translated into pennies at the rate of one penny for each point. On completion of the conditioning task the subjects were presented with another set of cards containing verbs that differed from the verbs of the conditioning trials and the other half of the Rosenzweig Picture Frustration Test.

Both experimental groups gave evidence of conditioning, and both experimental groups showed an increase in the frequency of hostile verbs in the generalization task over the frequency of selection of hostile verbs on the operant level measure. The measure of generalization of the Rosenzweig Test, however, showed that the group of subjects reinforced with points and pennies gave an increase in extrapunitive responses, but the verbally reinforced group of subjects failed to show an increase.

Research on the generalization of a reinforced verbal response has failed to provide consistent results. It would be expected that reinforced verbal behavior would be as amenable to generalization as any other form of behavior. Most of the research has used relatively simple generalization tasks in which the variable of similarity of task and conditions has not been measured. Since similarity is assumed to be a critical variable in generalization of nonverbal behavior, it should play an important role in the generalization of verbal behavior. There is enough evidence to suggest that generalization does occur with reinforced verbal behavior to warrant additional investigation of this variable.

Punishment and verbal responding

There has been relatively little research involving the use of punishment in the verbal conditioning paradigm. The use of physical stimuli as punishing stimuli has been reported in the literature for some years. The use of verbal punishing stimuli has not received very much attention. Thorndike used "right" and "wrong" in many experiments, but the effects of the punishing stimulus "wrong" are confused by being used in conjunction with "right." Buss and Buss (1956) have conducted a series of experiments in concept formation in which "right" and "wrong" together and separately have been manipulated. He has reported results that indicate that "wrong" for the incorrect response and saying nothing for the correct response is more conducive to acquisition of the correct response than the use of "right" for the correct response and saying nothing for the incorrect response.

Greenspoon (1951) used a verbal stimulus, "huh-uh," that was presumed to have punishing properties; for example, the frequency of a response followed by a punishing stimulus is suppressed. He found that the effects of "huh-uh" were dependent on the magnitude of the response class. When "huh-uh" was introduced following responses of a narrow response class, plural nouns, there was a tendency for the frequency of the response to decline. However, when the same stimulus was introduced following members of a broader response class, nonplural noun responses, there was a tendency for the frequency of the response to rise. It would appear that the punishing effects of "huh-uh" were extinguished through the extensive usage of the stimulus in the case of the larger response class. Kirman (1958) also reported a decrement in the frequency of responses that was followed with the verbal stimuli, "not so good." Whereas Greenspoon eliminated the subjects who indicated awareness of the contingency, Kirman analyzed separately the results of his subjects who were aware, partially aware, or unaware. He found that there was a significant decline in the frequency of the response for all three levels of awareness. The partially aware subjects showed the greatest decline and the unaware and aware subjects showed the least decline.

Sandler (1959) manipulated the schedule of punishment to determine the effect on rate of response. Neuropsychiatric patients were instructed to respond to Thematic Apperception Test cards. Following a period of no punishment, a period to obtain an operant rate of response, the experimenter introduced the punishing stimulus, "unh-uh." Three different experimental groups were used in which different schedules of punishment were used. An FI-20 Sec., an FI-40 Sec., and a VI-20 Sec. schedule of punishment were used. All subjects received the same number of punishments before the punishment was omitted for a period of time. All groups showed a marked decline in rate of response with the introduction of the punishing stimulus. The subjects who received punishment on the VI-20 Sec. schedule showed the greatest decline. With omission of punishment, the subjects who received punishment according to the FI-20 Sec. or FI-40 Sec. schedule showed a marked and rapid rise in response rate. The subjects on the VI-20 Sec. schedule showed an increase in response rate but had not attained their operant level by the end of the period of unpunished responding.

Walder (1959) examined three postacquisition procedures on a verbal avoidance response. Subjects in the training procedure had to respond to critical numbers with the verbal color response, orange, to avoid being informed they were wrong, e.g., the experimenter said "wrong" if the subject responded to the critical numbers with a color response other than orange. The criterion of conditioning was a 35 per cent increase in the orange response over the operant level. On reaching criterion, subjects were assigned to three groups that differed in the postacquisition procedures.

In one group of subjects, no further information was given but punishment was omitted during the next 200 trials. Subjects in the second group were informed that it was no longer possible to be wrong or punished but they were to respond with one of the three colors. In the third group, subjects were given no additional instructions, but before beginning the postacquisition trials the experimenter read 200 additional numbers. Half of these numbers had been designated as critical. All responses to the critical numbers were punished with "wrong" regardless of the responses. Then an additional 100 numbers were administered without punishment.

The groups were comparable on the operant and the acquisition trials. The discontinuance of punishment seemed to decrease frequency of previously nonpunished response but not to the operant level. The intermittent punishment of the avoidance response itself resulted in the response returning to the operant level. Telling subjects that punishment would be discontinued had an effect that was similar to the omission of punishment without informing subjects.

This review of the literature on the effect of verbal punishing stimuli on verbal behavior indicates that only a few of the variables of punishment have been investigated. However, the results of the research appear to be consistent with the research involving other forms of punishment and nonverbal behavior. At the same time, it is apparent that relatively few verbal stimuli have been examined to determine if they have punishing effects. The effects of punishing stimuli on verbal behavior should be a profitable area of research, especially since so much verbal behavior may be under the control of punishing stimuli.

Verbal conditioning and testing procedures

Since the responses to many test items are verbal responses, some researchers hypothesized that test performance may be modified by verbal conditioning techniques. One of the earliest experiments in verbal conditioning and test performance was conducted by Fahmy (1953). She investigated the effects of three different contingencies on the frequency of human responses on inkblots constructed by the experimenter. The first eight inkblots had the highest probability of eliciting human responses. The remaining 22 cards were randomly presented to the subjects. The three contingent stimuli were, "that's a good one," "give another one please," and repeating the subject's response. The group of subjects who received "that's a good one" made a significantly greater number of human responses than the two other experimental groups and the control group. The two other experimental groups and the control group did not differ significantly in number of human responses. In a second experiment in which the contingent stimulus was omitted after 40 trials, there was no evidence of a reduction in the frequency of the critical response.

Essman (1956) investigated the effect of schedule of reinforcement on the acquisition and extinction of responses to nonsense inkblots. Subjects were asked to put the inkblots into one of four categories. The verbal stimulus "good" was presented if the subject placed the inkblots into two of the four categories. One group of subjects received 100 per cent reinforcement, another group received 50 per cent reinforcement, and the third group was a control group. Both reinforced groups were superior to the control group in acquisition but did not differ from each other. Neither reinforced group showed much decrement in responding with omission of reinforcement, but the 50 per cent reinforcement group showed less decrement than the 100 per cent reinforcement group.

Wickes (1956) used verbal and nonverbal stimuli as contingent stimuli for human movement responses on an inkblot test. The verbal stimuli were "fine," "good," and "all right"; the nonverbal stimuli were nodding the head three times, a smile, and leaning forward in the chair and returning to the original position. The stimuli, whether

verbal or nonverbal were used in sequence for successive critical responses. He found that both kinds of stimuli were effective in increasing the frequency of the critical response, but the verbal stimuli
were more effective.

Nuthmann (1957) pretested three groups of subjects on a personality test and matched them on the basis of self-acceptance responses.
For one group of subjects, the contingent stimulus was a light, for
another it was "good," and the third group was a control. The frequency of self-acceptance responses was increased with the use of
"good," but not by the light. There was no significant difference between subjects who were aware or unaware of the reinforcement contingency. The results obtained by Gross (1959) are somewhat in
agreement with Nuthmann. Three groups of psychiatric patients were
administered the Rorschach. Human content responses were reinforced
with "good" in one group of subjects, a nod of the head in a second
group, and the third group was a control. Both contingent stimuli
were effective in increasing the frequency of human content responses,
but there was not a significant difference in effectiveness of the two
contingent stimuli.

The most extensive and comprehensive examination of verbal conditioning procedures in the testing situation was conducted by Simkins
(1959). He investigated the effects of two different contingent stimuli
on three different response categories of the Holtzmann Inkblot Test.
The two contingent stimuli were "good," or "that's fine" with a
smile, and "mmm-hmm" with a nod of the head. The former stimuli
were designated as strong reinforcement, and the "mmm-hmm" with
a head nod was designated as weak reinforcement. The three response
categories were a content category, a determinant category, and a
location category. Each subject received 15 cards on each of five
daily sessions. Thus, each subject received a total of 75 cards. No
reinforcement was administered to the experimental subjects on the
first and last days; the control subjects received no reinforcement on
all five days. The experimental subjects showed a significant increase
over the control subjects on the determinant and content response
classes, but not on the location response class. Though there was not
a significant difference between the two types of reinforcement, the
weak reinforcement tended to be somewhat more effective for the
location and content response classes and somewhat less effective
with the determinant response class.

Level of awareness was evaluated on a six-point scale derived
from a questionnaire. More content reinforced subjects were aware
than location or determinant reinforced subjects. There was not a
significant difference in level of awareness of subjects who received
strong or weak reinforcement. The correlation between level of aware-

ness and amount of change was only + .13. Experimental subjects were significantly more anxious than the control subjects, but the anxiety levels of the three response class groups or the kind of reinforcement groups did not differ significantly.

In a second experiment, Simkins (1959) investigated the effect of weak reinforcement on a content response as a function of set. Positive set, negative set, or no set was created by special instructions. A procedure similar to the procedure of the preceding experiment was used. The subjects with positive set and no set showed significantly greater change than the subjects with negative set. The subjects with negative set showed a significantly greater reduction in frequency of critical responses than their matched controls.

There was not a significant difference in level of awareness of the three groups of subjects. The three experimental groups did not differ with respect to level of anxiety.

The results of research concerned with the effects of reinforcement on test performance indicate that test performance can be modified by the judicious administration of contingent stimuli. However, the results of the studies by Fahmy (1953) and Nuthmann (1957) indicated that not all contingent stimuli may be effective in inducing change of response probabilities in the testing situation. The results of the research by Simkins (1959) indicate that the location category on the Rorschach may not be as amenable to modification as the other two response categories. In general, however, contingent stimuli of one form or another have been found to be effective in changing the frequency of responses in a test situation. These results have considerable import for testing procedures and, more importantly, for the personality theories that are assumed to underlie some personality tests.

Verbal conditioning and the interview

It is not too surprising that psychologists have examined verbal conditioning techniques with special reference to the interview. The essence of the interview is verbal behavior, and it seems logically consistent to apply verbal conditioning procedures to the interview.

Ball (1953) attempted to create a situation that resembled the clinical interview. His subjects were instructed to make up a story that would take about ten minutes to tell and would include a reference to a man, a woman, and an animal. There were five sessions, each separated by about two days, for each subject. The independent variable was the type of contingent stimulus that was introduced following each animal response. The contingent stimulus was "mmm-hmm" for one group of subjects, "huh-uh" for a second group, a buzzer for the third group, and a light flash for the fourth group. The control group of subjects received no contingent stimulus.

The results indicated that the groups differed with respect to frequency of animal responses, but the group that received "mmm-hmm" as the contingent stimulus accounted for most of the difference. The verbal stimulus "huh-uh" had two opposite effects, increasing the frequency of the response for some subjects and decreasing the frequency for others. The nonverbal stimuli tended to increase the frequency of animal responses, but not significantly.

Hildrum and Brown (1956), however, found that the verbal stimulus "good" was effective in increasing the frequency of pro- and anti-responses in an opinion interview, but the verbal stimulus "mmm-hmm" was not effective.

Salzinger and Pisoni (1958) obtained evidence that the verbal stimulus "mmm-hmm" was effective in increasing the frequency of affect responses in schizophrenic patients. They also reported that the sex of the experimenter was not related to the conditioning of the affect responses, and omission of the stimulus resulted in a decrement in the frequency of affect responses to the level of the control group.

Results similar to Salzinger and Pisoni were obtained by Quay (1959). He reinforced subjects for recall of family or nonfamily memories. The contingent stimulus was "uh-huh." He found that "uh-huh" was effective in increasing the frequency of family or nonfamily memories.

Hagen (1959) used an interview situation similar to that of Salzinger and Pisoni. He used two different diagnostic groups, chronic undifferentiated schizophrenics, and paranoid schizophrenics. The critical response was affect responses and the contingent stimulus was "mmm-hmm" accompanied by a nod of the head. The concept of affect response was broadened to include any affectional statement that involved the subject. Affect responses were divided into four different classes. One class included statements by the patient that evaluated his own affectional state. A second class of affect statements reflected intellectual private events. The third class included generalized feelings about his surroundings, and the fourth class consisted of statements that were not a direct expression of the patient's affect but referred affect to the patient by another person.

The subjects who received the contingent stimulus for affect statements showed a significant increase over the control subjects in all response categories except references to intellectual private events. There was not a significant difference between the diagnostic categories, but the undifferentiated schizophrenics tended to demonstrate a higher degree of conditioning.

Mock (1957) used a story telling situation in which the patient-subject was to include mother, father, child, and animal. Four groups of subjects were used. In one group of subjects, references to mother were followed by "mmm-hmm" and a nod of the head. In another group, mother responses were followed by "huh-uh" and a shake of the head. Two control groups of subjects were used, one in which the experimenter was present, and the other in which the experimenter was absent during the subject's telling of the story. There was a total of 20 sessions, each 15 minutes long, distributed over a five week period. Experimental subjects received no contingent stimuli during the sessions of the first, third, and fifth weeks and received the contingent stimuli during the sessions of the second and fourth weeks.

The trend of the data tended to follow the expected results, but significant differences were not obtained. The subjects who received positive contingent stimuli showed an increase in the frequency of the critical response during the second and fourth weeks and a decrease in the third and fifth weeks. There was a decrease in the frequency of the critical response of the subjects who received negative contingent stimuli in the second and fourth weeks. There were indications that the effectiveness of the positive contingent stimuli decreased during the second week in which they were used.

Rogers (1960) created a situation that resembled the clinical interview, though the subjects were college students. There were six ten-minute free responding interview sessions. The subjects were assigned to three different groups. One group of subjects received the contingent stimuli "mmm-hmm" for each positive self-referral statement, a second group received the contingent stimulus for each negative self-referral statement, and the third group was a control group.

The subjects reinforced for positive self-reference statements differed significantly from the two other groups, but the difference was due mainly to a reduction in the frequency of the critical response by the two groups rather than an increase by the reinforced group. However, the significant difference in the frequency of negative self-reference statements was due to an increase by the subjects reinforced for such statements.

There was no relationship between conditionability and anxiety level or emotional adjustment test score. There was not a significant reduction in anxiety level following the quasitherapy activities. There was a tendency for both experimental groups to show some improvement in adjustment as measured by the Q-Sort Adjustment Test, but they were not significantly improved over the control group. The conditioning of self-references did not affect self-references outside the therapy setting as measured by pre- and post-measures on the Adjective Self Description Test.

Waskow (1960) reflected three different kinds of verbal material in a quasitherapy setting. In one group she responded to feelings and attitudes, in a second group she responded to content, and in a third group she responded to feelings as they were attached to specific content. There were four 30-minute sessions conducted over a two-week period.

The subjects who had content responses reflected showed a significant increase in content responses, but the increase occurred in the first session. The subjects who had feelings or content with attached feelings reflected failed to show an increase in the frequency of their respective responses.

Rickard, Dignam, and Horner (1960) attempted to manipulate the amount of delusional speech in a 60 year old man who had spent 20 years in an neuropsychiatric hospital. Contingent stimuli were a smile, a nod of the head, or verbal stimuli. Contingent stimuli were introduced following nondelusional verbalizations. Delusional responses were responded to by turning away from the subject, gazing at the floor, or looking out the window. Under a high rate of contingent stimuli the nondelusional responses increased, but a reduction in the frequency of contingent stimuli resulted in a reduction in the amount of nondelusional verbalizations. Changes of experimenters resulted in a sharp drop in the amount of nondelusional verbalization, but the rate rose rapidly with the introduction of contingent stimuli.

Ullman, Krasner, and Collins (1961) investigated the effect of reinforcement of emotional words in an individual verbal conditioning situation with respect to changes of ratings of the patients in group psychotherapy. One group of patients received "mmm-hmm" and a nod of the head following each verbal emotional response during four story telling sessions. Another group of patients received a click and the patients could observe a change in a counter. The third group of patients received nothing during the story telling session. The patients who received "mmm-hmm" and the nod of the head made greater improvement in terms of group therapy ratings than the other two groups that did not differ from each other.

The use of verbal stimuli in the group therapy setting was investigated by Dinoff, Horner, et al. (1961). Patients in groups of five were reinforced for references to the patient himself or for references to the group. The two groups of patients were seen for six sessions in which the experimenter reinforced responses appropriate to the group. To insure reinforceable responses the experimenter would ask questions. After the six sessions of reinforcement, there were three sessions of the groups in which the experimenter was absent. Then there were five more sessions in which counterconditioning was used, e.g., the appropriate response class of the two groups were interchanged. The results were in the expected direction, but the effects of the conditioning procedures appeared to be rather unstable and very short lived.

Allyon and Michael (1959) have reported several interesting examples of successful applications of operant conditioning procedures to both the verbal and nonverbal behavior of hospitalized psychotic patients. This research was designed to deal with behavior that was pertinent to the psychosis of the patient. Shearn (1960) has also reported partial modification of the excessive talking of a psychotic patient by using a DRL (differential reinforcement low) schedule for silence.

The research on verbal conditioning in both the therapy and quasi-therapy settings generally suggest that the verbal behavior of the patient and/or subject can be modified. Krasner (1955) has suggested that psychotherapy be approached from the realm of experimental psychology. He suggested that the therapist is a source of manipulable independent variables, and the behavior of the patient is a source of measurable dependent variables. However, there is a major problem in the realm of treating psychotherapy within this framework. This problem is the effectiveness of verbal conditioning procedures in generalizing the appropriate verbal behavior to other settings. The research by Ullmann, Krasner, and Collins suggested that verbal behavior modification can generalize to other settings. It is critical that additional research be conducted to demonstrate this salient point. If generalization from therapy (verbal conditioning) settings to nontherapy settings can be reliably demonstrated, then it becomes necessary to conduct research that will isolate and measure the variables that contribute to this generalization.

Verbal conditioning in the group setting

Verbal conditioning in the group setting has received little attention from researchers in verbal conditioning. The methodological problems are very great and the number of uncontrolled and unspecified variables is increased over the individual setting. An initial effort to attack some of these methodological problems was made by Bachrach, Candland, and Gibson (1961). They created groups of three people, only one of whom was an actual subject. The other two members of the group were experimenters, though the subject did not know it. The group was instructed to decide the meaning of an ideogram. The experimenters talked a predetermined amount of time about the meaning of the ideogram during the operant phase. During the conditioning phase, one or both of the experimenters reinforced the subject for talking. Verbal reinforcements were used. During the extinction phase, the experimenters omitted reinforcement of verbalizations by the subject by changing the topic of conversation proposed by the subject. In a reacquisition phase, the procedures were the same as in original acquisition.

Though the results were characterized by great variability, there was a consistency of performance commensurate with the experimental operations. There was a sharp increase in the amount of time spent in talking by the subject during acquisition and re-acquisition. During extinction there was a sharp decline in the subject's talking time.

In a second experiment, the effect of the sex of the purveyor of re-inforcement and/or punishment was investigated. In the first phase, both experimenters positively reinforced the subject for speaking. During the second phase, the experimenters maintained normal speech without specific reinforcement of the subject. The male or female experimenter positively reinforced, and the female or male experimenter punished the subject during the third phase. The fourth phase was the same as the second phase, and the fifth phase was the same as the third phase except that the experimenters reversed positions so that the female or male experimenter provided reinforcement and the male or female experimenter provided punishment of the subject for talking. The positive reinforcers were the same as in the first experiment, and the punishing stimuli were expressions of disagreement, e.g., "I think you are wrong." The five phases were conducted consecutively and each phase lasted ten minutes.

There was an increase in time spent talking by the subject during the initial phase when both experimenters positively reinforced the subject. However, the subject showed a marked decrement in amount of talking during the second phase when reinforcement was omitted but the experimenter maintained normal amounts of speech. During the third phase, when the female experimenter positively reinforced and the male experimenter punished the male subject for talking, the subject showed an increase in amount of talking as measured by time spent in talking. The fourth phase, which was the same as the second phase, did not produce the same results as the subject maintained about the same amount of talking as in the third phase. When the two experimenters reversed their roles—the female experimenter punished the subject—there was a sharp drop in the amount of talking by the subject. It would appear that the sex of the purveyor of reinforcement is an important variable in the reinforcement of a subject in a group setting.

In a third experiment, a subject was reinforced only during the last 30 seconds of each successive one-minute period. A definite cyclic effect was produced. The amount of talking in the reinforced time period was much greater than during the nonreinforced time period.

Bachrach and his associates have indicated some of the methodologi-cal difficulties involved in investigating verbal conditioning in the group setting. They are continuing their research efforts (this informa-tion was gained via personal communication) with special emphasis on building in the reinforcement history of the subjects in individual verbal conditioning sessions before the subjects are put into the group setting. Additional research efforts are oriented toward determining the S^D value of individuals in the group setting. The S^D value of an individual may be reflected in the reinforcement value of stimuli presented by the individual.

The exploratory efforts by Bachrach and his associates may have tremendous import, especially for the social psychologist. As the methodological problems are resolved, this area of research in verbal conditioning may become one of the most important contributors to the understanding of the verbal behavior of the human because so much of his verbal behavior occurs in the presence of groups of people.

SOME PASSING OBSERVATIONS

This review of the literature on verbal conditioning leaves many issues in doubt, including the issue of the legitimacy of the phenomenon of verbal conditioning. The weight of numbers would tend to support the view that the probability of making a verbal response can be changed through the introduction of various kinds of stimuli following the occurrence of the response. That is, most of the research has demonstrated the phenomenon of verbal conditioning. However, there are relatively few additional issues that have been resolved, particularly what variables have a significant effect on the amount of change of the critical response. Various variables, including the kind of contingent stimuli, the response class, and personality characteristics of the experimenter and subjects have been investigated, but there is a definite lack of consistency in the results.

It appears to the writer that some questions may be raised concerning the inclusion of research using the Taffel-type situation with the operant conditioning paradigm. The writer has serious doubts about its conclusions because an essential element of operant conditioning is missing. Skinner (1935) emphasized the importance of the generic nature of the concept of response. The essence of Skinner's approach to the concept of response is that a single response is unique and it is necessary to conceive of a class of responses, the members of which have certain common characteristics. The Taffel-type situation in which a specific personal pronoun is reinforced certainly does not provide for generalization within a class of responses. The modification of the Taffel-type situation in which hostile verbs, bodily active verbs, etc., are reinforced does provide opportunity for generalization within the class of hostile or bodily active verbs. Some of the confusion in the results of research in verbal conditioning may be a product of apparatuses, materials and procedures that do not fit within the operant conditioning paradigm.

Other issues also remain unresolved. Such issues as extinction and generalization have not generated consistent experimental results. An issue that has received much research attention but still remains unresolved is the issue of the role of awareness in verbal conditioning. Of course, this issue remains unresolved in nonverbal learning, at least as evidenced by Adams' (1957) review of the research on this topic.

At the same time, it appears that the clinical psychologist has seized the verbal conditioning paradigm and is using it extensively in research related to clinical psychology. Though the verbal conditioning paradigm has provided the clinical psychologist with a seemingly valuable research tool, it should be viewed and examined with great caution. It should be recognized that efforts to reduce behavior disorders to some facet of verbal conditioning may represent a great oversimplification of the many variables that may be involved in the development and maintenance of a behavior disorder.

The available evidence, however, does indicate that the verbal conditioning paradigm may be a valuable weapon in the armamentarium of the clinical psychologist. It does provide a method for bridging the gap between the clinical psychologist and the general-experimental psychologist. Much of the research reviewed in this chapter has been done by clinical psychologists, but the problems and the methodology reflect the problems and methodology of the general-experimental psychologist. In this way, the verbal conditioning paradigm provides a bridge across the gap between clinical and general-experimental psychology. This situation may make it possible for more of the research of general-experimental psychology to be utilized by the clinical psychologist. At the same time there is the danger that the clinical psychologist may attempt to investigate relationships before the basic research has been completed. This situation represents a danger because the formulation of general behavior theory will depend upon research conducted with the so-called normal population. Theories that have evolved from clinical populations leave much to be desired, both as theories and in accounting for the abnormal behavior. It appears that more and more research in verbal conditioning has a clinical flavor, and the writer believes it is at least equally important that more basic research in verbal conditioning needs to be done. This review of the literature on verbal conditioning is strong evidence for this need.

A second important value of the verbal conditioning paradigm for the clinical psychologist is that it may lead to a re-examination of the psychodiagnostic tools that he uses. There is rather strong evidence that some response classes on some psychodiagnostic instruments are amenable to modification through reinforcement procedures. This result raises some questions about the theoretical structures that presumably underlie these instruments. It may also mean that the clinical psychologist in using such instruments must exercise great caution in administering the test and interpreting the results. At the same time it raises questions about whether these tests are measuring what they purport to measure, especially in the case of projective tests. It may be that the Rorschach does not provide an X-ray of the personality as Klopfer and Kelley (1942) have stated.

A third use of this verbal conditioning paradigm may be in the area of interviewing. Again the results of the research in verbal conditioning strongly suggest that the therapist may bring the verbalization of the patient under his control by the judicious usage of certain contingent stimuli. If subsequent research tends to support this contention, it may mean that the psychotherapist will be in a position to test various hypotheses about the patient at his discretion. For example, if the psychotherapist hypothesizes that sexual difficulties are involved in the behavior disorder of the patient, he may be able to control the verbal behavior of the patient so that this hypothesis may be tested.

This possibility also carries some grave consequences with it. It may mean that the psychotherapist, since he is in control of the verbalization of the patient, may have to be more aware of the variables involved in the development and maintenance of the behavior of humans. Psychotherapy may become a systematic probing of likely variables that are involved in the development and maintenance of the particular behavior in question. It may mean that the most important part of the education of a clinical psychologist will be time spent in an animal laboratory where he learns the methodology of controlling and shaping the behavior of infrahumans.

A fourth possible development may involve the entire conceptualization of psychotherapy. The emphasis may shift from the resolving of core problems to the development and maintenance of specific behaviors that may be used by the patient to cope with his environment. There is the tacit recognition here that the efforts in psychotherapy may have limited objectives, the development of specific behaviors that will enable the patient to cope better with his environment. The conceptualization of psychotherapy as a restructuring of the personality is not readily amenable to this position. The psychotherapist must assume the responsibility for the development of specific behaviors that will serve well the patient.

The importance of verbal behavior is also reflected by the fact that much of the behavior of the human, especially the adult human, is under the control of verbal stimuli. Verbal stimuli as S^Ds may represent the means whereby much of the human's behavior is controlled and manipulated. The S^D value of verbal stimuli has received little attention from researchers, but it may be that verbal stimuli as S^Ds represent the means by which self-control or self-regulation of behavior is achieved. The development of self-regulation of behavior is one of the most important aspects in the transition from childhood to adulthood. At the present time we know very little about this transfer of control from one individual to another. Verbal conditioning techniques may provide the methodological procedures to attack this problem.

Though there are many unresolved issues involved in verbal conditioning and the future of verbal conditioning is in question, it appears to the writer that the verbal conditioning paradigm has served a useful function in its brief history on the experimental scene. The verbal conditioning paradigm has suggested that verbal behavior may be construed within the rubric of general-experimental psychology, a possibility that has been suggested by Skinner (1957). Verbal conditioning may pass by the wayside—a definite possibility—but at the same time it has suggested that the marriage of experimental methodology and clinical psychology may be a happy and profitable one.

REFERENCES

Adams, J. Laboratory studies of behavior without awareness. *Psychol. Bull.*, 1957, 54, 383–405.

Allyon, T., & Michael, J. The psychiatric nurse as a behavioral engineer. *J. exper. anal. Behavior*, 1959, 2, 323–334.

Anderson, D. E. Personality variables and verbal conditioning. Unpublished Ph.D. Dissertation, Univ. of Nebraska, 1958.

Ball, R. S. Reinforcement conditioning of verbal behavior by verbal and nonverbal stimuli in a situation resembling a clinical interview. Unpublished Ph.D. Dissertation, Indiana Univ., 1953.

Bachrach, A. J., Candland, D. K., & Gibson, J. T. Experiments in verbal behavior. I. Group reinforcement of individual response. In I. Berg and B. Bass (Eds.) *Conformity and deviation*. New York: Harper, 1961, pp. 258–285.

Barnett, C. D., Pryer, M. W., & Ellis, N. R. Experimental manipulation of verbal behavior in defectives. *Psychol. Rpts.*, 1959, 5, 593–596.

Binder, A., McConnell, D., & Sjohelm, N. A. Verbal conditioning as a function of experimenter characteristics. *J. abnorm. soc. Psychol.*, 1957, 55, 309–314.

Branson, R. K. Ratio reinforcement of the superstitious mind in verbal behavior. Unpublished Ph.D. Dissertation, Ohio State Univ., 1959.

Buss, A. H., & Buss, E. H. The effect of verbal reinforcement combinations on conceptual learning. *J. exper. Psychol.*, 1956, 52, 283–287.

Buss, A. H., & Durkee, A. Conditioning of hostile verbalizations in a situation resembling a clinical interview. *J. consult. Psychol.*, 1958, 22, 415–418.

Campbell, J. M. Verbal conditioning as a function of the personality characteristics of experimenters and subjects. Unpublished Ph.D. Dissertation, Univ. of Washington, 1960.

Carpenter, J. Generalization in verbal conditioning. Unpublished Ph.D. Dissertation, Florida State Univ., 1959.

Caruth, E. G. The relationship of dependency to verbal learning without awareness. Unpublished Ph.D. Dissertation, Univ. of So. Calif., 1959.

Cohen, B. D., Kalish, H. I., Thurston,

J. R., & Cohen, E. Experimental manipulation of verbal behavior. *J. exper. Psychol.*, 1954, *47*, 106–110.

Cox, F. N., & Cox, M. J. Unconscious reinforcement of a verbal response in children. *Austral. J. Psychol.*, 1956, *8*, 140–151.

Cushing, M. C. Affective components of the response class as a factor in verbal conditioning. Unpublished Ph.D. Dissertation, Univ. of Nebraska, 1957.

Daily, J. M. Verbal conditioning without awareness. Unpublished Ph.D. Dissertation, State Univ. of Iowa, 1953.

Deering, M. F. A test of a training procedure designed to increase the intensity of angry verbalization. Unpublished Ph.D. Dissertation, Univ. of Pittsburgh, 1958.

Dignam, P. J. The effect of verbal and nonverbal reinforcement on the verbal behavior of geriatric subjects. Unpublished Ph.D. Dissertation, Florida State Univ., 1960.

Dinoff, M., Horner, R. F. Kurpiewski, B. S., & Timmons, E. O. Conditioning verbal behavior of schizophrenics in a group therapy-like situation. *J. clin. Psychol.*, 1961. In press.

Drennen, W., & Greenspoon, J. Instructions and verbal conditioning. Unpublished Research Report, Florida State Univ., 1960.

Dulany, D. E. Hypotheses and habits in "operant conditioning." Mimeographed paper, 1960.

Essman, W. B. Effect of reinforcement schedule on perceptual "learning without awareness." *Percept. Mtr. Skills*, 1956, *6*, 168.

Everstine, L., & Bendig, A. N. Conditioning neurotic verbalizations. Paper read at American Psychological Association Convention, Chicago, Ill., 1960.

Fadigan, J. Indirect verbal conditioning. Unpublished M.A. Thesis, Florida State Univ., 1961.

Fahmy, S. A. Conditioning and extinction of a referential verbal response class in a situation resembling a clinical diagnostic interview. Unpublished Ph.D. Dissertation, Indiana Univ., 1953.

Fattu, N., & Mech, E. V. Resistance to extinction of verbal responses following two patterns of reinforcement. *J. genet. Psych.*, 1955, *53*, 193–198.

Ferguson, D. C., & Buss, A. Operant conditioning of hostile verbs in relation to experimenter and subject characteristics. *J. consult. Psychol.*, 1960, *24*, 324–327.

Friesen, W. V., & Ekman, P. Conditioning of hostile and friendly responses to photographs of peers. Paper read at the American Psychological Association Convention, Chicago, Ill., 1960.

Gewirtz, J. L., & Baer, D. M. Deprivation and satiation of social reinforcers as drive conditioners. *J. abnorm. soc. Psychol.*, 1958, *57*, 165–172.

Greenspoon, J. The effect of verbal and nonverbal stimuli on the frequency of members of two verbal response classes. Unpublished Ph.D. Dissertation, Indiana Univ., 1951.

Greenspoon, J. The effect of two nonverbal stimuli on the frequency of members of two verbal response classes. Paper presented at the American Psychological Association Convention, New York, N.Y., 1954.

Greenspoon, J. The reinforcing effect of two spoken sounds on the frequency of two responses. *Amer. J. Psychol.*, 1955, *68*, 409–416.

Greenspoon, J., & Gersten, C. Delay of extinction on resistance to extinction of a reinforced verbal response. Unpublished Research Report, Florida State Univ., 1960.

Greenspoon, J., & Thompson, L. Generalization of a reinforced verbal response. Paper presented at Midwestern Psych. Assoc. Convention, Chicago, Ill., 1959.

Greenspoon, J., & Ward, C. Generalization of a reinforced verbal response across situations and experimenters.

Unpublished Research Report, Florida State University, 1960.

Gross, L. E. Effects of verbal and nonverbal reinforcement in the Rorschach. *J. consult. Psychol.*, 1959, *23*, 66–68.

Grossberg, J. M. The effect of reinforcement schedule and response class on verbal conditioning. Unpublished Ph.D. Dissertation, Indiana Univ., 1956.

Hagen, J. M. The conditioning of verbal affect responses in two hospitalized schizophrenics diagnostic groups during the clinical interview. Unpublished Ph.D. Dissertation, Univ. of Washington, 1959.

Hall, W. E. The effects of set and reinforcement in verbal conditioning. Unpublished Ph.D. Dissertation, Univ. of Connecticut, 1958.

Hartman, C. H. Verbal behavior of schizophrenic and normal subjects as a function of types of social reinforcement. Unpublished Ph.D. Dissertation, State University of Iowa, 1955.

Hildum, D. C., & Brown, R. W. Verbal reinforcement and interviewer bias. *J. abnorm. soc. Psych.*, 1956, *53*, 108–111.

Kanfer, F. The effect of partial reinforcement on acquisition and extinction of a class of verbal responses. *J. exper. Psychol.*, 1954, *48*, 424–432.

Kanfer, F. Verbal conditioning: reinforcement schedules and experimenter influence. *Psychol., Rpts.*, 1958, *4*, 443–452.

Kanfer, F., & Karas, S. Prior experimenter-subject interaction and verbal conditioning. *Psychol. Rpts.*, 1959, *5*, 343–353.

Kirman, W. J. The relationship between learning, with and without awareness, to personality needs. Unpublished Ph.D. Dissertation, Columbia Univ., 1958.

Klein, S. Conditioning and extinction of operant verbal behavior in neuropsychiatric patients. Unpublished

Ph.D. Dissertation, Indiana Univ., 1954.

Klopfer, B., & Kelley, D. M. *The Rorschach Technique.* Yonkers, N.Y.: World Book Co., 1942.

Krasner, L. Studies of the conditioning of verbal behavior. *Psychol. Bull.*, 1958a, *15*, 148–171.

Krasner, L. A technique for investigating the relationship between the behavior cues of the examiner and the verbal behavior of the patient. *J. consult. Psychol.*, 1958b, *22*, 364–366.

Krasner, L., Ullmann, L. P., Weiss, R. L., & Collins, B. J. A personality correlate of individual differences in responsivity to verbal conditioning as obtained by three examiners. Paper read at the Western Psychological Association Convention, San Jose, Calif., 1960.

Krasner, L., Weiss, R. L., & Ullmann, L. P. Responsivity to verbal conditioning as a function of two different measures of "awareness." Paper read at the American Psychological Association Convention, Cincinnati, Ohio, 1959.

Levin, S. The effects of awareness on verbal conditioning. Unpublished Ph.D. Dissertation, Duke Univ., 1959.

Mandler, G., & Kaplan, W. K. Subjective evaluation and reinforcing effect of a verbal stimulus. *Science*, 1956, *124*, 582–583.

Marion, A. J. The influence of experimenter status upon verbal conditioning. Unpublished Ph.D. Dissertation, UCLA, 1956.

Matarazzo, J. D., Saslow, G., & Pareis, E. N. Verbal conditioning of two response classes: Some methodological consideration. *J. abnorm. soc. Psychol.*, 1960. In press.

McNair, D. M. Reinforcement of verbal behavior. *J. exper. Psychol.*, 1957, *53*, 40–46.

Medini, S. Learning without awareness and its relationship to insight and the hysteric-obsessive dimension. Unpublished Ph.D. Dissertation, New York Univ., 1957.

Mock, J. F. The influence of verbal and behavioral cues of a listener on the verbal productions of the speaker. Unpublished Ph.D. Dissertation, Univ. of Kentucky, 1957.

Naumoff, H., & Sidowski, J. Variables influencing verbal conditioning. Paper read at Western Psychological Association, San Jose, Calif., 1959.

Nuthmann, A. M. Conditioning of a response class on a personality test. *J. abnorm. soc. Psychol.*, 1957, 54, 19–23.

O'Connor, N., & Rawnsley, K. Two types of conditioning in psychotics and normals. *J. abnorm. soc. Psychol.*, 1959, 58, 157–161.

O'Donnell, W. F., Jr. The effects of individual differences and hostility arousal on the expression of hostility in a verbal conditioning situation. Unpublished Ph.D. Dissertation, Univ. of Washington, 1959.

Prutsman, T. Magnitude of response class as a variable in verbal conditioning. Unpublished Ph.D. Dissertation, Florida State Univ., 1961.

Quay, H. The effect of verbal reinforcement on the recall of early memories. *J. abnorm. soc. Psychol.*, 1959, 59, 254–257.

Rechtschaffer, A., & Mednick, S. A. The autokinetic word technique. *J. abnorm. soc. Psychol.*, 1955, 51, 346.

Reidy, M. E. A study of the unconscious effects of approval and disapproval on verbal behavior. Unpublished Ph.D. Dissertation, Catholic Univ., 1958.

Rickard, H. C., Dignam, P. J., & Horner, R. F. Verbal manipulations in a psychotherapeutic relationship. *J. clin. Psychol.*, 1960, 16, 364–367.

Rogers, J. M. Operant conditioning in a quasi-therapy setting. *J. abnorm. soc. Psychol.*, 1960, 60, 247–252.

Rosenberg, L. I. A study of verbal conditioning and its relation to dependency. Unpublished Ph.D. Dissertation, Univ. of Kansas, 1957.

Rosenblum, J. Examiner presence, levels of anxiety, and verbal conditioning. Unpublished Ph.D. Dissertation, Florida State Univ., 1959.

Salzinger, K. Experimental manipulation of verbal behavior: a review. *J. genet. Psychol.*, 1959, 61, 65–95.

Salzinger, K., & Pisoni, S. Reinforcement of affect responses of schizophrenics during the clinical interview. *J. abnorm. soc. Psychol.*, 1958, 57, 84–90.

Salzinger, K., & Pisoni, S. Reinforcement of verbal affect responses of normal subjects during the interview. *J. abnorm. soc. Psychol.*, 1960, 60, 127–130.

Sandler, J. The effect of negative verbal cues upon verbal behavior. Unpublished Ph.D. Dissertation, Florida State Univ., 1959.

Sapolsky, A. Effect of interpersonal relationships upon verbal conditioning. *J. abnorm. soc. Psychol.*, 1960, 60, 421–426.

Sarason, B. R. The effects of verbally conditional response classes on postconditioning tasks. Unpublished Ph.D. Dissertation, Indiana Univ., 1956.

Sarason, I. G. Interrelationships among individual difference variables, behavior in psychotherapy, and verbal conditioning. *J. abnorm. soc. Psychol.*, 1958, 56, 339–344.

Scott, T. R. Social reinforcement of aggressive sentences. Unpublished Ph.D. Dissertation, Univ. of Nebraska, 1958.

Shearn, D. Excessive speech. Paper presented at American Psychological Association Convention, Chicago, Ill., 1960.

Sidowski, J. B. Influence of awareness of reinforcement on verbal conditioning. *J. exper. Psychol.*, 1954, 48, 355–360.

Simkins, L. D. Behavioral modification as a function of examiner reinforcement and situational variables in a projective testing situation. Unpublished Ph.D. Dissertation, Univ. of Houston, 1959.

Simkins, L. D. Generalization effects of hostile verb reinforcement as a function of stimulus similarity and type of reinforcer. *J. Personality*, 1961. In press.

Skinner, B. F. The generic nature of the concepts of stimulus and response. *J. genet. Psychol.*, 1935, *12*, 40–63.

Skinner, B. F. *The behavior of organisms*. New York: Appleton-Century-Crofts, 1938.

Skinner, B. F. *Verbal behavior*. William James Lectures, Cambridge, Mass.: Harvard Univ. Press, 1948.

Skinner, B. F. *Verbal behavior*. New York: Appleton-Century-Crofts, 1957.

Solley, C. M., & Long, J. When is "uh-huh" reinforcing? *Percept. Mtr. Skills*, 1958, *8*, 277.

Solley, C. M., & Santos, J. F. Perceptual learning with partial verbal reinforcement. *Percept. Mtr. Skills*, 1958, *8*, 183–193.

Spivak, M., & Papajohn, J. The effect of the schedule of reinforcement on operant conditioning of a verbal response in the autokinetic situation. *J. abnorm. soc. Psychol.*, 1957, *54*, 213–217.

Sullivan, M. W., & Calvin, A. D. Further investigation of verbal conditioning. *Psychol. Rpts.*, 1959, *5*, 79–82.

Taffel, C. Anxiety and the conditioning of verbal behavior. *J. abnorm. soc. Psychol.*, 1955, *51*, 496–501.

Timmons, E. O. Experiments in conditioning operant verbal behavior. Unpublished Ph.D. Dissertation, Univ. of Tennessee, 1959.

Ullmann, L. P., Krasner, L., & Collins, B. J. Modification of behavior through verbal conditioning: effects

in group therapy. *J. abnorm. soc. Psychol.*, 1961. In press.

Verplanck, W. S. The control of the content of conversation: reinforcement of statements of opinion. *J. abnorm. soc. Psychol.*, 1955, *51*, 668–676.

Walder, L. The effects of three postacquisition procedures on a verbal avoidance response. Unpublished Ph.D. Dissertation, Columbia Univ., 1959.

Waskow, I. E. The effect of selective responding by the therapist in a quasi-therapy setting. Unpublished Ph.D. Dissertation, Univ. of Wisconsin, 1960.

Webb, R. Suggestibility and verbal conditioning. Unpublished Research Report, Florida State Univ., 1960.

Weide, T. N. Conditioning and generalization of the use of affect-relevant words. Unpublished Ph.D. Dissertation, Stanford Univ., 1959.

Weiss, R. L., Krasner, L., & Ullmann, L. P. Responsivity to verbal conditioning as a function of emotional atmosphere and pattern of reinforcement. *Psychol. Rpts.*, 1960, *6*, 415–426.

Weiss, R. L., Ullmann, L. P., & Krasner, L. On the relationship between hypnotizability and response to verbal operant conditioning. *Psychol. Rpts.*, 1960, *6*, 59–60.

Wickes, T. A. Examiner influence in a testing situation. *J. consult. Psychol.*, 1956, *20*, 23–25.

Wilson, W. C., & Verplanck, W. S. Some observations of the reinforcement of verbal operants. *Amer. J. Psychol.*, 1956, *69*, 448–451.

Zedek, M. E. The conditioning of verbal behavior with negative cultural connotations. Unpublished Ph. D. Dissertation, Boston Univ., 1958.

16

The Experimental Foundations of Some New Psychotherapeutic Methods

JOSEPH WOLPE

Psychiatric thought with regard to the neuroses and their treatment continues to be dominated by psychoanalytic theory, even though such basic propositions of psychoanalysis as repression, castration anxiety, and resistance are still without scientific validation. In the practical matter of treatment of neurosis, psychoanalytic *therapy* is increasingly under fire. The evidence (e.g., Eysenck, 1952) shows that its results have been no better than those obtained by relatively simple traditional methods that consist mainly of reassurance, explanation, persuasion, and suggestion, either separately or in combinations. The claim of the psychoanalysts (e.g., Fenichel, 1945; Hendrick, 1958) that their methods alone can achieve recoveries that may with assurance be expected to endure, is in conflict with the facts revealed in a survey of follow-up studies (Wolpe, 1961a).

More research, therefore, is being directed toward the exploration of other approaches to the explication and control of neuroses. In keeping with what has been done in other fields of medicine, it has seemed appropriate to try to understand the "abnormal" in terms of the "normal." Understanding of the factors determining the acquisition and elimination of "normal" behavior might have application to our understanding of neurotic behavior.

We know three kinds of processes that can lead to lasting (i.e., habitual) changes of response to specified stimulus conditions: growth, lesions,* and learning. Because human neurotic habits of reaction can often be dated from particular experiences that involve stimuli to which the patient has come to react with anxiety, and because these habits can be altered through the techniques of psychotherapeutic interviews, there is a *prima facie* presumption that neurotic reactions owe their existence to the learning process.

Some years ago, investigations were initiated to examine this presumption, partly for its own sake, but mainly because of the practical possibility that we might develop more effective methods for treating neuroses. These investigations, which have been reported in detail in several communications (Wolpe, 1948, 1952a, 1952b, 1954, 1958, 1959), led to the conclusion that neurotic behavior consists of *persistent habits of learned (conditioned) unadaptive behavior acquired in anxiety-generating situations,* and that therapy depends upon the unlearning of this behavior.

In the great majority of instances, the core of neurotic behavior lies, not in any particular motor activity, but in anxiety. Anxiety refers specifically to those responses, *predominantly of the autonomic nervous system,* with which the individual characteristically reacts to noxious (painful) stimuli. Its commonest manifestations are rapid respiration (sometimes irregular), rapid pulse, raised blood pressure, increased palmar sweating, and more or less generalized elevation of muscle tension. Not all anxiety is neurotic. Anxiety in response to an objective threat, such as being held up by a gunman or faced by the loss of one's livelihood, is entirely appropriate. Anxiety is unadaptive when it is evoked where there is no real danger—for example, in an elevator, driving past a cemetery, or on entering a roomful of people.†

Observations by early workers with experimental neuroses suggested that neurotic behavior in the human being differs from that induced in laboratory animals only in such details as may be expected in an organism that is more complex and somewhat differently organized. Therefore, and because animal experiments offer far easier control of variables than is possible with human subjects (especially where illness is involved), it was logical first to explore in animals the applicability of principles of learning to neuroses and their treatment. The subsequent successful application to the human clinical situation of the lessons that were learned from the animal experiments vindi-

---

* This term is used here to mean either deviations from the normal physiological state in particular parts of the nervous system, or else generalized biochemical deviations such as may be produced by endocrine abnormalities.

† In certain circles, it has become customary to refer to anxiety as "fear" when it is appropriate to the evoking situation, and "anxiety" when it is not. Since the physiological response patterns are the same in both contexts, the words "fear" and "anxiety" are here used synonymously.

cated the operational assumption that the most highly organized behavior of men and cats might conform to the same general laws no
less than does the behavior of their respective digestive tracts.

EXPERIMENTAL NEUROSES[*]

Previous experiments

The first reports of neuroses induced in experimental animals came
from Pavlov's laboratories (1927). The earliest venture was the famous
"circle and ellipse" experiment, which depended upon subjecting the
animal to "difficult discrimination." A luminous circle was projected
on to a screen placed in front of a dog held by a harness on the laboratory table. Each projection was succeeded by the dropping of a piece
of food within easy reach of the animal. This cycle—appearance of
circle, appearance of food—was repeated until a food-seeking response
to the circle was firmly established. Then presentations of a luminous
ellipse with semi-axes in the ratio of 2:1 began to be interspersed
among the presentations of the circle. The ellipse was never followed
by food, so that it became a "negative alimentary stimulus"—that is,
salivation and other "anticipatory" responses associated with feeding
were inhibited. Quite soon, the difference of response to the two shapes
became "complete and constant."

> The shape of the ellipse was now approximated by stages to that
> of the circle (ratios of semi-axes of 3:2, 4:3 and so on) and the
> development of differentiation continued . . . with some fluctuation,
> progressing at first more and more quickly, and then again slower,
> until an ellipse with ratio of semi-axes 9:8 was reached. In this
> case, although a considerable degree of discrimination did develop,
> it was far from being complete. After three weeks of work upon
> this differentiation, not only did the discrimination fail to improve
> but it became considerably worse and finally disappeared altogether.
> At the same time, the whole behavior of the animal underwent an
> abrupt change. The hitherto quiet dog began to squeal in its stand,
> kept wriggling about, tore off with its teeth the apparatus for
> mechanical stimulation of the skin, and bit through the tubes con-
> necting the animal's room with the observer, a behavior which never
> happened before. On being taken into the experimental room, the
> dog now barked violently.

Apparently, the close resemblance of the 9:8 ellipse to the circle
resulted in what may be called "a state of conflict," the strong simultaneous activation of opposite action tendencies—the activation of
both the evocation and the inhibition of the alimentary response. Evidently this conflict engendered high intensity autonomic responses of

[*] For a fuller discussion of this topic, see Wolpe (1952, 1958).

the anxiety pattern which came to be conditioned to the environmental stimuli that made impact on the animal at that time. (The similarity of the autonomic reaction pattern accompanying conflict to that associated with noxious [electrical] stimulation has been demonstrated by Fonberg [1956].)

In subsequent years, many experimental neuroses were induced by methods that involved the use of conflict in variations of the above experiment. Jacobsen, Wolfe, and Jackson (1935), working with chimpanzees, used difficult discriminations based on the distance between two identical cups, under one of which food was hidden. Dworkin, Raginsky, and Bourne (1937), and Gantt (1944) produced neuroses in dogs by conflict-producing use of auditory stimuli. Krasnogorski (1925) did the same in children. An interesting and successful modification was the use of stimuli at, and just below, threshold (Dworkin, 1939; Dworkin, Baxt, and Dworkin, 1942). In addition, Karn (1938) reported a method in which the difficulty of discrimination depended on *internal* cues.

Another group of techniques for inducing experimental neuroses makes use of noxious stimulation, usually in the form of electric shock, to evoke the "unconditioned" anxiety responses to which "neutral" stimuli are conditioned. This method, too, had its inception in Pavlov's laboratories (Pavlov 1927, pp. 289–290). A mild electric current to a spot on the animal's skin was made a conditioned stimulus to food-seeking by delivering food immediately after each application of it. The current was then gradually intensified until it became "extremely powerful." Although frequently applied during many months, it did not evoke a defense reaction until it was systematically applied to a different spot daily. This eventually produced "a most violent defense reaction," and the animal was thereafter disturbed whenever exposed to stimuli related to the experiment. The fact that each of the original stages of training built up an inhibition of the defense reaction evidently distracted Pavlov's attention from the crucial role of the noxious stimulus and led him to conclude that the neuroses were due to "a clash between excitation and inhibition." This conclusion seems erroneous because, during the long period in which defense reaction was inhibited, while inhibition counterbalanced excitation, no disturbance appeared. The neurotic state was induced only when the electric current was applied in a way that outran the initial scope of the conditioned inhibition. Since, as will be seen below with respect to certain experiments on cats, shock alone can produce such neuroses, there is no need to compound the etiology. Similar comments apply to the neuroses produced by the Cornell group (e.g., Anderson and Parmenter, 1941; Liddell, 1944) using weak electric shocks, and Cook's rat neuroses (1939). It is only necessary to say here, that there is much evidence to indicate that all the effects for which complex explanations have been advanced can be produced by direct conditioning to "neutral" stimuli of the responses elicited by electric shock.

In another group of experimental neuroses, the effects were ascribed to motivational conflict between approach to food and avoidance of shock. This explanation was given by Dimmick, Ludlow, and Whiteman (1939) for the neuroses they produced in cats. Subsequently, Masserman (1943) advanced the same theory in respect to his much more extensive and elaborate series. The explanation was a consequence of the fact that the experiments of these workers were so set up that avoidance of shock did, in fact, interrupt approaches to food. However, it does not explain why much the same effects result when an animal is shocked in a confined space, even when there is an apparent absence of any other major motivation (see below).

Experimental neuroses as learned habits

The first experiment to indicate the learned basis of a persistent habit of unadaptive anxiety was Watson and Rayner's (1920) famous case of Little Albert. Finding that the child responded fearfully to the loud sound made by striking an iron bar behind him, the experimenters repeatedly struck the bar just as the child's hand touched a white rat. A fear reaction was conditioned to the rat and was found to have generalized to similar stimuli—a rabbit, a beaver fur, and a dog.

During the years 1947–1948, I conditioned neurotic behavior in cats (Wolpe, 1948, 1952) using an experimental cage similar to that of Masserman (1943)—40 inches long, 20 inches wide, and 20 inches high, with an electrifiable grid on its floor. I demonstrated that the neurotic behavior developed even when the animal had not had previous experience with food in the cage. It was sufficient merely to subject him to several high-voltage, low-amperage shocks soon after his first introduction to the experimental cage. The shocks evoked a variety of motor responses (e.g., crouching, clawing at the sides of the cage, howling) and autonomic responses (e.g., pupillary dilatation, erection of hairs, and rapid respiration). It was subsequently found that the autonomic responses (and certain of the motor responses) had become conditioned to the visual stimuli of the experimental situation and to an auditory stimulus (e.g., a buzzer) that had preceded each shock. This anxious behavior was consistently evocable at high intensity in the experimental cage, but some anxiety was also noted on the floor of the experimental laboratory; smaller measures were noted in other rooms that had features of similarity to the experimental laboratory. In several of these places, *anxiety was severe enough to prevent the*

animal from eating attractive food placed before him, even though he
had been starved for 24 hours, or longer.

Neurotic reactivity was extremely persistent, although the animal
was never again shocked. This was the case whether the animal was
kept away from the experimental cage for months, or was replaced in
it again and again, sometimes for hours. *The core of this persistent reactivity was always the autonomic complex of reactions.* For reasons
given below, motor responses were far less likely to be so persistent:
usually they diminished in strength and eventually disappeared.*

Two factors apparently contribute to the resistance to extinction of
the autonomic response of anxiety. First, a relatively low level of
muscle action is involved in autonomic responses, so that there is little
generation of the fatigue-associated process known as reactive inhibition (RI) upon which extinction seems to depend (Hull, 1943; Wolpe,
1952c). (It would appear to be for the same reason that conditioned
eyelid responses, involving very limited musculature, are unusually
resistant to extinction.) Second, each time an organism is removed
from an anxiety-evoking situation, there is a sharp reduction of an internal state of excitation that is conveniently termed anxiety drive. The
reinforcing effect that this drive-reduction has upon the anxiety response habit counteracts any fatigue-associated tendency toward extinction. That the mere cessation of an anxiety-evoking stimulus has a
reinforcing effect upon antecedent anxiety responses appears from an
experiment (Wolpe, 1958, p. 59) in which an auditory stimulus conditioned to anxiety was presented to a cat approaching a piece of food
dropped in a corner of a room. The animal recoiled, hair erect, pupils
dilated; and hesitated before again advancing. Repeating the procedure several times resulted in the establishment of anxiety and
avoidance reactions to that corner and also to the sight of food dropped
on any floor. The immediate response to the auditory stimulus was
anxiety and reversal of forward movement. The only reinforcing state
of affairs of which the situation contained evidence was the reduction
of anxiety following cessation of the stimulus. Similar findings have
been reported by other workers (e.g., Farber, 1948; Miller, 1948a).

Since autonomic responses are present continuously while the animal is in the experimental cage, they are inevitably reinforced at each
reduction of anxiety drive that follows removal of the animal from the
cage. Motor responses that happen sufficiently often to occur shortly

---

* The central role of autonomic responses is also apparent in most human
neuroses. While by such means as hypnotic suggestion particular motor responses
may be eliminated, the neuroses continue as long as neurotic *anxiety response*
habits persist. It may be predicted for the same reason that fundamental therapeutic effects would not as a rule result from therapist behavior that encourages
at the interview certain classes of statements made by the patient and not
others.

before drive reduction are also reinforced. Motor responses that are repeated infrequently are likely to occur only occasionally just before drive reduction, and therefore tend to undergo gradual extinction. That is why, in our experiments, infrequent motor responses were quite soon extinguished from neurotic constellations.

Basic therapeutic experiments

Only a few of the experimenters working with animal neuroses have concerned themselves with therapeutic measures. Pavlov (1927), Petrova (1938), and Dworkin, Raginsky, and Bourne (1937) explored the use of drugs, regarding which we shall have more to say in a later section. Masserman (1943) was the first to employ behavioral methods for overcoming experimental neuroses. His interpretations were in the psychoanalytic framework, however, and he did not analyze his experimental results in terms of the processes of learning with regard to either neurotic change or its reversal.

Some light was thrown on the role of learning in the therapy of experimental neuroses in the course of therapeutic experiments conducted by the present writer (Wolpe, 1948, 1952a, 1958). The resistance of neurotic anxiety responses to the ordinary process of extinction has already been noted. The fact that anxiety could prevent experimental animals from feeding despite prolonged deprivation of food suggested that, reciprocally, feeding might inhibit anxiety in conditions where the anxiety reaction was weak; and that thus to inhibit it might result in a weakening of the anxiety response habit. To test this possibility, we made use of the fact, mentioned above, that when the experimental animals were placed in other rooms, according to each room's degree of resemblance to the experimental laboratory, lesser degrees of anxiety were evoked. Each animal was offered food, first in the laboratory itself. If he refused to eat there, we proceeded on subsequent days to rooms successively more *unlike* the laboratory. When at last a room was found in which anxiety responses were so weak that feeding was not inhibited, the animal was presented with a succession of meat pellets. The feedings were accompanied by a gradual disappearance of all evidence of anxiety in the particular room. Tested the next day, the animal appeared free from anxiety in that room; and in the room next closest in resemblance to the experimental room showed relatively little anxiety and no longer refused food. Here, too, repeated feedings led to complete elimination of anxiety. Proceeding thus by stages, the animal was eventually induced to eat in the experimental cage, which also, in the same way, was finally deprived of all power to elicit anxiety.

However, the auditory stimulus that had regularly preceded the electric shocks in the original conditioning *could still evoke anxiety*. This was an important observation, for it indicated that neurotic responses are *stimulus-specific*. Similar specificity was subsequently noted in the treatment of human neuroses (Wolpe, 1961b). For example, the overcoming of a fear of the accoutrements of death did not, in a particular patient, ameliorate a claustrophobia. Further, clinical observation seems to confirm the expectation that, if all stimulus "triggers" to neurotic responses are "deconditioned" from the responses, the responses cease permanently (Wolpe, 1961b). They do not reappear spontaneously, as they would if there were a focus of irritation or of "dammed-up forces." Only relearning can be expected to re-establish responses to particular stimuli.

To overcome the residual neurotic habit of responding with anxiety to the auditory stimulus, we applied methods parallel to those used in the case of the visual stimuli. Theoretically, it would have been possible to work along several dimensions of generalization—time, distance, intensity, pitch. In fact, the first two of these were both applied with success. The distance dimension was used as follows:

The animal was offered food at increasing distances from the sound of the buzzer until eating occurred. One animal responded to the buzzer with anxiety so great that even at the distance of 30 feet the sound could inhibit him from taking food, although he had not eaten for twenty hours. However, at forty feet he hurriedly snapped up a pellet of meat. Pellets of meat were given repeatedly during the sounding of the buzzer, and overt anxiety at 40 feet gradually decreased to zero. When then tested at 30 feet, the animal had less anxiety than previously and accepted a pellet of meat, and after repeated feedings lost all signs of anxiety at that distance too. Increasingly close approaches were made by similar steps, with the eventual result that the animal had no anxiety with the buzzer sounding continuously only a few feet away—in fact, responded to the sound by looking around for food.

At this stage, we had to ask whether the anxiety response habit had been eliminated or was merely being suppressed by a more strongly conditioned feeding response. The matter was easily put to the test. The feeding response was extinguished by repeatedly presenting the buzzer without any further feeding. If the anxiety had been suppressed by the occurrence of feeding, the removal of the feeding reaction should have been followed by resurgence of anxiety to the sound of the buzzer. In no animal, as it turned out, was there any recurrence of anxiety to the sound of the buzzer upon the extinction of food seeking. This seemed to establish that the strength of the anxiety-response habit had been reduced to zero, and a basic method for overcoming neurotic reactions had become available.

A PSYCHOTHERAPEUTIC PRINCIPLE
AND ITS APPLICATIONS

The above therapeutic experiments led to the framing of a general hypothesis: *If a response inhibitory to anxiety can be made to occur in the presence of anxiety-evoking stimuli, it will weaken the connection between these stimuli and the anxiety responses.* This presumes the occurrence at a complex level of neural organization of the phenomenon of *reciprocal inhibition* first described by Sherrington (1906) in the context of spinal reflexes. A simple example of reciprocal inhibition is the reflex relaxation of the extensor muscles of the arm that accompanies contraction of the flexor muscles flexing the elbow, and the reciprocal relaxation of the flexors when the extensors contract. Modern neurophysiological research (e.g., Lloyd, 1946) has shown that such relaxation is brought about by impulses that directly block the synaptic transmission of excitatory impulses to the antagonists of actively contracting muscles.

At higher levels of organization, the performance of a given response often leads to the inhibition of all other responses that involve the same functional units. An obvious example is the articulation of a word. Ordinarily, this inhibits all simultaneous tendencies to articulate other words. Again, an attempt to do two mental tasks at the same time results in some degree of inhibition of the performance of each (Messerschmidt, 1927).

In certain circumstances, the intercurrent arousal of a relatively strong response incompatible with an ongoing response will inhibit the latter, at least in part, and a decrement may subsequently be noted in the strength of the habit that subserves the inhibited response.* The most extensive work on the weakening effects of new responses upon previously established habits has been in the area of verbal learning. An association between one word and another is weakened if a third word is repeatedly made to follow the first (stimulus) word. Osgood (1948) was the first to recognize that this phenomenon, known as retroactive inhibition, is an instance of reciprocal inhibition. The earliest study utilizing competing responses to weaken responses with powerful autonomic accompaniments was reported by Pavlov (1927). (It has been referred to above in another context.) A weak electric current was made a conditioned stimulus to feeding in a dog. During

---

* It is worth remarking that some psychologists, for example, Maatsch, Adelson, and Denny (1954) argue that even the process of experimental extinction depends upon competing responses rather than upon a fatigue-associated inhibitory state. It seems likely that, at the very least, in many instances competing responses are a contributory factor. The obscurity of the position is due to the fact that the great majority of studies on the weakening of habits have been concerned with extinction.

several experimental sessions, the strength of the current was increased by stages, and at each stage repeated feedings led to disappearance of all signs of anxiety and avoidance. Eventually, an extremely strong current elicited only a food approach response and no defense reaction at all. Apparently, at each stage of the experiment the occurrence of feeding was accompanied by a reciprocal inhibition of such mild defense reaction as the slightly intensified electrical stimulus tended to evoke. This conclusion is, of course, based on the findings, recounted above, of the therapeutic experiments on neuroses of cats.

RECIPROCAL INHIBITION IN THE TREATMENT OF HUMAN NEUROSES

Since neurotic responses in human subjects, no less than in animals, most typically have anxiety as their principal constituent, making use of the reciprocal inhibition principle implies finding responses that will inhibit anxiety. Observation alone can determine what responses will have this effect, for although it is possible that certain mutual inhibitory arrangements are immutably established in the course of the physical growth of the nervous system, in other instances such arrangements are modifiable by the learning process, and also perhaps by further growth. For example, while feeding often inhibits anxiety in children and has been used to overcome phobias (Jones, 1924; Lazarus, 1959), it usually seems to have lost this effect in adults.

Up to the present certain responses have been found most useful in deliberate efforts to overcome neurotic anxiety response habits: (1) relaxation responses; (2) sexual responses; (3) assertive responses; and (4) respiratory responses (carbon-dioxide-oxygen mixtures used for pervasive ["free-floating"] anxiety).

The employment of relaxation responses in systematic desensitization (see below) most clearly parallels the treatment of animal neuroses described above. Closer experimental analogues for the use of assertive and sexual responses are given below. There is as yet no direct experimental parallel to carbon dioxide therapy. However, experimental precedents are available for the adjuvant use of other drugs for fundamental therapy (therapy that changes habit patterns in contrast to symptomatic therapy that merely cloaks them), and also for two less frequently used conditioning methods. All these will be discussed.

It must always be remembered, when studying special methods of therapy of the neuroses, that the effects peculiar to a specific method must be separated from the more general effects of interviews that give a measure of success to all psychotherapy.

Systematic desensitization therapy

Systematic desensitization is an example of "gradual approach" therapy, closely parallel in its essentials to the already described method of overcoming experimental neuroses. It is applicable to treating the neurotic response habits related to a wide range of stimuli, but is generally not used in connection with neurotic responses that lend themselves to treatment by changing behavior in interpersonal situations. It is, however, especially valuable for treating phobias and habits of responding with anxiety to many relatively complex situations, such as being rejected or being watched, whose basic similarity to the phobias is far greater than is generally realized.

Systematic desensitization, which has been described in detail elsewhere (Wolpe, 1958, 1959, 1961b), involves three sets of operations: (1) training the patient in deep relaxation by an abbreviated form of the method described by Jacobson (1938) (who was the first to demonstrate [1939, 1940] that the autonomic effects of relaxation are the opposite of those of anxiety); (2) during the same sessions, identifying the "themes" of stimuli to neurotic reactions, e.g., heights, crowds, situations of rejection, listing a considerable number of situations on each theme, and then ranking these situations in order of the intensity of anxiety each arouses (the ranked list being called an *anxiety hierarchy*); and (3) at the session following the completion of the foregoing operations, causing the patient (usually hypnotized) to relax deeply and then asking him to imagine the least disturbing item in the list. If, according to expectation, the anxiety evoked is of low intensity, the strength of its evocation will progressively decrease, eventually to zero, in the course of several further presentations of the item. The next item in the list is then presented, likewise repeatedly, until it ceases to evoke anxiety. Proceeding in this manner, the therapist is eventually able to present the "strongest" item in the hierarchy without arousing any anxiety. At every stage it has been found that freedom from anxiety to an imagined stimulus confers freedom from anxiety upon confrontation with the real equivalent (though sometimes the latter lags behind).

It is crucial to note that, just as in the animal studies feeding can counteract only relatively weak anxiety, *relaxation can counteract anxiety only if the latter is relatively weak*. A stimulus that evokes anxiety strongly may be presented many times to the relaxed patient without the strength of anxiety diminishing in the least. But if the anxiety response is weak, then from one presentation of the stimulus to the next the anxiety declines in strength and at last ceases to be in evidence. There is, in fact, an inverse relationship between the magnitude of anxiety a stimulus evokes and the ease with which the anxiety-response habit can be overcome by the inhibiting effects of a given degree of relaxation.

Once a "weak" stimulus has stopped eliciting anxiety, a somewhat "stronger" one on the same theme presented to the fully relaxed patient will evoke less anxiety than it would have done before. Successive presentations diminish the anxiety aroused by this also to zero. Stimuli at ever-rising levels in the hierarchy are thus brought within the anxiety-inhibiting capacity of the subject's relaxation. To put the matter in another way: If there are ten stimuli which, in their variations along a dimension of generalization (see below), elicit in a subject quantities of anxiety which vary from one to ten, and if through the inhibiting effects of relaxation the anxiety aroused by the stimulus evoking one unit is reduced to zero, the stimulus that orginally evoked two units of anxiety will be found to be evoking only one unit. Take, for example, a subject who has a fear of heights in places where there is no danger of falling. He has one unit of anxiety on visualizing himself looking down from a height of ten feet, and two units when the height is 20 feet. Reduction of the anxiety from the ten-foot level to zero will have the result that the amount of anxiety evoked by 20 feet will be diminished to one unit. This in turn will drop to zero upon the repeated presentation of the 20-foot height to the imagination of the deeply relaxed subject; and then 30 feet will evoke one unit of anxiety. In this gradual fashion, anxiety responses can be eradicated from any height. It must be emphasized that these decrements of response are not transient, but lasting. As in the animal experiments, they are indicative of decrease of strength of anxiety-response habits.

Desensitization amounts to a systematic deconditioning of anxiety responses along a stimulus dimension of generalization (Hull, 1943) from a central conditioned stimulus. The applicability of the generalization principle to complex configurations was first demonstrated by Miller (1948b). Since each stimulus in a continuum shares features with "adjacent" stimuli, the elimination of anxiety responses to a stimulus remote from the central stimulus involves the elimination of whatever fraction of the anxiety evoked by related stimuli is attributable to the shared features. The situations to which the subject is "exposed" in desensitization are imaginary, but there is evidence that responses to imaginary stimuli are similar to real ones (Stone, 1955).

The use of systematic desensitization is not confined to "simple" classical phobias. It can be applied to almost every case where the subject is disturbed by the mere presence of stimulus situations which contain no objective threat. It will usually be found that each stimulus situation, however complex, is one of a class of situations whose members evoke anxiety in different degrees. The coherence of a class very often does not depend upon the outward similarity of the situations but upon some core or theme that they share. Themes commonly found are being rejected, being disapproved of, aggressive behavior of others, or being watched. In constructing hierarchies based on such themes, all situations that embody the theme are first listed; and then the patient ranks the situations in order of the magnitude of the reaction he anticipates he would have on exposure to each. The following is a young woman's hierarchy of situations on the theme of "devaluation by others," ranked in descending order of intensity of her reactions.

1. An argument she raises in a discussion is ignored by the group.

2. She is not recognized by a person she has briefly met three times.

3. Her mother says she is selfish because she is not helping in the house. (Studying instead.)

4. She is not recognized by a person she has briefly met twice.

5. Her mother calls her lazy.

6. She is not recognized by a person she has briefly met once.

In a recent survey of a randomly selected sample of 68 phobias and allied reactions in 39 patients treated by desensitization, it was found that 62 of the areas of disturbance were either totally overcome or markedly improved in a mean of 11.2 sessions per hierarchy (Wolpe, 1961b).

Experimental bases of other therapeutic techniques

Each of the experimental findings given below has a clinical parallel in the form of new psychotherapeutic techniques. Reciprocal inhibition appears to be the effective process in each of the instances in which lasting changes of response have been observed.

The addition of a stimulus increasing the probability of a response antagonistic to anxiety: The effectiveness of such a stimulus was first demonstrated by Masserman (1943) and confirmed by the writer (1952a). As already stated, hungry, neurotic cats will not eat meat pellets dropped in front of them in the experimental cage. But some of them *will* eat if the pellets are conveyed to them by a human hand, either directly or at the end of a rod. In my own experiments, the hand had become conditioned to evoke approach responses to food because food had been routinely given to the animals by the human hand in their living cages. These approach tendencies presumably summated with the approach tendencies evoked by the food itself, and in some cases the resultant drive strength was sufficient to overcome the anxiety-associated inhibition.

A summation of action tendencies analogous to the above is frequently operative in patients undergoing psychotherapy based on principles of learning (e.g., Salter, 1950; Wolpe, 1952b, 1954, 1958; Stevenson, 1959). Through such summation, the subject is enabled to perform certain acts previously impossible. For example, a patient may have been chronically inhibited by fear from expressing his resentment toward a person who has always taken advantage of him. The inhibition of its outward expression does not remove the resentment, which may have been evoked at every encounter with that person perhaps over many years. The therapist, having explained to the patient in a simple way the reciprocal inhibition principle, points out the value of assertiveness wherever there is undue fear in personal relationships. He increases the tendency to assertive action by making it clear that it is not "wrong" to stand up for one's reasonable rights or to hurt the feelings of those who flout these rights; by emphasizing the injustices that have been inflicted on the patient; and by pointing to the social unattractiveness of weak and poltroonish behavior. The action tendency aroused by changes in attitude thus directly brought about summates with that of the unexpressed resentment to produce a total action potential great enough to overcome the inhibiting effects of the fear. The patient can in consequence express his resentment outwardly. Such action leads to reciprocal inhibition of the anxiety response that had been invariable in this kind of interpersonal situation, and eventuates in a weakening of the anxiety-response habit. It is important for the patient to be carefully enjoined to be discreet—not to be assertive when the act might be punished, by the loss of his job, for example.

By contrast with the above, but to the same effect, in a technique employing sexual responses in actual sexual situations to overcome impotence (Wolpe, 1954, 1958), the therapist's intervention results in a *subtraction* of anxiety instead of an addition to the opposing impulse. It is made clear both to the patient and his partner that no particular level of performance must ever be *required* on any sexual occasion. A major source of anxiety is thus removed, and the sexual arousal is consequently more capable of inhibiting such anxiety as remains.

There is a feature of this technique that has another experimental analogue. According to the usual instructions, the patient lies with his partner in a relaxed way and waits for surges of sexual feeling as a basis for action. It would appear that these surges arise as a function of behavioral oscillation (Hull, 1943, pp. 304–321)—fluctuations in strength of different motivational states. Presumably, a high level of sexual drive now and then coincides with a low level of anxiety, and at such times sexual feelings "break through." The experimental analogue to this is a method of overcoming experimental neuroses described by Masserman (1943) and repeated by the present writer (1948, 1952a). This consists of placing a hungry, neurotic cat in the experimental cage, and then forcing it, by means of a sliding partition, toward the food box containing attractive food. After a delay, the animal may eat. Thereafter, eating takes place with increasing readiness and the neurotic reactions progressively decrease. It seems plausible that this technique succeeds because occasionally in some animals, through behavioral oscillation, the food-approach motivation momentarily exceeds the anxiety-*cum*-avoidance motivation in strength.

Diminishing the level of anxiety by drugs as an aid to reciprocal inhibition: Investigations in past years (Pavlov, 1927; Dworkin, Raginsky and Bourne, 1937; Masserman and Yum, 1946) have revealed that lasting improvement sometimes occurs in neurotic animals after more or less prolonged treatment with such sedative drugs as alcohol, bromides, or barbiturates. The first study to have isolated relevant variables is a recent one by Miller, Murphy, and Mirsky (1957). Using electric shock as the unconditioned stimulus, they conditioned a large number of rats to perform an avoidance response at the sound of a buzzer. The animals were then randomly divided into four groups for extinction studies. Two of the groups received injections of saline and the other two injections of chlorpromazine on each of four consecutive days. A saline-injected group (I) and a chlorpromazine injected group (II) received fifteen unreinforced presentations of the buzzer on each of the four days, while the other two groups were simply returned to the living cage. Group II made far fewer avoidance responses than Group I on these four days; and on the fifth and subsequent days, when *all* groups were given unreinforced trials without any injections, it was found that Group II had a much lower residue of avoidance conditioning than any of the other groups (as shown by a much smaller number of avoidance responses). That this outcome was related to autonomic effects of the chlorpromazine and not to a suppression of motor responses was indicated by repeating the experiment with injections of phenobarbital of a dosage that had previously been equated with chlorpromazine in terms of motor retardation effects. In animals given phenobarbital the level of avoidance responses was not diminished, in marked contrast to the chlorpromazine group.

The *lasting* consequences of completely or largely suppressing the autonomic responses conditioned to the buzzer may be accounted for as follows. Besides the buzzer, the experimental situation contained other stimuli that as a result of the animal's "life experience" had been previously conditioned to responses with autonomic accompaniments other than anxiety (e.g., curiosity responses [Berlyne, 1960]). Anxiety responses at full strength could inhibit these other emotions; but when chlorpromazine damped down anxiety to a low level, it permitted them to surge forth and reciprocally inhibit whatever anxiety or fraction of the anxiety-evoking process was activated. Each occasion of reciprocal inhibition of anxiety responses would leave behind some measure of conditioned inhibition of the anxiety response habit.

The clinical implications of Miller, Murphy, and Mirsky's experiments are likely to be considerable. There already are suggestive pieces of information regarding the effects of prolonged administration of chlorpromazine and other tranquilizing drugs. Winkelman (1954) found that after administration of the drug for six months or longer in doses sufficient to produce marked amelioration of neurotic symptoms, improvement persisted for six months in 35 per cent of patients in whom the drug was gradually withdrawn, even though they had received no psychotherapy. Unfortunately, no control study records the improvement rate in the same period among patients who, receiving no psychotherapy, were given a placebo instead of chlorpromazine; but the percentage of patients lastingly benefited seems greater than may perhaps be expected from the use of placebos.

In a number of exploratory tests with individual patients, I have found that after administering codeine, chlorpromazine, or meprobamate in such doses that the drugs inhibit any substantial degrees of neurotic anxiety even during repeated exposures to relevant stimuli, lasting improvement is often noted after discontinuing the drug. I have also observed that in certain patients in whom systematic desensitization is obstructed by an inability to procure sufficient muscle relaxation to produce emotional calm, the administration of a tranquilizing drug an hour or so before the session makes successful desensitization possible. The anxiety-suppressing action of the drug makes it easier for active muscle relaxation to inhibit the anxiety that verbal stimuli from the therapist tend to evoke.

Reciprocal inhibition of anxiety responses would be favored just as surely by chemical agents augmenting responses antagonistic to anxiety as by those selectively suppressing anxiety. In the case of neurotic anxieties elicited by sexual situations, it has proved possible preferentially to enhance the sexual response by the previous injection of testosterone so that the anxiety response is inhibited and its habit strength consequently weakened. A case illustrating this process was reported a good many years ago by Miller, Hubert, and Hamilton (1938); I have had two similar cases. An experimental rationale for using testosterone to heighten sexual drive is to be found in the observations of Beach (1942) that sexual arousal in relation to any of a variety of sexual objects increases with increases in circulating sex hormone.

Conditioned inhibition of anxiety through a dominating motor response: In 1948, Mowrer and Viek performed an experiment showing that when rats are repeatedly exposed to a continuous mild electric shock, those animals who are enabled to learn a definite motor response in relation to the termination of the shock develop very little anxiety when placed in the experimental situation minus the shock. In contrast to these, much greater anxiety is shown by animals who have no opportunity to learn such a motor response. In another context (Wolpe, 1953), I have explained this phenomenon as follows.

When an animal is subjected to continuous electric shock in a given situation, autonomic responses of anxiety and many musculo-skeletal (motor) responses are evoked. A similar variety of musculo-skeletal responses will accompany the autonomic responses at every repetition of the electric shock unless there is one motor response that is repeatedly followed by cessation of the shock. If there should be a response thus repeatedly reinforced, it will become increasingly dominant over all the other "competing" response tendencies. This implies a gradual weakening of the latter, probably by conditioned inhibition based on reciprocal inhibition. It is not unreasonable to suppose that the weakening of "competing" response tendencies extends also to the autonomic responses.

This suggested the therapeutic possibility that if a mild noxious stimulus is applied on repeated occasions in the presence of a stimulus evoking neurotic anxiety responses, and if this noxious stimulus is at the same time conditioned to produce a well-defined motor response, the neurotic anxiety may be gradually weakened. Since the practical application of this idea involves considerable difficulties, it has been considered only for certain cases that have not responded to simpler measures. Consequently, treatment based on this principle has been attempted in no more than half a dozen patients. Two of these have clearly benefited. One, reported in detail elsewhere (Wolpe, 1958), who had a fear of falling and a very severe agoraphobia, recovered completely and was still well four years later. The second, who had a fear of trembling while using cutlery or drinking tea in front of other people, experienced considerable improvement. In both cases, arm raising was used as the conditioned motor response to mild shock to the forearm, and graded neurotic anxiety-producing stimuli were presented to the patient's imagination.

Conditioning of "anxiety-relief" responses: Zbrozyna observed (1957) that if a stimulus is repeatedly presented to an eating animal just before the experimenter withdraws the food, that stimulus acquires the property of inhibiting feeding even when the animal is in the middle of a meal. This observation suggested that "anxiety-relief" responses may be directly conditioned to convenient stimuli and subsequently used to counter anxiety. By analogy, it was expected that if an uncomfortable induction shock were administered to a human subject for several seconds and were then made to cease immediately after a signal, that signal would become connected to such bodily responses as would follow cessation of the shock. Furthermore, these responses would be the negative of the anxiety that had been produced by the shock. This, it was hoped, would imply the acquisition of a weapon to combat anxiety due to *other* stimuli. The hope was encouraged by the fact that Coppock (1951) and Goodson and Brownstein (1955) had shown that when a stimulus is repeatedly presented at the moment of termination of an electric shock an approach response is conditioned to that stimulus.

The experimental facts have been applied therapeutically to some neurotic patients as follows. Silver electrodes connected to the secondary circuit of a Palmer inductorium are attached to the patient's left arm and forearm respectively. Using an inflow of 6 volts from a dry battery into the primary and starting with the secondary coil at 10 cms., we observe the patient's reactions to brief shocks whose intensity is increased step by step through approximating the secondary coil to the primary. When the shock is "very uncomfortable"— usually at about 7.0 cm.—a suitable level is considered to have been reached. After a pause, the patient is told that the shock will be turned on continuously. He is to endure it until he feels it quite unpleasant. It will be switched off the moment he says, "Calm." As soon as he says the word, the current is switched off. This is repeated ten to twenty times in a session. Some subjects report a feeling of relief at the cessation of shock that is out of proportion to the physical discomfort of the shock and seems attributable to termination of anxiety responses to the shock. After one to three sessions, these subjects find that using the word in disturbing situations or during their aftermath decreases the disturbed feeling.

I have used this method in a small number of cases, purely as a symptomatic measure, and in occasional individuals it has been a potent means of diminishing ongoing anxiety. Meyer (1957) has made an attempt to apply it to obtain conditioned inhibition of neurotic anxiety. The effects were not very impressive in his small-scale exploration, but the method seems to deserve more systematic study.

Concluding remarks

Experiments on the production and cure of neuroses in animals have resulted, as described above, in new methods of psychotherapy and also in a new theory of the crucial process conceived to operate in most psychotherapy—reciprocal inhibition of anxiety responses. It seems from a good many studies (e.g., Eysenck, 1952) that most other forms of psychotherapy yield favorable results in approximately 50 per cent of the cases treated, irrespective of the theoretical framework employed by the therapist. This suggests that a common process, perhaps generally unrecognized, is the real basis of success in all of them. On the ground of parsimony the possibility needs to be entertained that reciprocal inhibition is the basis of this common process, just as it seems to be the basis of the special effects described above. It has been proposed (Wolpe, 1958) that the source of inhibition of anxiety responses is the emotional responses other than anxiety that may be evoked in any kind of psychotherapeutic interview. It is presumed that these emotional responses reciprocally inhibit the neurotic responses evoked by verbal stimuli and thus gradually diminish the neurotic habit strength. If it is indeed the case that therapists who employ conventional therapies owe their successes not to the processes alleged by their theories but to learning mechanisms of which they are not cognizant, it will be a strong argument for the widespread use in psychotherapy of the specific techniques based on principles of learning. A number of studies are under way, and others are in prospect, which, it is predicted, will establish the position beyond reasonable doubt.

Increasing numbers of clinical reports, meanwhile, testify impressively to the efficacy of behavioral methods of therapy. I have reported (Wolpe, 1958) that nearly 90 per cent of 210 neurotic patients were either apparently cured or much improved after a mean of little over thirty sessions. Of forty-five patients followed up over two to seven years, only one relapsed. Eysenck (1960) has assembled more than thirty studies by many authors demonstrating successful elimination of neurotic habits by therapy based on principles of learning. Several further reports have recently appeared (Lazovik and Lang, 1960; Bond and Hutchison, 1960; Freeman and Kendrick, 1960; Walton, 1961).

The allegation is frequently made that such methods of treating neuroses are only symptomatic and do not "get to the root." This allegation springs from an assumption of the correctness of the psychoanalytic account of the nature of neurosis. Leaving aside the fact that psychoanalytic theory contains logical inconsistencies (Wohlgemuth, 1923; Salter, 1952) and that much of the evidence by which it has been bolstered is inadmissible (Wolpe and Rachman, 1960), the practical implication of the question is whether recoveries obtained by conditioning methods endure and are free from repercussions to the patient. The answer, based on the evidence so far obtained, would seem to be in the affirmative. Psychoanalytic theory postulates that, in general, recoveries from neurosis without psychoanalysis are unreliable; but in a survey of follow-up studies of such cases (Wolpe, 1961a) only four relapses were found among 249 patients. This finding accords well with conditioning theory, which holds that the elimination of a neurotic habit is permanent unless there is reinstatement by specific new conditioning.

REFERENCES

Anderson, O. D., and Parmenter, R. A long term study of the experimental neurosis in the sheep and dog. *Psychosom. Med. Monogr.*, 2, 1941, Nos. 3 and 4.

Beach, F. A. Analysis of the factors involved in the arousal, maintenance, and manifestation of sexual excitement in male animals. *Psychosom. Med.*, 1942, 4, 173.

Berlyne, D. E. *Conflict, arousal and curiosity.* New York: McGraw-Hill, 1960.

Bond, I. K., and Hutchison, H. C. Application of reciprocal inhibition therapy to exhibitionism. *Canad. Med. Assoc. J.*, 1960, 83, 23.

Cook, S. W. The production of "experimental neurosis" in the white rat. *Psychosom. Med.*, 1939, 1, 293.

Coppock, H. W. Secondary reinforcing effect of a stimulus repeatedly presented after electric shock. *Amer. Psychologist*, 1951, 6, 277.

Dimmick, F. L., Ludlow, N., & Whiteman, A. A study of "experimental neurosis" in cats. *J. comp. Psychol.*, 1939, 28, 39.

Dworkin, S. Conditioning neuroses in dog and cat. *Psychosom. Med.*, 1939, 1, 388.

Dworkin, S., Baxt, J. O., & Dworkin, E. Behavioral disturbances of vomiting and micturition in conditioned cats. *Psychosom. Med.*, 1942, 4, 75.

Dworkin, S., Raginsky, B. B., & Bourne, W. Action of anesthetics and sedatives upon the inhibited nervous system. *Curr. Res. Anesth.*, 1937, 16, 238.

Eysenck, H. J. The effects of psychotherapy: an evaluation. *J. consult. Psychol.*, 1952, 16, 319.

Eysenck, H. J. *Behavior therapy and the neuroses.* New York: Pergamon Press, 1960.

Farber, I. E. Response fixation under anxiety and non-anxiety conditions. *J. exper. Psychol.*, 1948, 38, 111.

Fenichel, O. *Psychoanalytic theory of neurosis.* New York: W. W. Norton, Inc., 1945.

Fonberg, E. On the manifestation of conditioned defensive reactions in stress. *Bull. Soc. Sci. Lettr. Lodz. Class III. Sci. Math. Natur.*, 1956, 7, 1.

Freeman, H. L., & Kendrick, D. C. A case of cat phobia. *Brit. Med. J.*, 1960, 2, 497.

Gantt, W. H. Experimental basis for neurotic behavior. *Psychosom. Med. Monogr.* 3, 1944, Nos. 3 and 4.

Goodson, F. A., & Brownstein, A. Secondary reinforcing and motivating properties of stimuli contiguous with shock onset and termination. *J. comp. physiol. Psychol.*, 1955, 48, 381.

Hendrick, I. *Facts and theories of psychoanalysis.* New York: Knopf, 1958.

Hull, C. L. *Principles of behavior.* New York: Appleton-Century-Crofts, 1943.

Jacobsen, C. F., Wolfe, J. B., & Jackson, T. A. An experimental analysis of the functions of the frontal association areas in primates. *J. Nerv. Ment. Dis.*, 1935, 82, 1.

Jacobson, E. *Progressive relaxation.* Chicago: Univ. Chicago Press, 1938.

Jones, M. C. Elimination of children's fears. *J. exper. Psychol.*, 1924a, 7, 382.

Jones, M. C. A laboratory study of fear. The case of Peter. *J. genet. Psychol*, 1924b, 31, 308.

Karn, H. W. A case of experimentally induced neurosis in the cat. *J. exper. Psychol.* 1938, 22, 589.

Lazarus, A. A. The elimination of children's phobias by deconditioning. *Med. Proc.*, 1959, 5, 261.

Lazovik, A. D., & Lang, P. J. A laboratory demonstration of systematic desensitization psychotherapy. *J. Psychol. Stud.*, 1960, *11*, 238.

Liddell, H. S. Conditioned reflex method and experimental neurosis. In J. McV. Hunt, *Personality and the behavior disorders*. New York: Ronald, 1944.

Lloyd, D. Facilitation and inhibition of spinal motoneurones. *J. Neurophysiol.*, 1946, *9*, 421.

Maatsch, J. L., Adelson, H. M., & Denny, M. R. Effort and resistance to extinction of the bar-pressing response. *J. comp. physiol. Psychol.*, 1954, *47*, 47.

Masserman, J. H. *Behavior and neurosis*. Chicago: Univ. Chicago Press, 1943.

Masserman, J. H., & Yum, K. S. An analysis of the influence of alcohol on experimental neuroses in cats. *Psychosom. Med.*, 1946, *8*, 36.

Messerschmidt, R. A quantitative investigation of the alleged independent operation of conscious and subconscious processes. *J. abnorm. soc. Psychol.*, 1927, *22*, 325.

Meyer, V. The treatment of two phobic patients on the basis of learning principles. *J. abnorm. soc. Psychol.*, 1957, *55*, 261.

Miller, N. E. Studies of fear as an acquirable drive. 1. Fear as motivation and fear-reduction as reinforcement in the learning of new responses. *J. exper. Psychol.*, 1948a, *38*, 89.

Miller, N. E. Theory and experiment relating psychoanalytic displacement to stimulus response generalization. *J. abnorm. soc. Psychol.*, 1948b, *43*, 155.

Miller, N. E., Hubert, E., & Hamilton, J. Mental and behavioral changes following male hormone treatment of adult castration hypogonadism and psychic impotence. *Proc. Soc. exp. Biol. & Med.*, 1938, *38*, 538.

Miller, R. E., Murphy, J. V., & Mirsky, I. A. Persistent effects of chlorpromazine on extinction of an avoidance response. *Arch. Neurol. & Psychiat.* 1957, *78*, 526.

Mowrer, O. H., & Viek, P. Experimental analogue of fear from a sense of helplessness. *J. abnorm. soc. Psychol.*, 1948, *43*, 193.

Osgood, C. E. An investigation into the causes of retroactive inhibition. *J. exper. Psychol.*, 1948, *38*, 132.

Pavlov, I. P. *Conditioned reflexes*. Translated by G. V. Anrep. London: Oxford University Press, 1927.

Salter, A. *Conditioned reflex therapy*. New York: Creative Age Press, 1950.

Salter, A. *The case against psychoanalysis*. New York: Henry Holt, 1952.

Sherrington, C. S. *Integrative action of the nervous system*. New Haven, Conn.: Yale Univ. Press, 1906.

Stevenson, I. Direct instigation of behavioral changes in psychotherapy. *A.M.A. Arch. Gen. Psychiat.*, 1959, *1*, 115.

Stone, D. R. Responses to imagined auditory stimuli as compared to recorded sounds. *J. consult. Psychol.*, 1955, *19*, 254.

Walton, D. Application of learning theory to the treatment of a case of somnambulism. *J. clin. Psychol.*, 1961, *17*, 96.

Watson, J. B., & Rayner, P. Conditioned emotional reactions. *J. exper. Psychol.*, 1920, *3*, 1.

Winkelman, N. W., Jr. Chlorpromazine in the treatment of neuropsychiatric disorders. *J.A.M.A.*, 1954, *155*, 18.

Wohlgemuth, A. *A critical examination of psychoanalysis*. London: Allen and Unwin, 1923.

Wolpe, J. An appproach to the problem of neurosis based on the conditioned response. Unpublished M.D. Thesis, University of the Witwatersrand, 1948.

Wolpe, J. Experimental neurosis as learned behavior. *Brit. J. Psychol.*, 1952a, *43*, 243.

Wolpe, J. Objective psychotherapy of the neuroses. *S. African Med. J.*, 1952b, *26*, 825.

Wolpe, J. The formation of negative habits: a neurophysiological view. *Psychol. Rev.*, 1952c, *59*, 290.

Wolpe, J. Learning theory and "abnormal fixations." *Psychol. Rev.* 1953, *60*, 111.

Wolpe, J. Reciprocal inhibition as the main basis of psychotherapeutic effects. *A.M.A. Arch. Neurol. Psychiat.*, 1954, *72*, 205.

Wolpe, J. *Psychotherapy by reciprocal inhibition.* Stanford, Calif.: Stanford University Press, 1958.

Wolpe, J. Psychotherapy based on the principle of reciprocal inhibition. In A. Burton *Case studies in counseling and psychotherapy.* Englewood Cliffs, N.J.: Prentice-Hall, 1959.

Wolpe, J. The prognosis in un-psychoanalyzed recovery from neurosis. *Amer. J. Psychiat.*, 1961a. In press.

Wolpe, J. The desensitization treatment of neuroses. *J. nerv. ment. Dis.*, 1961b, *112*, 189.

Wolpe, J., & Rachman, S. Psychoanalytic "evidence": a critique based on Freud's case of Little Hans. *J. nerv. ment. Dis.*, 1960, *130*, 135.

Zbrozyna, A. W. The conditioned cessation of eating. *Bull. Acad. Polonaise Sci.*, 1957, *5*, 261.

17

Patient-Doctor Relationships: Psychotherapist in the Therapeutic Process

HANS H. STRUPP

The human relationship between patient and doctor is central to contemporary conceptions of psychotherapy, which are deeply rooted in the discoveries of Sigmund Freud. In tracing the evolution of the doctor-patient relationship in terms of its historical context, Szasz, Knoff, and Hollender (1958) rightly call attention to the revolutionary notion of mutual participation and "partnership" inherent in the relationship between the modern psychotherapist and his patient. In his role of "participant observer" (Sullivan), the psychotherapist not only gains access to facets of the patient's personality and life which are unavailable by any other method (the above authors quote Breuer as saying that the patient's ". . . life became known to me to an extent to which one person's life is seldom known to another . . .") but also deliberately and systematically uses the doctor-patient relationship as the vehicle for therapeutic change.

This dual conception of the therapeutic situation as a unique laboratory situation for making observations about the motive forces in the living personality and the technical utilization of this situation for effecting profound changes in the patient's personality will undoubtedly be counted among the greatest contributions Freud made to the science of psychology. At the same time, the deepest insights regarding the therapeutic function of the transference relationship have come from clinical psychoanalysis. The primary objective of future research in this area is to attain increasingly objective and specific information about the most effective utilization of this relationship for maximum therapeutic gain. This statement implies the need for extending the frontiers of knowledge concerning the precise nature of the psychological influence exerted by the therapist in interaction with a particular patient, including data about the modes of interaction between the two participants, the technical operations employed by the therapist, and the effects of other social, cultural, and psychological factors impinging upon the therapeutic process.

Research in psychotherapy is extremely difficult, a major reason being the complexity and the interactive effects of a multitude of variables which, for convenience, are usually classified under the major headings of: (1) patient variables; (2) therapist variables; (3) psychotherapeutic method (or technique) variables; and (4) variables not directly a part of the therapeutic interaction but affecting the therapy relationship, such as extratherapeutic personal relationships, social class, intercurrent events, etc. Adequate isolation of a single or a few independent variables and experimental control of most of the others is obviously difficult to achieve, as has been pointed out by numerous authors who have addressed themselves to problems of experimental design during the last decade or so (see, for example, Frank, 1959b).

Whence the need for controlled, and preferably experimental, research in psychotherapy? Patently, the significant discoveries and contributions in this area have been made by clinician-scientists who have used the therapeutic situation as the laboratory for empirical observations, which in turn have given rise to the theoretical formulations which form the impressive body of knowledge contained in the literature of psychoanalysis and that of a variety of "schools," each advocating somewhat different therapeutic procedures and invoking divergent explanations for the *modus operandi* and the efficacy of their particular approach.

Broadly speaking, psychotherapy is as old as mankind, and the healing effects of a human relationship have always been recognized, at least implicitly (See Table 1). The conception of psychopathology as disturbances in man's relationships to his fellow beings, of neurosis as a problem in living, which can be resolved or ameliorated by deliberate and planful interpersonal interventions, is less than a century old. To the extent that psychotherapy attempts a systematic and self-conscious manipulation of variables in a human relationship and notes its effects, it has the makings of a scientific discipline. To the extent that the psychotherapist constructs a conceptual map of the patient's personality which he seeks to change by deliberate operations, he is

TABLE 1

Three Basic Models of the Physician-Patient Relationship

MODEL	PHYSICIAN'S ROLE	PATIENT'S ROLE	CLINICAL APPLICATION OF MODEL	PROTOTYPE OF MODEL
1. Activity-passivity	Does something to patient	Recipient (unable to respond or inert)	Anesthesia, E.C.T., acute trauma, coma, delirium	Parent-infant
2. Guidance-cooperation	Tells patient what to do	Cooperator (obeys)	Acute infectious processes, etc.	Parent-child (adolescent)
3. Mutual participation	Helps patient to help himself	Participant in "partnership" (uses expert help)	Most chronic illnesses, psychoanalysis, etc.	Adult-adult

Source: Szasz, Knoff, and Hollender (1958).

an experimental scientist. In this role he is an observer of the patient's attitudes, feelings, and patterns of behavior toward him. He tries to be aware of the impact of these variables upon him as a person and as a participant observer; he notes the immediate or long-range effects of his therapeutic interventions (the therapeutic method) as well as his attitudes, feelings, and behaviors upon the patient; and he is forever engaged in the process of refining his observations and specifying the nature of his influence. In this endeavor, the psychotherapist (as an applied scientist) joins hands with the psychologist (as a person concerned with the scientific study of psychological phenomena). Psychotherapy, therefore, is not only a method of vast practical importance for resolving problems in human living but also a unique laboratory situation for the study of the human personality in interaction with an observer-experimenter. Freud utilized the psychoanalytic situation in this dual sense, thereby revolutionizing man's knowledge about himself and evolving a therapeutic technique *second to none*, profound in penetration and impact. Admittedly, the psychoanalytic situation is a controlled laboratory situation only in a relative sense, since quantification, measurement, and experimental control are difficult to achieve. Nevertheless, it appears that research-minded psychologists have barely begun to exploit the rich potentialities of this setting for personality research.

RESEARCH IN PSYCHOTHERAPY

If psychotherapy as a scientific discipline is barely 75 years old, controlled research in this area is even more recent. Its starting date may be fixed around 1940, with an emerging interest, particularly by Carl Rogers and his students, in applying the methods of psychological research to the process of psychotherapy. Prior to that time, academic psychologists evinced considerable interest in "validating" or "proving" psychoanalytic propositions by the methods of experimental psychology. In a survey of "objective" studies of psychoanalytic concepts up to 1942, Sears (1943) noted significantly: "A few studies have been made of the psychoanalytic process itself, but since none of these was designed to test any theoretical point, they have . . . been excluded." Detailed longitudinal studies of the psychoanalytic process (that is, of intensive and prolonged therapy using the "classical" Freudian model) are still virtually nonexistent, although some important beginnings are being made, for example by Alexander and his group (Levy, 1960) and by Shakow (1960). With respect to other forms of psychotherapy, however, there has been since 1950 a steady increase, both in quantity and quality, of objective investigations of the therapeutic process. Such studies have taken precedence over so-called outcome studies, which were primarily concerned with demonstrating the effectiveness of particular methods of psychotherapy, or of psychotherapy in general.

The changing emphasis of research arises partly from a disillusionment with the methodological crudeness of outcome studies, which usually provide little detailed information about relevant characteristics of the doctor-patient relationship, the step-by-step process by which therapeutic results are achieved, criteria of change, etc., which lack adequate experimental controls and comparability with other patient and therapist populations as well as therapeutic methods, and which are seized upon as easy ammunition by critics (e.g., Eysenck, 1952) who wish to dispute the therapeutic effectiveness of psychotherapy. To be sure, the question of therapeutic effectiveness is important and should not be lightly dismissed. But it is pointless to compare percentage figures in the absence of precise information of what is being compared. The rising interest in studying the interpersonal processes of the doctor-patient relationship in the broadest sense reflects the more humble attitude of the scientist who patiently pursues knowledge for its own sake, who is not under obligation to defend at every juncture the practical utility of his inquiry. Concomitantly, a large number of studies have dealt with methodological problems, notably the development of measures by which the verbal and in some instances also the nonverbal content of therapist-patient communications can be quantified (see Auld and Murray, 1955, for a critical review of this literature to that time).

Other important foci of research include: specifications of personality changes in patients as a result of psychotherapy; exploration of situational variables, such as social class; experimentation with variations in treatment methods; and the influence of therapist variables upon the therapeutic relationship. This chapter is primarily concerned with objective research contributions to the last area, not because it is inherently of greater importance than any other, but because it is an example of one of the expanding frontiers of psychotherapy research. For a broad overview of contemporary efforts, the interested reader is referred to the recent volume edited by Rubinstein and Parloff (1959) as well as to the regular articles on the topic in the *Annual Review of Psychology*.

THE THERAPIST'S CONTRIBUTION TO THE THERAPEUTIC PROCESS

One of the important failings of studies concerned with the results of psychotherapy has been a lack of specific information about the method of treatment and the person of the therapist. To describe a therapeutic method by a shorthand label like "psychoanalysis" often conceals more than it reveals; moreover, it is clearly unsatisfactory, for scientific purposes, to treat a complex independent variable in summary fashion. The error is compounded as soon as the outcomes of therapy, even conducted by the same therapist, are compared. As early as 1938, in a questionnaire survey of British psychoanalysts, Glover (1955) demonstrated that the practices of a relatively homogeneous group of therapists could by no means be considered equivalent. Furthermore, the impression that therapists subscribing to different theoretical orientations appear to have roughly the same percentages of successes and failures, and that experience as a therapist seems to be reliably related to one's ratio of successes, encouraged speculation that individual differences between therapists might be a more important factor in determining treatment outcomes than theoretical orientation or even extent of training. Again, a therapist might work well with one patient, or with patients having similar personality structures, cultural backgrounds, etc., but not with others. Precise data on these questions have only recently begun to accumulate, and great lacunae still exist. An important contribution of research along these lines would be an improved ability to predict the course and outcome of psychotherapy for a particular patient with a particular therapist.

As early as 1910, Freud (1953) recognized that the personality of the therapist might play an important part in psychoanalytic therapy, and he introduced the concept of the countertransference to account for obstacles to therapy contributed by the therapist's personality. The resulting recommendation of a didactic or training analysis for all therapists was an ingenious attempt to eliminate as far as possible adverse influences arising from this source. Freud, however, never directly conceded the possibility that the personality of the therapist per se might represent an important therapeutic factor or exert a positive therapeutic force. To this day, analysts following the Freudian tradition adhere to the concept of the psychoanalytic situation *not* as the relationship between two participants but as the analysand's relationship to the analyst. Whereas in other forms of psychotherapy the therapist uses his person more freely and directly as a therapeutic force (through suggestion, reassurance, etc.), in psychoanalysis the major therapeutic factor is said to be the therapist's interpretations, which result in the ultimate resolution of the transference—that is, an understanding of infantile impulses, attitudes, fantasies, etc., which the patient unwittingly brings to bear upon his interaction with the analyst (see Macalpine, 1950).

This view may represent an unrealizable ideal, because, regardless of the theory or the technical desiderata, the therapist is a person with his own feelings, attitudes, and life history, and it is manifestly impossible to associate with another human being over a prolonged period of time without being affected by that person in some manner. At present, it is impossible to tell what part the personal influence of the therapist plays in any form of psychotherapy, and it is one of the important objectives of research to elucidate the effects of this variable. The question as to the nature of the therapeutic influence in psychoanalysis as well as in other forms of psychotherapy is obviously basic to an understanding of the therapeutic process, and it has far-reaching implications for all forms of interpersonal learning—education, child rearing, and interpersonal perception, to name but a few.

In recent years, numerous authors have attempted to conceptualize important aspects of the therapist's personality which might play a crucial part in the therapeutic relationship. Freud, despite his concern with countertransference, actually gave this problem scant attention (but see the quotation cited on p. 598). In formulating the concept of the "corrective emotional experience," Alexander (1950) stays within the psychoanalytic framework but gives explicit recognition to the important therapeutic function that the therapist performs when his attitude toward the patient is experienced as significantly different from those of the parents:

> No doubt, the most important therapeutic factor in psychoanalysis is the objective and yet helpful attitude of the therapist, something which does not exist in any other relationship. . . . To experience such a novel human relationship in itself has a tremendous therapeutic significance with cannot be overrated. . . . This attitude, combined with correct interpretation of material which is about to emerge from repression, together with the analysis of the ego's defenses is primarily responsible for the therapeutic effectiveness of psychoanalysis (pp. 487–488).
>
> The emotional content of the patient-physician relationship, the fact that the therapist's attitude is different from the original parental attitude, is the major dynamic factor which allows repressed material to become conscious (p. 496).

Alexander (1958) believes that the therapist's influence on the treatment process "by the virtue of being what he is: an individual personality, distinct from all other therapists," is the "most opaque area of psychoanalysis," and that the evaluation of this elusive element is at present quite beyond our ken. With this judgment the present writer is in full agreement.

Raush and Bordin (1957) advance the concept of "warmth" as a significant factor in psychotherapy, subsuming "commitment," "effort to understand," and "spontaneity." Rogers (1957) speaks of the therapist's "genuineness in the relationship," his "unconditional positive regard," and "empathy." He views the therapeutic relationship "as a heightening of the constructive qualities which often exist in part in other relationships, and an extension through time of qualities which in other relationships tend at best to be momentary." Unlike Alexander, however, Rogers feels that "the techniques of the various therapies are relatively unimportant." Frank (1959a) explores the hypothesis that the patient's attitude of trust or faith may play a significant part in his response to all forms of psychotherapy, and that this favorable expectation is fostered by the therapist's own confidence in his ability to help, by his caring deeply about the patient, and by his being able successfully to communicate this message. The present author (1960), basing his opinion on a study of psychotherapists in an experimental situation, regards the therapist's contribution as both personal and technical, the personal aspects probably representing a *sine qua non*, whose effects, however, may be deepened and maximized by appropriate technical operations.

As Fromm-Reichmann appropriately remarked, the patient is in need of an experience, not an explanation. The basic problem facing the psychotherapist is to enable the patient to have a constructive learning experience in interpersonal relations. Psychotherapy is aimed at undoing, to varying degrees, the damage caused by faulty or deficient interpersonal experiences in the patient's early childhood, by helping the patient to replace conflictual and self-defeating patterns of interpersonal relatedness by more adaptive ones. One of the primary obstacles confronting the therapist is the patient's unconscious resistance to change, which arises from the painful feelings which are inevitably stirred up in the process. Indeed, the degree and the persistence of his resistance is a fairly reliable measure of the depth and pervasiveness of the painful feelings he is warding off. The greater the original damage, therefore, the less the patient is able to profit directly from warmth, kindness, etc., when they are offered by the therapist. Thus, because of his defenses, he continually stands in his own way and is driven to defeat the therapist's best efforts. It appears that to help the patient relinquish these barriers, a high level of technical skill is needed on the therapist's part before he can begin to take advantage of a "good" human relationship with the therapist. It is not possible, within the confines of this chapter, to discuss different conceptions of what constitutes a neurosis, or the theories of psychotherapy (see, for example, Munroe, 1955; Menninger, 1958; Waelder, 1960) that are intimately bound up with these conceptions. My purpose is to forestall oversimplifications of the role and function of the psychotherapist and to point up the undeniable fact that, except in minor neurotic disturbances, "love is not enough."

At the same time, it should be clear from the preceding discussion that, from the beginning of any psychotherapy, the therapist must succeed in sparking strivings in the patient—sometimes called "the will to recovery," "motivation for therapy," the striving for "self-realization," and the like—which enable him to cooperate with the therapist and to oppose the neurotic forces within himself. Undoubtedly, no single combination of attributes will yield the answer. Much would depend, one suspects, on the patient's capacity to identify with the therapist as a "good parent." As yet, we know little about the dynamics of this process, in patients or in children, but it may well turn out to be the fulcrum upon which effective psychotherapy turns.

The assessment of such elusive variables at present defies our measuring instruments. The research findings, representative examples of which will be summarized in the following pages, are at best gross indicators of therapist qualities, aspects of the "good therapeutic relationship," and patient reactions to specific forms of intervention. If these results are taken for what they are—the beginnings in an extremely difficult area of psychological research—they may spur subsequent investigators to improvements in methodology, measurement, and design. The principal danger lies in an overconcern with "operational definitions," which are too often accepted as simple substitutes for closer naturalistic observation and which may prematurely close off painstaking inquiry into questions which, at present, are essentially unsolved.

Technique in psychotherapy may be viewed as a theory of psychotherapy translated into action. This translation, however, is not made in a vacuum, nor are techniques as a rule slavishly applied. The translation is made by the therapist who, as a sensitive participant-observer, is responsive to the patient's attitudes, mood, verbal and nonverbal communications, etc. The therapist's communications thus reflect his theoretical understanding of the clinical phenomena, the meanings he assigns to them, and the methods by which he seeks to influence the patient. But they also include, and are modified by, the therapist's attitudes, moods, hopes, defenses, life history, and a host of other variables, partly determined by the current situation, partly by more enduring attitudes. The point to be made is that the therapeutic technique and the therapist's personality are inextricably intertwined; however, by studying objectively therapeutic techniques, one may succeed in establishing systematic relationships with the therapist's personality.

Thus, a number of studies have taken the therapist's communications in actual interviews as a point of departure and investigated various correlates attributable to therapist variables (theoretical orientation, level of experience, etc.). Such studies have been facilitated by the advent of sound recording techniques, combined with a greater willingness on the part of therapists to tolerate external observers, who admittedly represent an intrusion into the privacy of a unique human relationship. From the standpoint of research operations, the development of a variety of systems permitting the quantification of the verbal (and, to some extent, the nonverbal) communication content of the messages exchanged between patient and therapist has rendered research more feasible. In addition to studies dealing with the naturally occurring events in psychotherapy, there have been experimental or quasi-experimental investigations of the therapist's contribution. While such work is more rigorous and permits a wider sampling of patient and therapist variables, its relevance (validity) to actual psychotherapy remains an open question.

Illustrations will be given of results from representative studies in this area. Of necessity, the presentation is selective rather than inclusive. Its principal foci are:

1. Methodological developments in quantifying therapeutic techniques.

2. Relationships between selected aspects of therapeutic technique to relevant therapist variables.

3. Interactions between patient and therapist variables (studies of the therapeutic relationship).

A large number of studies dealing with the assessment of patient changes as a function of psychotherapy will be omitted, unless there is a clear reference to one of the above topics. I will also exclude references to research on operant conditioning and experimental studies with structured interviews which may have relevance to psychotherapy, since these topics are considered elsewhere in this volume.

METHODOLOGICAL DEVELOPMENTS

Since communication between patient and therapist is mediated primarily by linguistic symbols, a first requirement for objective research is to devise conceptual tools which permit the investigator to abstract and quantify relevant aspects of the verbal interchange. Obviously, there are innumerable ways of accomplishing this end, and the measures upon which the investigator decides are as noteworthy for what they include as for what they leave out. The selection is dictated by theoretical as well as practical considerations, and in a sense it represents a prejudgment of what is important to measure. A content-analysis system is therefore not a neutral yardstick and the descriptive measures representing its yield are usually of limited value. Their meaning is enhanced when they are related to other variables, such as measures derived from patient communications, characteristics of the therapist's personality, and the like.

During the past 20 years a large number of content-analysis systems has been developed—some applicable to patient communications, some to therapist communications, some to both. A comprehensive, critical review of such systems as well as of substantive investigations based on them may be found in Auld and Murray (1955). Dittes (1959) may be consulted for additional references. Table 2 presents a few examples of typical content-analysis systems applicable to therapist communications.

Some systems are anchored in a particular theory of psychotherapy, others are theoretically neutral. The relevance of the latter type (such as Bales's system) to the goals and operations of psychotherapy is often not clear, although they have the advantage of not being contaminated by preconceptions about the efficacy of certain operations (such as interpretations or reflections of feeling). Ideally, one would like a system that is highly objective and equally sensitive to therapist activities irrespective of theoretical orientation. But these requirements are difficult to meet and perhaps in part mutually exclusive. In pointing out the limitations of my system for analyzing

TABLE 2

*Selected Systems of Content-Analysis Applicable to
Therapist Communications*

AUTHOR	DESCRIPTION	FEATURES
Bales (1950)	Interaction process analysis	12-category system for analyzing social interaction. Examples: agrees, shows solidarity, asks for opinion. Has built-in attitudinal dimension.
Porter (1943)	Measures of counselor activity	20+ categories. Examples: defining the interview situation, bringing out and developing the problem situation, developing client's insight and understanding.
Snyder (1945, 1953)	Counselor categories	20+ categories. Examples: defining the content, accurate clarification of feeling, forcing the topic, persuasion.
Harway *et al.* (1955)	Single scale measuring "depth of interpretation"	Seven-point rating scale, developed by Thurstone method (equal-appearing intervals); measures disparity between the view expressed by the therapist (interpretation) and patient's awareness.
Strupp (1957a)	Multidimensional system	Three a priori rating scales (degree of inference, initiative, "therapeutic climate") and 2 sets of categories (type of activity and dynamic focus).
Lennard & Bernstein (1960)	Measurement of therapist informational behavior	Eight categories to assess "informational stimulus values." Examples: therapist introduces a new proposition; therapist indicates that he is listening and passively encourages patient to continue; therapist limits patient to a single subject matter area.
Dollard & Auld (1959)	System of categories for scoring "human motives."	Six, mutually exclusive, "signs": D = drive ("raising" patient's motivation); *Interp* = naming, connecting, discriminating ("labeling") unconscious motives; M = mild agreement, assent, social facilitation; *Pretni* = serious error by therapist; R = reward (tension reduction); *Unsc* = unscorable.

TABLE 2 continued

THEORETICAL ORIENTATION (not necessarily explicit)	REMARKS
Social interaction as problem-solving sequence	Equally applicable to patient and therapist communications, but limited because of overinclusiveness and generality.
Client-centered	Descriptive scheme, mainly applicable to client-centered therapy.
Client-centered	Descriptive scheme, but embodies assumptions about therapeutic quality of communications, largely restricted to client-centered therapy or variants.
Psychoanalytic	Wide applicability to therapist communications in many forms of psychotherapy; disadvantage of any single measure of complex variable.
Psychoanalytic	Attempts to measure simultaneously several aspects of therapist communications, including attitudinal component (warmth-coldness); rating process is slow, dimensions show high degree of overlap.
Information-theory; sociology (therapy as a system of "role relations")	Relevance to clinical-therapeutic concepts and operations (such as transference, resistance, etc.) unclear or so far unexplored; appears to have general utility.
"Freudian-behavioral," i.e., an attempt to relate the principles of Hullian learning theory to psychoanalytic principles (Dollard & Miller, 1950)	Coördinated with a series of patient-categories. Seems to mix level of analysis; for example, signs M and *Interp* are descriptive; D and R require inferences, and *Pretni* involves a value judgment.

AUTHOR	DESCRIPTION	FEATURES
Leary & Gill (1959)	Analysis based on clinical evaluations *and* patient-therapist verbalizations	Using as a point of departure a combined psychological-psychotherapeutic model derived from psychoanalytic theory, the authors propose a comprehensive matrix for the classification of all statements in both clinical evaluation and patient-therapist content. Far too complex for brief description.
Murray (1956)	Major emphasis on *meaning* functions of patient's verbal behavior	Proposes preliminary set of categories for therapist remarks. Two general classes are distinguished: active remarks consist of: instructions to free associate, "labels," discriminations, similarities, strong approvals, demands, and directions. Passive subcategories include: mild probings, mild approvals and "Mm."

therapists' communications (1957a), I listed a number of points which apply equally to other systems of content-analysis:

1. Since the system is restricted to the *therapist's* activity, it provides only a one-sided picture of the interaction. The information must, therefore, be supplemented by data on the patient's behavior. The interactive elements are taken into account in coding the therapist's verbalizations, but the resulting measures must alway be considered in context. This illustrates the desirability of devising a parallel system for analyzing communications along similar lines, a task which seems quite feasible.

2. In its focus on the single communication the system is atomistic and disregards the idiosyncratic communication content. Therein lie both its strengths and weaknesses. On the positive side, it yields objective assessments of each intervention as it occurs, and is thus quite analytical. On the negative side, it does not throw light on the larger units of therapeutic interaction, such as themes and phases of the therapeutic work. Additional descriptions of the therapeutic process in terms of its idiosyncratic content undoubtedly mitigate this shortcoming, and are indeed indispensable. In this respect, the information yielded by this analysis is the direct antithesis of the

THEORETICAL ORIENTATION (not necessarily explicit)	REMARKS
Psychoanalytic	Preliminary trials suggest high reliability. While enormously complex, the system can be applied by "technicians." Extensive applications have not been reported.
"Freudian-behavioral" (Dollard & Miller, 1950); see above	High reliability. Found useful in substantive research (e.g., Murray, 1956).

typical case history found in the psychoanalytic literature, which stresses the larger sweep of dynamic events, but usually disregards the single interaction units. The two kinds of approaches may complement and supplement each other.

3. The analysis is relatively time consuming, requiring two to four hours for a typical therapeutic hour, and it requires highly qualified and trained raters.

4. Since the system is primarily descriptive and essentially nonvaluative, it makes no qualitative distinctions. Thus it provides no information as to whether an interpretation is "correct" or "incorrect," whether the therapist uses precise language, whether an intervention is properly timed, whether a remark is appropriate or anxiety provoking, and so on. Such evaluations are contingent upon adequate external criteria.

5. The system is restricted to the analysis of verbal symbolic messages and their emotional overtones; it largely omits from consideration nonverbal forms of interaction. This is not to deny their importance, but points up the need for developing further special methodologies.

6. There is an elusive but significant limitation which derives from the assumptions in any quantitative analysis. It is assumed that

each unit of analysis (therapist intervention) is equivalent to every other unit, that the units are additive, and that frequency of occurrence is an important heuristic indicator (pp. 305–306).

Of the technical problems inherent in measuring the content of the message exchanged between patient and therapist, probably none is more difficult than the assessment of latent motives and meanings. Just as the manifest content of a dream cannot be accepted at "face value," but must be interpreted if one wishes to understand the dreamer's underlying wishes, motives, and defensive operations, so the patient's verbal communications in the therapeutic session serve as a starting point for grasping the nature of the conflict with which he is struggling. Quantifications which are restricted to the surface meaning of communications are at best superficial and at worst grossly misleading. "Depth" interpretations, on the other hand, must necessarily go beyond the atomistic units of single communications, take into account contexts, nonverbal cues, associative trends, etc. Thus, objectivity is hard to achieve. One might almost say that ease of measurement and psychological meaningfulness are inversely related. A major problem facing the clinically sensitive researcher is that of achieving a reasonable balance, keeping compromises to a minimum.

Restating the problem in somewhat different terms, it might be said that a large part of the difficulty arises from the fact that (1) linguistic symbols are inadequate to deal with the phenomena to be described, defined, and measured; and (2) psychotherapy as a technique relies heavily on verbal symbols to bring about changes in the affective processes of another person. There is nothing unique about the first problem, which is common in science and which can often be successfully overcome. The second problem, on the other hand, is truly a stumbling block. I should like to point up the researcher's problem by means of a common example.

Patient X, let us say, comes to the psychotherapist and complains about marital difficulties. On the basis of various assessments the diagnosis is made that the difficulty cannot be "explained" by the "reality" of the situation. That is to say, the hypothesis is advanced that the problem lies in the way X structures the situation and the way he responds affectively to this structure (of which he is not aware); this state of affairs is mirrored in consciousness as "anxiety," "inhibition," or "unhappiness." The verbal symbols which X uses to communicate to the therapist his consciously experienced distress are in some manner related to an underlying structure (wish-defense), but neither participant at the beginning knows what "conflicts" in the underlying process give rise to the particular verbalizations. X wants to "solve" his problem—that is, he wants to change himself, the other person, or the situation in such a way that his affective processes signal greater "happiness" or less "conflict." Typically, he wants a cognitive solution to a noncognitive problem.

Now the therapist realizes that affective processes are not readily influenced in this manner, and he proceeds to approach the situation in different terms. He proceeds to do psychotherapy, that is, he helps the patient—the means need not concern us here for the moment—to restructure his wish-defense system. It is merely restating a commonplace to say that the structure of X's wish-defense system (psychic apparatus) is not directly observable, but must be inferred from his relationship to the therapist (transference). To an important degree—but by no means exclusively—this relationship is mediated by verbal communications. At some points, feelings toward the therapist are expressed directly (anger, rage, etc.), but for the most part, X's affects are bound (defended against). It is the current state of X's wish-defense system that the therapist is interested in, and he learns about it through clues from the patient's verbal and nonverbal communications. The clues may derive from a large variety of sources (gestures, inflection, associative trends, attitudes, bodily tensions, silences, etc.) but the inferential process is the therapist's. It is he who, on the basis of training, experience, clinical acumen, etc., sifts, arranges, and structures the data to form a hypothesis about the current state of affairs of the patient's emotional dynamics. His verbal communications are designed to alter the dynamics in ways which he judges to be therapeutic (permitting freer and more direct expression of feelings through enfeeblement of the defenses).

The grave difficulty, from the researcher's point of view, arises from the disparity between the verbal symbols (their syntactic meaning) and the underlying emotional process to which they (in part) refer. In other words, it is the difference between secondary and primary process. If we are interested in analyzing the content of the patient's communications, how can we identify and define measurable units? What metric can we use? Similarly, how can the therapist's communications be dealt with quantitatively? To call a communication an "interpretation" is of some value, but this is merely a beginning. To measure "depth" or "degree of inference" presently involves a host of difficulties. Even if such a judgment is made—and the experience of several investigators shows that it can be done with a fair degree of reliability—only a relatively superficial characteristic has been measured. Similar problems confront a group of external observers who may be called upon to describe and conceptualize the events in a given hour of therapy (see, for example, the work of Bellak and Smith [1956] and the more recent work of the group associated with Dr. Franz Alexander [Levy, 1960]).

In some exploratory work of my own, I devised a rating sheet which the therapist completes at the end of each hour. It calls for simple five-point ratings of such variables as anxiety, defensiveness, resistance, etc. Correspondingly, the therapist rates the relative frequency of his interventions and interpretations, the nature of his attitudes toward the patient, and so on. It is too early to evaluate the kinds of data generated by such a device. Since ratings must be made over an extended period of time, the statistical problems are quite complex. I suspect we shall find that the value of such ratings is fairly narrowly circumscribed, because they are at best only an epiphenomenon of the interplay of forces, which themselves undergo continual shifts during a single therapeutic hour. For example, what moment of the hour do the ratings represent? Often there may be several discernible shifts in a single hour. If this is so, how should one distinguish the units? The ratings may *to some degree* measure important aspects of the patient-therapist interaction, but their sensitivity is probably not very great. This is not to rule out the possibility that such ratings may illuminate some aspects of the interaction (such as relationships between therapist's attitude toward the patient, intensity of the patient's resistance, and depth of interpretations, etc.). They may also help to sharpen the therapist's powers of observation, if only because the rating procedure forces attention to a systematic assessment of important variables.

Theories of psychotherapy attempt to account for the changes occurring in the patient in terms of the therapeutic relationship or, more accurately, in terms of the patient-therapist interaction in the therapeutic relationship. Even in the psychoanalytic theory of psychotherapy, as I have tried to elaborate elsewhere (1960), opinion is divided concerning the precise nature of the therapeutic action. Clearly, a rearrangement of psychic forces does take place, and it is attendant upon a more or less intense emotional experience by the patient. There is strong reason to believe that (at least in intensive psychotherapy) the favorable therapeutic change is due to something more than the therapist's respectful, benevolent, tolerant, empathic, etc., attitude toward the patient. This "something" is usually (and undoubtedly correctly) subsumed under the heading of the therapist's technical operations (interpretations, analysis of resistances, etc.). The crucial question, however, remains as to the *precise* manner in which the communication of verbal symbols impinges upon, affects, and modifies the patient's psychic economy. Whatever changes take place, their effects can only be measured *indirectly*, as in changed attitudes of the patient toward himself and others, diminution of symptoms, greater subjective comfort, greater productivity, etc.

To be sure, psychological measures of many kinds are indirect, and are no less valuable on that account. As I have tried to indicate, the problem becomes acute in content-analysis studies of psychotherapy when, in quantitative indices derived from verbal symbols, a kind of isomorphism is assumed between the verbal symbols and the underlying psychic process. The training of the psychotherapist is largely aimed at sensitizing him to the metaphor in linguistic symbols—that is, it fosters the ability to read "between the lines"—an ability possessed to some degree by everyone. This clinical sensitivity, unfortunately, cannot be built into measurement instruments available today, nor can it be programed for electronic computers.

What are the uses to which content-analysis systems can be put? In listing a few specific applications, it should be kept in mind that no content-analysis system is an end in itself. Rather, it is a conceptual tool, a technique of ordering and—in a limited way—measuring scientific data, and its value is determined largely by the substantive research results to which it gives rise. A good system should prove useful in:

1. The comparative analysis of therapeutic protocols: comparisons between different theoretical orientations; comparisons between therapists of varying experience levels, degrees and kinds of training, backgrounds, professional affiliations, personality structures, and so on; comparisons between different forms of psychotherapy, such as psychoanalysis, psychoanalytically oriented therapy, nondirective therapy, supportive therapy, and so on.

2. Intratherapist analyses, such as comparisons of techniques used with patients of specific diagnostic categories—for example, different forms of neurotics, psychotics, and so on; longitudinal studies of single cases for the purpose of analyzing and comparing variations in technique as a function of the patient's problems, stage of therapy, therapeutic aims, and so on.

3. Validity studies in which techniques are related to therapeutic outcomes, eveluted by external criteria or by changes within the patient, judged independently.

4. The testing of specific hypotheses in so-called process studies. Examples would be reactions by the patient to, say, "deep" interpretations, focus on transference feelings toward the therapist, statements in which the therapist communicates "warmth," strongly assumes the initiative, and the like (Strupp, 1957a, p. 306).

CORRELATES OF THERAPIST VARIABLES

As already indicated, Freud and his immediate followers paid relatively scant attention to intertherapist differences, except to recognize that conflicts within the therapist might harm his ability to respond appropriately to problems within the patient to which the therapist might resonate defensively. It was assumed that countertransference problems, once they were resolved, would transform the therapist into a relatively "standard" therapeutic instrument. Clara Thompson (1956) succinctly formulates this problem when she states:

> In my early years as an analyst I was taught the idea that any well-trained analyst could do a good job on an analyzable patient. . . . I now believe that one analyst can sometimes take a particular patient further than another because his temperament and life experience fit him to understand this type of patient especially well (p. 534).

Few contemporary psychotherapists, I suppose, would take issue with this statement, until one tries to specify more stringently what is meant by "temperament" and "life experience." A decade earlier Fenichel (1945) had commented in a similar vein: "Any honest analyst will admit that even though he is very thoroughly analyzed he does better work with certain types of patients than with others" (p. 580).

If we consider that it was Freud who, more than any other single scientist, alerted the world to the enormous possibilities of self-deception and the effects of intersubjective factors upon perception, memory, affect, and surely also upon clinical operations, it is surprising that so little systematic research effort has as yet been expended by skilled clinicians toward the achievement of greater specificity about the problem. If such knowledge were available, one might assure a higher degree of compatibility between therapist-patient pairs, and perhaps thereby strengthen the therapeutic efficacy of available techniques.

A major reason for the slow progress of research is undoubtedly due to the overwhelming difficulties of defining, isolating, and measuring precisely those variables in the therapist's personality which probably make the largest difference. I am thinking of such characteristics as integrity, intellectual honesty, respect, humanity, tolerance—to name but a few. How can they be assessed? What psychological instruments available today provide a meaningful picture of these intangible but highly significant dimensions of a person's character? Unable to appreciate or to measure them, many investigators have simply ignored the existing complexities and confined their attention to more readily quantifiable variables, such as length of experience, theoretical orientation, and the like. There certainly can be no objection to a researcher's attempt to tackle an investigative problem as best he can, using the research techniques at his disposal. What in this writer's opinion has often earned the researcher the scorn of the perceptive clinician is the suspicion that the simplifications of the research design, rather than being dictated by the deficiency of the researcher's methodological tools, reflect his limited understanding of the subject matter. On the other hand, there are all too many published articles which suggest that their authors have become the slaves of the "operationalizing" mania sweeping American psychology today, which sacrifices psychological meaning to ease of measurement.

Whatever influence the therapist exerts upon the patient in psychotherapy, this influence is transmitted through his communications. The relative effects of verbal as opposed to nonverbal elements in the communicative content may not be measurable for a long time, but there can be little argument that the *verbal* aspects of the therapist's communications are exceedingly important. It makes good sense, therefore, to focus on the verbal aspects of the therapist's messages, keeping in mind that tone of voice, gestures, and other nonverbal elements may be equally important, if more difficult to measure. The first step in specifying the content of therapist's messages is some form of conceptual scheme, such as a system of content-analysis (see preceding section). The next step is to apply such a scheme to actual interviews or to quasitherapeutic situations, to measure the relative frequency of those variables one has decided to measure, and to seek correlates of these indices in the therapist's personality, training, experience, etc. Such analyses would help to answer empirically such questions as: How does an experienced therapist compare with an inexperienced therapist? How does a therapist adhering to one theoretical orientation compare with a therapist adhering to a different orientation? Are therapists of one theoretical persuasion more alike in their verbal communications than therapists of another school? If large individual differences exist, to what variables in the therapist's personality are they traceable? Again, let it be remembered that such investigations deal with relatively limited aspects of the therapist's performance, and they are a far cry from answering such global questions as to what makes a therapist "effective." At best, they may provide crude indices of perhaps superficial aspects of the therapist's performance. However—and this is equally important to recall—they do provide a starting point and possibly a foundation on which future generations of researchers can build.

The questionnaire survey of British analysts conducted by Glover (1955) in the late 1930's was perhaps the first attempt to determine empirically the extent to which therapists, whose training had been rather similar, subscribed *in a general way* to the technical rules and procedures they had been taught and how they carried them out in actual practice. Glover's questions ranged from major technical operations (such as free association, interpretations, handling of transference problems) to minor aspects (such as the patient's or the analyst's smoking, telephone conversations, etc.). He found general agreement regarding the analysis of the transference as the major therapeutic device, but his findings reflected wide variation in the technique of interpretation and in many other aspects of his questionnaire. As might be expected, there was greater agreement on general questions, and disagreement increased as the questions became more specific. Since many questions were essentially open-ended, there must have existed grave difficulties in coding the responses. Moreover, a verbal description of one's practices may or may not be an adequate account of what one actually does, generally or in specific instances. Regardless of their limitations, surveys of this kind provide very useful information, and it is regrettable that relatively little work along these lines has been done. Notable exceptions are Wolff's (1956) survey of a small sample of American psychotherapists representing different schools, and the researches of Meehl (1960), Fey (1958), and Moss, *et al.* (1960).

As part of a systematic effort to study the doctor-patient relationship in psychotherapy, nondirectivists (followers of Carl Rogers), focused upon the therapist's contribution, subjecting his communications during the therapeutic hour to systematic analysis. Snyder (1945) categorized 3600 statements made by nondirective counselors into 16 categories, which were then grouped into five broader classes representing a directiveness-nondirectiveness continuum. He found that 62.6 per cent of all responses were classifiable as nondirective. Seeman (1949) essentially repeated Snyder's study, using ten completely recorded cases comprising a total of 60 interviews. He found significant differences in counseling method, the largest shift being in nondirective responses. Seeman's figure was 85 per cent as compared with Snyder's 62.6 per cent. Contrary to these findings, Porter (1943) observed quite stable patterns in the use of counseling techniques from one interview to the next, and from one counselor to the next, in a given school of training.

The present writer (1955a) compared Rogerian and psychoanalytically oriented therapists, using their responses to a series of patient statements, presented to them on cards, and analyzing the data by means of Bales's (1950) system of interaction process analysis. As might be expected, Rogerians showed a strong predilection for reflection-of-feeling responses, whereas the second group preferred exploratory questions. In this sample, experienced Rogerians, as opposed to inexperienced Rogerians, showed a significant decline in reflection-of-feeling responses, with a concomitant increase in other response categories. Related comparisons (Strupp, 1955b, 1955c) showed that the response distributions of psychiatrists, psychologists, and social workers following psychoanalytical principles were markedly similar. Experienced therapists tended to give a larger number of interpretations, but their responses were more evenly distributed over a larger number of categories than were those of Rogerians. Therapists whose training had included a personal analysis gave fewer silent responses than nonanalyzed therapists gave. (There is reason to believe that the latter finding was a function of the experimental situation, because in a later study (Strupp, 1958a), involving therapists' responses to an entire filmed interview, the findings were reversed.)

Strupp (1957b) applied his system of content-analysis (1957a) to the therapist's interventions in ten actual interviews. These comprised a case of brief psychotherapy, reported by Wolberg. In a subsequent paper (Strupp, 1957c), the analysis of the Wolberg interviews was compared with a similar analysis of a case history reported by Rogers. The quantitative treatment essentially confirmed what would have been predicted from a knowledge of the theoretical orientations of the two therapists, their expertness, and their characteristic modes of interacting with patients. Nevertheless, the study is apparently a first attempt at comparing the verbal interventions of two therapists of different theoretical orientations.

Strupp (1958b, 1958c) has further documented the differences between therapists—in terms of clinical judgments as well as communications—attributable to level of experience, professional affiliation (psychiatrists vs. psychologists), theoretical orientation (Rogerians vs. psychoanalytically oriented therapists), and personal analysis.

Fey (1958), whose survey approach has already been noted, studied the responses of 36 therapists representing different theoretical orientations. His questions dealt primarily with common problems of technique. He found the greatest homogeneity among Rogerians (a finding confirmed by Strupp's studies) and the least homogeneity among analysts. Also, greater experience was found to be associated with greater flexibility (defined as a disinclination to give extreme responses).

Holt and Luborsky (1958), in their massive effort to predict the over-all competence of psychiatric residents, include a statement of the personality characteristics which a good psychiatrist, in the opinion of experts in the field, should possess. They found little specificity to the particular disciplines of psychiatry, psychotherapy, and psychoanalysis; likewise, little differentiation could be made between these characteristics and the qualifications of "the good clinical psychologist" drawn up by a committee of the American Psychological Association. Many statements seemed to characterize "the kind of man one might hope to encounter in any profession and who might be expected to do well in almost any type of work." Typical personality attributes were superior intelligence, capacity for understanding, empathy, flexibility, breadth of interests, respect for the dignity and integrity of the individual, etc. In one of his last papers Freud (1952) made a similar point:

Amongst the factors which influence the prospects of an analysis and add to its difficulties in the same manner as the resistances, we must reckon not only the structure of the *patient's* ego but the personal characteristics of the analyst. . . . The analyst, . . . because of the peculiar conditions of his work, is really impeded by his own defects in his task of discerning it in a manner conducive to cure. So there is some reason in the demand for a comparatively high degree of psychical normality and correct adjustment in the analyst as one of his qualifications for his work. And there is another point: he must be in a superior position in some sense if he is to serve as a model for his patient in certain analytic situations and, in others, to act as his teacher. Finally, we must not forget that the relationship between analyst and patient is based on a love of truth, that is, on the acknowledgment of reality, and that it precludes any kind of sham or deception (pp. 351–352).

The foregoing sampling of studies suggests that the importance of the therapist variable is being increasingly recognized, although objective research has thus far used relatively gross indices, such as theoretical orientation, level of experience, and the like. There is a noteworthy trend, in keeping with the emphasis upon an operational definition of variables, toward taking the actual transactions of the interview (or quasi-interview) situation as the point of departure rather than relying on secondhand reports. In this section I have for purpose of exposition focused primarily on research dealing with relatively "static" variables in the therapist's personality, realizing fully that such partitioning is artificial. I shall now turn to a discussion of selected studies dealing with interactive effects between therapist variables on the one hand, and patient and situational variables on the other. In accordance with the general orientation of this chapter, a somewhat disproportionate stress lies on the therapist's actions (or reactions) in the relationship.

INTERACTIONS BETWEEN PATIENT
AND THERAPIST VARIABLES

One of the major difficulties of research in psychotherapy is the necessity to deal simultaneously with the patient and the therapist. One should never lose sight of the fact that the two persons are engaged in an interactive relationship, and that the attributes and actions of one invariably influence the other. As soon as we arrest the interaction and take a cross-sectional reading on measuring instruments, such as rating scales, questionnaires, etc., we are in danger of losing sight of the interplay of forces. Unfortunately, neither our language nor our investigative procedures facilitate the task of keeping the *relational* aspects clearly in mind.

Nevertheless, unlike ordinary social interactions, the therapeutic relationship does not give equal "weight" to the contributions of the two participants. The psychoanalytic relationship in particular is a "tilted" relationship, to use Greenacre's (1954) phrase. The "tilt" is toward self-revelation on the part of the patient (discussion of his problems, subjective feelings and experiences, etc.), with *selective* participation by the therapist. There is, then, some justification in saying that the therapeutic relationship (its climate, conditions, procedural rules, etc.) is "created" by the therapist (compare Fiedler's studies, cited below). In a different sense—by projecting his feelings, attitudes, and the patterns acquired in past interpersonal relations upon the therapist—the patient is "creating" the prevailing emotional atmosphere. The degree of "tilt" undoubtedly varies from one form of therapy to another and depends largely upon the extent to which the therapist participates as a "real" person rather than as a therapist in the orthodox Freudian sense.

There are by now a few investigations which purport to study selected aspects of the therapeutic relationship and some of its determinants. The methodological difficulties surrounding this research are truly staggering and pose a continuing challenge to the researcher's ingenuity.

A pioneer effort was a series of widely quoted studies by Fiedler (1950a, 1950b, 1951a, 1953) which, unfortunately, have not been replicated or expanded. The measuring instrument was a Q-sort consisting of 75 statements describing the therapeutic relationship in terms of communication, emotional distance, and the role which the therapist maintained toward his patient. The items read, for example, "The therapist is well able to understand the patient's feelings," "The therapist maintains a friendly, neutral attitude throughout," "The therapist is hostile toward the patient," etc. Fiedler found that trained therapists as well as untrained judges agreed on the desiderata of a good therapeutic relationship. He then asked judges to rate, by means of the same Q-sort, early interviews conducted by ten therapists representing the psychoanalytic, the client-centered, and the Adlerian orientations. Within each group of therapists, half were nationally recognized experts, half beginners. Factor analyses of the ratings showed that therapeutic relationships created by experts, regardless of theoretical orientation, were more alike (more "ideal") than the relationships created by novices. From these findings and those of related studies, it was concluded that the quality of the therapeutic relationship is more basic to therapeutic success than the therapist's specific methods and techniques.

The results of this work do not warrant sweeping generalizations. The following criticisms, and possibly others, appear relevant: Therapeutic technique was not studied as such; the global descriptions elicited from the Q-sorts provided little more than the judgment that the relationship of some therapists was "good" and that of others less so; the descriptions were highly stereotyped; the number of therapists was extremely small and almost certainly atypical; patient variables were not controlled; no measures of outcome were available (these would appear to be mandatory if one would speak of "success"); the reputation of the expert therapists may have been a contaminating factor.

Whitehorn and Betz (1954) contributed a valuable piece of research in their study of therapist characteristics in relation to treatment outcomes. They analyzed the case records of one hundred schizophrenic patients treated at the Henry Phipps Psychiatric Clinic. Using ratings and similar measures of outcome as a criterion, they isolated one group of therapists whose patients had a high improvement rate and another group whose patients improved relatively little. Each group consisted of seven residents in psychiatry who were comparable in level of experience, number of patients treated, and related variables. On the basis of their successes with neurotic and depressed patients, the two groups differed very little; but they seemed to relate to schizophrenic patients in markedly different ways, as judged by abstracts of the case records, nurses' observations, conference reports, and the like. The more successful (Group A) therapists showed better understanding of the meaning and motivations of the patient's behavior; their diagnostic formulations went beyond mere clinical description and narrative biography; they appeared to place greater emphasis on the patient *as a person* rather than as an individual displaying a certain psychopathology; they appeared to focus on constructive aspects of the patient's behavior aimed at working out a better solution to his life problems, rather than on the mere decrease of symptoms or "better socialization." Interestingly, too, Group A therapists made greater use of "active personal participation" in their contacts with patients than did the less successful (Group B) ones, who were characterized by patterns of passive permissiveness, interpretation and instruction, and practical care. The authors' interpretation of their findings was that in the treatment of schizophrenic patients, those therapists are more successful who succeed in establishing a personal relationship characterized by trust and confidence, and who are more "active" in helping the patient to reorient himself in his personal relationships.

These results provide some empirical support for the view, espoused by Rogers, the existential analysts, and others, that stresses the uniqueness of the individual patient and requires on the therapist's part a deep understanding of the patient's self: "The therapist is assumedly an expert; but, if he is not first of all a human being, his expertness will be irrelevant and quite possibly harmful" (May *et al.*, 1958, p. 82).

The "successful" therapists studied by Whitehorn and Betz apparently were able to place technical considerations in the service of a truly collaborative relationship with the patient, with favorable results. Missing, unfortunately, are concrete data on the implementation of the relationship as well as the patient's perceptions of the therapist and the therapeutic experience. Also, the criterion of improvement was relatively gross, and the reliance on secondary data (case records, etc.) detracts from this otherwise excellent study. Corroboration of the results, particularly with patients who are less severely disturbed, is needed.* Recently, Whitehorn and Betz (1960) have reported some further correlates of "A" and "B" physicians in terms of differences in interest patterns on the Strong Vocational Interest Inventory. Their interpretation, however, is highly speculative.

Hiler (1958) studied characteristics of the therapist which might influence the patient to remain in therapy or to discontinue. Using an indirect measure of the patient's motivation for therapy (total number of responses on the Rorschach), he showed that therapists who were rated by colleagues as most warm and friendly tended to keep in therapy a larger percentage of unproductive patients. This finding seemed to apply particularly to female therapists. Furthermore, therapists who were rated as more competent tended to lose fewer productive patients. It made no difference whether the therapist was a psychiatrist, psychologist, or social worker. As Hiler points out, staying in therapy, while not synonymous with favorable outcome, is an indispensable prerequisite.

On the basis of a series of studies carried out at Pennsylvania State University, Snyder (1953) lists a number of therapist variables which seem to affect the patient-doctor relationship (self-insight, insight into others, adaptability, emotional control), but he confesses a lack of certainty as to which variables are the significant ones. Drawbacks of these studies are the relative inexperience of the therapists (graduate students in psychology) and brevity of the therapeutic contact (median 6.5 interviews).

Parloff (1956) investigated the degree to which the quality of the therapeutic relationships established by two equally expert therapists with the same patient sample is influenced by the therapist's personality and his perceptions of the patient. He found that the therapist who was able to establish the better social relationships also established the better therapeutic relationships; moreover, the therapist who perceived a patient as more closely approximating his "ideal

---

* In a recent (as yet unpublished) study, Lorr and his collaborators obtained contradictory evidence with neurotic Veterans Administration patients.

patient" concept created the better therapeutic relationship. Rosenthal (1955) showed that patients who improved in therapy tended to revise certain of their moral values in the direction of their therapist's values. These studies document the importance of the therapist's personality and cast some light on the all-important process of identification which seems to take place in successful therapy, but they are less explicit about the function of the technical operations used by the therapist.

Clearly, there is no simple answer to what makes a human relationship "click" and turns it into a productive experience for the patient (as well as for the therapist) or what leads to less favorable outcomes. A major source of variance obviously is the personality of the patient, the nature of his problems in living, and the manner in which they in turn affect the therapist. Sociological variables, such as social class, have also been shown to play a part. Some relevant research is reviewed in the following section.

THERAPIST RESPONSES IN RELATION
TO PATIENT VARIABLES

Every neurotic patient is unconsciously committed to maintaining the status quo; thus psychotherapy—particularly if aimed at confronting the patient with his inner conflicts—proceeds against powerful unconscious resistances. Unless there is a strong conscious desire to be helped and to collaborate with the therapist, the odds against a favorable outcome may be insuperable. "Motivation for therapy" is a global concept, which may include high intelligence, a "relatively intact ego," relative absence of strong secondary gains from one's neurosis, the ability and willingness to withstand frustration and suffering, a certain "psychological-mindedness," including a readiness to look within oneself for the causes of unhappiness, a strong desire to change coupled with subjective discomfort, freedom from crippling physical diseases, lack of interfering environmental factors, ample financial resources, youth, and others. In addition, such considerations as the nature and extent of the patient's symptomatology and the degree to which it permeates his personality structure enter into prognostic judgments. Because psychotherapy demands great investments of time and emotional energy from the therapist, it is hardly surprising that his willingness to enter into a therapeutic relationship with a particular patient becomes highly selective. Different therapists have highly individual preferences, which it would be important to elucidate. It seems reasonable to assume that therapeutic relationships in which the patient is highly motivated to seek therapeutic help and in which the therapist is highly motivated to put his skills at the patient's disposal have, other things being equal, the greatest chance of success. This is another area in which research may enhance specificity and thereby the effectiveness of psychotherapy.

Kirtner and Cartwright (1958), studying 42 cases treated at the University of Chicago Counseling Center, found a significant association between treatment outcome and the manner in which the client conceptualized and presented his problem in the initial interview. Unsuccessfully treated clients tended to intellectualize; they discussed external manifestations of internal difficulties. Successfully treated clients, on the other hand, tended to deal with feelings in the therapeutic relationship and were eager to discover how they were contributing to their inner difficulties. No doubt the second group would be considered more suitable for client-centered therapy. While it cannot be proved, it is entirely possible that those patients who felt they could be helped by client-centered therapy *and* client-centered therapists continued to work on their problems, whereas those who did not, dropped out. One may also speculate that the therapist's motivation to help the first group of patients was, for a variety of reasons, weaker. Thus, the therapist's attitude toward the patient may reinforce corresponding attitudes in the patient, which could lead to premature termination of therapy. There is no implication that this phenomenon is restricted to one form of therapy; the judgment of therapeutic failure, premature termination, therapeutic impasse, poor motivation for therapy, and the like, wherever it occurs, may indicate an unwillingness or inability on the part of the therapist to work with a particular patient, as much as it reflects limiting factors within the patient.

Indirect evidence bearing upon this problem was adduced by the author (1958) in a study, already cited, of the responses of over two hundred therapists to a sound film of an initial interview. Results showed considerable divergence in the respondents' clinical judgments, recommendations for treatment, attitudes toward the patient, and communications addressed to him. Systematic differences in therapist responses were traceable to such variables as level of experience and theoretical orientation. However, the therapist's attitude toward the patient, as rated by himself, seemed to be another important source of variance. For example, negative attitudes toward the patient were found to be correlated with a more unfavorable diagnosis and prognosis, with recommendations for greater strictness and activity on the part of the therapist, and with recommendations for less frequent interviews. Significantly, too, therapists who rated their attitude toward the patient as negative tended to show less empathy in their communications. This was particularly true of experienced therapists whose training had not included a personal analysis.

The findings clearly showed that therapists responded differently to the patient, depending on whether his hostile, angry, demanding attitudes stimulated anger (and rejection) in them. It was possible to differentiate two major groups of therapists, one who appeared more tolerant, more humane, more permissive, more "democratic," and perhaps more "therapeutic," and a second who emerged as more directive, more disciplinary, moralistic, and harsh. Those in the first group, too, were "warmer" in their communications to the patient; concomitantly, "cold," rejecting comments were relatively less frequent.

The results also suggested that, to some extent at least, therapists were aware of their positive or negative reaction to the patient and of their willingness or unwillingness to enter into a therapeutic relationship with him. Undoubtedly they were less aware of the manner in which their attitude interacted with their clinical evaluations. In the light of this evidence, one understandably begins to speculate about the extent to which the therapist's attitude, as conveyed by his communications to the patient, tends to bring about a realization of the therapist's expectations in actual therapy situations. For psychotherapy, the crux of the matter is not the perceptions and clinical evaluations, nor even the therapist's conscious attitude toward the patient; rather, it is the manner in which these variables influence and structure the therapeutic relationship. This, clearly, is an important problem requiring much further exploration.

A number of studies (Rubinstein and Lorr, 1956; Lorr, Katz, and Rubinstein, 1958; Frank et al., 1957; Imber et al., 1956) have presented converging evidence on those characteristics of patients which, actuarially, make them good candidates for psychotherapy. These people tend to be well educated, articulate, and socially responsible; they are members of the middle class, have a considerable measure of "ego strength," are not deriving excessive secondary gains from their neurotic difficulties via incapacitating somatic illnesses, are anxious, and are eager to do something about their problems. This does not mean, except in a superficial sense, that they are "well" or "normal." In fact, these people often are chronically disturbed in their interpersonal relations and extremely unhappy in their personal and professional lives. The trouble is that society—and "objective" science—has no adequate yardsticks for measuring personal unhappiness, nor does it usually pay much attention to it. Parenthetically, this is one of the flagrant shortcomings of the traditional "outcome" studies in psychotherapy—that they largely ignore the patient's subjective feelings of improvement. This is partly the patient's fault, if one may use this term, because frequently he is hard put, after significant therapeutic improvement, to recall his former state of distress.

The available evidence substantiates Freud's original dictum about the limited applicability of intensive forms of psychotherapy. Psycho-analysis, as the most ambitious and far-reaching attempt at restruc-turing the personality, makes the most stringent demands upon the "qualifications" of both the patient and the therapist. But other forms of psychotherapy, insofar as they are aimed at emotional insight, also presuppose a fairly intact ego in the patient, and most of the char-acteristics already mentioned. From everything that has been said, it is apparent then that psychotherapy, even with considerable modifica-tions, is applicable only to a relatively limited segment of the total population. It has been pointed out that most theories and principles of psychotherapy themselves embody middle-class objectives and values. Hollingshead and Redlich's (1958) investigations corroborate these assertions from a somewhat different vantage point. They demon-strate, among other things, that the form of therapy a patient receives tends to be correlated with social class membership. Thus, psycho-therapy is the therapy of choice for members of the upper middle class, whereas the somatic therapies (particularly in the case of psy-chotic patients) are more characteristic of the person belonging to the lower social classes. It must be remembered, however, that social class is merely one of the variables which enter into judgments of a patient's suitability for psychotherapy.

There can be little doubt that prospective patients are more likely to be accepted for psychotherapy if they meet most of the criteria char-acterizing the "good" psychotherapy patient. In addition, psychiatrists and psychologists subscribe to an implicit ranking of neurotic and characterological conditions according to their alleged treatability. Without attempting a thorough discussion of this complex problem it may be stated that, beginning with Freud, the "classical" neurotic conditions, like hysteria, are considered ideally suitable for psycho-therapy and psychoanalysis, whereas severe character disorders and the psychoses are generally considered unsuitable. Such subjective classifications reflect, in part, clinical experience; they may also reflect value judgments about the kind of persons psychotherapists "prefer" to work with, as well as an appraisal in socio-cultural terms of the con-ditions from which they are suffering. (The therapist's counter-anger in response to an angry patient mentioned above may be a minor but telling instance of this phenomenon.) Consequently, a patient meeting the psychotherapist's explicit as well as implicit criteria of a good or promising patient not only has a better chance of finding a competent therapist, but he may from the beginning elicit greater interest from the therapist, which may be reflected in greater willingness to make an emotional investment in the patient, to devote greater energy to the treatment, etc.

It is as yet unknown to what extent the patient may fulfill the therapist's unverbalized prophecy. This much, however, is clear: without a keen and abiding interest and dedication on the part of the therapist, the patient cannot marshal the necessary strength and energy to fight his way to a healthier adaptation. This is particularly true in those situations in which the therapist aims at a thorough reorganization of the patient's personality through the reliving of his childhood traumas. Too, the infinite patience which dedicated therapists like Frieda Fromm-Reichmann, Otto Will, Harold Searles, and others have invested in therapy with schizophrenic patients bears eloquent tribute to the proposition that therapeutic gains are often commensurate with the efforts expended by the therapist, provided the patient possesses basic personality resources.

On a smaller scale, numerous studies attest that patients who appear to be motivated for psychotherapy (however the therapist understands this term) tend to be better liked by therapists and the prognosis is seen as more favorable (Wallach and Strupp, 1960). Heine and Trosman (1960) have shown that mutuality of expectation is an important factor in the continuation of the therapeutic relationship. In this study, patients who continued in psychotherapy conceptualized their expectations of therapy in a manner more congruent with the therapist's role image, and may therefore have been more gratifying to the therapist. Similarly, Strupp and Williams (1960) found that patients who were judged nondefensive, insightful, likable, and well motivated for therapy were seen by therapists as most likely to improve. In the same vein, Sullivan, Miller, and Smelser (1958) summed up their findings by saying: "Those persons who are least equipped to meet life challenges are the ones who stand to gain least from psychotherapy."

COUNTERTRANSFERENCE

The phenomena usually classed under the heading of countertransference appear to be relatively gross deviations of the therapist from his role as an objective participant observer. Perhaps these deviations are viewed more fruitfully, not as a class of phenomena by themselves, but as extremes of continua underlying the emotional context of therapy. Thus, when the therapist responds to the patient's behavior in terms of the patient's distorted expectations, or when he views the patient in terms of cultural stereotypes, he restricts his therapeutic usefulness and in extreme cases may relinquish it completely. The therapist's distortions may be instigated by, and represent a response to, the patient's transference behavior; frequently, no doubt, this is the case. On the other hand, they may be distortions which the therapist would exhibit relatively independent of the patient's distortions. As Orr (1954) has shown, definitions of countertransference are unfortunately not very precise. Furthermore, it appears that most deficiencies in the therapeutic emotional context created by the therapist are not the gross phenomena which have traditionally been grouped under the heading of countertransference, but rather more subtle shortcomings in the therapist's contribution. Obviously, the experimental demonstration of such phenomena founders upon their extreme elusiveness. If one accepts a broader definition of the term, some of the studies cited in the preceding section might be more properly classified under the present heading. At any rate, a few investigations have been specifically addressed to the problem.

Bandura, Lipsher, and Miller (1960) studied therapists' reactions to expressions of hostility by the patient. They found that therapists who were rated as directly expressing their own hostility were more likely to respond with approach reactions when the patients expressed hostility. As might be expected, patients were more likely to continue the expression of hostile feelings when the therapist responded with an approach reaction. Perhaps as a function of the therapists' relative inexperience, they tended to discourage the patient's hostility when it was directed against themselves. Cutler (1958) defined operationally areas of "conflict" within the therapist in terms of discrepancies between self-ratings on a series of adjectives and ratings of the therapist by a group of judges. Studying these conflicts in relation to therapy interviews and therapists' reports, Cutler found that therapists tended to over- or under-report in areas related to their own conflicts. He also noted a tendency for therapist responses to be more "ego oriented" (less therapeutic) in these areas. Although these results are striking, it must be kept in mind that only two therapists were involved, and the complexity of the judgments entering into the statistical analyses was considerable. There is also a question of the extent to which discrepancy scores can be regarded as a true measure of inner conflict.

A somewhat similar approach to the quantification of countertransference attitudes was used by Fiedler (1951b). The steps include: a self-description by the patient via a Q-sort; the therapist's prediction of the patient's self-description; self- and self-ideal ratings by the therapist. The therapist's over- or underestimation of the similarity between his own and the patient's self-description, and the therapists "ideal" description is then used to estimate the nature and intensity of countertransference feelings. As Cronbach (1955) has pointed out, correlations between Q-sorts and discrepancy scores derived from such measures present complex statistical problems, which make meaningful psychological interpretations very difficult.

S TUDIES OF THE THERAPEUTIC
PROCESS

It is impossible within the confines of this chapter to do justice to the
many investigations which have been concerned with the effects of
selected therapeutic operations upon the patient's response in psychotherapy. The ascendancy of this kind of research, with its concomitant
de-emphasis of an arbitrary end point designated as "outcome," partly
represents a disenchantment with the traditional outcome studies,
which were more intent upon demonstrating whether a particular
technique "works" rather than the process by which a given result is
achieved. The latter kind of investigation is commonly considered to
have greater potential of advancing our knowledge about psychotherapy.

Credit for the most systematic pioneer effort must go to the group
affiliated with Carl Rogers. For comprehensive summaries of this work,
the reader is referred to Seeman and Raskin's chapter in Mowrer's
(1950) compendium, and to Rogers and Dymond (1954). In general,
these studies support Rogers' formulations—that a consistent attitude
of empathy, positive regard, warmth, and acceptance on the part of
the therapist, communicated primarily through reflections of the
client's feelings, lead to favorable therapeutic change. Some of the
concomitants of that change may be expressed as greater self-acceptance, self-awareness, subjective comfort, acceptance of others, and less
defensiveness. These studies do not prove conclusively that the results were due to the therapist's attitude, his technique, or to a combination of these. Nor do they claim that some other theoretical approach
or technique might not serve equally well or better. Another difficulty
is that of relating specific changes in personality and attitude to specific
therapeutic interventions. As Frank (1959a) has suggested, it is quite
possible that a general factor (favorable expectation, faith, "placebo
effect," or the like) may be operating in all forms of psychotherapy.
Answers to these questions and others may be forthcoming, as research
techniques and methodologies are sharpened and applied to a variety
of therapeutic situations and techniques.

A few examples of relevant research under this heading must suffice.
Dittmann (1952) investigated the kinds of therapist activities associated with therapeutic progress. Independent ratings were made of
the progressive and regressive movement reflected in the immediate
responses of a patient. Progressive therapeutic movement was found
to be associated with (1) a high level of participation on the part of
the therapist and (2) response by the therapist to either feelings or
interpersonal behavior, or to both, if they were consistent. Murray
(1956), working within the framework of learning theory, demon-

strated that in the course of psychotherapy those patient verbalizations which were mildly approved by the therapist (interpreted as
moves towards independence) tended to increase, whereas those
which were mildly disapproved (categorized as independence anxiety,
intellectual defenses, and sexual statements) tended to decrease. In a
related study, he showed that the frequency of statements about the
therapist increased reliably as therapy progressed. Bergman (1951),
in a study whose conclusions have been questioned, investigated the
manner in which therapists handled requests for "evaluation." Analyzing the patient's responses immediately following the therapist's intervention, he concluded that reflections of the patient's feeling by the
therapist led to continued self-exploration and "insight," whereas interpretations and structuring tended to lead to an abandonment of
self-exploration. Grossman (1952) found support for the hypothesis
that insight is greater following therapist responses that recognize
explicitly expressed feelings and attitudes. Speisman (1959) showed
that patient resistance was lowest following interpretations at a moderate level of "depth."

These researches may be criticized for dealing with microscopic
units of the therapist-patient relationship, a problem previously mentioned. Nevertheless, they represent noteworthy attempts at breaking
down the global complex of the patient-therapist interaction, thus making it amenable to scientific analysis.

The data of scientific psychology ultimately derive from self-observa-
tion, from the observations of one person by another, or from a combination of these. Contemporary American psychology, particularly in
those fields concerned with the study of nonclinical problems, heavily
emphasizes observations which can be made by external observers,
and often shows an almost phobic aversion to the subject's psychological experience, his "inner world," his personal frame of reference.
Despite increasing sophistication of the behavioristic approaches, there
is the implication that observable behavior can be studied by the
methods of science, whereas subjective experience cannot. There is a
widespread reluctance to accept Lord Russell's (1948) definition of
psychology as "the science which deals with private data, and with
the private aspects of data which common sense regards as public" (p.
45). He views psychology as

> . . . a science distinct from physics and physiology, and in part
> independent of them. All the data of physics are also data of
> psychology, but not vice versa; data belonging to both are made the
> basis of quite different inferences in the two sciences. Introspection
> is valid as a source of data, and is to a considerable extent amenable
> to scientific controls (p. 51).

If one wishes to deal with the patient's feelings, wishes, impulses, and inner conflicts—clearly a necessity if the objective is to help a patient by means of psychotherapy—he learns precious little and severely restricts his field of vision if he limits himself to observable behavior, such as emitted verbal responses, gestures, bodily movements, GSR traces, blood pressure, and the like. The alternative is to enlist the patient's cooperation in sharing with the therapist, via free association or related techniques, his personal psychological experience, thus making the therapist a working partner in a unique collaborative enterprise. Through this approach, Freud advanced to an unprecedented degree the frontiers of psychological knowledge about the mainsprings of interpersonal relations and their vicissitudes. He also provided the scientifically minded psychologist, no less than the clinician, with an exquisite research tool which, in sensitivity and potential penetration, has remained unequaled. I am, of course, referring to the experimental model of the psychoanalytic situation—the personal-impersonal relationship between a subject (patient) and a psychoanalytically trained observer-participant (therapist). It is my firm conviction that the rich possibilities of this instrument have been only dimly realized in controlled research concerned with the study of interpersonal processes.* It can be mentioned only in passing that the psychoanalytic theory of psychotherapy and personality has so far offered the most comprehensive and the most systematic formulations of the intrapsychic processes lying between stimulus and response, their subtle complexity, infinite ramifications, and unique laws (for systematic accounts, see Rapaport 1960a, 1960b).

If we are to proceed with the all-important task of studying psychological phenomena by techniques uniquely suited to their study, it is indispensable to take that study seriously. If we are to study the phenomena of psychotherapy and of doctor-patient relationships intelligently and productively, it is essential to have a thoroughgoing knowledge of the clinical findings, insights, and principles which clinical psychoanalysis and psychotherapy have distilled over the years. A major reason why psychologists have been more comfortable in accepting the S-R model for research as well as for theory is the conceptual and methodological difficulty of dealing with intrapsychic variables—what goes on in the organism's "black box" between sensory input and emitted responses. This problem is magnified when the researcher approaches the enormous complexities of the therapeutic interaction. By this I mean particularly the reciprocal influence between therapist and patient, the relative effects of the two personalities upon each other, including the planful therapeutic interventions

---

* This point is the basis of an excellent contribution by Janis (1958), with which I became familiar only after writing this chapter.

of the therapist, the manner in which he acquires information about the patient's inner state, how he operates upon the information he receives, and how his messages are perceived, dealt with, and integrated by the patient. Clearly, the researcher in psychotherapy deals with some of the most basic problems of psychological research—the conditions by which one human being influences another—which have far-reaching implications for child rearing, education, and propaganda, to name but a few.

This chapter has presented some examples of the steadily increasing research effort in this area. Clearly, research is at an early stage of development. It is groping, and it suffers from many conceptual and methodological deficiencies. At the same time, it continues to offer a momentous challenge to the clinically oriented experimental psychologist. However, as Rapaport (1960a) points out in a perceptive discussion, sophistication and advances in knowledge cannot be achieved by means of *ad hoc* quantifications based upon an inadequate understanding of complex processes, no matter how sophisticated one's methodology may be:

> If logic, methodology, and mathematics were the pacemakers of development in sciences, this development could be fast enough in psychology. But the pacemaker is not methodology—it is human invention. . . . Methodology, since it deals with relationships of concepts, all of which are potentially valid, can go on continuously, building ever-new "castles in Spain." But human invention consists of discontinuous events, each of which requires long preparation, since in it an individual's thought patterns must come to grips with patterns of nature, and only those rare encounters in which a unique human thought pattern actually matches a unique pattern of nature will matter. If the match is not specific and precise, or if the individual is not prepared to recognize it, or if he does recognize it but is not ready to use it, the moment is lost. (footnote, pp. 37–38.)

Mindful of Rapaport's injunction, research in this area should beware of pseudo-quantifications which often tend to close prematurely an area of inquiry and give rise to the illusion that a problem has been solved when the exploration has barely begun. In studying doctor-patient relationships in psychotherapy, there is as yet much room for patient, naturalistic observation and for a careful mapping out of variables. Morison's (1960) wise counsel to the scientist for "gradualness, gradualness, gradualness" (Pavlov) is likewise germane. Above all, it seems to this writer, the researcher should strive for a greater awareness of the proposition that research concerned with doctor-patient relationships and psychotherapy deals specifically and uniquely with *human* problems—with the complexities of human psychology and with the problems of human adaptation to other human beings. If this be true, there can be no simple substitutes or translations from laboratory research, animal studies, or conditioning experiments, much as these may advance psychological science in other respects.

REFERENCES

Alexander, F. Analysis of the therapeutic factors in psychoanalytic treatment. *Psychoanal. Quart.*, 1950, 482–500.

Alexander, F. Unexplored areas in psychoanalytic theory and treatment. *Behav. Sci.*, 1958, *3*, 293–316.

Auld, F., Jr., & Murray, E. J. Content-analysis studies of psychotherapy. *Psychol. Bull.*, 1955, 52, 377–395.

Bales, R. F. *Interaction process analysis.* Reading, Mass.: Addison-Wesley, 1950.

Bandura, A., Lipsher, D. H., & Miller, Paula E. Psychotherapists' approach-avoidance reactions to patients' expressions of hostility. *J. consult. Psychol.*, 1960, 24, 1–8.

Bellak, L., & Smith, M. B. An experimental exploration of the psychoanalytic process. *Psychoanal. Quart.*, 1956, 25, 385–414.

Bergman, D. Counseling method and client responses. *J. consult. Psychol.*, 1951, 15, 216–224.

Cronbach, L. J. Processes affecting scores on "understanding of others" and "assumed similarity." *Psychol. Bull.*, 1955, 52, 177–194.

Cutler, R. L. Countertransference effects in psychotherapy. *J. consult. Psychol.*, 1958, 22, 349–356.

Dittes, J. E. Previous studies bearing on content analysis of psychotherapy. In J. Dollard & F. Auld, Jr., *Scoring human motives.* New Haven, Conn.: Yale University Press, 1959, 325–351.

Dittmann, A. T. The interpersonal process in psychotherapy: development of a research method. *J. abnorm. soc. Psychol.*, 1952, 47, 236–244.

Dollard, J., & Auld, F., Jr. *Scoring human motives: a manual.* New Haven, Conn.: Yale University Press, 1959.

Dollard, J., & Miller, N. E. *Personality and psychotherapy.* New York: McGraw-Hill, 1950.

Eysenck, H. J. The effects of psychotherapy: an evaluation. *J. consult. Psychol.*, 1952, 16, 319–324.

Fenichel, O. *The psychoanalytic theory of neurosis.* New York: Norton, 1945.

Fey, W. F. Doctrine and experience: their influence upon the psychotherapist. *J. consult. Psychol.*, 1958, 22, 403–409.

Fiedler, F. A comparison of therapeutic relationships in psychoanalytic, nondirective, and Adlerian therapy. *J. consult. Psychol.*, 1950a, 14, 436–445.

Fiedler, F. The concept of an ideal therapeutic relationship. *J. consult. Psychol.*, 1950b, 14, 239–245.

Fiedler, F. Factor analyses of psychoanalytic, nondirective, and Adlerian therapeutic relationships. *J. consult. Psychol.*, 1951a, 15, 32–38.

Fiedler, F. E. A method of objective quantification of certain countertransference attitudes. *J. clin. Psychol.*, 1951b, 7, 101–107.

Fiedler, F. E. Quantitative studies on the role of therapists' feelings toward their patients. In O. H. Mowrer *et al.*, *Psychotherapy: theory and research.* New York: Ronald, 296–315.

Frank, J. D. The dynamics of the psychotherapeutic relationship: determinants and effects of the therapist's influence. *Psychiatry*, 1959a, 22, 17–39.

Frank, J. D. Problems of control in

psychotherapy as exemplified by the psychotherapy research project of the Phipps Psychiatric Clinic. In E. A. Rubinstein & M. B. Parloff (Eds.), *Research in psychotherapy.* Washington, D.C.: American Psychological Assoc., 1959b, 10–26.

Frank, J. D., Gliedman, L. H., Imber, S. D., Nash, E. H., Jr., & Stone, A. R. Why patients leave psychotherapy. *Arch. Neurol. Psychiat.,* 1957, 77, 283–299.

Freud, S. Analysis terminable and interminable. In *Collected papers.* Vol. 5. London: Hogarth, 1952, 313–357.

Freud, S. The future prospects of psycho-analytic therapy. In *Collected papers.* Vol. 2. London: Hogarth Press, 1953, 285–296.

Glover, E. Common technical practices: a questionnaire research. In *The technique of psycho-analysis.* New York: Internat. Univs. Press, 1955, 261–350.

Greenacre, Phyllis. Practical considerations in relation to psychoanalytic therapy (transference). *J. Amer. Psychoanal. Assn.,* 1954, 2, 671–684.

Grossman, D. An experimental investigation of a psychotherapeutic technique. *J. consult. Psychol.,* 1952, 16, 325–331.

Harway, N. I., Dittman, A. T., Raush, H. L., Bordin, E. S., & Rigler, D. The measurement of depth of interpretation. *J. consult. Psychol.,* 1955, 19, 247–253.

Heine, R. W., & Trosman, H. Initial expectations of the doctor-patient interaction as a factor in continuance in psychotherapy. *Psychiatry,* 1960, 23, 275–278.

Hiler, E. W. An analysis of patient-therapist compatibility. *J. consult. Psychol.,* 1958, 22, 341–347.

Hollingshead, A. B., & Redlich, F. C. *Social class and mental illness.* New York: Wiley, 1958.

Holt, R. R., & Luborsky, L. *Personality*

patterns of psychiatrists. New York: Basic Books, 1958.

Imber, S. D., Frank, J., Gliedman, L., Nash, E., & Stone, A. Suggestibility, social class, and acceptance of psychotherapy. *J. clin. Psychol.,* 1956, 12, 341–344.

Janis, I. L. The psychoanalytic interview as an observational method. In G. Lindzey (Ed.), *Assessment of human motives.* New York: Rinehart, 1958, 149–182.

Kirtner, W. L., & Cartwright, D. S. Success and failure in client-centered therapy as a function of initial in-therapy behavior. *J. consult. Psychol.,* 1958, 22, 329–333.

Leary, T., & Gill, M. The dimensions and a measure of the process of psychotherapy: a system for the analysis of the content of clinical evaluations and patient-therapist verbalizations. In E. A. Rubinstein & M. B. Parloff (Eds.), *Research in psychotherapy.* Washington, D.C.: Amer. Psychol. Assoc., 1959, 62–95.

Lennard, H. L., & Bernstein, A. *The anatomy of psychotherapy.* New York: Columbia Univ. Press, 1960.

Levy, N. Paper presented at annual meeting of the Academy of Psychoanalysis, May, 1960.

Lorr, M., Katz, M. N., & Rubinstein, E. A. The prediction of length of stay in psychotherapy. *J. consult. Psychol.,* 1958, 22, 321–327.

Macalpine, Ida. The development of the transference. *Psychoanal. Quart.,* 1950, 19, 501–539.

May, R. R., Angel, E., & Ellenberger, H. F. *Existence: a new dimension in psychiatry and psychology.* New York: Basic Books, 1958.

Meehl, P. E. The cognitive activity of the clinician. *Amer. Psychologist,* 1960, 15, 19–27.

Menninger, K. *Theory of psychoanalytic technique.* New York: Basic Books, 1958.

Morison, R. S. "Gradualness, gradualness, gradualness" (I. P. Pavlov).

Amer. Psychologist, 1960, *15*, 187–197.

Moss, C. S., Ourth, L., Auvenshine, C., & Shallenberger, Patricia. Attitudes of experienced psychologist-therapists. *Amer. Psychologist*, 1960, *15*, 414 (Abstract).

Mowrer, O. H. *et al. Psychotherapy: theory and research*. New York: Ronald, 1953.

Munroe, Ruth L. *Schools of psychoanalytic thought*. New York: Dryden Press, 1955.

Murray, E. J. The content-analysis method of studying psychotherapy. *Psychol. Monogr.*, 1956, *70*, No. 13, Whole No. 420.

Orr, D. W. Transference and countertransference: a historical survey. *J. Amer. Psychoanal. Assn.*, 1954, *2*, 621–670.

Parloff, M. B. Some factors affecting the quality of therapeutic relationships. *J. abnorm. soc. Psychol.*, 1956, *52*, 5–10.

Porter, E. H., Jr. The development and evaluation of a measure of counseling and interview procedures. *Educ. & Psychol. Measmt.*, 1943, *3*, 105–125; 215–238.

Rapaport, D. The structure of psychoanalytic theory: a systematizing attempt. *Psychol. Issues*, 1960a, *2*, No. 2.

Rapaport, D. On the psychoanalytic theory of motivation. In M. R. Jones (Ed.), *Nebraska symposium on motivation 1960*. Lincoln, Nebr.: Univ. of Nebraska Press, 1960, 173–247.

Raush, H. L., & Bordin, E. S. Warmth in personality development and in psychotherapy. *Psychiatry*, 1957, *20*, 351–363.

Rogers, C. R. The necessary and sufficient conditions of therapeutic personality change. *J. consult. Psychol.*, 1957, *21*, 95–103.

Rogers, C. R., & Dymond, Rosalind F. (Eds.). *Psychotherapy and personality change*. Chicago: Univ. of Chicago Press, 1954.

Rosenthal, D. Changes in some moral values following psychotherapy. *J. consult. Psychol.*, 1955, *19*, 431–436.

Rubinstein, E., & Lorr, M. A comparison of terminators and remainers in outpatient psychotherapy. *J. clin. Psychol.*, 1956, *12*, 345–349.

Rubinstein, E. A., & Parloff, M. B. (Eds.). *Research in psychotherapy*. Washington, D.C.: American Psychological Association, 1959.

Russell, B. *Human knowledge: its scope and limits*. New York: Simon & Schuster, 1948.

Sears, R. R. *Survey of objective studies of psychoanalytic concepts*. New York: Social Science Research Council, 1943.

Seeman, J. A. A study of the process of nondirective therapy. *J. consult. Psychol.*, 1949, *13*, 157–168.

Seeman, J., & Raskin, N. J. Research perspectives in client-centered therapy. In O. H. Mowrer *et al.*, *Psychotherapy: and research*. New York: Ronald, 1953, 205–234.

Shakow, D. The recorded psychoanalytic interview as an objective approach to research in psychoanalysis. *Psychoanal. Quart.*, 1960, *29*, 82–97.

Snyder, W. U. An investigation of the nature of non-directive psychotherapy. *J. genet. Psychol.*, 1945, *33*, 193–223.

Snyder, W. U. *Group report of a program of research in psychotherapy*. State College, Pa.: The Pennsylvania State College, 1953.

Speisman, J. C. Depth of interpretation and verbal resistance in psychotherapy. *J. consult. Psychol.*, 1959, *23*, 93–99.

Strupp, H. H. An objective comparison of Rogerian and psychoanalytic techniques. *J. consult. Psychol.*, 1955a, *19*, 1–7.

Strupp, H. H. Psychotherapeutic technique, professional affiliation, and experience level. *J. consult. Psychol.*, 1955b, *19*, 197–202.

Strupp, H. H. The effect of the psychotherapist's personal analysis upon his techniques. *J. consult. Psychol.*, 1955c, 197–204.

Strupp, H. H. A multidimensional system for analyzing psychotherapeutic techniques. *Psychiatry*, 1957a, *20*, 293–306.

Strupp, H. H. A multidimensional analysis of techniques in brief psychotherapy. *Psychiatry*, 1957b, *20*, 387–397.

Strupp, H. H. A multidimensional comparison of therapist activity in analytic and client-centered therapy. *J. consult. Psychol.*, 1957c, *21*, 301–308.

Strupp, H. H. The psychotherapist's contribution to the treatment process. *Behav. Sci.*, 1958a, *3*, 34–67.

Strupp, H. H. The performance of psychoanalytic and client-centered therapists in an initial interview. *J. consult. Psychol.*, 1958b, *22*, 265–274.

Strupp, H. H. The performance of psychiatrists and psychologists in a therapeutic interview. *J. clin. Psychol.*, 1958c, *14*, 219–226.

Strupp, H. H. Nature of the therapist's contribution to treatment process. *Arch. Gen. Psychiat.*, 1960, *3*, 219–231.

Strupp, H .H., & Williams, Joan V. Some determinants of clinical evaluations of different psychiatrists. *Arch. Gen. Psychiat.*, 1960, *2*, 434–440.

Sullivan, P. L., Miller, Christine, & Smelser, W. Factors in length of stay and progress in psychotherapy. *J. consult. Psychol.*, 1958, *22*, 1–9.

Szasz, T. S., Knoff, W. F., & Hollender, M. H. The doctor-patient relationship and its historical context. *Amer. J. Psychiat.*, 1958, *115*, 522–528.

Thompson, Clara. The role of the analyst's personality in therapy. *Amer. J. Psychother.*, 1956, *10*, 347–359.

Waelder, R. *Basic theory of psychoanalysis.* New York: Internat. Univs. Press, 1960.

Wallach, M. S., & Strupp, H. H. Psychotherapists' clinical judgments and attitudes towards patients. *J. consult. Psychol.*, 1960, *24*, 316–323.

Whitehorn, J. C., & Betz, Barbara J. A study of psychotherapeutic relationships between physicians and schizophrenic patients. *Amer. J. Psychiat.*, 1954, *111*, 321–331.

Whitehorn, J. C., & Betz, Barbara J. Further studies of the doctor as a crucial variable in the outcome of treatment with schizophrenic patients. *Amer. J. Psychiat.*, 1960, *117*, 215–223.

Wolff, W. *Contemporary psychotherapists examine themselves.* Springfield, Ill. Charles C Thomas, 1956.

18

In Conclusion

ARTHUR J. BACHRACH

In my introductory note, I suggested that we were going to evaluate experimental methods and clinical problems with an eye toward examining the mutuality of problems that may exist in the laboratory and the clinic. We hope that the title of the book prevented any misconception that this was to be a handbook for practitioners, for it is apparent that the current state of experimental psychology does not provide a coherent, immediately applicable body of knowledge on which to base a clinical practice. Nonetheless, I think it is fair to say that the stream of the book has yielded enough nuggets to warrant further panning, nuggets in the form of interesting problems for the research investigator as well as theoretical and methodological leads for the clinician. To the question regarding the relationship between clinician and investigator, the chapters vary in their answers; some are encouraging, others are not. Some clearly point to a significant experimental-clinical approach; others cannot.

At least part of this problem arises from the situation that exists in the field of psychology as a whole. There is no consistent and unified structure currently underlying psychological science; and although it is true that in any science different aspects of the same problems may be investigated from many and varied viewpoints, we would hope that people interested in the same problems could at least develop effective techniques for communicating with each other. I think that this has been successful to a degree in the present book, despite surface differences in method and terminology. Editorial judgment was responsible for the omission of a number of areas that might have been included, but beyond this selection process there was no attempt to formulate a central set of problems, to legislate agreement, or to provide a consistent orientation. The last is, again, a reflection of the situation prevalent in psychology.

To turn to the specific chapters we may first ask several questions: what reasons do the various authors give for the desirability of experimental-clinical collaboration, how much relevance do they see in these two areas, and what is the extent of their own involvement in such a collaboration?

The detached faith of the historian comes through clearly in Watson's chapter. He describes the historical roots of clinical psychology in biology and in experimental psychology, with the hope that a knowledge of their historical antecedents will act as an antidote to the impression held by many clinicians and experimentalists that they form two unrelated species. It is true, nonetheless, that the two groups have evolved in different directions; the mere fact that they are "kissin' cousins" with the same last name may lead to no closer collaboration than attendance at a joint annual convention.*

But the history-minded psychologist who also subscribes to a cyclic theory of history may see in some of the other chapters an interesting repetition of a phenomenon noted by Watson. Developing as it did from an experimental background, the initial problems in the clinical area were formulated by experimentalists. Clinical psychology has since formulated its own problems and has, at the same time, developed its own language, techniques, and philosophy. One consequence of this separate growth has been an increasing inability of the clinician to explain his problems to the experimentalist and to tell him what he would like to have from him. As a result, there seems to exist today a group of experimentalists who have clinical interests but who are unaware, for all practical purposes, that clinical psychology exists. Like the clinical precursors, these experimentalists are again formulating clinical problems on the basis of their own work in the laboratory, independently of any leadership or interest from the clinic.

Hefferline stands midway between those experimentalists who prefer to lead the clinicians and those who are able to find something of value in clinical formulations. The conflicts which his intermediate position generates are evident in his chapter. From a vantage point provided by his laboratory commitment to a nonclinical strict behaviorism and his personal interest in clinical problems, he simultaneously takes his experimental colleagues to task for ignoring the clinical relevance of their work, and scolds his clinical colleagues for

---

* Even here, there are obstacles erected by scheduling two halves of the annual American Psychological Association—three days for "experimental" and three days for "clinical" and "applied" papers. The contact between the two groups often occurs at the airport; as one leaves, the other arrives.

their failure to participate in the application of new developments in the laboratory. Hefferline formulates the clinical importance of his own and others' work on events under the skin in a way that is more closely related to his experimental orientation than to clinical conceptions of the same phenomena; yet he suggests that clinical application is more likely to develop if clinicians themselves will exploit the laboratory-derived tools, techniques, and research situations that are now available in this area.

Concentrating on "covert" behavior—skeletal muscle activity too small to be detected without special amplification techniques—Hefferline presents a lucid argument for its importance in problems of consciousness, thinking, "higher processes," and "neurotic tensions." But his conception of these traditionally subjective problems rests on a behavioristic and experimental analysis of the processes by which behavioral control is transferred from exteroceptive to internal stimuli —"internalization." Interestingly enough, the clinical formulation with which Hefferline finds himself in closest sympathy is the now offbeat "muscular armor" concept of Reich.

Although he is concerned with similar problems, Malmo stands somewhat more aloof from the clinic than Hefferline, resting his case for the clinical relevance of his work on the general faith that any major breakthrough in the basic science of psychology will eventually have its impact on clinical psychology. It is Malmo's interest in formulating a theoretical position that leads him to attempt a neurophysiological integration of his data where Hefferline rests content with the data and the manipulation of behavioral events.

The difference in emphasis observed in Malmo and Hefferline is marked and could easily prevent them from being recognized as true brothers under the skin. Malmo's concept of "activation," attributed to cortical bombardment by the ascending reticular activating system, is operationally close to Hefferline's concept of "set," attributed to muscular tension. The level of activation refers to an organism's general level of reticular activity, and forms the baseline from which specific behavior emerges; set is defined as a broad spectrum of behavior, largely tonic, which has extreme importance in determining the strength of more conspicuous phasic responses.

As Malmo points out in some detail, his conception is relevant to phenomena that have been classified under such headings as alertness, behavioral intensity or energetics, and drive. These phenomena have been of long-standing interest to clinicians; spurred on by recent developments in instrumentation, experimentalists are once again bringing them into the laboratory. Whether the clinician is encouraged or irritated by the experimentalists' conceptual applications, the lesson is clear. Hefferline reminds him that the instruments are available to all. This is another important lesson underscored by many of the authors—apparatus is here to stay and it is likely to render previously unapproachable problems investigable. Just as the electron microscope promises to bring significant breakthroughs to our sister field of neurology, so may the behavioral and physiological apparatus now humming in the psychological laboratories offer new data to render the covert overt.

Sidman moves still further away from Hefferline toward a purely laboratory-derived definition of clinical problems, and even suggests that clinical formulations based on the experimental analysis of operant behavior are unlikely to resemble any current schemes for classifying behavior pathologies. Like Malmo, he justifies the relevance of experimental investigation in terms of its future promise, drawing an analogy from medicine, in which laboratory sciences have contributed much to clinical practice.

Instead of emphasizing the clinical relevance of a specific problem area, Sidman's concern is largely with methodology and technique. If the experimentalist cannot provide the clinician with reliable techniques for modifying behavior, none of his other offerings is likely to prove fruitful. In an account that is at the same time confident and conservative, Sidman builds up a case for the applicability to human behavior of techniques derived from animal experimentation. Using this as a didactic platform as well, he tells the clinician that the techniques of behavioral control are basic tools for all psychologists, and invites the clinician to drink from the experimental cup. Sidman's review of the extent to which operant conditioning methods have entered the human laboratory makes it clear, however, that experimentalists are perfectly willing to go it alone and apply their own utensils to carving the clinical pie. The attempts thus far have been wide-ranging—from the practical management of patients in hospital wards to the restoration of behavior in autistic children—but, with their emphasis more on the control of variables than on content, the attempts have been necessarily limited in scope. If the clinician interprets this as an educative challenge, rather than as an indication that operant conditioners are not really interested in his problems, he may well hasten the appearance of a practitioner's handbook.

The point of view that Sidman expresses is interchangeable with Hefferline's as simply as by turning the finger of a glove inside out. Hefferline notes that an organism's operant behavior may be just as effectively controlled by its consequences on the environment of the internal receptors as when it operates on the environment of the exteroceptors. Brady's viewpoint is so close to these that it may well be considered to be the other glove of the pair, particularly insofar as he stresses the influence that behavior may exercise over internal events.

Brady is quite dubious about the likelihood that traditional laboratory formulations of emotional behavior can profitably be extended to the clinic. He observes that neither clinical nor experimental accounts of the psychophysiology of emotional behavior have provided a sound basis for applied efforts in this area, further noting that "In probably no other domain of psychological science has so little empirical data occasioned so much theoretical speculation as in the general area of the 'emotions.'"

The behavioral events involved in emotional processes have rarely been defined independently of the physiological events to which they are to be related, and only recently have neurological factors begun to be firmly specified anatomically and physiologically. Nevertheless, progress has occurred. If neurological theory has developed extensively without concomitant experimental analysis of the critical behavioral phenomena in the problems of emotion, the parallel development of operant techniques has provided methods for controlling individual behavior for psychophysiological analysis. Brady buttresses this point by reference to recent work on such obviously clinical problems as the effects of electroconvulsive shock, the influence of behavioral processes on autonomic and endocrinological activity, the experimental induction of ulcers by behavioral techniques, the relations between avoidance behavior and alcohol consumption, and others.

There is a subtle difference in emphasis between the approaches of Brady and Malmo to the neurophysiological correlates of behavior. Both are interested in objective behavioral controls. Malmo, however, concerned as he is with the formulation of a general neurophysiological theory, infers neurophysiological change from the behavior studied. Brady, on the other hand, eschews such inferences, preferring to specify and control the behavior and the internal events independently of each other.

If the previously mentioned authors are willing, to a greater or lesser extent, to formulate clinical problems in their own way, Festinger and Bramel are, by comparison, still bolder. They make only passing reference to clinical implications that might be derived from their work. In a token bow to clinical relevance, they state that their theory of dissonance is relevant to a wide variety of seemingly dissimilar situations, some of which are of interest to clinical psychologists. But they leave the task of extrapolation to anyone else who might be interested: "It is to be hoped, however, that any increased understanding of human behavior and human thought processes are potentially relevant to clinical psychology and that someone will see the relevance of these more remote areas also."

Frustrating though this attitude may be for the clinician, Festinger and Bramel are, of course, right. A clinical orientation is neither necessary for, nor a guarantee of, data of clinical interest.

Dissimilar as their subject matter may be, the closest relative of Festinger and Bramel in this book is Malmo. Like him, they are interested in the inferential development of a comprehensive theory in their chosen area. Also like him, they present a complexly interwoven set of experiments built around their theory. The reasoning is often intricate, and the clinical psychologist, who suffers no dearth of theories, may be unwilling to partake of it, but the experiments can also stand by themselves.

Their theory states that dissonance—inconsistency—gives rise to pressures to reduce the dissonance. The research is directed at specifying the factors that produce various amounts of dissonance, and at discovering the kinds of dissonance-reducing processes. The experiments have dealt with the way a person's values change as a consequence of dissonance-reducing decisions; changes in the attractiveness of behavioral consequences as a function of the exertion of effort or the endurance of inconvenience; the changes that occur in a person's opinions as a result of compliance or disagreement with conflicting opinions, and many others. Festinger and Bramel do point out that many of these processes go on in the therapeutic situation, and that there is a resemblance between some of the mechanisms of dissonance reduction and the classical defense mechanisms. The clinician who is in daily contact with the painful and often self-destructive stresses of his patients' lives may be impatient with Festinger and Bramel's assumption that they are getting at something real when they produce experimental stresses by instructions to their subjects. However, they have been successful in producing behavioral changes with this technique; whether the technique is powerful enough to produce clinically relevant behavioral effects is a problem that Festinger and Bramel reasonably leave for the clinician to answer.

Dews, a pharmacologist who has also contributed importantly to the experimental analysis of behavior, stands apart from clinical psychology with a truly Olympian detachment. Behavioral pharmacology has not, for him, advanced sufficiently to contribute in any important way to the problems of the clinic. His aim, therefore, in his chapter, is an educative one; to permit clinical psychologists to evaluate research in behavioral pharmacology in an appropriately critical manner, so that they will not place too much confidence in dubious conclusions. Lest the clinician feel an unintended slur here, he also aims his chapter at experimental psychologists, to prevent them from performing experiments that are invalidated by pharmacological misapprehensions or errors.

Dews' concerns are indeed basic ones, and the other authors might well have followed a similar course in presenting their own areas of research, to the benefit both of clinicians and other investigators. Some considerations of a similar nature were outlined by Sidman, with respect to operant techniques, and by Berg and Adams with respect to the use of rating scales. The evaluation of research in another area is always difficult; it is even more so for those who are not themselves engaged in research but who are eager to apply research findings.

Although he is mainly concerned with pharmacologic pitfalls in psychopharmacologic studies, Dews does have at least one novel and incisive comment to offer those psychologists who are interested in using drugs as a tool for psychophysiological analysis. He points out that drugs always affect any biological system along physiologically meaningful lines; this includes behavioral systems. If, therefore, behavior under the influence of a drug changes in ways that do not correspond to the postulations of a behavioral theory, it will be necessary to conclude that the theory does not bear any simple relation to the biological concomitants of behavior. Psychopharmacologic mysteries, in other words, are likely to reflect psychophysiologic misapprehensions.

In addition, Dews points out that a drug always has a multiplicity of actions; that a drug may act directly on the autonomic nervous system or may produce behavioral changes which then affect the autonomic nervous system—a point which derives additional validity from some of the experiments described in Brady's chapter—that individual differences in the effects of a drug do not necessarily reflect genetic differences; that a given type of drug action, e.g., stimulation or depression, does not occur in equal measure on all aspects of behavior; that the very behavioral modification produced by a drug may then generate additional behavioral changes, so that the effect we finally observe may be several steps removed from the original one.

It becomes obvious that the clinician or experimenter who wishes to make use of or to evaluate drugs must acquire a certain degree of pharmacological sophistication. Workers in an area like the one represented by this book, who reach for help in all directions, can consider themselves fortunate to have monitors like Dews looking over their shoulder as they work.

To round out the group, we have Goldiamond's chapter on perception. Instead of concentrating on a circumscribed research topic,

Goldiamond attempts to reorganize an area that forms one of the major divisions of psychology itself. In doing so, he repeats and amplifies many of the points that were made by the other contributors.

In accord with Hunt and Jones, Goldiamond observes that the logic and procedures of early laboratory investigations in perception underlie many of the diagnostic procedures currently used in the clinic; also, that perceptual theories are involved in much of the theoretical and methodological formulation of clinical psychology. These considerations, along with the sheer scope of his subject matter, form Goldiamond's justification for the clinical relevance of the material he presents. He then goes on to reformulate the logic, procedures, and theories of perceptual investigation in a manner distinctly different from current clinical conceptions.

Goldiamond takes as his points of departure the Theory of Signal Detection and principles derived from studies of operant behavior, both of which have developed outside the clinical area. He makes use of the theoretical model in a novel way, demonstrating that with a pair of dice as observer, he can generate any number of relationships whose properties have hitherto been interpreted as reflecting fundamental perceptual functions. If this were his sole use of the signal detection model, we might consider it a mere *tour de force*. But after going on to the conclusion that classical psychophysical functions hold only for particular settings of certain variables and do not constitute general sensory functions, be begins to pick up the pieces by pointing out that the model not only renders the variables explicit but can be used to systematize them. These variables then become the subject matter of perceptual investigation.

For example, the classical concept of sensory or perceptual thresholds becomes difficult to justify, since the response indicator is always under the control of other variables as well. Among these other variables are the consequences of the subject's responses, and it is here that Goldiamond makes contact with the material in Hefferline's and Sidman's chapters. The consequences of behavior are explicitly considered in operant conditioning, and Goldiamond equates psychophysical and perception experiments with operant conditioning experiments in discrimination and generalization. Operant phenomena supply the mechanisms through which the variables specified by Signal Detection Theory operate.

Differences in operant responses, including verbal reports, can reflect differences in conditioning history, the effects of reinforcement, general state variables, and other experimental conditions rather than the differences in discrimination or sensory thresholds that are usually inferred from them. Goldiamond suggests that a definition of perception in the restricted terminology of relevant variables may have more generality and utility outside the laboratory than a definition in intuitive experiential terms. Thus, from an entirely different starting point, Goldiamond arrives at the same conclusion with respect to the study of perceptual disorders that Sidman states with respect to other types of behavioral breakdown: Perceptual processes can be specified in terms of their controlling variables, and perceptual breakdown must be classified in terms of alterations in the nature of the control exercised by these same variables.

A book with a title like the present one might be expected to present an account of how people in the laboratory are contributing to the solution of problems that arise in the clinic. But we have just summarized the activities of a group of experimenters who are presenting problems, rather than solutions, to the clinical psychologist. Their work presents a challenge, because its relevance to clinical psychology is not in accord with the clinician's own conceptions of his problems. Some of these researchers are only minimally concerned, themselves, with clinical relevance. Although some of them may eventually make a deliberate effort to apply their findings and concepts, these are likely to be the exceptions. It will be largely up to the acknowledged clinicians to find and make the applications. To do this will require considerable reorientation and reformulation of their own conceptions.

This, then, is one type of relationship that currently exists between laboratory and clinic.

Clinicians will probably find the other large group of contributors to the book more congenial and, at the same time, more easily criticizable. This group may be characterized by its willingness to carry problems directly from the clinic to the laboratory for experimental investigation. Even here, however, we may make a further distinction—between those who take a clinical problem, e.g., the therapeutic interview, and study it on its own terms, and those who try to study the problem only indirectly, in terms of some more general process such as verbal interaction. Unless one realizes that the latter is being done, there may be unnecessary confusion between workers who are actually dealing with related problems.

One of the more unusual chapters in this volume is Pribram's provocative attempt to put Freudian theory back into its neurological cradle and to trace its development from that point. Freud is, of course, almost by definition, clinically relevant, but Pribram also rationalizes the utility of his chapter as an instance of the use of pathological material to illuminate questions of a basic theoretical nature.

Pribram's summary of Freud's "Project for a Scientific Psychology" need not be further summarized here. It is of interest to note, however, that one of the major problems that concerned Freud in this work, one whose unsatisfactory solution led him to turn in other directions, is also one toward which current research is being energetically directed. This is the problem of the organism's necessity to remain receptive to new stimulation, yet at the same time to develop the stabilities necessary to retain traces of prior stimulation. Malmo's concept of activation and Hefferline's concern with the storage function of implicit muscular activity are both occasioned in large measure by a similar concern.

Discussing work in the animal laboratory which deals with the effects of infantile experience on adult behavior, Levine suggests this type of experimental investigation as a potential source of verification of Freudian theory. His critical review reveals that the area has not yet developed a high level of internal consistency; the relevance of the stress stimuli also needs clarification.

Levine, too, recognizes that a convincing case has yet to be made, but he feels that there has been enough progress to define a valid research area. There is some support for the notion of critical periods —specific periods in development when the organism is particularly sensitive or vulnerable to certain types of stimulation. Instead of being discouraged by some of the conflicting findings, Levine suggests that the critical periods may vary not only for different species but for different types of behavior as well. The experimental evidence also leads him to the generalization that stimulation in infancy will permit the adult organism to adapt more effectively to novel situations, perhaps even reducing his emotional response to such experiences. If we are not yet aware of all the factors determining the extent and duration of the behavioral changes that occur with infantile experience, there is all the more need for experimental investigation.

Hunt and Jones do not, and need not, present any justification for the clinical relevance of their work, for they are concerned with the subjective decisions of the clinician himself. However, they find themselves in the strange position of having to justify, instead, the scientific propriety of their interest. Unlike Goldiamond, and Festinger and Bramel, who assume implicitly that judgment is a reasonable scientific issue, Hunt and Jones, more familiar with the territorial customs of clinical psychology, present a detailed discussion of this question.

The conclusion at which they arrive—"The clinician of today is on firm ground in viewing his judgmental processes as a natural behavioral phenomenon open to all the investigative procedures of experimental psychology"—also defines the scope of their own interest, which is to find approaches to clinical problems that will relate them to other psychological functions and areas of research. With respect to their own research interests, they find an analogy between clinical and psychophysical judgment. At this point, having started with an entirely different set of problems, Hunt and Jones find themselves standing on the same field as Goldiamond. In fact, they actually exchange tentative handshakes when Hunt and Jones suggest the potential applicability of learning theory and perception to the problem of clinical judgment.

Berg and Adams express concerns similar to those of Hunt and Jones, but in the area of personality measurement—also traditionally in the clinical sphere. In attempting a rigorous assessment of the techniques of personality measurement, Berg and Adams maintain only a despairing faith in the utility of most current methods. They state, essentially, "Look at how much has been tried and how little accomplished!"

Among the methods of personality measurement which they discuss are ratings, psychological tests, analysis of verbal behavior, physiological and organic measures, environmental and achievement measures, and the application of any or all of these to the experimental production of personality change. Berg and Adams retain enough respect for ratings to outline a number of conditions in which useful, reliable, and valid ratings may be obtained. They also observe that environmental and achievement measures of behavior in the social milieu are really the ultimate criterion for therapeutic success. Surprisingly enough, they are willing to climb much further out on the physiological limb than most of their laboratory oriented colleagues, and suggest that this area will eventually provide the basis of a science of personality.

Petrullo's coverage of the research in small-group behavior is intended less as a demonstration of clinical relevance than as a service to the clinician. He points out that the clinician wants both to understand his patients' behavior and to find methods to change it, whereas research people are usually content when they achieve understanding; the clinician, therefore, must make himself familiar with research progress if applications are to be developed. To this end, Petrullo reviews the literature on a group of concepts and techniques that have been applied to the analysis of interaction processes—equilibrium concepts, group dynamics, reinforcement, sociometric techniques, perceptual analysis, social influence, personality, etc. The wide range of coverage reveals points of contact between small-group research and almost every other chapter in this volume.

The small group is, for Petrullo, an important avenue through which individual behavior is influenced, and must be studied not only for its own sake but also as a way to understand the individual. Petrullo recognizes that one of the chief avenues of influence is verbal behavior, a topic that is given detailed attentions in Greenspoon's chapter.

Greenspoon's major suggestion to clinicians is that instead of trying to deal with the interpretative or symbolic aspects of verbal behavior, they might profitably treat verbal responses like any other responses, even like the lever pressing of the laboratory rat. In support of this suggestion, he reviews a number of experiments which show that verbal responses can, indeed, be controlled by their consequences. When these experiments, however, have been extended into more complex problems, such as conditioning in people with behavior disorders, the conflicting results lead Greenspoon to conclude that verbal conditioning requires the analysis of complexities beyond that which is usually undertaken in the lever-pressing situation.

Taking note of the fact that clinicians have seized upon verbal conditioning techniques and that this activity constitues a valuable experimental-clinical bridge, Greenspoon warns against the premature use of the techniques before basic research findings have been accomplished. But he whets the clinical appetite by hinting that verbal conditioning can operate in testing and therapy situations, and points out that generalization outside the therapy siuation is a critical problem for clinical application.

One of the basic problems that plagues research on verbal conditioning is the identification of response classes whose members will vary together lawfully when they are exposed to an experimental variable. Experimenters have defined classes in such terms as plurality, hostility, and self-reliance, but these specifications may not correspond at all with the structure of the subject's behavior. Greenspoon notes this as one of the major reasons for the variability of results in verbal conditioning and questions the future of such work. From Greenspoon's original research in this area, the experiments which in effect began the experimental study of verbal conditioning, there has been a significant shift in emphasis. The early research dealt with verbal response classes largely in terms of the acquired meaningfulness of words. Greenspoon now suggests that verbal behavior be studied independently of interpretative or symbolic aspects and offers provocative leads for strengthening the functional analysis of verbal behavior.

Partly in recognition of this problem, Matarazzo chooses to concentrate on the noncontent aspects of verbal behavior. His specific concern is with the verbal interaction that takes place in the interview situation, and he concentrates on the form rather than the content of interview behavior. By observing only the time relations in the interactions patterns of interview participants—for example, the amount of time a patient is silent and the amount of time he speaks—Matarazzo reveals a close methodological affinity to the work described by Sidman and Goldiamond.

Matarazzo finds that by standardizing the temporal characteristics of the interview, leaving the content free to vary, he obtains reliable and consistent individual interaction patterns. He has been able to show that predetermined changes in the interview will alter the interviewee's behavior and that these alterations will be different for various diagnostic groups. Although Matarazzo, too, recognizes the problem of generalization outside the interview situation, he suggests that it may be possible to change the patient's interview behavior therapeutically; for example, in the direction of speaking more often and in longer utterances.

In Wolpe's chapter we actually find a prescription for the translation of laboratory findings into therapeutic practice. The adequacy of the prescription will undoubtedly be debated, in terms of its derivation—largely from animal experimentation, its logical vulnerability (Are the therapeutic techniques a necessary consequence of the experimental data?) and its validity (Are the therapeutic techniques effective?). But these questions cannot be settled from the armchair.

Wolpe notes three sources of behavior modification: growth, lesions, and learning. He argues that the learning process is most important in neurosis and that here, as in other areas of medicine, it will be helpful to try to understand the "abnormal" in terms of the "normal." The normal learning processes upon which he leans most heavily are extinction and generalization. If he uses these processes differently from the other contributors to whom they are also important, we may hope that there will be a constructive reciprocity of influence and that both clinician and experimentalist will profit from the interaction.

Most of the authors, as active researchers, have tended to stress the laboratory as the appropriate scene of experimental action. Strupp's chapter presents a clear argument for the study of clinical problems in clinical settings. He is quite relaxed about his identification with Science: "To the extent that psychotherapy attempts a systematic and self-conscious manipulation of variables in a human relationship and notes its effects, it has the makings of a scientific discipline," and, in contrast to a good number of the other authors, he observes, "One might almost say that ease of measurement and psychological meaningfulness are inversely related."

Thus we come full circle, with Strupp, from the laboratory investigator who is only peripherally concerned with clinical relevance to the clinical investigator who feels that his problems are only minimally amenable to solution in the laboratory. Make no mistake about Strupp's research methodology, however—he is not a casual wallower in uncontrolled variables. Though he prefers the clinic for his stage, his techniques are developed with a care close to the laboratory. With respect to research in psychotherapy, in which his concern is with the influence of therapist variables upon the therapeutic relationship, Strupp makes some general points which are similar to the views of several of his experimental colleagues. He notes, for example, the changing emphasis of research from "outcome" studies to investigations of the processes involved in the therapist-patient interaction. And he points out that the therapist not only must possess certain defined personal behaviors but, like the laboratory investigator, also must develop a high level of technical skill with the operations that concern him.

Quite obviously, there exists no simple relationship between laboratory and clinic at the present time. Experimental psychology is approaching clinical from several directions. Sometimes the approach seems to be in a spirit of succor, sometimes of siege; sometimes the approach even seems to be accidental. There is relevance at many levels, from questions of methodology, through basic information about behavioral processes, to therapeutic practice. Workers in different areas are sometimes concerned, even unknowingly, with similar problems, and it may be useful to place these out on view for all to see. Similarly, research on seemingly different problems sometimes encounters similar difficulties. Some of these might best be solved by discarding certain clinical preconceptions, as a few authors suggest; others might profit from a more intensive consideration of clinical phenomena.

There is certainly sufficient clinical-experimental activity being carried out by able workers to warrant the optimistic prediction that the collaboration will increase, although at this moment the direction and extent of this collaboration cannot be predicted with certainty. In the belief that such a collaborative enterprise will be valuable and important and in the spirit of such collaboration this book is offered.

Index